ILLINOIS

CHRISTINE DES GARENNES

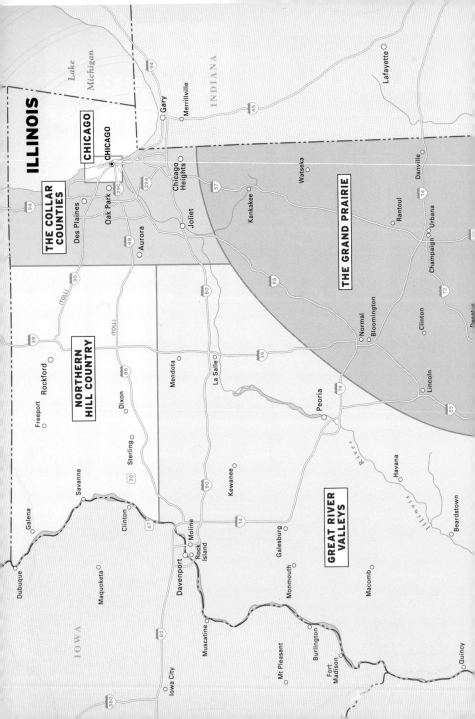

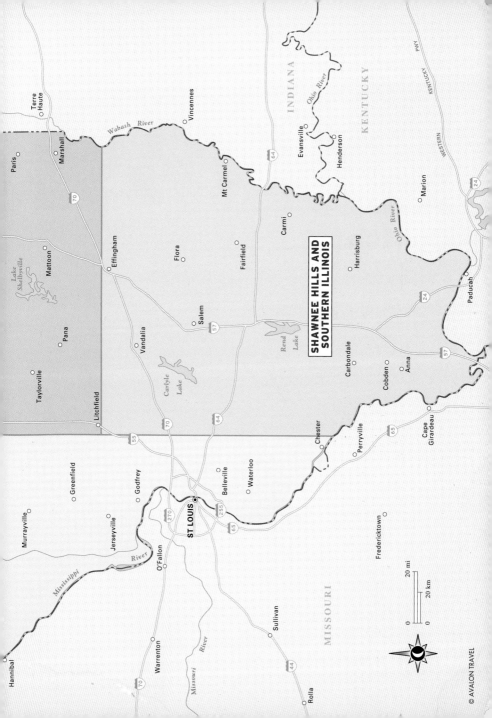

SHAWNEE HILLS AND SOUTHERN ILLINOIS

INDIANA

KENTUCKY

MISSOURI

Terre Haute
Paris
Marshall
Vincennes
Wabash River
Mt Carmel
Evansville
Henderson
Marion
Ohio River
Carmi
Flora
Fairfield
Harrisburg
Paducah
Effingham
Salem
Vandalia
Rend Lake
Carbondale
Cobden
Anna
Mattoon
Lake Shelbyville
Pana
Taylorville
Carlyle Lake
Litchfield
Chester
Perryville
Cape Girardeau
Greenfield
Godfrey
Belleville
Waterloo
Murrayville
Jerseyville
O'Fallon
ST LOUIS
Fredericktown
Hannibal
Mississippi River
Warrenton
Missouri River
Sullivan
Rolla

70
64
57
70
55
64
270
255
65
70
44
24
65
24

WESTERN KENTUCKY PKWY

20 mi
20 km
0
0

© AVALON TRAVEL

Contents

Discover Illinois

About 15 years ago I drove a Toyota Tercel south on I-94 toward Chicago. The skyline, framed by the Sears Tower and the John Hancock Center, appeared on the horizon, and I was on the edge of my seat. I couldn't help but accelerate.

Like many who come to Chicago and to Illinois, I carried with me images of Al Capone's Chicago (remember the Union Station scene in *The Untouchables*?) and Michael Jordan's United Center, and I imagined a place where winds whipped off the lakeshore, where beyond the city stretched endless corn and soybean fields, and in between were these things called grain bins. And of course I'd heard about Abe Lincoln.

I set off and over the years came to know classic Chicago places. On free admission days I headed downstairs to the photography exhibits at the Art Institute. I jammed to Lonnie Brooks and Big Time Sarah in blues clubs. I biked and jogged along the lakeshore path, and even swam in the harbor. I sampled more than my share of beer and pizza at city festivals. I even sat through a triple-overtime Blackhawks hockey game and an early April Chicago Cubs game. Yes, it is cooler by the lakeshore.

Eventually I started exploring beyond the city's borders. Illinois, I found out, is home to sweet-corn festivals, vintage car rallies, drive-in movie theaters – you'd be hard-pressed to find a more classic American place. I found myself saying, quite often, "Wow. I didn't know Illinois had

this." Frank Lloyd Wright's home; remains of pre-Columbian civilizations; cypress swamps; lush forests and river canyons; wineries; the juiciest peaches. There's space out here — space you might not be able to see or feel on the East or West Coasts. There's the beauty of the sun setting over a cornfield while a thunderstorm rolls in, or a red-winged blackbird calling out among the waving big bluestem grass. And there's the great history. This is where Abraham Lincoln grew to believe slavery was immoral, where Carl Sandburg wrote about the simple beauty of natural events such as the fog coming on, where Mother Jones fought for workers' rights, and where Ronald Reagan dreamed of Hollywood while working as a lifeguard.

So ride to the top of the Sears Tower or Hancock Building and take in the view. Cheer on the Cubbies. Bite into a hot dog. But don't forget there's more than corn and soybeans past the big city. Roll down the car window, slow down, and rumble down an old two-lane highway. Look beyond the bend. I guarantee you'll be surprised.

Planning Your Trip

▶ WHERE TO GO

Chicago

A city of nearly three million people stretching over 228 square miles, Chicago is one big city—the third largest in the country—with just about every ethnic neighborhood you can imagine. A packed agenda awaits. Cruise the Chicago River on an architectural boat tour. Get your groove on in a blues club. Bike or lounge in the sun along the Lake Michigan shoreline. Stroll through gorgeous Millennium Park with its Frank Gehry pavilion, gardens, and sculptures. Take your pick of one of the many world-class museums. Root for the home team at Wrigley Field.

The Collar Counties

Think Chicago is surrounded by sleepy, monotonous suburbs? It's time you caught a Metra train and started exploring the city's neighbors. To begin with, there's the awesome architecture of Oak Park, home to Frank Lloyd Wright's home and studio and Ernest Hemingway's birthplace. On the north shore, Evanston offers lakefront parks and a mix of restaurants and shops. Further north are the dazzling Baha'i Temple and the Chicago Botanic Garden. To the west are the picture-postcard Fox River villages. And to satisfy those consumerism urges, there's always Woodfield Mall and Gurnee Mills.

Northern Hill Country

Arguably one of the most scenic parts of the state, the hill country is quite bucolic, with small towns tucked into the valleys and farmsteads folded into the mix. Here are numerous state parks and trails for hiking along or atop cliffs near the Mississippi or Rock

Millennium Park, Chicago

IF YOU HAVE . . .

- **ONE WEEKEND:** Immerse yourself in Chicago and all its sights, but set aside a few hours for nearby Oak Park.

- **FIVE DAYS:** Expand your itinerary to include an overnight in the Starved Rock State Park area near Utica and another overnight in Galena.

- **ONE WEEK:** Head south toward Springfield, with side trips down Route 66 and east to Allerton Park in Monticello.

- **TWO WEEKS:** Become acquainted with the state of southern Illinois, with stops in and around Giant City State Park near Carbondale, the Cache River basin, and the Garden of the Gods.

Rivers. The jewel of the region is Galena with historic, well-preserved downtown, brick-lined streets, Ulysses S. Grant's home, artisans' shops, and opportunities for horseback riding and golfing.

Great River Valleys

From the Cahokia Mounds World Heritage Site near Collinsville to the well-preserved town of Nauvoo, the Mississippi and Illinois River valleys ooze history. The French were the first white people to settle in this area, and Fort de Chartres illustrates the state's early days. Two stars are Starved Rock State Park in Utica and Père Marquette State Park near Grafton, both with hiking trails, scenic overlooks, and historic lodges.

The Grand Prairie

What the midsection of the state lacks in hills and forests it makes up in awe-inspiring open spaces. The Grand Prairie is home to rural enclaves Arthur and Arcola, where the state's

Amish live, and larger cities like the capital, Springfield. Your itinerary should include trips to Abraham Lincoln sites, the university towns of Champaign-Urbana and Bloomington-Normal, and magnificent Robert Allerton Park in Monticello, with its formal gardens and trails.

Shawnee Hills and Southern Illinois

Leave your dress shoes at home. Four-star restaurants and hotels are rare here, but just around the bend is another hilly vista, hiking trail, winery, or barn full of antiques. Crowds? What are those? Go rock climbing or canoeing without running into mobs of other people. Fruit stands brimming with juicy peaches and hillside cabins with views of the Shawnee National Forest abound. Canoe the Cache River and its cypress and tupelo swamps, and you'd swear you were in Louisiana.

Robert Allerton Park, Monticello

▶ WHEN TO GO

You can visit Chicago anytime; the city never shuts down. As for the rest of the state, the ideal time to visit is mid-spring–mid-fall. Things don't shut down November–March, but the landscape is, quite frankly, dull. The festival season, from jazz concerts to pumpkin chucking, kicks in around June and continues through the fall. Summer in Chicago means air and water shows, outdoor music concerts, food markets, you name it. If you're sensitive to humidity, stick to the northern part of the state in July and August and leave the south to the spring or fall. The hiking trails in the Shawnee National Forest are especially inviting in fall when the leaves in the craggy ravines turn gold and red.

There are a few small ski hills and cross-country trails throughout the state's north and middle section, but snowfall can vary here. I wouldn't plan an entire trip around snow-centered activities. If you do visit in winter, make it a Chicago getaway. December is magical, with Michigan Avenue dazzled in white lights and outdoor markets of warm drinks and arts and crafts. If you're looking for bargain hotel rooms, come in February or March.

▶ BEFORE YOU GO

Getting Around

If you're sticking to Chicago and its inner-ring suburbs like Oak Park, it's possible to get by solely on public transportation. Elsewhere in the state, you're better off driving in your car or renting one. You can ride Amtrak from Chicago to cities like Springfield, but once you arrive there, it's best to rent a car.

Several interstates crisscross Illinois, and they're an efficient way to travel the state. The state, however, is deceptively long from north to south, and it can take a while to drive through here. (Chicago to Carbondale is a six-hour drive.) Two-lane highways are often more scenic, but remember it'll take longer to drive from one place to another. If you plan to veer off the main highways, DeLorme's Illinois Atlas and Gazetteer is a must-have. Winters in Illinois can feature heavy snowfall and freezing rain, so pack the emergency gear in your car.

Money

Most stores and restaurants will take major credit cards, and most gas stations have ATMs if you need cash fast. Bring along extra change for the toll highways that run through the north. Students should bring identification to receive discounts at attractions.

What to Take

Jeans and shorts are acceptable in most places, except nightclubs and better restaurants in the larger cities. Layering is a good idea. It's always cooler by the lake in the summer and warmer there in the winter.

entrance to Chicago's Red Line subway

Explore Illinois

▶ THE BEST OF ILLINOIS

So it's not as vast as Montana, but Illinois is a big state, from the hilly Shawnee National Forest in the south, the expansive corn and soybean belt in the middle, and the buzzing metropolitan Chicago in the northeast. It's chock-full of big-city museums, small-town antiques shops, and fancy and homespun restaurants. It might be asking a lot to see all this in two weeks, but load up the car, fill up the gas tank, and give it a shot. This is an ambitious tour that hits the state's must-sees. Be sure to set aside extra time for driving and for the occasional veering off for the flea market, fruit stand, or roadside restaurant that piques your interest.

Day 1
Begin your trip in Chicago, where you'll admire paintings and sculpture at the Art Institute of Chicago and get lost in other great museums downtown, such as the Field Museum or Shedd Aquarium. Take in an architectural boat tour or wander through Millennium Park and the lakefront.

Day 2
Still in Chicago, explore some of the city's eclectic neighborhoods such as Wicker Park, Chinatown, or Hyde Park. Spend the afternoon or evening in one of the historic inner-ring suburbs of Oak Park or Evanston.

Day 3
Drive northwest from Chicago toward the former mining town of Galena. On your way to Galena, stop at Castle Rock State Park near Oregon and hike up the limestone cliffs to view the Rock River valley. Continue northwest, with another stop at the small but scenic Apple River Canyon State Park for another short hike through the woods. Drive along Highway 20 and through the little towns of Stockton and Elizabeth. Check into an inn, bed-and-breakfast, or resort in Galena.

Day 4
Spend the day in Galena. Tour Ulysses S. Grant's former home, have lunch in the

SIMPLY THE BEST . . .

- **Best place to show off your athletic skills:** Giant City State Park (for hiking, climbing); Chestnut Mountain Resort (for skiing), Galena.
- **Best place to take the kids:** Navy Pier, Chicago; Children's Discovery Museum, Bloomington.
- **Best place to escape from the kids:** Eagle Ridge Resort, Galena; Rim Rocks Dogwood Cabins, near Garden of the Gods.
- **Best place for antiquing:** Kane County Flea Market, St. Charles; Sandwich Antiques Market, Sandwich.
- **Best artisans' shops:** Bishop Hill.
- **Best roadside architecture:** Rocket man at the Launching Pad Drive-In, Wilmington.
- **Best place to break your travel budget:** Oak Street boutiques, Chicago.
- **Best place to hone your photography skills:** architectural boat tour, Chicago; Starved Rock State Park, Utica.
- **Best big museum:** The Field Museum, Chicago.
- **Best little museum:** Under the Prairie Museum, Athens.
- **Best place to see bison:** Wildlife Prairie State Park, west of Peoria.

the Launching Pad Drive-In's rocket man

- **Best place to people-watch:** Crown Fountain in Millennium Park, Chicago; Arlington Park racetrack, Arlington Heights.
- **Best place to pamper yourself:** Heartland Health Spa, Gilman.

---

historic DeSoto House Hotel, sample regional wines, and shop in the galleries downtown. See a play or musical.

Day 5

Depart Galena and drive south along Great River Road. South of the Quad Cities, go east to the former Swedish colony Bishop Hill. Spend the day browsing artisans' shops and admiring Swedish-American folk art. In the afternoon drive east through the river towns of Hennepin, LaSalle, and Peru toward Ottawa and the popular Starved Rock State Park. Check into the state park lodge or a private cabin.

Day 6

Hike the trails at Starved Rock State Park. Rent horses and explore the nearby Matthiessen State Park. Cruise the Illinois River on a paddle-wheel boat.

Day 7

Drive to scenic Nauvoo for a visit to the Joseph Smith Historic Site, the rebuilt Mormon Temple—the Nauvoo Illinois

Giant City State Park

Temple—and a nearby winery. Stay overnight in a hotel or lodge overlooking the Mississippi River.

Day 8

Head south along the Great River Road to the small but bustling river town of Grafton. Hop on your bike (or rent one) and ride along the Mississippi River and through Père Marquette State Park. Stay in the grand state park lodge.

Day 9

Continue south and west of St. Louis to the town of Collinsville for a must-see visit to Cahokia Mounds. Wander the museum, hike Monks Mound, and walk the nearby trails. Spend the afternoon driving the scenic back roads to Carbondale.

Day 10

Grab a hard hat and some tough boots. This morning you'll explore the wild Illinois Caverns State Natural Area near Red Bud.

Day 11

Hike or horseback ride along the bluffs of Giant City State Park. Try your hand at rock climbing. Dine and stay in the historic lodge or one of the state park's cabins. Browse boardwalk shops in Makanda.

Day 12

Canoe the Cache River, stroll along a floating boardwalk through wetlands, and amble along on a drive through the region, pausing at the occasional scenic overlook.

Day 13

Hike the stupendous trails on the eastern end of the Shawnee National Forest in the Garden of the Gods and Lusk Creek Canyon.

Day 14

Drive north to Springfield for a walk through the Lincoln Home and surrounding historic district, followed by a visit to the new Lincoln Presidential Library and Museum.

► CHICAGO: YOUR KIND OF TOWN

You could live in Chicago an entire year and still not see all there is to see in this constantly changing town. The standouts are the Art Institute and an architectural boat tour of the city's great buildings, but Chicago is often called a city of neighborhoods, so don't forget to spend a few hours strolling through one or two of them. It's here where you'll get a sense of the city, its residents, its vivacity, its realness, and its dreams.

Art Institute of Chicago

Day 1

MORNING
Start your weekend downtown in the "Loop" district with an architectural boat tour along the Chicago River. Follow that up with a visit through the gorgeous Art Institute of Chicago and a walk through nearby Grant Park, pausing for a stop in front of Buckingham Fountain. Then it's off to Millennium Park and its gardens and outdoor art.

AFTERNOON
Rent bicycles at Navy Pier and ride along the lakefront trail. Take off your shoes and test the Lake Michigan water. Head back to the pier and then over to fabulous Michigan Avenue to ogle at the shops.

EVENING
Watch the sunset from atop the Hancock Observatory or Sears Tower. Take in a show at the Goodman Theatre or Steppenwolf Theatre.

Day 2

MORNING
Spend the morning touring the Field Museum, Adler Planetarium, or Shedd Aquarium, all within walking distance of each other downtown.

AFTERNOON
Take off for the north-side neighborhood of Lincoln Park for a visit to the free Lincoln Park Zoo. From there head north to Wrigleyville and the friendly confines of Wrigley Field. Browse the bookstores and boutiques and duck into a coffee shop in Andersonville.

EVENING
At night dine in the Wicker Park or Southport neighborhoods. Then slip into a jazz, blues, or alt-rock club.

Hancock Observatory

Day 3

MORNING

Go south to the burgeoning Prairie District to visit the Clarke House, the oldest house in the city. Continue farther south to bustling Chinatown for lunch.

AFTERNOON

And onward to the Hyde Park neighborhood and the University of Chicago campus. Get lost in bookstores, and wander through the gothic quad. Finish with a tour of Frank Lloyd Wright's Robie House or a visit to the DuSable Museum of African American History.

EVENING

Stick around the Hyde Park neighborhood for a theater production or music concert at one of the University of Chicago's performance spaces.

► DAY-TRIPPING AROUND CHICAGO

Oak Park

Boasting more than a dozen Frank Lloyd Wright homes, Oak Park is a mecca for fans of Prairie-style architecture. Free shuttle buses between the major sights and shopping districts make this town easy to navigate. You can get there from downtown Chicago on the Chicago Transit District's elevated trains or the Metra suburban train line.

MORNING

Begin your visit with a tour of Wright's Home and Studio, followed by a walking, biking, or driving tour of the surrounding neighborhoods. From there you can walk to downtown Oak Park, grab lunch from a deli, and picnic in one of the many parks in the village.

AFTERNOON

Spend an hour or so browsing the shops along Lake Street, Harrison Street, or Chicago Avenue. Each district offers a mix of clothing and gift boutiques, secondhand music and book stores, and coffee shops. Next it's on to the birthplace of Ernest Hemingway, also within a short walking distance of downtown. When you've finished the home tour, walk down the street to visit a small museum dedicated to the writer.

EVENING

Top off your visit to Oak Park with dinner at one of the dozens of restaurants there, such as La Bella Pasteria or Khyber Pass. Then follow that with a play at Circle Theatre or, if you're visiting in the summer, an outdoor Shakespearean play at Festival Theater in Austin Gardens.

Evanston

Bordering Chicago on the north side, Evanston manages to be part college town (Northwestern University is here), well-to-do north-shore suburb (lots of grand homes

the Ernest Hemingway Birthplace home, in Oak Park

CHASING ABE

Before moving to Washington, D.C., in 1861 to become the country's 16th president, Abraham Lincoln spent two decades in Illinois, beginning from the time he crossed into the state as an eager 21-year-old. He plied several trades (surveyor, store clerk) before practicing law and fine-tuning his skills as a politician. You could say Illinois is the place where Abraham Lincoln came of age.

The definitive Lincoln trip should begin with Springfield, the state capital. It is there where his former home and neighborhood have been preserved, and where a comprehensive presidential museum details his life, political and personal. Once you've spent time in Springfield, you can then set out on day trips to visit other sites around the state where he left his mark. There's no shortage of buildings in which he may have walked and artifacts (pens, beds, desks) he may have touched.

bronze bust of Abraham Lincoln, located at his burial site in Springfield

SPRINGFIELD

First, visit the **Lincoln Home National Historic Site** where he lived with his family while he worked in Springfield as a lawyer and politician. A visit to the home and the neighborhood, complete with renovated homes and brick streets, can take about two hours. Next up is the **Abraham Lincoln Presidential Museum and Library**, which opened in 2005. Its artifacts and multimedia displays illustrate Lincoln's life, politics, and the country during his presidential tenure.

A few steps from the library and museum is the **Old State Capitol State Historic Site**, where Lincoln delivered his House Divided speech in 1858. It's also where he lay in state before his burial. Two nearby and short stops on the Lincoln trail are the **Lincoln-Herndon Law Office State Historic Site,** where Lincoln and William Herndon practiced law in the 1840s and early 1850s, and the **Lincoln Depot,** where Lincoln delivered a brief speech before departing for Washington, D.C., in 1861.

Complete your Springfield trip with a visit to Oak Ridge Cemetery, home to the **Lincoln Tomb.** The monument and tomb is where Lincoln, his wife Mary Todd Lincoln, and three of their children are buried.

NEAR SPRINGFIELD

The following sites are all about 30 miles or less from Springfield. **Lincoln's New Salem** near Petersburg is a village modeled after the one in which Lincoln lived and worked in the 1830s. In the town of Lincoln, the **Postville Courthouse** is a re-created courthouse where Lincoln tried cases in the 1840s. Over at the **Lincoln College Museum** you'll find exhibits such as a poem written by Lincoln, a ballot box he once used, and an 1860 campaign banner. The **Mt. Pulaski Courthouse State Historic Site** is the original building where Lincoln tried cases as a lawyer.

ELSEWHERE IN THE STATE

The **Vermilion County Museum and Fithian Home** in Danville contains a desk used by Lincoln and a bed in which he reportedly slept. The **Old City Hall and Courthouse** in Beardstown is where Lincoln successfully defended an accused murderer in the Almanac Trial. Lincoln began his state legislative career in Vandalia, home to the **Vandalia Courthouse State Historic Site,** before he and other legislators lobbied for the capitol to be moved to Springfield. In Lerna, the **Lincoln Log Cabin State Historic Site** consists of the reconstructed farmstead where Abraham Lincoln's father, Thomas, lived with his wife and Abe's stepmother, Sarah.

on the lakeshore), and a vibrant diverse community of progressive artists and other folks. Visitors are drawn to the lakeshore, which stretches for four miles in Evanston. There are plenty of sandy beaches and lakefront trails for walking, biking, jogging, or in-line skating. You can take the Chicago Transit Authority elevated train to Evanston or the Metra suburban train line.

MORNING
Begin your trip visiting the scenic lakeshore and Grosse Point Lighthouse, a National Historic Landmark on the north side of Evanston. Tour the adjacent Evanston Arts Center and lounge a while on the sandy beach. If you're feeling ambitious, walk along the lakeshore path.

AFTERNOON
Head back into town for lunch at one of dozens of restaurants within walking distance of the lakeside parks. Shop for used books, travel accessories, and music along Chicago and Orrington Avenues. Rest your feet in one of the many coffee shops. Check out exhibits at Kendall College's Mitchell

Grosse Point Lighthouse, in Evanston

Museum of the American Indian or wander through the château-like Charles Gates Dawes House.

EVENING
Indulge in a big meal at Davis Street Fish Market or Dave's Italian Kitchen. Catch a theater production or music concert at Northwestern University or at one of the community venues.

Fox Cities
Forty miles west of Chicago along the rolling Fox River, the villages of St. Charles, Geneva, and Batavia are postcard towns: tree-lined streets with tidy bungalows and ornate, renovated Victorians, as well as historic downtowns with shops, restaurants, and watering holes. All three are connected by the multi-recreational Fox River Trail, which meanders along the river. From downtown Chicago you can take the Metra train line to Geneva. Otherwise, follow I-88 west to Batavia or North Avenue west.

MORNING
Start on the south end with a stroll along Batavia's riverfront park, which allows you to get up close to the river and admire a collection of windmills.

AFTERNOON
Drive north to Geneva for lunch at a riverside restaurant, followed by an hour or so of browsing art galleries and gift shops.

EVENING
Continue your shopping in St. Charles, which has numerous antiques and home-decor shops. Rent a paddle-wheel boat or bike and hit the trails at Pottawatomie Park. Stroll along the riverfront and dine at one of the downtown restaurants or within the historic Hotel Baker.

ILLINOIS FLAVOR

In Illinois we tend to like our pizza thick, our meat topped with fries and melted cheese, and our pumpkins, well, catapulted through the air.

Here's the lowdown on some Illinois favorites. Some advice: take a break from counting calories, and don't forget the napkins.

CHICAGO AND COLLAR COUNTIES

Chicago-style pizza is a thick, cheesy pizza in which the top layer is chunky tomato sauce, not mozzarella (the cheese is packed on top of the dough). Chicago-style pizza has in recent decades been exported to cities around the country and world, but you've got to give it a try where it all started. Early purveyors of this dish, Pizzeria Uno and Pizzeria Due, in the tourist-driven section of Chicago's River North neighborhood, still serve up a good pie. (But expect long lines on weekends.)

Chicago-style hot dogs are all-beef wieners topped with green relish, chopped onions, sliced tomatoes, serrano peppers, yellow mustard, and celery salt. They're usually served in a poppy-seed bun. And they are especially good on game day. In the city, head to classic dog joints Superdawg and The Wiener's Circle.

GREAT RIVER VALLEYS

Burgoo is a stew-like concoction cooked over an open flame usually in a big honkin' kettle. Various sources define burgoo as a pioneer stew, and early versions were said to contain game such as venison. Some think it may have gotten its name from the French word *ragout* (French for stew, pronounced "ra-GOO") or bulgar wheat. The modern version of burgoo usually contains beef, chicken, veggies (potatoes, onions, celery, and tomatoes) cooked for 12 hours or more. It's not a dish exclusive to Illinois (Kentuckians also enjoy bowls of the stuff), but some Illinois towns and their residents are so gung-ho they hold burgoo festivals. Utica near Starved Rock State Park holds a burgoo fest in early October.

The farms in and around Morton, near Peoria, grow all those **pumpkins** that go into the Libby's cans (you know, the ones found in nearly every supermarket in the United States

a large kettle of burgoo at the burgoo festival in Utica

in November). In early September, Morton celebrates with a pumpkin festival (pumpkin weigh-offs, cooking contests, big-wheel races) and the punkin chuckin' event held a little later in the fall when area teams haul out their homemade contraptions in a contest to see who can fling the cucurbits the farthest.

GRAND PRAIRIE

Oh, gluttonous joy! The **horseshoe sandwich** is an open-faced sandwich with toast, layered with meat (hamburger, ham steak, turkey, or corned beef), followed by a stack of French fries and melted cheese. It's often found on restaurant menus in and around Springfield (the local Springfield institution Norb Andy's Tabarin serves it up), to the dismay of dieters everywhere.

SHAWNEE HILLS AND SOUTHERN ILLINOIS

This being the state of southern Illinois, there's no shortage of **barbecue** joints. It's not unheard of to wake up at 8 A.M. and smell the apple wood burning behind a restaurant or someone's house.

The famous local favorite is 17th Street Bar and Grill. The original restaurant is in Murphysboro, west of Carbondale, but a new location also opened just off I-57 in Marion.

Chain O' Lakes

About 45 miles northwest of Chicago, the Chain O' Lakes region was formed by the last retreating glacier. The lakes and the parks along their shores provide lots of opportunities for boating, fishing, and hiking.

MORNING

Rent a rowboat or canoe at Chain O' Lakes State Park and explore the backwaters. Or lace up your hiking boots for a walk through the park.

AFTERNOON

After a picnic at Chain O' Lakes, drive to the rare Volo Bog, a National Natural Landmark, for a leisurely stroll. Look for orchids and listen for frogs.

EVENING

Take advantage of late-day discounts and take a spin on one of the many roller coasters at the Six Flags Great America in Gurnee.

Starved Rock

Craving fresh air and eager to exercise? About 1.5 hours west of Chicago along I-80

Volo Bog, in the Chain O' Lakes region

are several state parks packed with horseback riding and hiking trails.

MORNING

The largest and most popular state park in the region is Utica's Starved Rock State Park. Begin your visit with a tour of the visitors center, which has excellent exhibits on the region's Native American history. Hike up Starved Rock. Then take a trolley ride for an overview of the park or a paddle-wheel boat ride along the Illinois River.

AFTERNOON

Scout for eagles or admire the fall foliage of the region while on the back of a horse. Starved Rock Riding Stables offers several horseback-riding trips in the area.

EVENING

Visit nearby downtown Ottawa or Utica for dinner, followed by a walk through Washington Square in Utica where Abraham Lincoln and Stephen Douglas debated slavery. Or if you dine in Utica, wander along the Illinois & Michigan Canal State Trail. Before leaving, drop by Buffalo Rock State Park between Utica and Ottawa. The small park has an outstanding scenic overlook of the Illinois River Valley.

Wildcat Canyon, in Starved Rock State Park

▶ GET DIRTY: HIKING, BIKING, AND PADDLING IN SOUTHERN ILLINOIS

Day 1

Spend the morning exploring the only cave open to the public in the state, Illinois Caverns State Natural Area, near Redbud. The wild cave has several miles of trails to follow. They're lit only by the light of your flashlight.

After your time underground, drive southeast toward Carbondale and Giant City State Park. Pitch a tent or rent a room in the historic lodge in the heart of the Shawnee National Forest. Hike the Red Cedar Hiking Trail or take a brief jaunt along the Stone Fort Nature Trail. Otherwise, rent a horse at the park stables and follow one of the horse trails.

Day 2

After a full breakfast at the lodge, drive south through the Shawnee Hills to Natural Bridge Park for a short hike through woody ravines. Wind through the back roads and stop at Little Grand Canyon, also southwest of Carbondale. The steep, four-mile loop trail has several scenic overlooks of the forest. Unwind with a glass of wine at the nearby Pomona Winery or Von Jakob Vineyards.

Day 3

Drive east a short distance to Drapers Bluff and Vertical Heartland Climbing School, where instructors will teach you the ropes about rock climbing on their private outdoor course or take you to the best boulders and cliffs in the area, including those at Ferne Clyffe State Park.

Day 4

Today you'll turn south toward Metropolis. The shallow seas that once covered Illinois millions of years ago are long gone, but you've still got a chance to explore underwater life. Mermet Springs, between Vienna and Metropolis, is a spring-fed quarry that has been transformed into a scuba destination for beginner or experienced divers.

Day 5

Wake up early and rent a canoe in Ullin, and then paddle into the otherworldly Cache River State Natural Area near Belknap in the far southern part of the state. Reminiscent of the swamps in Louisiana and other Gulf states, the natural area has quiet canoe trails through tupelo and cypress swamps. Keep an eye out for orchids and egrets.

Day 6

Jog over to Karnak or north to Harrisburg, where you'll unload your bike for a trip down Tunnel Hill State Trail. The trail challenges riders for 45 miles from Harrisburg to Karnak. Pedal through tunnels, over trestles, and along the bottomlands of the Cache River basin.

Day 7

Discover remains of a Native American village and an ancient rock shelter while hiking along 80- to 100-foot-high bluffs at Lusk Creek Wilderness and Indian Kitchen, east of Eddyville in Southern Illinois. If you've got some strength left, go east toward the Ohio River for one final hike through the Garden of the Gods.

Garden of the Gods

CHICAGO

Let's be frank. Chicago winters can get wet, bitterly cold, and windy. Chicago "rush hour" traffic delays often develop as early as 3 P.M. And really, who likes to pay $20 a day to park their car?

But oh, I love this town. And I bet you will too. Step off the plane, train, or car, and Chicago rises before you. The lake stretches out to the east, and in the Loop, the birthplace of the skyscraper, steel and glass pierce the clouds. Down below you'll discover an array of dining, cultural, recreational, and shopping possibilities. Most visitors to Chicago tend to stick to the downtown Loop area and North Shore neighborhoods of Lincoln Park and Lakeview. But the city encompasses approximately 228 square miles and stretches for about 30 miles along Lake Michigan. In one corner of the city

a hot dog vendor sells juicy dogs, and in another a chef designs art nouveau cuisine. At the historic Lyric Opera, an internationally renowned singer takes stage; in a tiny storefront theater uptown, an actor reads from a new, groundbreaking script. From the popular Shedd Aquarium to the eco-friendly Notebaert Nature Museum, this rich city has it all.

Above all, Chicago is a fun city. Just take a look at the list of annual music and food festivals, where all walks of life from the Midwest gather every summer. Even if you aren't a sports fan, spending an afternoon in the bleacher seats in the friendly confines of Wrigley Field is a great way to experience the character of the city. For more refined tastes, Chicago has great opportunities for shopping in glitzy boutiques, dining in five-star

© CHRISTINE DES GARENNES

HIGHLIGHTS

LOOK FOR  TO FIND RECOMMENDED
SIGHTS, ACTIVITIES, DINING, AND LODGING.

◖ Museum Campus: A majority of Chicago's major museums lie within what is called Museum Campus, a cluster of huge buildings east of Lake Shore Drive and near the Lake Michigan shoreline. In particular, don't miss the Field Museum, the gigantic Oceanarium at the John G. Shedd Aquarium, and the historic Adler Planetarium and Astronomy Museum (page 30).

◖ The Art Institute of Chicago: Perhaps best-known for its extensive collection of 19th-century French impressionist art, the Art Institute, which contains more than 300,000 works of art, is also home to fine modern paintings (such as a few Picassos), contemporary photography, textiles, and a collection of medieval armor (page 33).

◖ Grant Park: Grant Park is where the city plays. You can watch vintage movies during the Chicago Outdoor Film Festival, listen to a blues concert, chomp on hot dogs, or smell the lilacs. During the summer the iconic Clarence Buckingham Memorial Fountain, a huge bronze and wrought-iron sculpture, displays a spectacular light and water show (page 35).

◖ Millennium Park: The newest and most stunning of Chicago's lakefront parks, with modern sculptures, an ice rink, native flowers, grasses, and walking trails, a Frank Gehry-designed pavilion, and the best views of the lakefront and downtown. What more could you want (page 36)?

◖ Wrigley Field: The "Friendly Confines," as the baseball stadium is known around town, was built in 1914 and is one of the few remaining ballparks in the country that can boast ivy-covered brick walls. An evening or afternoon game here is a treat even for people who aren't fans of the sport (page 46).

◖ Garfield Park Conservatory: On the National Register of Historic Places, this some-times-overlooked conservatory is a jewel box of a complex. Built in 1906, the conservatory was renovated in 2003 and features art glass by Dale Chihuly (page 49).

◖ Hyde Park: A great way to spend the day is walking through the diverse Hyde Park neighborhood on the city's south side. Take a peek inside the university's Gothic Rockefeller Memorial Chapel and Quadrangle. Go ice-skating or picnicking at Midway Plaisance, the extrawide and extralong parkway at the southern edge of the campus. Take a tour of Frank Lloyd Wright's Robie House and browse local bookstores (page 50).

◖ Lake Michigan Beaches: This isn't Santa Monica, California, but Chicago has plenty of parks and beaches along the Lake Michigan shoreline for dozing in the sun, jogging, bicycling, or engaging a stranger in a game of chess (page 58).

restaurants, or just strolling along tree-lined residential streets. Walk down to the lower level of the Art Institute of Chicago and view a moving photography exhibit. Check out the ornate architecture of the Pullman National Historic District on the far south side, the historic Garfield Park Conservatory to the west, or the bookshops and cafés in Andersonville on the far north end of the city. Board a boat for a fascinating tour of the Chicago River and a look at some of the city's most notable buildings. Bring your bike (or rent one), pedal along the lakeshore path, and unwind for about an hour or so on a rock ledge or sandy beach. Take in a show at one of the dozens of award-winning Broadway or storefront theaters. And if you want to eat like the locals, be sure to drop by a hot dog stand for a beefy dog or into a pizza joint and bite into the cheesiest, thickest pizza you could ever imagine.

PLANNING YOUR TIME

Like other major urban areas in the United States, Chicago has become much more of a welcoming place for visitors in recent years. Recreation trails have been expanded, parks have been remodeled, farmers markets have been added, and trolleys shuttle tourists from one attraction to the other. Public transportation in the city is usually swift and reliable (although L construction and accidents in recent years have caused some headaches for commuters and visitors). You should be able to ride an elevated train or bus to all the sights highlighted in this chapter. Driving will most likely take longer and just cause headaches. Construction, it seems, is always occurring on some highway.

You can do Chicago in a weekend, but chances are you might not be able to walk afterward. But if you do it all in two or three days, stick to the downtown and near north area. Museums and attractions such as the **Art Institute of Chicago** and **Shedd Aquarium** are huge and you could spend hours upon hours admiring their collections. Pick up interior maps of these places and hit the exhibits you're interested in first.

© CHRISTINE DES GARENNES

Shedd Aquarium

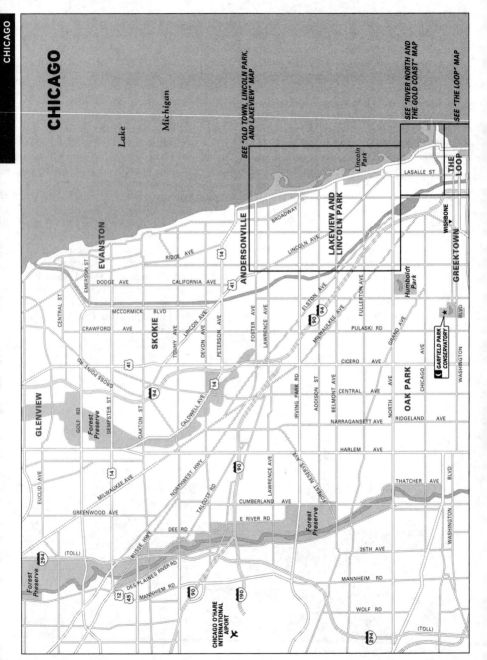

CHICAGO

Lake

Michigan

SEE "OLD TOWN, LINCOLN PARK, AND LAKEVIEW" MAP

SEE "RIVER NORTH AND THE GOLD COAST" MAP

SEE "THE LOOP" MAP

Lincoln Park

LASALLE ST

THE LOOP

WISHBONE

GREEKTOWN

EVANSTON

ANDERSONVILLE

BROADWAY

LINCOLN AVE

LAKEVIEW AND LINCOLN PARK

Humboldt Park

GARFIELD PARK CONSERVATORY

RIDGE AVE

EMERSON ST

DODGE AVE

CALIFORNIA AVE

CENTRAL ST

MCCORMICK BLVD

CRAWFORD AVE

SKOKIE

LINCOLN AVE

TOUHY AVE

DEVON AVE

FOSTER AVE

LAWRENCE AVE

PETERSON AVE

ELSTON AVE

MILWAUKEE AVE

FULLERTON AVE

PULASKI RD

GRAND AVE

CHICAGO AVE

WASHINGTON BLVD

GROSS POINT RD

GOLF RD

DEMPSTER ST

Forest Preserve

CALDWELL AVE

OAKTON ST

IRVING PARK RD

ADDISON ST

BELMONT AVE

CENTRAL AVE

CICERO AVE

NORTH AVE

OAK PARK

CHICAGO AVE

RIDGELAND AVE

NARRAGANSETT AVE

HARLEM AVE

GLENVIEW

EUCLID AVE

MILWAUKEE AVE

GREENWOOD AVE

NORTHWEST HWY

TALCOTT RD

LAWRENCE AVE

FOREST PRESERVE AVE

CUMBERLAND AVE

E RIVER RD

DEE RD

Forest Preserve

THATCHER AVE

WASHINGTON BLVD

25TH AVE

BUSSE HWY

DES PLAINES RIVER RD

MANNHEIM RD

MANNHEIM RD

WOLF RD

(TOLL)

Forest Preserve

(TOLL)

CHICAGO O'HARE INTERNATIONAL AIPORT

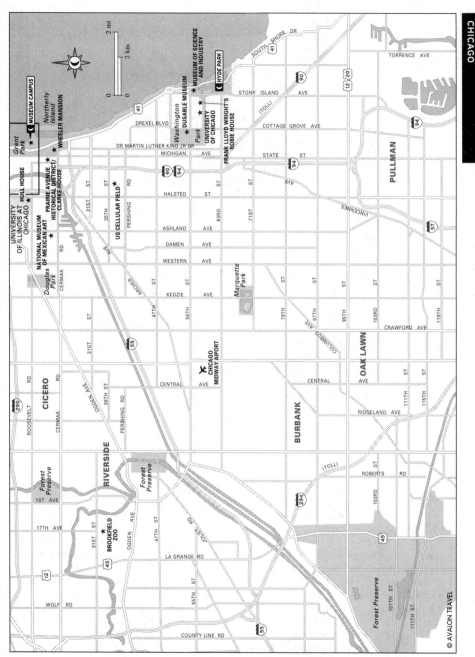

2 mi

2 km

MUSEUM CAMPUS

Northerly Island

WHEELER MANSION

SOUTH SHORE DR

TORRENCE AVE

MUSEUM OF SCIENCE AND INDUSTRY

DUSABLE MUSEUM

HYDE PARK

Grant Park

STONY ISLAND AVE

DREXEL BLVD

Washington Park

UNIVERSITY OF CHICAGO

FRANK LLOYD WRIGHT'S ROBIE HOUSE

COTTAGE GROVE AVE

DR MARTIN LUTHER KING JR DR

MICHIGAN AVE

STATE ST

PULLMAN

UNIVERSITY OF ILLINOIS AT CHICAGO

HULL HOUSE

PRAIRIE AVENUE HISTORICAL DISTRICT/ CLARKE HOUSE

NATIONAL MUSEUM OF MEXICAN ART

31ST ST

35TH ST

PERSHING RD

HALSTED ST

63RD ST

71ST ST

US CELLULAR FIELD

ASHLAND AVE

DAMEN AVE

WESTERN AVE

Douglas Park

CERMAK RD

VINCENNES

VINCENNES

ARCHER

Marquette Park

KEDZIE AVE

79TH ST

87TH ST

95TH ST

103RD ST

119TH ST

CRAWFORD AVE

47TH ST

55TH ST

COLUMBUS AVE

CICERO

ROOSEVELT RD

CERMAK RD

31ST ST

36TH ST

PERSHING RD

OGDEN AVE

CENTRAL AVE

CHICAGO MIDWAY AIPORT

CENTRAL AVE

OAK LAWN

BURBANK

111TH ST

116TH ST

RIDGELAND AVE

RIVERSIDE

Forest Preserve

1ST AVE

17TH AVE

31ST ST

BROOKFIELD ZOO

Forest Preserve

OGDEN AVE

47TH ST

JOLIET RD

ROBERTS RD

103RD ST

45

LA GRANGE RD

WOLF RD

55TH ST

Forest Preserve

107TH ST

111TH ST

COUNTY LINE RD

© AVALON TRAVEL

Chicago is a city of neighborhoods, and it's a good idea to see the city neighborhood by neighborhood. Start downtown and then move north one day, then south on another day. Plan for traffic delays and long lines in front of popular museums such as the **Field Museum.**

Access

Chicago is fairly easy to navigate. It's laid out like a grid. If you ride to the top of the Sears Tower or John Hancock Center, or arrive via airplane and fly above during a clear day or a clear night, you'll be able to see this extensive grid system. Madison Street downtown is the dividing line between north and south; State Street divides east and west. East-west streets south of Congress Parkway, which is at the south end of the Loop, are numbered in descending order as you drive or walk south. A handful of avenues, such as Lincoln, Grand, and Milwaukee, run diagonally to and from the Loop. These streets, it seems, are always flooded with cars.

As in any major metropolitan city, driving in Chicago is a hassle, despite the ongoing expansions of the area's highways and tollways. Chicago is served by a number of interstates and tollways. I-294, otherwise known as the Tri-State Tollway, skirts the western edge of the city and the western suburbs. I-290, the Eisenhower or Ike, runs from Congress Parkway in downtown Chicago west to the western suburbs and places such as the Brookfield Zoo and Oak Park. Traffic backs up in both directions of the Ike starting at 6 A.M., tapers off around 9 A.M., and starts up again at 3 P.M. The main highway through town is I-94, called the Dan Ryan Expressway from the south side to downtown, and the Edens Expressway on the north side. I-90 runs from the Loop out to O'Hare, Rockford, and beyond. It is notorious for long travel times.

Don't bother driving through the city unless you have to. Drivers aren't necessarily as speedy or territorial as they are in Los Angeles, but they aren't exactly considerate either. It's common for drivers to roll through stop signs and honk at those in front of them who have come to a complete stop. And unfortunately, it's not uncommon for cars to drive in a bicycle lane to pass other cars. If you do drive through here, don't forget to obey the traffic lights. Starting in 2003, the city started installing red-light camera systems. Run a red light and you'll receive photographs of your car disobeying the light with a $100 fine from the city.

Parking in the Loop can cost you at least $20 per day. You can usually find parking in the city lots near Grant and Millennium Parks. There are some metered spaces on the streets, but these are almost always taken and they're strictly monitored, so be sure to put in enough coins. Sometimes you can find available metered spaces in the South Loop (say, south of the Harold Washington Library) on weekend days. So if you don't want to pay the steep parking rates in a garage and don't mind walking, try looking for a spot there. On-street parking is restricted in some areas, such as the neighborhoods around Wrigley Field and Lincoln Park. Parking there will require residential zone stickers and city stickers. Read the signs before you park anywhere. Don't even think about parking illegally around Wrigley Field or U.S. Cellular Field during a game day. Parking enforcers will hunt you down, and tickets are expensive. If you park during street cleaning, expect a $50 ticket.

Your best bet is to avoid traffic and parking problems by riding on Metra, the suburban train line, or L trains and buses run by the Chicago Transit Authority. Trains and buses are fairly regular and reliable. One-way tickets cost $1.75.

Resources

Pick up sightseeing and attraction brochures (including free Chicago Transit Authority system maps) at the Tourist Information Centers throughout the city: **Chicago Water Works** (163 E. Pearson Ave.) and the **Chicago Cultural Center** (78 E. Washington St.).

The **Chicago Convention and Tourism Bureau** manages the tourism hotline 877/CHICAGO (877/244-2246) and the website www.choosechicago.com. The **City of Chicago Office of Tourism** is also helpful, and the city's website, www.cityofchicago.org, has tons of information about festivals like Taste of Chicago, farmers markets, and other events.

Several neighborhoods within the city also have chambers of commerce or neighborhood groups that have some useful information such as maps, events listings, and shopping directories. They include, for example, the Lincoln Square Chamber of Commerce on the far north side of the city (www.lincolnsquare.org), the Andersonville Chamber of Commerce also on the far north side (www.andersonville.org), the Chinatown Chamber south of the Loop (www.chicagochinatown.org), Wicker Park and Bucktown on the West Side (www.wickerparkbucktown.com), and Lincoln Park (www.lincolnparkchamber.org).

ORIENTATION
Neighborhoods

Many visitors to Chicago start their vacations here in **the Loop,** or downtown. All highways, subway lines, and elevated train lines lead to the Loop. The **Greyhound Bus Station** is here. So is **Union Station,** where suburban and Amtrak train lines depart and embark. The Loop is the area south and east of the Chicago River, north of Congress Parkway, and west of Lake Michigan. If you take a look at a Chicago Transit Authority Map, you'll see the train lines make a circle around this area. If you transfer bus or L (what we call the elevated trains) lines, chances are you'll transfer lines downtown.

The Loop is where the city does its business and where most convention and business travelers stay. It's easy to get around (plenty of taxis, trains, and buses) and boasts amazing architecture. But it clears out in the evening and lacks some of the charm that other areas of the city have.

North of the Loop are **River North** and the **Gold Coast** neighborhoods, home to the Museum of Contemporary Art, galleries, slick bars and restaurants, ritzy condominium buildings and hotels, department stores on Michigan Avenue, and chic boutiques and salons on Oak Street. West of there is **Bucktown** and **Wicker Park,** once an affordable neighborhood popular among artists, musicians, and

© CHRISTINE DES GARENNES

Wicker Park

antiques dealers and now an increasingly expensive district—still with great music venues and a mix of clothing and art shops. North of the Gold Coast are **Old Town** and **Lincoln Park,** gentrified areas home to Lincoln Park Zoo and several neighborhood parks, remodeled brownstones and Victorians, and a mix of storefront theaters, sports bars, and white-tablecloth restaurants frequented by the 20- and 30-something crowd. Other neighborhoods to explore are **Wrigleyville,** home to the world-famous Wrigley Field (and plenty of recent college graduates), and **Andersonville** and **Rogers Park** on the far north side, where a mix of people with Southeast Asian, Indian, Jewish, and Swedish roots live. To the south of downtown, and easily accessible via public transportation, is **Chinatown,** followed by **Hyde Park,** home to the University of Chicago campus, Frank Lloyd Wright's Robie House, and the Museum of Science and Industry. Finally, at the southern tip of the city is the historic **Pullman** neighborhood, a must-see for preservationist buffs.

When to Go

Anytime! Chicago is always pulsing, no matter what time of day or season. In May, the city streets, cafés, and lakeside beaches become packed with residents who have been itching to soak up the sun's rays. In early summer the city is bursting with activity, and into July and August it seems there's a festival every weekend. The average high in July is 83°F and in August 82°F. But sometimes it can get quite humid and hot in August. (In fact, a heat wave was blamed for hundreds of deaths in 1995.) When the humidity and temperatures rise, stick by the lakeside, where it's cooler in the summer (and warmer in the winter). Chicago is splendid in the fall, but the weather tends to be fickle in October and November. One day it could be 70°F, the next day it could be in the 40s.

Chicago tends to attract frugal and hardy travelers during the winter. The average high in January is 29°F and the low is 14°F. Average snowfall in January is about two inches;

however, in 1967 it snowed 23 inches in 29 hours. The museums are still open, and there are still a few excellent festivals, such as the outdoor Christkindlmarket downtown. Visit during this time and you'll get a lot more for your money. Hotels offer decent deals during the chilly and snowy months of January and February. During this time of year check out the city's historic pubs and load up on comfort food. Snow storms don't shut down the city, but folks who like to travel on foot might have a tough time walking along sidewalks where residents and businesses are slow to shovel. On snowy days, it's best to avoid the expressways and keep to the elevated trains and the Metro suburban trains.

HISTORY

Chicago gets its name from the Potawatomi Indian word *checagou,* which has been translated to mean wild onion and swamp grass. Before the settlers, the flat marshland area was home mainly to members of the Potawatomi tribe, who migrated from Michigan and the northeast region of the continent. Indians, fur traders, and explorers passed through the area, including Father Jacques Marquette and Louis Jolliet, who journeyed through the area on their way back from traveling down the Mississippi River. Most of the early pioneers to the state settled hundreds of miles south of Chicago, near Shawneetown.

It wasn't until the opening of the Erie Canal in 1825 that Chicago (and other parts of the former Northwest Territory) began to see their populations grow. From 1830 to 1840 the city's population increased from 100 residents to 4,470. They came via steamboats and the railroad. Another boon to development was the opening of the Illinois and Michigan Canal in 1848, which connected the Great Lakes to the Mississippi River. At the same time the first railroad—the Galena and Chicago Union—linked Chicago with the Galena lead mines in the northwestern part of the state.

As the city grew, officials realized that they would need to make major changes to the infrastructure to keep pace with its growth. In

1855 the city undertook the huge task of raising the street level by several feet. Until that point most of the city's buildings were constructed hastily on swampy ground, leaving no room for sanitary sewers (which did not bode well for the health of the residents). That year crews moved through the city, lifting buildings, adding foundations, building sewer lines, and planking the streets. The result was a more modern and cleaner city.

By that point the city was really taking off and emerging as an industrial center with McCormick's reaper factory, the Pullman Palace Car factory, textile factories, lumber companies, grain-storage facilities, and food companies. In 1865 the Union Stock Yards opened on the southwest side. The businesses employed thousands of workers, mostly German and Irish immigrants, and eventually included Eastern Europeans, Mexicans, and African-Americans. As chronicled by Upton Sinclair in *The Jungle,* these workers toiled long days at their tasks in unsanitary conditions. The yards were surrounded by miles and miles of railroad lines, which is how most of the animals were transferred into the city. Nearby was a branch of the Chicago River, dubbed Bubbly Creek because of what was dumped into the river from the plants. Beyond the yards were meat-packing and meat-byproduct plants such as Armour, and finally, the neighborhoods where the workers lived: Back of the Yards, Whiskey Point, and Packingtown.

Then one night in early October 1871, after a long, hot, and dry summer, a fire was ignited in a barn on the city's West Side. (Legend says Mrs. O'Leary's cow kicked over a lantern.) Within hours the flames migrated to the city's south side and eventually leapt the Chicago River and struck the north side. By the time it was extinguished the following day, the fire claimed the lives of 300 people and left about 90,000 without homes. The fire, however devastating it was to the city, would provide Chicago the opportunity to rebuild itself in grand style. Architects such as Daniel Burnham, Louis Sullivan, Jens Jensen, Frank Lloyd Wright, and others devised lofty plans for the city. They built lavish hotels, music halls, and early skyscrapers.

But the quality of life for the city's working class people and the poor was pretty grim. The Gold Coast and Prairie Avenue District flourished with mansions, parks, and department stores, but much of the city was mired with muddy, dirty streets and houses for drinking, gambling, and prostitution. Throughout the 19th and early 20th centuries residents battled smallpox, cholera, typhoid fever, tuberculosis, scarlet fever, and more. Hours at the factories or rail yards were long, and wages were often cut.

It was during these years that social activists came onto the scene. Among them were Mary Harris "Mother" Jones, a union and labor organizer who founded the Industrial Workers of the World, and Jane Addams, who founded Hull House in 1889. Addams and her staff taught English to recent immigrants, organized social and recreation opportunities, and lobbied for the city to improve services to the poor areas of town, such as demanding regular garbage collection.

In the decades that followed the Depression and World War II, Chicago became a modern city. Richard J. Daley ruled as mayor 1955–1976. While he was mayor, O'Hare Airport was built and a number of expressways developed, further ensuring the city's place as a transportation hub. The 912-foot-tall Prudential Building was erected in 1955, then the John Hancock Center in 1969, followed by the Sears Tower in 1974. During these years the city built massive housing projects on the south and west sides, many of which have been razed in recent years.

After Daley's death in 1976, the city's residents went on to elect their first female mayor, Jane Byrne, in 1979, followed by the first African-American mayor, Harold Washington, in 1983. Daley's son, Richard M., took control in 1989 and started his sixth four-year term in 2007.

Sights

THE LOOP

The Loop is where much of the city does its business. Many city, county, and state offices are here. The area is mobbed during weekdays, generally 8 A.M. to 6 P.M., but is a bit quieter on weekends. Many of the big must-see sights are here: Museum Campus, Millennium Park, Grant Park, The Art Institute of Chicago—plus it's home to a Broadway theater district.

Museums

MUSEUM CAMPUS

Home to the Field Museum, Adler Planetarium, and Shedd Aquarium, Museum Campus is a cluster of three amazing museums on the lakefront. You can get there by walking along the sidewalks from Michigan Avenue or by bus, taxi, or car. (There are some street parking spaces by Adler Planetarium, plus a lot by Field Museum. If you want a space, go in the morning as early as possible.)

The vast **Field Museum** (1400 S. Lake Shore Dr., 312/922-9410, www.fmnh.org, 9 A.M.–5 P.M. daily, $15–25) was built to house many of the anthropological and biological items that were on display during Chicago's Columbia Exposition in 1893. More than 15 million artifacts are stored here, including meteorites, seed vials, Aztec pottery, Papua New Guinean dance masks, Egyptian mummies, and dinosaur fossils—the most impressive of which is Sue, reportedly the largest, most complete, and best-preserved *Tyrannosaurus rex* in the world. The newer PlayLab area invites children to dig for dinosaur bones, play musical instruments, and have a go at other hands-on activities. It's a great spot for taking those restless preschoolers. And aside from the museum's permanent collections, the Field hosts several world-class visiting exhibits (a recent hit was on King Tutankhamen) throughout the year. Note: The museum typically closes

downtown Chicago, the Loop

© CHRISTINE DES GARENNES

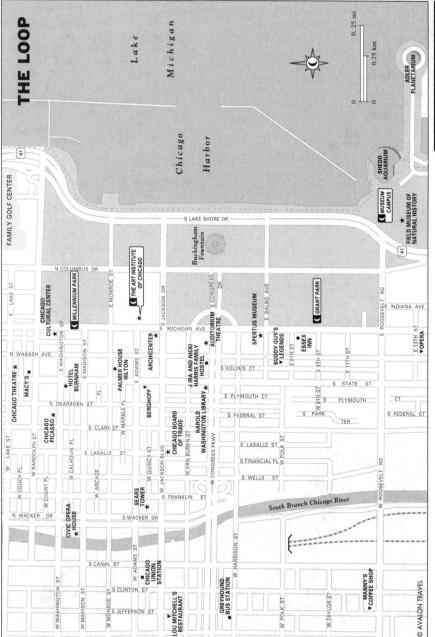

THE LOOP

Lake Michigan

Chicago Harbor

FAMILY GOLF CENTER

ADLER PLANETARIUM

SHEDD AQUARIUM

◀ MUSEUM CAMPUS

FIELD MUSEUM OF NATURAL HISTORY

S LAKE SHORE DR

Buckingham Fountain

N COLUMBUS DR

◀ MILLENNIUM PARK ★

◀ THE ART INSTITUTE OF CHICAGO ★

E MONROE ST

E LAKE ST

CHICAGO CULTURAL CENTER ★

S JACKSON DR

S MICHIGAN AVE

E CONGRESS DR

E BALBO AVE

SPERTUS MUSEUM ★

AUDITORIUM THEATRE ★

◀ GRANT PARK ★

E ROOSEVELT RD

S INDIANA AVE

E 13TH ST

▼ OPERA

BUDDY GUY'S ▼ LEGENDS ●

ESSEX INN ●

E 8TH ST

E 9TH ST

E 11TH ST

N WABASH AVE

CHICAGO THEATRE ★

MACY'S ■

HOTEL BURNHAM ●

E WASHINGTON PL

E MADISON ST

PALMER HOUSE HILTON ●

ARCHICENTER ▶

E ADAMS ST

J IRA AND NICKI HARRIS FAMILY HOSTEL

S HOLDEN CT

S STATE ST

S PLYMOUTH CT

S PLYMOUTH

CT

S FEDERAL ST

S FEDERAL ST

N DEARBORN ST

CHICAGO PICASSO ★

S CLARK ST

BERGHOFF ▼

S MARBLE PL

CHICAGO BOARD OF TRADE ●

HAROLD WASHINGTON LIBRARY ★

S PARK

W 9TH ST

S PLYMOUTH

PL

S LASALLE ST

W QUINCY ST

W VAN BUREN ST

W CONGRESS PKWY

S LASALLE ST

S POLK ST

N WACKER DR

W LAKE ST

W RANDOLPH ST

N COUCH PL

W COURT PL

W CALHOUN PL

N DEARBORN ST

W ARCADE PL

SEARS TOWER ★

S FRANKLIN ST

S FINANCIAL PL

S WELLS ST

W ROOSEVELT RD

CIVIC OPERA ★ HOUSE

S WACKER DR

South Branch Chicago River

W WASHINGTON ST

W MADISON ST

W MONROE ST

W ADAMS ST

S CANAL ST

CHICAGO UNION STATION ■

S CLINTON ST

S JEFFERSON ST

W HARRISON ST

LOU MITCHELL'S RESTAURANT ▶

GREYHOUND BUS STATION ■

W POLK ST

W TAYLOR ST

MANNY'S ▼ COFFEE SHOP

© AVALON TRAVEL

0   0.25 mi

0   0.25 km

around 5 P.M., but the last admission for visitors is at 4 P.M. Also for those with full travel itineraries, the museum does stay open late on some nights throughout the year. These days change year to year; check the Field's website for updated information. Admission fees can also vary quite a bit depending on whether or not you want to see the permanent collections and additional shows. Discount days are also scheduled throughout the year.

When it opened in 1930, the **Adler Planetarium and Astronomy Museum** (1300 S. Lake Shore Dr., 312/922-7827, www. adlerplanetarium.org, 9:30 A.M.–6 P.M. daily Memorial Day–Labor Day, 9:30 A.M.–4:30 P.M. daily Labor Day–Memorial Day, 9:30 A.M.– 10 P.M. first Fri. of the month, $8–23), was the first planetarium of its kind in the western hemisphere. Since then it has expanded quite a bit. The historical astronomical exhibit with its sundials and astrolabes is still stunning, but there are also the interactive digital StarRider Theater and an interactive computer graphic theater. Planetarium shows have focused on topics such as black holes and time travel. Don't forget your camera: You can't beat the views of the Chicago skyline from the planetarium.

Designers didn't hold back when planning exhibits at the **John G. Shedd Aquarium** (1200 S. Lake Shore Dr., 312/939-2438, www. sheddaquarium.org, $8–27.50), particularly the $45 million Pacific Northwest exhibit, which opened in 1991. The three-million-gallon Oceanarium is home to seals, dolphins, and Beluga whales. Then there's the Wild Reef exhibit, which features sharks, including blacktip reef and zebra sharks, in a 400,000-gallon shark habitat. The place is pretty amazing. Listen as divers swim through the tanks and chat with visitors about the biology and social habits of passing fish and mammals via underwater microphones. One of the newer permanent exhibits focuses on invasive species in the Great Lakes. The museum is open 9 A.M.–6 P.M. Memorial Day–Labor Day, and until 10 P.M. on Thursdays June–August. It is open 9 A.M.–5 P.M. weekdays and 9 A.M.–6 P.M. weekends Labor Day–Memorial Day.

The Art Institute of Chicago

◖ THE ART INSTITUTE OF CHICAGO
The Art Institute (111 S. Michigan Ave., 312/443-3600, www.artic.edu, 10:30 A.M.–5 P.M. Mon.–Wed. and Fri., 10:30 A.M.–8 P.M. Thurs., 10 A.M.–5 P.M. Sat.–Sun., $12, 5–8 P.M. Thurs. free) is probably best-known for its collection of 19th-century French impressionist art, including a number of Claude Monet paintings. You'll see Vincent van Gogh's self-portrait, Georges Seurat's *A Sunday on La Grande Jatte,* Pablo Picasso's *The Old Guitarist,* and Grant Wood's *American Gothic.* But the Institute contains more than just paintings. The collection of armor, including swords and iron helmets, from the 15th–19th centuries is awe-inspiring. The museum plans to open a huge north-wing addition in 2009; it will feature about 65,000 more square feet of exhibit space specifically focusing on modern and contemporary art.

OTHER MUSEUMS
The Spertus Institute of Jewish Studies (610 S. Michigan Ave., 312/322-1747, www.spertus.edu, 10 A.M.–6 P.M. Sun.–Wed., 10 A.M.–7 P.M. Thurs., 10 A.M.–3 P.M. Fri., $7), reopened in a schnazzy new building in 2007. With its hundreds of windows of hundreds of different shapes, the building has one of the coolest facades on Michigan Avenue. The Spertus Museum inside hosts cultural events, lectures, exhibits, and other programming. The museum's collection includes Jewish artifacts, such as silver Torah cases, 19th-century paintings depicting Jewish life, and items such as funerary objects and drinking vessels from as far back as the Bronze Age. The museum also contains a kosher café run by chef Wolfgang Puck.

History and engineering buffs may be intrigued with the new **McCormick Tribune Bridgehouse** (southwest bridge tower on the Michigan Avenue bridge over the Chicago River, www.bridgehousemuseum.org, 10 A.M.–5 P.M. Thurs.–Sun. summer months only, $3). This museum is housed in the tower of an actual Chicago River bridge house on the south side of the river. Open since the summer of 2006 and run by the river advocacy group Friends of the Chicago River, this little museum's exhibits show what Chicago and the river were like over 100 years ago. Learn about the city's 37 moveable bridges (32 are on the Chicago River), how the bridges work, as well as the great feat of reversing the river's flow back around the turn of the 20th century.

Architecture and Historic Buildings
SEARS TOWER
The art deco Board of Trade is an eye-catcher, the Art Museum is famous for its lions perched outside, but the most dominant building downtown is the Sears Tower (233 S. Wacker Dr., 312/875-9696, www.the-skydeck.com, 10 A.M.–10 P.M. Apr.–Sept., 10 A.M.–8 P.M. Oct.–Mar., $13, audio tours extra), which houses a variety of financial companies. When it was built in 1973, the 110-story Sears Tower was the tallest in the world at 1,450 feet. Owners can no longer make that claim, but it's still a trip to ride on the speedy elevator to the observatory. The best time to visit is before sunset, when the lines are shorter. Exhibits explain the building and the city's history, and telescopes will help you pinpoint various city landmarks. Don't waste your time or money here on overcast foggy days.

CHICAGO CULTURAL CENTER
Another grand building is the Chicago Cultural Center (78 E. Washington St., 312/346-3278, www.chicagoculturalcenter.org, 8 A.M.–7 P.M. Mon.–Thurs., 8 A.M.–6 P.M. Fri., 9 A.M.–6 P.M. Sat.–Sun., free). The center acts as one of the city's official visitors centers and is stocked with free maps and brochures for tours and hotels. (Visitor info is on the first floor.) But it is also a stunning beaux arts building where hundreds of free concerts, art exhibits, lectures, and readings are held every year. Built in 1897 as a library for the city, the building contains sparkling mosaics on the floors and ceilings, marble stairways, and a Tiffany stained-glass dome estimated to be worth $35 million. Free architectural tours of the building are typically

LOOK UP

Chicago is often called the birthplace of the skyscraper. Landmarks from the early days include **the Rookery** (209 S. LaSalle St.), built in 1888 and later renovated inside by Frank Lloyd Wright; the splendid 1889 **Auditorium Building** (430 S. Michigan Ave.), designed by Louis Sullivan; and the art deco **Chicago Board of Trade** (141 W. Jackson Blvd.), built in 1930.

In the 20th century the city saw the development of the **John Hancock Building,** at 100 stories and 1,127 feet tall, in 1969. The **Lakeshore Building** (875 N. Michigan Ave.) still affords visitors some of the best views of Lake Michigan and the city. Not long after the Hancock building debuted, another tower would change the Chicago skyline: The **Sears Tower** (233 S. Wacker Dr.), built in the early 1970s, comes in at 108 or 110 stories (depending on whether or not you count the roof and the mechanical units on top). In 1998 the Sears Tower lost its claim to fame as the world's tallest building when the Petronas Twin Towers were completed in Kuala Lumpur, Malaysia.

The Sears Tower still holds the title of the tallest building in the United States, although that may change in the coming years: **The Spire** is rising to its east. Located at 455 North Cityfront Plaza in Streeterville, west of Navy Pier, the Spire, a twisting, turning building of 150 stories, is planned to top out at 2,000 feet. Construction on the building, designed by architect Santiago Calatrava, began in the summer of 2007.

Other notable towers in the city include the new **Trump International Hotel and Tower,** a modern glass skyscraper that reaches 92 stories on the north side of the Chicago River. At 401 North Wabash Avenue, it was built in place of the old Sun-Times building. Nearby, also on

the riverfront, are those iconic corncob-like buildings, called **Marina City.** The mixed-use complex, built in 1964, is home to parking on the lower levels, restaurants, condos, a health club, and more.

The city also boasts several other tall and architecturally significant buildings, including the **Aon Center,** at 200 East Randolph Street, northeast of Millennium Park. Built in the early 1970s and formerly the Amoco Building and the Standard Oil Building, it is 83 stories tall. The Gothic 26-story **Tribune Tower** at 435 North Michigan Avenue was built in the in 1920s. On the same block is the **Wrigley Building,** noted for its white terra-cotta tiles and clock tower.

© CHRISTINE DES GARENNES

Wrigley Building

held at 1:15 P.M. on Wednesday, Friday, and Saturday. They begin in the building's lobby off Randolph Street.

CHICAGO ARCHITECTURE FOUNDATION

The place to go to catch one of the city's top architecture tours is the Chicago Architecture Foundation's **ArchiCenter** (224 S. Michigan Ave., 312/922-3432, www.architecture.org, 9:30 A.M.–5 P.M. Mon.–Sat., free). Here you can buy tickets for the foundation's boat, bus, and walking tours and check out scale models of Chicago's beautiful landmark buildings and hot new ones. Make sure you set aside some extra time in your day to view the foundation's rotating exhibits on architecture. Previous exhibits have been about topics like the city's trolleys and on historic preservation. A shop (9 A.M.–6:30 P.M.) is stocked with Prairie-style design items such as coasters and clocks.

FINANCIAL LANDMARKS

The financial center is mainly along LaSalle Street, which leads to Jackson Boulevard and the **Chicago Board of Trade** (141 W. Jackson Blvd., 312/435-3590, www.cbot.com, 8 A.M.–4 P.M. Mon.–Fri., free), where millions of commodities and bonds are traded every day. Founded in 1848, it is the world's oldest and largest futures and options exchange. Look for the statue of Ceres, the goddess of grain, at the top of the art deco building. Regular folks are not allowed to visit the gallery to view the trading floor, but you can stop by a visitors center on the building's first floor and watch the trading in the pits via television screens. There's also a gift shop.

Along Wacker Drive there's the **Chicago Mercantile Exchange** (30 S. Wacker Dr.), where more futures are traded. The smaller **Chicago Stock Exchange** (440 N. LaSalle St.) and **Chicago Board of Options Exchange** (400 S. LaSalle St.) are nearby.

OTHER NOTABLE BUILDINGS

Many workers and visitors arrive downtown in **Union Station,** the train station on Canal Street, between Jackson Boulevard and Adams

the Financial District

Street. Built in 1925, the station's best feature is the Great Hall, with its marble floors, wooden benches, and high ceilings. The room has appeared in films such as *The Untouchables* and *The Fugitive.* Even if you don't travel through Union Station, take a peek at this room. It's a great spot for watching people.

Built in 1991, the **Harold Washington Library Center** (400 S. State St., 312/747-4876 or 312/747-4300, www.chipublib.org, 9 A.M.–9 P.M. Mon.–Thurs., 9 A.M.–5 P.M. Fri.–Sat., 1–5 P.M. Sun., free) caused quite a stir among residents. The red-brick neoclassical building has more than 750,000 square feet and humongous ornamental owls at the corners of the building. You'll find plenty of warm cozy spots to read or write in your travel journal, such as the sunny Winter Garden on the ninth floor.

Parks and Plazas
GRANT PARK

East of the Loop, beyond Michigan Avenue, is Grant Park, a huge park where concerts, festivals, impromptu soccer games, and picnics take place. The park district calls Grant Park the city's front yard. You can spend hours strolling through here. The most distinctive feature of the park is the iconic **Clarence Buckingham Memorial Fountain and Garden** at Lake Shore Drive, Balbo Drive, Columbus Drive, and Jackson Boulevard. The 1927 beaux arts–style fountain is made of wrought bronze and depicts sea horses. Sculptor Marcel François Loyau modeled it after the fountains at the Palace of Versailles in France. The fountain's water runs 10 A.M.–11 P.M. daily. A water and light show starts around 7 P.M., lasts about 20 minutes, and continues every hour on the hour until 11 P.M. City Hall turns off the water during the winter but decorates the fountain with holiday lights.

◖ MILLENNIUM PARK

The most recent addition to Chicago's park scene, Millennium Park (northwest corner of Grant Park at Michigan Ave., between Randolph and Monroe Sts., www.millennium-park.org) boasts an outdoor music concert hall designed by Frank Gehry, gardens, fountains, sculptures, a restaurant, and an ice-skating rink. The long-awaited (and controversially over-budgeted) park should be at the top of your to-see list.

Start with the eye-catching **Crown Fountain,** a multimedia-type water fountain made of glass blocks and LEDs. A variety of different faces are shown on a giant block-like screen rising from the ground. Designed by Spanish artist Jaume Plensa, the sculpture is at the southern edge of the park at Michigan and Monroe Streets. Another not-to-miss artwork in the park is **Cloud Gate,** the big shiny sculpture on the west end of the park. Locals call it "the bean," and you'll see why: It looks like an overgrown chrome kidney bean. Anish Kapoor's elliptical sculpture is actually made of stainless steel, and it's 66 feet long—and it's stunning.

The Gehry-designed **Jay Pritzker Pavilion** is just east of the sculptures. This outdoor auditorium houses a few thousands seats, but thousands more can crowd in on the green lawn surrounding the stage. The pavilion hosts the

the gardens in Millennium Park

free Grant Park Music Festival in the summer along with dozens of other performing arts events throughout the year. Gehry also designed the **BP Bridge** (yes, corporation names like Chase Promenade and the Boeing Galleries can be found all over the park), a really cool stainless steel walking path. You can catch it just east of the pavilion and follow it over Columbus Drive toward Lake Michigan. Don't forget your camera: Some of the best views of Chicago can be seen from the bridge.

South of the pavilion is the **Lurie Garden,** which has been planted with flowers like asters, native plants like echinacea and phlox, plus graceful sedges and grasses. They're not arranged formally in colorful rows but grow organically throughout beds planted along winding paths.

During the winter months, head to the **McCormick Tribune Plaza and Ice Rink,** just off Michigan Avenue and Randolph Street. Skating at the ice rink is free, but skate rentals will cost about $9. The rink is open mid-November–mid-March. Call 312/742-5222 for conditions.

To learn more about Millennium Park, consider attending a free tour courtesy of the city's Chicago Greeter program. For more information about these tours, see *Tours* in the *Information and Services* section. The website www.millenniumpark.org also offers audio tours of the park that you can download onto an MP3 player.

PLAZAS AND OUTSIDE ART

Perhaps the most well-known and most-photographed sculpture in Chicago is Picasso's 50-foot-high 167-ton structure outside Richard J. Daley Plaza (Washington and Dearborn Sts., 312/744-6630), known simply as *The Chicago Picasso.* Installed in 1967, the steel structure resembles a woman's face (or, some say, a horse's head). Throughout the year, Daley Plaza hosts free noontime concerts on some weekdays. It is also the spot of a farmers market.

Built in 1985 and designed by Helmut Jahn, the glass and steel **James R. Thompson Center** (100 W. Randolph St., 312/814-6660)

contains mostly State of Illinois offices, but it also holds the **Illinois State Museum gallery,** which spotlights art by Illinois artists. Outside the shiny modern building is Jean Dubuffet's *Monument with Standing Beast,* a black-and-white fiberglass project completed in 1985.

Marc Chagall depicts scenes from the Russian countryside in his *Les Quatre Saisons,* a glittering mosaic at First National Plaza on Dearborn Street, between Madison and Monroe Streets. With plenty of benches and stairs on hand, this plaza makes a good spot for a picnic lunch.

The sloping red steel structure *Flamingo* at **Federal Center Plaza** (Dearborn and Adams Sts.) was designed by Alexander Calder and erected in 1974.

RIVER NORTH AND THE GOLD COAST

The area immediately north of the Chicago River consists of skyscraper hotels, headquarters for businesses such as the *Chicago Tribune,* and a dizzying array of shops and restaurants. Michigan Avenue is lined with shops and hotels. River North is chock-full of galleries and loft apartments. This is an area of the city where you can find plenty of million-dollar townhouses and mansions (including the former Playboy Mansion at State Street and Lake Shore Drive) and plenty of beautiful people. The tanned and toned shop at Barney's on Oak Street and sun themselves on the Oak Street beach, at Oak Street east of Lake Shore Drive. Just south and east of Oak Street is Navy Pier, an indoor and outdoor entertainment complex that tends to attract families and conventioneers.

Navy Pier

Opened in 1916, Navy Pier (600 E. Grand Ave., 312/595-7437, www.navypier.com), formerly known as Municipal Pier, is where Navy ships docked during World Wars I and II. Before it fell into disrepair in the 1970s, it contained a hospital, streetcar line, and the University of Illinois campus. Mayor Richard M. Daley authorized a massive redevelopment in the 1990s, and now much of the pier feels like a shopping mall. You'll

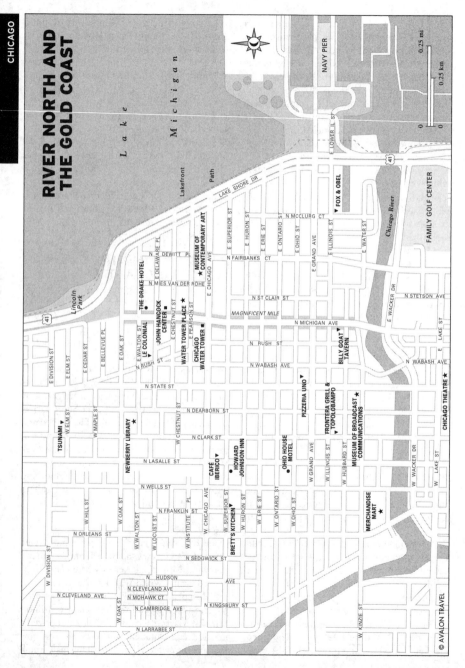

RIVER NORTH AND THE GOLD COAST

Lake Michigan

Lincoln Park

Lakefront Path

NAVY PIER

FAMILY GOLF CENTER

Chicago River

MUSEUM OF CONTEMPORARY ART ★

THE DRAKE HOTEL ●

LE COLONIAL ▼

JOHN HANCOCK CENTER ■

WATER TOWER PLACE ★

CHICAGO WATER TOWER ■

▼ FOX & OBEL

MAGNIFICENT MILE

BILLY GOAT TAVERN ▼

TSUNAMI ▼

NEWBERRY LIBRARY ★

CAFÉ IBERICO ▼

HOWARD ● JOHNSON INN

● OHIO HOUSE MOTEL

PIZZERIA UNO ▼

FRONTERA GRILL & ▼ TOPOLOBAMPO ★

MUSEUM OF BROADCAST COMMUNICATIONS

CHICAGO THEATRE ★

BRETT'S KITCHEN ▼

MERCHANDISE MART ★

© AVALON TRAVEL

0   0.25 mi
0   0.25 km

find souvenir shops, an IMAX theater, and restaurants like the Bubba Gump Shrimp Company. Sightseeing boats also dock here. Oddly enough, not all of it feels commercial. The pier is home to the **Chicago Shakespeare Theatre** and **SOFA Chicago** (Sculpture Objects and Functional Art), an event in the fall at which modern and contemporary artists sell their stuff.

The 150-foot-tall Ferris wheel offers some of the best views of the city and sunsets. The wheel is actually modeled after the first Ferris wheel, which debuted at the World's Fair in 1893 in Chicago. In addition to the Ferris wheel, the pier has a minigolf course, a carousel, and other rides for kids and adults. In the middle of the pier is **Amazing Chicago** (888/893-7300, www.amazingchicago.com, $10), part funhouse, part maze. Take another 15 minutes to walk through the **Smith Museum of Stained Glass Windows** (open when the pier is open, free), also located in the middle of the pier. It spotlights over 100 different stained glass windows, large and small, from traditional devotional glass to modern and Prairie-style stained glass.

Toward the front of the pier is the **Chicago Children's Museum** (312/527-1000, www. chicagochildrensmuseum.org, 10 A.M.–5 P.M. Mon.–Wed. and Fri., 10 A.M.–8 P.M. Thurs. and Sat., $9). Like other children's museums, this one is very hands-on. Kids are invited to explore an art studio, learn about the natural world around them, climb a tree, hunt for dinosaur bones, or fly an airplane. As of this writing, museum backers have proposed a new 100,000-square-foot museum to be built in Daley Bicentennial Plaza, which is on the north end of Grant Park. Check the website for updates on the new museum or to find out about the occasional days and evenings the museum offers free admission.

Crowd-averse travelers, take note: the pier is mobbed in the summertime, day and night. And rightly so: On summer evenings, bands play for free at the far eastern end. You can buy beer and stroll along the pier. A free fireworks show is held offshore Wednesday and Saturday evenings in the summer. To get to the pier, you can walk from Michigan Avenue or take a bus or cab. Just head east on Illinois Street. The pier's summer hours are 10 A.M.–10 P.M. Sunday–Thursday, 10 A.M.–midnight Friday and Saturday. Fall hours are 10 A.M.–9 P.M. Monday–Thursday, 10 A.M.–11 P.M. Friday and Saturday, 10 A.M.–7 P.M. Sunday. Winter hours are 10 A.M.–8 P.M. Monday–Thursday, 10 A.M.–10 P.M. Friday and Saturday, 10 A.M.–7 P.M. Sunday.

Chicago Water Tower and Michigan Avenue

One of the most recognizable landmarks on the city's north side is the old water tower in the 800 block of North Michigan Avenue. The cream-colored castle-like tower was the only structure in the area that survived the 1871 fire. The minipark surrounding it attracts buskers, school groups, and couples waiting for one of the horse-drawn carriages that tend to park nearby. Inside the tower is a city-sponsored gallery that features photographs of Chicago. A few years ago the **Lookingglass Theatre** (821 N. Michigan Ave., 312/337-0665, www.lookingglasstheatre.org)

© CHRISTINE DES GARENNES

the historic Chicago Water Tower

CHICAGO FOR CHEAPSKATES

So not everyone has the dough to check into the Drake, reserve a table at Charlie Trotter's, or buy – not browse – at the Oak Street boutiques. This section is for them.

Free or Reduced Admission: Most major museums have specific days or times where admission is free. The Art Institute, for example, is free on Thursday evenings. For most museums these days tend to change every couple of years, so be sure to check with the museums before setting your trip itinerary. If you don't make it in on a free day, be sure to ask if the museum or attraction offers discounts for students or seniors. Many, including the popular and must-see Field Museum, do.

If you plan on hitting a lot of museums and major tourist destinations (think the Sears Tower and Navy Pier), look into a GO Chicago Card (www.gochicagocard.com), a card that covers general admission to dozens of attractions for one to seven days. Whether or not this is a good deal will depend on what attractions you plan on visiting. Most major sites are included in the program, but if you're someone who can spend an entire morning at the Field Museum and the afternoon at the Art Institute, and not someone who will try to fit in visits to the Field, Shedd Aquarium, Adler Planetarium, Sears Tower, and a ride on the Navy Pier Ferris Wheel all in one day, well, this may not be for you. In other words, it's only a deal if you plan to check off as many sites as possible. CityPass (www.citypass.com) is a similar discount program, but instead of buying a one-day or three-day pass to dozens of attractions, you buy a pass to five attractions and then visit them within a certain time period, such as 10 days.

Entertainment: Half-price theater tickets are available from Hot Tix, run by the League of Chicago Theatres. You can buy tickets online at www.hottix.org or drop by the Chicago Water Works Visitors Information Center (163 E. Pearson St.) or the Chicago Tourism Center (72 E. Randolph St.). Chicago's big city festivals, such as Taste of Chicago, Blues Fest, Jazz Fest, and Venetian Nights, are all free. Other events such as the Chicago Outdoor Film Festival are also free. The Chicago Park District also holds tons of free concerts at its parks throughout the summer.

Lodging: Hotels in Chicago, not surprisingly, are cheaper in months like January and March. The cheapest places to stay, outside of your Aunt Barb and Uncle Terry's house, are hostels. Two hostels to try are the newer J. Ira and Nikki Harris Family Hostel in the Loop or the Arlington House International Hostel in Hyde Park on the south side. In addition to the standard dorm rooms, the Arlington also has private rooms. Both accept guests of all ages.

Tours and Transportation: The city's Chicago Greeter program connects visitors with locals. This means you can explore the city on foot (or by train or bus) for several hours with someone who really knows his or her stuff. The city also runs free trolleys (not to be confused with the privately operated trolley tours) between major attractions such as Museum Campus, Navy Pier, and the Sears Tower. Routes and hours have expanded in recent years (and so has their popularity, especially during the holiday shopping season; expect some lines during those times). As for riding trains, if you plan to ride the Metra to suburbs such as Oak Park or Evanston, buy the $5 weekend pass. Rides are unlimited.

moved into the adjacent and renovated Chicago Water Tower Water Works. Up and down Michigan Avenue from the tower are vertical malls and upscale shops such as Burberry's, Sak's Fifth Avenue, or Tiffany's. (See *Shopping* for more information.)

John Hancock Center

The **Hancock Observatory at John Hancock Center** (875 N. Michigan Ave., 888/875-8439, www.hancockobservatory.com, 9 A.M.–11 P.M. daily, $10) offers views of the city and the lake. The lines here are usually shorter than those at the Sears Tower. The view from the top—1,000 feet high—can span 80 miles. (Unlike the Sears, you can actually go outside at the top.) The annual Hustle up the Hancock, held in February, challenges runners to see how fast they can climb 1,632 stairs, or 94 floors. If you want to take in the sights but don't want to wait in line and pay the admission fee, order drinks or dinner or stop by for brunch at the **Signature Room,** a restaurant and bar on the building's 95th floor. Instead of paying about $10 to visit the observatory room, you can pay a little more than that for a glass of wine and a seat in a cushy lounge.

Museum of Contemporary Art

Shows at the MCA (220 E. Chicago Ave., 312/280-2660, www.mcachicago.org, 10 A.M.–5 P.M. Wed.–Sun., 10 A.M.–8 P.M. Tues., $10, free Tues.) just keep getting more impressive and evocative every year. Open since 1945, the museum, one block east of the water tower, contains paintings, sculpture, photography, and video installations by artists such as Chuck Close, Sol Lewitt, Ann Hamilton, and Andreas Gursky. The museum's store is one of the best places to buy original, functional art such as dinner plates, jewelry, and vases. Another reason to visit: Wolfgang Puck has opened a restaurant and lunch counter here.

Chicago History Museum

Writers and historians may spend hours researching the archives in the Chicago History Museum (1601 N. Clark St., 312/642-4600,

Hancock Observatory

© CHRISTINE DES GARENNES

www.chicagohistory.org, 9:30 A.M.–4:30 P.M. Mon.–Wed. and Fri.–Sat., 9:30 A.M.–8 P.M. Thurs., noon–5 P.M. Sun., $14, free Mon.), but it's also a great spot for visitors. Formerly known as the Chicago Historical Society, a renovated museum reopened in 2006. The new-and-improved museum has impressive rotating and permanent exhibits that highlight items from the museum's collection of 20 million or so artifacts, such as the bed on which Abraham Lincoln died and letters Lincoln penned to his rival Stephen A. Douglas and first-hand military man Ulysses S. Grant. Multimedia exhibits reveal stories about the city's many diverse neighborhoods. (Spend some time here before venturing out to places like Devon Avenue, Little Italy, or Chinatown.) Exhibits also show off items such as jerseys worn by baseball player Ernie Banks and basketball star Michael Jordan. The museum staff has covered everything from the rise of the Chicago suburbs to the rise of the band Chicago. There's also a children's area. In addition, the museum sponsors numerous walking, bus, or boat tours and

© CHRISTINE DES GARENNES

Museum of Contemporary Art

seminars throughout the year. Tag along with an expert and visit some of the city's architecturally stunning churches or get the scoop on famous Chicagoans from John Dillinger to George Pullman. The museum's store has vintage photographs and posters for sale, eclectic accessories, and a good book selection for those interested in reading more about the city.

Newberry Library

Bibliophiles will fall in love with the historic Newberry Library (60 W. Walton St., 312/943-9090, www.newberry.org, free). Founded in 1887, it houses 1.5 million books and an impressive map collection. It attracts scholars of Chicago history, Native American history, genealogy, Renaissance studies, and other subjects. The Newberry is a noncirculating library, but you can request a book and take it with you into the reading room, where you can lounge for hours. Don't leave without taking a stroll through the exhibit galleries for a look at the historic maps. Throughout the year you can catch the Newberry Consort chamber ensemble. To visit the library, you'll need

to show identification and fill out a registration form. The lobby and exhibit galleries are open 8:15 A.M.–5:30 P.M. Monday, Friday, and Saturday, and 8:15 A.M.–7:30 P.M. Tuesday–Thursday. Public tours are at 3 P.M. Thursday and at 10:30 A.M. Saturday.

If you're looking for a place to rest your feet or munch on some snacks, head to **Bughouse Square,** a small park (formally called Washington Square Park) across from the library. Before the days of televised debates, politicians and aspiring politicians stumped here.

Merchandise Mart

Another building of note is the hulking Merchandise Mart (Kinzie and Wells Sts., 312/527-4141, www.merchandisemart.com). With 4.2 million square feet of space, the Mart is reportedly the world's largest commercial building. You'll fit right in if you're outfitted in Prada or shopping for pricey designer furniture and home decor items (or are an interior designer yourself). The first and second floors, which contain various boutiques, are open to the public. Most of the other floors are showrooms and are open to shoppers accompanied by a designer. With almost 100 acres of space, it's so huge it's worth a look if you're in the neighborhood or if you need to mail some postcards (there's a U.S. Postal Service branch, and the building has its own zip code). For tours of the building, call 312/527-7762.

Museum of Broadcast Communications

Originally in the Chicago Cultural Center, the Museum of Broadcast Communications (State and Kinzie Sts., 312/629-6000, www.museum. tv) is planning a new River North building. The museum will contain tens of thousands of square feet of exhibit space for its collection of antique radios, televisions, and broadcast equipment. The Radio Hall of Fame pays homage to oldies such as Gene Autry and the folks from National Public Radio's *All Things Considered.*

OLD TOWN, LINCOLN PARK, AND LAKEVIEW

It's safe to say most of the city's young professionals live within the neighborhoods immediately north of the Gold Coast. Old Town, as its name implies, has an old-school feel to it. It's from Division Street north to the start of Lincoln Avenue. There are a handful of cafés, neighborhood pubs, florists, and clothing and accessories shops. Lincoln Park and Lakeview have countless restaurants, bars, theaters, parks, boutiques, plus the Old Town School of Folk Music and Wrigley Field.

Lincoln Park

Arguably the best park on the north shore, Lincoln Park is a sprawling public green space that winds along the Lake Michigan coastline from North Avenue to Hollywood Avenue. Once a cemetery containing the graves of people who died of diseases like cholera and smallpox (the bodies were moved to other cemeteries in the late 1800s), the popular park now contains the Lincoln Park Zoo, Conservatory, Theater on the Lake, softball diamonds, soccer fields, beaches, areas for playing chess, and more.

LINCOLN PARK ZOO

Lincoln Park Zoo (2200 N. Cannon Dr., 312/294-4660, www.lpzoo.com, free) is one of the few free zoos in the country. You'll find polar bears, monkeys, gorillas, and elephants here. But to be frank, it doesn't compare to other larger zoos such as the San Diego Zoo. (Some of the small cages don't exactly look comfortable for the animals.) But it's good for a walk through, and if you're traveling with kids, they should enjoy the Farm-in-a-Zoo. The place is definitely kid-friendly. Treat the tykes to a minitrain ride, a spin on the carousel, or a trip around the pond on a paddle boat. In fact, a summer day with children in Chicago should include a trip through the zoo. Cafés and concession stands sell plenty of fare like ice cream and hot dogs. And the area surrounding the zoo has plenty of green space for picnicking, throwing the Frisbee around, sunning, and napping. It's also a short walk to the beach or west to restaurants in the Lincoln Park neighborhood. In the winter, the zoo produces ZooLights, a fantastic light display. Buildings and trees are draped with gazillions of twinkling lights. A drive through ZooLights is also free. The Lincoln Park Zoo grounds are open 9 A.M.–6 P.M. daily. The buildings and the farm are open 10 A.M.–5 P.M. weekdays and 10 A.M.–7 P.M. weekends Memorial Day–Labor Day. Buildings close at 4:30 P.M., grounds at 5 P.M. November 1–March 31.

Near the main entrance to the Lincoln Park Zoo, you'll find the **Lincoln Park Cultural Center** (2045 N. Lincoln Park W., 312/742-7726, www.chicagoparkdistrict.com). The park district hosts numerous free concerts throughout the year at sites around the city, and this building often hosts evening musical performances (along with other park district activities). If you're looking for good cheap entertainment, drop by and pick up a copy of the events listings while you're in town or check the online calendar.

NOTEBAERT NATURE MUSEUM

Open since 1999, the Peggy Notebaert Nature Museum (2430 N. Cannon Dr., 773/755-5100,

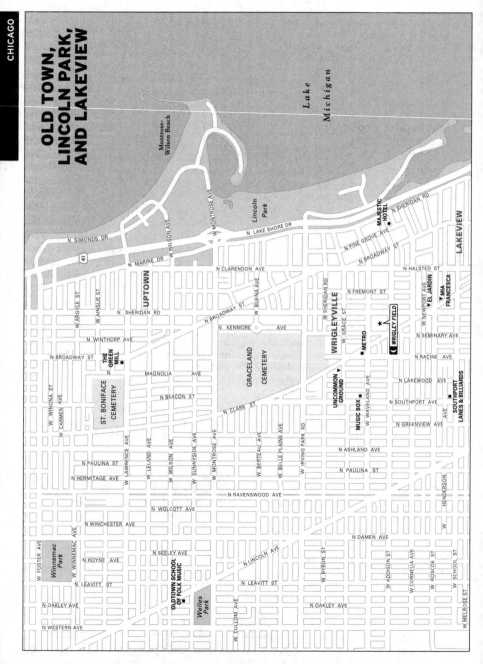

OLD TOWN, LINCOLN PARK, AND LAKEVIEW

Lake Michigan

Montrose-Wilson Beach

Lincoln Park

MAJESTIC HOTEL

LAKEVIEW

N SIMONDS DR

41

N MARINE DR

N WILSON AVE

W MONTROSE AVE

W WILSON AVE

W LAKE SHORE DR

N LAKE SHORE DR

N PINE GROVE AVE

N SHERIDAN RD

N BROADWAY ST

N CLARENDON AVE

N HALSTED ST

UPTOWN

N ARGYLE ST

W AINSLIE ST

N SHERIDAN RD

N BROADWAY ST

W BUENA AVE

N FREMONT ST

N NEWPORT AVE ▼ EL JARDIN

▼ MIA FRANCESCA

W SHERIDAN RD

WRIGLEYVILLE

W GRACE ST

W SCHOOL ST

N SEMINARY AVE

N WINTHORP AVE

N KENMORE   AVE

★ ■ WRIGLEY FIELD

■ METRO

N RACINE AVE

W WINONA ST

N BROADWAY ST

THE GREEN MILL ■

MAGNOLIA   AVE

GRACELAND CEMETERY

UNCOMMON GROUND ▼

N LAKEWOOD AVE

SOUTHPORT LANES & BILLIARDS ■

ST. BONIFACE CEMETERY

N BEACON ST

MUSIC BOX ■

W WAVELAND AVE

N SOUTHPORT AVE

W CARMEN   AVE

N CLARK ST

MUSIC BOX ■

N GREENVIEW AVE

N LAWRENCE AVE

N LELAND AVE

N WILSON AVE

N SUNNYSIDE AVE

N MONTROSE AVE

W BERTEAU AVE

W BELLE PLAINE AVE

W IRVING PARK RD

N PAULINA ST

N HERMITAGE AVE

N ASHLAND AVE

N PAULINA ST

N RAVENSWOOD AVE

N WOLCOTT AVE

HENDERSON

W

N WINCHESTER AVE

N DAMEN AVE

W FOSTER AVE

Winnemac Park

W WINNEMAC AVE

N HOYNE   AVE

N SEELEY AVE

N LINCOLN AVE

W BYRON ST

W ADDISON ST

W CORNELIA ST

W ROSCOE ST

W SCHOOL ST

N LEAVITT ST

OLDTOWN SCHOOL OF FOLK MUSIC ■

N LEAVITT ST

Welles Park

W CORNELIA AVE

N OAKLEY AVE

W CULLOM AVE

N OAKLEY AVE

N WESTERN AVE

W MELROSE ST

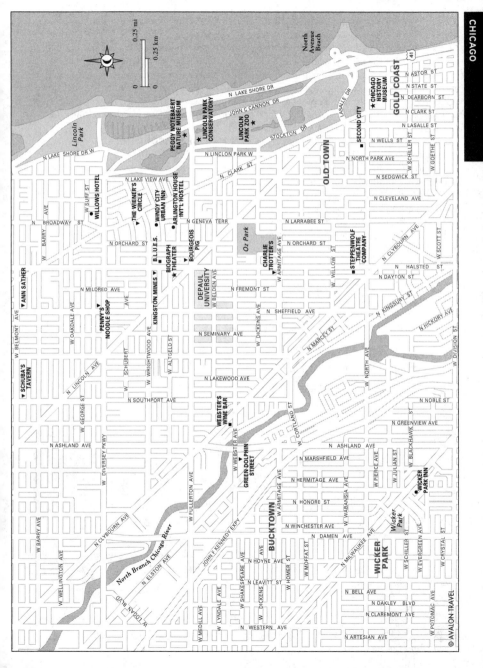

www.naturemuseum.org, 9 A.M.–4:30 P.M. Mon.–Fri., 10 A.M.–5 P.M. Sat.–Sun., $9, free Thurs.) in Lincoln Park promotes green living and awareness of the natural world. The building, some of it made with solar panels, contains exhibits on composting, high-speed rail, and water conservation. It also houses excellent visiting exhibits, one of which focused on primatologist Jane Goodall's research. Permanent exhibits are on prairies, wetlands, and rivers, and the animals and wildlife that live in them. The "butterfly haven" exhibit is a greenhouse stocked with hundreds of butterflies from as close as within Illinois and as far as Africa and South America. This exhibit doesn't just show you how pretty and delicate these creatures are; it also informs visitors about their involvement in the pollination process as well as what goes on during metamorphosis.

LINCOLN PARK CONSERVATORY
Lincoln Park Conservatory (2391 N. Stockton Dr., 312/742-7736, www.chicagoparkdistrict. com, 9 A.M.–5 P.M. daily, free), built in 1891, is right out of the Victorian age. The conservatory is a good place to take a break from touring; it's always peaceful here. The glass and iron building contains several different rooms that feature different types of plants: palms, ferns, and orchids. A show house is home to annual flower shows, such as the winter azalea and model train show, which are worth checking out.

North of Lincoln Park
🄲 WRIGLEY FIELD
To get a feel for what Chicagoans are like, spend an afternoon within the "Friendly Confines," Wrigley Field (1060 W. Addison St., 800/843-2827, www.cubs.com). Take in the lake air, view the city's rooftops, and listen to a guest sing "Take Me out to the Ball Game."

GRACELAND CEMETERY
Many of the city's elite are buried within Graceland Cemetery (4001 N. Clark St., 773/525-1105, www.gracelandcemetery.org, gates open 8 A.M.–4:30 P.M. daily, free), a quiet oasis just northwest of Wrigley Field. The

Lincoln Park Conservatory

© CHRISTINE DES GARENNES

© CHRISTINE DES GARENNES

Lorado Taft's *Eternal Silence* statue at Graceland Cemetery

cemetery, which dates back to 1860, is the final resting place of famous Chicagoans like retailer Marshall Field, railroad scion George Pullman, meatpacker Phillip Armour, and reaper inventor Cyrus McCormick. Architects Daniel Burnham (who is buried on a little island in the cemetery), Louis Sullivan, and Ludwig Mies van der Rohe are also buried here. It's a lush place in the spring and summer with ivy-covered chapels and mausoleums, a pond with plenty of ducks, and lots of winding paths.

The many mausoleums and tombs, representing Egyptian, Grecian, beaux arts, and Prairie-style designs, are all quite impressive because of their sheer size and the decoration. Don't miss artist Lorado Taft's *Eternal Silence,* a bronze sculpture of a cloaked figure at Dexter Graves's burial site. (It's especially eerie in the winter.) The Chicago Architecture Foundation, Chicago History Museum, and Chicago Cultural Center all offer guided tours of the cemetery throughout the year. Otherwise, tours are on your own. Historical maps are available from the cemetery office for $5.

ANDERSONVILLE

The **Swedish American Museum Center** (5211 N. Clark St., 773/728-8111, www.samac. org, 10 A.M.–4 P.M. Tues.–Fri., 11 A.M.–4 P.M. Sat.–Sun., $4) is a little museum in the heart of Andersonville filled with photos of the area that show how the area has changed throughout the decades, along with arts and crafts by Scandinavian artists. The third floor is dedicated to the Children's Museum of Immigration and contains items such as a model of a Viking ship, a log cabin, and a steamer ship.

UPTOWN

Another diverse neighborhood in the far north is Uptown, sometimes called "Chicago's United Nations." Walk or drive along Devon Avenue and you'll come across Jewish butcher shops and fabric stores selling material for saris. Free weekly events and changing exhibits on Native American culture and history are always on tap at the **American Indian Center** (1630 W. Wilson Ave., 773/275-5871, www.aic-chicago. org, 9 A.M.–5 P.M. Mon.–Fri.).

THE WEST AND SOUTH SIDES
West Side
GREEK TOWN

Clustered around Halsted Street and Jackson Boulevard, the small West Loop neighborhood of Greek Town thrives with cafés, gyro stands, and restaurants. You can spend a day sampling Mediterranean fare with all the restaurants packed into this area. Two of the best places to sample affordable Mediterranean fare and hear Greek being spoken is at the **Pan Hellenic Pastry Shop** or **Artopolis,** where you can nibble on sesame cookies and indulge in strong coffee. Both are in the 300 block of South Halsted Street.

DIVISION STREET RUSSIAN AND TURKISH BATHHOUSE

You can hear a number of foreign languages being spoken in the Old World–style Division Street Russian and Turkish Bathhouse (1916 W. Division St., 773/384-9671). Lounge around here and you might run into Mike Ditka or Jesse Jackson. Take your pick from hot and cold baths, showers, and massage areas. Men and women are welcome but are separated into their own areas.

HARPO STUDIOS

Famed and beloved media personality Oprah Winfrey once hosted a morning television talk show in Chicago before establishing her own production facility in the West Loop and eventually becoming a household name. Over two decades since moving to Chicago to make it big in television, the big O still produces *The Oprah Winfrey Show* in Harpo Studios (1058 W. Washington Blvd., 312/591-9222, www.oprah.com). Not surprisingly, tickets are tough to come by. You'll have to get through on the studio's audience phone line to make reservations. Taping schedules vary, but the season runs August through November and January through May. You must be at least 18 years old to attend a taping. Last-minute reservations are sometimes available by sending an email from Oprah's website.

NATIONAL MUSEUM OF MEXICAN ART

Many Chicagoans seemed to have first learned about the National Museum of Mexican Art (1852 W. 19th St., 312/738-1503, www.nationalmuseumofmexicanart.org, 10 A.M.–5 P.M. Tues.–Sun., free) during its hugely successful Frida Kahlo and Diego Rivera exhibit back in 2003. But the center, formerly known as the Mexican Fine Arts Center Museum, has been around since the late '80s. In recent years, however, perhaps thanks to its new building and the Kahlo show, it has become quite the destination for visitors and Chicagoans. Located on the city's southwest side in Pilsen, a thriving Hispanic neighborhood, the National Museum of Mexican Art has become the place to see and learn about Mexican culture through visual and performing arts. It has a permanent collection of paintings, photographs, drawings, sculptures, and textiles. And it hosts performances by musicians, readings by writers, and shows films. A gift shop sells arts and crafts by Mexican artists from the United States and Mexico.

© CHRISTINE DES GARENNES

Oprah Winfrey's Harpo Studios

◖ GARFIELD PARK CONSERVATORY

The Garfield Park Conservatory (300 N. Central Park Ave., 312/746-5100, www.gar-field-conservatory.org, 9 A.M.–5 P.M. Fri.–Wed., 9 A.M.–8 P.M. Thurs., free) is a gem within one of Chicago's struggling West Side neighborhoods. The conservatory, along with its weekend market during the summer, is one of the best free outings Chicago offers. Designed by landscape architect Jens Jensen in 1906, the 3.5-acre conservatory (within 184-acre Garfield Park) is listed on the National Register of Historic Places. A total of six enormous greenhouses (their rounded tops are said to evoke the image of haystacks) contain such rare items as a 44-pound seed from the double coconut palm and a cycad, thought to be one of the oldest plant species on earth. These are gorgeous buildings, with vaulted ceilings and even an indoor lagoon in the fern house, filled with gorgeous plants and flowers: palm trees, cinnamon plants, blooming azaleas, and more. Four major flower shows and special exhibits are held here every year. An exhibit showcasing art glass by Dale Chihuly was hugely popular. The conservatory also has a children's garden with touchable plants, a toddler slide, and kid-friendly programs such as scavenger hunts. The **Garfield Market Place** is a weekend market held in the park from late May to late October during which vendors sells glassware, pottery, and produce. It is open 11 A.M.–5 P.M. Sat.–Sun. The conservatory is west of downtown, just off I-290 toward Oak Park.

Prairie Avenue Historic District

© CHRISTINE DES GARENNES

Prairie Avenue Historic District

The Prairie Avenue District, about two miles south of downtown, is where you'll find the oldest house in Chicago, the **Clarke House** (1827 S. Indiana Ave., 312/745-0041, www.clarkehousemuseum.org, tours noon and 2 P.M. Wed.–Sun.) and the **Glessner House Museum** (1800 S. Prairie Ave., 312/326-1480, www.glessnerhouse.org, tours 1 and 3 P.M. Wed.–Sun., $10 for either house, $15 combined ticket, free Wed.). The stately Greek-revival Clarke House was built by Henry and Caroline Clarke in 1836. Since then the sandstone

structure has survived two moves and two fires. The house, renovated in recent years, is surrounded by a quiet, wonderfully tended and gated garden filled with prairie plants. Nearby is the Glessner House, a National Historic Landmark built in 1886 for John and Frances Glessner by Boston architect Henry Hobson Richardson. The style is unadorned English arts and crafts, and the house's presence in a district crowded with elaborate Queen Anne mansions annoyed many neighbors when it was built. Now these two homes are surrounded by posh new mansions built to resemble those built more than a century ago. The Glessner house has quite a collection of decorative arts, specifically ceramics.

While you're in the neighborhood, consider taking a **guided walking tour** of the Prairie Avenue Historic District. The tour center is in the Glessner House's coach house, at the west end of the building at 18th Street. Call the house for tour dates and times.

Jane Addams and Helen Gates Starr founded Hull House in 1889 on the near

West Side of the city. It was at Hull House that Addams fought for immigrant and worker rights. During her lifetime the pacifist won a Nobel Peace Prize, helped found the National Association for the Advancement of Colored People, and helped establish the American Civil Liberties Union. Owned and operated by the University of Illinois at Chicago, the **Jane Addams' Hull House Museum** (800 S. Halsted St., 312/413-5353, 10 A.M.–4 P.M. Thurs.–Fri., noon–4 P.M. Sun., free) consists of two original Hull House buildings (out of 13). They are the Charles J. Hull mansion, the first building Addams used as a health and education center for the neighborhood, and the residents' dining hall. The museum is closed during university breaks.

◖ Hyde Park

On the city's south side, the historic neighborhood of Hyde Park is home to college students, professors, young professionals, and some working-class families. It runs from 60th Street and the Midway Plaisance on the south to Hyde Park Boulevard on the north, between the lakeshore and Washington Park.

THE UNIVERSITY OF CHICAGO

The University of Chicago is in the center of it all, and it's surrounded by bookstores jam-packed with new and used books. Two bookstores to get lost in are **57th Street Books** (1301 E. 57th St., 773/684-1300, 8:30 A.M.–9 P.M. Mon.–Fri., 10 A.M.–6 P.M. Sat., noon–6 P.M. Sun.) and **Seminary Co-op** (5757 S. University Ave., 773/752-4381, 10 A.M.–10 P.M. Mon.–Sat., 10 A.M.–8 P.M. Sun.).

FRANK LLOYD WRIGHT'S ROBIE HOUSE

Another highlight of Hyde Park is Frank Lloyd Wright's Robie House (5757 S. Woodlawn St., 773/834-1847, www.wrightplus.org, $12). Frank Lloyd Wright referred to the house, built in 1909, as "the cornerstone of modern architecture." (He never was a modest fellow; neither was the original owner, Frederick C. Robie, a millionaire bicycle manufacturer.) The

Frank Lloyd Wright's Robie House

Prairie-style home features Wright's trademark low-pitched roofs, balconies, and art glass. (There are 174 art-glass windows and doors.) After the Robie family sold it to the Chicago Theological Seminary in 1926, the mansion was transformed into a dorm. Thanks to the University of Chicago, the National Trust for Historic Preservation, and the Frank Lloyd Wright Foundation, the mansion is undergoing an extensive renovation project begun in 1997. The exterior work has been completed and work has now moved to the inside of the home. Like those given at Wright's home in Oak Park, tours here are comprehensive and given by knowledgeable guides. They can last about an hour, but you'll leave the house well-versed in Prairie-style architecture and you'll be able to identify Wright's trademark style. If you can, buy your tickets in advance, as the museum limits the number of people allowed in each tour. Visitors have a few different tour options, including interior only, the neighborhood, and combo tours. Tours start every 30 minutes 11 A.M.–3 P.M. Saturday and Sunday, and at 11 A.M., 1 P.M., and 3 P.M. weekdays.

MUSEUMS
Affordable and informative, the **DuSable Museum of African-American History** (740 E. 56th Pl., 773/947-0600, www.dusablemuseum .org, 10 A.M.–5 P.M. Mon.–Sat., noon–5 P.M. Sun., June–Jan., $3, free Sun.) has friendly staff and well-done exhibits. Here you can learn about subjects such as the late Harold Washington, the city's first (and so far only) black mayor, and blacks in aviation, such as the Tuskegee Airmen. Rotating exhibits can feature notable African-Americans such as chemist Percy Julian or notable events such as the Montgomery, Alabama, bus boycott. Movies and lectures are also held throughout the year. DuSable is one of the few remaining museums in Chicago that doesn't cost double-digit entrance fees.

The **Museum of Science and Industry** (57th St. and Lake Shore Dr., 773/684-1414 or 800/468-6674, www.msichicago.org, 9:30 A.M.–4 P.M. Mon.–Sat., 11 A.M.–4 P.M. Sun., $13, Omnimax tickets extra, occasional

free days throughout the year) boasts some fairly significant and large mechanical equipment from history. Exhibits include the sleek 1934 Pioneer Zephyr, a high-speed streamliner; a Boeing 727, where you can check out the fuselage and engine; a working coal mine shaft elevator; the *Aurora 7* Mercury spacecraft, one of the first manned spacecraft to orbit the Earth; and a German U-505 submarine captured in 1944. In the spring of 2005 the museum reopened the exhibit after spending millions on restoring the U-boat and putting together an elaborate multimedia display. In addition to the science exhibits and artifacts, the museum has an Omnimax theater.

Pullman
Historic preservation buffs will fall in love with the buildings within the **Pullman National Historic Landmark District** on the city's far south side. Start your visit to the district by touring the **Historic Pullman Foundation Visitor Center** (112th St. and Cottage Grove Ave., 773/785-8181, www.pullmanil. org, 11 A.M.–3 P.M. Tues.–Sun.) Tours are at 12:30 P.M. and 1:30 P.M. on the first Sunday of each month May–October.

Pullman was established as a town in 1880 by railroad car executive George M. Pullman and annexed to Chicago in 1889. It was the first planned community in the United States, owned by stockholders and managed by the Pullman Land Association. It was here that most of Pullman's workers lived and worked. Pullman envisioned it to be an idyllic model community. There were flower gardens and open-air markets. But things didn't turn out as well as he planned. After Pullman laid off part of his workforce, cut back hours, and refused to lower rents on his workers' homes, employees went on strike. After troops marched in to quell the strikers, the town was eventually annexed into the city and the homes sold to their tenants.

In all, there are about 1,000 properties in the Pullman National Historic Landmark District. Some have been renovated and others are in need of a visit from the guys from the

PBS show *This Old House*. There's the grand and ornate Hotel Florence, which is being renovated; Market Hall, where the produce markets were originally held; stables; and executive homes. A standout is the Romanesque Greenstone Church, made of green serpentine stone and unlike any other found in Chicago. Annual tours include the Pullman House Tour in October and the Christmas Candlelight House Walk.

Entertainment and Events

PERFORMING ARTS
Live Theater and Music Venues

The Loop theater district has had its ups and downs throughout the years. It was the place for entertainment in the 1920s, languished a bit in the 1980s, and has become a vibrant spot in the late 1990s and the 21st century after several theaters were renovated. The showy 1921 **Chicago Theatre** (175 N. State St., 312/462-6363, www.thechicagotheatre.com), most noticeable for its glittering marquee and vertical CHICAGO sign, is a former movie palace. Its lobby was supposedly modeled after a chapel

Chicago Theatre, in the Loop theater district

in the Palace of Versailles, and a grand staircase was built to resemble the one in Palais Garnier, the Grand Opera House in Paris. The Chicago Theatre tends to host music concerts, musicals, and some comedians. Musicians including John Prine and Michael McDonald have taken the stage here. The modern yet classical **Goodman Theatre** (170 N. Dearborn St., 312/443-3800, www.goodman-theatre.org) has presented plays by August Wilson and Mary Zimmerman. The **Ford Center for the Performing Arts** (24 W. Randolph St., 312/855-9400, www.broadwayinchicago.com), formerly known as the Oriental, and the 1906 **LaSalle Bank Theatre** (22 W. Monroe St., 312/977-1700, www.broadwayinchicago.com), formerly known as the Shubert, present Broadway shows such as *Thoroughly Modern Millie* and Monty Python's *Spamalot* in gilded venues where Orpheum stars like Harry Houdini and Jack Benny performed. The nearby **Cadillac Palace Theatre** (151 W. Randolph St., 312/986-5853, www.broadwayinchicago.com) is another ornate French-inspired theater from the 1920s. It also shows Broadway productions.

Another rich and stunning venue is the Louis Sullivan–designed **Auditorium Theatre** (50 E. Congress Pkwy., 312/922-2110, www.auditoriumtheatre.org) in the south Loop. A young Frank Lloyd Wright worked on the project when he was employed by Sullivan. The Auditorium has had dancers with the Joffrey Ballet cross its stage as well as singers such as Erykah Badu.

Lookingglass Theatre (821 N. Michigan Ave., 312/337-0665, www.lookingglasstheatre.org) moved into the renovated Chicago

Water Tower Water Works space, an $8 million structure. Cofounded by *Friends* star David Schwimmer, Lookingglass has developed a loyal local following for its cutting-edge thoughtful plays.

In addition to the theaters in the Loop, there are a number of award-winning theaters around town. Featuring ensemble members such as John Malkovich and Gary Sinise, the **Steppenwolf Theatre** (1650 N. Halsted St., 312/355-1650, www.steppenwolf.org) stages productions such as *Hedda Gabler* and *A Streetcar Named Desire.*

Expect swift biting comedy at the **Neo-Futurarium** (5139 N. Ashland Ave., 773/275-5255, www.neofuturists.org) on the north side of the city.

Originally started by a group of University of Chicago students in 1955, the improv comedy theater **Second City** (1608 and 1616 N. Wells St., 312/337-3992, www.secondcity.com) has become a Chicago institution. It has helped launch the careers of comedians such as Jerry Stiller and the late Chris Farley. Skits involve some audience participation, are usually related to current events, and the troupe members almost always poke fun at the country's current president.

Like other major cities, Chicago has dozens of other theaters, from the storefront variety like Prop Thtr, to larger ones such as DePaul University's Merle Reskin Theatre. Here's a sampling of other theaters you might want to check out while in town: Apollo Theatre, Athenaeum, Bailiwick Repertory, Chicago Shakespeare Theatre Company, Royal George, and Stage Left. The University of Chicago, University of Illinois at Chicago, and Columbia College also have theater departments that produce plays during the year. For current theater listings, pick up a copy of the free weekly paper *Chicago Reader.*

Rising on the west end of the Loop near the Chicago Mercantile Exchange and other financial centers is the massive Civic Opera House, home of **Lyric Opera of Chicago** (20 N. Wacker Dr., 312/332-2244, wwww.lyricopera.org), where great operatic performers have taken the stage and symphonies and musicals

have been presented to its adoring (and almost always well-dressed) audience.

Not just folk music is on tap at the **Old Town School of Folk Music** (4544 N. Lincoln Ave. and 909 W. Armitage Ave., 773/728-6000, www.oldtownschool.org). Local, national, and international jazz, Latin, and South American musicians stop by for concerts. Dance and music lessons are also offered here. Stop by for a lesson in flamenco dancing or on how to play the banjo.

Dance

Established in 1956, the touring dance company **Joffrey Ballet** (312/902-1500, www.joffrey.com) presents, year after year, cutting-edge classical dance productions at venues throughout the city. The choreography, costume designs, and music scores have the ability to inspire and infuse joy into audiences.

To find out the latest on what the dance world is talking about, look up **Hubbard Street Dance Chicago** (1147 W. Jackson Blvd., 312/850-9744, www.hubbardstreetdance.org). For over three decades, this contemporary dance company has been performing original productions for audiences in Chicago and around the world. The West Loop neighborhood is their new base, but the company performs in venues throughout Chicago.

Movies

A few blocks from Wrigley Field is a lovely old movie theater, the **Music Box** (3733 N. Southport Ave., 773/871-6604, www.musicboxtheatre.com). The 1929 movie palace shows midnight movies, new art-house films, and classic Hollywood movies. Check out the cool ceiling—blue sky with stars and moving clouds.

Resources

Want to attend a show but don't want to pay full price? Visiting town at the last minute? The **League of Chicago Theatres** (312/554-9800, www.chicagoplays.com) offers a limited number of reduced-price tickets on the day of the show. These tickets are sold in person at select locations, such as the Chicago Water Works Visitors

Information Center (163 E. Pearson St.). For more information, visit www.hottix.org.

To find out about upcoming concert performances, contact the **Chicago Fine Arts Hotline** (312/346-3278, www.chicagomusic.org).

EVENTS

The majority of Chicago's free festivals take place in Grant Park and are sponsored by the city. If you're looking for more information about an event, check with **The Mayor's Office of Special Events** (312/744-3370, www.cityofchicago.com). Otherwise, the *Chicago Reader* (11 E. Illinois Ave., 312/828-0350, www.chireader.com), a weekly alternative newspaper, keeps track of happenings. You can pick up a copy at any convenience store, casual restaurant, or café.

Chicago's largest event is probably **Taste of Chicago** (312/744-3370), a snacking extravaganza held around the Fourth of July every year. Dozens and dozens of restaurants and food vendors pitch tents in Grant Park, hocking everything from cheesecake slices and ribs to egg rolls. As people chow down, blues, rock, and country bands perform.

Grant Park also plays host to a wide variety of free musical festivals in the summer. One popular event is **Blues Festival** (312/744-3370), or as some people refer to it, Booze Fest, because the crowds tend to get a little sloppy in the evening. Musicians such as Charlie Musselwhite, Otis Rush, and Bonnie Raitt have taken the stage here. Blues Fest is held in June.

A more subdued atmosphere can be found at the **Grant Park Music Festival** (312/742-4763), where the celebrated Grant Park Orchestra plays for free on various evenings late June–late August in Millennium Park. Other free music events at Grant Park include **Viva Chicago,** a Latin music festival at the end of August, and the **Jazz Festival** in early September.

Also at Grant Park during the summer is the popular **Chicago Outdoor Film Festival** (877/244-2246), which features films such as *It Happened One Night* and *In the Heat of the Night* on a huge screen. Arrive early to stake out a spot on the lawn by Butler Field. Films

the Taste of Chicago food festival in Grant Park

start at sunset and are shown on Tuesday evenings in July and August.

Pilots and parachutists with the U.S. Air Force and other flying groups such as the Blue Angels breeze into town in mid-August for the **Chicago Air and Water Show.** While helicopters and fighter jets zoom through the air there are WaveRunner and wakeboarding demos at the lake. Another spectacular water-related event is **Venetian Night** in July, when boats parade through Monroe Harbor with twinkling white lights.

Inland, the Printers Row District, in the south Loop area, hosts the largest free outdoor book show in the Midwest, the **Printer's Row Book Fair** (on Dearborn St. from Congress Pkwy. to Polk St., 312/222-3986, www.printersrowbookfair.org) in June. There are author readings, book signings, and antiquarian and out-of-print books for sale.

On the north side, Lincoln Square hosts a jolly **Oktoberfest,** with draft beer, fish sandwiches, and oompah bands.

Tons of parades are held throughout the city every year. Some of the best ones are the **Chinese New Year Parade** in January, the **South Side Irish Parade** in March, Little Village's **Mexican Independence Parade** in September, and Andersonville's **St. Lucia Festival of the Lights** in December.

During December, residents and tourists flock to **Christkindlmarket Chicago** (Daley Plaza, Washington, Clark, and Dearborn Sts., open daily from Thanksgiving to a few days before Christmas, www.christkindlmarket.com). Modeled after the outdoor Christmas market in Nuremberg, Germany, Christkindlmarket Chicago is a four-week event at which you can shop for nutcrackers, munch on pretzels, sip dark beer, watch glass-blowing demonstrations, and listen to choirs singing carols.

NIGHTLIFE

Dance clubs come and go in the Windy City, but a select few jazz, blues, and yes, polka clubs have persevered throughout the decades. The places listed below are almost always hopping, especially after midnight, and attract colorful audiences ranging from Northwestern University students to white-haired couples.

Live Music

One of the best late-night spots for music is the intimate **The Green Mill** in Uptown (4802 N. Broadway, 312/878-5552), which hosts regular poetry jams in addition to smooth jazz quartets.

The author's personal favorite is the easy-to-miss **Underground Wonder Bar** (10 E. Walton St., 312/266-7761), literally below street level in the Gold Coast. Cover charges are reasonable (usually less than $10) and the drinks strong. The staff is professional and not there to look good. The Wonder Bar features local and visiting talent, and it's not uncommon for musicians to walk in for impromptu sessions.

Regional bands such as Wilco play for enthusiastic crowds at the **Abbey Pub** (3420 W. Grace St., 773/478-4408, www.abbeypub.com) on the northwest side of the city. The Lambay Island Dining Room next door serves decent Irish fare for lunch and dinner in a surprisingly quiet atmosphere, considering it's next to a bar and small concert venue. The Abbey hosts St. Patrick's Day doings to write home about.

Green Dolphin Street (2200 N. Ashland Ave., 773/395-0066) is part restaurant, part jazz club, with a Latin bent. It's suitable for couples on dates or small groups who want to have conversations while listening to music.

Drinks at **B.L.U.E.S.** (2519 N. Halsted St., 773/528-1012, www.chicagobluesbar.com) tend to be overpriced, but you can't beat the up-close-and-personal atmosphere of these small-stage venues.

If you're in the mood to dance and don't mind the sweaty crowds, **Kingston Mines** (2548 N. Halsted St., 773/477-4646) is the place to go in Lincoln Park to listen to energetic blues.

If you're lucky, Buddy Guy himself will take the stage at his club and soul food restaurant, **Buddy Guy's Legends** (754 S. Wabash Ave., 312/427-0333).

CHICAGO

CHICAGO BLUES

On the stage of a south Loop club, Buddy Guy wails on Lucille, his electric guitar. In a north-side club, Big Time Sarah, in a brilliant red sweat suit, belts out the notes. On the Red Line train a busker entertains riders with the always popular tune "Sweet Home Chicago." Welcome to the Chicago blues scene, with its blend of performers and clubs, where you can hear a little bit of everything, from classic Delta blues to the electrified Chicago version. Name the major blues musicians – Junior Wells, Muddy Waters, Buddy Guy – and just about all of them have lived, recorded, or played in Chicago.

Chicago blues originated during the Great Migration, when Southern blacks moved north beginning in the 1920s in search of better jobs

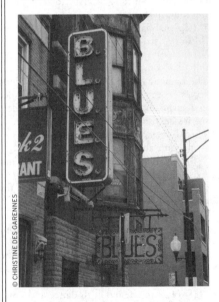

© CHRISTINE DES GARENNES

and opportunities. It came of age in the 1940s and 1950s when musicians from the Missis-sippi Delta region and Southern cities such as Memphis moved to Chicago. They hooked up with other musicians, plugged in their guitars, and added drums, piano, and other instru-ments to the mix. Early musicians performed in clubs along Madison Street and at outdoor markets such as the old Maxwell Street Market. Recording studios, such as Chess and Alligator Records, set up shops here. (Alligator still pro-duces blues music with the likes of Koko Taylor and Luther Allison.) In 1980, John Belushi and Dan Aykroyd introduced a younger generation to the city of the blues with their movie *The Blues Brothers*. Today, Buddy Guy still per-forms occasionally at his club. Regulars like Big Time Sarah draw a loyal crowd. And the Blues Festival is still going strong after more than 20 years: During the huge weekend-long music and food event held in early June, local and national blues artists such as Charlie Mus-selwhite and Bonnie Raitt take the stage. Most of the festival's concerts, which are held in Grant Park, are free.

While in Chicago you can catch a blues show at clubs such as Buddy Guy's Legends, Blue Chicago, Rosa's Lounge, Kingston Mines, or House of Blues. To find out who's playing where and for a more comprehensive listing of clubs, check concert listings in the free week-lies the *Chicago Reader* or *Newcity Chicago* or in the daily newspapers the *Chicago Tribune* and the *Chicago Sun-Times*.

Serious blues aficionados might want to set aside some time to peruse the **Chicago Blues Archives in Harold Washington Library.** The archives contain live recordings of shows from the Chicago scene that date back decades. The library also hosts blues concerts.

The kitschy **Baby Doll Polka Club** (6102 S. Central Ave., 773/582-9706) is always festive. Even if you're not a fan of the accordion, somehow you'll find yourself stomping your way across the packed dance floor.

The Wrigleyville club **Metro** (3730 N. Clark St., 312/549-3604, www.metrochicago.com) showcases up-and-coming alternative and retro bands. The Smashing Pumpkins, the Flaming Lips, the Dandy Warhols, and the Assassins all played here.

The bar and stage at **Double Door** (1572 N. Milwaukee Ave., 773/489-3160, www.double-door.com) are nothing to write home about, but the place tends to book some great bands that you might not otherwise get to see in a small venue. The Rolling Stones stopped by on their 1997 tour.

Both **Schuba's Tavern** (3159 N. Southport Ave., 773/525-2508, www.schubas.com) and the nearby **Southport Lanes and Billiards** (3325 N. Southport Ave., 773/472-6600) were Schlitz Brewery buildings. (Look for the vertical Schlitz signs.) Schuba's attracts a 20- and 30-something crowd for its live rock, alt-rock, alt-country, and sometimes bluesy concerts. Inside Schuba's is the surprisingly good Harmony Grill, which serves solid American and Southern food for lunch and dinner. Southport Lanes is an old-school four-lane bowling alley with real live pin-setters working in the back.

Bars

The subdued **Webster's Wine Bar** (1480 W. Webster, 773/868-0608, www.websterwinebar.com) has more than 400 wines by the bottle and 30 available by the glass. If you're not sure what you like, drop by for one of the tastings throughout the week or order a wine flight. Different wines are featured every month, focusing on a wine region or grape variety. A growing selection of food is available, such as plates of triple-cream Brie or Stilton. A small entrée will cost about $9. Live music every Monday night completes the mood.

Shopping

MAGNIFICENT MILE

The city's largest (and probably best-known) shopping district is the Mag Mile, the stretch of glamorous department stores on Michigan Avenue north of the Chicago River. Most of the stores in this area are national chain stores such as Nieman Marcus and boutiques such as Tiffany and Burberry. The wide sidewalks and extravagant plant and flowerbeds make shopping here easy and pleasant. During the holidays the street gleams with twinkling white lights. If it's February and blustery out, take cover in one of the street's vertical malls, such as the 900 North Michigan Avenue Shops, which is anchored by Bloomingdale's.

Just a few blocks north and west of Michigan Avenue is **Oak Street,** where the überrich shop for clothing and home decor in shops such as Barneys New York and unwind in day spas. See how many limousines or chauffeured town cars you can count.

STATE STREET AND THE LOOP

State Street, "that great street" (as the 1922 song "Chicago" goes) is still pretty great. The landmark **Marshall Field's** building, now **Macy's** (111 N. State St., 312/781-1000, www.visitmacyschicago.com, hours vary by season but are generally 10 A.M.–8 P.M. Mon.–Sat., 11 A.M.–6 P.M. Sun.) has been around since 1868. During the Christmas shopping season it's nearly impossible to walk down the sidewalk because everyone is checking out the store's extravagant window displays. Inside, the atrium is also lavishly decorated, and many shoppers take a break in the fabled Walnut Room, a touristy but decent lunch spot.

You'll find affordable items sold in stores

© CHRISTINE DES GARENNES

Macy's on State Street, in the landmark Marshall Field's building

known as **Jeweler's Row,** where you can often find bargain prices for engagement rings, cuff links, or rare coins.

ARTS, ANTIQUES, AND BOUTIQUES

Treasure hunters can get lost in the maze of antiques stores lining **Belmont Avenue,** west of Clark Street to I-90/94, and along Lincoln Avenue, north of Fullerton Avenue to Irving Park Road.

A number of gift shops, home decor shops, and the independent bookstore Women and Children First are in the northern neighborhood of **Andersonville,** along the 5000 block of North Clark Street.

Retro clothing shops (along with gay-friendly cafés, bars, and salons) dominate the **North Halsted Street** business district from Barry Street to Sheridan Road. More vintage and one-of-a-kind clothing shops are also packed into the West Side neighborhoods of **Bucktown** and **Wicker Park,** around the 1500 block of North Milwaukee Avenue and 2000 block of North Damen Avenue. These areas also have a number of galleries and framing shops. **River North,** from Chicago Avenue south to Illinois Street, has countless photography, home decor, and fine art galleries.

such as Sears along State Street from Lake Street to Jackson Boulevard. The discount chains TJ Maxx and Filene's Basement also have locations along State Street. One block east of State Street is Wabash Avenue, also

Sports and Recreation

PARKS

In addition to the popular Millennium Park, Grant Park, and Lincoln Park, the **Chicago Park District** (312/742-7529, www.chicagoparkdistrict.com) oversees dozens of parks and beaches throughout the city.

◖ Lake Michigan Beaches

On the city's far north side, the family-friendly **Montrose Avenue Beach,** at Montrose Avenue and the lake shore, has sandy beaches, picnic areas, soccer fields, a bathhouse, nature trail, and fishing pier. That blue-and-white ocean liner on **North Avenue Beach** is actually a

beach house where you can change into your swimsuit, buy ice-cream cones, rent volleyballs, or talk to the lifeguards. This beach, east of the zoo, tends to attract the college-age set. Less than a mile south is the chichi **Oak Street Beach,** which really is just another beach. You can travel between all these beaches via bicycle, in-line skates, skateboards, or on foot on the multiuse recreational **Lakefront Trail.**

Columbus and Jackson Parks

Columbus Park (500 S. Central Ave., 312/746-5046) and **Jackson Park** (6401 S. Stony Island Ave., 312/747-6187) may not have

A CITY BY ANY OTHER NAME

"The Windy City." "The Second City." "The City of Big Shoulders." "City on the Make." "My Kind of Town." "Chitown." Chicago has been called many things in the 200 or so years since pioneers started making their way to the southwest corner of Lake Michigan. One of the more common ones is the Windy City moniker. Although it's not unusual for the city to experience gusty days, Chicago does not rank at the top (or even close to the top) of the National Weather Service's list of windy metropolitan areas in the United States. What's behind the nickname? The tireless politicians and promoters who bragged endlessly about how fabulous the city was around the time of the Columbia Exposition in 1893 (which prompted another nickname: "The White City" named for all the white-painted buildings on the fairgrounds).

The second-most-common nickname is "The Second City," the name now used by the leg-endary north side comedy club. Before Los Angeles came into the picture, Chicago was the second-largest city in terms of population, after New York City. It was New York writer A. J. Liebling who popularized the term. Liebling lived in Chicago in 1952 and penned a series of essays for *The New Yorker* magazine about life in the city. Essentially he thumbed his nose at Chicago's residents and their habits, politics, restaurants, theater scene – you name it.

The nicknames "City of Big Shoulders" and "Hog Butcher to the World" were coined by Galesburg, Illinois, native Carl Sandburg in his *Chicago Poems* in 1916. And in the song "My Kind of Town," Frank Sinatra describes Chicago as being full of "people smiling at you." It tugs at his sleeve and is calling him home. It's a town that "won't let you down." I think Blue Eyes said it best.

---

beaches, but they are historic parks worth a visit. Famed architect Jens Jensen designed the West Side Columbus Park in 1912 in full Prairie style with walking paths, waterfalls, and an outdoor stage. Today there are also a golf course, tennis courts, and baseball diamonds. Frederick Olmsted and Calvert Vaux designed the grand South Park in the 1870s, part of which would become Jackson Park. During the 1893 Columbia Exposition some exhibits were held in Jackson Park. When you visit today you'll find a lagoon, bicycle path, baseball diamonds, tennis courts, and a golf course.

Northerly Island

In the middle of the night in March 2003, a crew of workers driving backhoes and other heavy equipment tore up the runway at Miegs Field, a small airstrip on an island east of the Loop. The controversial decision by Mayor Richard M. Daley to close Miegs and disable the runway caused an uproar among pilots and many Chicagoans. Daley wanted the island, site of the 1933 World's Fair, to become a park, and that's just what he did. It's still a work in progress:

The island (it's actually a peninsula) is currently home to some walking trails and a temporary 7,500-seat venue, Charter One Pavilion (www.charteronepavilion.com), that has hosted performances by bands like Chicago and the Doobie Brothers. A prairie restoration is also underway in the park. The park is on South Linn White Drive just south of Adler Planetarium and east of Soldier Field, north of McCormick Place. More information on the park is available at www.chicagoparkdistrict.com.

BIKING

Mayor Richard M. Daley is a big fan of bicycling, and as a result the city has become much more bike-friendly during his tenure, renovating trails, widening bridges, and installing bike racks. For a free map of bicycling trails and lanes, contact the City of Chicago Department of Transportation (312/742-2453, www.cityofchicago.org). The Chicagoland Bicycle Federation (312/427-3325, www.chibikefed.org) also publishes bicycling maps and sponsors rides.

The **Lakefront Trail,** maintained by the park district, runs along the shore of Lake

Michigan past sunbathers, volleyball players, chess players, and anglers. The asphalt-paved path is not used only by bicyclists but also by walkers, joggers, and in-line skaters. The trail is accessible from any major east-west street.

The **North Branch Trail Connection** (708/771-1050, www.fpdcc.com), a partly paved, partly gravel bike path, runs through Cook County Forest Preserve land on the far northwest side of the city and north to the suburbs. This trail is accessible at the corner of Milwaukee and Devon Avenues.

Several city streets have bicycle lanes. A word of caution when riding in the bicycle lane: It is designated for bicycles only, but as you will find, particularly during peak traffic times, cars will speed past others by using the bicycle lane. Biking in this lane does not necessarily mean worry-free biking. Here are some streets with bike lanes: Elston Avenue, which runs diagonally from the far northwest side to the near north end of the city; parts of Southport Avenue south of Belmont Avenue; Lincoln Avenue south of Diversey Parkway; Milwaukee Avenue south of Chicago Avenue; Damen Avenue from Irving Park Road to Summerdale; Wells, Clinton, and Canal streets; South Wabash Avenue from south of the Loop to Chinatown; and along parts of Lawrence Avenue.

You'll also find a smattering of bicycle paths through parks along the Chicago River, such as Horner Park and Legion Park on the city's north side.

Bike Chicago (at North Avenue Beach, Navy Pier, and South Dock, 800/915-2453, www.bikerental.com)and **Bike and Roll** (1600 N. Lake Shore Dr., 773/327-2706, www.bikeandroll.com) rent bicycles and offer tours of the lakefront and the city's neighborhoods.

The Chicago Transit Authority has installed some bike racks on buses serving 63rd Street and North Avenue. Bikes are allowed on the L trains at any time during the weekends and on weekdays during nonpeak hours. For more information about bringing your bike on buses and trains, call 888/YOUR-CTA (888/968-7282) or visit www.transitchicago.com.

GOLF

The Chicago Park District has one 18-hole course, five nine-hole courses, three driving ranges, and a miniature golf course. The 18-hole golf course is on the south side in **Jackson Park** (6401 S. Stony Island Ave., 63rd and Lake Shore Dr., 312/747-2763 or 312/747-6187). Fees range from about $20 to $26 for a weekend round. In addition there are five nine-hole courses: **Columbus Park** (500 S. Central Ave., 312/746-5573 or 312/746-5046), **Marquette Park** (6734 S. Kedzie Ave., 312/747-2761 or 312/747-6469), **South Shore Cultural Center** (7059 S. South Shore Dr., 312/747-2536), **Robert A. Black** (2045 W. Pratt Ave., 312/742-7931 or 312/742-7888) in Warren Park, and **Sydney Marovitz** (3600 N. Recreation Dr., 312/742-7930) along Lake Michigan. Prices for nine-hole courses range from about $17 to $24 for a weekend round.

Driving ranges are at Jackson Park, Marquette Park, and in Lincoln Park at the **Diversey Driving Range and Miniature Golf Course** (141 W. Diversey Pkwy., 312/742-7929). For more information on the park district's golf courses, visit www.cpdgolf.com. You can book tee times online.

CANOEING AND KAYAKING

Yes, people do paddle down the Chicago River. In fact, canoeing the river has grown in popularity in recent years, and it is a different way to see the city. You can rent canoes or kayaks and get tips on canoeing the area from the folks at **Chicagoland Canoe Base** (4019 N. Narragansett, 773/777-1489, www.chicagolandcanoebase.com, 9 A.M.–5 P.M. Mon.–Wed. and Fri.–Sat., 9 A.M.–9 P.M. Thurs.). It'll cost about $40 per day to rent a canoe, more if you need to rent a trailer, clothing, or other accessories. If canoeing along the Chicago River intimidates you, head just north of the city to Skokie and the quiet Skokie lagoons.

ICE-SKATING

During the winter the Chicago Park District maintains a number of outdoor ice-skating rinks. Two popular spots are at **Daley Bicentennial**

Wrigley Field

© CHRISTINE DES GARENNES

Plaza (337 E. Randolph St., 312/742-7650) and **Millennium Park** (55 N. Michigan Ave., 312/742-5222). Depending on the weather conditions, the rinks are open from the end of November to the end of February. Admission is $4 for residents, $5 for nonresidents, except at Millennium Park, where admission is free. Skate rental is available at all parks, and costs $5 at Millennium Park and $4 elsewhere.

SPECTATOR SPORTS
Baseball

The two baseball teams are the **Chicago Cubs** and the **Chicago White Sox.** Most north side residents are fans of the Cubs, and most south-siders adore the Sox. The hottest tickets during the baseball season, which runs April–September, are for the games when these teams play against each other. The Cubs play at **Wrigley Field** (1060 W. Addison St., 800/843-2827, www.cubs.com), which was built in 1914 and is one of the oldest ballparks in the country. Diehard fans tend to sit in the sometimes raucous (but always a good time) bleacher seats. If you can't find tickets at the box office, take a walk on the streets leading up to the stadium on game day and you'll find plenty of scalpers hoping to unload.

The Chicago White Sox play in **U.S. Cellular Field** (333 W. 35th St., 312/831-1769), formerly Comiskey Park, on the south side. Game-day tickets are usually available, although they tend to be in the nosebleed seats. Stick around after a weekend game; the stadium's management often puts on a fireworks show.

Football

The city's professional football team, the **Chicago Bears,** a team that dates back to the 1920s, still has a loyal following. You can catch a game in the renovated **Soldier Field** (3425 E. McFetridge Dr., 312/559-1212, www.chicagobears.com).

Basketball

Chicago Bulls games are still fun, even though stars such as Michael Jordan have been gone for years. The Bulls play at the **United Center** (1901 W. Madison St., 312/455-4000) on the city's West Side.

Hockey

The United Center is also home to the city's professional hockey team, the **Blackhawks** (312/445-4500, www.chicagoblackhawks. com).

If you love hockey but can't find tickets to a Blackhawks game (or can't afford a ticket), try the **Chicago Wolves,** a semiprofessional team that plays in the **Allstate Arena** (6920 N. Mannheim Rd., 800/843-9658, www.chicagowolves.com).

Soccer

The **Chicago Fire,** the city's major league soccer team, is developing a strong fan base. After playing in Soldier Field downtown and in the far west suburb of Naperville, the Fire are now at home in a multimillion-dollar soccer stadium called **Toyota Park** (71st and Harlem Ave., Bridgeview, 888/657-3473, www.chicago-fire.com). It's just outside the city limits in the town of Bridgeview. Tickets start around $12 per person and run up to $45.

Roller Derby

With team names like Hell's Belles and The Fury, who wouldn't want to check out the **Windy City Rollers** (Cicero Stadium, 1909 S. Laramie Ave., www.windycityrollers.com), the city's Roller Derby league for ladies. Imagine girls donning helmets, arty eyeglasses, tattoos, and attitudes skating around a flat track. The season usually runs from the end of January to the end of May.

Accommodations

Rates tend to vary quite a bit, depending on the day and time of year. Chicago tends to be a big convention town, and when these groups (retailers, accountants, farmers) are here, it's tough finding rooms, and when you do, expect to pay top dollar. Hotel rooms usually start around $150 per night. On summer weekends it's not uncommon for hotel rooms at standard national chains (think Best Western, Holiday Inn) in and around the Loop and north neighborhoods to go for $200 or more. In addition to the hotels listed here, you can expect to find most major hoteliers in Chicago, including Hampton Inn, Marriott, Ramada, and so on.

THE LOOP
Under $50

One of the best lodging deals in Chicago, the **❰ J. Ira and Nikki Harris Family Hostel** (24 E. Congress Pkwy., 312/360-0300, www. hichicago.org, $28–34) has single-sex dorm-style 14-bed rooms and four-bed rooms. This clean, hip hostel opened in 2000, although the building dates to the 1800s. The seven-story complex has a kitchen, coffee shop, luggage storage, and a library, and is near a number of L stops and the Amtrak and Greyhound stations. You don't need to be a member of Hostelling International to stay here, but members do receive cheaper rates. Rates are also cheaper if you book a room 30 days in advance. Beds rates depend on whether or not you want to stay in a room with a bathroom in it.

$150-250

If you're planning to spend most of your time at Museum Campus, Grant Park, or the Art Institute and don't want to shell out a lot of money, a good bet is the **Essex Inn** (800 S. Michigan Ave., 312/939-2800 or 800/621-6909, www.essexinn.com, $179–260). You won't get the plush robes, but the rooms are clean and have been updated. It's not a bad option for people who don't plan to hang out in a hotel room.

Along with the Drake, dignitaries often find their way to the **Palmer House Hilton** (17 E. Monroe St., 312/726-7500, $179–260) while in town. The lobby is dazzling at this 1920s hotel, named for developer Palmer Potter. Some complain the rooms are small and outdated, but the location can't be beat. And renovations have

© CHRISTINE DES GARENNES

Palmer House Hilton

million later, it opened as a high-end boutique hotel. The 103 rooms and 19 suites are gorgeous, decorated in muted gold and royal blue colors. Architecture and history buffs will love the place, with its dark mahogany woodwork, mosaics, and marble touches throughout the building. It's a pretty pampering experience to stay here: There's free wine in the evening, and if you've got your dog or cat in tow, the hotel provides pet beds and kitty litter service.

RIVER NORTH AND THE GOLD COAST
$100-150

Chain restaurants such as Planet Hollywood have come and gone, but the **Ohio House Motel** (600 N. LaSalle St., 312/943-6000, www.ohiohousemotel.com, around $100) has become a bit of a landmark in the River North area, with its kitschy white 1950s-style design. No Egyptian cotton sheets here, but if you're looking for a cheap hotel room in a central location, this one delivers. And parking is free.

been underway. At the Palmer House, you're steps from L stops, the Art Institute, and State Street.

Over $250

If you're all about details, try the **W Chicago City Center** (172 W. Adams St., 312/332-1200, www.starwoodhotels.com, around $280), where the rooms have features like cushy robes, pillow-top mattresses, and high-thread-count sheets, and where they don't frown on guests with pets (they'll even provide you with things like litter boxes and scoops). The W City Center is within walking distance of the Sears Tower, Art Institute, and theater district.

Before it was renovated (transformed, really) into the (**Hotel Burnham** (1 W. Washington St., 312/782-1111 or 877/294-9712, www.burnhamhotel.com, $219–285), the building at the corner of Washington and State Streets was known around town as the Reliance Building, a National Historic Landmark designed by Daniel Burnham's firm. In 1999, $28

$150-250

Another neighborhood icon is the **Howard Johnson Inn** (720 N. LaSalle St., 312/664-8100 or 800/446-4656, www.hojo.com, from $170), a genuine motor lodge right smack in the middle of tony River North. This place is a bargain. It's safe, clean, and best of all, there's free parking.

Gold Coast Guest House B&B (113 W. Elm St., 312/337-0361, www.bbchicago.com, $130–230) is an 1873 town home with four guest rooms in the chichi Gold Coast neighborhood. Big, comfy beds await you and allow you to catch up on sleep after a day of touring. Breakfasts are served in a quiet little ivy-laden backyard.

The Flemish House of Chicago (68 E. Cedar St., 312/664-9981, www.chicagobandb. com, $155–225) is in the heart of Gold Coast, steps away from Oak Street Beach and the Oak Street shops. The renovated 1890s building contains four smartly designed studio and three one-bedroom apartments. The owners have decorated the rooms in English arts and crafts style. Rooms feature private baths, kitchens, hardwood floors, and fireplaces. You'll feel part of the neighborhood if you stay here.

If it's views of Lake Michigan you're after, book a room at the **W Chicago Lakeshore** (644 N. Lake Shore Dr., 312/943-9200, www.starwoodhotels.com, $155–225), a stunning contemporary hotel overlooking the lake. Here you're within walking distance to Navy Pier, Water Tower Place, and Michigan Avenue shops. But with its spacious rooms, spa, indoor pool, fitness center, the hotel restaurant Wave, and the glamorous Whiskey Sky rooftop bar, it's possible to spend an entire weekend here in indulge-yourself mode and rarely leave the place.

Over $250

The historic **Drake Hotel** (140 E. Walton Pl., 312/787-2200 or 800/553-7253, www.thedrakehotel.com) is where most celebrities, dignitaries, and royalty (from Bono to Prince Charles) stay when they're in town. It's opulent, and according to some, snooty. If you've got money to throw around, spend it on a lake-view room at the Drake. As with many Chicago hotels, rates can vary widely depending on when you are in town and what type of room you stay in.

One of the best features of the **Four Seasons Hotel** (120 E. Delaware Pl., 312/280-8800 or 800/332-3442, deluxe rooms $250 and up) is the stunning 50-foot indoor pool. People wearing togas strut around, and there is a domed glass ceiling and palm trees. The Four Seasons is a superclean classy joint above the fancy-schmancy 900 North Michigan Avenue shops. It's one of the best bets along the Magnificent Mile.

LINCOLN PARK TO UPTOWN
Under $50

The Arlington House International Hostel (616 W. Arlington Pl., 773/929-5380 or 800/467-8335, www.arlingtonhouse.com, dorm beds $28–33, private rooms $60–80) is within walking distance of Lincoln Park and all the shops and eateries along Lincoln Avenue and Clark Street. The hostel has basic single-sex dorm rooms and some private rooms available for extra. A kitchen is on-site.

On the far north side of the city you'll find **Chicago International Hostel** (6318 N. Winthrop Ave., 773/262-1011, $26) near the colorful Devon Avenue neighborhood and the inner-ring suburb of Evanston. Loyola University of Chicago is also nearby, and the place tends to attract the college set. Private single rooms, dorm-style, and four-bed rooms are available. The hostel has lockers, a laundry room, and a kitchen.

$100-150

Owned by local TV news reporter Andy Shaw and his wife, **Windy City Urban Inn** (607 W. Deming Pl., 773/248-7091, www.chicago-inn.com, $150, suites $225 and up) has five guest rooms in the main house, plus three suites in the coach house (named after Illinois authors). Some suites have whirlpool baths and fireplaces. The 1886 brick home has an enclosed garden and common room with books, television, and a refrigerator. It is a great deal for the neighborhood.

Over $150

Neighborhood Inns of Chicago runs a handful of boutique hotels within residential areas on the city's north shore. Two good options are the 55-room **Willows Hotel** (555 W. Surf St., 773/528-8400 or 800/787-3108, www.cityinns.com, $179–319) and the 52-room ◖ **Majestic Hotel** (528 W. Brompton St., 773/404-3499, www.cityinns.com, $179–319). The Willows is a bright French-style hotel blocks from the lake. The Majestic is an English-style hotel in northern Lakeview, within walking distance of home-decor boutiques, cafés, and intimate neighborhood restaurants. A highlight is tea and cookies served throughout the day.

GREEKTOWN TO AUSTIN
$100-150

The House of Two Urns (1239 N. Greenview Ave., 773/235-1408 or 877/896-8767, www.twourns.com, $109–215) is in the heart of the artsy Wicker Park and Bucktown neighborhoods, surrounded by galleries, restaurants, nightclubs, and boutiques. There are three options here: a one-bedroom room with a fireplace and whirlpool bath, a two-bedroom suite, and a three-bedroom apartment that can sleep up to five adults. A little backyard patio and garden offer respite after a day of traveling.

The Wicker Park Inn (1329 N. Wicker Park Ave., 773/486-2743, www.wickerparkinn.com, $129–189) is another option for staying in hip Wicker Park. The three rooms here are modern, clean, and feature private baths, hardwood floors, and homey touches such as quilts on the beds. It's by the Blue L line.

CHINATOWN TO PULLMAN
$150-250
Wooded Isle Suites (5750 S. Stony Ave., 773/288-5578, www.woodedisle.com, $162–225) consists of 14 apartment units in a courtyard building between the University of Chicago and the Museum of Science and Industry in Hyde Park. Some of the units are studio apartments with Murphy beds and kitchens.

The Benedictine Bed and Breakfast (3111 S. Aberdeen St., 773/927-7424 or 888/539-4261, www.chicagomonk.org, $165–225) is run by the Roman Catholic Monastery of the Holy Cross in Chicago's Bridgeport neighborhood (less than two miles from the Chicago White Sox's Comiskey Park). In Gothic and Renaissance-style buildings, the complex includes a two-bedroom loft with a kitchenette and living room, and a one-bedroom garden apartment.

Over $250
Built in 1870, the **(Wheeler Mansion** (2020 S. Calumet Ave., 312/945-2020, www.wheelermansion.com, $235–365) is a Second Empire–style Chicago landmark. It's south of Chinatown, by McCormick Place in the up-and-coming Prairie Avenue Historic District. For a real treat, check in here, where each one of the 11 rooms is different—some with claw-foot bathtubs, sleigh beds, and floor-to-ceiling windows. In the morning you'll be treated to a heavenly gourmet breakfast with nice touches, such as fresh-squeezed orange juice. Other pluses: a rose garden, bikes for rent, and free parking.

Food

Given Chicago's large number of residents with German and Polish ancestry, it's no surprise that the city's restaurants serve an ample supply of comfort food. There are steak-and-potatoes establishments such as Gene and Georgetti's Italian steakhouse. But because of its diverse population, you can find numerous Asian restaurants, particularly Thai spots, and Latin and South American restaurants. Some places do serve heart-healthy and dieter-friendly dishes, but for the most part, portions are large and butter-laden.

Two quintessential Chicago foods that are certainly not for the dieting type are pizza and hot dogs. A **Chicago-style hot dog** is robust, juicy, and spicy. It's an all-beef wiener placed in a poppy-seed bun and topped with green relish, chopped onions, sliced tomatoes, and serrano peppers. A good place to sample this Chicago favorite is at Superdawg (see listings). **Chicago-style pizza** has thick, dense crust and is incredibly cheesy. You need a fork and a knife to dive into a slice. Even if you've worked up an appetite, don't be surprised if you can eat only 1–2 slices. Here is how Chicago-style pizzas tend to be made, from bottom to top: a sprinkling of cornmeal, followed by pressed dough (lots of it), layers of mozzarella (lots of it), ingredients such as sausage or spinach (lots of it), then tomato sauce. Although always crowded with tourists, Pizzeria Uno serves a pie that never misses the mark.

If you want to sample some of the city's best cuisine, head over to one of Rick Bayless's restaurants, Frontera Grill or Topolobampo, which serve Mexican-American fare; Italian bistro Mia Francesca; Swedish spot Ann Sather for the massive gooey cinnamon rolls; Manny's Coffee Shop and Deli for a turkey club sandwich; and the expensive but outstanding Charlie Trotter's, for innovative cuisine.

THE LOOP, RIVER NORTH, AND THE GOLD COAST
Casual

Manny's Coffee Shop and Deli (1141 S. Jefferson St., 312/939-2855, 5 A.M.–4 P.M. Mon.–Sat., lunch $8) is a clattering, boisterous institution in the South Loop. It's been around for decades serving traditional deli food for breakfast and lunch. Try the corned beef on rye.

Actor John Belushi is credited with making the **Billy Goat Tavern** (430 N. Michigan Ave., 312/222-1525, 7 A.M.–2 A.M. Mon.–Fri., 10 A.M.–3 A.M. Sat., 11 A.M.–2 A.M. Sun., $5) famous when he parodied the owner on a *Saturday Night Live* skit, shouting "cheezborger, cheezborger, no fries, chips!" Decades later, the grill has spawned a handful of other locations around the city. The food isn't spectacular, it's just greasy grill food, but the owners and the crowd (newspaper people, tourists, construction workers) is true blue. The Billy Goat is also the subject of local legend. The story goes that Billy Sianis, the tavern's original owner, and his goat were turned away from Wrigley Field during the 1945 World Series. A rebuffed Sianis cursed the team, saying it wouldn't ever play in the series again. Open for breakfast, lunch, and dinner.

Before they embark on a drive down Route 66, road-trippers often fuel up on pancakes at **Lou Mitchell's Restaurant and Bakery** (625 W. Jackson Blvd., 312/939-3111, 5:30 A.M.–3 P.M. Mon.–Sat., 7 A.M.–3 P.M. Sun.). Some say the place is overrated, but like Manny's, it's a good place to people-watch. They serve free doughnut holes, and you can't beat the omelets and French toast. You'll spend a little less than $10 for breakfast or lunch here.

Breakfast and lunch sandwiches at

Brett's Kitchen (223 W. Superior St., 312/664-6354, 6 A.M.–4 P.M. Mon.–Fri., 8 A.M.–4 P.M. Sat., sandwiches about $5) are so satisfying. Everything is great: the toasted bagels, fried egg sandwiches, veggie pitas, and brownies, which are available only on Fridays. The cooks are always smiling.

Steaks

Chicagoans tend to love or hate **Gene and Georgetti** (500 N. Franklin St., 312/527-3718, 11:30 A.M.–midnight daily, dinner entrées $30), an Italian steakhouse that has been in the River North neighborhood (and within sight of the Brown Line L train) since the 1940s. The clientele tends to be mostly salt-and-pepper–haired men in suits, and the servers usually reflect the clientele. The lunch and dinner menus feature items such as lamb chops and a 32-ounce T-bone. You can usually spot celebs and dignitaries here.

Many Illinois politicians rub elbows at **Gibson's** (1028 N. Rush St., 312/266-8999, www.gibsonssteakhouse.com, entrées $25) during lunch or dinner. (Mayor Daley and Bill Clinton have dined here.) Gibson's is a place to see and be seen, but unlike some other trendy places in Chicago, the restaurant serves mouthwatering food. Come for the scene or the food. Not surprisingly, the menu focuses on red meat, such as porterhouse steaks and London broils. For something "lighter" there are pork chops and wild salmon. Gibson's is open for lunch at 11:30 A.M. Friday, Saturday, and Sunday. Dinner is served 3–11 P.M. Sunday–Saturday.

Asian

The chic sushi restaurant **Tsunami** (1160 N. Dearborn St., 312/642-9911, www.tsunamichicago.com, 5–10 P.M. Sun.–Wed., 5–10:30 P.M. Thurs., 5–11 P.M. Fri.–Sat.) has two levels: a sushi bar and dining room on the first floor and a hip sake bar on the second floor. There are also some tables set up on the sidewalk. The sushi selection (nigiri, maki rolls, etc.) is extensive, and there are some nonseafood entrées such as beef tenderloin and rack of lamb.

Either way, the food's fresh, colorful, and beautifully prepared. Prices can range $2.50–4.50 per nigiri piece, and maki rolls range around $4.50–13.50. Entrées can cost about $18–34.

Le Colonial (937 N. Rush St., 312/255-0088, www.lecolonialchicago.com, lunch 11:30 A.M.–2:30 P.M. daily, dinner 5–11 P.M. Mon.–Wed., 5 P.M.–midnight Thurs.–Sat., 5–10 P.M. Sun.) is a French-Vietnamese restaurant. Diners can nibble away at dishes like ginger-marinated duck, barbecued pork with a lime garlic sauce, or tofu stir-fried with vegetables in a room with slowly circulating ceiling fans, potted banana and palm trees, and shutters on the walls. A bar is on the second floor. Dinner entrées are about $25.

Mexican American

Celebrated chef Rick Bayless and his wife, Deann, run **Ⓒ Frontera Grill** and its upper-end sibling, **Topolobampo** (445 N. Clark St., 312/661-1434, www.fronterakitchens.com). Both feature fresh artistic dishes for lunch and dinner, such as chipotle-glazed scallops, stews, and chilis featuring homemade tortillas and organic ingredients. A dinner entrée at Frontera, the more casual of the two, will cost about $20. A five-course tasting menu at Topolobampo costs around $75. Topolobampo is open for lunch 11:45 A.M.–2 P.M. Tuesday, 11:30 A.M.–2 P.M. Wednesday–Friday. It is open for dinner 5:30–9:30 P.M. Tuesday–Thursday, 5:30–10:30 P.M. Friday and Saturday. Frontera Grill is open for lunch 11:30–2:30 P.M. Tuesday–Friday, for brunch 10:30 A.M.–2:30 P.M. Saturday, and for dinner 5:30–10 P.M. Tuesday, 5–10 P.M. Wednesday–Thursday, 5–11 P.M. Friday and Saturday.

German

A Loop landmark, the **Berghoff** (17 W. Adams St., 312/427-3170, www.berghoff.com, café 11 A.M.–2:30 P.M. Mon.–Fri., $6–15) opened in 1898. A popular lunch and afterwork spot, the Berghoff sold traditional German fare such as sauerbraten and strudel, plus American dishes such as broiled halibut, for over a century. In December 2005, however, the venerable

Berghoff restaurant

restaurant closed after the owner decided to focus on catering. But good news: The café on the lower level remains, and you can still order classic Berghoff meals, like wiener schnitzel and sauerbraten, there. Upstairs, 17/west is the formal restaurant that serves a greater variety of dishes.

Spanish

The sangria is always flowing at **Ⓒ Café Iberico** (739 N. LaSalle St., 312/573-1510, www.cafeiberico.com, 11 A.M.–11 P.M. Mon.–Thurs., 11 A.M.–1:30 A.M. Fri., noon–1:30 A.M. Sat., noon–11:30 P.M. Sun.), a busy tapas restaurant in River North serving lunch and dinner. Little plates of red potatoes, marinated pork loin, or goat cheese range in price $3.75–5.95. If you're in a hurry, try the deli inside the restaurant and pack a picnic lunch to take with you to a park.

Italian

Scoozi (410 W. Huron St., 312/943-5900, www.leye.com, 5:30–9 P.M. Mon.–Thurs.,

5:30–10 P.M. Fri., 5–10 P.M. Sat., 5–9 P.M. Sun., entrées about $12) is a large, fun, sometimes loud Italian restaurant that serves big heaping dishes of pasta for lunch and dinner. Dine in the outdoor seating area if you're in River North sightseeing during lunch time.

Chances are you'll have to wait for a table at either **Pizzeria Uno** (29 E. Ohio St., 312/321-1000, 11:30 A.M.–1 A.M. Mon.–Fri., 11:30 A.M.–2 A.M. Sat., 11:30 A.M.–11:30 P.M. Sun.) or **Pizzeria Due** (619 N. Wabash Ave., 312/943-2400, 11 A.M.–1 A.M. Sun.–Thurs., 11 A.M.–2 A.M. Fri.–Sat.), and you'll have to wait for more than 30 minutes for your Chicago-style pizza to cook. Once you've had your fill (the cooks at these places whip up some heavy-duty pie), you probably won't be able to get up from the table.

Ranalli's (1925 N. Lincoln Ave., 312/642-4700; 24 W. Elm St., 312/440-7000; 337 S. Dearborn St., 312/922-8888; 11 A.M.–2 A.M. Sun.–Fri., 11 A.M.–3 A.M. Sat.) is a popular dining spot, particularly the Lincoln Avenue location because of its huge outdoor patio. Ranalli's serves crunchy thin-crust pizza and has a good beer selection.

Continental

Booth One is where celebs such as Judy Garland and Humphrey Bogart hung out when they dined at **The Pump Room** (in the Omni Ambassador East Hotel, 1301 N. State Pkwy., 312/266-0360, www.pumproom.com, breakfast 6:30–11 A.M. Mon.–Fri., 7–11 A.M. Sat.–Sun., lunch 11 A.M.–2 P.M. Mon.–Sat., dinner 6–10 P.M. daily, brunch 11:30 A.M.–2 P.M. Sun.). The restaurant, lounge, and cigar saloon scream old-school; it has been around since the 1930s. Black-and-white celebrity photographs are plastered throughout the restaurant, and chandeliers dangle from the ceiling. The chefs serve European and Midwestern fare (king salmon, veal porterhouse) and arrange them so artfully on your plate that you're not sure how to begin eating. Dinner entrées are around $30; lunch is half that. The Sunday champagne brunch is about $30.

The **Bin 36** (339 N. Dearborn St., 312/755-9463, www.bin36.com) complex includes a restaurant, café, wine bar, and wine shop. It's a light and airy modern place where you can choose from more than 50 wines by the glass and dine on items such as tuna tartare. Arrive early and have a seat at the cool red and zinc bar. Breakfast, lunch, and dinner are served here daily. A five-course tasting menu is about $40; wine flights are approximately $15.

If you'd like to sample fine French dining, try the early dining menu option at **Kiki's Bistro** (900 N. Franklin, 312/335-5454, www.kikisbistro.com, 11:30 A.M.–2 P.M., 5–9 P.M. Mon.–Thurs., 11:30 A.M.–2 P.M., 5–10 P.M. Fri., 5–10 P.M. Sat.). Founded by a native Frenchman, Kiki's is a beautiful restaurant in the River North neighborhood. With warm touches like hardwood floors and wooden beams on the ceiling, it's a nice setting for a quiet date. And the early dining menu option is a great deal: From 5–6:30 P.M. you can choose an appetizer, entrée, and dessert from a menu for $25. It's a great way to try great French food. Kiki's also has wine flights and cheese platters in the evenings. The regular menu tends to include appetizers like mussels, French onion soup, and duck liver pâté, classic French dishes like coq au vin (chicken cooked in red wine sauce), and desserts like the heavenly chocolate mousse. Dinner entrées are about $17.50–29.

LINCOLN PARK AND LAKEVIEW
Casual

Late at night, Cubs fans pack into ◖ **The Wiener's Circle** (2622 N. Clark St., 773/477-7444, 11 A.M.–4 A.M. daily, $5), where the sassy cooks serve Chicago-style dogs and extra-thick milk shakes. Don't hem and haw when you order, or expect a few expletives shouted your way.

Costello Sandwiches and Sides (2015 W. Roscoe Ave., 773/929-2323, 11 A.M.–9 P.M. Mon.–Sat., 11 A.M.–6 P.M. Sun., lunch or dinner about $8) is crowded for a reason. The sandwiches are big, and there are veggie-friendly pasta dishes.

Stanley's Kitchen and Tap (1970 N. Lincoln Ave., 312/642-0007, 11:30 A.M.–11 P.M. Mon.–Thurs., 11:30 A.M.–midnight Fri.–Sat., 11 A.M.–11 P.M. Sun., brunch 11 A.M.–4 P.M. Sat.–Sun.) serves food just like your mom and grandma used to make in a dining room out of the early 1970s. Stanley's serves fun dishes such as meatloaf and Tater Tots. Another location is on South Race Street.

The best fish and chips in the city are at **Duke of Perth** (2913 N. Clark St., 773/477-1741). Wash down your meal with some top-shelf scotch whiskey.

The mascarpone-stuffed French toast at **Toast** (746 W. Webster Ave., 773/935-5600; 2046 N. Damen Ave., 773/772-5600; 7 A.M.–3 P.M. Mon.–Fri., 8 A.M.–4 P.M. Sat.–Sun.) is just incredible, and the breakfast burritos will tide you over until dinner. You can expect to spend less than $10 on breakfast or lunch at this popular and often-crowded Lincoln Park restaurant.

Southport Grocery and Cafe (3552 N. Southport Ave., 773/665-0100, 8 A.M.–7 P.M. Mon.–Fri., 8 A.M.–5 P.M. Sat., 8 A.M.–3 P.M. Sun.) sells gourmet treats like cupcakes and a few sandwiches like tilapia and unusual items for breakfast and lunch (consider the arugula-tomato omelet; the prosciutto, salami, and fig salad; or something called the "grown-up Pop-Tart made with real berry preserves and mascarpone cheese"). The café is child-friendly: You can order peanut butter and jelly sandwiches or buttered noodles for your little one.

Asian

Penny's Noodle Shop (3400 N. Sheffield Ave., 773/281-8222; 950 W. Diversey Pkwy., 773/281-8448; and 1542 N. Damen Ave., 773/394-0100; 11 A.M.–10 P.M. Tues.–Thurs. and Sun., 11 A.M.–10:30 P.M. Fri.–Sat.) is always bustling, no matter what time of day or day of the week. The dishes—pad thai, spicy basil noodles—are not only yummy and large but affordable. A bowl or plate will cost about $7 for lunch or dinner.

The neighborhood and the building in which you'll find **Arun's** (4156 N. Kedzie Ave., 773/539-1909, 5–10 P.M. Tues.–Sat., 5–9 P.M. Sun.) are pretty unspectacular, but the cuisine, primarily Thai, gets rave reviews by restaurant critics from all around every year. Don't be surprised if you spend about $75 on dinner here.

Ethiopian

At **Ethio Café** (3462 N. Clark St., 773/929-8300, 3–11 P.M. Tues.–Thurs., 3 P.M.–midnight Fri., 1 P.M.–midnight Sat., noon–11 P.M. Sun.), as a live band jams, diners sit together around one large platter and scoop lentil and split pea stew-like concoctions onto *injera* bread (instead of using utensils). Lunch and dinner (about $10) is served on weekends, dinner on weekdays. Nearby are several other Ethiopian restaurants worth trying, including **Mama Desta's Red Sea** (3216 N. Clark St., 773/935-7561).

Mexican

In the shadow of the L tracks and a short walk from Wrigley Field is **El Jardin Cafe** (3401 N. Clark St., 773/935-8133, 4–10 P.M. Mon–Wed., 11 A.M.–10 P.M. Thurs., 11 A.M.–midnight Fri.–Sat., 11 A.M.–9 P.M. Sun., entrées $7–10), a boisterous (particularly on weekends and on Cubs game days) restaurant. Their claim to fame? El Jardin is home to the most "wicked" margaritas in Wrigleyville. They're not kidding: Whether they're served on the rocks or slushed, these margaritas do have some serious punch. Dishes are mostly traditional Mexican meals like carne asada and flautas, and dinners come with the usual side helpings of beans and rice, or potatoes. Groups (and this is a good place to bring the extended family or the troupe of girlfriends) can order family-style portions of fajitas. The restaurant also has a decent selection of vegetarian dishes. If you're in the burbs, El Jardin also has a restaurant at 1831 Tower Drive in Glenview (847/729-9888, www.eljardin-norte.com).

Spanish

Hot and cold Spanish tapas are on the menu at **Café Ba-Ba-Reeba!** (2024 N. Halsted St., 312/935-5000, www.leye.com, noon–10 P.M. Sun.–Thurs., noon–midnight Fri.–Sat., tapas

$2.95–7.95), a festive restaurant with an outdoor patio. Try one of the heaping steaming dishes of paella (rice dishes originally from Valencia, Spain).

Italian

The focus is on Northern Italian cuisine at ▐ **Mia Francesca** (3311 N. Clark St., 773/281-3310, 5–10:30 P.M. Sun.–Thurs., 5–11 P.M. Fri.–Sat., entrées $20). The bruschetta always tastes fresh and the pasta rich. The little courtyard is a great spot on summer evenings.

Unlike Mia Francesca, **Sabatino's** (4441 W. Irving Park Rd., 773/283-8331, 11 A.M.–midnight Mon.–Thurs., 11 A.M.–12:30 A.M. Fri.–Sat., noon–10:30 P.M. Sun., dinner around $10) isn't necessarily a scene with up-and-coming young professionals. It's an old-school Italian restaurant in the Old Irving Park area with the look and feel of a supper club. The dining rooms are a bit cramped, but you can't beat the piano player welcoming you, the crunchy warm bread, and the gracious hosts.

Fine Dining

Housed in a renovated townhouse on well-to-do Armitage Avenue, **Charlie Trotter's** (816 W. Armitage Ave., 773/248-6228, www.charlietrotters.com, 6–10 P.M. Tues.–Thurs., 5:30–10 P.M. Fri.–Sat.) is often called the best restaurant in the city. Trotter and his staff create French and Asian dishes using organic free-range meat and heirloom vegetables. The menu changes all the time, but here's a sampling of what you might dine on: cold smoked sturgeon with citrus crème fraîche or warm soufflé of acorn squash. It's easy to drop more than $100 on dinner here.

For a romantic night out, Chicago couples love to nuzzle in **Geja's Café** (340 W. Armitage Ave., 773/281-9101, 5–10:30 P.M. Mon.–Thurs., 5 P.M.–midnight Fri.–Sat., 4:30–10 P.M. Sun.), an intimate fondue spot near Lincoln Park.

Coffee Shops

Tucked into a residential area within Wrigleyville, ▐ **Uncommon Ground** (1214 W. Grace St., 773/929-3680, 9 A.M.–11 P.M. Sun.–Thurs., 9 A.M.–midnight Fri.–Sat.) is a great spot to visit any time of day. You can drop by in the afternoon for a latte or sip on hot toddies while listening to a jazz band or folk singer in the evening, or dive into an omelet during Sunday brunch.

The only **Julius Meinl Café** (3601 N. Southport Ave., 773/868-1858, www.meinl.com, 6 A.M.–10 P.M. Sun.–Thurs., 6 A.M.–11 P.M. Fri.–Sat.) in the United States is on North Southport Avenue, just by the Brown Line stop. The Austrian café sells its world-renowned coffee here in addition to pastries such as apricot strudel, some sandwiches, and soups. Classical or jazz groups perform for customers on some days.

The homey ▐ **Bourgeois Pig** (738 W. Fullerton Pkwy., 773/883-5282, www.bpigcafe.com, 7 A.M.–10 P.M. Mon.–Sat., 8 A.M.–10 P.M. Sun., $8) is the kind of place where on a rainy day you can pick out some loose-leaf tea, order a pot, have a seat at a well-worn table or couch, and read the paper or write letters back home. A favorite of students from nearby DePaul University or young families from the neighborhood, the Bourgeois Pig sells sandwiches, baked goods, plus a ton of coffees and teas. Indulge in a cup of extra-rich hot chocolate made with steamed milk and Ghirardelli chocolate. They've got stuff like omelets, but the sandwiches (many with names inspired by great works of literature) are out of sight. Some of the towering sandwiches include the Catcher in the Rye (corned beef, cabbage on rye) and the Walden (honey walnut curry chicken salad).

UPTOWN
Casual

Breakfast is just delightful at ▐ **Ann Sather** (5207 N. Clark St., 312/217-6677; 929 W. Belmont Ave., 773/348-2378; and 3416 N. Southport Ave., 773/404-4475; www.annsather.com, $6–10). The cinnamon rolls are enormous, the brownies fresh, the eggs fluffy, and the potatoes done just right.

Blue-haired ladies tend to frequent **Lutz**

© CHRISTINE DES GARENNES

Superdawg, home to Chicago-style hot dogs

Continental Café (2458 W. Montrose Ave., 773/478-7785, www.lutzcafe.com, 11 A.M.–8 P.M. Sun.–Thurs., 11 A.M.–10 P.M. Fri.–Sat., lunch or dinner about $12), which has been open since 1948, for the coffee cakes. But the menu also features crepes, homemade ice cream, goulash soup, and warm sandwiches such as the broiled ham sandwich on rye bread.

As its name implies, the **Fireside** restaurant (5739 N. Ravenswood Ave., 773/561-7433, 10 A.M.–4 A.M. Sun., 11 A.M.–4 A.M. Mon.–Fri., 11 A.M.–5 P.M. Sat., lunch or dinner about $10) boasts a warm hearth for you to sit beside during your meal. Or have a seat on the deck, a great spot during the winter or summer; the roof retracts. The kitchen serves barbecued ribs, burgers, pizza, and pasta.

You can recognize ◖ **Superdawg** (6363 N. Milwaukee Ave., 773/763-0660; 3344 N. Kimball Ave., 773/478-7800 or 773/478-7214; www.superdawg.com, 11 A.M.–1 A.M. Sun.–Thurs., 11 A.M.–2 A.M. Fri.–Sat., $6) by the two giant fiberglass hot dogs dancing on the roof. Superdawg wieners are solid Chicago hot dogs (all-beef dogs topped with green relish,

onions, serrano peppers, and celery salt). The crinkly fries are salty and crunchy.

The first **Fluky's** hot dog stand (6821 N. Western Ave., 773/274-3652; and on the fourth floor of the Shops of Northbridge, 520 N. Michigan Ave.; www.flukys.com) opened on the city's West Side in 1929. The dogs are beefy, salty, and smoky.

Middle Eastern
Reza's (5255 N. Clark St., 773/561-1898; 432 W. Ontario St., 312/664-4500; entrées about $10) serves primarily Persian cuisine, such as kebabs, hummus, and thick creamy yogurt. Whatever dinner you choose, top it off with a cup of Persian tea.

Coffee Shop
Bring a book and slide into a window seat at ◖ **Kopi** (5317 N. Clark St., 773/989-5674, 9 A.M.–11 P.M. Mon.–Thurs., 9 A.M.–midnight Fri.–Sat., 10 A.M.–11 P.M. Sun., $7), where you can watch people, sip great coffee, and nibble on chocolate cake or order a sandwich. Kopi is a place where you can lounge away the afternoon unnoticed.

© CHRISTINE DES GARENNES

Wishbone restaurant

WEST SIDE
American
Wishbone (1001 W. Washington St., 312/829-3597; 3300 N. Lincoln Ave., 773/549-2663; breakfast and lunch 7 A.M.–3 P.M. Mon.–Fri., 8:30 A.M.–2:30 P.M. Sat.–Sun., dinner 5–10 P.M. Tues.–Fri. and Sun., 5–11 P.M. Sat.) is the kind of place some people can visit every day and not grow tired of the food. The corn cakes and crab cakes are superb, the eggs and breakfast burrito fresh and satisfying. There's a reason they call it soul food.

One of the best Sunday brunches in Chicago is at ◖ **Flo** (1434 W. Chicago Ave., 312/243-0477, breakfast 8:30 A.M.–2:30 P.M. Tues.–Fri., brunch 9 A.M.–2:30 P.M. Sat.–Sun., dinner 5:30–10 P.M. Tues.–Thurs., 5:30–11 P.M. Fri.–Sat., $5–15), which cooks up great Southwestern-style food. Try the Southwestern-style breakfast burritos. The chicken and green chili enchiladas are also really tasty.

Crust (2056 W. Division St., 773/235-5511, www.crustchicago.com, 11 A.M.–10 P.M. Sun.–Wed., 11 A.M.–1 P.M. Wed.–Sat., $10–13) is essentially a pizza joint, but the pizza they cook here is not exactly the traditional thick, cheesy, saucy pizza Chicago is known for. Crust creates flatbread pizzas using all organic ingredients and cooks them in a wood-fired oven. Everything is organic here; the restaurant is the Midwest's first certified organic restaurant. And their ingredients on the various flatbreads are something else: fresh-pulled buffalo mozzarella, shaved cremini mushrooms, pea shoots, caraway seeds. The Italian sausage flatbread pizza, for example, is made with wild-boar sausage. Some soups and sandwiches are on the menu too. But go there to try the flatbreads. There's also a patio out back for warm-weather dining.

French
If you're in the mood for innovative French cuisine, head to the West Loop brasserie **Marché** (833 W. Randolph St., 312/226-8399, www.marche-chicago.com, lunch 11:30 A.M.–2 P.M. Mon.–Fri., dinner 5:30–10 P.M. Sun.–Wed., 5:30–11 P.M. Thurs., 5:30 P.M.–midnight Fri.–Sat., entrées $18). The dining room is colorful (umbrellas hang from the ceiling), and so is

the food. Dinner entrées can include monkfish medallions and duck confit strudel.

Greek

Traditional Greek pastries such as *diples* (fried pastry) are baked daily at the **Pan Hellenic Pastry Shop** (322 S. Halsted St., 312/454-1886).

The casual café **Artopolis** (306 S. Halsted St., 312/559-9000, www.artopolischicago.com, 9 A.M.–11 P.M. Mon.–Thurs., 9 A.M.–1 A.M. Fri.–Sat., 10 A.M.–11 P.M. Sun.) is a gathering place for many residents of the area. Sip on a latte in this bustling joint or dine on a Greek sandwich such as *kotosalata:* walnut bread topped with mesclun, chicken salad, pine nuts, and pesto. Wood-fired pizza is also available. Sandwiches, made from fresh wholesome breads baked on-site, cost approximately $7.

If you're traveling with a large party or family, spend the evening at the festive **Greek Islands** (200 S. Halsted St., 312/782-9855, 11 A.M.–midnight Sun.–Thurs., 11 A.M.–1 A.M. Fri.–Sat.). Feast on fresh seafood, lamb, and favorites such as *spanakopita,* which is spinach and feta cheese wrapped in pastry.

Polish

Hearty stick-to-your-ribs food is dished up at the **NorthPoint Café and Grill** (2234 W. North Ave., 773/395-1111, 7:30 A.M.–8:30 P.M. Mon.–Sat., 9:30 A.M.–3 P.M. Sun.), an unpretentious restaurant that serves Polish and (yes) Mexican food, such as pierogi, borscht, and *tortas* that never disappoint.

Culinary School

See what the next Wolfgang Puck is conjuring by dining at one of the dinners presented by the **Kendall College School of Culinary Arts** (900 N. Branch St., 312/752-2328, www.kendall.edu). This notable culinary school trains students who present themed meals (vegetarian, Mexican). These are prix fixe menus with several courses and tend to be meat- and seafood-heavy, with such offerings as lobster risotto and braised lamb shank. Prices are about $20 per person.

SOUTH SIDE
Asian

Bubble teas have made Chinatown's **Joy Yee's Noodle Shop** (2159 S. China Pl., 312/328-0001, www.joyyee.com, 11 A.M.–9:30 P.M. daily) famous. The affordable, youthful pan-Asian restaurant also has spring rolls, noodle dishes such as black mushroom chow mein, and Korean barbecued ribs. Lunch or dinner will cost about $7 per dish.

For great dim sum, try **The Phoenix** (2131 S. Archer Ave., 312/328-0848) in the heart of Chinatown. The restaurant is upstairs, the more casual café downstairs.

The ambience at **Opera** (1301 S. Wabash Ave., 312/461-0161, www.opera-chicago. com, 5–10 P.M. Sun.–Wed., 5–11 P.M. Thurs., 5 P.M.–midnight Fri.–Sat., dinner entrées about $20) is definitely romantic and much like an opera house (imagine lots of silky red drapes throughout the dining rooms). Meals are cooked in Cantonese, Szechuan, Shanghai, and Hunan styles.

Southern

Cajun and Creole fare is on the menu at **Dixie Kitchen and Bait Shop** (5225 S. Harper Ave., 773/363-4943, 11 A.M.–10 P.M. Sun.–Thurs., 11 A.M.–11 P.M. Fri.–Sat.). Try the fried green tomatoes.

Island

Sometimes in the dead of winter when the snow and wind won't stop, Chicagoans need a pickup. In Hyde Park that place is the colorful **Calypso Cafe** (5211 S. Harper Ave., 773/955-0229, www.calypsocafechicago.com, 11 A.M.–10 P.M. Sun.–Thurs., 11 A.M.–11 P.M. Fri.–Sat.), where diners can wile away a dreary evening with mango daiquiris or mojitos. The menu features sandwiches and pastas, but this is a Caribbean joint, so try the jerk chicken or specialty entrées like salmon with tequila sauce.

FOOD MARKETS

If you dig fresh local foods, make a point of visiting the independently run **Green City Market** (south side of Lincoln Park off Clark St., a few blocks north of North Ave., 773/435-0280, www.chicagogreencitymarket.org), where you can find farmers from Illinois and nearby states such as Wisconsin and Indiana selling fresh herbs, cheese, meats, and other goodies. Green City Market Cooking also holds special events and programs, including cooking demonstrations by the city's top chefs. The Green City Market is held 7 A.M.–1:30 P.M. Wednesdays and Saturdays from roughly mid-May to the end of October.

Depending on the location, you can expect to find a variety of other vendors selling flowers, fruits, veggies, and arts and crafts from mid-May or mid-June through early October at locations throughout the city. Downtown on Thursdays you can find **farmers markets** at Daley Plaza (Washington and Dearborn Sts.) and at the Sears Tower (Jackson Blvd. and Wacker Dr.) as well as at a handful of other locations. For a complete listing of farmers markets, contact the Mayor's Office of Special Events (312/744-3370, www.cityofchicago.com).

The site of the original **Maxwell Street Market** has been cleared (not without controversy) for town houses and boutiques, but the tradition of an open-air market continues somewhat on Desplaines Street between Roosevelt Road and Harrison Street, southwest of the Loop. Vendors sell everything from *churros* to zucchini, T-shirts to toasters. The market is held 7 A.M.–3 P.M. Sunday year-round. For more information, contact the Mayor's Office of Special Events (312/744-3370, www.cityofchicago.com).

Warm fresh breads and imported meats and cheeses are on display at **Fox and Obel** (401 E. Illinois St., 312/410-7301), a gourmet food market in River East (from Michigan Ave. to Navy Pier). The shop's café also sells mugs of coffee and glasses of beer and wine.

If you have plans to picnic, you'll find plenty of supplies at **Treasure Island** (3460 N. Broadway, 773/327-3880; 680 N. Lake Shore Dr., 312/664-0400), which stocks food, wine, and beer from around the world.

Information and Services

TOURISM AGENCIES

The **Chicago Convention and Visitors Bureau** manages the tourism hotline 877/CHICAGO (877/244-2246) and the website www.choosechicago.com. Its offices are in McCormick Place (2301 S. Lake Shore Dr.). The city of Chicago also has a tourism office in the Chicago Cultural Center (78 E. Washington St.) and has a helpful guide to visitors on the city's website, www.cityofchicago.org.

You can pick up sightseeing and attraction brochures and free Chicago Transit Authority system maps at the Tourist Information Centers throughout the city: Chicago Water Works (163 E. Pearson Ave.), Chicago Cultural Center (78 E. Washington St.), and the James R. Thompson Center (100 W. Randolph St.).

MEDIA

Two newspapers dominate the Chicago market: the *Chicago Tribune* (www.chicagotribune.com) and the *Chicago Sun-Times* (www.sun-times.com). The *Trib* is a broadsheet that costs $0.75, and the *Sun-Times* is a tabloid-size paper that costs $0.50. Both are fairly conservative in their political views, publish Thursday entertainment sections, and are available at newsstands throughout the city and in L stations, grocery stores, and coffee shops.

The Tribune Company also owns *Chicago* magazine (www.chicagomag.com), a slick monthly magazine that often highlights the best and the worst restaurants, most attractive bachelors and bachelorettes, most successful businesspeople, and other list-driven articles. It is available at grocery stores, drug stores, and convenience marts.

The most comprehensive entertainment and

dining listings are in the weekly alternative paper *The Chicago Reader* (www.chireader.com). The other alternative weekly is the *Newcity Chicago* (www.newcity.com). Both are available at most convenience stores, casual restaurants, and bookstores.

The weekly newspaper *Windy City Times* (www.wctimes.com) focuses its coverage on the city's gay, lesbian, and bisexual population. The newspaper and its website have plenty of listings on the city's gay and gay-friendly restaurants, bars, and nightclubs.

You'll find NBC on channel 5, ABC on channel 7, CBS on channel 2, Fox on channel 32, WGN on channel 9, and WTTW, the Chicago PBS affiliate, on channel 12.

WBEZ 91.5 FM is Chicago Public Radio, WXRT FM 93.5 plays classic and alternative rock, and WFMT 98.7 FM is the classical music station. On the AM dial the *Tribune's* news and talk radio station is WGN 720 AM. You can also get the scoop on local news by listening to WBBM 780 AM.

TOURS
Bus, Biking, and Walking Tours

If you're not comfortable exploring the city on your own, a great option is the free **Chicago Greeter** (877/244-2246, www.chicagogreeter.com) tour-guide service run by the City of Chicago. The program links you with a Chicago native or resident, and together you explore a neighborhood such as Lincoln Park or Chinatown. It is available for solo travelers and groups of up to six people.

For a formal tour of a neighborhood, hop aboard one of the **Chicago Neighborhood Tours** (312/742-1190, www.chgocitytours.com). Run by the Chicago Office of Tourism and Chicago Department of Cultural Affairs, these half-day bus tours highlight local landmarks, restaurants, and shopping enclaves, and focus on specific neighborhoods from Devon Avenue to Pullman. Tours are $25 for adults, $20 for seniors and students. A few select, more comprehensive tours are $50. Tours are by reservation only.

A good way to check out the downtown area on rainy or snowy days is on the free

Loop Tour Train. Docents from the Chicago Architecture Foundation provide stories about the history of the city and the elevated trains. It runs Saturday afternoons May–September. Even though it's free, you'll need a ticket, available at the Chicago Cultural Center (77 East Randolph St., 877/244-2246).

Guides with **Tour Black Chicago** (312/684-9034, www.tourblackchicago.com) will pick you up from one of the major hotels in the Loop and give you the African-American perspective on some of the city's sights.

There aren't that many sites related to Al Capone or mobsters left in Chicago—many buildings have been torn down or extensively remodeled—but the guys with **Untouchable Tours** (312/881-1195, www.gangstertour.com, $24) make a mafia-focused tour of the city a blast. As Italian singers croon on the radio, you'll drive past places such as the site of the St. Valentine's Day Massacre aboard a black-painted school bus. Tours depart from the 600 block of North Clark Street.

Bike rental companies such as **Bike Chicago** and **Bike and Roll** also offer guided tours of the city; see the *Sports and Recreation* section.

Boat Rides

If you're going to take a guided tour of Chicago, take an architecturally focused boat tour with the **Chicago Architecture Foundation** (224 S. Michigan Ave., 312/922-8687, 312/922-3432 for bus tours, www.architecture.org). Its boat tours win rave reviews every year. Boat cruises run April–mid-November. The 1.5-hour narrated river cruises spotlight historical buildings in the Loop, including the Sears Tower and the Wrigley Building, and docents give you the scoop on the city's most famous architects, such as Frank Lloyd Wright, Mies van der Rohe, Louis Sullivan, and others. Cruises cost $23–25.

A number of speedboats and cruise lines docked at Navy Pier and along the Chicago River offer shoreline cruises of Chicago. The best bet is to admire the skyline aboard the *Tall Ship Windy* (Navy Pier, 312/595-5555, www.tallshipwindy.com, $25 for a 1.5-hour cruise, $125 full-day tour), a 150-foot-tall majestic sailboat.

Carriage Rides

To catch a horse-drawn carriage ride, just head north on Michigan Avenue in the Gold Coast neighborhood. Along Michigan several companies offer rides in open-air or closed carriages for about $35–40 for a 30-minute ride. Most companies can also arrange to pick you up at a hotel or drop you off at a restaurant or theater; just call in advance. A carriage ride is a great way to see the Michigan Avenue holiday lights displays during the month of December.

Noble Horse (carriages based at Michigan and Chicago Aves., 312/266-7878, www.noblehorsechicago.com) offers horse-drawn carriage rides as well as live horse shows (such as *The Legend of Sleepy Hollow*) in a historic renovated stable. Tickets for the horse shows begin around $18 and will cost more if you want to include a meal with the show.

Other carriage companies are **Antique Coach** (carriages at Michigan Ave. and Huron St., 773/735-9400, www.antiquecoach-carriage.com) and **J. C. Cutters** (carriages at Chestnut St. and Michigan Ave., 888/664-6014, www.jccutters.com).

Trolleys

Chicago Trolley (www.chicagotrolley.com) offers a variety of different tour options, including a convenient "hop on, hop off" service which allows you to pick up the trolley at an attraction, such as Navy Pier, then take it an hour later to the Sears Tower or the Art Institute. Traditional and theme rides are also offered year-round, such as a holiday lights tour in December and a Haunted Chicago tour in the fall.

If just getting there is the main objective, the City of Chicago offers free trolley rides to and from places like Museum Campus and Millennium Park. These rides are not narrated like those offered by Chicago Trolley, however. (See *Getting Around* for more about the free trolleys).

HOSPITALS

On the West Side is **John H. Stroger Jr. Hospital** (1835 W. Harrison St., 312/633-3000), formerly Cook County Hospital, which opened in 2002 at a price tag of $551 million. The hospital, named after the head of the Cook County board, is the oldest public hospital in the country. It served as the model for the television show *E.R.* The original 1914 building still sits next door. You can reach Stroger Hospital on the Blue Line L's Forest Park branch; the stop is Medical Center.

In the Gold Coast is **Northwestern Memorial Hospital** (251 E. Huron St., 312/926-2000, www.nmh.org). In Lakeview and Lincoln Park there's **Advocate Illinois Masonic Medical Center** (836 W. Wellington Ave., 773/975-1600, www.advocatehealth.com). And on the south side is the **University of Chicago Hospitals** (5841 S. Maryland Ave., 773/702-1000 or 888/824-0200, www.uchospitals.edu). You can reach the university hospital on the Green Line; the stop is Cottage Grove.

POST OFFICES

Most of the major office buildings have U.S. Postal Service offices: the Sears Tower (233 S. Wacker Dr.), John Hancock Building (835 N. Michigan Ave.), and Merchandise Mart (Kinzie and Wells Sts.). In the Gold Coast you'll find an office at 540 North Dearborn Street; in Lincoln Park at 2405 North Sheffield Avenue and also at 2643 North Clark Street.

INTERNET ACCESS

Although a plan to offer free Wi-Fi in downtown Chicago has been scrapped, you'll still find Internet access widely available throughout the city. Most cafés (from chains like Starbucks to independents like Bourgeois Pig) offer wireless Internet access, as do all branches of the Chicago Public Library. You'll also find it available at most hotels and even B&Bs, where it's either free or will cost you an extra $10 or so. And there's also about a dozen FedEx Kinko's shops in and around the Chicago area where you can sit down at one of their computers and, for a fee, check your email account or do other business online.

LIBRARIES

The Chicago Public Library has branches throughout the city, but the main (and coolest) library is the **Harold Washington Library Center** (400 S. State St., 312/747-4876 or 312/747-4300, www.chipublib.org, 9 A.M.–9 P.M. Mon.–Thurs., 9 A.M.–5 P.M. Fri.–Sat., 1–5 P.M.

Sun., free). The huge red building, on the south end of the Loop, has a Winter Garden on the ninth floor. It also hosts events like author readings and art and history exhibits. A tip for Chicago residents: You can check out passes to the city's main attractions, like the Shedd Aquarium, at the library branches.

Getting There

AIR
O'Hare International Airport

Chicago is served by two major airports: O'Hare International and Midway. O'Hare International Airport (773/686-2200, www.ohare.com or www.flychicago.com) is one of the world's busiest airports, located about 19 miles northwest of the city. In 2006 there were 76.5 million passengers who traveled through its terminals. In 2002 the city started acquiring land for a massive redevelopment of O'Hare, including reconfiguring the runways, adding

more highway access and a new terminal, and extending the Blue Line L train. The city also plans to open a new runway, an expanded runway, and a new tower.

To get to the city from O'Hare, catch the Blue Line L train, which operates 24 hours a day, seven days a week. Trains leave about every 10 minutes from the lower level of the main parking garage. To get to the station, you'll have to schlep through the pedestrian tunnels from Terminals 1, 2, and 3 or hop on the Airport Transit System from

neon lights in a corridor of O'Hare International Airport

Terminal 5 to Terminal 3. A one-way ticket costs $1.75.

Parking at O'Hare can be ridiculously expensive—$9–45 per day depending on how close you want to park to the airport and whether or not you choose valet service. The free Airport Transit System shuttles people between the four terminals, long-term parking, and Metra (the suburban train line) station. It operates 24 hours a day. Traveling from Terminal 1 to Lot E (the economy parking lot) takes less than 10 minutes.

Metra's North Central Line (312/222-6777 or 312/836-7000, www.metrarail.com) serves northern Cook and Lake Counties between the northern suburb of Antioch and Union Station in downtown Chicago. You can catch a shuttle from its O'Hare stop to Remote Parking Lot F. A one-way fare between the shuttle stop and downtown costs close to $4. The Chicago Bicycle Federation is working to expand the program. Call Metra for additional information.

All the major rental-car companies have desks at O'Hare. They are on the lower level of the airport near the baggage claim in Terminals 1, 2, and 3. If you are in Terminal 5, head to the lower level, where you can call a rental-car agency on one of the free courtesy telephones stationed throughout.

You can catch a cab (fares run around $35 to the Loop, depending on traffic) from the lower levels of all terminals. If it's rush hour and traffic is backed up on the Kennedy (which is highly likely), expect a higher fare. You can also share a cab to and from downtown from either of the two airports through the **Shared Ride Program.** Up to four people can share a cab for a flat fee. In 2008 those rates were $19 per person from O'Hare, $14 per person from Midway, and $35 between the two airports.

Midway International Airport
Located about 10 miles from downtown on the city's southwest side, Midway (5700 S. Cicero Ave., 773/838-0600, www.flychicago.com) is a hub for economy carriers Southwest Airlines

and ATA. It's smaller than O'Hare, but by no means is it a small airport: 17 million passengers fly through here every year. Two new concourses opened in 2002, as well as a new parking garage.

To get to the city from Midway, take the CTA's Orange Line L train (312/836-7000, www.transitchicago.com), which runs between the airport and the Loop. It's about a 30-minute ride to downtown, and a one-way ticket will cost you $1.75. The first train to downtown departs at 3:55 A.M. and the last train to the city is at 12:55 A.M. Trains run about every 10 minutes during the day, more frequently during rush hours, and a little less often late in the evening or very early in the morning.

You can catch a taxicab into the city on the lower level of the arrivals area by door LL3. Taxi fare to downtown will run about $30 depending on traffic conditions. Most of the major rental-car companies have desks in the lower-level arrivals area. Parking at Midway costs about $14–28 per day. A free shuttle will take you from the economy parking lots to the airport. **Continental Airport Express** (312/454-7800 or 800/654-7871) offers rides to and from Midway and downtown Chicago and some suburbs for $16 per person 6 A.M.–11:30 P.M. Shuttles leave about every 15 minutes from outside door LL3.

If you need to travel between O'Hare and Midway Airports, **Omega** (773/483-6634) and **Coach USA Wisconsin** (877/324-7767) offer bus shuttles. Omega operates 7 A.M.–11:45 P.M. for $17. Coach USA Wisconsin runs 8 A.M.–10 P.M. for $12. Allow about one hour travel time. If you are staying at one of the hotels in the area, inquire about a shuttle; some offer this service.

TRAIN
The vast **Union Station,** at Canal and Madison Streets, is where suburban trains and Amtrak trains come and go. As of January 2004, **Amtrak** (225 S. Canal St., 800/872-7245, www.amtrak.com) had 13 train lines arriving and departing from Chicago, including

the California Zephyr, City of New Orleans, Michigan, Missouri, Southwest Chief, and Empire Builder.

At Union Station you can store your luggage, grab a bite to eat in one of the many fast-food joints, shop for trinkets, and rent a car. Three car-rental companies have offices in Union Station: Hertz (800/654-3131), Budget (800/527-0700), and Enterprise (800/736-8222). Short-term and long-term parking is available. You can catch a cab anywhere outside Union Station. The closest Blue Line stop is at Clinton and Congress Parkway, two blocks south of the station. The Orange, Blue, and Purple Lines are three blocks east at Quincy and Wells Streets.

BUS

The main **Greyhound Bus Terminal** (630 W. Harrison St., 312/408-5800 or 800/229-9424, www.greyhound.com) is in the South Loop and is open 24 hours a day, seven days a week. Greyhound buses also stop at 95th Street and the Dan Ryan Expressway (14 W. 95th St., 312/408-5999) and on the north side at Cumberland Avenue (5800 N. Cumberland Ave., 773/693-2474).

MegaBus (877/462-6342, www.megabus. com) now offers bus rides between Chicago and other Midwest cities like Kansas City, Minneapolis, and Milwaukee. Buses leave and arrive from the east side of Canal Street by Union Station downtown.

Getting Around

PUBLIC TRANSPORTATION

About two million people ride on the buses and trains of the **Chicago Transit Authority** (888/968-7282, www.transitchicago.com) every day. The quickest way around the city is aboard the **L, Chicago's elevated train system,** which consists of eight train lines (some run above ground, some below). All are designated by color: blue, red, purple, green, orange, brown, pink, and yellow. A sign on the front of each train shows its final destination. Stations can be found at all the major attractions and neighborhoods: Wrigley Field, State Street, Old Town, the University of Chicago, as well as in the inner-ring suburbs of Oak Park and Evanston.

Schedules vary per line, but trains generally run every 5–10 minutes. Most lines operate 4 A.M.–1 A.M., seven days a week. There are some exceptions: The Blue Line's Forest Park branch, which travels to and from O'Hare Airport and the western suburb of Forest Park, and the Red Line, which travels from the northern part of Chicago all the way south to 95th Street, operate 24 hours a day, seven days a week. The Yellow Line, a short route from the northern edge of the city to the suburb

of Skokie, does not operate on weekends. One ride costs $1.75 for adults, and a transfer is $0.25. If you spend $10 on a Chicago or

entrance to Red Line subway

© CHRISTINE DES GARENNES

Transit card, you'll receive a 10 percent discount. A one-day pass is $5 and a seven-day pass is $20. You can buy passes at places such as the city's visitors centers, airports, and museums. In recent years the CTA has hinted that it will raise rates again.

The City of Chicago's Department of Transportation (877/244-2246, www.city ofchicago.org) offers **free trolley rides** in the summer and during the winter holidays. The trolleys run between major tourist destinations downtown such as Museum Campus, Navy Pier, and Union Station. Don't confuse these trolleys with paid operators that run sightseeing tours. Schedules change every year.

REGIONAL RAIL AND BUS

To travel to the near and far suburbs, ride on the commuter rail line called **Metra** (312/836-7000, www.metrarail.com), which has 11 lines to six neighboring counties that depart from Ogilvie Transportation Center (Madison and Canal Streets) and Union Station in downtown Chicago, and from Randolph Street Station between Michigan Avenue and Grant Park. Metra allows passengers to bring bicycles aboard some of its train lines at various times

by reservation for an additional $5. Ogilvie Center has a currency exchange, ATMs, luggage storage, and phones.

The suburban bus line is **Pace** (847/364-7223, www.pacebus.com).

TAXIS

There are more than 20 **taxicab companies** in Chicago. You can hail a taxi on the street or call one of the cab companies. Some companies include Yellow Cab (773/907-0020), Jitney Cab (773/548-6391), Checker Taxi Association (312/733-4790), and Chicago Carriage Cab (312/326-2221). Meters start at **$2.25** and then increase for each additional mile. Each additional passenger is $1. A ride to O'Hare from downtown is about $35; to Midway it's around $25. Tipping is optional.

DRIVING

It's fairly easy to navigate the city; it's set up like a grid. But it's one thing to find your way to Point A or Point B, and it's another dealing with traffic and finding or paying for a parking space. For more information on driving and parking in the city, see *Access* under *Planning Your Time.*

THE COLLAR COUNTIES

Like many communities surrounding big cities, Chicago's suburbs sometimes face an image problem. When most people think of suburbs they think of monotonous subdivisions, strip malls, and golf courses. Sure, this region has some of those things, but Chicago's towns are surprisingly diverse places with rare, beautiful landscapes—from Volo Bog in the northwest, where you can stroll along a boardwalk, look for orchids, and listen for herons, to Illinois Beach State Park in the northeast, where you can hike past sand dunes. The inner-ring suburb of Oak Park boasts the nation's largest collection of Frank Lloyd Wright–designed homes, plus an Ernest Hemingway home and museum (he was born here). The far west villages of Geneva, St. Charles, and Batavia are a string of arts and

shopping villages on the Fox River connected by a riverfront trail.

The range of sights and activities in the collar counties is impressive. In the shopping nexus of Schaumburg, there's sprawling Woodfield Mall, but there's also Lynfred Winery, a winery and bed-and-breakfast. There's a lot to see and do other than shop—although that is a big thing to do out here. You can catch a Kane County Cougars game for about $10 or an off-Broadway play at the Metropolis Center in Arlington Heights for about $20, cast a fishing line in a Lake County park, or view a multimedia art installation in Schaumburg.

PLANNING YOUR TIME

There's quite a lot to see and do in the collar counties. You'll need a week to hit all the best

THE COLLAR COUNTIES

HIGHLIGHTS

LOOK FOR ◖ TO FIND RECOMMENDED SIGHTS, ACTIVITIES, DINING, AND LODGING.

◖ **Ernest Hemingway Birthplace and Museum:** In 1899 Hemingway was born in a Victorian home on a tree-lined street in Oak Park. In recent years his birth home was restored and filled with furniture, books, letters, and displays about the writer's early years in the village (page 85).

◖ **Frank Lloyd Wright Home and Studio:** Built in 1889, Wright's renovated home and studio is where the architect launched his Prairie style of design (page 87).

◖ **Brookfield Zoo:** The family-friendly zoo in Chicago's western suburb of Brookfield has constructed several different habitat areas, from Illinois marshes and prairies to African savanna, for hundreds of animals (page 96).

◖ **Grosse Point Lighthouse:** This National Historic Landmark has been standing tall on the north side of Evanston since 1873. Climb the 113-foot-tall tower to take in views of Lake Michigan, stroll through the surrounding gardens, and visit the adjacent art center (page 100).

◖ **Chicago Botanic Garden:** English walled gardens, Japanese gardens, colorful spring bulb displays, vegetable gardens, waterfalls — you name it, the botanic garden (based in Glencoe, not Chicago) has got it. Add to the mix tram rides, walking trails, and indoor and outdoor cafés and you've got a great way to spend a morning or afternoon (page 108).

◖ **Baha'i House of Worship:** Built in 1953, this stunningly beautiful building in Wilmette, near the Lake Michigan shoreline, is the first of its kind in the western hemisphere. Learn about the Baha'i faith or sit back and admire the architecture of the 135-foot-high dome and the surrounding rose gardens (page 108).

◖ **Historic Village of Long Grove:** In an area where most of the land has been developed into sprawling modern mansions or town-house developments, Long Grove is a picture-postcard town complete with a covered bridge, mill pond, and turn-of-the-20th-century buildings home to boutiques and casual restaurants (page 120).

◖ **Morton Arboretum:** Once the estate of a Morton Salt executive, Morton Arboretum in Lisle is one of the best places in Chicago's western suburbs for taking a stroll. Choose among numerous trails through formal rose gardens and woodland trails past vibrant maple and birch trees into tallgrass prairies or along a marsh boardwalk (page 133).

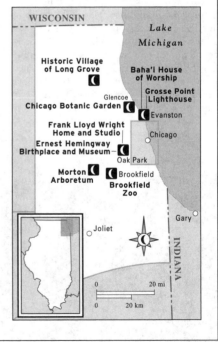

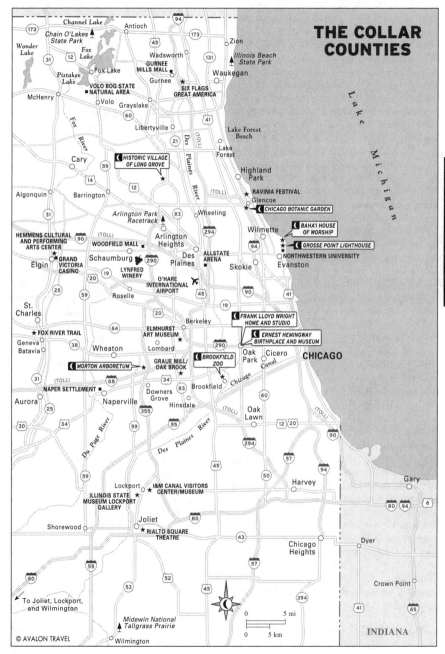

THE COLLAR COUNTIES

spots. If your time is limited to 2–3 days, focus your visit on one geographic area: the north shore, the near west and south, or the far west. If you're staying in Chicago and have a day or two free to explore outside the city limits, head to nearby Oak Park or Evanston. You can pack the north shore into a weekend, including a day in **Evanston** at the **Grosse Point Lighthouse,** lakeshore parks and beaches, downtown shops and restaurants, and a walk through Northwestern University, followed by a day driving north along **Sheridan Road** to the grand **Baha'i House of Worship** in Wilmette, and a walk through the **Chicago Botanic Gardens** in Glencoe. To the near west, don't miss the impressive **Brookfield Zoo** in Brookfield or **Morton Arboretum** in Lisle. To the far west the Fox River towns of **Geneva, St. Charles,** and **Batavia** boast riverside paths and parks, dozens of artisan and antiques shops, galleries, and storefront restaurants.

If you've got shopping on the brain, make tracks to Schaumburg's **Woodfield Mall** and the enormous **Gurnee Mills** in the northwest. While planning your trip, check to see if the towns you plan to visit are on commuter train lines. You can waste a lot of time in traffic if you take the highways, especially in the summer.

Chicagoland covers a large area, roughly 30–40 miles from Chicago's city limits in all directions except east. It stretches north along Lake Michigan into northern Cook County and Lake County, and to the west and south along the Des Plaines, DuPage, and Fox Rivers into DuPage County, and beyond that, Kane County. South of the city the suburbs extend into Will County.

If you plan to spend more than a day in the suburbs, particularly in towns that are within an hour's drive of the city, consider basing your vacation in lively **Oak Park,** which has plenty of attractions for literary and architecture buffs, boutique hotels, affordable top-rated restaurants, and independently owned shops. Also, keep in mind that restaurants in the suburbs tend to close earlier than those in Chicago (around 9–10 P.M.) and most shops (other than malls) keep bankers' hours (9 A.M.–5 P.M. daily). Sunday evenings are pretty quiet out here.

Access

If you plan to explore the inner-ring suburbs, you don't need to drive your car or hire a rental car. Suburbs such as Oak Park, Forest Park, and Evanston are on **Chicago Transit Authority** train lines (888/968-7282, www.yourcta.com), so you could even stay in Chicago and take the L (elevated train) out to these cities for the day. The commuter train line **Metra** (312/836-7000, www.metrarail.com) runs a regular train schedule from downtown Chicago to the inner-ring cities as well as to towns in the collar counties of DuPage, Lake, Kane, and Will. Many of these towns have revitalized downtowns that you can explore right off the train.

If you want to visit sites beyond the downtowns situated along train lines, you will have to take one of the buses run by the suburban bus line **Pace** (847/364-7223, www.pacebus.com). Schedules for Pace buses vary per suburb, day, and time of year. With that said, you might be better off driving your car or renting one. But be warned: Driving through the suburbs will take time. On the map, Elmhurst and Naperville are about 15 miles apart and connected via interstate highway, but make this drive in the morning or early evening and it could easily take you 30 minutes. Sometimes, traffic out here is just as snarly as it is in Chicago. I-290 is notorious for backups, as is I-55 from Chicago to Joliet. The "Hillside Strangler," where I-290, I-294, and I-88 intersect near the west suburban town of Hillside, was reconfigured in recent years to relieve congestion, but drivers still encounter delays there.

Resources

The **Chicago Plus Regional Tourism Development Office** (60 W. Randolph St., Suite 204, Chicago, 312/795-1700, www.chicagolandtravel.com) has information on attractions and accommodations within a 60-minute drive of Chicago, including to Lake County on the north, west to Elgin and St. Charles, and southwest to Joliet and other southern suburbs. It can send you tons of brochures, maps, and itinerary suggestions.

Oak Park, Forest Park, and River Forest

Known for their grand and decorative Victorian homes and Prairie-style mansions, Oak Park and River Forest are picturesque old towns, with streets lined with tall oak and elm trees, busy downtowns along commuter train lines, thriving arts scenes, and great little restaurants. Divided by Harlem Street, which runs north and south, Oak Park and River Forest share a high school and are often referred to together or as one town. Oak Park native Ernest Hemingway supposedly (the quote may be apocryphal) referred to his hometown as the city of "broad lawns and narrow minds." That image was probably true when Hemingway was living there at the turn of the 20th century, when Oak Park was home to many conservatives, but today that statement is pretty far from the truth. Since the 1970s the city has been proactive about maintaining diversity and building a community where all races and sexes can coexist. Forest Park, which borders both towns to the south, is home to more working-class people and smaller homes. It is a bit livelier and less polished than its neighbors to the north. In recent years Forest Park has emerged as a diverse village with colorful and friendly young professionals, families, and older residents who were born and raised there.

SIGHTS

Although they comprise a relatively small area (Oak Park is about 4.5 square miles), the near west suburbs of Oak Park, Forest Park, and River Forest boast quite a few attractions, restaurants, and shops. Together they have become quite the tourist destination. What draws most folks to Oak Park is the village's connection to two famous former residents: novelist and short-story writer Ernest Hemingway, who was born here in 1899, and Frank Lloyd Wright, who built a home and studio in Oak Park in 1889.

◀ Ernest Hemingway Birthplace and Museum

Let's start with Papa Hemingway, whom many residents (lots of whom are writers) adore. To

© CHRISTINE DES GARENNES

THE COLLAR COUNTIES

Ernest Hemingway Birthplace, Oak Park

commemorate his 100th birthday in 1999, local devotees scrounged up lots of money to renovate the **Ernest Hemingway Birthplace** (339 N. Oak Park Ave., Oak Park, 708/848-2222, www.hemingway.org, www.ehfop.org, 1–5 P.M. Sun.–Fri., 10 A.M.–5 P.M. Sat., $8, includes admission to the Hemingway Museum).

The birth home and nearby **Hemingway Museum** (200 N. Oak Park Ave., same hours and admission as the birthplace) are in a historic area of Oak Park, along tree-lined streets and near other Victorian or Prairie-style homes.

Hemingway was born in the home on Oak Park Avenue and lived there with his family until 1905, when they moved to a house on Grove Street, followed by one on North Kenilworth Avenue. He graduated from the nearby Oak Park and River Forest High School in 1916 (it's still standing and producing writers, such as Jane Hamilton). Hemingway left

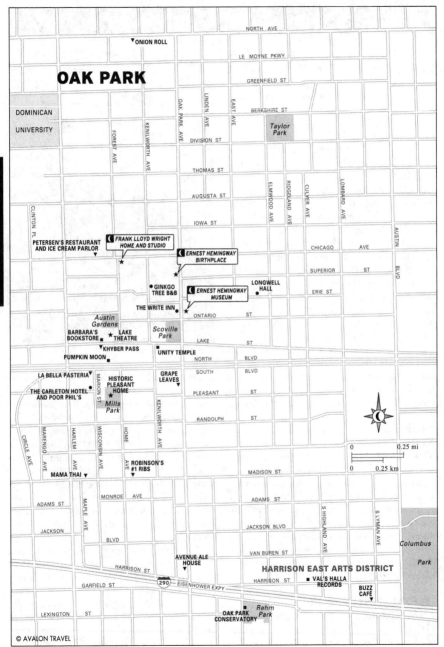

NORTH AVE

▼ ONION ROLL

LE MOYNE PKWY

GREENFIELD ST

OAK PARK

DOMINICAN

UNIVERSITY

BERKSHIRE ST

Taylor Park

OAK PARK AVE

LINDEN AVE

EAST AVE

DIVISION ST

FOREST AVE

KENILWORTH AVE

THOMAS ST

AUGUSTA ST

IOWA ST

ELMWOOD AVE

RIDGELAND AVE

CULVER AVE

LOMBARD AVE

CLINTON PL

PETERSEN'S RESTAURANT AND ICE CREAM PARLOR ▼

★ 🌙 FRANK LLOYD WRIGHT HOME AND STUDIO

🌙 ERNEST HEMINGWAY BIRTHPLACE
★

● GINKGO TREE B&B

🌙 ERNEST HEMINGWAY MUSEUM
★ THE WRITE INN

CHICAGO AVE

LONGWELL HALL ●

SUPERIOR ST

ERIE ST

AUSTIN BLVD

Austin Gardens

BARBARA'S BOOKSTORE ■ ★ LAKE THEATRE

Scoville Park

ONTARIO ST

LAKE ST

▼ KHYBER PASS

PUMPKIN MOON ■

■ UNITY TEMPLE

NORTH BLVD

LA BELLA PASTERIA ▼

THE CARLETON HOTEL AND POOR PHIL'S ●

HISTORIC PLEASANT HOME
★

GRAPE LEAVES ▼

SOUTH BLVD

PLEASANT ST

MARION ST

Mills Park

RANDOLPH ST

MARENGO AVE

HARLEM AVE

WISCONSIN AVE

HOME AVE

KENILWORTH AVE

CIRCLE AVE

MAMA THAI ▼

● ROBINSON'S #1 RIBS

MADISON ST

MONROE AVE

ADAMS ST

ADAMS ST

JACKSON

JACKSON BLVD

MAPLE AVE

BLVD

VAN BUREN ST

S HIGHLAND AVE

S LYMAN AVE

Columbus Park

AVENUE ALE HOUSE ▼

HARRISON EAST ARTS DISTRICT

HARRISON ST

HARRISON ST

■ VAL'S HALLA RECORDS

BUZZ CAFÉ ■

GARFIELD ST

🛣 290 EISENHOWER EXPY

LEXINGTON ST

OAK PARK CONSERVATORY ■

Rehm Park

0   0.25 mi

0   0.25 km

© AVALON TRAVEL

the village in 1919. The birth home is decorated with period furniture from the era when he lived there. (You'll see the nursery that Ernest shared with his sister Marcelline.) Among the items you will see displayed in the house and museuvm are toys donated by Hemingway's sister, a few family pieces such as a vase and rocking chair, Army fatigues, lots of photos and letters, and various editions of his many books.

◖ Frank Lloyd Wright Home and Studio

About five blocks from Hemingway's birthplace is the Frank Lloyd Wright Home and Studio (951 Chicago Ave., Oak Park, 708/848-1976, www.wrightplus.org, guided tours only 11 A.M., 1 P.M., 3 P.M. weekdays, every 20 minutes 11 A.M.–3 P.M. weekends, $12). Like Hemingway's birthplace, Wright's home has been restored. Built in 1889, the home and studio is where Wright crafted Prairie-style architecture, which would become his trademark style. The buildings and the accents

in them, such as the art-glass windows, have been painstakingly and lovingly renovated by Wright devotees.

To see the house, you have to join a guided tour given by docents who know their stuff. Visitors have a couple of different options for touring the place, including guided interior tours but also self-guided audio exterior tours and tours geared toward families. Special tours are also organized throughout the year, such as a beautiful holiday tour in December. Tickets are sold first-come, first-served, and on weekends there are often folks lined up before the first tour of the day. You need to buy your tickets at the Under the Ginkgo Tree Bookshop adjacent to the home and studio (or better yet, buy them online in advance). The bookshop has every product you could possibly imagine related to Wright and the Prairie style. You can even buy a CD-ROM of a Wright-designed font for computers. The bookshop is open 10 A.M.–5 P.M. daily.

Wright's home and the Hemingway birthplace are in the heart of Oak Park, so take some

© CHRISTINE DES GARENNES

Frank Lloyd Wright Home and Studio, Oak Park

THE COLLAR COUNTIES

time to wander through the neighborhood, dubbed the Frank Lloyd Wright Prairie School of Architecture Historic District. Thirteen more Wright-designed homes can be found in the surrounding area. This area is also marked by other impressive homes (one after the other, in fact) of Victorian, Tudor, and Greek-revival styles. Several guided and self-guided walking and bicycling tours are offered throughout the year via the Oak Park Visitors Center and the Wright Home and Studio. You can pick up maps or cassette players at both spots.

Unity Temple

The roof does not look stable and there are cracks in the walls, but Unity Temple (875 Lake St., Oak Park, 708/383-8873, www.unitytemple-utrf.org, 10:30 A.M.–4:30 P.M. Mon.–Fri., 1–4 P.M. Sat.–Sun., Mar.–Nov.; 1–4 P.M. daily Dec.–Feb., $8) is still a must-see for Frank Lloyd Wright aficionados. The architect reportedly said it was with this building that modern architecture was launched (he was never a modest man). Back when it was built in 1908, the cubicle-style building, made with reinforced concrete, was definitely different as far as church designs went. (For a contrast, check out the Gothic St. Edmund Church at 188 South Oak Park Avenue, about a 10-minute walk away). In recent years Unity Temple, a National Historic Landmark, has been undergoing a multimillion-dollar renovation, but you can still visit. If you can't make it for a visit during the hours the temple is open, a good way to see the inside (the highlight is its auditorium) is by attending one of the temple's concerts held on various Saturday evenings October–April.

Historic Pleasant Home

Another example of early Prairie-style architecture can be found in the historic Pleasant Home (217 S. Home Ave., Oak Park, 708/383-2654, www.pleasanthome.org, tours 12:30 P.M., 1:30 P.M., 2:30 P.M. Thurs.–Sun., $5, Fri. is "pay what you can day"), a 30-room mansion designed by George Maher in 1897. The National Historic Landmark features many of

the telltale Prairie-style accents, such as decorative art glass and low-pitched roofs.

The second floor of the mansion is home to the **Historical Society of Oak Park and River Forest** (708/848-6755, call for hours). Rooms pay tribute to all the celebrated people who grew up in Oak Park or lived there at some point in their lives. There's a decent exhibit on Edgar Rice Burroughs, who created Tarzan while living in Oak Park from 1914 to 1919. The historical society runs an excellent cemetery walk in Forest Park every year near Halloween. The museum store is open 12:30–2:30 P.M. Thursday–Sunday.

South of the Pleasant Home and historical society is **Mills Park,** which stretches for several acres. There are numerous tall elm trees to recline under or open spaces for sunning.

Oak Park Conservatory

Another good little rest stop can be found in the Oak Park Conservatory (615 Garfield St., Oak Park, 708/386-4700, www.oakparkparks.com, 10 A.M.–4 P.M. Tues.–Sun., 2–4 P.M. Mon., $1 donation). Stop by this beautiful Edwardian-style conservatory in the middle of the afternoon and you may be the only person there. Just off I-90 in Oak Park, the conservatory is small compared to the Garfield Park Conservatory and Lincoln Park Conservatory in Chicago, but this one costs only $1 for admission and has stunning exhibits. Built in 1929, the conservatory has three different rooms: the tropical, fern, and desert. About 3,000 plants and flowers are on display here, from exotic birds of paradise to more common begonias.

Children's Museum

Wonder Works (6445 W. North Ave., Oak Park, 708/383-4815, www.wonder-works.org, 10 A.M.–5 P.M. Wed.–Sat., noon–5 P.M. Sun., $5) is a relatively new children's museum on the north side of Oak Park. A good place to take the kids on rainy days when they need to expend some energy, Wonder Works has a variety of hands-on educational exhibits. They can paint, learn about nature and how food grows, and build towers.

Scoville Park

Situated in the heart of Oak Park, the four-acre Scoville Park always seems to have some event going on in it, whether it is a food festival or a group of high school students playing with a Frisbee. The park, designed by landscape architect Jens Jensen, is on a little hill overlooking the town. One of the best ways to enjoy Scoville is by dropping by early Sunday evenings in the summer with a blanket or a few lawn chairs and listening to one of the **free music concerts,** where local jazz, bluegrass, or rock bands perform.

Trailside Museum

If you find an injured bird or squirrel while on your bike ride or walk through the woods, you can call forest preserve staff at the Trailside Museum (738 Thatcher Ave., River Forest, 708/366-6530, 10 A.M.–5 P.M. daily, donation); the staff rehabilitate wildlife at the River Forest office. Trailside also houses a child-friendly nature center housed in a historic building. Built in 1874, the museum was once a finishing school for girls and a private residence before the Forest Preserve District of Cook County bought the building to use as offices.

ENTERTAINMENT AND EVENTS
Theater

Most nightlife in the near west suburbs is centered in Oak Park and Forest Park. Both host a number of well-attended community events throughout the year (both villages have spectacular Fourth of July fireworks shows), plus thriving community theater troupes and arts groups.

A troupe of professional actors performs Shakespeare's plays under the stars in Oak Park's Austin Gardens as part of the annual **Festival Theatre** (Austin Gardens, Forest Ave. one block north of Lake St., Oak Park, 708/524-2050 or 708/660-0633) on evenings July–mid-August.

For top-notch theater indoors, try **Circle Theatre** (7300 W. Madison St., Forest Park, 708/771-0700, www.circle-theatre.org). Circle

was founded in the mid-1980s with the goal of presenting innovative theater to the western suburbs. Twenty years and many Jefferson awards (the Chicago version of the Tony award) later, the intimate theater is still producing smart and professional productions, such as *When You Comin' Back Red Rider?* and David Mamet's *American Buffalo.* In 2008 the theater announced it would eventually be moving to a new space on Harrison Street in Oak Park.

Movies

The **Lake Theatre** (1022 Lake St., Oak Park, 708/848-9088, www.classiccinemas.com) is a beautifully renovated art deco movie theater in the heart of downtown Oak Park. It shows first-run films.

Events

The Oak Park and River Forest Historical Society hosts the popular **Tale of the Tombstones in Forest Home Cemetery** (863 Des Plaines Ave., Forest Park, 708/366-1900) every year in October. Local actors dress up as the deceased, share stories about life in the Chicago area back in the 1700s–1900s, and highlight tragic events such as the Haymarket Riot and the Iroquois Theatre Fire. Forest Home is the final resting place for a number of names that will ring a bell, such as members of Ernest Hemingway's family.

The big to-do for Wright aficionados is the **Wright Plus** house walk, held every year in Oak Park. For about $70 you get to tour the insides of about 10 homes designed by Wright, many of them private residences.

SHOPPING
Downtown Oak Park

The largest shopping district is downtown Oak Park, also known as the Lake Street shopping district. It lies along Lake Street from Harlem Avenue to Oak Park Avenue and is anchored by national chain stores Gap and Old Navy on the west end and independent and regional shops throughout. Here's a sampling of some of the shops you'll find in the district.

Earthy scents abound in **Penzeys Spices**

© CHRISTINE DES GARENNES

the Lake Theatre, in the heart of downtown Oak Park

(1138 Lake St., Oak Park, 708/848-7772, www.penzeys.com), a Midwest distributor of fine spices, herbs, and all kinds of goodies you need to make soups and sauces. Items such as tarragon, mint leaves, ginger, chili peppers, and saffron are stored in glass jars with recipe cards nearby to give you ideas on what to make with the stuff.

A few doors down from the Borders store is **Barbara's Bookstore** (1100 Lake St., Oak Park, 708/848-9140, www.barbarasbookstore. com), a regional independent bookshop where staff write passionate and witty reviews about books on little cards on the shelves for you. Barbara's has a good selection of locally published periodicals and regional books.

Marion Street
South of downtown Oak Park is a little sub–shopping district called Marion Street, formerly an outdoor pedestrian mall. You can get to Marion Street (which is closed to vehicular traffic) from Lake Street to the north or North Boulevard to the south. Marion Street is a few blocks east of Harlem Avenue. Here you will find a few casual restaurants, an antiques mall, and two great little shops: **Fitzgerald's Fine Stationery** (131 N. Marion St., Oak Park, 708/445-8077) and **Pumpkin Moon** (1028 North Blvd., Oak Park, 708/524-8144, www.pumpkinmoon.com). Fitzgerald's has beautiful handmade journals, letter-writing paper, and greeting cards, and the designs are not all pastel and flowery. Pumpkin Moon carries whimsical tin toys and retro lunch boxes and action figures.

Harrison Street
Once a string of empty dilapidated storefronts, Harrison Street is now a lively arts district, home to art galleries and home-decor shops featuring many original designs. (The Harrison East Arts District runs roughly from East Avenue to Austin Boulevard in Oak Park; Harrison Street is parallel to the Eisenhower Expressway, or I-290, on the north side.) One of the original locally owned stores that has been around since the district started flourishing in the early 1990s is **Bead in Hand** (145 Harrison St., Oak Park, 708/848-1761, www.

beadinhand.com). The shop sells semiprecious stones, African beads, glass beads, and bead kits for people who are new to the art of jewelry-making.

Val Camiletti has stashed away thousands of 45s, LPs, cassettes, and compact discs in her music store, **Val's Halla Records** (239 W. Harrison St., 708/524-1004, www.valshalla.com). A fixture on South Boulevard near downtown Oak Park for over 30 years, Val's moved to the Harrison Street location in 2007. You'll find all music genres here, from Neil Diamond to the Pixies.

River Forest

Across Harlem Avenue in River Forest, the upscale tea shop **Todd and Holland Tea Merchants** (7577 Lake St., River Forest, 800/747-8327, www.todd-holland.com) has attracted quite a following in recent years for its wide selection of teas from all over the world, including white tea from Sri Lanka or green tea from China. Prices range $20–220 for a quarter pound of tea. Bulk teas, teapots, cozies, and other accessories are for sale here.

ACCOMMODATIONS
$50-100

Built in 1890, **Under the Ginkgo Tree Bed and Breakfast** (300 N. Kenilworth Ave., Oak Park, 708/524-3237, $75–90) is an affordable B&B tucked into a mature and leafy residential neighborhood. The house has a huge wraparound porch for spending time in the morning and evening. There are three rooms available here, each with a private bath.

$100-150

Another good bet for Hemingway fans is **Longwell Hall** (301 N. Scoville Ave., Oak Park, 708/386-5043, www.oakparkbnb.com, $75–100), which is in a beautiful residential area within a few blocks of Hemingway's birth home. Like the Ginkgo Tree, Longwell Hall is an affordable bed-and-breakfast in a beautiful residential area, decorated in English style and with a touch of femininity (white down comforters). Each room has

a private bathroom, and one of the rooms has a screened-in porch.

The gorgeous **Harvey House Bed and Breakfast** (107 S. Scoville Ave., Oak Park, 708/848-6810, www.harveyhousebb.com, $175 and up) is a brick Victorian in a residential neighborhood south of the Green Line L. There are five suites, with two of them geared toward people staying around for longer stays with kitchenettes and other features. Expect extras like marble bathrooms, luxurious seating areas, wireless Internet access, and (in some rooms) fireplaces.

€ **The Carleton** (1110 Pleasant St., Oak Park, 708/848-5000, www.carletonhotel.com, $100 and up), a boutique hotel steps from the Green Line L stop and downtown Oak Park, has several lodging options for guests. Depending on how much money you are willing to spend and what kind of space you need, you can rent a room in the main boutique-style hotel, which was built in 1928; rooms in the adjacent Plaza Hotel, which was built in 1892 for visitors to the Columbia Exposition; or the economical option of staying at the motor lodge in the rear of the hotel. Two restaurants (one casual, one upscale) are downstairs. Rooms are clean and comfortable, with nice accents such as cherry-finished desks and armchairs for reading.

The other boutique hotel in town is the € **Write Inn** (211 N. Oak Park Ave., Oak Park, 708/383-4800, www.writeinn.com, $100 and up), also near downtown Oak Park and a short walk to Hemingway's birth home, the Green Line L stop, restaurants, and shops. There are 66 rooms here; some are suites that come with refrigerators, sinks, and microwaves. (Suites can cost up to $126.) Rooms are decorated sparsely, but with antiques and furniture from the 19th and early 20th century. A French bistro is on the first floor.

The **Best Western** (4400 Frontage Rd., Hillside, 708/544-9300, around $100) doesn't have the charm of the boutique hotels in Oak Park, but with a spot just off I-290 it's not a bad deal if you're breezing through the area.

FOOD AND DRINK

Oak Park can be paradise for foodies. There are so many wonderful restaurants in this town, with chefs cooking cuisine from all around the world, from Italy to India, from pancakes to pad thai. In recent years more national and local chain restaurants have opened, but there's still no shortage of good local independently run restaurants that have had Oak Park addresses for decades.

Breakfast

Oak Parkers pack into the **Maple Tree** (1034 Lake St., Oak Park, 708/848-8267, 7 A.M.–10 P.M. daily) on Saturdays and Sundays. At this casual restaurant downtown you can rub noses with local activists and politicians while noshing on blintzes, big pancakes, and cheesy omelets.

Fast Food

Plump, juicy Chicago-style hot dogs and crispy fries are the specialty at ◖ **Parky's** (329 Harlem Ave., Forest Park, 708/366-3090, 10 A.M.–9 P.M. Mon.–Thurs., 10 A.M.–10 P.M. Fri.–Sat., 11 A.M.–9 P.M. Sun., $4), located on the main drag between Forest Park and Oak Park.

Mmm . . . the meatball sandwiches at **Starship Subs** (7618 Madison Ave., Forest Park, 708/771-3016, 8 A.M.–8 P.M. Mon.–Sat., 10 A.M.–6 P.M. Sun., $5) will fill you up. Starship, on Forest Park's main drag, whips up Italian and American-style hot and cold subs and is well known for its homemade soups, such as cream of asparagus, split pea, and tamale.

Café

Owned and operated by Laura and Andrew Maychruk, ◖ **The Buzz Café** (905 S. Lombard Ave., Oak Park, 708/660-0894, www.thebuzzcafe.com, 6 A.M.–9 P.M. Mon.–Fri., 7 A.M.–9 P.M. Sat., 8 A.M.–2 P.M. Sun.) is the place to go to hear the latest news in the village, controversy swirling about a new development, or ravings about a music or theater performance. The Maychruks have made this place welcoming for everyone. It manages to

The Buzz Café, Oak Park

© DEREK TAYLOR/WWW.OAKPARKDINING.COM

be bustling and relaxing at the same time. The main fare is coffee, but they also serve traditional coffeehouse fare (bagels, turkey sandwiches) with a focus on organic ingredients.

American

A popular local hangout, **Poor Phil's Shell Bar** (139 S. Marion St., Oak Park, 708/848-0871, www.poorphils.com, 7 A.M.–1 A.M. Mon.–Thurs., 7 A.M.–2 A.M. Fri., 8 A.M.–2 A.M. Sat., 8 A.M.–midnight Sun.) is known mostly for its seafood. The fried calamari, mussels, and crab cakes are all good bets. The place is casual, loud (lots of gabbing going on at all the tables), and a bit messy (much of the restaurant's free popcorn ends up on the floor on busy Friday nights). During the summer a table in its outdoor patio is a great spot to watch people. The Carleton Hotel is upstairs and the Green Line L is just down the block. If you want a quiet, more continental atmosphere, try **Philander's** (708/848-4250, 5–10 P.M. Sun.–Thurs., 4–11:30 P.M. Fri.–Sat., bar open later), the restaurant adjacent to the lobby.

Try a slice of warm apple pie and cinnamon ice cream at **Petersen's Restaurant and Ice Cream Parlor** (1100 Chicago Ave., Oak Park, 708/386-6131, www.petersenicecream.com, 11 A.M.–10 P.M. Mon.–Thurs., 11 A.M.–11 P.M. Fri., 8 A.M.–11 P.M. Sat., 8 A.M.–10 P.M. Sun., $7), a friendly spot where the ice cream (made here since 1919) is rich in butterfat, calories, and everything else you're not supposed to eat while on a diet. In addition to ice cream sundaes, milk shakes, and other cool treats, Petersen's serves American food such as tuna melts and chicken salads in a diner-like environment.

Walk into the **Onion Roll** (6935 North Ave., Oak Park, 708/383-2548, 6 A.M.–4:30 P.M. Tues.–Sat., 6 A.M.–2:30 P.M. Sun.–Mon.), a Jewish deli and bakery, and you'll be comforted by the smell of fresh-baked bread and a cup of the shop's chicken noodle soup.

Back in the early 1980s the late Chicago newspaper columnist Mike Royko held a rib cooking contest. Charlie Robinson's ribs earned first place, and since then Robinson's ribs and sauces have been winning contests and raves

from diners (note his website address). At his casual restaurant, **Robinsons No. 1 BBQ Ribs** (940 Madison St., Oak Park, 708/383-8452, www.rib1.com, 11 A.M.–10 P.M. Mon.–Thurs., 11 A.M.–11 P.M. Fri.–Sat., noon–5 P.M. Sun.), the ribs are marinated and slow-cooked in a hickory smoker. Got a big appetite? Try the rib and shrimp combo. If you're not up to trying a slab or half slab of ribs, there are great messy barbeque sandwiches, burgers, chicken, and sausage sandwiches. Sides include slaw, collard greens, corn bread, and a few desserts such as peach cobbler and sweet-potato pie are also on the menu. If you're not comfortable licking your fingers in public, order at the counter and take the goods back to your hotel room. Also, if you're traveling with a vegetarian, no worries— Charlie's cooks up veggie burgers and wraps.

Italian

For lunch, try **Cucina Paradiso** (814 North Blvd., 708/848-3434, www.cucinaoakpark. com, 5–9:30 P.M. Mon.–Thurs., 5–10:30 P.M. Fri.–Sat., 5–9 P.M. Sun., $10), for the fresh pastas and personal pizzas. The shop puts a spin on plain old pepperoni; try the pear or artichoke pizzas.

A local favorite is 【 **La Bella Pasteria** (109 N. Main St., Oak Park, 708/524-0044, www. labellapasteria.com, 4–10 P.M. Mon.–Wed., 11 A.M.–10 P.M. Thurs., 11 A.M.–11 P.M. Fri., 4–11 P.M. Sat., 4–9 P.M. Sun., lunch $6–19, dinner $9–25). This light and airy restaurant serves fine food in an atmosphere that is not too casual and not too pretentious. The menu is extensive and the dishes impressive. You can't go wrong with any dish. You've got plenty of pastas to choose from and sauces that are a little bit out of the ordinary (how about marinara with jalapeño peppers and prosciutto?). Then there are filet medallions, chops, chicken dishes, and seafood specials. For an appetizer try the bruschetta.

Indian and Middle Eastern

The affordable lunch buffet at 【 **Khyber Pass** (1031 Lake St., Oak Park, 708/445-9032, www.khyberpassrestaurant.com, lunch

11:30 A.M.–3:30 P.M. daily, dinner 5–10 P.M. daily, $7–17), which runs about $7, features a variety of fresh, authentic Indian food, such as kebabs, fish curry, and fresh naan bread. The restaurant, a favorite of area food critics, is know for its *dumbac* and tandoor *khana* cooking, which are techniques of cooking in a pot or over charcoal, respectively.

The cooks at **Ⓒ Grape Leaves** (129 S. Oak Park Ave., Oak Park, 708/848-5555, 11:30 A.M.–10 P.M. daily, $7) know how to pack a falafel sandwich. The food is fresh and yummy at this small, cheap, and casual restaurant near the Oak Park Avenue Green Line L stop. Try the signature dish, stuffed grape leaves.

Thai

At **Mama Thai** (1112 Madison St., Oak Park, 708/386-0100, www.mamathai.com, 11:30 A.M.–9:30 P.M. Tues.–Thurs., 11:30 A.M.–10 P.M. Fri.–Sat., noon–9 P.M. Sun., $9), the food delivered to your table is fresh, the dishes are affordable, and the atmosphere and staff are pleasant. The restaurant does traditional Thai well: spicy basil, pad thai, fish cakes, hot-and-sour soup, and so on. Expect a variety of salads, noodle and rice dishes, and curries.

Greek

At the festive **Papaspiros Grecian Taverna** (733 W. Lake St., Oak Park, 708/358-1700, www.papaspiros.com, 11 A.M.–11 P.M. Mon.–Thurs., 11 A.M.–midnight Fri.–Sat., noon–10 P.M. Sun., $13) the cooks whip up lamb, seafood, chicken, and veggie dishes. You can get kebabs, spanakopita (spinach-stuffed phyllo dough), and of course saganaki, cheese set aflame with brandy.

Markets

Although it started as a grocery store catering to the West Siders with Italian roots, **Caputo's Fresh Markets** (2560 N. Harlem Ave., Elmwood Park, 708/453-0155, 7 A.M.–10 P.M. Mon.–Fri., 6 A.M.–9 P.M. Sat., 6 A.M.–8 P.M. Sun.) also sells Hispanic and Asian groceries. Here you will find a variety of pastries, produce, deli meats, and wine. The Elmwood Park store is just north of Oak Park and River Forest; stores are also in the suburbs of Addison and Hanover Park.

Stop by the **Oak Park Farmers Market** (Pilgrim Church parking lot, 460 Lake St., Oak Park, 7 A.M.–1 P.M. Sat. June–Oct.) for homemade doughnuts, juicy peaches, and fresh-cut flowers.

Stilton, Gouda, Brie, cheddar, you name it: The **Marion Street Cheese Market** (101 N. Marion St., Oak Park, 708/848-2088, www.marionstreetcheesemarket.com), an inviting little shop in the Marion Street shopping district, stocks it all. Wines are also available here for the picking.

Going picnicking? **River Forest Market** (7761 Lake St., River Forest, 708/366-7400, www.riverforestmarket.com, 8:30 A.M.–6:30 P.M. Mon.–Fri., 8:30 A.M.–5 P.M. Sat., 10 A.M.–2 P.M. Sun.) has deli meats and is a neat place to visit. It's an old-fashioned kind of meat market, with butchers who know their regular customers by name and who create extravagant crown roasts.

The national health-food chain **Whole Foods** (7245 W. Lake St., River Forest, 708/366-1045, 8 A.M.–10 P.M. Mon.–Sat., 8 A.M.–9 P.M. Sun.) has a River Forest store at the town center at the southwest corner of Lake Street and Harlem Avenue. There are a salad bar, coffee bar, bakery and deli sections, and a decent wine and beer selection.

Bars

As far as watering holes go, Forest Park contains the most bars because of an Oak Park ordinance that limits certain types of drinking establishments in the village. The majority of Forest Park's bars (most are Irish and sports bars) are just west of Harlem Avenue on Madison Street. **Healey's West Side** (7321 Madison St., Forest Park, 708/366-4277, 11:30 A.M.–2 A.M. Sun.–Thurs., 11:30 A.M.–3 A.M. Fri.–Sat.) is a neighborhood bar where you can watch a ball game and play a game of darts.

The **Avenue Ale House** (825 S. Oak Park Ave., Oak Park, 708/848-2801, www.

avenuealehouse.com, 11 A.M.–10:30 P.M. Mon.–Thurs., 10:30 A.M.–midnight Fri., 9 A.M.–midnight Sat.–Sun.), located in south Oak Park, just north of I-290, is a good place to watch a football or basketball game or unwind with a brew in between visits to area attractions. The food is also better than your standard pub fare: grilled salmon, pork tenderloin, veggie wraps, and lots of burger options. Outdoor seating is available on the rooftop.

INFORMATION AND SERVICES

The **Oak Park Area Convention and Visitors Bureau** (158 N. Forest Ave., Oak Park, 708/848-1500 or 888/625-7275, www.visitoakpark.com, 10 A.M.–5 P.M. daily Mar.–Dec., 10 A.M.–4 P.M. Jan.–Feb.) maintains a visitors center just off Lake Street in downtown Oak Park. Here you can rent self-guided audio tours, pick up maps, and shop for Wright and Hemingway paraphernalia.

The main branch of the **Oak Park Post Office** (901 Lake St., Oak Park, 708/848-7901, www.usps.com, 8 A.M.–5 P.M. weekdays, 8 A.M.–1 P.M. Sat.) is right next to Unity Temple in downtown Oak Park. Like many buildings in the city, it's quite beautiful to look at. Inside the 1930s-era art deco building are murals depicting scenes from Illinois history designed by Works Progress Administration employees.

GETTING AROUND
Train

Base your vacation in lively Oak Park, which has the most sights, with day trips or side trips to neighboring Forest Park for a visit to the innovative Circle Theatre or Brookfield Zoo, which is about five miles southwest of Oak Park.

Oak Park and Forest Park are connected to Chicago through the Green and Blue Lines of the L train (888/968-7282, www.yourcta.com). The **Green Line** runs parallel to Lake Street with stops at Austin Boulevard, Ridgeland, Oak Park, and Harlem Avenues. The **Blue Line** runs between the eastbound and westbound lanes of the Congress Expressway (I-290) with stops at Austin Boulevard, Oak Park Avenue, and Harlem Avenue in Oak Park. The Blue Line ends in Forest Park at 711 South Des Plaines Avenue. Trains run about every five minutes during rush hour and every 10–15 minutes during the rest of the day. One-way rides cost $1.75 per person. There is a CTA parking lot adjacent to the Forest Park station. It will cost $1.50 to park there for 12 hours.

Metra's Union Pacific Western Line (312/836-7000, www.metrarail.com) runs between downtown Chicago (Madison and Canal Sts.) and the far west suburb of Geneva on the Fox River. Generally, these trains run once an hour on weekdays and every two hours on weekends. A one-way ticket to or from Chicago costs $2.35. If someone is staffing the ticket booth, you will need to buy your ticket there. Otherwise you will have to pay the conductor a $2 fee. If no one is on duty, you can buy your ticket on the train. The Oak Park Metra stop is at 1115 West North Boulevard. An agent is on duty 5:15 A.M.–1:15 P.M. Monday–Friday.

Bus

The suburban bus line **Pace** (847/364-7223, www.pacebus.com) operates buses in the suburbs, including Oak Park, River Forest, and the surrounding towns. Regular fare is $1.50; transfers and other specials cost less. The **free Oak Park Shuttle** (Pace Route 906), run by the village of Oak Park, is a free passenger van service to major tourist attractions and destinations, such as the Hemingway Museum, Carleton Hotel, and CTA train stations. The vans now run year-round, however hours vary each year. You can download an updated map and schedule from the visitor bureau's website, www.visitoakpark.com.

Bicycle

Because of its compact size (it's less than 5 square miles) and scenic residential streets, Oak Park is a bike-friendly town. Bring your bike or rent one at **Oak Park Cyclery** (1113 Chicago Ave., Oak Park, 708/524-2453).

Riverside, Brookfield, and Vicinity

Like the other inner-ring suburbs of Oak Park and Evanston, the towns of Riverside and Brookfield, about 12 miles west of downtown Chicago, are older, leafy burbs along the commuter train line. Designed by Frederick Law Olmsted, Riverside has walking trails along the Des Plaines River and gas lamp–lit winding roads. Nearby Brookfield offers an impressive zoo and the Salt Creek Bicycle Trail, a wooded trail that runs north and west of the zoo. A trip to the zoo is worth the drive out here, but try to fit in an extra half hour or so to explore Riverside's historic neighborhoods and picnic or stroll through the parks.

SIGHTS
◖ Brookfield Zoo

From the aardvark to the white-cheeked gibbon in Tropic World, the 216-acre Brookfield Zoo (1st Ave. and 31st St., Brookfield, 708/688-8000, 866/468-6966, or 800/201-

0784, www.brookfieldzoo.com, open daily, hours vary each year, $10, free Tues. and Thurs. Oct.–Feb., parking, children's zoo, and some shows and activities extra) has a huge variety of amphibians and other animals from all over the world. Every year it seems the zoo updates or alters its exhibits and brings in new animals either from other countries or from breeding programs. The family-friendly zoo has plenty of feeding demonstrations throughout the day year-round. The dolphin shows are usually a good bet. Most major animal habitats are represented here, such as the African savanna and Asian rainforest. Less exotic but just as educational is the Salt Creek Wilderness area, which focuses on the state of Illinois's environment during the last two centuries. This area comprises the cool Dragonfly Marsh and some walking trails through wetland areas. If your feet get tired, climb aboard the tram for $3 and see the park that way.

Brookfield Zoo

After you buy your ticket you can get on and off when you want.

Riverside Historic District

Unlike Chicago and the majority of its surrounding suburbs, the village of Riverside was not designed on a grid system. Situated along the shore of the Des Plaines River (about a 10-minute drive south of Oak Park and River Forest), the village has streets that weave through old neighborhoods. The town has over 350 gaslit street lanterns, more than 40 little parks, and historic arts and crafts, Georgian revival, and Victorian homes. The brain behind the plan was Frederick Law Olmsted, who would go on to design New York City's Central Park.

The **Riverside Landscape Architectural District** (which is clustered around downtown Riverside, east of the Brookfield Zoo) has 56 local landmarks. The entire village was designated a National Historic Landmark in 1970 because of its community and landscape plans. Downtown Riverside features numerous historic and renovated buildings. To learn more about Olmsted and the Riverside plan, stop by the **Riverside Historical Museum** (10 Pine Ave., Riverside, 708/447-2574, 10 A.M.–2 P.M. Sat.), in the historic Victorian Gothic pump house next to the water tower. In a storefront near the water tower is the **Riverside Arts Center** (32 E. Quincy Rd., Riverside, 708/442-6400, www.riversideartscenter.com, 11 A.M.–5 P.M. Wed. and Sat., 11 A.M.–7 P.M. Thurs.–Fri.), where a mix of contemporary art is always on display. While you're walking through town, stop by **Grumpy's** (1 Riverside Rd., across from the Metra station, Riverside, 708/443-5603), a neighborhood catch-all shop and café for a cup of coffee, sandwich, or milk shake or sundae made with Petersen's of Oak Park's ice cream.

Cernan Earth and Space Center

Laser light shows are the specialty at Cernan Earth and Space Center (Triton College campus, 2000 5th Ave., River Grove, 708/583-3100, www.triton.edu, shows Fri.–Sun., $4–10), where staff have produced cool shows

the Riverside water tower, one of many historic structures and landmarks in Riverside

for all types of visitors. Take your pick from shows set to Pink Floyd and Jimi Hendrix music, pop, R&B, country, New Age, or even winter holiday music. The monthly earth and sky shows (schedules change monthly) highlight things such as planetary movements, moon phases, or changes in the weather. Before the show, stop by the lobby to check out various artifacts from the Apollo space missions, a spacesuit donated by astronaut Gene Cernan, spacecraft models, and telescopes.

Chicago Portage National Historic Site

History buffs might want to make a quick detour to the Chicago Portage National Historic Site (4800 S. Harlem Ave., Lyons, 773/267-0948, www.civiccenterauthority.org, free). A statue of the explorers Louis Jolliet and Father Jacques Marquette marks the spot where the two came to the conclusion in 1673 that there should be a canal built to connect Lake Michigan to the Illinois River to facilitate water travel.

SPORTS AND RECREATION
Biking
The best trail in the near west suburbs is the **Salt Creek Bicycle Trail,** a 6.6-mile paved trail between Brookfield Woods, just north of the zoo by 31st Street, and Bemis Woods, which is north of the town of Western Springs, on Wolf Road between 31st Street and Ogden Avenue. The wide trail wanders along Salt Creek, through woods and meadows and under a railroad underpass.

If you didn't bring your bicycle with you on your trip, you can rent one at **Oak Park Cyclery** (1113 Chicago Ave., Oak Park, 708/524-2453).

Canoeing
So it may not be as scenic or thrilling as, say, the Colorado River, but the Des Plaines River does offer fun easygoing opportunities for canoeing. You don't have to be an expert to canoe here, just a solid canoer. The **Forest Preserve District of Cook County** (headquarters 536 N. Harlem Ave., River Forest, 708/366-9420, www.fpdcc.com) comprises thousands of acres along both the east and west sides of the Des Plaines River. In Riverside you can launch your canoe at the preserve's Stony Ford ramp, by 1st Street, and float down to the Columbia Woods stop, which is 7.5 miles to the southwest by Willow Springs Road in Willow Springs.

Kiddieland
A fixture on the north side since 1929, Kiddieland (8400 W. North Ave., Melrose Park, 708/343-8000, www.kiddieland.com, mid-Apr.–Oct., weekends only Apr.–May, Sept.–Oct., hours vary by day and by year, $22.50 ages six and up, $19.25 after 5 P.M.) is what amusement parks used to be: midway games, skee ball, train rides, and a roller coaster. The oldest amusement park in Chicago, Kiddieland has a carousel from the 1920s. It is just west of River Forest in nearby Melrose Park, about 10 minutes from downtown Oak Park.

Horse Racing
Maywood Park (8600 W. North Ave., Melrose Park, 708/344-4800, www.maywoodpark.com) has live harness horse racing Thursday and Friday January–June and August–December. The park is west of the Des Plaines River, a few minutes from River Forest.

It is not as glamorous as Arlington Park, but **Hawthorne Race Course** (3501 S. Laramie Ave., Cicero, 708/780-3700, www.hawthorne racecourse.com) can offer visitors an entertaining glimpse of the Illinois horse-racing industry as well as the colorful and sometimes unpolished West Side culture. Harness and thoroughbred races are held on the one-mile track.

FOOD AND DRINK
The pub-like **Irish Times** (8869 Burlington Ave., Brookfield, 708/785-8787, www.irish-timespubchicago.com, 11 A.M.–1:30 A.M. Sun.–Thurs., 11 A.M.–2:30 A.M. Fri.–Sat.), where the all-you-can-eat fish dinners draw loyal regulars, is hopping on Friday nights during Lent. During the winter this place can't be beat, with its cozy fireplace and live Irish music. Most dishes are around $10.

FitzGerald's (6615 Roosevelt Rd., Berwyn, 708/788-2118, www.fitzgeraldsnightclub. com, doors open 7 P.M. Tues.–Sat. and 5 P.M. Sun.) is a former hunting club and jazz club that has been transformed into a great spot to hear local, regional, and national acts. The performance schedule changes monthly, but on any given night you could hear soul, alt-country, rock, or blues. Next door the fabulous **Wishbone** (6611 Roosevelt Rd., Berwyn, 708/749-1295, www.wishbonechicago.com) recently opened a restaurant, and FitzGerald's customers can order from there and bring the food on over. Wishbone serves up Southern food (they call it "Southern reconstruction" food) like French toast dipped in corn flakes or a jambalaya omelet.

For more than three decades **Hala Kahiki** (2834 N. River Rd., River Grove, 708/456-3222, www.hala-kahiki.com, 7 P.M.–2 A.M. Mon.–Tues., 4 P.M.–2 A.M. Wed.–Thurs. and Sun., 4 P.M.–3 A.M. Fri.–Sat.) has been serving a dizzying array of stiff rum-laden tropical concoctions. Drinks are reasonably priced (about $5) and served in a relaxing, somewhat amusing atmosphere (lots of bamboo and palm trees). There are hot and cool drinks, elaborate and simple drinks, and some made specially for couples that require you to drink out of the same bowl. Hala Kahiki is about five miles northwest of Oak Park.

INFORMATION AND SERVICES

The Frederick Law Olmsted Society (tours depart from the Riverside Train Station, 90 Bloomingbank Rd., Riverside, 708/447-2311, www.olmstedsociety.org, $7 donation includes Riverside map and brochure) hosts walking tours of Riverside on the last Sunday of the month May–October. During the biennial house walk in May, people can tour inside several of the village's grand homes.

For more information about the village of Riverside, its history, and architectural landmarks, visit the community website, www. riverside-illinois.com. You can also get more information from the Oak Park Area Convention and Visitors Bureau; see *Information and Services* under *Oak Park.*

Evanston

Evanston, like Oak Park, is a diverse village with a mix of wealthy residents, professors, day laborers, and up-and-coming artists. However, because Northwestern University is here, you can always find college students running down the Lakeshore Path and talking in coffee shops, lending energy to the town. The downtown is busy with a variety of restaurants, from hot dog stands to upscale cuisine. The lakeshore is lined with parks and stately historic homes. Over on the campus in the northeastern part of town, students or visiting artists stage poetry readings, opera performances, and other performing arts events.

SIGHTS
Northwestern University Campus

The only private university in the Big Ten, Northwestern University (633 Clark St., Evanston, 847/491-3741, www.northwestern. edu) is one of the most prestigious universities in the Midwest. Although it has a Chicago campus in addition to the Evanston one, the 240-acre campus on Evanston's north shore is the more scenic of the two and designed like a college campus should be: situated along the lakeshore with Gothic buildings and spacious modern ones, with plenty of walking paths and trees.

The university was chartered in 1851 and was the university for the Northwest Territory, which included land west of the Appalachian Mountains. It opened in 1855 with 10 male students. It was later one of the first universities to admit women, in 1869. Today there are about 17,000 students, including undergraduates, graduates, and part-time students in its business school, journalism school, liberal arts college, and other colleges. Alums include producer Garry Marshall, playwright Mary Zimmerman, politician Dick Gephardt, plus numerous business leaders and intellectuals. A great time to visit Northwestern is early fall, when you'll walk among eager students and under the canopy of large colorful trees. However, during the summer, crowds are fewer.

The best way to tour Northwestern is on foot, and a good start is at the iron **Arch,** a gate erected in 1993 at the southern edge of the campus, on the north side of Sheridan Road at Chicago Avenue (where Sheridan curves to the north). From there you can walk north along the sidewalk to **University Hall,** the oldest building on campus. This Gothic limestone building was completed in 1869 and held dormitory rooms, classrooms, offices, you name it. Renovated in the early 1990s, University Hall now contains seminar rooms, English Department offices, and other offices for students and professors.

Just outside University Hall is the iconic **Rock,** a former fountain that students now coat with paint to promote various campus events and to honor graduating classes. This is a good spot to sit and watch people.

Another little architectural treasure nearby is **Annie May Swift Hall,** the building northeast of University Hall. Built in 1895 to house the school of oratory, the building is a little bit Romanesque, a little bit Gothic. (It has a striking red-tile roof.) Annie May Swift Hall now contains the campus radio station, WNUR, 89.3 FM.

Continuing north, past the theological seminary and Dearborn Observatory, you'll reach **Shakespeare Garden,** near Annenberg Hall (where the School of Education and Social Policy is housed). Listed on the National Register of Historic Places, this garden was designed by noted landscape artist Jens Jensen in 1915, the 300th anniversary of William Shakespeare's death. In it are flowers, herbs, and other plants mentioned in the playwright and poet's writings, such as roses, daisies, and poppies. The traditional English garden features a fountain and a sundial.

From there you can walk farther north to the quads and east toward the lakeshore. Heading back south you can follow along the lakeshore multipurpose trail for views of the campus (the library and arts buildings) and Chicago in the distance. You'll travel past athletic fields, a boathouse, and plenty of spots for sunbathing.

This tour sounds time-consuming, but the Evanston campus is fairly compact. Stopping by the aforementioned buildings should take no longer than two hours.

While you're on campus, consider a visit to the **Mary and Leigh Block Museum of Art** (40 Arts Circle Dr., Evanston, 847/491-4000, www.blockmuseum.northwestern.edu, 10 A.M.–5 P.M. Tues., 10 A.M.–8 P.M. Wed.–Fri., noon–5 P.M. Sat.–Sun., free) located on the southeast side of campus near Pick-Staiger Hall. The Block museum has permanent collections of photographs and prints, and it organizes temporary exhibitions. For example, one previous exhibition was on Roy Lichtenstein's work. Block Cinema within the museum shows new and vintage films as well as international films. Tours of the building and the collection are offered at 2 P.M. Saturday and Sunday.

◖ Grosse Point Lighthouse

Just off scenic Sheridan Road, which curves along the Lake Michigan coast, is Grosse Point Lighthouse (2601 Sheridan Rd., Evanston, 847/328-6961, www.grossepointlighthouse. net, grounds open daily, tours of the keeper's quarters museum 2, 3, 4 P.M. Sat.–Sun. June–Sept., $6), a National Historic Landmark. Built in 1873, the white and black lighthouse is surrounded by a beautiful park with wildflower and butterfly gardens, right near the shoreline and a great sandy beach. You can climb the 113-foot tower (it's 141 steps to the top) and tour the lighthouse keeper's house, which has been made into a little museum with photos and blueprints of the lighthouse.

Next door to the lighthouse is the **Evanston Art Center** (2603 Sheridan Rd., Evanston,

Grosse Point Lighthouse

© CHRISTINE DES GARENNES

847/475-5300, www.evanstonartcenter.org, 10 A.M.–10 P.M. Mon.–Thurs., 10 A.M.–4 P.M. Fri.–Sat., 1–4 P.M. Sun., $3 donation), a well-respected place where contemporary regional artists display their paintings, drawings, and photographs, and budding artists take classes.

Charles Gates Dawes House

Another stunning building near the lakeshore in Evanston is the Charles Gates Dawes House (225 Greenwood St., Evanston, 847/475-3410, www.evanstonhistorical.org, 1–4:30 P.M. Fri.–Sun., $5), a château-like home that just exudes wealth. The place was home to Charles Dawes, Calvin Coolidge's vice president in 1925. The house, built in 1894, is quite impressive. Don't miss the gorgeous mahogany library with its historic books, Tiffany lamps, and paintings. But what's fascinating is learning about all this man accomplished during his life. Dawes was a banker and a businessman (he owned numerous power companies), he raised money to support the World's Fair in 1933, earned a Nobel Peace Prize, and in his spare time played the flute and piano and composed music. The home now contains exhibitions about the town's past.

The Mitchell Museum of the American Indian

This museum (3001 Central St., Evanston, 847/475-1030, www.mitchellmuseum.org, 10 A.M.–5 P.M. Tues.–Sat., Thurs. until 8 P.M., noon–4 P.M. Sun., closed last two weeks of Aug., $5 donation) highlights the history and culture of Indians from the Great Lakes, Plains, Southwest, and other regions in North America. Thousands of items are on display here (and the collection is always growing), including beadwork, blankets, dolls, and silver and turquoise jewelry. There's also a kid-friendly area where visitors can reach out and touch things such as birch bark.

Ladd Arboretum and Nature Center

Ladd Arboretum and Nature Center (2024 McCormick Blvd., Evanston, 847/864-5181, www.laddarboretum.org, ecology and nature center open 9 A.M.–4:30 P.M. Mon.–Sat., mid-Sept.–May, closed Sat. June–early Sept.) is a gem of a park (park complex, really). The park stretches for about a mile along the North Shore Channel of the Chicago River. There are plenty of walking trails through woods of birch, maple, and oak trees, past the community gardens, and a little bird sanctuary. You'd hardly know you are about two miles from the Edens Expressway (I-94). In the middle of the arboretum (at Bridge Street) is the Evanston Ecology Center, where community events are held. Many of the activities are geared toward children, but some will be enjoyed by adults, such as birding by canoe. You don't need to be an Evanston resident to take advantage of its classes (many of them one-day classes), so check with the center in advance. There may be a yoga workshop or similar type of activity there while you're in town.

ENTERTAINMENT AND EVENTS
Theater

Evanston has a thriving theater scene, with municipal theater groups like Fleetwood-Jordain and professional groups like the Next Theatre Company. Pick up a copy of the *Evanston Review* or the *Chicago Reader* to find out about theater performances when you're in town.

Next Theatre Company (Noyes Cultural Arts Center, 927 Noyes Ave., Evanston, 847/475-1875, www.nexttheatre.org, box office noon–6 P.M. Mon.–Fri., and two hours before curtain on days of performances) is a professional off-Loop troupe that produces dramas that prompt audience members to ponder social and political issues. Next has won a slew of Jefferson awards, a local version of the Tonys.

Gilbert and Sullivan musicals are often presented by the community theater group **Light Opera Works** (Noyes Cultural Arts Center, 927 Noyes St., Evanston, 847/869-6300, www.light-opera-works.org). The group, around since the early 1980s, performs shows such as *The Mikado* and *The Fantasticks*. Shows are presented at either the Cahn Auditorium (600 Emerson St.) or McGaw YMCA (1420 Maple Ave.).

Concerts and performances in Northwestern University's 1,000-seat **Pick-Staiger Concert Hall** (50 Arts Circle Dr., 847/467-4000 or 847/491-5441, www.northwestern.edu, 10 A.M.–6 P.M. Mon.–Fri., noon–3 P.M. Sat., hours change during academic breaks) feature students, faculty, and visiting artists. On any given evening you could see the opera *La Bohème,* a jazz concert, brass band performance, or choral concert.

Other local theater groups include the Piccolo Theatre, Evanston Children's Theatre, Fleetwood-Jordain Theatre, Piven Theatre, and Actors Gymnasium.

Movies

The **Century Evanston 12/CineArts 6** (1715 Maple Ave., Evanston, 847/491-9751, www.cinemark.com) shows new blockbuster films and art house films.

Events

Originally designed clothing, pottery, and fine art are for sale at **Custer's Last Stand Art Fair** (Custer St., parallel to the Metra and CTA train lines, Evanston, 847/328-2204, www.custerfair.com, mid-June, free), a giant arts festival that has been held in Evanston for more than 30 years. The fair showcases the work of about 350 artists, dozens of food tents, and almost nonstop live music, including jazz, blues, and folk music. Other well-attended arts fests include the **Lakeshore Arts Festival** held in early August in Dawes Park and the **Ethnic Arts Festival** held in mid-July also in Dawes Park.

The music of Johann Sebastian Bach and other baroque composers are highlighted every May during **Bach Week Festival** (concert locations vary each year throughout Evanston, www.bachweek.org, tickets $10–35 per concert). Chamber orchestras and choruses play in venues such as historic churches.

You can't beat free music. The city's **Starlight Concert Series** is a free outdoor evening music series held every summer in Evanston's parks. Check www.cityofevanston.org for listings.

SHOPPING
Downtown Evanston

Not surprisingly Evanston is home to college-town standards such as Urban Outfitters, The North Face, and Borders Books and Music. But there are also dozens of local or regional chains specializing in women's or children's clothing, a handful of galleries, home decor shops, hobby stores, and more. You can browse for hours along Davis and Church Streets and Sherman Avenue. Here are a few highlights.

Get lost amid the stacks at **Bookman's Alley** (in the rear of 1712 Sherman Ave., Evanston, 847/869-6999, noon–8 P.M. Tues.–Thurs. and Sun., noon–6 P.M. Fri., 10:30 A.M.–6 P.M. Sat.) where about 40,000 used and rare books are for sale. Tucked between the stacks are antiques such as rare records, prints, and uniforms from the armed services, as well as armchairs and tables and chairs where customers are welcome to lounge for as long as they like. Another local used book store that focuses on collectible books is **Amaranth Books** (828 Davis St., Evanston, 847/328-2939).

At **Uncle Dan's** (700 W. Church St., Evanston, 847/475-7100, www.udans.net, 10 A.M.–8 P.M. Mon.–Thurs., 10 A.M.–7 P.M. Fri.–Sat., 11 A.M.–5 P.M. Sun.) you can browse for camping and hiking gear, clothing and shoes, bags and bottles for bicycling, gloves and hats for winter, and more. It has additional locations in Lincoln Park and Southport in Chicago and in another lakeshore suburb, Highland Park.

Everything from earth-friendly mattresses to mosquito spray are available from **Healthy Green Goods** (702 Main St., Evanston, 847/864-9098, www.healthygreengoods.com, 10 A.M.–5 P.M. Mon.–Wed. and Fri.–Sat., 10 A.M.–7 P.M. Thurs.).

Skokie

Westfield Shoppingtown Old Orchard (Skokie Blvd. and Old Orchard Rd., Skokie, 847/673-6800, www.westfield.com, 10 A.M.–9 P.M. Mon.–Sat., 11 A.M.–6 P.M. Sun.), or Old Orchard, as it's known locally, is a ritzy open-air shopping center. There are

THE COLLAR COUNTIES

© CHRISTINE DES GARENNES

downtown Evanston

the usual suspects, such as Nordstrom and Marshall Field's, but also Brooks Brothers, known mostly for its men's suits, Christian Bernard jewelry, and Kate Spade purses.

RECREATION
Parks and Beaches

Evanston stretches for about four miles along Lake Michigan, with several city parks and sandy beaches along the way (Evanston Parks Department, 847/866-2900, www.cityof evanston.org). Listed from north to south, there are five public beaches in Evanston: **Lighthouse Beach** (at Central St. and Sheridan Rd.), **Clark Street Beach** (at Clark St. and Sheridan Rd.), **Greenwood/Dempster Street Beach** (Greenwood St. at the lakeshore), **South Boulevard Beach** (South Blvd. at the lakeshore), and **Lee Street** (at Lee St. and Lakeshore Blvd.). You need a token to get onto the beach mid-June–Labor Day. Daily passes cost $7 and are sold at each beach. You can't go wrong with any of these beaches. At the **Dempster Street Beach** you can rent a sailboat or kayak (the phone number for the

Dempster Beach office during the season is 847/866-4167). Lighthouse Beach is probably the most scenic, but it can get crowded.

Burnham Shores (between Dempster and Hamilton Sts.) park is on the lakefront and has a sailboat launch (but no beach). Burnham is a nice quiet spot to picnic, take in the Chicago skyline, and look out onto the lake. Occasionally the city closes the beaches to swimming because of high winds, inclement weather, or (gulp) high *E. coli* levels.

Merrick Park (at Lake St. and Oak Ave.), in downtown Evanston, is another good spot to take a break and read the newspaper for a while or take in the downtown scene. There's a fountain and rose garden. **Dawes Park** is the big lakeside park where several festivals are held every year. It's between Dempster and Church Streets.

Biking, Hiking, and Jogging

The **Evanston Lake Shore Trail,** which extends the city limits, is the closest you'll get to Lake Michigan while riding your bicycle. Most of the trail is on blacktop. Parallel to the

© CHRISTINE DES GARENNES

Evanston has a number of public beaches along Lake Michigan.

trail is a gravel trail for joggers and walkers. The southern end the trail links with Chicago's Lakefront Trail, so if you're not satisfied with the 3–4 miles in Evanston, you can head south. There are plenty of signs pointing you to the trail near Sheridan Road. Otherwise, you can head northwest to the **Green Bay Trail,** which runs along the Metra line starting near Shorewood Park in Wilmette, the suburb to the north.

Ice-Skating

Take a spin on the ice at **Robert Crown Community Center and Ice Rink** (1701 Main St., Evanston, 847/448-8258, www.cityofevanston.org, 8 A.M.–6 P.M. Mon., 8 A.M.–8 P.M. Tues.–Thurs., 8 A.M.–9 P.M. Fri., 8 A.M.–10 P.M. Sat., noon–4 P.M. Sun.). You can rent ice skates at this indoor ice-skating rink. Ice skating is also possible, weather permitting, on the Dawes Park lagoon at Sheridan Road and Church Street.

Big Ten Sports

You can watch everything from fencing to football on Northwestern University's campus. The main attraction during fall and winter are Wildcats football games in the 40,000-seat Ryan Field, which can get a little rowdy with flying marshmallows. Contact the **Athletic Ticket Office** (1501 Central St., Evanston, 847/491-2287, www.nusports.com, 9 A.M.–5 P.M. Mon.–Fri. Aug.–Apr., 9 A.M.–4 P.M. Mon.–Fri. May–July).

ACCOMMODATIONS

In addition to the hotels and inns listed below, the city of Skokie, which borders Evanston to the north, has several chain hotels along Skokie Boulevard, Touhy Avenue, and Old Orchard Road. They include the Hampton Inn, Comfort Inn, Holiday Inn, and Doubletree.

$100-150

If you're tired of chain hotels where all the rooms look the same, but you're not exactly a fan of bed-and-breakfasts, a good compromise is the ⟨ **Margarita Inn** (1566 Oak Ave., Evanston, 847/869-2273, www.margaritainn.com, $120), which bills itself as a European-style hotel. It's a boutique hotel with 42 rooms and five floors. The cheap rooms (about $80) require you to share a bathroom with other hotel guests on your floor. The more expensive suites (including mini and two-room suites) come with private bath. They cost up to $170. Standards come with a single queen or two twins. You don't have to spend much time in your room, though. The hotel has a rooftop deck, parlor, and a gorgeous English-style library with built-in bookcases and armchairs. Extras are continental breakfast and high-speed Internet access, which is available in the lobby, library, and parlor.

The **Best Western University Plaza** (1501 Sherman Ave., Evanston, 847/491-6400 or 800/382-6786, www.bestwestern.com, $140) is a good bet because of its location, plus it has an indoor swimming pool and fitness room.

$150-250

If you plan to stay around for several days, try ◖ **The Homestead** (1625 Hinman Ave., Evanston, 847/475-3300, www.thehomestead. net, $140–255), which offers studios with kitchens and one- and two-bedroom apartments. This is a fancy (there's a doorman) superclean hotel a few blocks from downtown, shoreline parks, and Northwestern's campus. Downstairs the well-reviewed **Quince** restaurant (847/570-8400, www.quincerestaurant.com, 5:30–9:30 P.M. Tues.–Thurs., 5:30–10 P.M. Fri., 5–10 P.M. Sat., 5–9 P.M. Sun.) serves high-end contemporary American food. Choose à la carte or multicourse prix fixe menus.

The **Orrington Omni** (1710 Orrington Ave., Evanston, 847/866-8700 or 888/529-9100, www.hotelorrington.com, $199–239) is perhaps one of the more exclusive spots to stay in the area, if you have money to throw around. The 269-room renovated hotel has restaurants and a fitness room inside.

Located in the heart of Evanston, the **Hilton Garden Inn** (1818 Maple Ave., Evanston, 847/475-6400, www.hiltongardeninn.com, $150–230) has an indoor pool and fitness center for guests. The rooms also come with extras like little fridges and Internet access.

FOOD
Italian
There are many pizza joints in and around the Evanston area, but **Carmen's** (1012 Church St., Evanston, 847/328-0031, 11 A.M.–10 P.M. Mon.–Thurs., 11 A.M.–11 P.M. Fri.–Sat., noon–10 P.M. Sun.) is one of the best because you can sample all different styles and flavors (stuffed, deep-dish, and thin) during the affordable lunch buffet.

◖ **Dave's Italian Kitchen** (1635 Chicago Ave., Evanston, www.davesik.com, 4–9:30 P.M. Sun.–Thurs., 4–10:30 P.M. Fri.–Sat., $6.75–12.75) is another popular place for college students, locals, and visitors. And no wonder: You get a lot of good food for a reasonable price. A heaping plate of pasta averages $8. Options include the traditional spaghetti Bolognese with carrots and onions in a beefy red sauce, but also the tantalizing and unique dishes such as spaghetti carbonara (bacon and onion bits in a cream and egg sauce) or spaghetti calamari (with squid and garlic and olive oil). The pizza and homemade calzones are also yummy.

American
The veggie-friendly **Blind Faith** (525 Dempster St., Evanston, 847/328-6875, www.blindfaith-cafe.com, breakfast, lunch, and dinner daily, under $10) cooks tempeh, tofu, textured vegetable protein, and soy smoothies for vegans and those dabbling in vegetarianism. There's also a self-serve section in the restaurant.

When you visit the **Dixie Kitchen and Bait Shop** (825 Church St., Evanston, 847/733-9030, 11 A.M.–10 P.M. Mon.–Thurs., 11 A.M.–11 P.M. Fri.–Sat., 9 A.M.–10 P.M. Sun., $8), don't hold back, especially if you're there for its famous Sunday brunch. You could be there for hours stuffing yourself with sizzling Cajun food: catfish strips, gumbo, crawfish étouffée, shrimp, and grits. (Dixie Kitchen also has a location in the Hyde Park neighborhood of Chicago.)

There's something about a pulled-pork sandwich that is just so satisfying. At ◖ **Merle's** (727 Benson Ave., Evanston, 847/475-7766, www.merlesbbq.com, 4:30–9:30 P.M. Mon.,

11:30 A.M.–9:30 P.M. Tues.–Thurs., 11:30 A.M.–11 P.M. Fri.–Sat., noon–9 P.M. Sun., $10–20) the kitchen staff barbecue pork, beef, and chicken for days, it seems. The meat is so tender, and there's a wide variety of barbecue sauce flavors. If you're hungry (and not concerned about getting barbecue sauce stains around your mouth), try the baby back ribs or share the jumbo-size "barnyard platter," which is made for two. Otherwise, you won't be disappointed by a bowl of Brunswick stew (made with tomatoes, corn, potatoes, and pulled meats) and a side of potato salad.

The menu changes daily at **《 Davis Street Fish Market** (501 Davis St., Evanston, 847/869-3474, www.davisstreetfishmarket. com, 4:30–10 P.M. Mon., 11:30 A.M.–10 P.M. Tues.–Thurs., 11:30 A.M.–midnight Fri.–Sat., 11:30 A.M.–9 P.M. Sun., bar open later on weekends, $13–22), one of the best places in the Chicago area to eat fresh fish. Seafood dishes may include Lake Superior whitefish or grouper, or oysters from the beautiful raw bar. There's a reason the Cajun brunch on Sundays is always packed.

The motto for **Prairie Moon** (1502 Sherman Ave., Evanston, 847/864-8328, www.prairiemoonrestaurant.com, lunch 11:30 A.M.–2 P.M. Wed.–Sat., dinner 4:30–10 P.M. Sun.–Thurs., 4:30–11 P.M. Fri.–Sat., brunch 9:30 A.M.–1:30 P.M. Sun., $8 average lunch, a bit more for dinner) is "All-American Dining." That means cheeseburgers and sides of macaroni and cheese, but also surprising entrées such as tilapia fish tacos with avocado salad and Chesapeake blue crab cakes. Prairie Moon is big, with several dining rooms, two bars, and a patio, but it's friendly. Each month the restaurant celebrates a festival occurring somewhere in the United States.

Asian

After opening in a small storefront and expanded into a new space in 2003, **《 LuLu's Dim Sum and Then Sum** (804 Davis St., Evanston, 847/869-4343, www.lulusdimsum.com, 11 A.M.–10 P.M. Mon.–Thurs., 11 A.M.–11 P.M. Fri.–Sat., 11 A.M.–9 P.M. Sun., $7.95–14.95) serves contemporary pan-Asian food, including stir-fries and noodle bowls. Don't leave without trying one of the funky drinks, such as a Singapore sling (gin, vermouth, ginger ale) or a frozen spiked lemonade.

Cafés

One of the coolest places in town to load up on java (or muffins and scones) is **《 Kafein** (1621 Chicago Ave., Evanston, 847/491-1621, 11 A.M.–1 A.M. Sun.–Thurs., 11 A.M.–2 A.M. Fri.–Sat.). Service is not exactly stellar here, but Kafein is one of those places where you can feel free to pull out *Moby Dick* and read for hours. Occasional spoken-word performances are held here.

If you see a tiny table open at the often-crowded **The Unicorn Café** (1723 Sherman Ave., Evanston, 847/332-2312, 7:30 A.M.–11 P.M. Sun., 7 A.M.–11 P.M. Mon.–Thurs., 7 A.M.–midnight Fri., 7:30 A.M.–midnight Sat.), grab it. This busy café offers original art on the walls (for sale), hot and cold coffee and tea drinks, plus a few panini options.

Ice Cream

Stop by this ice cream shop for a cone or shake, and then head to the lakeshore or downtown for a stroll. **Hartigan's Ice Cream Shoppe** (2909 Central St., Evanston, 847/491-1232, 11 A.M.–11 P.M. daily June–mid-Sept., 11 A.M.–10 P.M. daily mid-Sept.–May) not only has good cones but also a variety of drinks such as rich thick milk shakes and sherbet coolers.

Markets

Dozens of produce and flower vendors set up tents every Saturday at the **Evanston Farmers Market** (University and Oak Aves., 847/866-2936, 7:30 A.M.–1 P.M. Sat., mid-May–early Nov.).

INFORMATION AND SERVICES
Visitor Information

You can pick up hotel and event info from the **Chicago's North Shore Convention and**

Visitors Bureau (8001 Lincoln Ave., Suite 715, Skokie, 847/763-0011, www.visitchicagonorthshore.com). The CVB maintains listings for Evanston and surrounding towns.

Media

The weekly *Evanston Review* (1601 Sherman Ave., Evanston, 847/866-6501, www.pioneerlocal.com) has decent entertainment and events listings for the region, in addition to movie and stage reviews. It's published on Wednesdays by Pioneer Press, which runs a chain of weeklies in the Chicago region.

The Daily Northwestern (1999 Campus Dr., Evanston, 847/491-3222, www.dailynorthwestern.com) is published daily during the school year and weekly on Thursdays during the summer. It has a good city section for local news in addition to campus happenings. You can pick up a copy at most convenience stores and cafés.

The Reader's Guide to Arts and Entertainment (11 E. Illinois St., Chicago, 312/828-0350, www.chireader.com) is published by the Chicago weekly *The Reader* on Thursdays. It's free and available in cafés, restaurants, and convenience stores.

Hospital

Evanston Northwestern Healthcare (2650 Ridge Ave., Evanston, 847/570-2000, www.enh.org) operates Evanston Hospital, a full-service hospital in Evanston, as well as several others in the region, including Highland Park Hospital to the north (718 Glenview Ave., Highland Park, 847/432-8000).

GETTING AROUND

The Chicago Transit Authority's **Purple Line** elevated train (312/836-7000, www.yourcta.com) runs from Evanston to downtown Chicago and has several stops in Evanston (from north to south): Linden, Central, Noyes, Foster, Davis, Dempster, Main, and South Boulevard. Trains run about every 15 minutes 6 A.M.–1 A.M. on Sundays, 5 A.M.–1 A.M. weekdays, and 5 A.M.–2 A.M. Saturdays. A one-way ticket costs $1.75.

CTA operates the **"Evanston Circulator"** bus route Monday–Friday. The bus operates roughly 6 A.M.–7 P.M. along Ridge and Dodge Streets, with stops at the Metra Station. A one-way fare is $1.75.

Metra's Union Pacific Line stops at several locations in Evanston (Central Ave., 847/869-3622; 901 Davis St., 847/492-5066; and 600 Main St., 847/492-5066, www.metrarail.com). Trains run about every hour. During weekday rush hours they run about every 15 minutes. A one-way ticket to or from Chicago's Ogilvie Transportation Center costs $3.35, and you must buy the ticket at the station if it is staffed. (Otherwise, you'll pay an extra $2 on the train.)

The North Shore

As the name implies, the North Shore region consists of towns along Lake Michigan. Most of them are quite elite, with mansions, well-manicured lawns, clean downtowns with boutiques and little cafés, and impressive schools. As you drive north on Sheridan Road, the scene might look familiar. Director John Hughes set many of his films here, including *Ferris Bueller's Day Off, Sixteen Candles,* and *Home Alone.* The towns have been home to bigwigs such as advertising mogul Leo Burnett, the Walgreens drugstore family, basketball player Michael Jordan, 1980s television star Mr. T, and many others. If you don't have time to visit the sights here, at least drive north along Sheridan Road (which follows Lake Michigan) to gawk at some mansions or have fun taking the curves.

SIGHTS
€ Chicago Botanic Garden

A trip to the Chicago Botanic Garden (1000 Lake Cook Rd., Glencoe, 847/835-5440, www.chicagobotanic.org, 8 A.M.–sunset daily, free admission, parking $15 per car, tram tours extra) can last all day. The constantly evolving gardens (there are 23) are larger than they seem. Footpaths wind through Japanese and English gardens, onto little islands (accessible by little bridges), above miniature waterfalls, by vegetable gardens, formal flower gardens (in spring the tulips are dazzling), and through prairie and woodlands. Take the narrated tram tour if your feet tired. Season-specific tours are also available. These highlight the spring flowers, herb collections, and even what's going on during the winter. Flowers and plants aren't just on display here. The garden has a research and breeding center, where staff recently developed an orange echinacea plant. Throughout the gardens you will find tons of spots for writing, reading, or chatting. Don't miss the recently renovated dwarf conifer garden with its meticulously maintained spruces, cypresses, and more. There's also an indoor and outdoor

café and a well-stocked gift shop. If you want to avoid paying the $15 per-car admission fee, you can ride the Metra train to the Braeside stop or park at the Braeside train station (10 N. St. John's Ave.). From there you can bike to the botanic garden. Head west from the train station on County Line Road; the botanic gardens are just west of Green Bay Road on the east side of County Line.

€ Baha'i House of Worship

As you drive north on Sheridan Road, the view of the Baha'i House of Worship (100 Linden Ave., Wilmette, 847/853-2300, www.us.bahai.org, gardens and auditorium 7 A.M.–10 P.M. daily, visitors center 10 A.M.–5 P.M. daily Oct.–late Apr., 10 A.M.–8 P.M. May–Sept., free) is just amazing. Built in 1953 not far from the Lake Michigan shoreline, it has a 135-foot-high lacy white dome and is surrounded by colorful rose gardens. This building is the first Baha'i

© CHRISTINE DES GARENNES

Baha'i House of Worship, Wilmette

MADE IN ILLINOIS

Here's a sampling of movies filmed in Illinois:

- *About Last Night*
- *Backdraft*
- *Barbershop*
- *Batman Begins*
- *The Blues Brothers*
- *Ferris Bueller's Day Off*
- *The Fugitive*
- *Groundhog Day*
- *High Fidelity*
- *Home Alone*
- *I, Robot*
- *Meet the Parents*
- *National Lampoon's Vacation*
- *Natural Born Killers*
- *Never Been Kissed*
- *Ordinary People*
- *Prelude to a Kiss*
- *Risky Business*
- *The Road to Perdition*
- *Save the Last Dance*
- *Sixteen Candles*
- *Spiderman II*
- *Uncle Buck*
- *The Untouchables*
- *Wayne's World*
- *While You Were Sleeping*

House of Worship built in the western hemisphere. The religion was founded by a Persian man by the name of Bahá'u'lláh in the 1800s, and it teaches tolerance, acceptance, and peace. Some of his writings appear on the walls of the dome. There is no cross to which people kneel, nor are there statues lining all the walls. People tend to pick a seat (no pews, either) and sit quietly amongst others, looking upward. Curious? You can learn more about the religion and its followers in the building's visitors center on the lower level.

Skokie Sights

Another quiet place for reflection can be found west of Wilmette and the Baha'i temple in the town of Skokie. When residents of Skokie, home to a large Jewish population, heard that a neo-Nazi group planned to hold a rally in the town, they banded together and prevented it. Afterward the group formed the **Holocaust Memorial Foundation** (847/677-4640, www.hmfi.org), which aims to educate the public about the Holocaust through educational programs, classroom visits, and exhibits at the Skokie center. At the center, visitors can hear firsthand accounts from survivors of the Holocaust and view artifacts from that era, including photographs, letters, and Jewish identification cards. The center on Main Street has closed and a new 50,000-square-foot museum and center, the **Illinois Holocaust Museum and Education Center** (9603 Woods Dr., Skokie), is scheduled to open in 2009.

Skokie also contains a great little **Sculpture Park** (just east of McCormick Blvd. from Dempster St. to Touhy Ave., 847/649-4265, www.sculpturepark.org, free). More than 70 sculptures line a two-mile walking and bicycling path along the north branch of the Chicago River. The sculptures are abstract figures, animals, and people and are made of material such as steel, bronze, and wood.

ENTERTAINMENT AND EVENTS

Ravinia Festival

The quintessential evening for North Shore residents includes a gourmet candlelight picnic of wine and cheese on the lawn of Ravinia Park, followed by a concert by the Chicago Symphony Orchestra, Tony Bennett, or Peter, Paul, and Mary. The Ravinia Festival (Green Bay and Lake-Cook Rds., Highland Park, 847/604-2414 or 847/266-5100, www.ravinia.org, lawn tickets $10, more for seats in the pavilion, discounts for college students for certain concerts) is a summerlong series of outdoor concerts in Ravinia Park. You can buy seats in the 3,200-seat pavilion or the less-expensive lawn seats. Each season tends to focus on a specific composer, such as Sergey Rachmaninoff, a recent highlight. Visiting artists run the gamut and include legendary figures such as Itzhak Perlman and up-and-coming young artists. People can bring a picnic basket or buy food and drink at one of the many restaurants in the park (fare varies from basic hamburgers to fillets).

Lawn spaces fill up quickly. For a concert that starts at 8 P.M., you will want to stake out a spot at 6 P.M. Tickets go on sale starting at the end of May. The box office is open at 9 A.M. daily and 1 P.M. Sunday until the time of the show. Parking is available at the park, but those spots fill up rapidly. A good bet is to park around downtown Highland Park and take the free "park 'n' ride" shuttle. It runs every evening there is a concert, before and after the concerts. You can pick it up at the Metra Station. If you're staying in Chicago, you can take the Metra Union Pacific line on concert days; the train stops right at the park entrance. Ravinia's season typically runs June–September; its Rising Stars series, however, featuring up-and-coming artists, holds concerts in the park's indoor venues during the fall through spring. College students with identification receive free admission to concerts by the Chicago Symphony Orchestra.

Theater and Film

If you want to avoid large crowds and are on a budget, one summer concert series you won't want to miss is the Park District of Wilmette's **Starlight Theatre** (Gillson Park, Michigan and Washington Aves., Wilmette, www.wilmettepark.org, 847/256-9656, weekend evenings July–Aug., concert free, parking $7–8). Held in the Wallace Bowl, an outdoor stage and seating area in Wilmette's lakeside Gillson Park, Starlight concerts may feature '50s music, Polynesian music, or a patriotic big band show.

The **North Shore Center for the Performing Arts** (9501 Skokie Blvd., Skokie, 847/679-9501, www.northshorecenter.org) is not far from I-94 and a slew of ordinary shopping malls, but you can always find original entertaining events here. The arts complex is home to the **Northlight Theatre Company, Skokie Valley Symphony Orchestra,** and **Centre East,** an arts programming company at the center. Centre East brings in a variety of performers, including Al Franken and Victor Borge. Northlight stages new musicals and plays, such as *Studs Terkel's The Good War,* and some revivals, such as Oscar Wilde's *Lady Windermere's Fan.* Prices vary per show.

Since it began in 1993, **Writers' Theatre** (in the Glencoe Woman's Club, 325 Tudor Ct., Glencoe; and the rear of Books on Vernon, 664 Vernon Ave., Glencoe, 847/242-6000, www.writerstheatre.org) has been staging moving works of art in its intimate theaters. From its inaugural production, an adaptation of Anton Chekhov stories, the theater has been warmly received from critics and local theatergoers. Writers' Theatre has produced work from writers such as William Blake and William Shakespeare.

You can catch an art film or second-run movie at the **Highland Park Theatre** (445 Central Ave., Highland Park, 847/432-3300, $3.50–5). Free parking is available in the lot next door.

SHOPPING

Downtown Highland Park and Lake Forest have a number of upscale boutiques, including locally owned and international chain stores. Lake Forest's town square near Western Avenue and Westminster Road has a miniature Macy's (formerly Marshall Field's) department store. Highland Park's downtown shopping district is clustered around Central Avenue, between Green Bay Road and Saint Johns Avenue. You'll find a number of clothing stores, such as Gap, as well as a handful of upscale children's boutiques, plus home decor such as Restoration Hardware.

Lake Forest and Highland Park

The **Lake Forest Book Store** (680 N. Western Ave., 847/234-4420) is a crowded little bookshop near the Metra train station. The friendly, frank staff of this independent store are always eager to make recommendations.

Kids aren't the only ones gawking at the toys and trains in **The Toy Station** (270 Market Sq., Lake Forest, 847/234-0180, www.trains-toys-horses.com). Model-train enthusiasts can check out a variety of trains here—streamliners, locomotives, you name it. In addition to trains, the store carries a seemingly inordinate number of stuffed animals and dolls, including Madame Alexander dolls.

RECREATION
The Skokie Lagoons

The Skokie Lagoons are a series of seven interconnected lagoons along the Skokie River, totaling about 200 acres. They were constructed in the 1930s and 1940s by the Civilian Conservation Corps to control spring flooding in the area and to build a water recreation area for residents. The river runs parallel to the Lake Michigan coastline and the lagoons are situated from roughly Willow to Lake-Cook Roads. (Eventually the Skokie River runs into the Chicago River.) The lagoons are a popular spot for fishing (bass, walleye, northern pike) and for canoeing. There's a public boat launch just south of Tower Road, east of the Edens Expressway, between the towns of Wilmette to the east and Northbrook to the west. Or you can rent a canoe, kayak, or trailer from the **Chicagoland Canoe Base** (4019 N. Narragansett Ave., Chicago, 773/777-1489, www.chicagolandcanoebase.com, 9 A.M.–5 P.M. Mon.–Wed. and Fri.–Sat., 9 A.M.–9 P.M. Thurs., $45 per day, trailers extra).

THE COLLAR COUNTIES

© CHRISTINE DES GARENNES

downtown Highland Park

Beaches

One of the best beaches on the Lake Michigan coastline is **Forest Park Beach** (Deerpath and Lake Rds., Lake Forest, 847/615-4284 or 847/615-4320, www.cityoflakeforest.com, Memorial Day–Labor Day). There are long stretches of sandy beaches (peach colored, not white), a large stone fishing pier that is not only good for fishing but also for picnicking, boulders that jut into the water that are great for sunbathing, a concession stand, a playground, a shelter for picnics, and a place to wash your sandy feet. It's nearly perfect, except beachcombers who are not Lake Forest residents cannot park at the nearby parking lot or along nearby residential streets. Your best bet is paying a few bucks to park in town in the Metra Lot (Deerpath Rd. and Western Ave.) and walk a little less than one mile along Deerpath Road to the beach. It's an easy stroll, through a residential neighborhood and past Lake Forest College.

The 60-acre **Gillson Park** (Michigan and Washington Aves., Wilmette, 847/256-9656, www.wilmettepark.org) has a sandy beach and spots on the lawn for lounging in the sun, plus a pavilion called the Lakeview Center. Admission for nonresidents of Wilmette is $7.50 per person, $3 after 6 P.M. Sailboats and kayaks are available for rent ($35–75 per hour). On weekend evenings July–August, the park district holds free concerts in the Wallace Bowl, a little stage by the lake.

Skokie River Nature Preserve

The quiet Skokie River Nature Preserve (from Green Bay Rd. turn west on Laurel Ave. until it ends, Lake Forest, 847/234-3880, www.lfola.org, 6:30 A.M.–sunset) has four miles of wood-chip trails through woodlands and meadows, with plenty of benches and spots along the way to picnic or watch for wildlife. There's a swinging bridge over the river. The preserve is managed by Lake Forest Open Lands, a land trust organization.

ACCOMMODATIONS
$100-150

Located just off Highway 41 (the Edens Expressway) and not far from the Chicago Botanic Garden, the **Courtyard Chicago Highland Park** (1505 Lake Cook Road, Highland Park, 847/831-3338, www.marriott.com, $89–187) is in a central spot for north shore tripping. Its prices aren't too bad either. The 149-room hotel has an indoor pool and restaurant, plus a free shuttle will take you to the garden and shops near the hotel.

$150-250

Located at the site of a former hunting lodge in Lake Forest, the **⟪ Deer Path Inn** (255 E. Illinois Rd., Lake Forest, 800/788-9480, www.dpihotel.com, $170) was built in 1929. Designed by Chicago architect William Jones, who also designed a number of buildings for the Chicago World's Fair, the Deer Path is an English manor type of inn. There are 54 rooms in a variety of layouts, including regular rooms, suites, and executive-level suites. Suites can cost up to about $300 per night. Depending on which room you stay in, you'll receive slippers and robes, turn-down service, and whirlpool baths. Each guest is treated to a breakfast buffet, but the Sunday champagne brunch is quite an extravagant feast and worth the $35.

FOOD
Casual

Try the crispy thin-crust pizza at **Buffo's** (431 Sheridan Rd., Highwood, 847/432-0301, 11 A.M.–11 P.M. Mon.–Sat., 11 A.M.–10 P.M. Sun., $5–10), a casual spot to grab a bite to eat. Buffo's is a kid-friendly place, popular among local softball and soccer teams.

You can't beat the cheese steaks (or cheese fries or chocolate shakes) at **Hoagie Hut** (555 Bank Ln., Highwood, 847/432-3262, 10:30 A.M.–10 P.M. Mon.–Sat., 11 A.M.–7 P.M. Sun.), a casual and friendly little place near the Metra line.

⟪ The Lantern (768 N. Western Ave., 847/234-9844, kitchen open 11 A.M.–11 P.M., bar until midnight, $6) is where the locals go when they are not in the mood for foie gras. At this casual intimate bar and restaurant you'll meet a mix of millionaire business professionals, college students, and folks who work in nearby towns. On the menu are burgers, sandwiches such as Reubens, and roast chicken. Right by the Metra station, it's a good place to hang out before you catch the train.

Most dishes at **The Silo** (625 Rockland Rd., Lake Bluff, 847/234-6660, 11 A.M.–10 P.M. Mon.–Thurs., 11 A.M.–midnight Fri.–Sat., 4–10 P.M. Sun., pizzas $5–24, sandwiches $7), right off the Edens Expressway, seem to ooze cheese (the chili, the pizza, the patty melts). Portions are large, and the atmosphere is welcoming to everyone—families, college students, and couples. Deep-dish pizzas are the specialty, but you'll also find some more unusual menu items, such as ostrich burgers.

Cafés

The apple pancakes are out of this world at **Walker Brothers Pancake House** (620 Central Ave., Highland Park, 847/432-0660, 7 A.M.–10 P.M. Sun.–Thurs., 7 A.M.–11 P.M. Fri.–Sat., $6–10). They're several inches thick, supersweet, dense, and chunky. They're worth the wait on a weekend morning. Other breakfast foods here, such as the waffles, are also able to fill you up and make you want to unfasten your belt a notch.

On a sunny morning, the outdoor patio at **C Southgate Café** (655 Forest Ave., Lake Forest, 847/234-8800, www.southgatecafe. com, 11:30 A.M.–8:30 P.M. Mon.–Thurs., 9 A.M.–9 P.M. Fri.–Sat., 9 A.M.–8 P.M. Sun., $12–25) is a great spot to read the paper and feast on French toast or scrambled eggs.

Regional chain restaurant **Egg Harbor** (512 N. Western Ave., 847/295-3449, Lake Forest, www.eggharborcafe.com, breakfast and lunch daily, $7), which features breakfast and lunch, is probably better-known for its big rich breakfasts, such as open-faced omelets, eggs Benedict, and oatmeal-raisin French toast.

Mexican

For this writer, a perfect day would include time spent in the outdoor sidewalk café at **C Hot Tamales** (493 Central Ave., Highland Park, 847/433-4070, 11 A.M.–2 P.M.

Mon.–Sat., 5–9 P.M. Sun.–Thurs., 5–10 P.M. Fri.–Sat., $10), munching on chips and *salsa verde* and sipping a cold beer. This brightly colored, lively restaurant serves amazingly fresh dishes (the tomatoes and peppers taste as if they were picked from a garden that morning), including corn chowders, quesadillas, and of course tamales.

Fine Dining

Former astronaut and Lake Forest resident Jim Lovell and his son, Jay, a chef, are behind the fancy **Lovell's of Lake Forest** (915 S. Waukegan Rd., Lake Forest, 847/234-8013, www.lovellsoflakeforest.com, 11 A.M.–2 P.M. Mon.–Fri., 5–9 P.M. Sun.–Thurs., 5–11 P.M. Fri.–Sat., lunch entrées $12–22, dinner entrées $32 and up). There's a manly man bent to this restaurant, with a martini and cigar bar, cognac list, and a menu that includes game, such as antelope loin. It's not too clubby, though; after all, there is a children's menu, which features chicken fingers. Lovell's last trip into space, by the way, was aboard Apollo 13 (Tom Hanks played him in the movie named after the mission).

Carlos and Debbie Nieto's French restaurant **C Carlos'** (429 Temple, Highland Park, 847/432-0770, www.carlos-restaurant.com, 5:30–9 P.M. Sun.–Fri., 5:30–9:45 P.M. Sat., $80) has been receiving rave reviews since it opened. It's a lovely restaurant, and eating here is a carefully and beautifully designed multi-course event. Here's a sample from a recent degustation menu: rabbit loin wrapped in prosciutto di Parma with purple potato rosettes, black truffle and leek spaghettini and a natural jus. If only you could eat like this every night. The food is French, and in addition to an extensive degustation menu you can choose from a regular menu.

Nearby is **Café Central** (455 Central, Highland Park, 847/266-7878, 10:30 A.M.–9 P.M. Tues.–Thurs., 11:30 A.M.–10 P.M. Fri.–Sat., 8 A.M.–10 P.M. Sun., $10), also run by the Nietos. Like Carlos', Café Central serves French food, but this restaurant is more casual (you can sit at a sidewalk table) and less expensive. Dishes are less artsy but still great-tasting items such as a *croque monsieur* (a French version of grilled cheese).

Candy Shop
Colorful 【 Sweets (284 E. Deerpath Rd., Lake Forest, 847/295-1111) in downtown Lake Forest has jars stocked with all the goodies you can imagine, from Gummi Bears to flavored licorice.

Markets
Don's Finest Foods (850 N. Western Ave., Lake Forest, 847/234-2700) in downtown Lake Forest sells fresh fruits and vegetables, deli meats and salads, chocolates, wines, and a variety of organic and healthy food products.

INFORMATION AND SERVICES
Visitor Information
The **Chicago's North Shore Convention and Visitors Bureau** (8001 Lincoln Ave., Suite 715, Skokie, 847/763-0011, www.visitchicagonorthshore.com) keeps track of what's doing in towns from Evanston to Lake Bluff.

The **Highland Park Chamber of Commerce** (508 Central Ave., Suite 206, Highland Park, 847/432-0284, www.ehighlandpark.com) publishes a decent shopping and dining guide.

The **Lake Forest/Lake Bluff Chamber of Commerce** (695 N. Western Ave., near Metra train line, Lake Forest, 847/234-4282, www.lakeforestonline.com) also maintains a shopping and dining guide, plus information about things to do in the two communities.

Media
North Shore Magazine (www.northshoremag.com) is a colorful glossy monthly with restaurant reviews, performing arts information, and profiles of famous current and past residents. You can pick up copies at drugstores such as CVS, convenience stores such as White Hen, and bookstores such as Borders.

Pioneer Press (www.pioneerlocal.com) publishes weekly newspapers on Wednesdays in several North Shore towns, including Lake Forest and Highland Park.

Services
Not feeling well? Pay a visit to the **Highland Park Hospital** (718 Glenview Ave., Highland Park, 847/432-8000) or **Lake Forest Hospital** (660 N. Westmoreland Rd., Lake Forest, 847/234-5600).

If you are not a resident of Lake Forest, you won't be able to check books out of **The Lake Forest Library** (360 E. Deerpath Rd., Lake Forest, 847/234-0636, www.lakeforestlibrary.org, 9 A.M.–9 P.M. Mon.–Thurs., 9 A.M.–5 P.M. Fri.–Sat., 1–5 P.M. Sun. Sept.–May), but that's no reason not to stop by this building. The library has an impressive collection of American art, including John James Audubon engravings. On a cold winter day you won't want to leave the reading room, with its crackling fireplace and armchairs.

While you're waiting to catch your train, drop by a neat little barbershop in the Lake Forest train station: **Michael's Barber Shop** (950 Northwestern, Lake Forest, 847/234-9752).

GETTING AROUND
Metra's Union Pacific North Line (312/496-4777, www.metrarail.com), which runs from Chicago to Kenosha, stops at most North Shore towns. Trains run about every hour 5 A.M.–1 A.M. Monday–Friday, except during rush hours, when they run about every 15 minutes. Trains run about every two hours 5 A.M.–1 A.M. Saturday and Sunday.

Lake County

With sand dunes on the Lake Michigan coastline, a rare bog to the west, a historic village to the south, and a chain of lakes to the north, Lake County contains some of the most picturesque landscapes in all of Chicagoland. You can walk the nature trails in popular Illinois Beach State Park or Volo Bog. Rent a rowboat and paddle out on one of the Chain O' Lakes. Or, for a change of pace, drain your checking account at the huge Gurnee Mills mall and test your will at Six Flags Great America.

CHAIN O' LAKES AND GRAYSLAKE
Chain O' Lakes State Park

Formed by retreating glaciers thousands of years ago, the lakes that make up this region all came about naturally, unlike many of the big lakes in the rest of the state. Chain O' Lakes State Park (8906 Wilmot Rd., Spring Grove, 847/587-5512, www.dnr .state.il.us, 6 A.M.–9 P.M. daily in the summer, 8 A.M.–sunset in the winter), a few miles south of the state line, has about 3,000 acres of woods and prairie and nearly 6,500 acres of water. Most of that is freshwater bog over peat deposits. The state park offers access to some of these lakes, including Grass Lake, a 44-acre lake that was famous for its blooming lotuses (you can still see some in the backwater areas), plus Maria and Nippernik lakes. These lakes lead to the Fox River, which runs south through the eastern part of the park and connects to seven other lakes. You could spend a lot of time in your boat exploring these lakes. Fishing and boating is the thing to do for area residents, and the lake can get a little loud as speedboats zoom by on sunny summer days.

Instead, take the quiet route. One of the most relaxing ways to see the park is by renting a canoe or rowboat from the park's concession stand and paddling out through some of the low-lying grassy areas of the lake, where you can listen to frogs and birds singing. Another great option is renting a horse from the park's stables and hitting the eight-mile-long equestrian trail on the west side of the park. Other trails include a 2.5-mile nature trail near the campgrounds and a bicycle (or in-line skating) trail throughout much of the park. You'll trek through oak, hickory, and birch forests, restored prairie, and bogs. These trails, by the way, can be used for cross-country skiing in the winter.

Chain O' Lakes State Park offers what the Department of Natural Resources calls "rent a tent." For a fee you camp in a tent or rent a cabin, and the park supplies you with the necessary camping accessories (lanterns, etc.). Cabins come with bunk beds and a double bed and rent for about $25 per night plus various camping and utility fees. Renting a tent costs $8–12, plus camping fees. There are also electrified campsites for RVs. A word of caution: The park is open only to deer and waterfowl hunters early November–mid-December.

Volo Bog State Natural Area

South of Chain O' Lakes State Park is a treasure of a natural area, Volo Bog State Natural Area (28478 W. Brandenburg Rd., Ingleside, 815/344-1294, www.dnr.state.il.us). A National Natural Landmark, Volo Bog is a quaking bog: It has a floating layer of moss at the edges and fresh water in the middle. Like the nearby lakes, the bog was formed when the Wisconsin glacier (the last glacier in the region) started melting and retreating, depositing sand, rocks, and blocks of ice. The ice eventually melted and formed marshes, ponds, and lakes. Volo Bog was originally a deep lake, but because of poor drainage several thousand years ago, vegetation such as sphagnum moss started growing in it, eventually forming a layer of peat around the edges. Eventually cattails, sedges, shrubs, and tamaracks grew around it. In the 1960s the bog was almost plowed over for development, but area citizens rallied to protect it and helped the Illinois Department of Natural Resources buy the land.

THE COLLAR COUNTIES

© GEOFFREY POCIASK

Volo Bog State Natural Area

The total site is about 1,100 acres; Volo Bog itself is a little less than 50 acres. There are also two smaller bogs nearby. A half-mile interpretive trail on a floating boardwalk has signs that explain how bogs form. The tamarack view trail, almost three miles long, weaves throughout the site, up and down sloping areas, through woods and wetlands. Because the bog's water is acidic (due to the presence of moss), rare plants thrive here—look for orchids. You might also be able to spot some herons and sandhill cranes. Before you hit the trail, stop by the visitors center (9 A.M.–3 P.M. Wed.–Sun.) in a dairy barn to learn a little about the bog's history (natural and otherwise).

Winery
At the **Glunz Family Winery** (888 E. Belvidere Rd., Grayslake, 847/548-9463, www.gfwc.com, 10 A.M.–6 P.M. Mon.–Sat., noon–5 P.M. Sun.) you can sample red and white table wines made from California grapes as well as wines made from raspberries, plus a few other concoctions such as sangria and mulled wine.

Events
Watch dogs perform tricks, listen to 1980s bands play music, and ride a camel: You can do all these things at the **Lake County Fair** (Lake County Fairgrounds, U.S. 45 north of Hwy. 20, Grayslake, www.lakecountyfairassoc.com, end of July, $7). The classic county fair has carnival rides, horse shows, a petting zoo, 4-H exhibits, and lots of fried and sugar-laden food. Almost 200,000 people visit this weeklong fair.

Information
Check with the **Fox Waterway Agency** (5 S. Pistakee Lake Rd., Fox Lake, 847/587-8540, www.foxwaterway.state.il.us) for lake and river conditions, information about underwater fish cribs, and other hunting and fishing information.

LAKE MICHIGAN SITES
Illinois Beach State Park
Sandy beaches, nature and bike trails, marshland, campgrounds, and a resort—Illinois Beach State Park (main entrance at Sheridan and Wadsworth Rds., Zion, 847/662-4828 or 847/662-4811, www.dnr.state.il.us) seems to have it all. It is a great park, but Illinois Beach has a past and some neighbors that it just cannot run away from. The park is divided into two sections, north and south, and between them is the Zion nuclear power plant. Towering nuclear reactors (the plant was shut down in 1998) are not exactly a pretty sight while you're sunbathing or on a nature walk. Then to the south is a federal Superfund site where asbestos was once processed. Asbestos has washed up on the shore in recent years. Oh, and the northern part of the park was a prisoner-of-war camp during the Civil War. If you can get past these things (and apparently many people have, as it's the most-visited state park in Illinois), it is quite beautiful. The 4,000-acre park has trails that weave through wetlands, dune habitat, and woodland areas, free sandy swimming beaches, fishing ponds, and more.

In the northern section, between 7th and 21st Streets, you'll find North Point Marina, beaches, and picnic areas. The southern section, between just north of Greenwood Drive and 29th Street, contains more beaches, the resort, campground, interpretive center, and nature center. A bike trail connects the two sections. The campground has 224 electric sites, and some are wooded. Reservations are not required, but this is a popular campground and sites fill up fast. Call the park office to reserve a place. As mentioned, chunks of asbestos have been known to wash up on the shore of the beaches, sometimes closing the beach. Just how this type of asbestos affects folks hiking and swimming in the area is up for debate.

Illinois Beach Resort and Conference Center (Lake Front Dr., Zion, 847/625-7300 or 866/452-3224, www.ilresorts.com) is a modern hotel in the southern part of the park. Rooms there start around $105 during tourist season. If the beach is closed or it's cool outside, you can swim in the Olympic-size swimming pool or warm up in the sauna. The restaurant, which has tables looking out onto the park, serves breakfast, lunch, and dinner daily. Dinner entrées such as fillets and seafood dishes are around $15.

North Point Marina

You can also swim or sun yourself at the beaches at North Point Marina (701 North Point Dr., Winthrop Harbor, 847/746-2845), a marina and park north of the state park. The marina has 1,500 boat slips, a fishing pier, fish-cleaning facilities, picnic tables and grills, plus two restaurants. Several fishing-boat charter tours depart from North Point Marina (see *Fishing* in the *Essentials* chapter).

GURNEE, LIBERTYVILLE, AND WADSWORTH
Six Flags Great America

What's a summer if you haven't spent at least one day riding roller coasters? At Six Flags Great America (Hwy. 134 and I-94, Gurnee, 847/249-4636, www.sixflags.com) you have your pick of a dozen roller coasters, from the vintage Viper, a wooden coaster, to Raging Bull, a coaster that zips along at as much as 73

© CHRISTINE DES GARENNES

Illinois Beach State Park

Six Flags Great America

© CHRISTINE DES GARENNES

miles per hour and drops as much as 200 feet. And then there's Vertical Velocity, one of those terrifying spiraling coasters on which riders' feet dangle in the air. Six Flags Great America has plenty of stuff for little kids too—low-to-the-ground coasters, carousels, and people dancing around dressed up like cartoon characters. The biggest change to the park in recent years has been the opening of a separate area called **Hurricane Harbor Water Park,** which opened in spring 2005. It's got the standard water-park features, such as a wave pool, water playground, flume rides, and mat slides.

The park is open May–October. Hours vary each year, but generally during the peak summer season, late June–mid-August, the park is open 10 A.M.–10 P.M. daily. Tickets are $55 and include admission into the theme park and water park. Early-season tickets (for May) are a few bucks cheaper, and the website also offers online deals. Children under three get in free. If you buy and print your tickets from the website, you won't have to wait in line at the ticket counter. You can leave and come back the same day; just make sure you stop at the booth and

get your hand stamped. There are bank machines in the park. No coolers, food, drink, or other picnic items are allowed. There are restaurants and concession stands in the park. You can rent strollers and wheelchairs.

Gurnee Mills

With more than 200 stores, restaurants, a movie theater, game arcade, and more, Gurnee Mills Mall (6170 W. Grand Ave., just off I-94, Gurnee, 847/263-7500 or 800/937-7467, www.gurneemillsmall.com, 10 A.M.–9 P.M. Mon.–Fri., 10 A.M.–9:30 P.M. Sat., 11 A.M.–7 P.M. Sun.) is an exhaustingly large complex. Highlights include **Rink Side Sports** (6152 W. Grand Ave., Gurnee, 847/856-1064, www.rinksidesports.com), where you can play with pretend guns (laser tag, video games) until the cows come home, and **Bass Pro Shops Outdoor World** (6112 W. Grand Ave., 847/856-1229, www.basspro.com), a 125,000-square-foot store where you can shop for real guns, stop by the archery range, check out fish in giant aquariums, and see how you look in blaze orange.

Horse Show

Even if you're not a horse owner or horse admirer, the dressage shows at **Tempel Lipizzans** (17000 Wadsworth Rd., Wadsworth, 847/623-7272, www.tempelfarms.com, Sun. and Wed. during summer, $18) are amazing. A quick explanation: Lipizzans are a European breed of stallion (they're white horses, although they are born brown and gradually turn white) and dressage is a French style of riding or performing. After attending a performance where horses and riders demonstrate medieval battle techniques, jump, and dance, you can tour the stables and view antique carriages and other equestrian accessories.

Lamb's Farm

Families with young children should plan a trip to Lamb's Farm (Hwy. 176 and I-94, 847/362-4636, www.lambsfarm.org, 10 A.M.–5 P.M. daily late Mar.–late Oct., $5), a petting zoo, pet shop, country restaurant, and game complex just off the interstate and not far from Great America. The whole project is to benefit children and adults with disabilities by providing them with places to live and opportunities for work. The petting zoo, called the Farmyard, has standard farm animals such as chickens and bunnies. Then there are a pet-supply shop, miniature golf course, miniature train ride around the 72-acre campus, and other games. The restaurant serves American country food such as fried chicken and mashed potatoes (in heaping portions). A country store and bakery sells fresh bread, jams, chocolates, and other goodies made by the staff. The farmyard, country shop, and pet shop are open 10 A.M.–5 P.M. daily and the restaurant is open for breakfast and lunch 7 A.M.–3 P.M. Tuesday–Friday, 8 A.M.–3 P.M. Sunday. Admission into the farmyard, where the animals are, is $5; however, you'll have to pay a few bucks extra for each minitrain ride, carousel ride, and other games. If you plan to do all these things, opt for the unlimited children's daily pass for $12 and adult pass for $6.

Cuneo Museum and Gardens

A Venetian-style mansion built for millionaire businessman John Cuneo, Cuneo Museum and Gardens (1350 N. Milwaukee Ave., Vernon Hills, 847/362-3042, www.cuneomuseum. org, guided tours 11 A.M., 1 P.M., and 3 P.M. Tues.–Sat. summer, self-guided tours fall–spring, $12) is an extravagant estate hidden off Highway 21 (Milwaukee Avenue). The pink main house and its contents exude wealth (it's like Italian Barbie's dream house). Rich tapestries hang on the walls, a chapel has ornate stained-glass windows, and there are a greenhouse, an indoor swimming pool, and an amazing marble-floored ballroom that Cuneo's children actually used as a playroom. Outside are colorful rose gardens. Tour prices are a little steep, so if you're on a budget or don't want to spend much time inside the house, pay the $7 parking fee and hang out in the lush gardens. The grounds are open 10 A.M.–5 P.M. Tuesday–Sunday.

Events

Downtown Libertyville (along Milwaukee Ave.), with its city park, boutiques, and restaurants, transforms itself into a Norman Rockwell town at Christmas by organizing evening caroling events, offering horse-drawn carriages, and holding a tree-lighting ceremony. It's called **Dickens of a Holiday** and is held from the end of November until a few days before Christmas.

Accommodations and Food

Families or groups will appreciate the huge **(KeyLime Cove Water Resort** (1790 Nations Dr., Gurnee, 847/406-3993, www.keylimecove.com, $200 and up), a new hotel and water park complex that has everything you, your spouse, your parents, and your kids could need for a weekend. The water park has the required wave pool, kiddie pool, and lazy river, but also several slides and an activity pool for playing games like water basketball. The 400-plus-room hotel also has several shops (including one for swimming trunks and similar items), several restaurants (ice cream, coffee, burgers, seafood), an arcade, and a spa. The water park, typically open 10 A.M.–9 P.M. Monday–Friday,

9 A.M.–10 P.M. Saturday–Sunday, is available only to hotel guests.

The new **Hotel Indigo** (450 N. Milwaukee Ave., Vernon Hills, 847/918-1400, www.hotelindigo.com, $110 and up) boasts modern decor (no Victorian-style wallpapered rooms here), an indoor pool, fitness center, and one feature not many hotels have any more: You can actually open the room's windows for fresh air.

The **Econolodge** (3740 Grand Ave., Gurnee, 847/623-7777, traditional rooms $60–70, themed rooms around $140) is a hoot with its themed rooms and indoor swimming pool. Choose from rooms decorated like an igloo, a bamboo shack, a Roman bathhouse, a carousel, and a variety of other, ahem, interesting decor.

If you'd rather spend your money shopping at the mall or at Six Flags Great America, book a room at the **Gurnee Grand Hotel and Suites** (5520 W. Grand Ave., Gurnee, 847/249-7777 or 866/874-7263, www.gurneegrandhotel.com, $50–140), a budget hotel with a few amusing fantasy suites of its own.

Other mid-price hotels in Libertyville include a **Holiday Inn Express** (77 Buckley Rd./Hwy. 137, Libertyville, 847/863-4780). **Candlewood Suites** (1000 N. Hwy. 45, Libertyville, 847/247-9900), is an extended stay–type of hotel with little kitchens in the rooms.

◖ Mickey Finn's (412 N. Milwaukee Ave., Libertyville, 847/362-6688, www.mickeyfinnsbrewery.com, 11 A.M.–11:30 P.M. Mon.–Thurs., 11 A.M.–1:15 A.M. Fri.–Sat., noon–9 P.M. Sun., $9), a lively brew pub and restaurant on Main Street, is a great spot to fill up on big sandwiches such as stacked turkey clubs or classic burgers and fries. Or just have a seat at the 100-year-old bar and order a homemade beer such as oatmeal stout or root beer. Upstairs the Amber Room hosts live music concerts Thursday–Saturday.

Information
Downtown Libertyville (Milwaukee Ave., 847/680-0370, www.mainstreetlibertyville.org) organizes events such as weekly food tastings in the park during the summer. For a list of shops and restaurants, call or visit its website.

◖ HISTORIC VILLAGE OF LONG GROVE
Long Grove is a rarity in this part of Illinois. Surrounded by modern subdivisions, golf courses, and shopping centers, the village is a flashback to life more than 100 years ago, with whitewashed frame houses, a mill pond, and a covered bridge. First settled in the 1830s by immigrants from the Alsace-Lorraine region between France and Germany, the village has preserved many of the original buildings, such as a community church and a one-room schoolhouse. How much time you spend here depends on how much you love historic towns and shopping. Housed inside the vintage buildings are several boutiques where local residents sell imported French furniture, antiques, Scandinavian gifts, gourmet food, and more. The core business district is centered around Old McHenry Road and Robert Parker Coffin

© CHRISTINE DES GARENNES

Historic Village of Long Grove

Road, near Highways 53 and 83. You have to drive to get here.

Shopping

Buckets of molded chocolates and chocolate-dipped strawberries are sold at **Long Grove Confectionery Co.** (220 Robert Parker Coffin Rd., Long Grove, 847/634-0080, www.long-grove.com). When the company started years ago, the chocolate concoctions were actually made in the Long Grove schoolhouse. Now the schoolhouse is a retail shop, and the cooking operations are housed in a factory to the south in Buffalo Grove. (You can tour the candy factory in Buffalo Grove; for tour information call 847/459-3100 or 888/459-3100. The one-hour tours are held during hours of production and cost $2.)

Old-fashioned popcorn (meaning no artificial flavorings) is the specialty at **Long Grove Popcorn Shoppe** (318 Old McHenry Rd., Long Grove, 847/921-9101, www.thelong-grovepopcorn.com, 10 A.M.–5 P.M. Mon.–Sat., 11 A.M.–5 P.M. Sun.). See how good the stuff tastes with real butter and real caramel. Load up on bags or tins.

Coffee and tea are sold by the pound and the cup at **Beans and Leaves** (320 Old McHenry Rd., Long Grove, 847/844-9450, 7:30 A.M.–5 P.M. Mon.–Fri., 9:30 A.M.–5 P.M. Sat., 10:30 A.M.–5 P.M. Sun.), a bustling little coffee shop downtown.

Looking for some shiny accessories for your diner-like kitchen? **Nifty 50s** (327 Old McHenry Rd., Long Grove, 847/821-7047) sells art deco and art nouveau decor (including neon items), jukeboxes, Betty Boop memorabilia, and lots of other imaginative pieces.

Nickelby's (219 Robert Parker Coffin Rd., Long Grove, 847/634-6552, 10:30 A.M.–5 P.M. Mon.–Sat., 11:30 A.M.–5 P.M. Sun.) sells fine stationery, greeting cards, stamps, and more.

Events

The Historic Village of Long Grove is a festival-happy village with several tourist-friendly events held throughout the year. The best ones are the **Strawberry Festival** at the end of June, at which you can eat as much strawberry shortcake and strawberry pie as you want. Another culinary extravaganza takes place in May. At **Chocolate Fest,** chefs demonstrate all the fabulous dishes you can create with chocolate, and you can nibble to your heart's content on samples and load your trunk with boxes of truffles. Both festivals are held in downtown Long Grove.

Accommodations and Food

There's a wholesome country-charm feel to the ◖ **Round Robin Inn** (231 E. Maple Ave., Mundelein, 847/566-7664, www.roundrobininn.com, $60–160), south of Long Grove. Pick from seven rooms with names such as "Stars and Stripes Forever" and "Camelot." Rooms contain large beds covered with quilts and are decorated with items such as a portrait of Abraham Lincoln.

Open since 1849, the ◖ **Village Tavern** (135 Old McHenry Rd., Long Grove, 847/634-3117, 11:30 A.M.–3 P.M. and 5–9 P.M. Mon., 11:30 A.M.–9 P.M. Wed.–Thurs., 11:30 A.M.–10 P.M. Fri.–Sat., 9 A.M.–9 P.M. Sun., bar open later, under $10) has a friendly pub-like atmosphere with American food entrées such as meatloaf and pizza. Its all-you-can-eat dinners throughout the week always attract a crowd.

Housed in a restored Victorian home, ◖ **Enzo and Lucia's Ristorante** (343 Old McHenry Rd., Long Grove, 847/478-8825, 11 A.M.–9:30 P.M. Mon.–Thurs., 11 A.M.–midnight Fri.–Sat., 11 A.M.–9 P.M. Sun., $14–25) is a white-tablecloth restaurant. Here it's all Italian all the time. Enjoy fresh homemade pasta, fresh calamari, and desserts while sitting outside.

Information

The shops and restaurants within the **Village of Long Grove** (visitors center 847/634-0888, www.longgroveonline.com) have put together a detailed brochure and website that contain information on the town's festivals, attractions, and more. Also, a little visitors center is near a parking lot south of the fountain square, between Old McHenry and Robert

Parker Coffin Roads. Most shops in the town are open 10 A.M.–5 P.M. Monday–Saturday, 11 A.M.–5 P.M. Sunday.

NEAR LONG GROVE
Lake County Discovery Museum and Curt Teich Postcard Archives

Not many people may recognize the name Curt Teich, but what about vintage postcards with "Greetings From . . ." written in large letters across a blue sky or street scene? The enormously popular postcards from the first half of the 20th century were created by the Curt Teich Postcard Company, formerly of Chicago. Hundreds of thousands of these postcards are stored and some of them are on view at the Lake County Discovery Museum and the Curt Teich Postcard Archives (27277 Forest Preserve Dr., Wauconda, 847/968-3400, www.lakecountydiscovery-museum.org, 11 A.M.–4:30 P.M. Mon.–Sat., 1 A.M.–4:30 P.M. Sun., $6, $3 Tues.), about 15 miles northwest of Long Grove in the Lakewood Forest Preserve. The museum's postcard exhibits detail the history of postcards but also Teich's technique. After establishing a studio in Chicago in 1898, he traveled around snapping black-and-white photographs of towns, monuments, and landscapes and jotting down notes about what colors appeared in them. Later, artists would draw in the colors and blot out anything unsightly in the images.

In addition to the postcards on view and the historical exhibits, the Lake County Museum has a well-organized and educational exhibit about the history of the county, focusing on how the landscape has changed through the decades due to residential and commercial development. It also has a gallery that showcases photography and works of area artists. Follow signs to the museum from Highway 176.

INFORMATION

The main tourism bureau promoting the region is the **Lake County Convention and Visitors Bureau** (5465 W. Grand Ave., Gurnee, 847/662-2700 or 800/525-3669, www.lakecounty.org).

GETTING AROUND

Metra (312/322-6777, www.metrarail.com) operates several commuter train lines that serve Lake County seven days a week. Times vary by line and day of the week. Fares also vary, but you can buy a $5 weekend pass that's good on all trains Saturday and Sunday. The Union Pacific North Line runs from Chicago's Ogilvie Transportation Center to Kenosha with stops in Zion and Winthrop Harbor along Lake Michigan. The Milwaukee District Line connects Chicago's Union Station to Fox Lake with stops in Grayslake, Libertyville, and other towns. And the North Central Service goes from Chicago's Union Station to Antioch (a town just south of the Wisconsin border), with stops in Round Lake Beach, Vernon Hills, and other towns.

Northwest Suburbs

Connected to Chicago via commuter train lines and I-90, the northwest suburbs are a string of solid suburban communities—not quite the sprawling suburbs of Schaumburg or Hoffman Estates farther out west, but not quite as eclectic as inner-ring suburbs such as Oak Park and Evanston. Homes here are well-kept, streets are mostly quiet, and the schools are good. This is where many young families live. Highlights include the racehorse track Arlington Park and the performance venues in Rosemont, which seems to cater to the conventioneer set.

DES PLAINES AND NILES
"First" McDonald's

So, technically it is not the first McDonald's restaurant, and no one serves hamburgers or milk shakes here, but the **McDonald's #1 Store Museum** (400 N. Lee St., Des Plaines, 847/297-5022, www.mcdonalds.com, roughly Memorial Day–Labor Day, free) is a neat stop to drop by for a quick visit. The original store was actually torn down long ago, but this is a nifty recreation spot, complete with shiny cars from the 1950s outside the store. Mannequins model how McDonald's employees used to prepare food decades ago (by gosh, they used to cut up potatoes before frying them). A video on the lower level tells the story of Ray Kroc, the creator, and how the empire got its start. If you're itching for a cheeseburger after your visit, there's a working McDonald's just across the street.

Golf

Even in April, the Chicago area can be chilly, and temperatures of 45°F (or even snow) are not unheard of. With that said, golfers will appreciate the chance to get their golf games in gear at the **Golf Center of Des Plaines** (353 N. River Rd., Des Plaines, 847/803-4653, www.desplainesparks.org, 8 A.M.–10 P.M. daily, $7–15). The center has 80 heated stations at its three-level driving range.

Leaning Tower of Niles

Fool your friends back home by having your photo taken in front of the **Leaning Tower of Niles** (6300 W. Touhy Ave., Niles, 847/647-8222). This tower, a much smaller version of the original, was built in 1932 as part of a recreational complex. As it happens, Niles and Pisa, Italy, are sister cities. The building now belongs to the YMCA, and the village hosts evening concerts here outside in the summer.

Food

A favorite among the kids and older train buffs, the **C Choo Choo Restaurant** (600 Lee St., Des Plaines, 847/391-9815, www.thechoochoo.com, 10:30 A.M.–8 P.M. Mon.–Fri., 7 A.M.–3 P.M. Sat., $6) has food delivered to some lucky customers on a toy train. Open since 1951, this breakfast and lunch spot serves milk shakes, pecan Belgian waffles, egg salad sandwiches, and chili dogs (a beef dog with turkey chili). Try the freight car of onion rings.

Another northwest side institution is **Affy Tapple** (7425 Croname Rd., Niles, 847/588-2900, www.affytapple.com, 9 A.M.–5 P.M. Mon.–Fri., 9 A.M.–2 P.M. Sat.) which also dates back more than 50 years. Visit the factory store and load up on caramel apples covered with peanuts.

ROSEMONT
Donald E. Stephens Museum of Hummels

In a town where the name Donald E. Stephens appears on almost every major building (Stephens was mayor here from when the town was incorporated in the 1950s until his death in 2007; his son Bradley Stephens is now mayor), perhaps it shouldn't be too surprising there is a Hummel museum named after him. The Donald E. Stephens Museum of Hummels (555 N. River Rd., Rosemont, 847/692-4000, www.stephenshummelmuseum.com, call for appointment) has thousands of those little ceramic figurines: cherub-faced boys and girls carrying umbrellas, books, and flowers with ceramic birds always perched nearby, on the fence post, or on top of the child's hat. Surprise—some Hummels and other figurines are for sale.

Performance Venues

The **Allstate Arena** (6920 N. Mannheim Rd., Rosemont, 847/635-6601, www.allstatearena.com) is a 19,000-seat arena that holds major rock, pop, and country concerts as well as events such as the Harlem Globetrotters and national circus shows.

The more intimate **Rosemont Theatre** (5400 River Rd., Rosemont, 847/671-5100, www.rosemont.com, 11 a.m.–7 p.m. Mon.–Fri., noon–5 p.m. Sat.) has 4,300 seats. You can catch a wide variety of stars here, including Tom Jones and Tori Amos.

Movies

The new, enormous (it's over 100,000 square feet) **Muvico 18** (9701 W. Bryn Mawr Ave., Rosemont, 847/447-1030, www.muvico.com) is not your typical movieplex. The VIP Theatre, for moviegoers 21 years old and up, has free popcorn, bigger seats, and cocktails. You can even dig into a salad or a fillet while watching the movie; a full-service restaurant is on-site. The complex also has a playroom and child care for kids age 3–10.

Sports

The semiprofessional hockey team the **Chicago Wolves** (6920 N. Mannheim Rd., Rosemont, 800/843-9658, www.chicagowolves.com) play in the Allstate Arena in Rosemont, just off I-90. The season runs mid-October–mid-April.

Information

Rosemont is packed with national chain hotels and restaurants. Just about every hotel chain has a location here. For lodging or dining information, contact the **Rosemont Convention Bureau** (9301 W. Bryn Mawr Ave., Rosemont, 847/823-2100, www.rosemont.com).

ARLINGTON HEIGHTS
Arlington Park

Open since 1929, Arlington Park (2200 W. Euclid Ave., Arlington Heights, 847/385-7500, www.arlingtonpark.com, $6–7 admission, reserved seating and program guide extra) is a premier park to watch and bet on thoroughbred horse racing in the Midwest. After ownership changes, a fire in 1985 (which forced races to shift to Hawthorne Racetrack for a while), and then a few years of closure in the late 1990s, Arlington Park now seems to attract a good mix of regular bettors, young couples, and even families out for a day. The park itself is well-maintained, with plenty of flowers planted around the track area and staff cleaning up after bettors. Races are held every day except Tuesday mid-May–mid-September. If you're a novice, Arlington has special betting windows for beginners, plus a tutorial on its website.

Metropolis Performing Arts Center

Audiences can be treated to anything from a cabaret performance to a *Peter Pan* musical at the **Metropolis Performing Arts Center** (111 W. Campbell St., Arlington Heights, box office 847/577-2121, www.metropolisarts.com, 10 a.m.–5 p.m. or until show time on the day of an event Tues.–Sun.). This 350-seat theater is one block from the Arlington Heights Metra stop.

The Metropolis Performing Arts Center is part of a village development called the Metropolis. In addition to the theater, you'll also find a club called The Boiler Room on the building's lower level, as well as a supper club, shops, and apartments.

Janus Theatre (www.ahpd.org), affiliated with the Arlington Heights Park District, stages summer outdoor productions throughout the northwest suburbs.

Water Park and Hotel

Near Arlington Park is the newer **CoCo Key Resort** at the Sheraton Chicago Northwest (3400 W. Euclid Ave., Arlington Heights, 847/394-2000, www.cocokeyresort.com), a hotel with a substantial water park adjacent to it. The park has a wave pool, several water slides, whirlpool, sun deck, plus activities such as water basketball and a separate area (complete with plenty of slides) for younger children. Also on hand: an arcade, snack bar, restaurant, and bar. In the dead of the Chicago winter, this hotel can be a welcome oasis, particularly if you're traveling with kids. If you stay at the hotel water park, admission is included in the cost of your room. Day passes are available for people not staying in the hotel, but just how many nonhotel guests are admitted into the park will depend on capacity. The water park is typically open 10 A.M.–8 P.M. Sunday, 11 A.M.–8 P.M. Monday–Thursday, 11 A.M.–10 P.M. Friday, and 10 A.M.–10 P.M. Saturday.

Food

Irish pubs are a dime a dozen in Chicago and Chicagoland. **Peggy Kinnane's Irish Restaurant and Pub** (8 N. Vail Ave., Arlington Heights, 847/577-7733, www.peggykinnanes.com, 11 A.M.–1 A.M. Mon.–Thurs., 11 A.M.–2 A.M. Fri.–Sat., 10 A.M.–1 A.M. Sun.) has developed quite a following among northwestern residents. With its prime location and outdoor seating in downtown Arlington Heights, Peggy Kinnane's is a good place to hang out in the sun on an afternoon and have a brew. There are plenty of beers available on tap, plus sandwiches and meals served in large portions, such as fried cod fillets, fish and chips, traditional Irish dishes such as shepherd's pie, and a decent selection of non-Irish food such as pasta and sandwiches. There is live music Friday and Saturday evenings.

If you want to splurge on some glorious food, spend a few hours at ◖ **Le Titi de Paris** (1015 W. Dundee Rd., Arlington Heights, 847/506-0222, www.letitideparis.com, 5–9:30 P.M. Tues., 11:30 A.M.–2:30 P.M. and 5–9:30 P.M. Wed.–Thurs., 11:30 A.M.–2:30 P.M. and 5–10 P.M. Fri.–Sat., 5–9 P.M. Sun.). Here are just two examples of its beautiful creations: grilled striped bass with wilted spinach, shaved fennel, red onions, carrot mousseline, shallot essence, and garlic aioli. Or how about a duo of pheasant sausage and quail served with a wild mushroom and sweetbread mousse? Lunch entrées are around $20 and dinner

entrées $35, but this really is a place to order the whole shebang: appetizers, wine, and dessert, which is appropriately called the grand finale.

GLENVIEW

A fairly typical northwest suburb, Glenview is home to plenty of subdivisions and shopping centers, not to mention a business park or two (Kraft Foods has its headquarters here). As most suburbs go, it's chock-full of middle-class and upper-middle-class families, and if you're traveling with a load of kids in the van or wagon, you might want to schedule a stop here. Among the many parks and programs the Glenview Park District runs are two family-friendly and educational properties, the Wagner Farm and the Grove. **The Grove** (1421 Milwaukee Ave., Glenview, 847/299-6096, www.thegroveglenview.org, 8 A.M.–4:30 P.M. Mon.–Fri., 9 A.M.–5 P.M. Sat.–Sun.) is a 123-acre park and estate once belonging to a horticulturalist. There are several buildings here for kids to explore, including the former owner's estate, a greenhouse, log cabin, interpretive center, and more. In a similar vein, the hands-on **Wagner Farm** (1510 Wagner Rd., Glenview, 847/657-1506, 9 A.M.–5 P.M. Mon.–Sat., 9 A.M.–3 P.M. Sun.) is a place where clueless city kids can learn where milk comes from with a visit to the farm's milking parlor and how plants grow with a visit to a greenhouse.

Other educational activities are lined up for the little ones (specifically those up to eight years old) at the **Kohl Children's Museum of Greater Chicago** (2100 Patriot Blvd., Glenview, 847/832-6600, www.kohlschildrensmuseum.org, 9:30 A.M.–noon Mon., 9:30 A.M.–5 P.M. Tues.–Sat., noon–5 P.M. Sun., $7.50). Visitors can learn about gravity, electricity, and simple machines, and how to run a grocery store or doll day care.

INFORMATION

For tips on traveling to the region, contact the **Prospect Heights Convention and Visitors Bureau** (664 N. Milwaukee Ave., Suite 213, Prospect Heights, 847/577-3666 or 800/955-7259, www.chicagonorthsuburbs.com).

Busse Woods and Woodfield Corridor

At first glance, tourism activities along I-90 and I-290 seem to center on shopping, shopping, and shopping, especially at the gigantic Woodfield Mall, where you can buy everything imaginable. However, there are some other sights worthy of a visit, namely Lynfred Winery and Busse Woods.

SIGHTS
Lynfred Winery

A few miles from huge shopping complexes such as Woodfield Mall, Lynfred Winery (15 S. Roselle Rd., Roselle, 630/529-9463, www.lynfredwinery.com, 10 A.M.–7 P.M. daily, free) offers a nice little respite for folks looking for a break from the mall scene. Founded in the 1970s by the Koehler family, Lynfred Winery produces 25,000 cases of sweet red and white wines and some fruit wines. Some are made from Illinois grapes such as the chambourcin and chardonnel. The winery is housed on a renovated, approximately 100-year-old one-acre estate (it's a winery; there's no vineyard here). It holds tastings daily, tours on the weekends, and new-release parties and culinary events that pair food and wine throughout the year. A gift shop has boutique dipping sauces and jams. Seven dollars gets you a taste of seven different wines; dozens are featured in the tasting room. A bed-and-breakfast is on-site.

Rolling Meadows Historical Museum

It may seem silly to have a historical museum for a town that has been around for about 50 years, but the Rolling Meadows Historical Museum (3100 Central Rd., Rolling Meadows, 847/577-7086, 10 A.M.–2 P.M. Wed., 1–4 P.M. Sun., donation) is what it is, a surprisingly interesting museum (a house, really) that tells the story of how Rolling

The Streets of Woodfield shopping center

Meadows, a planned community, came to be. The house, a rebuilt 1950s ranch-style home, with furniture and decorations from that era, is a trip to visit.

ENTERTAINMENT AND EVENTS
Live Theater and Music

At **Medieval Times** (Roselle Rd. and I-90, Schaumburg, 888/935-6878, www.medievaltimes.com, $40–66, includes dinner), men with long hair and long swords wield spiked balls and other such weapons and attempt to outmaneuver each other while riding well-trained Andalusian stallions. All the while, guests dine on chicken, potatoes, and assorted vegetables with their hands (this is medieval times, after all) and cheer for their favorite knight. It's all a bit unreal, but the kids will get a kick out of it.

The **Prairie Center for the Arts** (201 Schaumburg Ct., Schaumburg, 847/895-3600, www.prairiecenter.org, galleries 8 A.M.–6 P.M. Mon.–Fri. and during events and performances, box office 9 A.M.–4 P.M. Mon.–Fri. and 1.5 hours before shows) is the major performing arts venue for the Schaumburg area. Regional dance, music, and theater groups stage shows in its 442-seat theater, and local art students and professional artists exhibit their work in the gallery. The center also brings in a number of national touring musicians and the occasional speaker.

Even if you are not a fan of opera, you might be surprised by a visit to **Opera in Focus** (Rolling Meadows Park District Headquarters Theater, 3000 Central Rd., Rolling Meadows, 847/818-3220, www.operainfocus.com, shows 1:30 P.M. Wed., Thurs., Sat., $12). Dedicated and talented volunteers bring rod puppets to life during a series of musical numbers choreographed on a small-scale but ornate and intricately designed stage. Each month they choose the best music and scenes from different operas and musicals; you won't sit through a three-hour production. Previous selections have included music from *Carmen, Faust, Porgy and Bess,* and *Fiddler on the Roof.*

Events

In the beginning, organizers of **Dodgeball Days** (Olympic Park, 1675 Old Schaumburg Rd., Schaumburg, 847/985-2115, www.dodgeballusa.com, mid–late July) were really just looking for something different to do other than getting together and playing softball or volleyball. The relatively new National Amateur Dodgeball Association's Championship annual tournament has really taken off. Teams of 6–10 players play with foam balls for enthusiastic crowds that grow every year. The annual event is run by the Schaumburg Park District.

Christkindlesmarkt (Towne Square, Roselle and Schaumburg Rds., Schaumburg, 847/895-3600, free) is an open-air market with traveling minstrels, crafts booths, carolers, and visits from Santa Claus.

The **Prairie Arts Festival** (Prairie Center for the Arts, Schaumburg, Memorial Day weekend) includes a juried artists show with watercolor paintings, ceramics, glassware, sculptures, and photography, plus live music (jazz, flamenco, you name it) and typical festival food such as ice cream and funnel cakes.

SHOPPING

Woodfield Shopping Center (Golf Rd. and Hwy. 53, Schaumburg, 847/330-1537, www.shopwoodfield.com, 10 A.M.–9 P.M. Mon.–Fri., 10 A.M.–9 P.M. Sat., 11 A.M.–6 P.M. Sun.) has big-name department stores such as Lord and Taylor, Nordstrom, and Sears as well as chain after chain of clothing and knickknack stores and entertainment outlets. Name brands are well represented here, including Apple, Coach, and Lucky. One of the mall's biggest newcomers is **LegoLand** (847/517-1640, www.legolanddiscoverycentre.com), which opened in August 2008. The company's only "discovery center" in the United States, the Woodfield Lego store is much, much more than a store: It's part amusement park and part museum. Kids can learn how Lego is made, meet model makers, and ride a dinosaur made of Lego in addition to buying as much Lego as mom or dad will allow.

Woodfield Mall is surrounded by several

shopping centers and megastores. They include **The Streets of Woodfield** (600 block of N. Martingale Rd., Schaumburg, www.the streetsofwoodfield.com), which is marketed as an urban-style shopping center (the stores all have exterior facades resembling a Disneyfied Main Street). Part of the complex is a Loews Theatre, chain restaurants and cafés (yes, there's a Starbuck's), plus **Galyan's Trading Company** (847/995-0200, www.galyans.com), a giant sports equipment and sportswear store complete with an indoor climbing wall.

The massive, just massive Schaumburg **Ikea** (1800 E. McConnor Pkwy., Schaumburg, 847/969-9700, www.ikea-usa.com) is always packed. The vast complex includes several levels of furniture and accents (for home or office) on display. Decide what you want and staff will find it on the warehouse shelves on the bottom level. It's chaotic, with bargains on random items such as coat hangers and terracotta pots. The folks at Ikea made it easy for you to spend hours here. For example, there's the café upstairs that serves yummy Swedish meatballs. And there's the nursing room for mothers and babies.

Had it with new stuff? Make tracks to the **Antiques Mart of Elk Grove Village** (800 S. Rohlwing Rd., Elk Grove Village, 847/895-8900, 11 A.M.–6 P.M. Mon.–Fri., 11 A.M.–5 P.M. Sat.–Sun.) where 150–200 dealers sell their wares, including Depression glass, china, furniture, and collectibles.

SPORTS AND RECREATION
Nature Centers and Forest Preserves
Spring Valley Nature Sanctuary (1111 E. Schaumburg Rd., 847/985-2100, www. parkfun.com, museum and visitors center 9 A.M.–5 P.M. daily summer; site 8 A.M.–8 P.M. Apr.–Oct., 8 A.M.–5 P.M. Nov.–Mar.) has 135 acres through woodlands, a lake, wetlands, and prairie, plus a log cabin and 1880 farmstead the children will enjoy. A highlight of this park is its wheelchair-accessible trails; there are about three miles of them.

Ned Brown Forest Preserve, also known as **Busse Woods** (Golf and Arlington Heights Rds., Elk Grove Village, 708/366-9420, www. fpdcc.com) is a sprawling 6,000-acre park just east of I-290 and south of I-90. Park your car at the lot at Higgins and Arlington Heights Roads, near the elk pasture (yes, an elk pasture). Then hop on your bike and hit the 11-mile trail around the park. The route is easy and fairly quiet (although you can hear the rumbling of cars on the nearby expressways). In the center of the park is Busse Lake Boating Center, where you can rent rowboats and fish. You can also reach the boat area off Higgins Road.

Baseball
The **Schaumburg Flyers** team (1999 Springinsguth Rd., Schaumburg, 847/891-2255, 847/891-4545, or 877/691-2255, www. flyersbaseball.com, $5–11) is a member of the independent Northern League and a relative newcomer to the minor leagues. Since the team started playing in Schaumburg (the stadium, Alexian Field, was built in 1999), the Flyers have attracted quite the loyal following, much like the Kane County Cougars to the west. Unlike at major league games, tickets are affordable here (less than $10), parking is free, and you can relax in the bleachers, lawn seats, or bucket seats. Or for a more private experience, fans can watch the game from within the Schaumburg Club, a glass-enclosed restaurant in view of first base. Alexian Field is just across the street from Metra's Milwaukee District West line.

Airplane Rides
Slip into a bomber jacket and strap on a pair of goggles—you are going flying in a bona fide biplane with **Red Baron Rides** (Schaumburg Regional Airport, 905 W. Irving Park Rd., Schaumburg, 847/466-3848, www.redbaron-rides.com, Apr.–Nov.). Rides last 20, 40, or 60 minutes.

Golf
Indian Lakes Resort (250 W. Schick Rd., Bloomingdale, 630/529-0200, www.indian-lakesresort.com) has a little bit of something

for everyone: two golf courses, indoor and out-door pools, a miniature golf course, spa, plus more than 300 hotel rooms if you plan to make it a weekend visit. At the resort's hilarious Bad Pants Open, locals strut their finest and most obnoxious golf pants.

Two public courses worthy of a stop are **Schaumburg Golf Club** (401 N. Roselle Rd., Schaumburg, 847/885-9000, www.parkfun. com) and **Walnut Greens** (1150 N. Walnut Ln., Schaumburg, 847/490-7878, www.park-fun.com). The Schaumburg Golf Club has one 18-hole course and a nine-hole course, putting green, and driving range. Walnut Greens has a nine-hole course and a putting green. Both are run by the Schaumburg Park District.

Water Parks

Schaumburg is a good three hours from Wisconsin Dells and all of its water parks, but a good substitute on hot days is **Rainbow Falls Water Park** (Elk Grove Blvd. and Lions Dr., Elk Grove Village, 847/437-9494, www. parks.elkgrove.org, hours vary each year, Memorial Day–Labor Day, $14, miniature golf an extra $3), a public water park with tons of activities: flume slides, paddleboat rides, and a place called the Fun House. Here water squirts out at you when you least ex-pect it (although gauging by the squealing kids ahead of you, you get an idea of when to expect the water spray). Rainbow Falls also has **miniature golf.**

The Schaumburg Park District's **Water Works** (Springinsguth Rd., 0.5 mile north of Schaumburg Rd., Schaumburg, 847/490-2505, www.parkfun.com, $9) is an indoor pool com-plex with a water playground, several slides, a lap pool, and a lazy river. Call or visit the website to find out open swim hours; hours vary each year.

Skiing

Here in the Midwest we make do with what we have. There are no mountains to speak of, at least not any of significance in Illinois, but come winter, when the snowy stuff starts to fall and skiers feel the urge to move, they head

to **Villa Olivia Golf Course Ski Area and Country Club** (1410 W. Lake St., Bartlett, 630/289-1000, www.villaolivia.com). Not everyone can afford to fly often to Colorado or drive six hours to northern Wisconsin and Michigan. Villa Olivia is relatively cheap for an afternoon of downhill skiing, snowboard-ing, or snow tubing. As for skiing, the "moun-tain" has a 180-degree vertical drop, 12 lighted downhill runs, a chair lift, and several tow lifts. In addition to downhill skiing and snowboard-ing, there are groomed cross-country ski trails and a tubing hill.

The hill is open daily during the winter, even when snow has not fallen, thanks to snowmaking machines. Downhill skiing is 1–10 P.M. Skiing Monday–Thursday, Sunday, and holiday evenings cost $29 for adults plus $26 for equipment rental. Skiing during the day Friday, Saturday, and Sunday costs $37 for skiing plus $26 for equipment rental. Slopes are closed for grooming 4:45–5:45 P.M. daily.

Snowboarding board rental is $16.25 for one hour, $31 for 2–6 hours. Boot rental for snow-boarders is $12.75 for one hour or $17.50 for 2–6 hours. Snow tubing costs $14–20. During the warmer months, Villa Olivia maintains an **18-hole golf course.**

ACCOMMODATIONS

Because Schaumburg has countless office parks and numerous business conferences every year, there are dozens of chain hotels here (Amerisuites, Marriott Courtyard, Comfort Suites, Hampton Inn, and Holiday Inn, to name a few), and many cater to the business traveler. Continental breakfasts, fitness rooms, and Internet access are fairly standard. What follows is just a sample of the hotels in the Schaumburg area.

$50-100

Super 8 Chicago-O'Hare (2951 Touhy Ave., Elk Grove Village, 847/827-3133, $70) has standard accommodations for the budget-minded traveler. A block from Woodfield Mall, **Quality Inn** (600 N. Martingale Rd., Schaumburg, 847/517-7737, $90) is a good option if you want to be close to the shops. It has an indoor pool, fitness center, and a decent-size breakfast buffet. The **Wingate Inn** (50 E. Remington Rd., Schaumburg, 847/882-5000, $80) is also a good bet for shoppers and offers shuttle service to Woodfield Mall. It also has some suites in addition to standard rooms.

$150-250
Eaglewood Resort and Spa (1401 Nordic Rd., Itasca, 630/773-1400, www.eaglewood resort.com, $150, suites more) is a cool retreat in the middle of the suburbs. There are almost 300 rooms here, some with balconies and views of the resorts' golf course and nearby woods. Extras are terry cloth robes, high-speed Internet access, a spa and fitness center, plus restaurants on the grounds. You really don't have to leave the resort. There are also an 18-hole golf course and a six-lane bowling alley.

Over $250
Lynfred Winery (15 S. Roselle Rd., Roselle, 630/529-9463, www.lynfredwinery.com, $300–385) has four extravagant suites at its winery south of Schaumburg. Expect luxurious Italian-themed decorative accommodations such as marble fireplaces and bathtubs.

FOOD
A good place to fuel up before a marathon shopping day is **Richard Walker's** (1300 N. Roselle Rd., Schaumburg, 847/882-1100, www.richardwalkers.com, 6 A.M.–9 P.M. Sun.–Thurs., 6 A.M.–10 P.M. Fri.–Sat.), a pancake house located near Woodfield Mall. A variety of breakfast fare is served here—omelets, crepes, waffles—but the restaurant's real specialty is the baked pancakes and flap jacks. Choose from banana nut, cherry, pecan, blueberry, and more. Bring a newspaper for weekend mornings; you may have to wait for a table.

INFORMATION AND SERVICES
Visitor Information
More information about the area is available by contacting the **Greater Woodfield Convention and Visitors Bureau** (1430 N. Meacham Rd., Suite 1400, Schaumburg, 847/490-1010 or 800/847-4849, www.visitgw.com or www.chicagonorthwest.com).

Media
The *Daily Herald* (www.dailyherald.com) covers northwest and west suburban news. You can find it at most gas stations, convenience stores, grocery stores, and news stands.

Tours
Village Trolley and Tours (847/228-7662, www.villagetrolley.com) organizes tours throughout Elk Grove Village, through historic districts, to shops, and past homes lit up for the holiday season.

Hospital
St. Alexius Hospital (1555 N. Barrington Rd., Hoffman Estates, 847/843-2000, www.alexianbrothershealth.org) is near I-90 and the suburbs of Hoffman Estates, Schaumburg, and Barrington.

Library
The **Schaumburg Public Library** (130 S. Roselle Rd., Schaumburg, 847/985-4000, www.stdl.org) seems more like a Borders books and music store than a library. It is huge and often crowded with students and families, but it is staffed by friendly librarians and has a great periodicals and reference section, not to mention a coffee and sandwich café in the building.

GETTING AROUND
Train
Metra's Milwaukee District West Line (312/322-6777, www.metrarail.com) operates between Chicago's Ogilvie Transportation Center and Elgin, with stops in Itasca, Roselle, Schaumburg, and other northwest suburbs. Catch it at the Schaumburg station (2000 S. Springinsguth Rd., 847/895-9260, ticket office 5 A.M.–12:45 P.M. Mon.–Fri.). A ticket to or from Chicago to Schaumburg costs $4.75. Trains run more frequently during rush hour weekdays and less frequently on holidays.

You need to buy your ticket at the depot office when it is open; otherwise you will have to pay the conductor an additional $2. When the ticket office is closed, buy your ticket on the train from the conductor. There's plenty of parking at the depot.

Bus
From the Metra station, you can board a **Pace** bus (847/364-7223, www.pacebus.com, $1.50), which can take you into Schaumburg and its neighboring town Roselle. Pace Northwest Transportation Center near Woodfield Mall is a hub of sorts for most of the bus system's suburban lines. There you can transfer to other lines, which run to most of the area's major shopping and hotel areas.

Trolley
The free Schaumburg Trolley connects Woodfield Mall and all the outlying shopping centers, in addition to the Pace Northwest Transportation Center. Known as Route 905, it operates daily.

I-88 Corridor: Naperville to Elmhurst

Out here, there's much more space compared with some of the inner-ring suburbs or even those in Lake County. There are plenty of forest preserves, golf courses, and well-manicured subdivisions and shopping centers. DuPage County, in which most of the towns in this section are situated, is conservative and for the most part more quiet compared with other suburbs. There are lots of families and stereotypical suburban activities of soccer games, nights at the movie complex, and mornings spent shopping. The wholesomeness of this area has attracted more and more families, and the area is booming.

NAPERVILLE
Riverwalk
The Riverwalk (500 W. Jackson Ave., 630/848-5000, www.napervilleparks.org) is an easy, popular way to spend time strolling on weekday evenings and weekend mornings. The 3.5-mile brick path follows the DuPage River and local landmarks such as the **Moser Tower Millennium Carillon** (www.naperville-carillon. org), which, with its musical bronze bells, soars to almost 160 feet tall. You can tour and climb the tower, but hours vary each year. Check the website for updates. The Riverwalk is close to downtown. It's accessible at **Centennial Beach** (500 W. Jackson Ave., Naperville, 630/848-5000, www.napervilleparks.org, end of May–early Sept., $10 nonresident daily fee, $3 after 3 P.M.), where there is a quarry filled with water. The city has built a little beach here for residents, and it rents paddleboats.

Naper Settlement
The big attraction in downtown Naperville is a historical village called Naper Settlement (523 S. Webster St., Naperville, 630/420-6010, www.napersettlement.org, 10 A.M.–4 P.M. Tues.–Sat., 1–4 P.M. Sun. Apr.–Oct., 10 A.M.–4 P.M. Mon.–Fri. Nov.–Mar., $8 spring and summer, $4.25 fall and winter). It is one of those "living museum" types of places where people are dressed up in costumes resembling clothes worn in the village Naperville once was (although the stone carvers and blacksmiths look a little too clean for living in the 1800s in a frontier town). The 13-acre site is pretty impressive as far as historical villages go. There are about 30 structures, including a schoolhouse, chapel, meetinghouse, and the town's first post office, built in 1833. Throughout the year the settlement hosts numerous events popular with area families, such as Maple Sugar Days. Don't forget to check out an art gallery on the lower level of the Pre-Emption House Visitor Center (formerly a hotel and tavern in the town); fans of folk-art paintings will like the collection. During the winter the settlement grounds are open but the buildings are not.

Children's Museum

Rainy day? Load the kids in the car and spend an hour or three at the **DuPage Children's Museum** (301 N. Washington St., Naperville, 630/637-8000, www.dupagechildrensmuseum.org, 9 A.M.–1 P.M. Mon., 9 A.M.–5 P.M. Tues.–Wed. and Fri.–Sat., noon–5 P.M. Sun.). The colorful building is filled with activities to keep them occupied: a giant Lite-Brite, a drawing and painting area, bubble games, a building workshop, wind tunnel, toddler area, and more.

Events

Naperville hosts several free outdoor concerts in the summer. The **Rolling on the River** concerts (630/848-5000, www.napervilleparks.org) are held at Civic Plaza, at the Riverwalk and Webster Street in downtown Naperville. They are held usually 7–9 P.M. on Wednesday and Friday nights. At around 7:30 P.M. on Tuesdays in the summer, you can hear the bronze bells of the carillon play. The concerts are free and last about one hour. The **Naperville Municipal Band** (55 Concert Ln., Central Park between Benton and Jefferson Aves., west on Van Buren Ave., Naperville, 630/778-9994, www.napervilleband.org) plays around 7:45 P.M. on Thursday evenings at the Community Concert Center, an outdoor band shell. The municipal band (the organization has been around since the mid-1800s) plays big-band tunes from the 1940s, music composed by John Philip Sousa, Broadway music, and other festive selections.

Accommodations

In the shadow of huge fancy hotels you'll find the **Stardust Motel** (890 E. Ogden Ave., Naperville, 630/355-3467, $50), a 70-room motor lodge with basic clean rooms, coin-operated laundry, and a glittering sign in the shape of a star, reminiscent of the days when the Stardust opened back in the 1950s.

Bed-and-breakfasts are rare in the west suburbs, but a fine one can be found in Naperville at the **(Harrison House B&B** (26 N. Eagle St., Naperville, 630/420-1117,

www.harrisonhousebb.com, $178–228). Most hotels lie along the interstates out here, but Harrison House is less than a mile to Naperville's Riverwalk and Centennial Beach. Renovated in 2002, the bed-and-breakfast has four light and airy romantic rooms with modern touches such as high-speed Internet access. As expected, guests are treated to a full breakfast in the morning.

At 24,000 square feet, the **Holiday Inn Select** (1801 N. Naper Blvd., Naperville, 630/505-4900, www.holidayinnselect.com, over $200) is one of the largest, if not the largest, hotels in DuPage County. If you've got money to throw around in the suburbs, stay overnight in one of the rooms on the Concierge Floor, where you have a choice between two-room suites or king studios. Free cocktails and appetizers are offered in the evenings.

About half a dozen other chain hotels can be found in Naperville. They include, for example, the **Best Western** (617 Naperville Rd., Naperville, 630/505-0200); **Fairfield Inn and Suites** (1820 Abriter Ct., Naperville, 630/577-1820); and the **Hampton Inn** (1087 E. Diehl Rd., Naperville, 630/505-1400). Rates tend to vary depending on how far in advance you book, which weekend you're in town, and whether or not you carry discount cards from groups like AAA or AARP. Typically a standard room in Naperville at one of these chain hotels will run $60–100.

Markets

Naperville hosts a **farmers market** at the 5th Avenue Station (5th Ave. just east of Washington St., Naperville, 630/369-5638, 7 A.M.–noon Sat., June–late Oct.).

Information and Services

The **Naperville Trolley and Tours** (630/420-2223, www.naperville.net) offers one-hour tours of downtown Naperville and the nearby Naper Settlement.

For information about Naperville, try the **Naperville Convention and Visitors Bureau** (212 S. Webster, Naperville, 630/305-7701 or 877/236-2737, www.visitnaperville.com).

© CHRISTINE DES GARENNES

wandering through the maze at Morton Arboretum, Lisle

THE COLLAR COUNTIES

WHEATON, LISLE, AND GLEN ELLYN
◖ Morton Arboretum

During the fall, a walk or drive through the Morton Arboretum (4100 Hwy. 53, Lisle, 630/719-2400, www.mortonarb.org, 7 A.M.–7 P.M. daily during daylight saving time, 7 A.M.–5 P.M. during central standard time, $9, $6 Wed., tram tours extra) is a sight to behold: red maple trees, silver and yellow birch trees, and rusty oaks. Then again, it's gorgeous in spring with all the blooming crab apples, and in the summer with the rosebushes.

About a dozen trails wind through this 1,700-acre park, once the estate of a Morton Salt company executive. Trails cut through woodland areas and restored prairies that feature trees, shrubs, and flowers native to Illinois. During a trip down the boardwalk and Bur Reed marsh, you can hear what sounds like hundreds of frogs singing. There's also an herb garden on-site and a restaurant called the Ginkgo.

Cantigny Park

The former estate of *Chicago Tribune* publisher Colonel Robert McCormick has also been transformed into a place for the public to enjoy. Cantigny Park (1S151 Winfield Rd., Wheaton, 630/668-5161, www.cantignypark.com, parking $4–8) contains formal gardens, a war museum, a golf course, and hosts outdoor concerts. You could spend hours upon hours here. First, you can learn a little about the history of the estate by stopping by the former horse stables, which have been converted into a visitors center. There you can watch a 10-minute film and pick up a map. Next are the park's two museums. The McCormick museum is basically a tour of some rooms of the main house. The second is a museum extolling the bravery of the soldiers in the First Division (McCormick commandeered the First Battalion during World War I, part of the division).

Finally, the gardens: Staff and volunteers maintain about 40 acres of gardens. In the spring literally thousands of tulips are

THE COLLAR COUNTIES

DRIVE-IN THEATERS OF ILLINOIS

THE COLLAR COUNTIES

- **Cascade Drive-In** (1100 E. North Ave., 1.5 miles east of Hwy. 59, West Chicago, 630/231-3150 or 630/231-3151, www.cascadedrivein.com)

GREAT RIVER VALLEYS

- **Clark 54 Drive-In** (U.S. 54 W., Summer Hill, 217/285-2805, www.clark54drivein.com)
- **Galva Autovue Theatre** (8 James B. Young Rd., off Hwy. 5, Galva, 309/932-2919, www.galvaautovue.com)
- **Skyview Drive-In** (5700 N. Belt W., Belleville, 618/233-4400, www.skyview-drive-in.com)

THE GRAND PRAIRIE

- **Harvest Moon** (Hwy. 47, Gibson City, 217/784-8770 or 877/54-MOVIE – 877/546-6843, www.harvestmoondrivein.com)

- **Route 66 Drive-In** (Knight's Action Park, 1700 Recreation Dr., Springfield, 217/698-0066, www.route66-drivein.com)
- **Skyview Drive-In** (Route 66, Litchfield, 217/324-4451, www.litchfieldskyview.com)

NORTHERN HILL COUNTRY

- **C You at the Movies McHenry Outdoor Theater** (1510 N. Chapel Hill Rd., McHenry, 815/385-0144)
- **Midway Drive-In** (91 Palmyra Rd., Sterling, 815/288-8700 or 815/622-2900)
- **34 Drive-In** (Old Hwy. 34, Earlville, 815/246-9700, www.rt34drivein.com)

SHAWNEE HILLS AND SOUTHERN ILLINOIS

- **Fairview Drive-In** (16045 Hwy. 33, Newton, 618/455-3100)

---

blooming, and in the summer the scent of about 800 roses fills the air. In addition to the flowers, staff has added wispy ornamental grasses, vegetable and herb gardens, ponds, a fountain, and a gazebo. Because of its beautiful gardens, Cantigny is a great place to spend half a day. It's rarely mobbed with people, and chances are you can find a quiet spot in the gardens to read or write. When you get hungry, head to the Tack Room Café, an equestrian-themed café that serves sandwiches in indoor and outdoor seating areas. Throughout the summer, at various times and days, the park hosts concerts in the estate's band shell or First Division museum. Concerts are free, but you still have to pay for parking.

In February, the park and grounds are open 9 A.M.–sunset Friday–Sunday, and the museums are open 10 A.M.–4 P.M. Friday–Sunday. March–Memorial Day, the park and grounds are open 9 A.M.–sunset Tuesday–Sunday, and the museums are open 10 A.M.–4 P.M. Tuesday–Sunday. June–August, the park is open 9 A.M.–sunset and the museums 10 A.M.–5 P.M. Tuesday–Sunday; September–December the museums close at 4 P.M. Cantigny Park is closed in January.

Adjacent to Cantigny Park is its golf course, containing three nine-hole courses (27w270 Mack Rd., Wheaton, 630/668-3323, www.cantignygolf.com, $30 for nine holes, $85–90 for 18 holes).

Forest Preserves

At **Herrick Lake Forest Preserve** (Butterfield and Herrick Rds., just west of Arrowhead Golf Course and 1 mile west of Naperville Rd., Wheaton, 630/933-7200, www.dupageforest.com, one hour after sunrise–one hour after sunset), more than six miles of limestone trails wind through Herrick Lake, with additional trails connecting it to nearby Danada and Blackwell Forest Preserves. On these trails you can hike or bike past woodlands, meadows, and marshy areas. In the winter, several miles are groomed for cross-country skiing. At the center of the preserve is 21-acre Herrick Lake, surrounded by a handful of smaller lakes, where you can fish for bass and crappie. Herrick Lake rents canoes and rowboats by the hour, and a concession stand sells drinks and snacks during the summer.

Next to Herrick Lake is another large DuPage County forest preserve, **Danada Forest Preserve and Equestrian Center** (35501 Naperville Rd., Wheaton, 630/668-6012, www.dupageforest.com). Before it became a forest preserve Danada was the estate of a wealthy DuPage family that raised racehorses. The farm estate consisted of an apple orchard, mansion, greenhouse, and riding stables. Today much of the estate remains, and there is still a focus on horses. **Hayrides and sleigh rides** are offered throughout the year at the Equestrian Center (9 A.M.–5 P.M. daily). And at the annual Fall Festival in October, visitors show various breeds and demonstrate riding styles. The preserve has three miles of trails for riding horses, hiking, jogging, or cross-country skiing, plus a display farm contains agricultural machinery and exhibits about the agricultural history of the county. Like Herrick Lake, Danada has property that runs through prairie, woodlands, and wetland areas.

A hidden gem in Wheaton is the **Lincoln Marsh Natural Area** (accessible from Harrison, Jewel, and Gary Aves., Wheaton, 630/871-2857). With just over 130 acres, the marsh is not nearly as vast as some of the forest preserves nearby, but it's a good detour while in the area. There is a quiet, short boardwalk trail through the marsh and a side trail through the restored prairie and wooded areas. The Illinois Prairie Path connects to trails within the marsh.

Other Parks
Railroad aficionados will want to drop by the town of Lisle's **Lisle Station Park** (915-925 School St., Lisle, 630/968-0499 or 630/968-2747, wwww.lisleparkdistrict.com). The park contains an 1881 wooden caboose, a railroad depot that dates to 1874, model trains, and gardens.

Billy Graham and Wheaton College
Christian evangelist Billy Graham, who attended Wheaton College, is revered at the **Billy Graham Center Museum on the Campus of Wheaton College** (500 E. College Ave., Wheaton, 630/752-5905, www.wheaton.edu, 9:30 A.M.–5:30 P.M. Mon.–Sat., 1–5 P.M. Sun., donation). There's biographical information about Graham, but also plenty about evangelism in general and how it developed in this country. In another exhibit, *Walk through the Gospel,* visitors, as the name implies, walk through a series of displays that illustrate major events written about in the Gospels.

Entertainment
From June to August, several theater and music students from the College of DuPage and members of area community theater groups perform in the **McAnnich Arts Center** (College of DuPage campus, Fawell and Park Blvds., Wheaton, 630/942-4000, www.atthemac.org, prices vary but generally $10–30). Shows run the gamut, from Shakespeare's *As You Like It* to the musical *Into the Woods.*

Events
Held in early July, the **Eyes to the Skies Balloon Festival** (Community Park, Hwy. 53 and Short St., Lisle, 630/963-4281, www.eyestotheskiesfestival.com, $8) entails about 20 hot air balloons taking off from the festival grounds, captained by mostly Midwestern pilots. Balloons are in the shapes of footballs, the Energizer bunny, Felix the Cat, and yes, even a bottle of Jack Daniel's. They launch early in the morning (around 5:30 A.M.) and early evening (around 6:30 P.M.), when it tends to be less windy and the skies are clear. Around 8:30 P.M. organizers light balloons for the balloon glow. Also on the festival grounds are dozens of arts and crafts booths, carnival rides, food vendors, and musicians. Past performers have included Davy Jones of the Monkees and the Spin Doctors (remember them?).

Golf and Cross-Country Skiing

Run by the Wheaton Park District, **Arrowhead Golf Club** (26W151 Butterfield Rd., Wheaton, 630/653-5800, www.wheatonparkdistrict. com, 9 A.M.–dusk Mon.–Tues. and Thurs., 9 A.M.–9 P.M. Wed. and Fri., 8 A.M.–dusk Sat.–Sun.) has 27 holes plus a driving range. The courses are sandwiched between parks and wooded areas. Tee time bookings are required on weekends and holidays. During the winter, staff groom cross-country ski trails and rent skis here; it's a highly recommended way to spend a winter morning or afternoon.

Accommodations

A former Holiday Inn, the **Crowne Plaza Glen Ellyn** (1250 Roosevelt Rd., Glen Ellyn, 630/629-6000, $88–220) is a 120-room hotel with an outdoor heated pool. It's near I-88 and I-355, shopping centers, and grocery stores.

OAK BROOK
Graue Mill and Museum

Oak Brook is home to McDonald's, the sizeable Oak Brook Mall, and plenty of other shopping centers and office towers, so it does seem a bit odd that there is an actual operating gristmill there, just off I-294. The Graue Mill and Museum (York and Spring Rds., Oak Brook, 630/655-2090, www.grauemill.org, 10 A.M.–4:30 P.M. Tues.–Sun. mid-Apr.–mid-Nov., $3.50), listed on the National Register of Historic Places, is at Salt Creek in a brick building constructed in 1852. The mill itself is quite interesting (as are the demonstrations on stone- and grain-grinding techniques) and the park surrounding it is beautiful, but what happened under the mill is worthy of note. The miller, Frederick Graue, housed slaves here as they made their way across the United States on the Underground Railroad. An exhibit discusses this connection, as well as the claim that Abraham Lincoln stopped by the mill at one point. On the weekends you might catch one of the regional history lectures or talks on the Underground Railroad occasionally held at the mill. In addition, staff or guests conduct workshops on crafts such as weaving. Next to the mill is the house where the Graue family lived,

the historic Graue Mill, Oak Brook

© CHRISTINE DES GARENNES

an Italianate building renovated for its 150th anniversary in 2002. Fresh-ground cornmeal is for sale in the museum shop.

Czech Museum

A variety of crystal, dolls, and folk costumes are on view at the little **Czechoslovak Heritage Museum** (122 W. 22nd St., Oak Brook, 630/472-9909, www.csafraternallife. org, 10 A.M.–4 P.M. Mon.–Fri., donation). The museum has a research area for people searching for information on their Czech, Slovak, or Moravian ancestors, such as immigration documents and other historical documents.

Performing Arts

The flashy **Drury Lane Theatre** (100 Drury Ln., near Oakbrook Mall, Oak Brook, 630/530-8300, www.drurylaneoakbrook.com, $25–44) tends to host Broadway revivals such as *Fiddler on the Roof* or *Miss Saigon* along with well-known children's theater or Neil Simon comedies. The theater, which seats almost 1,000, is lavish, with plush red seats and several large chandeliers.

Shopping

Not as crowded or as large as Woodfield Mall, but with many of the same department stores, **Oakbrook Center** (Hwy. 83 and 22nd St., Oak Brook, 630/573-0700, www.oakbrookcenter. com, hours vary but generally 10 A.M.–9 P.M. Mon.–Sat., 11 A.M.–6 P.M. Sun.) is an upscale outdoor mall, much like Old Orchard on the North Shore. There are 160 shops and 18 restaurants. Department stores include Neiman Marcus, Lord and Taylor, Macy's; specialty shops include Banana Republic, J. Crew, Crate and Barrel, and an Apple Computer store. The shopping center is just off I-294 and I-88.

Polo

Sunday polo at the **Oak Brook Polo Grounds** (700 Oak Brook Rd., Oak Brook, 630/990-2394, www.chicagopolo.com, 1 P.M. Sun. mid-June–mid-Sept., $10) has been a tradition in Oak Brook since 1922. Local and international players compete on the grounds of the exclusive Oak Brook Sports Core, part of the Oak Brook Bath and Tennis Club. Some might consider the atmosphere to be clubby and preppy, but you don't need to be royalty or a member of the club to attend a match. So if you're in the area and have never seen a game of polo, here's your chance.

Accommodations

Shoppers will want to stay at the **Hilton Garden Inn Oakbrook Terrace** (1000 Drury Ln., Oakbrook Terrace, 630/941-1177, www. hiltongardeninn.com, $92–169). Oakbrook Center is just steps away from this hotel, as is Drury Lane, a dinner theater complex. Other national chain hotels such as Comfort Suites, Staybridge Suites, Holiday Inn, Marriott Courtyard, and La Quinta can be found in Oak Brook and Oakbrook Terrace.

ELMHURST
Wilder Park

In the 1990s the little (compared with the Chicago Art Institute or Milwaukee Art Museum) **Elmhurst Art Museum** (150 Cottage Hill Ave., Elmhurst, 630/834-0202, www.elmhurstartmuseum.org, 10 A.M.–4 P.M. Tues., Thurs., Sat., 1–8 P.M. Wed., 1–4 P.M. Fri. and Sun., $4, free Tues.) scored quite the collector's piece: the **McCormick House,** designed by famed modern architect Ludwig Mies van der Rohe. The house, with its telltale Van der Rohe qualities of low ceilings, straight lines, and plenty of floor-to-ceiling windows, once belonged to reaper inventor Robert H. McCormick and was eventually transported to Wilder Park, where the art museum is. In addition to the McCormick House, the Elmhurst Art Museum has a decent collection of contemporary American art, including large-scale mixed media and watercolor paintings. The museum has a number of exhibitions each year, plus talks by visiting artists. At the annual Art in the Park event in early May, more than 100 artists sell their work in Wilder Park.

Also in Wilder Park is the unusual **Lizzardo Museum of Lapidary Art** (220 Cottage Hill, in Wilder Park, Elmhurst, 630/833-1616, www. lizzadromuseum.org, 10 A.M.–5 P.M. Tues.–Sat., 1–5 P.M. Sun., $4, free Fri.). Lapidary art involves cutting, polishing, and arranging stones. It was a popular hobby in the 1950s–1970s, and Joseph Lizzardo was one of the most prominent lapidary hobbyists and collectors. His collection encompasses more than 200 carvings made from jade and other stones. There's a cool exhibit on fluorescent rocks, plus other small exhibits showing pieces of ivory or fossils.

York Theatre

A highlight of downtown Elmhurst is the York Theatre (150 N. York Rd., Elmhurst, 630/834-0675, www.classiccinemas.com), a Spanish-influenced theater that also features pipe-organ music before weekend movies are played. The theater opened in 1924, and since then it has been extensively renovated and keeps Elmhurst's city center alive into the evening, long after the boutiques have closed. It's a beautiful theater and worth a visit, especially for old-movie-theater buffs. The York shows first-run films, and the Tivoli shows second-run movies (about a month or so after they first

THE COLLAR COUNTIES

hit theaters). On the second floor of the theater is the **American Movie Palace Museum** (152 N. York St., Elmhurst, 630/782-1800, www. historictheatres.org, 9 A.M.–4 P.M. Tues.–Fri. and sometimes Sat., free) run by the Theatre Historical Society of America. Volunteers have collected oodles of vintage movie posters, photographs of movie palaces from across the country, and pictures of shows performed in these historic theaters. Included in the collection is a scale model of the Avalon, a Chicago movie palace built in 1927.

Water Park and Hotel

Every year it seems a new hotel in the suburbs opens an indoor or outdoor water park. One of the newer ones in the western burbs is the **Mayan Adventure Indoor Water Park** at the Holiday Inn (624 North York Rd., Elmhurst, 630/279-1100, www.mayanindoorwaterpark. com or www.hielmhurst.com, $119–200) at I-290 and York Road. Lazy river? They've got it. Pools, fountains, water games, toddler play areas? It's all here, plus some nice extras like cabana rooms. As for the hotel rooms, you've got your pick of the traditional rooms with double or king beds, but this hotel also has some kid suites available with bunk beds, and get this—gaming systems. Call ahead if you just want to come to use the water park. Day passes are available depending on capacity. If you're not staying at the hotel, park admission can cost $15–30 per person. Hours vary by season.

Food

The **Red Dragon** (117 W. 1st St., Elmhurst, 630/832-8326, www.reddragontogo.com, 11:30 A.M.–9:30 P.M. Mon.–Thurs., 11:30 A.M.–10:30 P.M. Fri.–Sat., 4–9:30 P.M. Sun., lunch about $7, a bit higher for dinner) serves affordable Cantonese, Mandarin, and Szechuan dishes for lunch and dinner. The restaurant, not exactly casual and not yet fine dining, has comfortable red booths where you can enjoy your meal of beef with broccoli, lemon chicken, or a bowl of noodles. Couples will appreciate the "dinner for two" options in which you can share several dishes.

Gourmet wines, chocolates, and teas are featured at **Tannins** (112 N. York Rd., Elmhurst, 630/834-4800, 11 A.M.–6 P.M. Tues.–Wed., 11 A.M.–7 P.M. Thurs.–Fri., 11 A.M.–5 P.M. Sat.), a storefront shop near the York Theatre. If you are lucky, you will stop by during one of the tastings held here occasionally. Have a seat in an armchair, flip through catalogs, and test your senses.

For a quick burger and soda, but not the chain restaurant kind, try **Hamburger Heaven** (281 N. York Rd., Elmhurst, 630/832-3535, 10:30 A.M.–10:30 P.M. Mon.–Fri., 10:30 A.M.–9 P.M. Sat. Mar.–Nov., $6), a local institution. Hot dogs, double cheeseburgers, fries, and root beer are served in a nostalgic atmosphere.

DOWNERS GROVE AND LOMBARD

During the first part of the 20th century, mail-order giant Sears, Roebuck and Co. sent out not only countless articles of clothing and appliances, but also kits for homes. These self-assembled mail-order kit homes came with tens of thousands of parts and were shipped by the railroads to neighborhoods across the country. The idea really caught on in the town of Downers Grove, about 18 miles west of Chicago. More than two dozen were built here, many of which are in good shape. Most of these homes are within 1–2 miles of the downtown, which is centered around Main and Curtiss Streets.

Downtown Downers Grove

Downtown Downers Grove, like most downtowns in the Chicago suburbs, is clustered around the Metra station. In Downers Grove it can be found at the intersection of Main and Curtiss Streets. Most of the shops are along Main Street. Downtown Downers Grove is nice in that it is not especially trendy, and it has quite a mix of shops, a few slightly upscale boutiques, and a few crafts stores in which Grandma should feel comfortable shopping. Along the way you'll find casual Italian restaurants, a hot dog and pizza joint, and a brewery.

Classic Cinemas operates several restored movie theaters in downtowns throughout the suburbs. The **Tivoli Theatre** (5021 Highland Ave., Downers Grove, 630/968-0219, www.classiccinemas.com) is a French and 1920s-style movie palace where you can listen to the music of a Wurlitzer pipe organ on weekends before the movies roll.

For bibliophiles, downtown Downers Grove has **Brain Snacks** (5239 Carpenter St., Downers Grove, 630/241-1040), a small shop that stocks primarily mystery and history books, many of them in paperback, and **Anderson's Book Shop** (5112 Main St., Downers Grove, 630/963-2665, www.andersonsbookshop.com, which also has a shop in Naperville (123 W. Jefferson St., Naperville, 630/355-2665). Anderson's has a decent collection of new fiction and nonfiction, much of it reviewed by staff; a decent travel section, literary journals and magazines, plus children's toys and puzzles. Both stores host frequent author visits and readings.

St. Therese Shrine
South of Downers Grove is the **National Shrine of St. Therese and Carmelite Visitors Center** (8501 Bailey Rd., Darien, 630/969-3311, www.saint-therese.org, 10 A.M.–4 P.M. daily), a shrine to Therese Martin, a French Carmelite nun who wrote *Story of a Soul.* Martin, who died at age 24 of tuberculosis, is known best for her writing about "doing the ordinary with extraordinary love." Her admirers travel here from around the world to see photographs of her as a child and to lay eyes on her prayer book and a chair she sat on while in the convent.

Events
Sometimes referred to as Lilac Village, Lombard hosts a popular festival, **Lilac Time,** in early May in the lovely **Lilacia Park** (Parkside and Park Aves., near the Metra train line, Lombard, www.lombardparks.com). This 8.5-acre horticultural park was part of the estate of a family that planted lilac bush after lilac bush after seeing them in Europe in the 1800s. In addition

to the lilac bushes, the park, designed by landscape architect Jens Jensen, also contains a butterfly garden. During the annual festival you can buy lilac flowers and bushes and other plants, watch a parade, and listen to a variety of concerts in the park. You can monitor the flowers' progress on the "Bloom O' Meter" on the park district's website.

Shopping
With department stores such as JCPenney and Target, **Yorktown Shopping Center** (Highland Ave. and Butterfield Rd., Lombard, 630/629-7330, www.yorktowncenter.com, 10 A.M.–9 P.M. Mon.–Fri., 10 A.M.–7 P.M. Sat., 11 A.M.–6 P.M. Sun.) is slightly less ritzy than the Oakbrook mall. Here you can expect international chain shops such as Gap and the Disney Store, plus a movie theater and several restaurants, such as Bucca di Beppo, a regional chain of family-style Italian restaurants.

Whirlyball
What do you get when you cross bumper cars with a sport resembling lacrosse? Why, Whirlyball (800 E. Roosevelt Rd., Lombard, 630/932-4800 or 800/894-4759, www.whirlyball.com, noon–10 P.M. Sun.–Thurs., noon–1 A.M. Fri.–Sat., walk-in $12 per person per 30 minutes or $180 per hour for court rental Mon.–Thurs., $200 per hour Fri., Sat., holidays). Imagine two teams with players driving bumper cars, carrying scoops, and shooting a Wiffle ball at a backboard. That's Whirlyball. Although many corporations reserve courts for "team building," Whirlyball is also frequented by people in their 20s stopping by after work for a pickup game (followed by a little time spent at the bar there). Courts are rented out in advance; walk-ins are allowed, however. If you know you want to give Whirlyball a shot, you might want to call in advance to reserve a court or find out when a good time would be to walk in. Children younger than 12 are not allowed to play.

Accommodations
The 121-room **Comfort Inn of Downers Grove**

(3010 Finley Rd., Downers Grove, 630/515-1500, www.comfortinn.com, $75–130) is a couple of miles from Morton Arboretum and all its trails, as well as several major highways (I-355 and I-88). Rooms come with coffeemakers, irons, data ports, and continental breakfast.

Downers Grove and Lombard are also home to about a dozen other national chain hotels, such as Holiday Inn, Doubletree, Hampton Inn, Fairfield Inn, and more. Most hotels can be found along 22nd Street, Butterfield Road, and Finley Road.

THE ILLINOIS PRAIRIE PATH

One of the best bicycling trails in the Chicago region is the Illinois Prairie Path (630/752-0120, www.ipp.org, free), an approximately 60-mile trail along a former railroad bed. The trail (much of it is crushed limestone) attracts serious bicyclists who race by you or parents toddling along with young children. Scattered along the way are picnic tables, benches, restrooms, water fountains, and garbage cans. The trail starts about 20 miles west of Chicago, just west of Maywood, and continues to Wheaton, where a northern section follows through to Elgin and another branch jogs south to Aurora through Naperville. There are dozens of access points along the path. Most DuPage County Forest Preserves have trails that connect to the trail, including Herrick Lake (see *Forest Preserves* in the *Wheaton, Lisle, and Glen Ellyn* section) and Blackwell (Butterfield Rd., just west of Winfield Rd.). These are good spots to park because there's always plenty of parking available and there are restrooms nearby. To reach the path from Herrick Lake, you can park at the lot at the southeast corner of Butterfield and Herrick Roads. Otherwise, a good spot to start is in Wheaton at Liberty Drive and Carlton Street, near the Metra train line, or at Kline Creek Farm (County Farm and Geneva Rds., Wheaton), where you can bike along the Illinois Prairie Path or backtrack eastward to the Great Western Trail, which runs parallel to St. Charles Road from Carol Stream to Villa Park.

INFORMATION AND SERVICES
Visitor Information
DuPage County Convention and Visitors Bureau (915 Harger Rd., Suite 240, Oak Brook, 800/232-0502, www.dupagecvb.com) is the umbrella tourism organization for most western suburban towns. It publishes an annual travel guide, which contains numerous lodging lists, plus a calendar of events brochure. It does not maintain a visitors center.

Media
Sun Publications publishes weekly and daily newspapers in several suburbs, such as Elgin, Antioch, and Naperville. *The Naperville Sun* (1500 W. Ogden Ave., Naperville, 630/355-8015, www.suburbanchicagonews.com) covers news in Naperville, Downers Grove, and other western suburbs.

Hospital
If you're in need of immediate care, you can go to **Advocate Good Samaritan Hospital** (3815 Highland Ave., Downers Grove, 630/275-5900, www.advocatehealth.com).

Libraries
At both of the following libraries you can use the Internet, flip through magazines, and more: **Downers Grove Library** (1050 Curtiss St., Downers Grove, 630/960-1200, www.downersgrovelibrary.org, 9 A.M.–9 P.M. Mon.–Fri., 9 A.M.–5 P.M. Sat., 1–5 P.M. Sun.), and **Naperville Library** (2035 S. Naper Blvd., Naperville, 630/962-4100, www.naperville-il.org, 9 A.M.–9 P.M. Mon.–Thurs., 9 A.M.–5 P.M. Fri.–Sat., 1–5 P.M. Sun.).

GETTING AROUND
Train
Metra's Burlington Northern Santa Fe Line (312/322-6777, www.metrarail.com) runs from downtown Chicago's Union Station to Aurora, with stops in Brookfield, Hinsdale, Downers Grove (5001 Main St., 630/969-0013), Lisle (1000 Front St., 630/968-3916), Naperville (105 E. 4th Ave.,

630/355-4409), and other towns. A one-way ticket from the Downers Grove Main Street station to Chicago's Union Station is $4.30. **Metra's Union Pacific Western Line** runs from downtown Chicago to Geneva with stops in Elmhurst (128 W. 1st St., 630/834-2923), Lombard (9 S. Main St., 630/627-0099), Glen Ellyn (551 Crescent Blvd., 630/469-0353), Wheaton (402 Front St., 630/668-0176), and others. A one-way ticket from Wheaton or Elmhurst to Chicago's Ogilvie Transportation Center runs $3.80–4.30. On both lines, trains leave about every hour, with more during weekday rush hours, and about every 1–2 hours on weekends and holidays.

Bus

Pace (847/364-7223, www.pacebus.com) runs several bus lines through the western suburbs. Schedules and routes vary by town. Fares generally run $1.50 per ride.

Fox River Villages

Situated about 40 miles west of Chicago, the communities along the Fox River until recently were not considered suburbs. These charming villages, especially Geneva and St. Charles, attracted people first for their shops (Geneva has a lot of galleries; St. Charles has plenty of antiques shops). People discovered old homes, tree-lined streets, and opportunities for recreation along the river. (Out here the topography changes and is a bit more hilly than, say, the Wheaton or Elmhurst areas.) Each town has a slightly different character. Geneva could be called the most yuppified of the three with its trendy boutiques and white-tablecloth restaurants. St. Charles, while also quite trendy and wealthy (the historic Hotel Baker is here) is a tad more youthful because it has more bars and restaurants with outdoor seating. Batavia, on the southern end, is probably the most diverse of the three. It's got a beautiful riverside park, but also a few fast-food restaurants.

SIGHTS
Fermi National Accelerator Laboratory

The fastest particle accelerator in the United States is housed in Fermi National Accelerator Laboratory (Kirk Rd. and Pine St., Batavia, 630/840-3000, www.fnal.gov, 8 A.M.–6 P.M. daily, free). It's called the Tevatron, and using this along with other high-tech equipment at Fermi, scientists are essentially examining matter in its smallest form. You can't actually go into any working laboratories, but Fermi does have a science center that explains some of the work being done there. If you don't have any interest in particle acceleration, Fermi is a great place to go for a quiet hike. The laboratory is on a site measuring about 10 acres. You can hike, bike, or ride horses through the property's many trails, go fishing in one of several ponds, or even check out the herd of buffalo on the restored prairie. In the winter, locals go cross-country skiing through the site.

Downtown Batavia

Just off Wilson and Houston streets in downtown Batavia, the **Batavia Riverwalk** (Houston St. and Island Ave., Batavia, 630/879-5235, www.batpkdist.org) consists of a few nature trails winding through a 3.2-acre park on an island in the middle of the Fox River. The area has a few secluded spots for visitors to fish, admire wildflowers, or dip their toes in the water. During the winter the park district maintains an outdoor ice rink here.

Perhaps the most noticeable attractions along the Riverwalk are several windmills dating from the 1880s to the 1940s. Batavia was once home to several windmill manufacturers, and the ones in the park represent steel and wooden models manufactured here. On

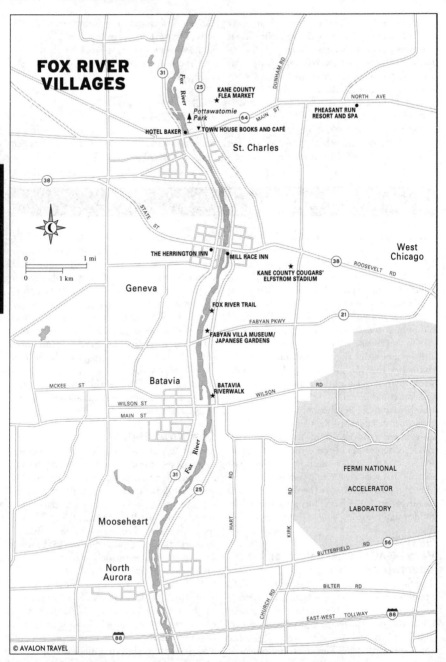

FOX RIVER
VILLAGES

Fox River

③①

②⑤

KANE COUNTY
FLEA MARKET

DUNHAM RD

NORTH AVE

Pottawatomie
Park

⑥④

MAIN ST

PHEASANT RUN
RESORT AND SPA

HOTEL BAKER

▼ TOWN HOUSE BOOKS AND CAFÉ

St. Charles

③⑧

STATE ST

West
Chicago

THE HERRINGTON INN

MILL RACE INN

③⑧

ROOSEVELT RD

KANE COUNTY COUGARS'
ELFSTROM STADIUM

Geneva

FOX RIVER TRAIL

②①

FABYAN PKWY

FABYAN VILLA MUSEUM/
JAPANESE GARDENS

MCKEE ST

Batavia

BATAVIA
RIVERWALK

WILSON

RD

WILSON ST

MAIN ST

Fox River

③①

②⑤

HART RD

KIRK RD

FERMI NATIONAL

ACCELERATOR

LABORATORY

Mooseheart

⑤⑥

BUTTERFIELD RD

North
Aurora

CHURCH RD

BILTER RD

EAST-WEST TOLLWAY

⑧⑧

⑧⑧

0   1 mi
0   1 km

© AVALON TRAVEL

a sunny, windy day, the red, white, and blue mills are quite a sight.

Homes, Gardens, and Parks

Founded by Colonel Fabyan and his wife, Nelle, **Fabyan Villa Museum and Japanese Gardens** (Hwy. 31, Geneva, 630/232-4811, 1–4 P.M. Wed., 1–4:30 P.M. Sat.–Sun.) within the **Fabyan Forest Preserve** was built at the turn of the 19th century. The star of this 600-acre estate (known as Riverbank before the county turned it into a preserve) is the villa, redesigned by Frank Lloyd Wright in 1907, and the surrounding gardens. The house contains some local photographs of the area from decades ago. Also within the preserve but on the east side of the river across from the villa is a 68-foot-tall **Dutch-style windmill** that Colonel Fabyan brought to Geneva in 1914. The restored windmill is now listed on the National Register of Historic Places.

The picturesque **LeRoy Oaks Forest Preserve** (37W330 Dean St., St. Charles, 630/584-5988) is tucked among 29 acres of woodlands and wetlands and along the babbling Ferson Creek (a perfect spot for cooling off in midsummer). There are six miles of trails here, with one of those miles paved. Inside the preserve is an 1843 farmhouse, known as the **Durant House Museum** (Hwy. 31, 630/377-6424, 1–4 P.M. Sun. June 15–Nov. 1, 1–4 P.M. Thurs. June 1–Aug. 31, and some Sun. in Feb., $3). This small house contains a smattering of remnants from the mid-1800s, such as a stove and kitchen table. Also in the preserve is the **Pioneer Sholes School** (1–4 P.M. Sun., June 15–Oct. 15), a one-room schoolhouse containing old school textbooks and other antique educational items.

ENTERTAINMENT AND EVENTS
Film and Performing Arts

A vaudeville playhouse built in 1926, the **Arcada Theatre** (105 E. Main St., St. Charles, 630/845-8900, www.o-shows.com) has been transformed into a multipurpose venue in downtown St. Charles. Local and touring musicians play here and organ concerts have been held at the Arcada.

Headliners at the **Norris Cultural Arts Center** (1040 Dunham Rd., St. Charles, 630/584-7200, www.norriculturalarts. com, gallery 10 A.M.–4 P.M. Mon.–Fri., 11 A.M.–4 P.M. Sat., gallery free, show prices vary) have included jazzman Ramsey Lewis, the U.S. Air Force band, and the touring company of the comedy troupe Second City. This modern theater seats 1,000 people, and there's an art gallery that tends to highlight the work of regional artists.

The **Steel Beam Theatre** (111 W. Main St., St. Charles, 630/587-8521, www.steel-beamtheatre.com) is a 79-seat theater presenting community theater productions such as Steven Sondheim musicals and Noël Coward comedies.

Pheasant Run Resort and Spa (4051 E. Main St., St. Charles, 800/474-3272, www. pheasantrun.com), hosts dinner theater performances, musicals, comedian visits, and productions from Chicago's Noble Fool Theater Company.

Events

The highlight of the St. Charles **Scarecrow Festival** (Lincoln Park, Main and 4th Sts., and throughout downtown St. Charles, www. scarecrowfest.com, early Oct., free) is row after row of scarecrows (more than 100 every year) crafted by area residents. In addition to the scarecrows, expect fall goodies such as apple muffins, along with arts and crafts booths.

For more than two decades **Pride of the Fox RiverFest** (throughout St. Charles, 630/584-8415, www.prideofthefox.com, free) has featured live music, dance groups, carnival rides, and food tents. But perhaps the most interesting part of the fair is the dragon-boat racing. A Chinese tradition, dragon-boat racing involves teams of 18 paddlers racing along the river in hand-painted boats with dragon heads. They race for about 3,330 yards, with the participants paddling the water and beating drums. The river festival is held in early June.

SHOPPING
Geneva
Geneva's main shopping district is around 3rd Street, although you will find little storefront boutiques or galleries inside the first floors of restored homes from the 19th century throughout the town.

Like many shops in Geneva, **The Little Traveler** (404 S. 3rd St., 630/232-4200, www. littletraveler.com) is set up in a Victorian home. Each room is stocked with clothing and home-decor items from countries around the globe.

You can rent a bike, have your tire fixed, or buy tools and travel kits at **Mill Race Cyclery** (11 E. State St., 630/232-2833, www.millrace. com, 10 A.M.–6 P.M. Mon.–Fri., 10 A.M.–5 P.M. Sat., noon–5 P.M. Sun.). Another shop is in Oswego.

St. Charles
Whereas the town of Geneva has countless boutiques and galleries, St. Charles has antiques shops and street-side shopping malls.

About two dozen shops are housed under one roof on the first block of 3rd Street. Known as the **3rd Street Shops**, they contain, for the most part, antiques dealers. You can find used books, furniture, china collections, and other collectibles here.

St. Charles Century Corners (Main St. and 2nd Ave., www.centurycorners.com) is a string of beautiful shops along the east side of the Fox River from Highway 64 to State Avenue. One of those beautiful shops is **Stone House on Cedar** (201 Cedar Ave., 630/762-0762, 10 A.M.–5 P.M. Mon.–Wed. and Fri., 10 A.M.–8 P.M. Thurs., noon–5 P.M. Sun.) specializes in functional art. This includes modular colored glass vases, primitive antiques, and writing journals made with handmade paper.

Another favorite is **Town House Books and Café** (105 N. 2nd Ave., 630/584-8600 or 630/584-8603, www.townhousebooks.com, 9 A.M.–5 P.M. Mon.–Sat., 9 A.M.–8 P.M. Thurs., 10:30 A.M.–4 P.M. Sun.), an independent bookseller with a homey and collegiate atmosphere (within walking distance of other shops and restaurants). The shop features staff picks and the usual author signings. But Town House will take the author visits one step further, such as an inclusive dinner with an author. Inside it has a café that cooks up more than just good shots of espresso; it also offers sandwiches and brunch fare. Try the roasted chicken with apricots. In the evenings the café becomes a wine bar. Have a seat in the outdoor courtyard to begin reading that new book or magazine.

West of the Fox River is the old town commercial district known as **Old St. Charles** (Main and 3rd Sts.) where more antiques markets have set up shop.

Flea Market
You could spend hours browsing over the oodles and oodles of antiques and collectibles for sale at the **Kane County Flea Market** (Hwy. 64 and Randall Rd., St. Charles, 630/377-2252, www.kanecountyfleamarket. com, noon–5 P.M. Sat., 7 A.M.–4 P.M. Sun., schedule varies each year but is generally the first weekend of the month, $5). Hundreds and hundreds of vendors set up tables under tents and in the buildings of the Kane County Fairgrounds for this hugely popular flea market. The event is one great treasure hunt for thousands of people each month. You can find everything from high-end furniture, linens, and glassware to boxes of cassette tapes from the 1980s. Parking is free, but you have to pay to get in.

SPORTS AND RECREATION
Multiuse Recreation Trails
The Fox River Trail runs along the river for roughly 30 miles between Algonquin and Aurora and is used by bicyclists, runners, in-line skaters, and walkers. The northern half is on the eastern shore of the Fox. At Fabyan Parkway, halfway between Geneva and Batavia, it crosses the river and follows the west shoreline until Aurora. In Geneva it connects with the Illinois Prairie Path, an approximately 60-mile trail through the western suburbs. As it snakes along the river, the Fox River Trail passes through several Kane County forest preserves and municipal parks. To rent a bike for

© CHRISTINE DES GARENNES

fishing along the Fox River in St. Charles

an hour or a day, try **Mill Race Cyclery** in Geneva (see *Shopping*), **Bicycle Heaven** (505 W. Main St., St. Charles, 630/444-7450, www. bicycleheavenstcharles.com), or **The Bike Shop** (1 West Illinois St., St. Charles, 630/587-5335, www.thebikeshopge.com).

Parks

Tekakwitha Woods (35W06 Villa Marie Rd., St. Charles, 847/741-8350, www.kaneforest. com, 8 A.M.–sunset daily, free) is a 65-acre park at a bend in the Fox River. Before it became a county forest preserve, Tekakwitha, which is on the east side of the river, belonged to the Catholic Church, and for decades retreats were held in its secluded setting. Because of its secluded nature, this park is a good quiet spot for birders (staff also have set up several bird feeders). There's also a nature center here and about six miles of trails through the woods and ravines.

The first public park in Illinois, **Pottawatomie Park** (0.5 mile north of Main St. on 2nd Ave., St. Charles, 630/584-1028, www.st-charlesparks.org) is on the east side of the Fox River near downtown St. Charles. At Pottawatomie you can catch a ride on a paddlewheel boat, rent canoes, play nine holes of golf, or sun alongside the swimming pool.

Baseball

You can't beat a baseball game in the summertime, and the **Kane County Cougars** (Elfstrom Stadium, 34W002 Cherry Ln., Geneva, 630/232-8811, www.kccougars.com, $8–12) never disappoint, even if they don't win a game. For one thing, an afternoon or evening here won't empty your bank account. Parking is free, and the pork chops and beer for sale in the concessions are not outrageously priced. There are several amusing side shows that are a hit with college kids and those of elementary-school age. Human bowling, for example, entails a person's being strapped inside a giant foam ball and rolled into six-foot plush pins. Roaming through the stands are cartoon characters such as "Clammy Sosa" (a talking clam) and "Harry Canary" (a talking bird). The Cougars are affiliates of the Oakland A's, and some of the players have gone on to major league teams in the region, including Joe Borowski of the Chicago Cubs. Take your pick of lawn seats, which are sold as general admission on a first-come, first-served basis, bleacher seats, or box seats. More than two dozen games throughout the summer are concluded by free fireworks shows.

Amusement Parks

Just off I-88, **Funway Entertainment Center** (1335 S. River St., Batavia, 630/879-8717, www.funwaybatavia.com, Apr.–Sept.) has all the makings of paradise for preteens: go-carts, bumper boats, miniature golf, and batting cages.

ACCOMMODATIONS

Accommodations aren't cheap in the Fox River valley, but you get a lot for what you pay for. For options cheaper than the ones listed below, you'll find a slew of chain hotels in St. Charles. They include the **Best Western** (1635 E. Main St., St. Charles, 630/584-4550), **Country Inn and Suites** (155 38th Ave., St. Charles, 630/587-6564), **Courtyard by Marriott** (700 Courtyard Dr., St. Charles, 630/377-6370) and several more.

$150-250

Overlooking the Fox River and within walking distance of parks, antiques shops, and a variety of restaurants is (**Hotel Baker** (100 W. Main St., St. Charles, 630/584-2100, www.hotelbaker.com, $169 and up). Listed on the National Register of Historic Places, it opened in 1928 and has had notables including Louis Armstrong and John F. Kennedy stop by. It's a brick building with a patio and rose garden. Rooms come with data ports and whirlpool tubs. Luxury suites are also available. The Trophy Room restaurant serves steaks and seafood in a dining room overlooking the Fox River. It's awe-inspiring.

The **Herrington Inn** (15 S. River Ln., Geneva, 630/208-7433, www.herringtoninn. com, $164 and up) is a 61-room riverside spa inn, if you can imagine such a wonderful place. With fireplaces, nightly turn-down service,

the historic Hotel Baker and the Fox River, St. Charles

© CHRISTINE DES GARENNES

and whirlpool tubs, this is a place for relaxation. The cheapest room ($164 during the week) is certainly not skimpy. It comes with a whirlpool and private balcony that overlooks the courtyard. Premiere suites can cost up to almost $400 per night. The hotel's restaurant, Atwater, also overlooks the Fox River.

Designed in Prairie style, **Pheasant Run Resort and Spa** (4051 E. Main St., St. Charles, 800/474-3272, www.pheasantrun. com, $159 and up) is a golf and spa resort with 473 rooms (some with whirlpools), performance spaces, and several restaurants on-site. Brush up on the sticks by hitting the 18-hole golf course, order massages and pedicures, and lift some weights at the fitness center. The latest dining addition to the resort is **Harvest,** a restaurant and bar serving American food in a renovated barn.

The former country estate of a Chicago banker was transformed into a bed-and-breakfast called the **Oscar Swan Inn** (1800 W. State St., Geneva, 630/232-0173, www.oscarswan. com, $99–169), a large brick home with an expansive lawn and eight rooms, some with private baths. Decorated modestly, it's along the Lincoln Highway (Hwy. 38) on the west end of town.

FOOD
American

🄲 Mill Race Inn (4 E. State St., Geneva, 630/232-2030, www.themillraceinn.com, 11:30 A.M.–9 P.M. Mon.–Thurs., 11:30 A.M.–10 P.M. Fri.–Sat., 10 A.M.–9 P.M. Sun., lunch $7–17, dinner $18–25) dates as a restaurant (it started as a tea room, actually) to 1933. With views of the river, this not-too-fancy country restaurant has great views of the Fox River. Lots of good comfort food here: slow-roasted pot roast that's great during the cold months, simple open-faced sandwiches, and more complex pecan-encrusted fish fillets.

A good quick place to grab a turkey or ham sandwich is **Smitty's on the Corner,** a deli in downtown St. Charles (15 E. Main St., St. Charles, 630/762-1080, 8 A.M.–7 P.M. Sun.–Thurs., 8 A.M.–10 P.M. Fri.–Sat., $6).

During the warm months, **🄲 The Filling Station Pub and Grill** (300 W. Main St., St. Charles, 630/584-4414, www.filling-station.com, 11 A.M.–1 A.M. Mon.–Thurs., 11 A.M.–2 A.M. Fri.–Sat., 11 A.M.–10 P.M. Sun., $6–9) is a decent spot to chow down on big hamburgers, lots of crispy fries, and share a pitcher of beer with friends. Near downtown St. Charles, within walking distance of the river and shops, the Filling Station is a casual festive place with good food and good prices. It's reminiscent of roadside eateries that were common along the Lincoln Highway. As a tribute to that era, try the '58 Edsel Dog, a beef hot dog loaded with cheese, onions, and chili.

In addition, Hotel Baker, the Herrington Inn, and the Pheasant Run Resort and Spa all have well-appointed restaurants on their grounds.

Mexican

El Taco Grande (6 N. River St., Batavia, 630/406-8415, lunch and dinner) is a casual spot near the Fox River where you can buy large plates of cheesy enchiladas or *tortas* (sandwiches).

Markets

You can buy picnic supplies at the **Blue Goose** (164 S. 1st St., St. Charles, 630/584-0900, www.bluegoosemarket.com), on the west side of the Fox River near downtown and the Fox River Trail. Blue Goose stocks juicy, ripe produce and has a good selection of deli meats and cheeses.

INFORMATION AND SERVICES
Visitor Information

The following chambers of commerce maintain shopping, dining, and lodging guides to their towns, as well as links to local festival information: **Geneva Chamber of Commerce** (8 S. 3rd St., Geneva, 630/232-6060 or 866/443-6382, www.genevachamber.com); **St. Charles Convention and Visitors Bureau** (311 N. 2nd St., Suite 100, St. Charles, 630/377-6161 or 800/777-4373, www.visitstcharles.com); and **Batavia Chamber of Commerce** (100 N. Island Ave., Batavia, 630/879-7134, www.bataviachamber.org).

Tours

Admire the Fox River aboard a paddlewheel boat. The *St. Charles Belle* and the *Fox River Queen* (Pottawatomie Park, 2nd St., just north of State Ave., St. Charles, 630/584-2334, www.st-charlesparks.org) offer tours May–October and depart from the east side of the river.

GETTING AROUND
Train

Metra's Union Pacific Western Line runs from downtown Chicago to Geneva (station at 328 Crescent Pl., 630/232-0852, www.metra-rail.com) with stops along the way in Lombard, Elmhurst, and other western suburbs. A one-way ticket from Geneva to Chicago's Ogilvie Transportation Center is $5.65. Trains leave about every hour, with more during weekday rush hours, and about every 1–2 hours on weekends and holidays.

Elgin

A diverse city on the Fox River, Elgin suffered from an image problem for many years. North of the Fox River Villages of St. Charles, Geneva, and Batavia, Elgin is not only a bigger city, it has an industrial and manufacturing past (Elgin watches were made here) that doesn't make this blue-collar city as quaint as its neighbors to the south. In recent years, however, economic development has picked up a bit, and people are rediscovering the city, especially taking to the affordable Victorian-style homes and refinishing them. Downtown, the main highlight is the riverboat casino, a blessing or a curse (depending on who you talk to) to the city and the region.

SIGHTS
Parks and Museums
You name it, **Lord's Park** (100 Oakwood, Elgin, 847/931-6120) has got it: a museum, petting zoo, pavilion, swimming pool, tennis courts, and more. This park, more than 100 years old, is named after a manager of the Elgin National Watch Factory and a former mayor. During the summer the park district sponsors free concerts on occasional Sunday afternoons at the Lord's Park pavilion. Also inside the park is the **Elgin Public Museum of Natural History and Anthropology** (Lord's Park, 225 Grand Blvd., Elgin, 847/741-6655, www.elginpublicmuseum.org, call for hours, $2).

Listed on the National Register of Historic Places, the **Elgin Area Historical Society and Museum** (360 Park St., Elgin, 847/742-4248, www.elginhistory.org, noon–4 P.M. Wed.–Sat., Mar.–Dec., $3) is in the former Elgin Academy (once connected to Northwestern University). Here you'll find a number of local-history exhibits, including lots of information on the watch company as well as amusing and intriguing photographs of the city from the past, such as a bridge collapsing from the weight of a herd of cattle in 1896. Got an Elgin watch and curious how much it's worth? The society will appraise it for a fee.

Fire Barn No. 5 (533 St. Charles St., Elgin, 847/931-1960, call for hours, weekends) is an unexpected gem of a museum south of Elgin's downtown. Built in 1904, the classical-revival–style firehouse was decommissioned in 1991 and has been remade into a little museum with restored fire engines, vintage firefighter uniforms, and photographs.

The **South Elgin Trolley Museum** (361 S. LaFox St., South Elgin, 847/697-4676, www.foxtrolley.org, 11 A.M.–5 P.M. Sun. May–Nov., 11 A.M.–5 P.M. Sat. end of June–Aug., open Memorial Day, Fourth of July, and Labor Day, $2–7) has an impressive collection of vintage street cars, Pullman cars, engines, and cabooses. Highlights of the collection include a street railcar used to deliver mail in Chicago, Chicago Transit Authority cars from the 1950s, and a Soo Line caboose from 1887. Visitors board a train and take a four-mile ride along the Fox River Line, a line that used to run for 40 miles from Carpenter to Yorkville along the Fox River. The museum holds special events throughout the year, such as on Father's Day. The museum is located just off Highway 31 south of Elgin, but north of St. Charles.

Grand Victoria Casino
You won't see it actually cruising down the Fox River, but Grand Victoria Casino (250 S. Grove Ave., Elgin, 847/468-7000, www.grandvictoria-elgin.com, 8:30 A.M.–6:30 A.M.) is technically a riverboat casino. Inside are rows upon rows of slot machines (more than 1,000), video poker machines, and tables of blackjack, craps, and roulette. If you need a break from gambling there are several restaurants (a steak and seafood restaurant, a buffet, and a sandwich café) and some shops. You must be 21 years old to enter the casino.

ENTERTAINMENT AND EVENTS
Performing Arts
The **Hemmens Cultural and Performing**

Arts Center (150 Dexter Ct., 45 Symphony Wy., Elgin, 847/931-5900, www.hemmens. org, box office 10 A.M.–4 P.M. Mon.–Fri., noon–4 P.M. Sat.) has had jazz, country, blues, rock, and bluegrass musicians such as David Sanborn and the Cowboy Junkies play here, as well as comedians such as Paul Rodriguez. The 1,200-seat theater is on the Fox River and within walking distance of downtown shops and restaurants.

There are several other community theater and music groups that perform around the area. These include **Elgin Community Theatre** (355 E. Chicago St., Elgin, 847/741-0532) and the **Symphony Orchestra** (20 DuPage Ct., Elgin, 847/888-4000). Throughout the year students and visiting musicians take the stage in **Elgin Community College's Visual and Performing Arts Center** (1700 Spartan Dr., Elgin, 847/622-0300).

Talisman Theatre (Wing Park band shell, 1000 Wing St., Elgin, 847/622-0300, www. talismantheatre.org) produces Shakespeare in the Park during the summer.

Events
Held in mid-August, Elgin's **Fine Arts Fest** (Civic Center Plaza, 150 Dexter Ct., Elgin, 847/692-4000) brings out hundreds of juried artists, local food vendors, and music performers.

SHOPPING
State Street Market Shops (701 N. State St., Elgin, 847/695-3066, www.statestreetmarketshops.com, 10 A.M.–5 P.M. Tues.–Wed. and Fri.–Sat., 10 A.M.–8 P.M. Thurs., 11 A.M.–5 P.M. Sun.) has a little more than 30 specialty shops, including gourmet food, costume jewelry, kitchen supplies, and a few collections such as cookie jars and glassware.

Schock's Greenhouse (508 N. McLean Blvd., Elgin, 847/742-7635) lies alongside a creek. You can buy flower bouquets and plants here. Also on the property: Our House Antiques, in the former home of one of the original owners of the greenhouse, which sells antiques but also serves coffee,

cookies, and slices of cake. Schock's also hosts occasional events on the property, including musical concerts, theater productions, and weddings.

RECREATION
The Fox River Trail follows the river for about 30 miles from Algonquin to Aurora. For more information, see *Sports and Recreation* under *Fox River Villages*. Canoeists can launch their boats at **Blackhawk Forest Preserve** (35W003 Hwy. 31, South Elgin, 847/741-7883, www.kaneforest.com), another park along the Fox River. From Blackhawk you can float southward to St. Charles's Ferson Creek Park, about four miles downriver, where there is also a boat launch. Or you can go all the way to Les Arends on the west shore or Glenwood Park on the east shore in North Aurora. Otherwise, there's plenty to do at Blackhawk, a 289-acre park with three miles of trails, including a mowed grass trail for horseback riding. Plus the Fox River Trail comes through here.

ACCOMMODATIONS
The bulk of Elgin's lodging options are clustered around the city's exits at I-90. Rates run $60–125 per night. Here are a few: **Country Inn and Suites by Carlson** (2270 Point Blvd., Elgin, 847/426-6400); and **Hampton Inn** (Airport Rd., Elgin, 847/931-1940).

Camping
Burnidge and Paul Wolff Forest Preserve (campground is one mile west of Randall Rd. on Big Timber Rd., Elgin, 847/888-1361, www.kaneforest.com) has 67 campsites (19 tent, 48 trailer), and the tent sites are in an area separate from the trailers. The forest preserve has 12 miles of mowed trails for horseback riding and a pond stocked with fish.

FOOD
With some of the best malts, milk shakes, and phosphates in the area, ◖ **Al's Cafe and Creamery** (43 DuPage Ct., Elgin, 847/742-1180, www.alscafe.com, 11 A.M.–8 P.M.

Mon.–Thurs., 11 A.M.–9 P.M. Fri.–Sat., $7) has been whipping up thick, rich dairy treats for decades. But there's more than just ice cream here: Al's sells sandwiches (with some veggie options) and sides such as sweet potato fries. The café is within walking distance of the river.

INFORMATION

You can find out more about Elgin or order brochures from the **Elgin Area Convention and Visitors Bureau** (77 Riverside Dr., Elgin, 847/695-7540 or 800/217-5362, www.enjoyelgin.com).

GETTING AROUND
Train
Metra's Milwaukee District Western Line runs from Union Station in downtown Chicago to Elgin (station at 109 W. Chicago St., Elgin, www.metrarail.com) with stops along the way in Schaumburg, Roselle, Itasca, and other northwestern suburbs. A one-way ticket from Elgin to Union Station is $5.65. Trains leave about every hour, with more during weekday rush hours, and about every 1–2 hours on weekends and holidays.

Upper I&M Canal Corridor

While exploring the region in the late 1600s, Frenchman Louis Jolliet envisioned a grand canal that would connect Lake Michigan on the east with the Illinois and Mississippi rivers to the west. This canal would pave the way for commerce and settlement of the region. Two hundred years later construction of the Illinois and Michigan Canal, or I&M Canal, got under way. The process started in 1836 but stalled for several years because of lack of money. The expensive project, which cost an amazing $6.5 million, did indeed spark development of the region, but the canal ended up being eclipsed by the railroads and other waterway projects not long after it was finished. The building of the nearly 100-mile-long and 60-foot-wide canal, however, did open the area to settlers who otherwise would have traveled here on wagons and stagecoaches. Building it also required a huge labor force and a heck of a lot of tools and materials. Immigrant Germans and Irish came out to work on the project, and towns such as Lockport and Joliet popped up along the canal.

Joliet became known as the city of steel and stone after canal workers uncovered limestone there. Most downtowns, like Lockport's, have several buildings made from this limestone. Quarrying provided some jobs to workers after the canal was completed, but after a series of violent labor strikes in the 1880s and the discovery of limestone in Indiana, the industry started to decline. Stone is still quarried here, but it's mostly crushed limestone and gravel. Steel and iron works were also the big industries and eventually so were gas refineries, which are still operating today. Joliet is still very much a working-man and woman's town. Driving through town and along I-80, you'll notice one warehouse or factory after another. Today the upper canal corridor comprises towns from southwestern Cook County to Morris and toward Starved Rock—towns that were once shipping ports, manufacturing centers, and home to immigrant workers. The I&M Canal, the Des Plaines River, and the Chicago Sanitary and Ship Canal (which was built after the I&M Canal) all run southwest through here.

The Illinois River begins by Channahon, where the Des Plaines and Kankakee meet. The canal towns, many of them surrounded by hills and filled with historic limestone buildings and a growing number of restaurants, are great towns to visit for a day. Look for the yellow and orange signs depicting a boy and a mule. These signs will point you to the towns and any historic sites or parks along the way. For quick vehicle access through the area, I-80 is north of the canal and runs east-west through the region. U.S. 6 runs parallel to I-80 west of Joliet and is for the most part south of the canal. In the 1970s the Illinois Department of Natural Resources took control of the canal and started converting land along the canal into parks. In 1984 the federal government designated the 97-mile region as the I&M Canal National Heritage Corridor. A multipurpose trail follows the canal from Lockport to LaSalle with other spurs being developed in towns such as Lockport, Romeoville, and Lemont.

JOLIET
Sights

Instead of paving over the remains of an old iron factory, the Forest Preserve District of Will County saved a piece of Joliet's history by buying the land and turning it into a park. Visitors to the **Joliet Iron Works Historic Site** (Columbia and Scott Sts., Joliet, 815/727-8700, www.fpdwc.org, 8 A.M.–8 P.M. daily summer, 8 A.M.–5 P.M. winter, free) follow a one-mile-long walking trail past blast furnaces and stove ruins. Along the way are signs that explain how iron is produced and the history of the site, which was home to ironworks from roughly the 1860s to the 1930s. The park hooks up with the I&M Canal Trail, a paved or crushed limestone path.

The star of downtown Joliet is the **Rialto Square Theatre** (102 N. Chicago St., Joliet, 815/726-6600, www.rialtosquare.com, box office 9 A.M.–5 P.M. Mon.–Fri., 9 A.M.–noon Sat. and before shows), a restored 1926 hall. Once a vaudeville theater, it brings in national touring musical and dance troupes, comedians, and musicians including Merle Haggard and Carrot Top. Listed on the National Register of Historic Places, the theater features intricate plaster work, arched ceilings, and a historic pipe organ. A handful of art galleries are located near the theater, mostly along Chicago Street.

West of the theater along the Des Plaines River is **Bicentennial Park** (201 W. Jefferson St., Joliet, 815/740-2399, www.bicentennial-park.org), a riverside park with a walkway along the river, views of the bridge, a fountain, and a band shell where local theater groups and bands perform throughout the year.

Route 66

A relatively new attraction in the city is the **Joliet Area Historical Museum** (204 Ottawa St., Joliet, 815/723-5201, www.jolietmuseum.org, 10 A.M.–5 P.M. Tues.–Sat., noon–5 P.M. Sun., $5, except the Route 66 Experience, which is free), located in a former church. The museum not surprisingly has several exhibits on local history such as the city's steel and stone industries and its connection to the I&M Canal. It also has something called the Route 66 Experience, which attempts to take visitors back to Route 66's heyday. With a faux drive-in, a motel, and murals, there are plenty of photo ops here. Too bad there aren't any genuine drive-ins or diners along Route 66 in the area anymore. The route originally ran through Chicago Street in Joliet, and it now jogs down Route 53, a usually congested artery with modern-day shopping centers. The **Route 66 Park** is a section of the Broadway Greenway, a stretch of parkland along the Des Plaines River and Broadway, that has several sculptural nods to Route 66's past, including statues of Jake and Elwood Blues of *Blues Brothers* movie fame. You'll also notice several recreated vintage gas pumps placed at sites, such as the Will County Courthouse and the Rialto, throughout Joliet. The website www.jolietkicks.com lists tour suggestions in Joliet for Route 66 travelers.

Sports

Sports enthusiasts will want to put Joliet at the top of their lists. Here you can scale vertical walls, hunt down your friends in a game of paintball, or ride in a 600-horsepower race car.

First up is **CPX Sports** (2903 Schweitzer Rd., Joliet, 815/726-2800, www.cpxsports.com, 9 A.M.–5 P.M. Sat.–Sun.), an all-outdoors park southwest of Joliet near the Illinois River. Round up some friends and spend the morning or afternoon hunting each other down during a round of paintball or airsoft, a similar combat game. Don't worry about bringing any special equipment. You can rent all the goggles and pads you'll need. The park is open on weekdays by reservation only.

For more thrills, head to the **Chicagoland Speedway** or the adjacent **Route 66 Raceway** (500 Speedway Blvd., Joliet, 815/727-7223, www.chicagolandspeedway.com or www. route66raceway.com, race times and admission vary), both relatively new tracks south of Joliet. The Chicagoland Speedway is the larger of the two, with a 75,000-seat arena. It hosts the ever-so-popular NASCAR speed races. The Route 66 Raceway, a dirt track, is for drag racing and other events. If you've got a lot of dough and fantasize about being a race-car driver, you can ride or drive in a race car with an instructor at the Chicagoland Speedway. Prices vary from about $100 to more than $1,000, depending on whether or not you drive the car yourself and how many laps you log on the track.

Gambling

Because it's situated on the Des Plaines River, perhaps it was no surprise when Joliet became the site of two casinos after riverboat gambling became legal in the state. The two casinos (Harrah's is downtown, Empress is southwest of downtown) certainly have brought more people to the town, and the downtown has cleaned up quite a bit since they opened. But with thousands of slots, several restaurants, and lounge acts, these casinos make it nearly impossible for guests to want to leave their complexes and explore the rest of the area. Both offer a mix of slots and table games and charge a few dollars for admission. **Harrah's Joliet Casino** (151 N. Joliet St., Joliet, 815/740-7800 or 800/427-7247, www.harrahs.com, 8 A.M.–6 A.M. daily) has more than 1,000 slot machines and table games such as blackjack, craps, roulette, three-card poker, and Caribbean stud poker. There are several restaurants, including a diner-type restaurant, a fine-dining steak and seafood joint, a buffet restaurant, a coffee shop, and a sports café. Adjacent to the casino is a 200-room hotel, which has rates around $100 if you

book in advance. (Expect to pay more for the weekends, though.) The hotel offers standard and luxury rooms. And, yes, rooms come with blackout draperies, so if you're up until 5 A.M. gambling, you should have no problem sleeping away the morning. Only people 21 years or older are allowed to stay in the hotel.

The 50,000-square-foot Mediterranean-themed **Argosy's Empress Casino Joliet** (2300 Empress Dr., Joliet, 815/744-9400 or 800/436-7737, www.argosy.com, 8:30 A.M.–6:30 A.M. daily) has about 1,000 slots and dozens of game tables, such as mini baccarat, three-card poker, craps, and other games. Like Harrah's, this casino also has several dining options, including a steakhouse, a café, a buffet restaurant, and a lounge that often features live music. The hotel also features an indoor pool, exercise room, and standard and luxury rooms that vary in price depending on the day of the week and the time of year. For a weekend in the summer you can expect to pay about $89–99 for a room. Outside the hotel is an RV park that has shower facilities.

Accommodations and Food

Hotels in and around Joliet are primarily chain hotels centered around the I-80 exits. All cost basically $70–100 per night and offer two-double-bed rooms or king beds. Here's a roundup: the 62-room **Best Western** (4380 Enterprise Dr., Joliet, 815/730-7500); the 64-room **Comfort Inn North** (3235 Norman Ave., Joliet, 815/436-5141); the 67-room **Comfort Inn South** (135 S. Larkin Ave., Joliet, 815/744-1770); **Fairfield Inn North** (3239 Norman Ave., Joliet, 815/436-6577); and **Fairfield Inn South** (1501 Riverboat Center, Joliet, 815/741-3499). The casinos also have hotel accommodations.

A highlight of downtown Joliet is **Belle Amici's** (201 N. Ottawa St., Joliet, 815/722-0907, lunch Mon.–Fri., dinner Tues.–Sat.), an Italian restaurant with a welcoming dining room. The walls are painted in warm red and yellows and the windows look out onto the street. This white-tablecloth restaurant has casual lunchtime fare, such as hearty Italian meatball sandwiches, and fine dinners, including chicken, beef, and seafood dishes. Try the grilled tuna or gnocchi.

Al's Steak House (1990 W. Jefferson St., Joliet, 815/725-2388, www.alssteaks.com, 11 A.M.–midnight Mon.–Sat., 10 A.M.–midnight Sun., lunch $5–12, dinner $10–47) is an old-school lounge and steakhouse that specializes in charbroiled steaks. The menu is quite extensive and wide-ranging in selection and prices, from tenderloin sautéed with mushrooms and a wine sauce to fried calamari and lobster tail.

Just down the block from the Rialto Square Theatre is the homey **Jitters** coffee house (178 N. Chicago St., Joliet, 815/740-0048), where you can grab an espresso or sit down with a cappuccino before taking in a show or before getting back on Route 66.

Dan's Candies (1003 Plainfield Rd., Joliet, 815/722-0712) is locally famous for its caramel apples, caramel candies, and other homemade goodies.

Information

The Joliet Visitors Bureau (30 N. Bluff St., Joliet, 877/456-5438, www.visitjoliet. org) can provide you with the scoop on local happenings, maps, and other information. The **Heritage Corridor Convention and Visitors Bureau** (81 N. Chicago St., Joliet, 800/926-2262, www.heritagecorridorcvb.com) has tourism information for towns along the canal from southern Cook County and into Will and Grundy Counties, including cities such as Lockport, Joliet, and west to LaSalle. Another great resource is the **Canal Corridor Association** (Gaylord Bldg., 200 W. 8th St., Lockport, 815/588-1100 or 800/926-2262, www.canalcor.org), a group that promotes the region as a historic and recreational destination. It publishes an excellent driving tour brochure that highlights historic places from Lemont westward. Call and the association will send you a free copy, or pick one up at the Gaylord Building in downtown Lockport.

LOCKPORT

Once the headquarters for the I&M canal, Lockport is an increasingly picturesque town with several restored limestone buildings in its downtown. It's a must-see stop for travelers along the canal as it's home to a visitors center and museum that feature exhibits about the canal's history, plus some top-notch restaurants. All are near the intersections of Highways 7 and 71 near State Street, south of the canal.

Sights and Activities

A former limestone warehouse for storing construction materials for the I&M Canal has been converted into a history and information center about the canal. The three floors of the **Gaylord Building** (200 W. 8th St., Lockport, 815/588-1100, 11 A.M.–5 P.M. Tues.–Sat., noon–5 P.M. Sun., free), owned by the National Trust for Historic Preservation, acts as a visitors center about the canal. It contains historical photographs, a mural, and displays about the building (which dates to 1838 and has housed a carpentry shop, brass foundry, and other businesses), the canal's history, and the towns along it. The building also contains **Public Landing** (11:30 A.M.–2:30 P.M. and 5–9:30 P.M. Tues.–Sat., noon–7 P.M. Sun., dinner entrées $16–50), which serves regional cuisines such as lamb chops, steaks, and pasta.

For more comprehensive historical information about the canal and the Illinois River, visit the **I&M Canal Museum** (803 S. State St., Lockport, 815/838-5080, call for hours, free). In the former canal commissioner's home and office, a white frame building from the 1830s, this museum contains furnishings from that time, plus photographs and more stories about the building of the canal. Behind the building is the Will County Historical Society's pioneer settlement, a group of various buildings moved here through the years to save them from demolition.

More historic photographs of the canal are on view in the **Gladys Fox Museum** (231 E. 9th St., Lockport, 815/838-1183, 1–4 P.M. Mon.–Fri.), another quick stop for folks who like old buildings. The museum is within an

1839 Old Congregational Church and is run by the Lockport Park District.

In an old grain-storage building adjacent to the I&M Canal, the **Illinois State Museum Lockport Gallery** (201 W. 10th St., Lockport, 815/838-7400, www.museum.state.il.us, 9 A.M.–5 P.M. Mon.–Fri., noon–5 P.M. Sun., free) features the work of Illinois artists on three floors. The beautiful limestone building with hardwood floors has about 3,000 square feet of exhibit space for rotating exhibits of textiles, drawings, photographs, and other creations. Outside the building is a courtyard and nearby is the canal trail.

Food

One of the best restaurants, if not the best one in the southwestern suburbs, **Tallgrass** (1006 S. State St., Lockport, 815/838-5566, www.tallgrassrestaurant.com, dinner Wed.–Sun., reservations only, beginning at 6 P.M. with last reservation at 8 P.M. on weeknights and 8:30 P.M. on Sat., $45–65) has been reaping praise from restaurant critics since it opened in a stone and brick building in downtown Lockport in the 1980s. Diners choose from three-, four-, or five-course menus featuring locally and organically raised products when possible. The menu changes often, but here's an example of the alluring food served there: grilled bobwhite quail with toasted barley, pecans, prosciutto, and current sauce. Or how about this: grilled organic pork tenderloin with slow-roasted bacon, carrot loaf, pickled red grapes, Dijon herb vinaigrette, and natural juices. The wines are mostly from France, Oregon, and Sonoma Valley, California. Tallgrass is an intimate, classy place. You don't have to wear a suit and tie or an evening gown here, but leave the tennis shoes and jeans at the hotel. Reservations are required.

ROMEOVILLE

In the middle of the Des Plaines River between Lemont and Lockport is a small island, home to **Isle a la Cache Preserve and Museum** (501 Romeo Rd., Romeoville, 815/866-1467, www.fpdwc.org, 10 A.M.–4 P.M. Tues.–Sat.,

noon–4 P.M. Sun., free). The island's name refers to a local legend that a French fur trader stashed his goods on the island to hide them from other traders and potential looters. A kid-friendly museum on the island contains pelts (which visitors are encouraged to touch), a birch bark canoe, and other artifacts, recreations, and exhibits about the fur trade in North America. The park itself and a nearby lagoon provide habitat for egrets and waterfowl. If you've got a canoe, you can launch it here. There's also a fishing pier and picnic area.

LEMONT

Surrounded by hills, Lemont is a scenic river town with a mix of antiques shops and two great restaurants, the slightly upscale Stonecutters and the down-home White Fence Farm, famous for its fried chicken.

Popular among locals and hungry travelers along Route 66, **White Fence Farm** (11700 Joliet Rd., Lemont, 630/739-1720, www.whitefencefarm.com, 5–9 P.M. Tues.–Fri., 4–9 P.M. Sat., noon–8 P.M. Sun., $12) has been serving food like Grandma used to make ever since Grandma was a young girl. Established in the 1920s by an area coal baron, White Fence Farm was back then and still is a place for delicious comfort food. The signature meal is fried chicken made from fresh chicken, corn fritters, potatoes (mashed, baked, or fries), cole slaw, and other fixings. The dining rooms (there are several) are fairly basic, some with outdated wooden paneling. And it can get pretty busy, especially on weekends. But the chicken is so good, it's worth it. White Fence has also become quite the tourist attraction, with a petting zoo for the kids and antique cars on display.

TINLEY PARK

For a quintessential summer music concert (crowds, beer, lawn seats) check out the lineup at **First Midwest Bank Amphitheatre** (19100 Ridgeland Ave., Tinley Park, 708/614-1616), formerly known as the Tweeter Center and before that the New World Music Center and the World. Country acts like Brad Paisley and

Brooks and Dunn and pop music acts like Maroon 5 have all taken the stage here. The 20th anniversary Farm Aid concert was also held here in 2005. Take your pick from lawn or pavilion seats.

WILMINGTON

A popular stop along Route 66, the quiet town of Wilmington lies on the eastern shore of the Kankakee River, a few miles south of Goose Lake Prairie and about seven miles south of the I&M Canal and the Des Plaines River, and is surrounded by strip mines. Just north of the downtown is the huge Midewin National Tallgrass Prairie. Downtown Wilmington has a host of antiques shops and one of the icons of Route 66 in Illinois: the Launching Pad Drive-In.

Midewin National Tallgrass Prairie

Established in 1996 on the site of a former arsenal, Midewin National Tallgrass Prairie (30239 S. Hwy. 53, Wilmington, 815/423-6370, open one hour before sunrise–one hour after sunset daily, free) is the country's first national tallgrass prairie. The entire site is about 19,000 acres. For the most part, the area has been closed to visitors while the Army cleans the site of the explosive TNT, which was manufactured here (along with many other things). In 2004, however, about 6,300 acres on the east and west sides were opened to the public. Another 1,000 or so acres have opened since, and one day the entire area, which is managed by the U.S. Department of Agriculture's Forest Service, will be open to the public. Over 7,000 acres is just fine for now, though. There are about 22 miles of trails to explore here.

Begin your visit with a stop at the welcome center off Highway 53, two miles north of Wilmington. (This is the only place in the park with water and flush toilets.) The welcome center is open 8 A.M.–4:30 P.M. daily during the summer and Monday–Friday the rest of the year. There you can pick up some maps and some tips for exploring the region. You can explore Midewin by hiking, biking, or horseback

riding along dirt roads or mowed grass trails. What makes Midewin so great is not only its enormous size but that it's rustic: No paved roads, no fancy campgrounds—just the sound of grassland birds singing and blades of grass swishing against each other in the wind. The tallgrass prairie once covered 60 percent of the state, and a walk through Midewin, like the nearby Goose Lake Prairie, can give you a sense of what the region might have looked like when the pioneers came through in the 1800s.

Where to go? You can park your car at the Hoff Road Trailhead and choose from miles of trails for hiking, mountain biking, and horseback riding. The shorter pedestrian-only trail off Explosives Road is another option. Another option is joining a guided tour. The park's staff offers hiking, biking, and horseback-riding tours throughout the year. Some tours focus on the birds of Midewin or the agricultural history of the area, and others highlight ongoing work to restore the prairie.

Shopping

Bargain hunters and treasure seekers could spend an entire weekend hopping from one antiques store to another. Shops can be found downtown on Water Street or on the outskirts of town along Highway 102. Here's a sampling of area shops; most are open daily. The multidealer shop **Water Street Antique Mall** (121 N. Water St., Wilmington, 815/476-5900) boasts 15,000 square feet of antiques. **Mill Town Market** (508 N. Kankakee St., Wilmington, 815/476-0386) sells primitives and collectibles in a turn-of-the-20th-century lumberyard near downtown Wilmington. And in a century-old barn south of town, you'll find **Forked Creek Trading Company** (1763 S. Water St., Wilmington, 815/476-1810), a gift shop with home-decor items, Amish furniture, gourmet food, and other items.

Food

With the 26-foot-tall iconic Gemini Giant standing guard outside, the **Launching Pad Drive-In** (810 E. Baltimore, Wilmington, 815/476-8535, open at 9 A.M. daily, $4) has

THE COLLAR COUNTIES

© CHRISTINE DES GARENNES

the Polk-a-Dot Drive-In, Braidwood, southwest of Wilmington

been serving the Route 66 crowd since 1960, when it was called Dairy Delite. The attraction is the fiberglass space man (who looks a little like Superman with a helmet) grasping an eight-foot-long faux rocket, but the food, particularly the Italian beef sandwiches and ice-cream drinks, is another reason to stop by. It's fast food—barbecued ribs or grilled sandwiches—and it's cheap food, costing a few bucks a sandwich. Though the name might imply otherwise, the Launching Pad isn't a true drive-in; it's an indoor restaurant with carry-out service and a drive-through.

For a quick pick-me-up while antiquing in Wilmington, stop by **Cool Beans Coffee House** (110 N. Water St., Wilmington, 815/476-5943, daily).

Just a short drive southwest of Wilmington is the town of Braidwood and the **Polk-a-Dot Drive-In** (222 N. Front St., Braidwood, 815/458-3377, www.polk-a-dot.com, 11 A.M.–9 P.M. daily, $5), another favorite stop for Route 66 travelers. A drive-in with an indoor restaurant and an outdoor eating area furnished with picnic tables, the Polka Dot

(or "The Dot" as some call it) was initially a school bus with polka dots painted on it and a makeshift kitchen on the bus. But that was more than 50 years ago. The Dot today is a fun gathering place for roadies and foodies. Cruise Night, on the first Saturday in August every year, brings them all here. Inside you'll eat in a black-and-silver–themed dining area surrounded by walls covered with photographs of celebrities from the 1950s and 1960s and antique cars. The food is Midwestern drive-in food: corn dogs, pizza burgers, and French dip sandwiches. Don't leave without trying the signature dish, a heaping order of chili cheese fries. It goes well with a shake.

MORRIS

Before Midewin National Tallgrass Prairie came onto the scene a few years ago, the 2,500-acre **Goose Lake Prairie State Natural Area** (5010 N. Jugtown Rd., Morris, 815/942-2899) was the best place to walk on a tallgrass prairie in northern Illinois. Though some may say it has been eclipsed by the sprawling Midewin to the south, Goose Lake is still worth a visit.

The walking trails are certainly scenic, with towering cord grass (which can grow up to 12 feet tall) and other native grasses, but it's an interesting site historically and environmentally speaking. It has been through a lot in the last 150 years. Situated southeast of Morris, about a mile or so south of the confluence of the Des Plaines and Kankakee Rivers, where the Illinois River begins, the site did indeed have a lake. Settlers drained the 1,000-acre lake to farm the area and to get at the clay. They dug out this clay and sent it to Joliet and other areas, where it was made into bricks. Even though the area was drained, it was still often wet—too wet to grow some crops. The area was also strip-mined for coal for many decades.

Today the site is made up of tallgrass prairie, ponds, and other wetland areas. There are several miles of trails of varying length up to 3.5 miles long. The Tall Grass Nature Trail is a beautiful trail showing you what the prairie may have looked like 200 years ago, with big blue stem grass and switch grass growing on all sides and the occasional sighting of a pheasant or fox. The marsh loop includes a boardwalk over a pond. Also on the site is a cabin built to resemble those that the pioneers built in the 1830s. Adjacent to the park's north end is Heidecke Lake, a 1,300-acre lake that provides cooling water for a nearby power plant. You can rent a rowboat and go fishing there.

On the west side of Morris is **Gebhard Woods State Park** (401 Ottawa St., Morris, 815/942-0796, www.dnr.state.il.us), a small state park that makes a good launching point

for a canoe trip down the I&M Canal or a bicycle ride along the I&M Canal Trail. There's a canoe launch here, and you can paddle up and down to Channahon State Park to the north. And the bike trail is also nearby, so you can start the bike ride here if you want. Also, if you're itching to put in some fishing time, the 30-acre park has three fishing ponds. A backpack campground is 0.3 mile from the parking area.

Accommodations and Food

As in Joliet, lodging options around here are limited to national chain hotels near I-80, including a **Comfort Inn** (70 W. Gore Rd., Morris, 815/942-1433, $85–95), which has an indoor pool and offers guests continental breakfast; and **Morris Inn** (I-80 and Hwy. 47, Morris, 815/942-6600, $85), which has an outdoor pool, restaurant, and cocktail lounge.

The vintage **Rockwell Inn** (2400 W. U.S. 6, Morris, 815/942-6224, lunch 11:30 A.M.–2:30 P.M. Mon.–Sat., dinner from 5 P.M. Tues.–Fri., from 3 P.M. Sat., and from 1 P.M. Sun., lunch $7–16, dinner $10–45) offers diners a hodgepodge of cuisine, from chicken piccata to Wiener schnitzel, plus sandwiches, steaks, and seafood. This family supper club–like restaurant contains several different dining rooms and a gallery of Norman Rockwell paintings. The coolest thing in the place is an opulent mahogany and red oak bar from the 1893 World's Fair in Chicago. It was used for the Anheuser-Busch display. Closing times vary depending on traffic, typically around 8:30 P.M.

THE COLLAR COUNTIES

NORTHERN HILL COUNTRY

Every time I visit northern Illinois, particularly in and around towns such as Galena and Savanna, I find myself saying, as I look out over the rolling hills or drive through the lively downtowns, "Yup. I could live here." It's a fetching region of the state (and one of the best places to choose a road and follow it through the country). Galena, in the far northwest corner, is the state's tourism gem, a place every small town's tourism office would love its town to become. Situated along the Galena River and a few miles from the Mississippi, the former mining town and steamboat hub was once home to Ulysses S. Grant. It's filled with historic sites and museums and home to artisans, performing artists, and engaging entrepreneurs who run restaurants, antiques shops, or gift shops. South of Galena about 25 miles is one of the best state parks, Mississippi Palisades, in Savanna. Drive or hike up the steep bluffs, then pick a spot at one of the many scenic overlooks to scout for eagles. In addition to Mississippi Palisades State Park, the region has the small but scenic Apple River Canyon State Park near the Wisconsin border, where visitors are treated to an excellent example of driftless geology. The glaciers bypassed this part of the state, and as you'll see when driving through here, it can be a rugged, rolling land. This part of the world is rural, with dairy farms nested in and among the valleys and a fruit orchard here and there. Spend an afternoon picking apples or pumpkins or sampling wine.

As you drive along the old stagecoach road east of Galena, you'll understand why Black Hawk did not want to give it up so easily to

HIGHLIGHTS

LOOK FOR  TO FIND RECOMMENDED
SIGHTS, ACTIVITIES, DINING, AND LODGING.

(Ulysses S. Grant Home State Historic Site: Grateful for General Ulysses S. Grant's role in defeating the Confederate Army, residents of Galena presented him with a brick Italianate home upon his return to Galena, a lead-mining and steamboat town where Grant had lived before the war. Today Galena is still chock-full of historic homes such as Grant's (page 162).

(Apple River Canyon State Park: Just below the Wisconsin border, this state park, with its river canyons and rocky hilltops, offers visitors a good look at the geology of the driftless region, an area untouched by the glaciers (page 172).

(Mississippi Palisades State Park: Another top-notch park with several endurance-building hiking trails through steep wooded bluffs. This Savanna-area park is perched atop a bluff overlooking the Mississippi River, and it boasts several lookout points with awesome views of the river and the many eagles that call the area home in the winter (page 173).

(Castle Rock State Park: This 2,000-acre park south of Oregon is perhaps best known for the sandstone bluff and viewing platform above the rambling Rock River, but it also has several miles of excellent hiking trails that wind through quiet native forest and prairie west of the river (page 178).

(John Deere Historic Site: After Grand Detour blacksmith John Deere invented a plow in 1837 that could handle the thick prairie soil, farming in Illinois and the Midwest would never be the same. The Rock River historical complex, comprising an archaeologi-

cal site, a re-created (and working) blacksmith shop, and the Deere family home, highlight the significance of that invention, not to mention the art of blacksmithing (page 179).

(Woodstock: Located about 60 miles northwest of Chicago in the heart of McHenry County, the town of Woodstock, with its Courthouse Square, Gothic revival-style opera house, festivals (including one in honor of Mozart), cafés, and shops, makes for a packed day-trip from Chicago or stop on the way to Galena (page 192).

NORTHERN HILL COUNTRY

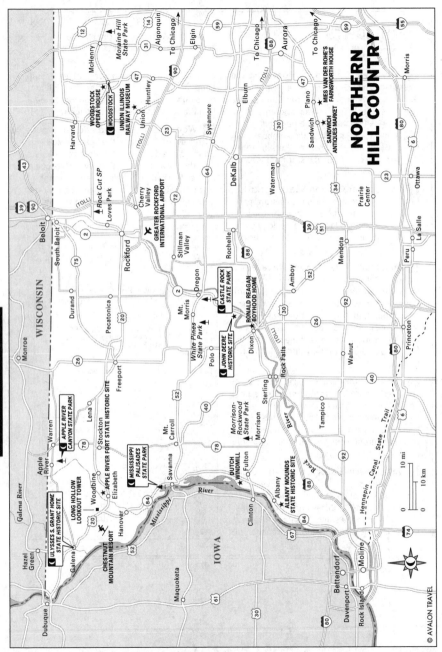

NORTHERN HILL COUNTRY

WISCONSIN

IOWA

NORTHERN
HILL COUNTRY

To Chicago

To Chicago

To Chicago

Moraine Hill
State Park

Rock Cut SP

Loves Park

Greater Rockford
International Airport

Woodstock Opera House

WOODSTOCK

Union Illinois
Railway Museum

Mies van der Rohe's
Farnsworth House

Sandwich
Antiques Market

Castle Rock
State Park

Ronald Reagan
Boyhood Home

John Deere
Historic Site

White Pines
State Park

Morrison-
Rockwood
State Park

Dutch
Windmill

Mississippi
Palisades
State Park

Apple River Fort State Historic Site

Apple River
Canyon State Park

Long Hollow
Lookout Tower

Ulysses S. Grant Home
State Historic Site

Chestnut
Mountain Resort

Albany Mounds
State Historic Site

Hennepin Canal State Trail

Apple River

Galena River

Mississippi River

Rock River

McHenry
Algonquin
Elgin
Aurora
Morris
Harvard
Union
Huntley
Sycamore
Elburn
Plano
Sandwich
DeKalb
Waterman
Ottawa
Cherry Valley
Stillman Valley
Rochelle
Mendota
La Salle
Peru
Prairie Center
Beloit
South Beloit
Rockford
Oregon
Mt. Morris
Dixon
Rock Falls
Amboy
Walnut
Princeton
Monroe
Durand
Pecatonica
Polo
Sterling
Morrison
Tampico
Freeport
Mt. Carroll
Lena
Stockton
Warren
Savanna
Fulton
Clinton
Albany
Woodbine
Elizabeth
Hanover
Galena
Hazel Green
Maquoketa
Dubuque
Bettendorf
Moline
Davenport
Rock Island

© AVALON TRAVEL

10 mi
10 km
0

12
14
31
59
55
43
39
90
2
75
26
20
52
84
61
30
67
74
80
6
23
34
52
92
88
51
39
26
30
40
92
88
64
72
47
90
30
23
59

the United States. It's a beautiful part of the world. The Sauk and Fox Indian tribes lived in this region until 1730, when they were forced to move westward. Years later the Sauk leader Black Hawk tried to reclaim parts of the land, and despite a few victorious battles with U.S. militia, his tribe was eventually forced west of the Mississippi River for good.

PLANNING YOUR TIME

Visiting **Galena** should be at the top of your to-do list. A three-day weekend is fine for hitting the town's major sights, such as **Grant's home** and a few other historic homes, allowing time for shopping downtown, strolling along the river, and visiting the small towns on the outskirts. A week, however, is definitely doable with all the vacation homes available for weekly rentals. In fact, you could base your vacation in Galena, then explore towns beyond Galena, such as **Scales Mound** and **Apple River,** basically following the **Old Stagecoach Trail** northeast of Galena or U.S. 20 eastward. You can also drive south to **Savanna** for a day. The only downside is that staying in Galena will drain your checking or credit card account faster than if you choose to stay in some of the smaller outlying towns.

Another road trip option is to start near Chicago's southwestern suburbs and spend a three-day weekend visiting towns near or along U.S. 34. You can begin with **Plano** and Mies van der Rohe's **Farnsworth House,** followed by a visit to **Sandwich's huge flea market.** Then it's on to the town of **Princeton,** near

the **Hennepin Canal.** Spend a day or part of a day biking along the supremely quiet and not-at-all crowded bicycle trail that follows the canal. One more scenic route to follow is the **Rock River** from southwest of **Rockford to Dixon.** Drive along Highway 2 through towns such as Oregon, visiting **Castle Rock State Park** near the river and the **John Deere Historic Site** in Grand Detour, where the blacksmith forged the plow that would make him a famous and rich man. Finally, this is **Ronald Reagan country.** Begin with a visit to the apartment where he was born in **Tampico** and continue to his boyhood home in **Dixon.**

Resources

The umbrella tourism organization for the region is the **Northern Illinois Tourism Development Office** (200 S. State St., Belvidere, 815/547-3740, www.visitnorthern illinois.com). Its territory includes the majority of the towns and counties covered in this chapter.

In addition, the **Blackhawk Waterways Convention and Visitors Bureau** (201 N. Franklin Ave., Polo, 815/946-2108 or 800/678-2108, www.bwcvb.com) covers Carroll, Lee, Ogle, and Whiteside Counties in the northwestern part of the state, including towns such as Savanna, Morrison, and Dixon.

Most towns featured in the chapter have local convention and visitors bureaus or chambers of commerce that publish maps and guides to their towns.

Galena

In this author's opinion, Galena is Illinois's most picturesque town. Driving into the town from the east or west on U.S. 20, you'll see white church steeples poking out among tall oak trees, a Main Street lined with historic and beautifully preserved brick buildings, and dotted about the hills above the Galena River are the steamboat captains' Italianate mansions, many of which have been converted into bed-and-breakfasts.

Galena can thank two industries for its growth in the early to mid-1800s: river travel and lead mining. The town was actually named after the type of lead ore that was mined in the region: galena lead ore. The area's lead-mining era lasted from about the early 1820s until the 1850s, when many miners left town after learning that gold had been discovered in California. Today you can visit the Vinegar Lead Mine north of town to learn more about lead mining and Galena's mining past. Galena was also home to steamboat captains and businesses that serviced boats and barges. The Galena River, you see, leads directly to the Mississippi River. In the 1840s there were 14,000 people living in Galena. Today year-round residents number around 3,500.

Galena today is a popular weekend destination for Chicago-area residents (it's about 150 miles from the city). Potters, painters, weavers, and other artists have shops in and around the town. Ulysses S. Grant's former home is open to the public, as well as the town's old market house and several other historic mansions and museums. And don't forget to pack your clubs: Eagle Ridge Resort, east of town in The Galena Territory, has 63 holes set amid rolling fairways near woodlands, ravines, and bunkers.

ORIENTATION

Most likely you'll enter Galena off U.S. 20. This will take you directly through the center of town. The Galena River runs diagonally through downtown. Most of the shops and restaurants are on the west side of the river along Main Street. Ulysses S. Grant's home is on the east side of the river, just off Bouthillier Street, which also leads to the river but does not cross it. Historic homes and bed-and-breakfasts are scattered all throughout town. The mansions tend to be up on the hills overlooking the town. Even though downtown Galena has well-marked public parking lots, spaces can be hard to come by, especially on sunny summer weekends. Your best bet is to find a space several blocks away and then walk to downtown. About six miles east of town is a 6,800-acre resort community called **The Galena Territory.** This is where the famed Eagle Ridge Resort is located as well as dozens of condominiums, townhouses, cottages, and mansions tucked into the woods, in valleys, and on the sides of hills.

SIGHTS
◖ Ulysses S. Grant Home State Historic Site

Before he went off to fight in the Civil War, Ulysses S. Grant (who had decided to leave the Army and enter civilian life again) moved his family to Galena, where he had planned to work in one of his family's leather shops. They moved here in 1860 and rented a home. Then the Confederates fired at Fort Sumter in South Carolina in 1861. He left his job and family and was appointed colonel of the Illinois Volunteer Infantry Regiment. He was credited with organizing the successful victory at the battle of Vicksburg, Mississippi, in 1863, was promoted, and later led the U.S. Army to defeat the Confederacy and General Robert E. Lee. When he returned to Galena, the city was just plain thrilled and presented him a brand-new house, a big brick Italianate home.

A few years later, in 1868, Grant was elected president, and he and his family visited Galena only occasionally after that. In 1904 his children returned the home to the city of Galena, which later sold it to the state. The Ulysses S. Grant Home State Historic Site (500

COURTESY OF GALENA AREA CONVENTION AND VISITORS BUREAU

Ulysses S. Grant Home State Historic Site

Bouthillier St., Galena, 815/777-3310, www. granthome.com, 9 A.M.–4:45 P.M. Wed.–Sun. Apr.–Oct., 9 A.M.–4 P.M. Wed.–Sun. Nov.–Mar., $4) appears much like it may have been back in the 1860s and 1870s, as much of the furniture placed throughout the house once belonged to the Grant family and was original to the house.

Other Historic Sites

A few blocks west of Grant's home is the former estate of one of his pals, Elihu Washburne. At the **Washburne House State Historic Site** (908 3rd St., Galena, 815/777-9406, 10 A.M.–4 P.M. Fri. May–Oct., free) you can tour a grand 1843 Greek-revival home and learn a little about the local attorney and U.S. congressman who would become a friend and political adviser to Abraham Lincoln and Grant. Grant appointed him ambassador to France. Washburne, by the way, didn't speak too fondly of Galena, calling its residents litigious and the town itself dull.

Just west of the Galena River is the **Old Market House State Historic Site** (123 N. Commerce St., Galena, 815/777-3310, 9 A.M.–4:45 P.M. Fri.–Sat. Apr.–Oct., 10 A.M.–4 P.M. Fri.–Sat. Nov.–mid-Dec., $2). Opened in 1846, the building was something of an early mall: The first floor contained several different stalls where vendors sold food and goods. Later it housed jail cells and some city offices, including the town's surveyor. The Market House today often features local-history exhibits, including a long-running one about Grant. One of the highlights of that exhibit is a buggy used by Grant's family. During Old Market Days, held throughout the year, locals sell flowers, bread, and other food.

Housed in an 1858 Italianate mansion on a hill just west of Main Street, the **Galena/Jo Daviess County History Museum** (211 S. Bench St., Galena, 815/777-9129, www.galenahistorymuseum.org, 9 A.M.–4:30 P.M. daily, $4.50) has an impressive and wide-ranging collection of historical artifacts and exhibits about the town and county's past. One of the oddest items may be a cigar butt that Grant reportedly threw into the gutter after learning he didn't win the 1880 presidential nomination.

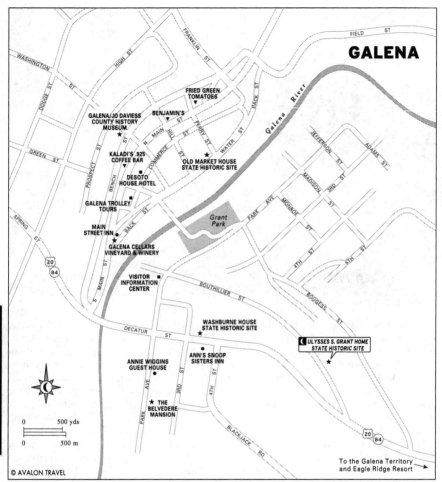

The museum has plenty of guns, earthenware pottery made in the area during the second half of the 19th century, quite a lot of clothes from the 19th century, and some portraits of Galena's residents from the past, including one of Grant's wife. Visit the gift shop to browse for books about Grant, the Civil War, and lead mining, plus maps and other souvenirs. The historical society leads walking tours through downtown Galena May–October (for more information see *Tours*).

The historical society also runs the

Blacksmith Shop (254 Commerce St., Galena, 815/777-9129, www.galenahistorymuseum. org, 10 A.M.–4 P.M. Fri.–Mon. May–Oct., $2), a blacksmithing museum in a former blacksmith shop. It rebuilt the forge, and occasionally the shop holds demonstrations. Hanging on the walls of this 1897 building are dozens of tools used to make iron products as well as tools made during the process. At the gift shop you can buy items made by the resident blacksmith.

If you can't get enough of touring old homes,

here are two other old homes to visit: **The Belvedere** (1008 Park Ave., Galena, 815/777-0747, $12), like many other homes in town, is a brick Italianate mansion from the 1850s. It's filled with antique furniture and some unusual collectibles, such as the green drapes from the set of *Gone with the Wind*. The **Dowling House** (220 Diagonal St., Galena, 815/777-1250, $9), an old stone house near downtown that dates to 1826, is the oldest home in the city. Dress up in 19th century garb and have your photo taken here. Buy a combo ticket for both houses and save a buck or two. Hours vary for both; call ahead.

Arts

Galena is home to many visual artists and artisans. Galleries and gift shops along Main Street and its side streets sell everything from landscape oil paintings to jewelry and pottery. A good first stop is the **Old Market House Square** on the 100 block of Commerce Street which contains the Hello Galena shop. It features photography, paintings, pottery and other work by area artists.

Working artists behind the **Galena Artists Guild** (324 Spring St./Hwy. 20, Galena, www.galenaartists.com, 10 A.M.–5 P.M. Thurs.–Mon.) host events like gallery walks throughout the year. The organization's gallery on Highway 20 showcases local talent.

One of the most recent additions to Galena's art scene is the **Chicago Athenaeum Museum of Architecture and Design** (601 S. Prospect St., Galena, 815/777-4444, noon–5 P.M. Fri.–Sun.), located in an old brewery building. The museum showcases contemporary design, photography, sculpture, and other media or artwork, such as weaving. The museum has headquarters in Chicago and has a branch in Schaumburg as well.

Other Sights and Activities

In addition to Grant's home and the DeSoto House Hotel, a visit to the **Galena Cellars, Winery, and Vineyard** (shop 515 S. Main St., vineyard 4746 N. Ford Rd., Galena, 815/777-3300 or 800/397-9463, www.galenacellars.

com) should be high up on your tour itinerary. It has two locations, a shop housed in an renovated granary barn in downtown Galena, and the actual vineyard with its own shop and tasting room about six miles northeast of Galena. The vineyard is in a bucolic setting north of the Galena Territory. It's worth the short drive. Before you go out there, call and find out when it's offering tours of the winery; that way you can see how it all comes together, in addition to sampling some of the wines while sitting on a deck overlooking the vineyard. You can't beat it. Want to stick around for a while? The winery rents a one-bedroom suite above the tasting room. The shop is open 9 A.M.–5 P.M. Monday–Thursday, 9 A.M.–8 P.M. Friday–Saturday, 9 A.M.–6 P.M. Sunday January–May; 9 A.M.–8 P.M. Monday–Saturday, 9 A.M.–6 P.M. Sunday Memorial Day–Labor Day.

Linmar Gardens (504 S. Prospect Rd., Galena, 815/777-1177, www.linmargardens.com, tours 10 A.M. and 2 P.M. daily mid-May–Oct., $8) is a privately owned 3.5-acre garden on a hill overlooking downtown Galena complete with a waterfall, sunken garden, flagstone pathways, and sculptures.

ENTERTAINMENT AND EVENTS
Theater

Several community theater groups present productions each year at locations around town. To find out what's on tap for the season contact the **Main Street Players Theatre Company** (815/777-2787), **Galena Art Theatre** (815/777-3288), **Galena Trolley Depot** (815/777-1248), or check the local newspaper entertainment listings.

Events

Galena is home to many artists, so perhaps it's not surprising that it has several art-related events throughout the year. Grant Park hosts the **Galena Country Fair** (www.galenacountryfair.org) in October, where more than 100 nonjuried artists sell arts and crafts (paintings, photography, jewelry, you name it). Come mid-June, hot-air balloonists race across the sky, and area gardeners open up their gates and allow visitors to take a peek at their projects. During Galena's **Festival of the Performing Arts** in mid-July, area musicians perform in the Galena Public Library and area churches. On select weekends in the fall, visitors are invited to tour Grant's home by lamplight.

RECREATION
Horseback Riding
Tucked into the rolling hills of the Galena Territory east of town, the **Shenandoah Riding Center** (200 N. Brodrecht Rd., Galena, 815/777-2373, www.shenandoahridingcenter. com) offers Territory guests and nonguests guided trail rides. (The Territory has about 40 miles of trails through green hills, woods, and along creeks.) The one-hour rides are offered daily year-round. Call to make a reservation.

Canoeing and Kayaking
Sometimes visitors to Galena get so caught up with all the town's historic sites that they forget that running through town is not only a scenic rambling river, but one that is navigable and friendly to canoeists and kayakers. **Fever River Outfitters** (525 S. Main St., Galena, 815/776-9425, www.feverriveroutfitters.com) takes people out on guided canoe or kayak adventures on the Galena River. Trips can last 2–4.5 hours and cost around $40. If you prefer to canoe or kayak at your own pace and navigate your own way, you can just rent the canoe or kayak. The sports store also rents bicycles, scooters, and snowshoes.

Golf
One of the finest places to golf in northern Illinois is **Eagle Ridge Inn and Resort** (800/892-2269, www.eagleridge.com), just off U.S. 20 east of downtown Galena. The resort's golfing options include three 18-hole courses plus a nine-hole course; there are 63 holes in all. The resort's pride and joy is the General course (109 Eagle Ridge, Galena, 815/777-4525). Other options include the North course (400 Eagle Ridge Dr., Galena, 815/777-2500); the South course (10 Clubhouse Dr., 815/777-

2280); and the nine-hole East course (100 E. Point Dr., Galena, 815/777-5200).

The surrounding region (up to about a 20-mile radius) is home to about a dozen more courses. Here are a few: **Galena Golf Club** (11557 U.S. 20, Galena, 815/777-3599), a par-71 course with yardages 5,339–6,623; **Woodbine Bend** (3500 E. Center Rd., Stockton, 815/858-3939, www.woodbinebend. com), a par-72 course with yardages 5,280–6,755; and **Blackhawk Run Golf Course** (3501 S. Golf Rd., Stockton, 815/947-3011), a par-72 and 76 course with yardages 5,591–6,378.

Chestnut Mountain
For Illinois, **Chestnut Mountain Resort** (8700 W. Chestnut Rd., Galena, info and ski conditions 800/798-0098, reservations 800/397-1320, www.chestnutmtn.com), which is south of downtown Galena, has some of the best skiing around. The "mountain," with its 475-foot drop, overlooks the Mississippi River. You can downhill ski or snowboard down the 17 trails, some of which are labeled for advanced skiers and others for novices. The resort has set aside an area for beginners (called Beginners' Bowl and Rookies Ridge) where, if you're new to the whole skiing thing, you don't have to worry about looking ridiculous as you fall down over and over. A magic carpet, like a moving sidewalk, shuttles you from one area to another as you stand.

The resort has a cafeteria, game room, and lounge. The resort rents not only equipment for downhill skiing but for snowboarding too. Fees vary depending on the time and day you visit. It's cheaper to ski in the evenings during the week. Ski passes are $29–43 and equipment runs $23–28. The ski shop is open 9 A.M.–9 P.M. Monday–Thursday, 9 A.M.–10 P.M. Friday–Saturday, 9 A.M.–midnight Friday in January and February.

In the summertime the resort doesn't shut down; instead it opens what's called an alpine slide, an open-air tube slide that you fly down for $7 ($20–30 for unlimited rides). There's also an 18-hole miniature golf course. You can also rent mountain bikes for $25 per day.

COURTESY OF CHESTNUT MOUNTAIN RESORT

one of the overlooks at Chestnut Mountain Resort

ACCOMMODATIONS

Galena has an enormous number of bed-and-breakfasts, inns, condominiums, and vacation homes available to guests. Outside of Chicago this is probably the most expensive town to stay in Illinois. Some homes are in downtown Galena, a block or three from shops, and others are a few miles from town on private estates amid gardens, hills, and wooded areas. This is a popular town to visit, especially from spring to fall. It's a good idea to make your reservation as soon as you know when you'll be visiting Galena.

In addition, several companies and private families offer small to large vacation homes for long-term rental (a week or more) in the area. For a list, contact the visitors bureau.

If you prefer to go the chain hotel route, there's the **Best Western Quiet House** (9923 Hwy. 20, Galena, 815/777-2577, $100–170) and the kid-friendly **Country Inn & Suites** (11334 Oldenburg Ln., Galena, 815/777-2400, $87–200), which has an indoor pool complete with a tube slide and games like air hockey.

$50-100

The **Grant Hills Motel** (9372 U.S. 20, Galena, 815/777-2116, www.granthills.com, from about $50) is a clean, comfortable 34-room motel a mile or so east of downtown Galena. The motel, which overlooks the hills and valleys of the driftless region, has an outdoor pool.

One of the best things about **Ann's Snoop Sisters Inn** (1000 3rd St., Galena, 815/777-3062, www.snoopsistersinn.com, $69–155) is its location. The 1858 brick home is within a few blocks of Main Street's shops and restaurants and a block from Grant's home. The friendly inn has four rooms for rent.

$100-150

Similar to the Snoop Sisters Inn, the **Huckleberry Inn** (515 Mars Ave., Galena, 815/281-1113, www.huckleberryinngalena. com, $120–135) is a historic brick home within walking distance of downtown Galena. The home sits on a hill above town, surrounded by a white picket fence and a few gardens. There are three cozy rooms. Each is tailored toward those who love to read and write and include writing tables, journals, and stationery.

If you prefer to be where the action is, you can't get any closer to downtown than the **Main Street Inn** (404 S. Main St., Galena, 815/777-3454, www.mainstinn.com, $85–130). The 1850s-era inn is right smack in the heart of Galena's shopping and restaurant district. There are six rooms available, and all come with private baths and continental breakfast.

If you're visiting the region during the winter and skiing is on your agenda, book a room at the **Chestnut Mountain Resort** (8700 W. Chestnut Rd., Galena, 800/397-1320, www.chestnutmtn.com, $84–200, more for suites), a ski resort that has a 120-room lodge. Lodge rates vary according to the day of the week you visit and the season. Winter, of course, is when rooms are on the pricey side. Consider this lodge during the summer if you're looking for some good deals, or if you want to stay near the Mississippi River.

On the east side of the Galena River, across the street from Grant's home, is **The Stillman Inn** (513 Bouthillier St., Galena, 866/777-0557, www.stillmaninn.com, $120–280), an 1858 brick mansion with seven guest rooms and some suites with fireplaces and whirlpool tubs. Rooms contain minifridges, CD players, and televisions. Outside the house are gardens and plenty of places to sit.

Over $150

Stay overnight in a hotel where Abraham Lincoln, Mark Twain, and Teddy Roosevelt have all stayed. The ◖ **DeSoto House Hotel** (230 S. Main St., Galena, 815/777-0090 or 800/343-6562, www.desotohouse.com, $170 and up in summer), a grand brick hotel built in 1855, is in the center of downtown Galena, steps from shops, restaurants, historic sites such as the Old Market House, and the Galena River. Named after Hernando DeSoto, reportedly the first European to discover the Mississippi River, this hotel has quite a past. Lincoln delivered a speech from a balcony inside the hotel on July 23, 1856, and Ulysses S. Grant had his presidential campaign

the DeSoto House Hotel

COURTESY OF GALENA AREA COVENTION AND VISITORS BUREAU

NORTHERN HILL COUNTRY

headquarters here. A range of rooms is available: a standard room with one double bed, two doubles, a king, a parlor suite that comes with a private parlor or sitting room with a fireplace, or a suite with a king bed. Some rooms overlook the inner courtyard.

South of Galena a few miles, overlooking the Mississippi River, is **The Goldmoor Inn** (9001 Sand Hill Rd., Galena, 815/777-3925 or 800/255-3925, www.goldmoorinn.com, $135–345), with four suites, two rooms, cottages, and a cabin. Each is decorated differently (French country, Irish cottage, etc.). Rooms come with amenities such as fireplaces, microwaves, minifridges, stereos, and more. In some you can soak in a hot tub and look out a window at the Mississippi River. Guests have use of bicycles.

Also on the outskirts of town are **Allen's Log Cabin Guest Houses** (11661 W. Chetlain Ln., Galena, 815/777-2043 or 866/847-4637, www.galena-illinois-lodging.com, $179–275) a cluster of five log cabins from the 1830s. They've all been renovated with modern decor and amenities such as double whirlpool tubs and minifridges. The cabins range in size from one that sleeps two people to a larger model that can sleep six.

Many people, when they visit Galena, tend to stick around the town or maybe venture east for a drive along the Stagecoach Trail. Unless they're headed to Iowa, not many drive through East Dubuque, a small Illinois town about 15 minutes west of Galena on the Mississippi River. But the **C Captain Merry Guest House and Fine Dining** (399 Sinsinawa, East Dubuque, 815/747-3644, www.captainmerry.com, $99–329) is worth the short drive. The rooms are huge and absolutely gorgeous. The 1867 Italianate mansion, once home to a successful ferry captain, has five suites (one has 800 square feet). Each has been exquisitely and tastefully designed in muted earthy colors and according to a different theme (Mediterranean, Egyptian, etc.). The owners have added some great amenities to the guesthouse, such as a fine-dining restaurant and a movie room with oversized armchairs (for guests only), plus a spa.

About six miles east of Galena, at the edge of the resort community the Galena Territory, is **Eagle Ridge Inn and Resort** (444 Eagle Ridge Dr., Galena, 815/777-2444 or 800/892-2269, inn $129–289, villas and homes $169–1,129). The resort, just off U.S. 20, has 80 rooms, plus it rents an array of one- to eight-bedroom homes, town houses, and condominiums. Nearby are four golf courses, exercise and dining facilities, a spa, and a horseback-riding center. Consider this resort for longer stays.

FOOD
American
In the mood for some fine chops? **Backstreet Steak and Chophouse** (216 S. Commerce St., Galena, 815/777-4800, www.backstreet-galena.com, dinner daily), in the old Galena State Bank, serves everything from grilled lamb chops to pepper-crusted fillets or salmon and other seafood items. Try the New York strip with a crawfish cream sauce. Choose your steak for about $30, and then pick sides such as grilled mushrooms for about $5 more. Most entrées are $15–30; however, the restaurant also offers a few large high-end dishes such as a 28-ounce New Zealand lobster tail and Kansas City strip for more than $100.

The historic **C DeSoto House Hotel** (230 S. Main St., Galena, 815/777-0090, www.desotohouse.com) has three places where you can dine. The Green Street Tavern (11 A.M.–11 P.M. Sun.–Thurs., 11 A.M.–1 A.M. Fri.–Sat.) is a bar and grill that serves lunch and dinner daily. Its brats and burgers will run you about $7. The Courtyard restaurant (7 A.M.–2 P.M. Sun.–Thurs., 7 A.M.–3 P.M. Fri.–Sat.) in the atrium serves breakfast and lunch daily. If you're looking for a place to indulge in breakfast, put the Courtyard on your list. Its raspberry pancakes, stuffed omelets, and skillet breakfast will make you want to skip lunch. If you come by during lunchtime, try a Cornish pasty. Breakfasts and lunches are around $8. The General's Restaurant (5–9 P.M. Sun.–Thurs., 5–10 P.M. Fri.–Sat.) is the hotel's fine-dining operation, serving dinner daily with a range of steak, seafood, and chicken options.

NORTHERN HILL COUNTRY

Italian

Another great place to eat because of its location (and tasty dishes) is **✪ Fried Green Tomatoes** (213 N. Main St., Galena, 815/777-3938, www.friedgreen.com, dinner from 3 P.M. Fri.–Sun., from 5 P.M. Mon.–Thurs., $15–30). The intimate dining room in downtown Galena, with its exposed brick and stone walls, is in a building that has seen just about every possible use, including a theater, courthouse, and shop. The food is primarily traditional Italian, such as fettuccine Alfredo and lasagna, lots of pasta dishes, plus seafood, veal, beef, and chicken dinners. You must save room for dessert; the restaurant's resident pastry chef prepares the treats daily. On Sundays singers meander around the room crooning jazz and cabaret tunes.

Vinny Vanucchi's Little Italy (201 S. Main St., Galena, 815/777-8100 or 815/777-8140, www.vinnyvanucchis.com, lunch and dinner daily, lunch $7, dinner $15) also cooks traditional hearty Italian fare, such as chicken cacciatore and veal marsala. For lunch, go for the Italian beef or Italian sausage sandwich. With its hardwood floors, checked tablecloths, and outdoor dining deck, this restaurant is comfortable, and you might want to prolong your lunch or dinner as you drink some red wine or a glass of beer. If you're traveling with a group, Vinny's is an option—in addition to preparing single-plate servings, the restaurant can serve meals family-style.

Bar and Grill

Benjamin's (103 N. Main St., Galena, 815/777-0467, www.benjaminsgalena.com, lunch and dinner daily, lunch $7, dinner $15) is a lively pub and grill on the corner of Hill and Main Streets housed in two buildings that date to the 1850s. You'll find standard pub fare here, such as pizza and pita sandwiches, but also quite a surprising selection of not-so-standard tavern food, such as apple pork chops, fried tilapia, and lemon pepper chicken. On some weekend evenings a band strikes it up in the bar.

Coffee Shop

✪ Kaladi's 925 Coffee Bar (309 S. Main St., Galena, 815/776-0723, 7 A.M.–9 P.M. Mon.–Sat., 7 A.M.–7 P.M. Sun., sandwiches around $7) is the perfect place to go for your morning espresso or cappuccino and plan the day's itinerary or simply read the newspaper. Return in the afternoon for panini sandwiches and gelato. Kaladi's is quite the hotspot on the weekends, and the counter line can get long, but usually everyone, including the staff, is in a cheery mood.

Wine Bar

The chichi **Grape Escape** (233 S. Main St., Galena, 815/776-9463, www.grapeescapegalena.com, 5 P.M.–1 A.M. Mon.–Fri., noon–1 A.M. Sat.) is a wine and martini lounge in downtown Galena that also offers accompaniments such as appetizers and cheese spreads and often features live music (the smooth jazz kind) on the weekends.

Markets

For gourmet food, walk down Main Street to **Galena River Wine and Cheese** (420 S. Main St., Galena, 815/777-9430), which stocks domestic and imported cheese, sausage, beer, and wine. Another option is **The Great Galena Cookery** (in the Galena Art Center's Artists' Annex, 412 Spring St., Galena, 815/777-1556), which sells soapstone cookware and holds cooking classes, and its sister shop, **The Great Galena Peddlery** (116 N. Main St., Galena, 815/777-2307), where you can browse the collection of herbs and teas from around the world.

For fresh produce, head on over to the **Old Market House Square** (123 N. Commerce St., Galena, 7 A.M.–noon daily May–Oct.), where area farmers sell freshly picked tomatoes, beans, and other items.

On the outskirts of town is **Wooded Wonderland** (610 Devil's Ladder Rd., Galena, 815/777-1223, mid-July–late Aug.), a pick-your-own blueberry farm southeast of Galena just off U.S. 20; and **Murphy's Gardens** (12550 W. Norris Ln., Galena, 815/777-1177, weekends Aug.–Sept.), which grows raspberries, flowers, and produce. Murphy's is northwest of town, south of U.S. 20.

INFORMATION AND SERVICES
Visitor Information
The **Galena and Jo Daviess County Convention and Visitors Bureau** (877/464-2536, www.galena.org) operates a visitors information center in the Old Train Depot at 101 Bouthillier Street in Galena.

Media
The weekly community newspaper is the *Galena Gazette* (716 S. Bench St., Galena, 815/777-0019, www.galenagazette.com), a good source for events listings. Its offices are in downtown Galena, just south of U.S. 20 on the west side of the river.

Tours
With all the hills and circular narrow streets, not to mention traffic, a good way to tour Galena is on a trolley. **Galena Trolley Tours** (314 S. Main St., Galena, 815/777-1248 or 877/425-3621, www.galenatrolleys.com) has day or evening tours that last an hour or more. Prices can vary from about $18 to $36. Some tours include admission to historic sites. **Tri-State Trolley** (220 S. Main St., Galena, 800/779-4869) also offers a narrated tour of the town for about $18.

The **Jo Daviess County Historical Society** leads one-hour walking tours of downtown Galena on Saturdays May–October. The cost is $5 per person. Tours depart from the DeSoto House Hotel. The historical society (815/777-9129) also offers various themed tours (gardens, houses, cemeteries) throughout the year.

Set off at sunrise or sunset and take in awesome views of the Galena River valley aboard a hot-air balloon thousands of feet up in the air. **Galena on the Fly** (815/777-2747, www.buy-aballoonride.com) organizes one-hour flights for visitors by reservation only. Flyers meet at Eagle Ridge Resort and then head to a departure point, which can vary.

For the paranormal perspective on Galena, join the **Annie Wiggins Ghost Tour** (1004 Park Ave., Galena, 815/777-0336, www.anniewiggins.com), a 1.5-hour walking tour of the village. They're offered on weekend evenings May–October and cost $10 per person.

Iowa-based **Mississippi Explorer Cruises** offers scheduled trips along the Upper Mississippi River. A 1.5-hour-long river tour, at $25 per person, departs from Chestnut Mountain Resort, south of Galena. For more information contact the cruise company at 563/586-4444, www.mississippiexplorer.com, or Chestnut Mountain Resort at 800/397-1320, www.chestnutmtn.com.

THE APPLE RIVER VALLEY
Believe it or not, there's more to Jo Daviess County than Galena. In fact, when the summer crowds swell in downtown Galena, you can escape for a day or afternoon by driving along a rolling two-lane highway through towns where the populations are well below 1,000. Southeast of Galena by about 15 miles is Elizabeth, home to the Apple River Fort State Historic Site, where Sauk leader Black Hawk battled with early miners in 1832. Elizabeth is also a Main Street town where a few artists have opened galleries, and on the hilly outskirts is the Massbach Winery. The Old Stagecoach Trail northeast of Galena leads to tiny border towns such as Apple River and to the scenic Apple River Canyon State Park, where you can hike through canyons.

Apple River Fort State Historic Site
In 1804 the Sauk Indians sold millions of acres of land to the United States, including land in northwestern Illinois, where they had lived and hunted for many years. Under the agreement, the Sauk could continue to hunt on the land until the government sold it to settlers. Several years later, after returning from the West, Sauk Indians returned to northwestern Illinois and encountered lead miners, who had built a camp on the Apple River. The Indians were ordered to go west of the Mississippi River. But the

leader Black Hawk wanted to return to his native land and led a group of Sauk up the Rock River to reclaim the land. After hearing about Black Hawk's arrival in the state and about the tribe's skirmishes with white settlers, the miners erected a wall of timber around their settlement, now called the Apple River Fort State Historic Site and Interpretive Center (311 E. Myrtle St., Elizabeth, 815/858-2028, 9 A.M.–4 P.M. Wed.–Sun., $3). On June 24, 1832, Black Hawk and his warriors attacked the fort. The settlers managed to keep them at bay, and Black Hawk moved on. Eventually, however, the tribe was defeated in the brutal Battle of Bad Axe in Wisconsin.

The original Apple River Fort didn't last for more than a dozen years. What you see when you visit is all reconstructed—the log cabins and the firing stations. The whole site, which is actually quite small (around 3,500 square feet), was built in the mid-1990s based on excavations and historical documents. An interpretive center has exhibits on the background of the Sauk Indians, the area's mining history, and the Black Hawk War. If you want to understand more about the region's history, this is a great place to do it. It shouldn't take you more than an hour to tour the site.

Other Sights and Activities

While in the area, history buffs might want to pay a visit to the **Great Western Railroad Museum** (111 E. Myrtle St., Elizabeth, www.elizabethhistoricalsociety.org, 11 A.M.–3 P.M. Sat.–Sun., May–Oct., free). In an old depot on one of the earliest rail lines in the state—the Chicago Great Western Railroad—the museum highlights the railroad's history and the development of Elizabeth and other area towns. Nearby is a local history museum and former lead miners' cottages.

Downtown Elizabeth (along Main St./U.S. 20) is home to a handful of galleries, antiques shops, and gift shops, including **Studio Work** (130 N. Main St., Elizabeth, 815/858-3588) which shows pottery, paintings, and other works of art by locals, and **Eshelman Pottery** (238 N. Main St., Elizabeth, 815/858-2327,

www.eshelmanpottery.com). This store features red stoneware creations such as mugs, teapots, and bottles.

Massbach Ridge Winery (8837 S. Massbach Ridge Rd., Elizabeth, 815/291-6700, www.massbachridge.com, noon–6 P.M. Fri.–Sun. May–Oct., noon–5 P.M. Sat.–Sun. Nov.–Apr.) is tucked among 20 acres of hills south of town. It produces more than a dozen wines—red, white, and some fruit wines, such as apple wine. It has a tasting room and gift shop. Winery tours are available.

Scenic Overlook

Just off U.S. 20, just west of Elizabeth and before you come to Galena, is the **Long Hollow Tower.** Climb the tower for splendid views of the surrounding valleys, farmland, and small towns. Actually, you don't even need to climb the tower to admire the pastoral views: Just pull off into the parking lot and look north, and leaf-peepers should be satisfied.

Accommodations

Marcotte's Family Motel (2156 U.S. 20, Elizabeth, 815/858-2217, $60–85) is not a luxurious hotel (no marble shower stalls here), but the rooms are clean, with homey touches such as quilts. It has just about every type of room: one king bed, one queen and a double, or two doubles in a room, plus two- or three-room units with kitchens.

Information

The **Elizabeth Chamber of Commerce** (P.O. Box 371, Elizabeth, 815/858-2221, www.elizabeth-il.com) can help with any questions about what to see and do in the area.

◀ APPLE RIVER CANYON STATE PARK

At about 300 acres, Apple River Canyon State Park (8763 E. Canyon Rd., Millville, 815/492-2477, www.dnr.state.il.us) is one of the smaller state parks in Illinois, but it's definitely one of the most scenic. The rambling Apple River runs through here, past 250-foot-high limestone cliffs, bottomland,

and upland forests. Thousands of years ago the Illinois glacier stopped short of this region. While much of Illinois was scraped over by the glacier, the driftless region in far northwest Illinois remained relatively unscathed. The Illinois glacier actually halted its advance a few miles from the state park and ended up blocking water flow in the Apple River, causing the water to rise and the river to change direction. This high water gradually eroded the limestone and dolomite and created the canyon visitors see today. The park is just off the old stagecoach route and a little town called Millville that used to be

here; you can see remains of a gristmill and sawmills. Five hiking trails through the park will take you along the river, through the canyon, and atop the bluffs. Along the way are ferns, the rare woodland white violets, and other wildflowers as well as trees such as birch, aspen, and chestnut. The park has a campground with tent sites.

While you're in the area, give the folks at **Stage Coach Trails Livery** (5656 Stagecoach Trail, Apple River, 815/594-2423, by reservation) a call. They organize stagecoach rides pulled by draft horses, and sleigh rides in the winter.

Great River Road: Albany to Savanna

Follow Highway 84, the Great River Road, south of Galena. Here the land turns a bit more dramatic the closer you get to the Mississippi River. For outstanding views of the river, not to mention some excellent hiking, head to Mississippi Palisades State Park, one of the best parks we've got in the state. The towns here are small (none bigger than 4,000 people), and the restaurants homey. The focus is on outdoor activities: biking, fishing, hiking, and watching birds, particularly eagles in the winter. Fulton, a historically Dutch village about 15 miles south of Savanna, is right on the Great River Road Bike Trail, and is a good place to launch your ride. The town is also home to a genuine working windmill on the riverfront. South of there is the even smaller town of Albany, which was once home to an ancient mound-building Indian tribe.

SAVANNA AND THOMSON
◖ Mississippi Palisades State Park
One of the best state parks in Illinois, Mississippi Palisades State Park (16327 Hwy. 84, Savanna, 815/273-2731, www.dnr.state. il.us) is a hiker's delight, especially for hikers who love steep hills and wooded bluffs.

The 13-mile trail system is essentially divided into two areas: the northern section and the southern section. The southern trails are more rugged and steep than those on the northern side. Novice hikers or hikers who want a more

Mississippi Palisades State Park in Savanna

© CHRISTINE DES GARENNES

NORTHERN HILL COUNTRY

THE GRAND ILLINOIS TRAIL

The Grand Illinois Trail is a series of bicycle trails and street routes that loops around the northern section of the state. The 535-mile trail begins in Chicago and moves northwest and then westward to the Mississippi River. It then turns south along the Mississippi before heading back east along the Hennepin and I&M Canals to Chicago again. The idea for such a trail was floated around for several years. But only since 2003, after more trails were linked to each other and an annual weeklong ride was launched, has the idea of traveling the trail really taken hold with bicyclists.

The trail essentially allows you to bike from downtown Chicago through the rolling hills around Rockford to Rock Island, with side trips to some of the state's best state parks, such as Mississippi Palisades, Starved Rock, and the Kankakee River State Park. Depending on where you begin your ride, you could be peddling on crushed limestone along rails-to-trails paths or on paved road routes (with di-

rectional signs that guide riders). Some of the trails along the way include the Old Plank Road Trail southwest of Chicago, the Illinois Prairie Path in the western Chicago suburbs, the Great River Trail along the Great River Road and the Mississippi River, and the east-west I&M and Hennepin Canals state trails, which are just north of I-80.

More information is available from the **Illinois Department of Natural Resources** (www.dnr.state.il.us) or the **League of Illinois Bicyclists** (www.bikelib.org). Most visitors bureaus in northern Illinois have pamphlets on the trail. Or you can request a copy of the detailed users guide to the trail from the DNR or League of Illinois Bicyclists. The guide divides the trail into 10 different segments and lists bike repair shops, lodging options including campsites, and other tips on riding the trail. Both organizations also have information on the annual Grand Illinois Trail and Parks Ride in June.

relaxing walk will enjoy the Aspen and Deer trails in the north by the primitive campsites. In the south, Sunset Trail will test your calf muscles, but you'll be rewarded with an awesome view of the Mississippi River at Lookout Point at the top. The Sentinel Trail takes you around a giant 200-foot-tall column of dolomite. So you're not up for a challenging hike? Drive the roads and pull off at one or all of the scenic overlooks. The sheer number of vistas in Palisades is amazing. Some are quite accessible, even for those who have trouble walking. Handicapped parking spaces for those are close to some vistas with benches, such as Oak Point. Because of the many overlooks, benches, and views of the river, this is a good park for eagle-watching in January and February. Throughout the 2,500-acre park are small caves (including one called Bat Cave), sinkholes, steep cliffs, rock outcroppings, and wildflowers such as trilliums and lady's slippers. The park has several campgrounds (see *Accommodations* for more information).

Boating

To cruise the Mighty Mississippi or embark on a fishing expedition, you'll want to launch your boat at the public launch across from the state park's northern entrance. Chances are you'll hook a catfish, bluegill, carp, or bass. There's a boat launch on the Mississippi River on Highway 84, just across from Mississippi Palisades State Park's northern entrance. There's also one on Spring Lake, a backwater lake that's part of the **Upper Mississippi River National Fish and Wildlife Refuge,** just off Highway 84 south of Savanna.

Other Sights and Activities

Spend an hour or so browsing **Pulford Opera House Antique Mall** (324 and 330 Main St., Savanna, 815/273-2661, 9:30 A.M.–5:30 P.M. Mon.–Thurs.), a downtown Savanna antiques shop where several dealers showcase their wares.

The fertile soil in and around Savanna has been great for growing melons. Savanna, which calls itself the Watermelon Capital of the World, celebrates its melon growers and melon-producing history with **Melon Days.** The festival is held annually during Labor Day weekend and features watermelon-eating contests and plenty of watermelon to eat. During the summer various farms set out stands along the main roads. Try **McGinnis Melon Market** (2200 Hwy. 84/Great River Road, Thomson), south of Savanna.

For those of you traveling on the back of a Harley-Davidson or other motorcycle, Savanna has two biker-friendly bars: The **Iron Horse Social Club** (314 Main St., Savanna, 815/273-2600), which has a collection of motorcycle memorabilia inside; and **Poopy's** (1030 Viaduct Rd., Savanna, store 815/273-2363, restaurant 815/273-4516, www.poopys.com), which also serves a decent lunch buffet.

Accommodations
Adjacent to Mississippi Palisades State Park, ◖ **The Nest at Palisades Cabins** (Scenic Ridge Rd., Savanna, 815/273-7824, www.thenestatpalisades.com, $138–168) rents cabins with kitchens (fridges, microwave ovens), wood-burning stoves, whirlpool tubs, porches, and pluses such as satellite television if the mosquitoes are biting and you'd rather not sit outside. The location can't be beat if you're in town for some serious hiking: A trail leads directly to the park. The owners also provide bicycles for guests.

For standard hotel or motel accommodations, try the **Super 8** (101 Valley View Dr., Savanna, 815/273-2288, under $100), a newer hotel with an indoor pool.

Whatever your fancy, whether it's private wooded campsites or sites large enough to accommodate your new RV, **Mississippi Palisades State Park** has got it. There are more than 240 campsites for RVs (105 sites have electrical hookups), tent campers, and people who want to pack into a primitive site. Some sites are well-manicured and lawn-like; others are more rustic. Pack-in sites are about 0.5 mile from the parking area. Latrines are scattered throughout the campgrounds. In

addition, there are three shower buildings that have running water May–October. A camp store that sells food, snacks, and camping tools can be found near the northern entrance to the park. It's open May–mid-September. The campgrounds, at the northern end of the park, fill up quickly in summertime, especially on holiday weekends. If you plan to camp then, stake your claim early. Campsites are first-come, first-served. Camping is $13–15 per day.

Food and Drink
Poopy's (1030 Viaduct Rd., Savanna, store 815/273-2363, restaurant 815/273-4516, www.poopys.com) in downtown Savanna serves up decent bar food like cheese curds, nachos, burgers, BLTs, and sandwiches that taste good despite their stomach-churning names: "The Big Poop," (a one-pound beef patty), "The Poopy Melt" (a cheeseburger), and "The Porker" (pork tenderloin).

The island-themed **Java Hut** (734 Viaduct Rd., Savanna, 815/273-4528, www.javahut.biz, 7 A.M.–5 P.M. Mon.–Fri., 8 A.M.–3 P.M. Sat.) combines coffee drinking with tanning—cheap lattes, 10-minute tanning booths.

Information and Services
The **Savanna Chamber of Commerce** has a tourist information center next to its offices on Main Street. You can't miss it: The offices are in an old train car, and the brochures and maps are at a center next to the car. You can park your car at the lot there and hop on the Great River Bike Trail, if you like. Otherwise, you can visit their website, www.savanna-il.com.

MT. CARROLL
Raven's Grin Inn
After working as a plumber, the eccentric Jim Warfield decided he was ready for a career change. He bought a creepy 1870 Italianate mansion in Mount Carroll (less than 10 miles east of Savanna) and transformed it into the enormously popular Raven's Grin Inn (411 N. Carroll St., Mount Carroll, 815/244-4746, www.hauntedravensgrin.com, call for hours,

open year-round, $12). The tour, which usually lasts 1.5 hours, can vary according to who you are (curious child, fearless teen, skeptical adult). Gather some strength and ride the "bad dream bed slide." Strapped to a mattress, you'll drop four stories into the wine cellar, also known as the freaky torture chamber. If you're going to visit during October, call ahead to reserve a spot. The entrance line can wind down the sidewalk.

Timber Lake Resort

Just south of Mt. Carroll, among woods and alongside a 10-acre lake, the Timber Lake Resort (8216 Black Oak Rd., Mt. Carroll, 800/485-0145, www.timberlakeresort.com, tent camping $22–28, RV sites $32–37, cabins $139–149) is home to the **Timber Lake Playhouse.** The professional summer stock theater group stages a mix of comedies, musicals, and dramas (think *West Side Story* and *The Producers*) throughout the summer months. Their performances often win rave reviews from the local press. The resort itself is quite a

complex, with tent and RV camping, one- and two-bedroom cabins, an outdoor swimming pool, a camp store, and a recreation center.

FULTON

Christened "De Immigrant," **Fulton's Dutch Windmill** (10th and 1st Sts., Fulton, 815/589-4545, www.cityoffulton.us, 10 A.M.–5 P.M. Sat., 1–5 P.M. Sun. May and Oct., 10 A.M.–3 P.M. Mon.–Fri., 10 A.M.–5 P.M. Sat., 1–5 P.M. Sun. Sept.; 10 A.M.–5 P.M. Mon.–Sat., 1–5 P.M. Sun. June–Aug., free) is the city's pride and joy (and biggest attraction). Many immigrants settled here in the late 1800s, and this is a tribute to the city's Dutch heritage. The windmill sits atop a flood-control dike overlooking the Mississippi River and is adjacent to flower gardens. The site, with its river views and benches, makes for a good rest stop if you're traveling along the Great River Road. The windmill is authentic (built in the Netherlands), but it's not exactly historic. The 90-foot-tall structure dates back a few years rather than centuries. Still, it's fully operational and there are

the working Dutch Windmill in Fulton

© CHRISTINE DES GARENNES

NORTHERN HILL COUNTRY

grinding stones inside. (Stone-ground flour is for sale in the gift shop.) You can check out the exterior any time of year, but if you want to tour the welcome center or climb into the windmill to see how it works, you'll have to visit in the spring through the fall.

At the top of the dike near the windmill runs the **Great River Bike Trail,** a path that follows the river for more than 60 miles from the Quad Cities on the south to the northern town of Savanna. There's a parking lot here if you want to start your bike ride from here.

The other main attraction in Fulton is **Heritage Canyon** (515 N. 4th St., Fulton, 815/589-4545, 9 A.M.–5 P.M. daily Apr.–mid-Dec., donation), a limestone quarry that one local couple transformed into a little historical village. It's within steps of the Mississippi River in a residential neighborhood. Now owned by the city, the unusual site is open for visitors who wish to take a self-guided walking tour through the 12-acre site, past buildings mainly from the mid-1800s. They include a log cabin, a one-room schoolhouse, a church, and other buildings.

Vendors sell kitchen gadgets, tools, glassware, and an assortment of tchotchkes at **Great River Road Antiques** (23080 Hwy. 84, Fulton, 815/589-3355, 10 A.M.–6 P.M. daily Apr.–Oct.). Outside are sale tables; inside are more antiques plus some food and drink for sale.

ALBANY

Another example of the ingenuity of ancient Native Americans can be found at **Albany Mounds State Historic Site** (Cherry St. and 12th Ave., Albany, 309/887-4335, sunrise–sunset daily, free), one of several sites in Illinois where a mound-building village was situated. The inhabitants were from the Middle Woodland Period (about 2,000 years ago) and they built nearly 100 mounds overlooking the Mississippi River. In some of them they buried their dead along with their possessions. Previous excavations of the mounds have turned up items such as obsidian, copper, and sea shells, suggesting the villagers traded with people from the western United States, south to Mexico, and north to the Great Lakes. The present-day site, now listed on the National Register of Historic Places, is about 200 acres, and you can see the remaining mounds (ranging in height from a few feet to 15 feet) by walking along a mowed grass path. You can also get to the Great River Bike Trail from the parking lot.

Along the Rock River

The Mississippi and Illinois Rivers garner quite a lot of attention in Illinois because of the bluffs that often jut above their shorelines and because of the fishing and wildlife-viewing opportunities in the parks that border the rivers. Sometimes residents forget about the Rock River, which runs south from Wisconsin through Rockford and southwesterly to the Mississippi River. It's a river just as scenic as the other two, with its own bluffs and parks here and there. Highway 2 follows much of the river from Rockford south through towns such as Oregon, where you can board a paddlewheel boat for a cruise of the river. Just south of Oregon, brake for some hiking or picnicking at Castle Rock State Park, where a sandstone bluff rises above the river's west bank. From there, it's on to the even smaller town of Grand Detour, where blacksmith John Deere forged a plow that would make farming the thick prairie soil a much more manageable chore. And beyond Grand Detour you'll come to Dixon, a river town known for the thousands of petunias that residents plant each year, as well as a local boy who went on to become a Hollywood actor and U.S. president, Ronald Reagan.

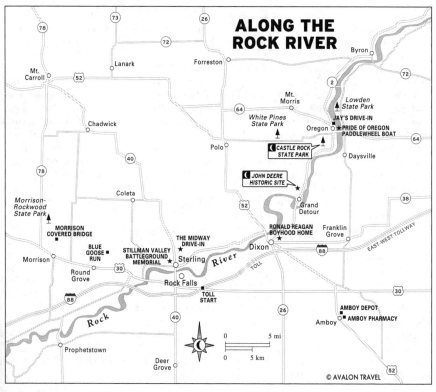

ALONG THE ROCK RIVER

© AVALON TRAVEL

OREGON
◖ Castle Rock State Park

Right smack in the middle of the Rock River hills region, the 2,000-acre Castle Rock State Park (1365 W. Castle Rd., Oregon, 815/732-7329, www.dnr.state.il.us) is a riverside park with land right along the river as well as up on the hills west of Highway 2. Castle Rock, after which the park is named, is a sandstone bluff east of Highway 2. You can climb up a few sets of stairs to a platform that looks eastward over the river. Near the rock are a few picnic tables and areas for bank fishing. The trails—there are six miles through prairie and native forest—are on the west side of the park, west of Highway 2. Part of this area is set aside as a nature preserve. A layer of glacial till blankets the area, making it a hospitable region for

diverse species of flora and fauna. Castle Rock is three miles south of Oregon.

White Pines State Park

If you're tired of staying in hotels or bed-and-breakfasts and prefer a more rustic experience, but are not exactly ready or willing for full-fledged tent camping, make tracks to **White Pines State Park** (6712 White Pines Rd., Mount Morris, 815/946-3717, www.dnr.state.il.us or www.whitepinesinn.com, cabins $85–105), a 385-acre park west of Oregon. In the 1930s the Civilian Conservation Corps built the log lodge that now houses a restaurant and the 25 cabins near it. The log cabins come with a queen-size hand-hewn log bed with a trundle underneath, a private bathroom, air-conditioning, and heat. If you prefer camping, the park has a 110-site campground with tent and RV sites. The **White Pines Inn Restaurant** (815/946-3817, lunch and dinner Mon.–Sat., brunch Sun., $10) serves steak, seafood, and chicken dishes. The restaurant also hosts dinner theater productions.

The park, as the names suggests, is home to native pine forest. A little more than five miles of trails, ranging in length up to 1.4 miles, wind through the forest and along creeks. (Try the lookout trail, which takes you along Pine Creek.) The park is about six miles east of U.S. 52 off County Highway 6.

Other Sights and Activities

While you're in the area, take a quick detour to visit **Lowden State Park** (1411 N. River Rd., Oregon, 815/732-6828, www.dnr.state.il.us), a small park just north of Oregon on the east side of the Rock River. The park contains a nearly 50-foot-tall statue of Black Hawk. The concrete statue, sculpted by Illinois artist Lorado Taft after the turn of the 20th century, looks out over the river valley. The statue is actually hollow, but visitors are not allowed inside.

Docked at Maxson Riverside Restaurant north of Oregon, the **Pride of Oregon** (Hwy. 2, north of Oregon, 815/732-6761 or 800/468-4222, www.maxsonrestaurant.com, lunch and dinner Mon.–Sat., brunch Sun., Apr.–Oct.) is a 100-foot-long paddlewheel boat that cruises along the Rock River, including past Lowden State Park. It offers lunch and dinner cruises and Sunday brunch rides, plus sightseeing-only rides. Tickets start at $12.

An old piano factory has been converted into a series of shops called the **Conover Square Mall** (201 N. 3rd St., Oregon, 815/732-3950, www.conoversquare.com, 9:30 A.M.–5:30 P.M. Mon.–Fri., 9:30 A.M.–5 P.M. Sat., 1–5 P.M. Sun.). Among the businesses are an antiques shop, cheese shop, bakery, and pottery store.

Accommodations and Food

The recently remodeled **Patchwork Inn** (122 N. 3rd St., Oregon, 815/732-4113, $75–115) is a two-story brick inn in downtown Oregon. The inn, more than 150 years old, has been a

hotel for most of its years. Abraham Lincoln reportedly slept here. Today there are 10 rooms modestly decorated with homemade quilts. Continental breakfast is served in a sun room.

As noted above, the **White Pines Inn** in White Pines State Park has cabins available for rent plus a campground with tent and RV sites.

A bona fide drive-in with teenage carhops, **Jay's Drive-In** (107 W. Washington St., Oregon, 815/732-2396) is an old-school drive-in near the Rock River. The menu is extensive, varying from plain hamburgers for under $2 to chicken dinners for $8, gyros, grilled chicken sandwiches, and chicken wings. The main attraction is the drive-in's grilled butter burgers and fries (zesty twisty fries or cheddar fries). Cones and shakes are also available.

GRAND DETOUR

Named for the bend in the Rock River nearby, Grand Detour is a tiny town with a smattering of white frame houses and flower beds, a place where you'll see older folks on walks. More than 160 years ago an entrepreneurial man came into town, established a blacksmith shop, and would invent an item that would change how farming was done in Illinois and the United States.

⟨ John Deere Historic Site

The John Deere Historic Site (8393 S. Main St., Grand Detour, 815/652-4551, www.deere.com, 9 A.M.–5 P.M. daily Apr.–Nov., $3), just west of Highway 2 and the Rock River, comprises an archaeological site, re-created blacksmith shop, and the Deere family home. Deere arrived in town in 1836 and developed the plow in 1837. The original is in the Smithsonian, but there are plenty of other old plows and blacksmith tools on view throughout the site. What was so remarkable about Deere's invention is that it was a self-scouring plow. Farmers could drive it through the thick prairie soil and instead of sticking to the blade, the soil would brush off. This meant farmers could cut down on the amount of time they'd spend in the field scraping the soil off their plows. Farmers loved it, of course, and it was such a success that eventually Deere moved his operation closer to the Mississippi River and Moline, where he could easily ship the plows across the country.

You can see the foundations of Deere's original blacksmith shop by touring a building that was constructed around the excavation site. After walking through, visitors are treated to a demonstration of the art (by the site's engaging resident blacksmith) at a re-created but fully functioning blacksmith shop. The shop was modeled after Deere's shop. (You can buy items made by the blacksmith in the gift shop, where, incidentally, there's also no shortage of green-and-yellow Deere collectibles.) Also on the site is the six-room two-story white frame house where Deere lived with his family. Staff has set it up as though the Deere family were still living there. Throughout the summer the site often hosts vintage tractor shows.

Food

A short walk from the Deere site is the **Colonial Rose** (8320 S. Green St., Grand Detour, 815/652-4422, www.colonialroseinn.com), a B&B and restaurant housed in a brick Italianate home. Surrounded by plenty of gardens, the inn has four different rooms, each with a private bathroom. The restaurant, which is also open to people not staying in the B&B, serves entrées such as fillets, ribs, and duck for about $15–30. It's open for dinner Wednesday–Saturday.

DIXON, ROCK FALLS, AND STERLING

Former Hollywood actor and late U.S. President Ronald Reagan grew up in northern Illinois, including Tampico and Dixon. It was in Dixon where he spent his so-called formative years attending school and spending summers working as a lifeguard at a Rock River park.

The family moved to Dixon from Tampico in 1920 when Reagan was nine years old. The **Ronald Reagan Boyhood Home and Visitors Center** (816 Hennepin Ave., Dixon, 815/288-5176, www.ronaldreaganhome.com, 10 A.M.–4 P.M. Mon.–Sat., 1–4 P.M. Sun.

Apr.–Oct., 10 A.M.–4 P.M. Sat., 1–4 P.M. Sun. Mar., $5) has been restored to a 1920s-era home complete with all the furnishings. Next to the home is a small garden with a statue of Reagan and a few benches. (Reagan and his pals used to play football in the side yard.) Also on Hennepin Avenue is the former South Side School, which now houses the Dixon Historic Center and contain exhibits about Dixon's favorite son.

For about 50 years, residents of Dixon have been planting thousands and thousands of flowers in beds along roads and in boxes, earning the nickname "the Petunia Capital of the World." The town's popular **Petunia Festival** (www.petuniafestival.org), held for several days in late June through early July, is the quintessential Midwestern festival, complete with a parade, the coronation of the petunia queen, country music concerts, a pancake breakfast, fishing derby, and craft show.

The **Midway Drive-In Movie Theater** (Prairieville Rd., Sterling, 815/625-4099, www.themidwaydrivein.net) has been showing films for about five decades. All you need is an FM radio in your car to be able to listen.

About 10 minutes east of Dixon is the **Franklin Creek State Natural Area** (1872 Twist Rd., north of Hwy. 84, Franklin Grove, 815/456-2878, www.dnr.state.il.us), a park marked by the scenic creek, ravines, bluffs, and the occasional fox or heron. Inside the over 650-acre site is a working grist mill. It's not the original 1847 mill, but it works just like grist mills did back then. On weekends visitors can go inside and see how it works. It's open noon–4 P.M. Saturday–Sunday. Otherwise the park has several scenic and quiet walking trails. A short wheelchair-accessible trail takes you to the mill spring.

Accommodations and Food

There are several national chain hotels in Dixon and Rock Falls. Standard hotel rooms are around $75, more for suites. In Dixon there's the **Comfort Inn** (136 Plaza Dr., Dixon, 815/284-0500) and near that is the newer **Quality Inn & Suites** (154 Plaza Dr., Dixon, 815/288-2001), which has two indoor

"DUTCH": THE PRE-HOLLYWOOD AND WASHINGTON, D.C., YEARS

Even before Ronald Reagan died in 2004, it was not uncommon for Illinois folks to wax nostalgic about the former president's time here, from birth to college. In fact, stories about Reagan, such as his days as a lifeguard at a Rock River beach, sound almost mythical. For example, during the summers he worked at the beach in Dixon, the hunky lifeguard reportedly saved 77 lives. (And how many of them were teenage girls who wanted to attract his attention?)

When he was a child, Reagan's family moved around a lot, beginning in Tampico, where he was born, and continuing through Galesburg, Monmouth, and Dixon. From there Reagan was off to college in Eureka, east of Peoria. Not only did the family live in several towns, but they lived in different houses too. There's no shortage of Reagan destinations in Illinois. The state has placed a series of highway signs featuring his silhouette throughout the region. They direct travelers to Reagan sites. More information is available from the state-sponsored website, www.ronaldreagantrail.net, which offers lodging and dining suggestions in towns where Reagan once lived or passed through.

Reagan was born on February 6, 1911, in a simple apartment above a bakery in Tampico, where his father worked as a store clerk. The restored **Ronald Reagan Birthplace** (111 S. Main St., Tampico, 815/438-2130), which is open to visitors, is decorated as though it were still 1911. From there, the Reagans moved to Galesburg when Ron was five years old. Ironically, Nancy Davis, whom Ron would later meet in Hollywood and marry, also often spent time in Galesburg visiting relatives. After Galesburg came Monmouth, and finally Dixon in 1920.

It was in Dixon, a medium-size Rock River town, where Dutch developed into an all-star football player, got the acting bug with the school's drama club, and worked as a lifeguard at Lowell Park. The family lived in what is now the **Ronald Reagan Boyhood Home and Visitors Center** (816 Hennepin Ave., Dixon, 815/288-5176, www.ronaldreaganhome.com) for only several years before moving into another one, but no matter. Like the Tampico apartment, it

© CHRISTINE DES GARENNES

Ronald Reagan's boyhood home, in Dixon

has been restored to reflect the years when the Reagans lived there and is filled with 1920s-era furnishings and photographs of Dutch from his years in Dixon and his visits back to the area.

In recent years the town of Dixon renovated South Side School, which Reagan attended. It's now home to the **Dixon Historic Center** (205 W. Fifth St., Dixon, 815/288-5508, www.dixonhistoriccenter.org, 9 A.M.-4 P.M. Mon.-Fri.), with installed displays on Reagan and local-history exhibits. The gift shop stocks some of Reagan's favorite treats, Jelly Belly jelly beans.

Before eventually leaving for Hollywood, Reagan studied economics and sociology at Eureka College, near the Illinois River to the south. There he also played every sport imaginable (football, track, swimming) and all the while continued to hone his acting skills. Exhibits in Eureka College's **Ronald Reagan Museum** (Donald B. Cerf Center, 300 E. Peoria Ave., Eureka, 309/467-3721, www.eureka.edu) highlight his years here, plus events from throughout his movie and political career. A large room is filled with about 2,000 items, such as photographs of him in his football uniform and books about his life and politics. Nearby is the peace garden with a piece of the Berlin Wall.

NORTHERN HILL COUNTRY

pools; the **Reagan Hotel and Suites** (443 Hwy. 2, Dixon, 815/284-1890); and in Rock Falls you'll find the **Country Inn and Suites** (2106 1st Ave., Rock Falls, 815/625-3200) and the **Holiday Inn** (2105 S. 1st Ave., Rock Falls, 815/626-5500).

In addition, up the hill from Dixon's downtown in a residential area above the Rock River you'll find the **Crawford House Inn** (204 E. 3rd St., Dixon, 815/288-3351, www.crawfordhouseinn.com, $65–85), an 1869 Italianate brick home. There are three bedrooms, two with king beds, one with a queen. All three are feather beds. The decor is Victorian with period antiques (dark wood, floral patterns). The stay includes a full breakfast. Guests share two full bathrooms; there's one bath on each floor. Common sitting areas include the library, parlor, and an expansive porch looking out over the town. Prices here are competitive with those at the chain hotels, up to about $85 a night.

If you like a little kick to your food, try the **Salamandra Restaurant** (105 W. 1st St., Dixon, 815/285-0874, 11 A.M.–9 P.M. Mon.–Sat., $9), an authentic Mexican restaurant in downtown Dixon. The colorful family-run restaurant features dishes from all regions of Mexico, including traditional fare such as *carne asada*, burritos, sandwiches, and salads, and also specialties such as the excellent potato and chorizo *sincronizada* (flour tortillas filled with chorizo, potatoes, jalapeño, cheese, and other ingredients).

A few feet away is another find, **Baker Street** (111 W. 1st St., Dixon, 815/285-2253, 7 A.M.–5:30 P.M. Mon.–Fri., 7 A.M.–2 P.M. Sat.), a coffeehouse and *boulangerie* (French for bakery).

Information

For more info about the region, contact the **Rock Falls Visitors Bureau and Chamber of Commerce** (601 W. 10th St., Rock Falls, 815/625-4500, www.rockfallsil.com). The city of **Dixon** has a visitors information center (106 W. River St., Dixon, 815/284-3496, www.discoverdixon.com). The **Lee County Tourism Council** (113 S. Peoria Ave., Dixon, 815/288-

1840, www.leecountytourism.com) can provide you with the scoop on Dixon, Amboy, and little towns in the Green River valley southeast of Dixon.

MORRISON

Just off U.S. 30, the Lincoln Highway, the town of Morrison has a surprisingly bustling downtown, where the casual restaurants are especially busy on Friday nights serving families and teens. North of town, take a quick detour to drive through a new covered bridge, then drop a fishing line in the lake at Morrison-Rockwood State Park for some R&R.

Morrison-Rockwood State Park

In the summer the focal point of the 1,100-acre Morrison-Rockwood State Park (18750 Lake Rd., Morrison, 815/772-4708, www.dnr.state.il.us) is Lake Carlton, a spring-fed reservoir stocked with a variety of fish. If you have a boat, you can launch it from a ramp here, or have a go at bank fishing. In the winter, this is a great place to go for some serious cross-country skiing or snowshoeing. Follow the 14-mile horse trail through the woods and along the rambling Rock Creek, a tributary of the Rock River. The park also has a campground.

On the way to Morrison-Rockwood State Park, look for signs to the **Covered Bridge** (Crosby Rd., follow signs north of Morrison, 815/772-5175). It's actually a new bridge that stretches almost 150 feet in length. Feel free to drive through it. It's full of light because dozens of spaces or windows line both sides of the bridge.

Food

◖ **Blue Goose Run** (14609 Blue Goose Rd., Sterling, 815/772-7200, www.bluegooserun.com, 5–9:30 or 10 P.M. Thurs.–Sat., 8 A.M.–2 P.M. Sun.) is a country farm that has become home to a fine-dining white-tablecloth restaurant and wine bar, banquet hall, corn maze, huge chess and checkers set, 3.5-acre gardens, and most recently, a vineyard. It's a great example of how some families have changed the way they see and operate their farms. (Blue Run was once a commodity farm.) Take some time before or after visiting Morrison-Rockwood State Park to walk through the gardens, order an appetizer and a glass wine, or get lost in the maze. You can find the farm just north of Highway 30, halfway between Sterling and Morrison.

At the casual and kid-friendly **Isle of Rhodes** (100 W. Main St., Morrison, 815/772-7431, 11 A.M.–9 P.M. Mon.–Thurs., 6:30 A.M.–10 P.M. Fri., 6 A.M.–10 P.M. Sat., 7 A.M.–9 P.M. Sun.), you can try the regional specialty called Chicken George. A plate of Chicken George usually consists of white chicken strips deep-fried in a slightly sweet batter. Some say the batter tastes like funnel cakes or elephant ears.

GREEN RIVER VALLEY
Tampico
An apartment where Ronald Reagan was born has been restored, and fans of the 40th president of the United States are welcome to tour the place. The **Ronald Reagan Birthplace** (111 S. Main St., Tampico, 815/438-2130, hours vary each year; call ahead, donation) also has a souvenir shop.

The Dutch Diner Family Restaurant (105 S. Main St., Tampico, 815/438-2096) serves good old American standards such as casseroles and homemade pies.

Amboy
If you're feeling nostalgic, drive south on U.S. 52 to the town of Amboy and pay a visit to the **Amboy Pharmacy** (202 E. Main St., Amboy, 815/857-2323, 8 A.M.–5 P.M. Mon.–Fri., 8 A.M.–10 P.M. Sat., 8 A.M.–2 P.M. Sun.), an actual pharmacy and soda fountain shop. A soda jerk mixes phosphates, milk shakes, and whips up sundaes. And if you're out of aspirin or bug spray, well, you can stock up on some of those too while you're here.

Near the pharmacy you can't miss the **Amboy Depot** (Main St., downtown Amboy, 815/857-4700, www.amboydepotmuseum.org, 1–4 P.M. Wed.–Thurs. and Sun., 10 A.M.–4 P.M. Fri.–Sat., donation), a two-story brick building that once was a busy depot and division headquarters for the Illinois Central Railroad. Amboy was once a stop along the Charter Line, which ran from Cairo down in southern Illinois to East Dubuque by Galena. But the depot closed in the late 1960s, the line shut down in the 1980s, and the building deteriorated. Residents eventually rallied around their dear old building, raised money, and spent thousands of hours renovating it. It's now filled with mementos about the railroad and life in a 19th-century railroading town. You'll find plenty of photos, maps, schedules, and more. Outside the depot are a hulking steam engine, a caboose, and a one-room schoolhouse.

NORTHERN HILL COUNTRY

Rockford and Vicinity

The largest city in Illinois outside of Chicago, Rockford is a diverse city of more than 155,000 people on the Rock River. Founded by a group of Galena residents in the 1830s, Rockford, halfway between Chicago and Galena, was once called Midway. For years travelers tended to think of Rockford as exactly that—a halfway point, a place to fill up your tank with gas while traveling to Galena or north to Madison, Wisconsin.

But a visit to Rockford can yield surprises,

especially for people interested in regional history and art. Because the city was quite a hub for manufacturing, thousands of immigrants migrated to the area, attracted by the hope of landing jobs at agricultural equipment factories, furniture makers, knitting mills, and other businesses. Swedes, Irish, and Eastern Europeans, followed by Southern blacks, all made Rockford their home. Several homes and buildings around town showcase photographs, furniture, and other items left behind

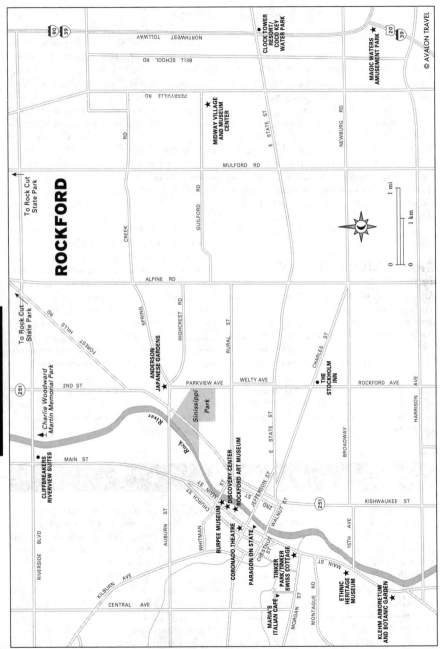

© AVALON TRAVEL

by many of the city's early residents. One of the finest is the Tinker Swiss Cottage, a home that looks as if it belongs in the Swiss Alps, not northern Illinois. On the west bank of the river is a museum park, home to the Rockford Art Museum, among other art organizations, which contains an impressive collection of American art; and the Burpee Museum of Natural History, a must-see for anyone curious about why Illinois is shaped the way it is and what kind of cultures lived here before the white settlers arrived.

Finally, Rockford should be on your list if you're a gardener or interested in horticulture. The town has an amazing collection of parks. Stroll through Anderson Gardens (formal Japanese gardens), Klehm Arboretum and Botanic Garden, plus riverside parks with walking and biking paths.

SIGHTS
Museums

Outside of Chicago's Field Museum, the place to learn about prehistoric life in Illinois is Rockford's **Burpee Museum of Natural History** (737 N. Main St., Rockford, 815/965-3433, www.burpee.org, 10 A.M.–4 P.M. Mon.–Fri., 10 A.M.–5 P.M. Sat., noon–5 P.M. Sun., $7, free Wed.). One of the more recent additions to the museum is a skeletal cast of a *Tyrannosaurus rex,* dubbed Jane. (Jane is Rockford's answer to the Field Museum's Sue, another famed *T. rex.*) Near the 10-foot-high and 40-foot-long skeleton is a reproduction of a wooly mammoth. A reminder: Things were big millions of years ago. The museum also has a cool recreation of what a coal forest may have looked like 300 million years ago, exhibits about glaciers and how they shaped the land, plus displays about Native American life in the region before the white settlers arrived.

How does air move? How does an airplane work? What's the best way to swing a bat or toss a football? The kid-friendly **Discovery Center Museum** (711 N. Main St., Rockford, 815/963-6769, www.discoverycentermuseum.org, 10 A.M.–5 P.M. Mon.–Sat., noon–5 P.M. Sun., 10 A.M.–7 P.M. Thurs. summer, $6 adults,

$5 children), also at the riverfront park, attempts to demystify science and explain theories to youth and the nonscientific set. In addition to the applied-science exhibits, the museum has a planetarium and an outdoor playground where kids can race boats and engage in other water play. Another fun exhibit explains the physics behind amusement park rides and invites visitors to build their own coasters.

Adjacent to the Discovery Museum is the **Rockford Art Museum** (711 N. Main St., Rockford, 815/968-2787, www.rockfordartmuseum.org, 10 A.M.–5 P.M. Mon.–Sat., noon–5 P.M. Sun., $6, free Tues.). It showcases 19th- and 20th-century American art by organizing rotating exhibits and highlighting pieces from its permanent collection. Expect everything from realist landscape paintings and portraits to abstract sculpture. Among the highlights: a Lorado Taft sculpture, a painting by Rudolph Ingerle, and an Ed Ruscha lithograph.

You'll find the **Tinker Swiss Cottage** (411 Kent St., Rockford, 815/964-2566, www.tinkercottage.com, tours 1, 2, 3 P.M. Tues.–Fri. and Sun., $5) in Rockford's historic west bank district. On the National Register of Historic Places, the cottage (it's more like a mini estate) was built in 1864. Rockford businessman Robert Tinker modeled it after homes he saw while traveling through Europe. (Tinker, by the way, was not born in Switzerland but in Hawaii). The home, which features intricate woodwork and plasterwork, also contains a conservatory and a rose garden. Inside, the house is furnished with period items, and on the walls hang portraits of the Tinker family's relatives.

If you enjoy touring old homes and want to learn more about Rockford's past, walk a block south from the Tinker Cottage to the **Ethnic Heritage Museum** (1115 S. Main St./Hwy. 2, Rockford, 815/968-6044, 2–4 P.M. Sun., $2). Each room in the 1850s-era home is devoted to a different ethnic group that helped build Rockford: African-American, Hispanic, Irish, Italian, Lithuanian, and Polish.

The folks behind the **Midway Village and Museum Center** (6799 Guilford Rd., Rockford, 815/397-9112, www.midwayvillage. com, 11 A.M.–4 P.M. Tues.–Sun. June–Sept., 11 A.M.–4 P.M. Thurs.–Sun. May and Oct., $5) have amassed quite the collection of historic and re-created buildings from the turn of the 20th century. Two dozen buildings are clustered around the 137-acre site to make visitors think they're visiting a town circa 1900. Walk into an old-time barbershop, general store, hotel, fire station, and other buildings. It looks pretty real except the grass here is kept nicely trimmed and some of the structures were rebuilt at three-quarter scale. Speaking of small scale, there's a doll museum on the grounds.

Water Parks

The Rockford Park District has a hit with its **Magic Waters** outdoor water park (7820 N. Cherryvale Blvd., Cherry Valley, 815/966-2442 or 800/373-1679, www.magicwaterswaterpark.com, $20, extra for tube rental, reduced prices afternoons and for kids, hours vary each year but typically about 10 A.M.–6 P.M. daily Memorial Day–Labor Day). In addition to the standard wave pool, the park has tube slides, raft rides, a children's play area, a lazy river that has waterfalls and other features, plus food stands and sand volleyball courts. The water park is at I-90/I-39 and Highway 20 in Cherry Valley, just north of Rockford.

During the winter, area visitors can spend a day or several hours at **CoCo Key Water Park** (7801 E. State St., Rockford, 815/398-6000, www.cocokeywaterresort.com), located on the grounds of the Clock Tower Resort on the east side of town. The indoor water park, which is open also to people not staying in the hotel, also has tube rides, a lazy river, waterslides, and a water play areas for younger children. Day passes are available from $16 for afternoon admission to $35 for an all-day weekend ticket.

Parks and Gardens

Though some of its downtown buildings could use some rehabbing, Rockford's parks are in tip-top shape. **Klehm Arboretum and Botanic**

Garden (2701 Clifton Ave., Rockford, 815/965-8146, www.klehm.org, 9 A.M.–8 P.M. daily Memorial Day–Labor Day, 9 A.M.–4 P.M. daily Labor Day–Memorial Day, $4) is a 150-acre park south of downtown where lots of trails curl past blooming flowers and trees. Walk among flowering dogwoods and crab apple trees and a 12-acre burr oak grove. Have a seat under a pergola and listen to the water fountain. Gather ideas for your own garden by visiting the demonstration garden, and check out the ornamental grasses, hostas, and daylilies. Tours of the gardens aboard a golf cart are also available for a small fee. The arboretum also is home to an evening farmers market on Mondays in the summer.

One of the best parks in the county is **Anderson Gardens** (318 Spring Creek Rd., Rockford, 815/229-9390, www.andersongardens.org, 9 A.M.–5 P.M. Mon.–Thurs., 9 A.M.–sunset Fri., 9 A.M.–4 P.M. Sat., noon–4 P.M. Sun. May–late Oct., $7), formal Japanese gardens along the riverfront that feature trickling waterfalls, a teahouse replica, and some sculpture. New to the gardens are a visitors center and restaurant.

Nearby are two more riverside parks. **Sinnissippi Park** (1300 N. 2nd St., Rockford, 815/987-8858, www.rockfordparkdistrict.org) is a good place to unwind, soak in the sun, or read a book or magazine. Pick a bench looking out onto the river or a spot under the trees or near the lagoons. Here you have access to the **Rock River Recreation Path,** a paved trail that follows the river for seven miles from downtown Rockford north to Loves Park. Sinnissippi also has a lagoon (home to mute swans) and a greenhouse. To the north is **Charlie Woodward Martin Memorial Park** (5600 Park Ridge, Loves Park), which is also on the Rock River Recreation Path. Here you'll find a pavilion, playground, and boat ramp.

Farther north of town, **Rock Cut State Park** (7318 Harlem Rd., Loves Park, 815/885-3311, www.dnr.state.il.us) is a 3,000-acre park just off I-90. (I-90 actually divides the park into two sections, connected by an overpass road). Fat-tire riders, rejoice: The park has 23 miles of designated mountain-biking trails that wind around lakes, oak and hickory forest, and prairie. Park your bike for a while and choose from more than 40 miles of hiking trails, and in the winter, go cross-country skiing and snowshoeing. The park also has a campground, wheelchair-accessible fishing piers, and a swimming beach on Olson Lake, which is on the east side of the park. The beach is open noon–7 P.M. daily, Memorial Day–Labor Day. Beach access costs $1 per person.

ENTERTAINMENT
Theater and Nightlife
More than a dozen performing arts groups call Rockford and the surrounding towns home. Some of the highlights include the baroque, gilded, and just plain opulent **Coronado Theatre** (314 N. Main St., Rockford, 815/968-0595, www.coronadotheatre.com), a renovated 1927 vaudeville house that hosts concerts and Broadway plays and musicals. It's also home to the **Rockford Symphony Orchestra** (815/965-0049, www.rockfordsymphony.com), **Rockford Dance Company** (815/963-3341, www.rockforddancecompany.com), and other companies.

The **MetroCentre** (300 Elm St., Rockford, 815/968-5222, www.centreevents.com) is a modern 10,000-seat venue that hosts music concerts and sporting events. This is where touring acts like Weird Al Yankovic or the band Poison perform when in town.

For a change of pace, head to **Octane Interlounge** (124 N. Main St., Rockford, 815/965-4012, www.octane.net), part coffee joint, restaurant, Internet café, and nightclub. Sink into a blue velvet couch with a newspaper, coffee, and muffin in the morning. At night, nibble on some Thai chicken kebabs or sip on a martini.

SPORTS
So they're not as famous as Chicago sports teams, but Rockford is home to several pro teams. And a night at a RiverHawks baseball game or an arena football game is a heck of a lot cheaper than a trip to Wrigley Field or Soldier Field. The **IceHogs** team

(815/986-6465, www.icehogs.com), part of the American Hockey League, is an affiliate of the Chicago Blackhawks. The team plays in the MetroCentre, and its season runs roughly October–May. The **Rock River Raptors** (815/965-7000, www.raptorsindoorfootball.com) are the town's arena football team. They play in the MetroCentre against teams from cities like Milwaukee and Flint, Michigan. The season runs late-winter–early summer. The Rockford **RiverHawks** are part of the Frontier professional baseball league. You can catch a game at Road Ranger Stadium (4503 Interstate Blvd., Loves Park, 815/885-2255), off Riverside Drive and east of I-90/I-39.

ACCOMMODATIONS
In addition to the hotels listed here, Rockford also has a dozen or so chain hotels off I-39/I-90 and U.S. 20 exits. Expect to pay about $75–125 per night. A sampling: **Comfort Inn** (7392 Argus Dr., Rockford, 815/398-7061); **Hampton Inn** (615 Clark Dr., Rockford, 815/229-0404); **Red Roof Inn** (7434 E. State St., Rockford, 815/398-9750); and **Sleep Inn** (725 Clark Dr., Rockford, 815/398-8900). For a complete list, contact the visitors bureau.

$50-100
Sweden House Lodge (4605 E. State St., Rockford, 815/398-4130 or 800/886-4138, www.swedenhouselodge.com, $60) is a 105-room Swedish motor lodge halfway between downtown Rockford and I-90. The cheery hotel has a mix of standard motel rooms and suites that come with kitchenettes. The lodge also has an indoor pool.

$100-150
Overlooking the Rock River and a few hundred feet from the Rock River Recreation Path, **C Cliffbreakers Riverview Suites Hotel** (700 W. Riverside Blvd., Rockford, 815/282-3033 or 800/478-9395, www.cliffbreakers.com, from about $100) is the best place to stay if you want to keep driving to a minimum. Bring your bikes along, and then ride across the bridge and head south to town and the

parks and museums. The hotel has a restaurant and indoor pool on-site.

For more of a retreat-like setting, try the ◖ **Best Western Clock Tower Resort** (7801 E. State St., Rockford, 815/398-6000, www.clocktowerresort.com, from about $110), just off I-90 and State Street (U.S. 20). The 247-room hotel complex has just about everything travelers could ask for: a large indoor water park for the kids, a fitness center with tennis and racquetball courts for the adults, plus a restaurant, lounge, and high speed Internet access.

FOOD

The usually busy **Maria's Italian Café** (828 Cunningham St., Rockford, 815/968-6781, 4:30–9 P.M. Tues.–Sat.) serves northern Italian dishes, heaping portions of pasta, polenta, and steak dinners. People keep going back to Maria's for the homemade pasta and sauces, which taste amazingly fresh. Most entrées are about $10, more for steaks.

Another popular eatery is the **Stockholm Inn** (2420 Charles St., Rockford, 815/397-3534, www.thestockholminn.com, 6 A.M.–8 P.M. Mon.–Fri., 6 A.M.–1:30 P.M. Sat., 7 A.M.–1:30 P.M. Sun.). The sunny Swedish restaurant and gift shop churns out traditional meals such as Swedish pancakes and meatballs, and some seafood dishes.

Housed in a refurbished brick building in Rockford's downtown river district, **Paragon on State** (205 W. State St., Rockford, 815/963-1660, www.paragononstate.com, lunch Tues.–Fri., dinner Tues.–Sun., lunch $5–12, dinner $19–32) is a modern restaurant and sushi bar with modular decor (cherry chairs and purple-painted walls). Dishes are creative here, such as shiitake mushroom salad, chicken bruschetta sandwich, and New Zealand rib chop.

INFORMATION AND SERVICES

The **Rockford Area Convention and Visitors Bureau** (102 N. Main St., Rockford, 815/963-8111 or 800/521-0849, www.gorockford.com) has comprehensive lodging, dining, and tour information for visitors.

Media

The daily newspaper is the **Rockford Register Star** (99 E. State St., Rockford, 815/987-1200, www.rrstar.com), available in most grocery stores and convenience stores.

Tours

The Rockford Park District operates open-air **trolley tours** departing from Riverview Park (324 N. Madison St., Rockford, 815/987-8894, www.rockfordparkdistrict.org). A ride, about 45 minutes long, will cost $4 per adult. The district was renovating its trolley in 2008, but expected to start up service again in 2009. From the same location the park district launches **riverboat rides** on the Rock River aboard the *Forest City Queen;* call for hours.

Hospital

For medical emergencies, contact **Rockford Memorial Hospital** (2400 N. Rockton Ave., Rockford, 815/971-5000, www.rhsnet.org), located east of Highway 70 and south of Riverside Boulevard.

GETTING THERE AND AROUND
Air

Chicago Rockford International Airport (Airport Dr./Hwy. 2, south of U.S. 20, Rockford, 815/969-4000, www.flyrfd.com) is a full-service airport south of town with free parking for fliers. The airlines that serve the airport include United to Denver; Southern Skyways to Denver and Myrtle Beach, South Carolina; Allegiant Air to Denver, Las Vegas, Phoenix, and the Florida cities Orlando, Clearwater/St. Petersburg, and Ft. Lauderdale; and Apple Vacations. The carriers that serve Illinois's regional airports tends to change often. Check with the airport's website to learn of any updates.

Car

Car-rental companies **Avis** (815/962-8447), **Hertz** (815/963-5318), and **National/Alamo** (815/965-4466) are all at the Rockford Airport.

Rockford has several taxicab services. They include **Reliable Cab** (815/968-2227), **Spee-Dee Taxi Cab Service** (815/963-3322), and **Yellow Line Cab** (815/962-5511).

Public Transportation

Rockford Mass Transit District (520 Mulberry St., Rockford, 815/961-9000, www.rmtd.org) buses run daily. Rides cost $1 per person.

DAY TRIPS FROM ROCKFORD
Cedarville and Vicinity

In honor of Cedarville native and humanitarian Jane Addams, founder of Chicago Hull House, the community helped develop the **Jane Addams Trail** (www.janeaddamstrail.com), a 13-mile crushed-limestone trail from north of Freeport to the Illinois-Wisconsin state line. A rails-to-trails project, the trail follows part of the Galena and Chicago Union Railroad line past oak groves, corn and soybean fields, and prairie. A section of the trail passes Cedarville Cemetery on Mill Street, where Addams is buried. In the winter it's open for snowmobiling and cross-country skiing. You can get to the trail north of Freeport off Fairview Road, which is south of U.S. 20. Other places to park your car and hit the trail are at the Richland Creek Trailhead on High Street, north of Orangeville; off Red Oak Road in Red Oak; and off McConnell Road in Buena Vista.

Rockton

One of the area's first white settlers was a man named Stephen Mack, a fur trader. His humble 1834 home, now listed in the National Register of Historic Places, is straight north of Rockford on the Pecatonica River. The **Stephen Mack Home and Whitman Trading Post** (Macktown Forest Preserve, 2221 Freeport Rd., Rockton, 815/877-6100, call for hours, $1) contains a few tools and pieces of furniture from the early 1800s, plus some Native American artifacts.

Information

For lodging, dining, and recreational options in towns west of Rockford, contact the **Freeport-Stephenson County Convention and Visitors Bureau** (2047 Ayp Rd./U.S. 20, Freeport, 815/233-1358 or 800/369-2955, www.stephenson-county-il.org).

U.S. 34 Corridor: Plano to Princeton

PLANO
The Farnsworth House

Far from the steel skyscrapers he designed for Chicago, Mies van der Rohe's Farnsworth House (14520 River Rd., Plano, 866/811-4111, www.farnsworthhouse.org, 10 A.M.–3 P.M. Tues.–Sun. Mar.–Nov., $20) is planted in a patch of woods along the Fox River. The white steel and glass home, built in 1951 for Chicago doctor Edith Farnsworth, is something else. Farnsworth ended up selling the house in the 1970s, and a British lord took ownership. In 2003 the National Trust for Historic Preservation, with the nonprofit Landmarks Illinois and a group of donors, purchased the 1,500-square-foot house for a reported $7.5 million. The modernist house is now on the National Register of Historic Places. Rising a little more than five feet off the ground, it's a completely unadorned house that directs visitors to look at the nearby Fox River instead of paintings on a wall. It's transparent; many of the walls are windows. It's a must-see for architecture and design buffs.

Accommodations

Less than three miles from the Farnsworth house is another notable home, **The Homestead** (611 E. Main St., Plano, 630/552-4322, $145–265), the former estate of a town founder. The Homestead, built in Italian cottage style, is now a B&B with a twist. The 1854 home is a

NORTHERN HILL COUNTRY

decorating firm's showcase house, meaning if you fall in love with any of the home decor or the house's furniture, you just might be able to buy it from the owners. There are five rooms here, some with private baths, and some with shared bathrooms. Outside is a lovely sculpture garden and labyrinth.

SANDWICH

Every year about 65,000 people wander up and down the aisles of the **Sandwich Antiques Market** (Sandwich Fairgrounds, 1401 Suydam Rd., Sandwich, 815/786-3337, www.antique-markets.com, 8 A.M.–4 P.M., third or fourth Sun. of the month, May–Oct., $5) to hunt for 19th- and 20th-century antiques. About 500 dealers set up tables and tents (some inside buildings and some outside).

Built in 1878, the **Sandwich Opera House** (140 E. Railroad St., Sandwich, 815/786-2555, 8:30 A.M.–noon, 1:30–4:30 P.M. Mon.–Fri., and during performances, www.sandwichoperahouse.com) once housed city hall on the first floor and a vaudeville theater on the second floor. Today the renovated performance space showcases everything from bluegrass to gospel music.

Take a drive into the country north of Plano and Sandwich to chomp on a sweet crunchy apple or slice into a warm apple fritter at **Honey Hill Orchard** (11747 Waterman Rd., Waterman, 815/264-3337, www.honeyhillorchards.com). Pick raspberries, search for pumpkins, shop for mums, and come hungry. The folks here bake cider doughnuts, apple pies and breads, and just about every other type of apple concoction you can dream up.

Accommodations

The newer **Best Western Timber Creek Inn & Suites** (3300 Drew Ave., Sandwich, 630/273-6000, $100–150) has a mix of rooms and suites for guests, plus a fitness center, indoor pool, wireless access, and other amenities.

Information

Any questions about the area? Contact the **Sandwich Chamber of Commerce** (815/786-9075, www.sandwich-il.org).

PRINCETON

A picturesque town south of the Hennepin Canal and I-80, Princeton in recent years has emerged to become a nice little detour for drivers along U.S. 6, the Grand Army Highway, and U.S. 34. Its downtown is lined with antiques shops and gift shops. The residential neighborhoods along Euclid Avenue and Church Street boast many restored turn-of-the-20th-century homes. And north of town is a red covered bridge.

Princeton is a railroad town, literally (the tracks are just north of U.S. 6) and figuratively: Slaves escaping to the north were said to have traveled through here. The **Owen Lovejoy Homestead** (E. Peru St., Princeton, 815/879-9151, www.lovejoyhomestead.com, 1–4 P.M. Fri.–Sun. May–Sept.), was a stop on the Underground Railroad. It was home to an abolitionist preacher. Near the home is a one-room schoolhouse also open to visitors. While you're in downtown Princeton, visit **Hoffman's** (513 S. Main St., Princeton, 815/875-1944, www.patternsofthepast.com), an antiques shop with a vast collection of discontinued china. A few doors down is **Eco Espresso** (437 S. Main St., Princeton, 815/875-3333), where servers whip up smoothies and coffee drinks. The 1863 **covered bridge** is a few miles northwest of Princeton off Highway 26. Signs will point you to the bridge.

Information

You can gather more traveling tips about the region from the **Bureau County Tourism Council** (Princeton, 815/454-2502 or 800/664-4420) or the **Princeton Chamber of Commerce** (815/875-2616, www.visitprinceton-il.com).

NORTH OF PRINCETON

One of the state's newest multiuse recreational trails runs alongside the **Hennepin Canal,** a nearly 100-year-old canal that connects the Illinois River with the Mississippi River near

© CHRISTINE DES GARENNES

downtown Princeton

Moline. The canal, now listed on the National Register of Historic Places, was mainly used as a shipping canal throughout the first half of the 20th century. In the 1950s it opened to boat traffic. In recent years the state developed a trail on one side and opened up the old tow path on the other side (which, because it's mostly grass, is good for hiking and fat-tire riding). Depending on where you go, the canal itself spans five counties, running through Bureau, Henry, Lee, and Whiteside, mostly through farmland and prairie, past locks and dams, some aqueducts, an old boat-repair yard, and parks. On some legs the trail is paved with oil and chip, and in other areas there's crushed limestone. All told, there are about 95 miles of trails. A visitors center (815/454-2328) is one mile south of I-80, just west of U.S. 34, in Sheffield.

Because of erosion and overgrazing, what was once cattle pasture is now a 200-acre park with dunes, prickly pear cactuses, and tall willowy prairie grasses such as big blue stem. The **McCune Sand Prairie** (5.5 miles north of Mineral on County Rd. AA, Mineral, 815/875-8732 ext. 3) is transforming itself back to prairie. It's a peaceful place, miles from any major highway, where several narrow walking paths crisscross over rolling hills and dunes. Managed by the local soil and water conservation district, it's open sunrise–sunset daily.

McHenry County

◖ WOODSTOCK

In the center of McHenry County, Woodstock (population 23,000) is a picturesque town surrounded by rolling hills and horse farms. With its courthouse square, opera house, park, and antiques and gift shops, it is a postcard-perfect Midwestern town. Remember the Bill Murray movie *Groundhog Day?* It was filmed in downtown Woodstock.

Sights and Activities

The 1889 **Woodstock Opera House and Performing Arts Center** (121 Van Buren St., Woodstock, 815/338-5300, www.woodstockoperahouse.com) is a gorgeous steamboat Gothic building that has seen everyone from Orson Welles to Paul Newman perform here. It hosts city band concerts, an opera festival, a Mozart festival, and other events. Visual art is also displayed here. Inside the opera house is the **Stage Left Café** (815/337-1395), open on Wednesday–Saturday evenings and two hours before performances.

Take an hour or two to walk around Courthouse Square in Woodstock to browse its clothing, gift and antiques shops, and galleries, or grab a cup of coffee or tea. Bibliophiles and related wordsmiths will enjoy a trip to the local independent bookseller, **Read Between the Lynes** (129 Van Buren St., Woodstock, 815/206-5967, daily). Fine stationery and other related gifts are sold at **Paper and Plumes** (132 Cass St., Woodstock, 815/338-6422, www.paperandplume.com, Tues.–Sat.). And the **Old Court House Arts Center** (101 N. Johnson St., Woodstock, 815/338-4525, www.oldcourthouseartscenter.com, 11 A.M.–5 P.M. Thurs.–Sat., 1–5 P.M. Sun.), located in the brick 1857 building on the square, contains a consignment gallery where several rooms feature work by photographers, potters, painters, and other area artisans. Courthouse Square is also home to a festive **farmers market** Tuesday and Saturday mornings until 1 P.M.

Accommodations and Food

For breakfast or lunch, you must head to **La Petite Creperie and Bistro** (115 N. Johnson St., Woodstock, 815/337-0765, lunch 11 A.M.–2:30 P.M. Mon.–Sat., dinner 5–9 P.M. Mon.–Thurs., 5–9:30 P.M. Fri.–Sat., breakfast and lunch 9 A.M.–2 P.M. Sun.), housed in the former sheriff's house as part of the old courthouse complex on the square. Have a seat in the house's dining room or at a table set on the front lawn and try one of the sweet or savory crepes. And there's more to choose from than crepes: omelets, sandwiches such as croque monsieur and madam, pâté, salads, fish, and my personal favorite, chocolate croissants. An hour on their lawn is a great way to spend a sunny Saturday or Sunday morning.

For dinner, it's **Courthouse Grill** (101 N. Johnson St., Woodstock, 815/337-1600, www.courthouseonthesquare.com, 11 A.M.–10 P.M. Mon.–Thurs., 11 A.M.–11 P.M. Fri.–Sat., 11 A.M.–9 P.M. Sun., $15). While you wait for your table you can have a beer or a glass of wine in its pub, the Groundhog. There you'll find some mementos of the movie *Groundhog Day,* filmed in Woodstock. Live music is also often featured on weekend evenings. Entrées here can include chicken pot pie, beef stew, fish and chips, and other hearty choices.

If you want to extend your stay, your best bets are trying one of two local B&Bs. The **Bundling Board** (220 E. South St., Woodstock, 815/338-7054, www.bundlingboard.com, $105–125) is a grand Victorian-style home a few blocks from the courthouse square. In addition to the three available rooms (each with a bathroom) the inn has a cozy library, and a gift shop is also on-site. The other independent lodging option in Woodstock is the **Town Square Inn** (112½ Cass St., Woodstock, 815/337-4677, www.townsquareinn.com, $140–175), an all-suites inn right on the scenic square.

Getting There

Woodstock is located about 60 miles from downtown Chicago. But with traffic on I-90 and Highways 12 or 14, it'll take much more than an hour to drive out here. Instead, if you're staying in Chicago and want to visit Woodstock, ride **Metra's Union Pacific Northwest Line** (312/836-7000, www.metrarail.com). A one-way ticket from the Ogilvie Station in downtown Chicago to Woodstock costs $7.05. But a weekend pass, which allows for unlimited rides on Saturday and Sunday, will set you back only $5. The Woodstock train station is at 90 Church Street, about a block from Courthouse Square.

MORAINE HILLS STATE PARK

Unlike other areas of the state where large bodies of water were created by people, the northeastern corner of Illinois is full of naturally formed lakes. Thousands of years ago when the last glacier was retreating from Illinois, a giant block of it broke off and melted. Thus we have Lake Defiance in **Moraine Hills State Park** (914 S. River Rd., McHenry, 815/385-1624, www.dnr.state.il.us). Moraine Hills, in the northeastern part of the county, has 1,690 acres, half of which is lakes or wetland areas. It's also home to a few nature preserves, such as Leatherleaf Bog and Pike Marsh. Follow the Leatherleaf Bog Trail to view the floating layer of sphagnum moss growing on the water's surface, and walk past willows, ferns, marsh marigolds, and other wetland plants.

Otherwise, the Fox River Trail, which takes visitors to the river on the west side of the park, has some wildlife-viewing platforms, so you can take a break from walking and watch ducks, beavers, and other animals. Finally, visit the nature center on Lake Defiance to learn more about how bogs develop. The park also has concession stands at the McHenry Dam and Lake Defiance, where you can rent fishing boats and buy some bait. In the winter you can rent cross-country skis at the Lake Defiance building.

UNION, ALGONQUIN, AND BARRINGTON
Sights and Activities

Hulking locomotives, sleek streamliners, and dozens of other railcars are open to the public at the **Union Illinois Railway Museum** (7000 Olson Rd., Union, 815/923-4000 or 800/244-7245, www.irm.org, call for hours, Apr.–Oct., $4–12). The 50-acre site is packed with steamers, diesels, and a variety of different railcars. Visitors take a 10-mile ride on an old intraurban line on a steam locomotive or diesel passenger train. Trolley rides are also available. Even though it has regular hours April–October, the museum hosts special events throughout the year for Mother's Day, Father's Day, and during the Halloween and Christmas seasons. On some days there's free admission to the grounds. Those are set ahead of time, and you can find out about those days on the museum's website.

You don't have to drive down to Branson, Missouri, if you want to take in a country music show or wander around a faux pioneer town. Rally up the kids for a day at **Donley's Wild West Town** (8512 S. Union Rd., Union, 815/923-9000, www.wildwesttown.com, 10 A.M.–6 P.M. daily Memorial Day–Labor Day, 10 A.M.–6 P.M. Sat.–Sun. Apr.–May and Sept.–Oct., $14), a Wild West playland of sorts. Ride through the park on a scale-model locomotive train, watch a dramatized shootout and country music shows, belly up to the bar at a re-created saloon, and pan for gold. But wait, there's more: pony rides, a blacksmith shop, an ice cream parlor, a steakhouse, and a cowboy museum.

During the winter **Raging Buffalo** (Hwy. 31 at the McHenry/Kane County Line, Algonquin, 847/846-7243, www.ragingbuffalo.com) is open for snowboarding only, and in the summer its staff offers wakeboarding lessons on the Fox River. During the winter you can bring your own board and hit the hills or take some lessons. Snowboarding admission costs $32–45; rentals are $19–45. Wakeboarding sessions vary.

Shopping

If you've got shopping on the brain, this area has several shopping centers, from **Prime Outlets** (I-90 at Hwy. 47, Huntley, 847/669-9100 or 888/545-7222, www.primeoutlets. com), which contains a mix of name-brand clothing, sporting goods, and housewares stores such as Calvin Klein, Corningware, and Reebok. You'll find designer clothing, jewelry, and other specialty shops in **Barrington's Ice House Village** (200 Applebee St., Barrington, 847/381-6661), a 1904 former icehouse in downtown Barrington. Finally, near the Fox River you can shop for neoclassic and country-style ceramic items at **The Haeger Potteries Museum and Shop** (7 Maiden Ln., south of Hwy. 72, East Dundee, 847/783-5420, www .haegerpotteries.com, 10 A.M.–6 P.M. Mon. and Thurs.–Fri., 11 A.M.–5 P.M. Sat.–Sun.). This family-owned business has been creating artistic vases, pitchers, plates, and sculptures since the 1800s.

Food

One of the best restaurants near the Fox River, C **Emmett's Tavern and Brewing Co.** (128 W. Main St., West Dundee, 847/428-4500, www.emmettstavern.com, 11:30 A.M.–11 P.M. Mon.–Thurs., 11:30 A.M.–12:30 A.M. Fri.–Sat., 12:30–10 P.M. Sun., lunch $5–13, dinner $13–25) is a slightly upscale tavern in West Dundee's historic district. It serves gourmet comfort food, including freshly baked pretzels, hand-crafted

beer (made in the copper tanks on display in the restaurant), whitefish sandwiches, and home-made bread. Other options include peppercorn sirloin and buffalo burgers. Emmett's is one of those places that you could never grow tired of. Locations are also in Downers Grove, Oswego, and Palatine.

A fixture on the Fox for decades, the **Port Edward** (20 W. Algonquin Rd., Algonquin, 847/658-5441, www.portedward.com, 11:30 A.M.–3:30 P.M. and 5–9 P.M. Tues.–Thurs., 11:30 A.M.–3:30 P.M. and 5–10 P.M. Fri., 5–10 P.M. Sat., 9:30 A.M.–1 P.M. and 3–8:30 P.M. Sun.) is probably known best for its seafood buffet on Friday or the Sunday champagne brunch. Menu items here include mussels (always a good bet), oysters, trout, stuffed mushrooms, and baked artichokes. The restaurant has some amusing seating areas for couples: a booth tucked into a windmill or a table inside the cabin of a 25-foot-long sailboat, which is actually floating on water inside the restaurant.

Part country-style restaurant and part entertainment complex, **The Milk Pail** (Hwy. 25, just north of I-90, Dundee, 847/742-5040, www.themilkpail.com, 4–9 P.M. Fri., 8 A.M.–2 P.M. Sat.–Sun.) always seems to be hosting some kind of event, whether it's a business meeting, wedding, murder mystery dinner, or flea market. One of the best times to dine at The Milk Pail is during the Sunday jazz brunch, when you can dive into some pancakes while a brass band plays some ditties.

GREAT RIVER VALLEYS

Packing list for western and west-central Illinois: a good pair of hiking shoes, jeans for horseback riding, binoculars, fishing pole, and a bicycle. With its limestone bluffs, prairies, savannas, and bottomland and upland forests, the Illinois and Mississippi River valleys offer quite the assortment of outdoor activities for visitors. As it flows southwest from Chicago, the Illinois River brushes past manufacturing centers such as Peoria, agricultural areas in the Imperial Valley, and wildlife preserves such as Chautauqua before it joins the Mississippi River, which runs along the western border of the state.

People have always been drawn to this region. Almost 1,000 years ago a Native American culture, the mound builders, established thriving villages near present-day Lewistown and Collinsville. In the 1600s the French staked their claim on the area and protected it by building Fort de Chartres near Prairie du Rocher. When Joseph Smith arrived in 1839 he envisioned Nauvoo as an Eden of sorts for himself and his fellow Mormons. In the same vein, the Swedish Janssonists prospered throughout the 1840s and 1850s at the Bishop Hill Colony. The region is steeped in history. Explorers Meriwether Lewis and William Clark set off on their journey westward from here. Abraham Lincoln debated with Stephen Douglas about slavery here. There's nothing like a drive along a historic river road or through a river town to remind you of the area's past and its connection to the development of Illinois. You can also get a feel for the richness of the region by hiking through one of the region's many natural areas, from the popular and majestic Starved Rock near Utica or the quiet Emiquon

© CHRISTINE DES GARENNES

HIGHLIGHTS

LOOK FOR **◖** TO FIND RECOMMENDED SIGHTS, ACTIVITIES, DINING, AND LODGING.

◖ Starved Rock State Park: Adjacent to the Illinois River near Utica, this popular state park was once the site of an early French fort and a battle between two Native American tribes. Hike the 125-foot-tall Starved Rock and watch barges chugging down the river and eagles searching for prey. Check into the historic lodge or one of the cabins (page 201).

◖ Bishop Hill Artisans' Shops: In the 1840s Swedish religious leader Erik Jansson and his followers established a commune near the Edwards River, a tributary of the Mississippi. The commune eventually dissolved, but many descendants of the colony and Sweden remained in the area and transformed the village into a bustling community with restaurants and artisans' shops (page 208).

◖ Joseph Smith Historic Site: Another remarkably well-preserved historic village is Nauvoo, perched above the Mississippi River. Smith and his fellow Mormons settled here in the 1840s, and the town soon became a thriving city. A visit to the Smith site includes walking tours of about a dozen restored homes and shops as well as Smith's homestead (page 243).

◖ Cahokia Mounds: Before the American pioneers, before the French and British, and even before the Illiniwek Indians, the Mississippi and Illinois River valleys were home to several mound-building cultures. The largest village, in existence roughly A.D. 700-1400, was near present-day Collinsville. Today the site includes several mounds, including the 100-foot-tall Monks Mound, and a comprehensive museum about Native American history (page 259).

◖ Fort de Chartres: To find out what it might have been like in the Illinois Territory during the 1700s, visit the remote, partially rebuilt French fort near Prairie du Rocher. The stone fort, which features musket ports, a powder magazine, and other structures, is near the Mississippi River (page 262).

◖ Illinois Caverns State Natural Area: The only cave open to the public in Illinois, Illinois Caverns near Red Bud is often called a wild cave. Guided by the light of flashlights and lanterns, visitors can expect to shinny through narrow, cool (and oftentimes wet) passages and stand up in awe in expansive rooms filled with stalagmites (page 265).

National Wildlife Refuge near Havana. And don't forget those binoculars: If there's an icon for this part of the state, it's the bald eagle.

PLANNING YOUR TIME

The Illinois and Middle-Mississippi Rivers region covers a large part of the state, from the southwestern suburbs of Chicago to south of East St. Louis. I-80 is a major east-west artery from the south side of Chicagoland to the Quad Cities (past Utica, Ottawa, and other destinations); however, most of the other highways are two lanes, meaning travel can be slow going. In some spots, this is a good thing. The Great River Road, for example, is a scenic drive near Grafton and Nauvoo, although it's uninteresting near industrialized East St. Louis and East Moline. The road, you will find, does not always hug the Mississippi River. And it does not always follow one particular highway. Instead, follow the pilot wheel signs.

One way to explore the region is to set off from Chicago and follow the Illinois River southwest to the East St. Louis region and then head back north along the Great River Road through Alton, Quincy, Nauvoo, and up to the Quad Cities. If your time is limited, there are some places along this route that you don't want to miss. They include **Starved Rock and Matthiessen State Parks** near Utica and Collinsville's **Cahokia Mounds.** (If you can't get there, visit a similar site, **Dickson Mounds** near Havana along the Illinois River.) The **Bishop Hill** colony southeast of the Quad Cities is a must-see. A lot of travelers spend a day in Bishop Hill, but because of the cozy restaurants, growing number of artisans' shops, and friendly residents, it's not a bad idea to stay a night or two in a bed-and-breakfast there. It's a long drive out to the remote **Fort de Chartres** near Prairie du Rocher and an even longer drive to Fort Kaskaskia, but for visitors who enjoy historic sites, these two are worth it. Naturalists will also want to put in some **eagle-watching** time at Meredosia or one of the refuges along the rivers.

Resources

The **Western Illinois Tourism Development Office** (581 S. Deere Rd., Macomb, 309/837-7460, www.visitwesternillinois.info) is the umbrella organization for several regional convention and visitors bureaus, including Galesburg, the Quad Cities, Peoria, Jacksonville, Quincy, and others. The office maintains an online guide to **Illinois Great River Road National Scenic Byway** (www.greatriverroad-illinois.org). In addition, you may want to contact **The Tourism Bureau of Southwest Illinois** (10950 Lincoln Tr., Fairview Heights, 618/397-1488 or 800/442-1488, www.thetourismbureau.org), which has visitor information for the area in and around Collinsville and south to Prairie du Rocher.

There are several tourist information centers throughout this region along major highways: at eastbound I-80 at Rapid City, by Rock Island; northbound I-55 by Hamel, just northwest of Edwardsville; and eastbound I-64 at New Baden, east of O'Fallon.

A few **ferries** shuttle passengers or cars across the Mississippi and Illinois Rivers. The Illinois Department of Transportation operates two free ferries in Calhoun County, where the Illinois and Mississippi Rivers meet. There's the **Brussels Ferry** (618/786-3636) which connects Highway 100 between the Grafton and Père Marquette State Park area with the town of Brussels; and the **Kampsville Ferry** (618/653-4518); which carries cars traveling along Highway 108 in Jersey County to Kampsville and Highway 100. In addition, there are several other toll ferries, such as the Modoc, Illinois–St. Genevieve, Missouri, ferry; the Golden Eagle, Illinois–St. Charles, Missouri, ferry; the Grafton Ferry Company between Grafton and St. Charles County Airport, Missouri; and the Canton, Missouri–Meyer, Illinois, toll ferry.

The *Spirit of Peoria* (309/636-6169 or 800/676-8988, www.spiritofpeoria.com) offers daylong and overnight cruises along the Illinois River between Peoria and Père Marquette State Park near Grafton, around the Starved Rock State Park region, plus overnight trips to St. Louis, which includes a ride on the Mississippi. Several themed cruises, such as fall colors tours or cruises featuring live jazz or bluegrass, are offered throughout the year.

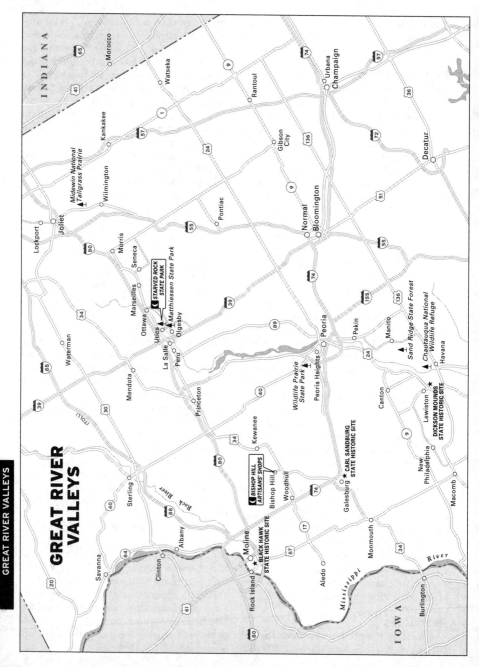

GREAT RIVER VALLEYS

GREAT RIVER VALLEYS

INDIANA

Morocco
Watseka
Rantoul
Urbana
Champaign
Decatur
Gibson City
Kankakee
Wilmington
Midewin National Tallgrass Prairie
Pontiac
Normal
Bloomington
Joliet
Lockport
Morris
Seneca
Marseilles
STARVED ROCK STATE PARK
Matthiessen State Park
Ottawa
Utica
Olgesby
La Salle
Peru
Peoria
Pekin
Manito
Sand Ridge State Forest
Chautauqua National Wildlife Refuge
Havana
Waterman
Mendota
Princeton
Wildlife Prairie State Park
Peoria Heights
Canton
Lewiston
DICKSON MOUNDS STATE HISTORIC SITE
Kewanee
Sterling
Rock River
BISHOP HILL ARTISANS' SHOPS
Bishop Hill
Woodhull
CARL SANDBURG STATE HISTORIC SITE
Galesburg
New Philadelphia
Macomb
Savanna
Albany
Clinton
Moline
Rock Island
BLACK HAWK STATE HISTORIC SITE
Aledo
Monmouth
Burlington
Mississippi River
IOWA
Waterman

(65) (41) (1) (57) (9) (24) (136) (9) (51) (55) (55) (74) (155) (136) (72) (57) (36) (89) (39) (80) (34) (88) (39) (30) (40) (88) (84) (20) (61) (80) (17) (67) (34) (9)

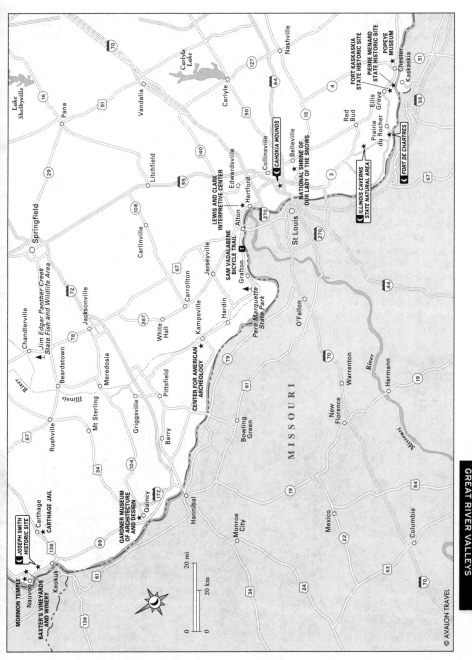

© AVALON TRAVEL

Starved Rock State Park Area

Because it is about a 1.5-hour drive from Chicago, the Quad Cities, Bloomington, and Rockford, the Starved Rock region is a popular weekend getaway for residents of those metropolitan areas. It is not uncommon for the parking lot of area parks to be almost full on summer weekends.

The star of the region is Starved Rock State Park near Utica, and it probably attracts such crowds because its topography is so sharply different from that of the prairie to the south and the slightly rolling hills to the north. When the glaciers receded thousands of years ago, the melting water surged through the region, eroding the sandstone, which itself dates back several hundred millions of years. The result was several picturesque canyons.

Hopewellian Woodland and Mississippian Native American tribes lived in the region for thousands of years, perhaps as early as 8000 B.C. And the Kaskaskian tribe of the Illiniwek

lived along the river from the 1500s through the 1800s. Taken with the region's beauty and the potential to convert some of the Indians, Father Jacques Marquette established a mission at a village near where Starved Rock State Park is now. The French built a fort on top of Starved Rock, but later left it for Peoria. It's been a public park since 1911.

You've got lots of outdoor adventure here, from horseback riding to hiking, biking, and camping. The Illinois River runs through here alongside towns such as Marseilles on the east, Ottawa, Utica, LaSalle, and Peru. Ottawa and Utica, on the north side of the river, have perhaps the best mix of restaurants, shops, and parks. Starved Rock is on the south side of the river, and Matthiessen State Park is south of it. Buffalo Rock, a small but scenic state park, is near Ottawa. The I&M Canal cuts a path through the region north of the Illinois River, with the bike trail along

GREAT RIVER VALLEYS

© CHRISTINE DES GARENNES

atop Starved Rock

its side. U.S. 6 connects towns on the north side of the river.

SIGHTS

◖ Starved Rock State Park

On the south side of the Illinois River near the town of Utica stands a 125-foot-tall sandstone bluff. It's a great lookout point. You can see up and down the river, the hills, and nearby farm fields. This bluff, after which Starved Rock State Park (Hwy. 178, Utica, 815/667-4726, www.dnr.state.il.us, park 5 A.M.–10 P.M. daily, visitors center 9 A.M.–4 P.M. daily, free) is named, was the scene of a tragic event in local Native American history. The story goes that after the leader of an Ottawa Indian tribe, Pontiac, was killed in 1769 by a member of another tribe, the Illiniwek, a war broke out between the two tribes. Allies of the Ottawa Indians, the Potawatomi reportedly drove a group of Illiniwek Indians to the bluff, where the Illiniwek stayed until they died of starvation. Before all this occurred, the area had been chosen as the site of a French fort, Fort St. Louis, in the late 1600s. The French would eventually abandon it in the 1700s.

It will take you about five minutes to climb to the top of Starved Rock. Half of the trail is paved concrete; the rest is up wooden stairs with a few deck-like areas to rest along the way. You won't be the only one making the trek up the stairs (it's often crowded), but the view is worth it. Off the shoreline from the visitors center is Plum Island (no biological research is conducted here as there is on Plum Island near New York). And across the way is Lover's Leap Overlook, which also offers great views and is sometimes not as crowded as the Starved Rock trail.

Hiking is the thing to do at Starved Rock State Park. All in all there are about 13 miles for hiking here. (Bicycling is not allowed.) Trails range in length from the 0.3-mile Starved Rock Trail to the 4.7-mile Illinois Canyon Trail. Pick any trail, and you can expect to work out your calves; some will take you up to scenic overlooks, along canyons and cliffs. Springtime in the park is an especially beautiful time as the melting snow and spring rains prompt water to trickle and tumble down the sides of canyons.

The visitors center has exhibits on Illinois's geologic past, Native American Indian tribes, and the history of the park and the La Salle fort. Staff is obliging to inquisitive visitors and armed with maps and brochures and recommendations on what to do in and outside the park. Starved Rock State Park also holds guided tours in the park in October to highlight the fall foliage, as well as guided hikes in January. The **Bald Eagle Watch Weekend** in late January is a good one. You can take tours of the park and scout for the birds of prey, and watch videos about their habits in the lodge.

The park also has a lodge with hotel room accommodations, cabins, and a campground.

Matthiessen State Park

About a mile or so south of Starved Rock State Park is the less-crowded Matthiessen State Park (Hwy. 178, Utica, 815/667-4868, www.dnr.state.il.us). The approximately 2,000-acre state park was originally a privately owned park developed by industrialist Frederick W. Matthiessen. The park is divided into two sections: the dells area to the north and the river area to the south, including land on the bluffs above the river and alongside an approximately one-mile-long canyon carved by the Vermilion River. If you travel to Matthiessen from the north, the first section you will come to is the dells, where a little more than three miles of trails weave through wooded areas above the Vermilion River. This set of trails will take you past waterfalls, mineral springs, and over bridges. Along the way you will see butterflies, ferns, jacks-in-the-pulpit, and black-eyed Susans. This section has plenty of picnic tables and grills, a shelter, and restrooms. The trails in the river section of the park can be a bit trickier to navigate, especially after a heavy rain or in the spring when the dirt hiking trails can get muddy. They are also a bit steeper as they snake through wooded ravines.

In addition to the hiking trials, there are miles and miles of horse trails through here. Plus, the park has made plenty of accommodations for visitors with horses. There's trailer parking and, for those who want to stick around overnight with their horses, a horse campground. It is off Highway 178, south of Highway 71 and before the dells entrance.

During the winter, park staff groom about six miles of cross-country ski trails through the park. You can rent skis on weekends December–March at the dells area of the park. Also, the Vermilion River section has a model airplane–flying field open to everyone.

Buffalo Rock State Park

If you cannot hike up all those stairs at Starved Rock State Park, but you still want to take in views of the Illinois River from on high, drive to Buffalo Rock State Park (Dee Bennett Rd., between Utica and Ottawa, 815/433-2220, www.dnr.state.il.us, 8 A.M.–sunset daily). It is on the north side of the Illinois River, just south of Ottawa Street and the I&M Canal trail. Before becoming a state park, the area was used as, among other things, a retreat site for a religious group and the site of a sanatorium for sick employees of the Crane Company. At 300 acres it's a nice little park, with a few unusual features such as a handful of grazing buffalo and an effigy tumulus, which is one artist's project to pay homage to the historic Native American practice of sculpting the earth into the shapes of animals. In addition, the park has a scenic overlook, a few trails along bluffs above the river, and picnicking spots.

Historic Sights

It was in Ottawa's **Washington Square** that the first debate between Abraham Lincoln and Stephen A. Douglas took place. The date was August 21, 1858, and about 10,000 people gathered to hear the two Senate candidates address the issue of slavery. Lincoln's position was that slavery was morally wrong. Douglas took the stance that each state should decide whether or not it should legalize slavery. Statues and historical markers commemorate the spot. The park, which features well-tended gardens, is a nice little spot to take a break from bicycling or sightseeing.

Vintage mansions open to the public can be found in almost every major town or former industrial town in Illinois, but perhaps none is as enormous as the 16,000-square-foot **Hegeler Carus Mansion** (1307 7th St., LaSalle, www.hegelercarus.org, free). The Second Empire-style home was built in 1874 by a businessman involved with an area zinc works. It stood on a full city block, complete with a greenhouse, pond, tennis courts, and gardens galore. Now undergoing a $12 million renovation, the mansion has had the slate roof and much of the exterior restored. Listed on the National Register of Historic Places, the mansion has some amazing and intricate woodwork and plasterwork on its ceilings, floors, and other areas throughout the house. While it's quite fun to tour this estate and admire the architecture, it should also be noted that it housed an academic publishing company here for decades. Open Court Publishing specialized in translations of Asian manuscripts and is credited by some for introducing many Americans to Japanese and other cultures, as well as to Buddhism. Until recently, a descendent of the family still lived in the home. Tours begin on the hour at noon, 1 P.M., 2 P.M., and 3 P.M. Wednesday–Sunday.

While you're in Utica for breakfast or lunch, drop by the **LaSalle County Historical Museum** (Canal and Mill Sts., on the I&M Canal, Utica, 815/667-4861, lasallecountymuseum.org, 10 A.M.–4 P.M. Wed.–Fri., noon–4 P.M. Sat.–Sun. Apr.–Nov., noon–4 P.M. Fri.–Sun. Dec.–Mar.) to tour the barn, blacksmith shop, and schoolhouse. The museum itself is located in an 1848 sandstone building and contains exhibits about local Native American and pioneer history.

The **Ottawa Scouting Museum** (1100 Canal St., Ottawa, www.ottawascoutingmuseum.org, 10 A.M.–4 P.M. Thurs.–Mon., $3) is a tribute to Ottawa native W. D. Boyce, who founded the Boy Scouts of America, as well as to the history of the Boy Scouts, Girl Scouts, and Camp Fire girls. There are also displays on the I&M Canal and Native American history of the region.

EVENTS

For the last several decades the LaSalle County Historical Museum has sponsored a fall **burgoo festival** that celebrates this hearty stew cooked on an open flame in giant kettles. Visitors can sample some of the concoction, brewed by none other than a "burgoomeister," listen to live music, and browse the arts and crafts booths. The event is held on a weekend in early October.

RECREATION
Horseback Riding

Starved Rock Riding Stables (Hwy. 71, Oglesby, 815/667-3026, Apr.–Nov.) offers one-hour guided trail rides and hayrides, bonfires, and other similar activities. Rides begin at noon, 2 P.M., and 4 P.M. Wednesday–Friday, and at 10 A.M., noon, 2 P.M., and 4 P.M. Saturday–Sunday.

About 15 minutes southwest of Starved Rock State Park, **Cedar Creek Ranch** (249 E. Hwy. 71, Cedar Point, 815/446-4105) also offers guided horseback riding along wooded trails.

© CHRISTINE DES GARENNES

horseback-riding and hiking trail in Matthiessen State Park, Utica

Boating

For an adventure in canoeing, call **Ayers Landing** (3494 E. 2089th Rd., Utica, 800/540-2394), which organizes canoe rentals and trips along the Fox River, which flows into the Illinois River from the north near Ottawa.

If you prefer clipping along at faster speeds on the Illinois River, **Starved Rock Adventures** (Starved Rock Marina, Dee Bennett Rd., Ottawa, 815/434-9200, www.srarock.com) rents Jet Skis, speedboats, pontoon boats, and fishing boats by the hour or by the day.

Water and Amusement Park

Grizzly Jack's Resort and Grand Bear Lodge near Starved Rock State Park operates a 24,000-square-foot indoor water park, **Grand Bear Falls,** for its hotel guests. The resort also runs an indoor amusement park called the Enchanted Forest, which has rides like bumper cars and a Tilt-A-Whirl. It's loud, and there are a lot of flashing lights. They kids will love it. (For more information see *Accommodations.*)

Biking

In downtown Utica you can park your car and access the **I&M Canal Trail.** The bike trail, which runs north of the Illinois River, links Rockdale, a town southwest of Joliet, to the LaSalle–Peru area, passing towns like Morris, Seneca, Marseilles, Ottawa, and Utica. Parking lots are just off Canal Street, Highway 178. You can rent bikes by the hour or by the day at **Mix's Trading Post** (602 Clark St., Utica, 815/667-4120), located a few blocks from the Canal on Highway 178.

ACCOMMODATIONS
$100-150

 Starved Rock Lodge and Conference Center (815/667-4227 or 800/868-7625, www. starvedrocklodge.com, $80–200) has a mix of cabins and lodge rooms. The cabins, located 150 feet from the lodge, come with one king bed or two double beds. They're great cabins, but they're not exactly in a secluded area. The 72 lodge rooms are within a cozy and rustic stone and log lodge. Rooms in the east wing are in the original part of the lodge that dates back to 1939. Other rooms are in the west wing, an addition to the lodge in 1989. All guests have use of a large indoor pool and children's pool.

Just north of Starved Rock State Park is the **Willows Hotel** (325 Clark St., Utica, 815/667-3400, www.thewillowshotel.net, $89–149) in downtown Utica. It's on the town's main drag, within walking distance to restaurants and shops. Rooms at this two-story hotel have separate outside entrances and have kitchens in them. Some have whirlpool tubs and some have fireplaces.

$150-250

Set on a 14-acre homestead near Starved Rock and Matthiessen State Park, the **Brightwood Inn** (2407 N. Hwy. 178, Oglesby, 815/667-4600 or 888/667-0600, www.brightwoodinn.com, $115–210) is a country inn with bed-and-breakfast rooms and elegant evening dining. Built in 1996, the Brightwood is a modern farmhouse type of building with eight rooms available, each with a private bathroom, gas fireplace, TV, and phone. One of the rooms is a 1,000-square-foot suite. Guests are also welcome to lounge in the library, which is stacked with books, unwind on the expansive veranda, or walk through the herb garden. Breakfast is included. Guests can also enjoy dinner at the inn Thursday–Sunday. The five-course meals can feature contemporary pasta, seafood, and meat dishes.

Grand Bear Lodge (2643 N. Hwy. 178, Tonica, 866/399-3866, www.grandbearlodge.com, family suite about $200, villa for up to nine people about $300, deluxe suites up to $400) rents a mix of lodge suites and what it calls "vacation villas," essentially townhouse and condo-like accommodations. The decor is called rustic, meaning exposed logs, but the amenities are pretty high-end with whirlpool bathtubs, DVD players, and lots of television sets. If you like hiking in the outdoors but aren't thrilled about spending the night in a sleeping bag, you'll like this place. It's adjacent to Starved Rock State Park. The three-story lodge has 92 suites, some with bunk beds for vacationing families, others with whirlpool suites for couples. Prices can vary depending on the weekend. All rooms include

admission into the indoor water park, Grand Bear Falls. The 24,000-square-foot indoor park has a wave pool, lazy river, and other rides. The resort also has an arcade, miniature golf, and indoor amusement park rides.

☾ Landers House (115 E. Church St., Utica, 815/667-5170, www.landershouse.com, $150, cottages $300), on the north side of the Illinois River, offers luxurious bed-and-breakfast rooms and cottages. If you're in town for a while and you're willing to spend a little more than $300 per night, the cottages are the way to go. (Otherwise, the regular rooms are $150.) The richly decorated cottages focus on one theme or another, such as the African-styled Serengeti cottage or the upscale hunting lodge decor of the Caribou cottage. They feature fireplaces, whirlpool tubs, living rooms, loft bedrooms, and a lot more. They're cottages that will make you want to spend the entire day and evening inside.

Who knew a Boy Scout camp could become so lovely? **Kishauwau on the Vermilion** (901 N. 2129 Rd., Tonica, 800/659-0627, www.kishauwau.com, $85–200) is an old Boy Scout camp turned cottage retreat. Located south of Matthiessen State Park, and right on the river as its name states, Kishauwau is the place to stay when you would like to be close to nature but you don't want to sleep in a tent or a cabin without air-conditioning or heat. Prices vary by weekend or weeknight. Some cabins are deluxe suites with whirlpool tubs; others are made for parents with small children. All come with kitchens.

If any of the above hotels or bed-and-breakfasts don't suit you or are not available, there's a slew of chain hotels near I-80 around Ottawa and the LaSalle–Peru area. Most cost $70–100 per night. They include the **Comfort Inn** (510 E. Etna Rd., Ottawa, 815/433-9600), **Baymont Inn** (5240 Trompeter Rd., Peru, 815/223-8585), **Days Inn** (120 N. Lewis Ave., Oglesby, 815/883-9600), **Hampton Inn** (4115 Holiday Ln., Ottawa, 815/434-6040), **Holiday Inn Express** (900 Holiday St., Oglesby, 815/883-3535; 120 W. Stevenson Rd., Ottawa, 815/433-0029), and **La Quinta Inn** (4389 Venture Dr., Peru, 815/224-9000).

Houseboating

Starved Rock Adventures (Starved Rock Marina, Dee Bennett Rd., Ottawa, 815/434-9200, www.srarock.com) rents houseboats for three-day trips up to seven-day trips. The boats sleep up to 10 people and feature sundecks, swimming platforms, kitchens, grills, ice chests, entertainment centers, phones, and radios. Houseboats rent for $1,200–3,200 and they're available April–mid-October for up to a week. You'll need to bring along an electric motor boat for the ride, which will cost extra, unless you bring your own boat. Starved Rock Adventures also rents one- and two-bedroom suites and villas for 3–7 days. Rates begin around $300 for a three-day rental in a one-bedroom and can go all the way up to $1,400 for a weeklong stay in a two-bedroom.

Camping

Starved Rock State Park (Hwy. 178, Utica, 815/667-4726, www.dnr.state.il.us) has 133 campsites with electric hookups, showers, flush toilets, and pit toilets. Because Starved Rock is a popular park, sites are snatched up quickly. The park takes reservations for about half of the sites. The others are available on a first-come, first-served basis. (Most of the wooded sites are ones that can be reserved.) You can find out which sites are available by stopping by the visitors center. The cost is $20 per site per night.

Matthiessen State Park has a campground for visitors with horses.

FOOD

Located in a sunny house, the 🄲 **Nodding Onion** (522 Clark St., Utica, 815/667-4990, 7 A.M.–3 P.M. daily, 5–9 P.M. Thurs.–Sun., average $7) boasts food made from scratch. Their motto is, "We put a lot of love in that." You can tell: The omelets are scrumptious, and the sandwiches and wraps couldn't taste fresher. Breakfasts are popular here, with French toasts, breakfast paninis, and fruit bread, but lunch is also a good bet. You can sit in the warm dining room near the fireplace or order out and take your gourmet sandwiches to the park for a picnic.

Louisiana native Ron McFarlain holds crawfish boils at **Ron's Cajun Connection** (897 U.S. 6, Utica, 815/667-9855, www.ronscajunconnection.com, 4–9 P.M. Thurs.–Sat., noon–6 P.M. Sun.). He cooks up dishes like crawfish étouffée and jambalaya, blackened catfish, and some more unusual items like frogs' legs. Don't forget the cornbread and pecan pie.

Just down the street from the Nodding Onion is **Country Cupboard** (402 S. Clark St., Utica, 815/667-5155, 11 A.M.–9 P.M. daily), a sandwich and ice cream joint with some outside seating.

If you've come to town with an appetite look into **Canal Port** (148 Mill St., Utica, 815/667-3010, 11 A.M.–8 P.M. Tues.–Thurs. and Sun., 11 A.M.–9 P.M. Fri.–Sat., $6–26), a restaurant and bar that serves entrées like fried walleye, pork chops, and strip steak, plus pastas and burgers.

Cheesy fries, pizza, burgers, and the excellent root-beer floats—the food at **Moore's Root Beer Stand** (225 N. Columbia Ave., Oglesby, 815/883-9254, 7 A.M.–about 10 P.M. daily, $4) is richly satisfying. Healthy? Probably not. Greasy? A little. But in the summertime, you can't beat a stop at a rare bona fide drive-in such as Moore's, just off I-39. The stand tends to close earlier in the evenings during the winter.

Thai Café (610 Columbus St., Ottawa, 815/431-8090, 11 A.M.–9 P.M. Mon.–Wed., 11 A.M.–10 P.M. Thurs.–Sat., 4–9 P.M. Sun., $8) is a storefront restaurant also near downtown Ottawa. The warm place (from the decor with its red-painted walls to its friendly wait staff) serves curry dishes, noodle soups, fried rice with vegetables, and beverages such as a delicious Thai ice tea, another good option on a hot summer day or evening.

Starved Rock Lodge (see *Accommodations*) also offers breakfast daily, lunch Monday–Saturday, dinner daily, plus a popular Sunday brunch. The lodge also has a lounge that features live music. Outside is a veranda overlooking the valley. Various bands often perform here in the summer.

The **Brightwood Inn** (see *Accommodations*) serves multicourse dinners Thursday–Sunday. Reservations are recommended if you plan to eat dinner at either Starved Rock or the Brightwood.

Coffee Shops

Need a coffee fix? Head to **Planet Java** (203 W. Main St., Ottawa, 815/433-6030, 7 A.M.–6 P.M. daily) or **Jeremiah Joe Coffee** (807 LaSalle St., Ottawa, 815/434-3507, 7 A.M.–10 P.M. Mon.–Sat., 7 A.M.–5 P.M. Sun.).

Common Grounds (723 S Clark St., Utica, 815/866-5167, 7:30 A.M.–3:30 P.M. Mon.–Fri., 7:30 A.M.–6 P.M. Sat.–Sun.) whips up Italian coffees, makes cheap sandwiches (an egg sandwich goes for $3), offers Internet access on a computer, and sells books too.

INFORMATION AND SERVICES
Visitor Information

The **Heritage Corridor Convention and Visitors Bureau** maintains an office in Utica (801 E. U.S. 6, Utica, 815/667-4356 or 800/746-0550, www.heritagecorridorcvb.com), where you can pick up brochures and maps of the region.

The **Ottawa Visitors Center** (815/434-2737 or 888/688-2924, www.visit-ottawa-il.com or www.experienceottawa.com, 9 A.M.–5 P.M. Mon.–Fri., 9 A.M.–4 P.M. Sat., 10 A.M.–2 P.M. Sun.) is in the Reddick Mansion (100 W. Lafayette St., Ottawa), just across the street from Washington Square, the Lincoln-Douglas debate site.

At the **Illinois Waterway Visitors Center** (Lock 14, Hwy. 351 and Canal Rd., near Utica, 815/433-2224, free) you can observe barges traveling along the river, learn about the history of water travel along the Illinois River, and how the whole locking process works. Call for hours; they vary according to the season.

Tours

If you're in a crunch or not up to hiking the park (it is hilly), you can see the park with **Starved Rock Trolley Tours** (815/667-4211 or 800/868-7625, $10). Tours run at 1:30 and 3 P.M. Wednesday–Thursday, and at noon, 1:30, and 3 P.M. Friday–Sunday. You can hop on the trolley at the state park lodge. This tour runs about 1.25 hours; you drive through the park, stopping at the visitors center, and over to the nearby lock and dam, where you can get out and walk around for a few minutes, followed by a drive through the town of Utica. Other trolley tours are offered throughout the year, such as a fall colors tour and a land-and-water tour package that includes a trolley tour, a ride on the *Belle of the Rock* boat, and lunch at the park lodge. These special tours run higher, around $28.

For water-only tours, you can catch a ride on the **Belle of the Rock boat** (1 Dee Bennett Rd., Ottawa, 815/434-9200, www.belleoftherock.com, $13) at Starved Rock State Park. Narrated tours aboard the *Belle* (a boat that looks part paddlewheel and part pontoon) depart on the hour 10 A.M.–5 P.M. on weekends and 11 A.M.–4 P.M. weekdays May–October. The tours last slightly less than an hour. You'll cruise by Starved Rock, Lover's Leap, the lock and dam, Plum Island, and hear about the history of the region.

If you've got the cash, another unusual way to see the rivers, the state parks, and their rock formations is from above. **Starved Rock Air Tours** (Illinois Valley Regional Airport, south of I-80 off Plank Rd., Peru, 815/791-6013 or 847/247-8687, www.starvedrockairtours.com) offers two different helicopter rides. For $95 you'll fly above Starved Rock, Buffalo Rock, and Matthiessen State Parks for about 30 minutes. For $200 you'll get to see the Illinois River valley for an hour.

Bishop Hill

Near the south branch of the Edwards River, a tributary of the Mississippi River, you'll find the extraordinary little village of Bishop Hill. With its artisans' shops, Swedish restaurants, and local-history museum, Bishop Hill is a fascinating place to visit. A religious commune from 1846 to 1861, the entire well-preserved village has been designated a National Historic Landmark. What makes Bishop Hill a great place to visit is that it's not a living history village, where old buildings have been brought in from around the state and assembled in a park where people dress up as if they were residents from the 1850s. This is an actual town with real residents. Former colony homes still stand and are home to gallery owners, gift shops, and restaurants.

HISTORY AND ORIENTATION

The village's story begins with Erik Jansson, a Swedish immigrant who walked all the way to this area from Chicago. He believed simplicity was the key to salvation. When he and his followers arrived in 1846, it was tough going. During the first winter 96 people died, probably because of the lack of nutritious food and adequate housing. But Jansson's followers got to work building the colony. They put up almost two dozen buildings and started farming thousands of acres of land. They crafted furniture from the black walnut trees in the area. And they were among the first people in the area to adopt new technology, such as the mechanical reaper. Not exclusionists, they built a hotel and invited noncolony members to visit. After erecting a mill, colonists offered to grind grain for area farmers (for every five bushels, the colony kept one). It was a tough life. They worked 14–16 hours a day, but their work did pay off. At its peak, the colony owned about 14,000 acres of land.

The ride at the top didn't last very long, though. The first hit was the murder of Jansson in 1850 in a dispute between him and the husband of one of the colony members who was also a relative of Jansson's. After he was shot and killed, Jansson lay in state for three days because his followers believed he was the second coming of Christ and that he would rise from the dead. That never happened. After some financial problems the colony dissolved in 1861 and many men left town to fight in the Civil War. Today about one fifth of the town's 120 residents are descended from colony members.

Bishop Hill is north of U.S. 34, a few miles southwest of Kewanee and about a 10-minute drive east of I-74. Most likely you'll enter from the south on Bishop Hill Street. The state historic site museum is one of the first buildings you'll see on the west side of the road. This is a good place to begin your visit. From there, continue downtown. Bishop Hill Park, surrounded by a white wooden fence, is in the center of town. Most historic buildings and restaurants are situated around the park and the side streets along Bishop Hill Street. All are within walking distance of each other.

SIGHTS
Bishop Hill Museum State Historic Site

The main feature of the Bishop Hill Museum State Historic Site (Bishop Hill St., Bishop Hill, 309/927-3345, 9 A.M.–5 P.M. Wed.–Sun. spring–fall, 9 A.M.–4 P.M. Wed.–Sun. winter) is Olof Krans, a folk artist who painted scenes of Bishop Hill. Krans moved here as a boy in 1850 and later painted images of the town from his memory. For example: a line of women sowing seeds in a field, and a group of women driving piles into the ground to build a bridge. Many of the paintings on view in the museum are portraits of the town's blue-eyed, grim-faced residents dressed in black. Look closely and you'll notice Krans's paintings are not exactly flawless. Some bodies and objects are out of proportion. And he forgot to finish painting some lines. At the museum you can pick up free brochures, a walking-tour guide, and other information.

The museum also has a decent video about the history of the town, plus it has on view furniture made by colony members.

Colony Church State Historic Site

Colony Church State Historic Site (Bishop Hill St., Bishop Hill, 309/927-3345, 9 A.M.–5 P.M. Wed.–Sun. Mar.–Oct., 9 A.M.–4 P.M. Nov.–Feb., free) served as a church for the Christian colonists, but it also functioned like a dormitory. There were rooms here for families plus a dining room. Rooms on the first floor are filled with a few straw beds, bare wooden tables, cradles, and other original colony furniture. Some rooms have other items salvaged from the town, such as the tin eagle that once stood outside the Bjorklund Hotel, and a collection of farm tools. Upstairs is where the men and women (on different sides of the church) listened to Jansson's sermons.

Other Sights

The **Colony Steeple Building Bishop Hill Heritage Association Museum** (Bishop Hill St., Bishop Hill, 309/927-3899, call for hours) is a large 1854 Greek-revival brick building downtown that colonists intended to be a hotel, but that ended up housing administrative offices, a school, and later a bank. Managed by the heritage association, the building today houses more historical exhibits and a video about the colony's past. The association also organizes guided tours of the town's sights. Tours last about 1.5 hours and cost $3.50 per person.

Renovated in 2005, the **Colony Hotel** (309/927-3345, 9 A.M.–5 P.M. Wed.–Sun. Mar.–Oct., 9 A.M.–4 P.M. Nov.–Feb., free) stands on the southwest corner of Bishop Hill Park. The building was first used to house colonists and later opened as the Bjorklund Hotel. In the 1900s it was converted into an apartment building and then restored back to a hotel.

EVENTS

Bishop Hill hosts several Swedish heritage festivals throughout the year. They include the **Midsommar Music Festival** in mid-June,

which features fiddlers, guitarists, and accordion players performing Swedish music concerts all day long, plus a barn dance. Feast on corn and apple dishes at **Jordbruksdagarna,** a harvest festival at the end of September. Finally, during **Lucia Nights,** the festival of lights in mid-December, area residents perform holiday choral music concerts.

◖ ARTISANS' SHOPS

Bishop Hill residents are a creative bunch. Area shops, inside historic and nontraditional buildings along Bishop Hill Street and nearby side streets, contain hand-crafted artisanal products such as jewelry, pottery, quilts, and furniture. Shops hours vary, but most in town are open 10 A.M.–5 P.M. April–December. Some of the town's shopping highlights include **Bishop Hill Street Colony Peddlers** (110 S. Bishop Hill St., Bishop Hill, 309/927-3130), which is a little complex featuring work by several artists. There is an 1870 house filled with antiques, candles, and other home decor; a blacksmith shop; a potting shed; and herb gardens. Just down the street is a red 1882 barn that is home to **Peasant Works** (205 N. Bishop Hill St., Bishop Hill, 309/927-3061), which sells handwoven baskets, herbs, and other items. Tucked off a side street, **Outsider Gallery** (409 Erickson St., Bishop Hill, 309/927-3314, www.bishophillgallery.com) is a little shop that sells jewelry and home-decor items made by regional and international artists. **Colony Store** (101 W. Main St., Bishop Hill, 309/927-3596) stocks smoked herring pâté, Swedish coffee, candy, drinks, books, and gift items such as Christmas ornaments.

ACCOMMODATIONS

◖ **The Colony Hospital Bed and Breakfast** (110 N. Olson St., Bishop Hill, 309/927-3506, www.bishophilllodging.com, $90–135) is in a yellow frame house that was once the town's hospital. There are four rooms, each with a queen-size bed, private bath, and a kitchenette that contains a little fridge, a microwave, and a coffeemaker. A library with a wood-burning stove is open for all guests to use. It's all a nice blend of old and new. The plank floors are original; the quilts on the bed are fresh and new.

The second floor of the **Bishop Hill Fine Arts** (109 N. Bishop Hill St., 309/927-3020, http://bishophillfinearts.com, about $90) building, an 1848 brick structure, has been converted into a loft apartment. The one-bedroom apartment comes with its own bathroom, kitchen, and living room. The first floor shop sells paintings, quilts, baskets, photographs, glassware, and other artwork made by Bishop Hill–area artists.

For a stay in the country—really out in the country—check into **Indian Creek Vineyard B&B** (County Rd. 550E, Toulon, 309/286-5302, www.indiancreekvineyard.com, $55–100). About 20 miles southeast of Bishop Hill, the bed-and-breakfast looks out over corn- and soybean fields and rows and rows of grapevines. There are four rooms in the "château" (a pleasant white frame house), including one room in which Lincoln reportedly stayed while campaigning in the area. Some rooms have shared baths. While you're here, sample Illinois wines in the tasting room in a remodeled red barn. The tasting room and wine shop is open 1–5 P.M. Saturday–Sunday. Look for directional signs to the vineyard and bed-and-breakfast from State Highways 17, 78, or 91.

FOOD

Try to spend a full day or a day plus one overnight in Bishop Hill. That way you can eat a meal at all the excellent restaurants. Begin at **Bishop Hill Colony Bakery** (103 S. Bishop Hill St., Bishop Hill, 309/927-3042, www.bishophillcolonybakery.com, 8 A.M.–5 P.M. Tues.–Sun.) for a cup of coffee and homemade granola or a cinnamon roll. Buy some Swedish rye or other Swedish specialty bread to take home with you.

For lunch, spend time in the cheery **The Red Oak** (106 Bishop Hill St., Bishop Hill, 309/927-3539, www.theredoak.com, 11 A.M.–2 P.M. daily, $6) dining room or outside at one of the tables on the deck. Scandinavian sandwiches are the specialty (such as open-faced sandwiches on rye bread). There's the Frikadellar,

a meatloaf served with dill sauce and beets. Or the Biff, thinly sliced roast beef on rye topped with cucumbers and a light mustard sauce. House sauces, by the way, are for sale by the register.

Swedish sandwiches are also served grandly at **P. L. Johnson's Dining Room** (110 W. Bjorkland St., Bishop Hill, 309/927-3885, 11 A.M.–3 P.M., dinner 5:30–8:30 P.M. daily May–end of Aug., $5). Inside a former home near Bishop Hill Park, P. L. Johnson's is a restaurant-gift store combo. Named after a former colony member, the building has several antique bicycles hanging from its ceiling. Apparently P. L. Johnson (a blacksmith, farmer, and jack-of-all-trades) often cycled through town. Here you can dine on dishes such as Swedish meatballs or chicken salad sandwiches.

More fresh-brewed coffee, homemade sandwiches, and smiling faces can be found at **The Filling Station** (303 N. Bishop Hill St., Bishop Hill, 309/927-3355, 11 A.M.–2 P.M. daily, dinner 5–8 P.M. Fri., breakfast 7–10 A.M. Sat.–Sun.), an antique-laden café also on the main drag.

INFORMATION

The first stop you should make is the **Bishop Hill State Historic Site Bishop Hill Museum.** Watch the short video, check out Olof Kranz's paintings, pick up some maps, and then head into town. This is the first building you see when you drive into town on Bishop Hill Street heading north.

Several groups and businesses in town maintain a resourceful website, www.bishophill.com. It lists lodging, dining, and attraction information. Otherwise, regional information is available from the **Henry County Tourism Council** (307 W. Center St., Cambridge, 309/937-1255, www.visithenrycounty.com).

JOHNSON-SAUK TRAIL STATE PARK

Situated on a glacial moraine, Johnson-Sauk Trail State Park (27500 N. 1200 Ave., Kewanee, 309/852-0709, www.dnr.state.il.us), was once a marshy area home to diverse wildlife and frequented by Native American tribes who hunted for game here. It's along part of the Sauk Trail, which they followed while traveling from Lake Michigan to where the Rock River meets the Mississippi River. Eventually the pioneers drained the area for farming. The park itself is about 1,365 acres with more than 12 miles of trails. They're fairly easy, relaxing trails along a few rolling hills and around the 58-acre lake. You can rent a fishing boat with a trolling motor on it from the concessionaire on the lake. Or just bring a picnic and choose a table under a tall pine. Within the park is the huge **Ryan's Round Barn** (309/852-4262, $2). At 85 feet in diameter and 80 feet tall, it's one of the largest round barns remaining in the country. The barn, listed on the National Register of Historic Places, contains a collection of antique farm machinery and tools. It's typically open 1–4 P.M. on the first and third Saturdays of the month and sometimes on additional days May–October. Call ahead before you go.

The park, about three miles north of Kewanee just off Highway 78, also has a campground with RV and tent sites.

Rock Island and Moline

Huddled together around the Mississippi and Rock Rivers, the Quad Cities are an assortment of river towns in Iowa and Illinois. Rooted in agricultural manufacturing, iron- and glass-making, coal mining, and other industry, the cities are solid Midwestern working towns. The Mississippi River has always been the focus of activity here, economically and entertainment-wise. In the past, tourists haven't exactly flocked here. But the cities are in riverfront revitalization mode and becoming much more diverse and vibrant, offering a surprisingly long list of things to do. The Rock Island entertainment district, with its nightclubs and watering holes, beckons on hot summer days and nights: Bicycle along the riverfront, watch giant barges pass through the locks from Arsenal Island, hop across the river to Iowa on a river taxi, spend hours checking out the vintage collection of John Deere tractors, order a malt at Lagomarcino's, or stroll through the botanic gardens.

HISTORY

The area around Rock Island and Moline was originally home to the Sauk and Fox Indians. The Sauk, in fact, had a bustling village of several thousand residents near present-day Rock Island, where the Rock River meets the Mississippi. After the defeat of Sauk warrior Black Hawk (see the *Background* chapter), settlers pushed the Indians westward, and more pioneers started moving into the region. Before the Army Corps of Engineers reconfigured the river, this section of the Mississippi was a notoriously dangerous area—the river was shallow, and there were rapids for roughly 14 miles. Several businesses came about to service the steamboats and ferries as they pulled over while navigating the rapids. After John Deere opened his plow factory in Moline in 1848, many immigrants, particularly Germans, Belgians, and Swedes, moved into the area. Soon the area was home to more and more agricultural equipment companies, lumber mills, rock quarries, breweries, and iron foundries. All these goods were shipped out along the river or on the railroads, which also prompted growth in the region.

ORIENTATION

The Quad Cities comprise Moline and Rock Island in Illinois (Moline is to the northeast, and Rock Island is south of it) and Davenport and Bettendorf across the Mississippi River in Iowa. Together the four cities have a population of about 400,000.

The Rock River comes in from the north and runs along the east end of Moline and south of Rock Island (just north of I-280) before it drains into the Mississippi River. In the

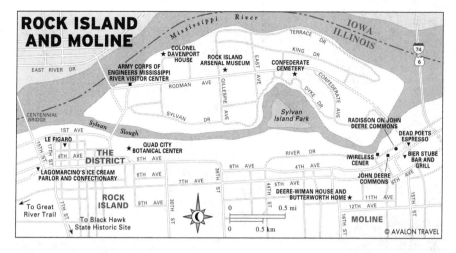

middle of the river between the cities is Arsenal Island. It has been home to an American fort during the Black Hawk War, a Confederate prison during the Civil War, as well as an armory. The John Deere sites are near Moline's riverfront. And the District in Rock Island, along with the riverboat casino and Quad City Botanical Center, are just south of the riverfront in northern Rock Island.

SIGHTS
Black Hawk State Historic Site

A good way to begin your visit to the Quad Cities is a tour of Black Hawk State Historic Site (1510 46th Ave., Rock Island, 309/788-9536, www.blackhawkpark.org), a small park and museum complex on a bluff above the Rock River in southwest Rock Island. Native Americans lived in this area for thousands of years. During the 1700s it was primarily the Sauk nation that was living in the area. Its capital was Saukenuk, which historians believe was near this site. Before it became a state historic site, the area was actually home to a popular amusement park during the late 1800s and early 1900s. It was called the Watch Tower Park and there were vaudeville shows, boat rides, a roller coaster, and a toboggan slide. (The toboggan was said to have been invented in Rock Island.) At about 200 acres, it's not a huge park, but

there are quite a few interesting sites, especially for those interested in history. In the park is the **Hauberg Indian Museum** (309/788-0177, 9 A.M.–noon, 1–5 P.M. Wed.–Sun. Mar.–Oct., 9 A.M.–noon, 1–4 P.M. Wed.–Sun. Nov.–Feb., donation), founded by John Hauberg, a Rock Island resident who collected Sauk baskets, jewelry, bowls, and other items. These types of artifacts are on view here as well as life-size dioramas of Indian homes. The museum is housed in **Watch Tower Lodge,** built by the Civilian Conservation Corps in 1939. Adjacent to the lodge is a picnic area and restored prairie; a trail leads to **Dickson Cemetery,** a two-ace pioneer graveyard. There is also a nature center where you can sit and watch birds.

John Deere Sites

On one end of the **John Deere Pavilion** (1400 River Dr., Moline, 309/765-1000, www.johndeerepavilion.com, 9 A.M.–5 P.M. Mon.–Fri., 10 A.M.–5 P.M. Sat., noon–4 P.M. Sun., free) you'll see a corn planter from 1884, and a few steps away a mammoth combine that retails for more than $100,000. A brief history of the company is outlined for guests with an illustrated timeline on the wall. This documents major events such as Deere's development of the plow in Grand Detour, his decision to open a factory in Moline to be on a shipping

the John Deere Collectors Center, Moline

© CHRISTINE DES GARENNES

route, and eventually the company's choice to branch out into computer-assisted farming in the 1990s. You can take a virtual tour of a tractor factory. And one enlightening exhibit for people who don't have an agricultural background is called *Cornucopia,* which attempts to demystify the whole seed-to-table concept and what happens in between. Adjacent to the pavilion is the **John Deere Store** (1300 River Dr., Moline, 309/765-1007, 10 A.M.–5 P.M. Mon.–Sat., noon–4 P.M. Sun. Jan.–Feb., 10 A.M.–6 P.M. Mon.–Fri., 10 A.M.–5 P.M. Sat., noon–4 P.M. Sun. Mar.–Dec.) where a slew of Deere merchandise is for sale, including toy tractors, hats, and mugs.

Just down the street is the **John Deere Collectors Center** (320 16th St., Moline, 309/748-7944, www.johndeerecollectorsctr. com, 9 A.M.–5 P.M. Mon.–Fri., 10 A.M.–5 P.M. Sat., noon–4 P.M. Sun., free), where the farm equipment on display is so shiny that it all looks brand new. Housed in a beautiful 1885 Italianate brick building, the center contains mostly Deere tractors from the 1920s to the 1950s. The antique equipment is certainly fun

to look at, but what might capture your attention even more is the area where workers are painting or tuning up the antique tractors. The center also has an area where you can buy old parts for your vintage tractor.

For those who want to hit everything Deere-related in Moline, you can also visit the company's **headquarters** (1 John Deere Rd., Moline, 309/765-8000, 9 A.M.–5 P.M. daily, free), which is off Highway 5, about 3–4 miles east of I-74. More new and old Deere equipment, including wagons, combines, and mowers, are on display in the lobby.

Sitting above the old Deere factories in the bluffs above the Mississippi River are two grand old homes, the **Deere-Wiman House** (817 11th Ave., Moline, 309/765-7970, free), where members of the Deere family once lived; and the **Butterworth Center** (1105 8th St., Moline, 309/765-7970, www.butterworth-center.com, free). Both were built by Charles Deere, John Deere's son, and are surrounded by acres of formal gardens. The Butterworth Center was actually a wedding present Charles Deere gave to his daughter. Not a bad gift!

During the summer, tours are given on the hour 1–4 P.M. Sundays. Music concerts, art exhibits, and other events are also held occasionally throughout the year in the homes.

Rock Island Arsenal

A long narrow island in the middle of the Mississippi, Arsenal Island, a National Historic Landmark, is quite a fascinating place. Start your visit on the northwestern side of the island at the **Colonel Davenport House** (follow signs from Rodman Ave., www.davenporthouse.org, noon–4 P.M. Thurs.–Sun. May–mid-Oct., by appointment mid-Oct.–Apr., $5). The yellow two-story clapboard house was built in 1835, before the area became a boomtown for agricultural factories, coal mining, and other industries. It belonged to George Davenport, a fur trader and supplier to Fort Armstrong, which the government built shortly after the turn of the 17th century to control the waterway.

Davenport earned the title of colonel by volunteering as quartermaster at Fort Armstrong. Eventually, after the Black Hawk War, the government dismantled the fort.

Next, head to the site of a former prisoner-of-war camp and the **Confederate Cemetery,** a striking, somber graveyard on the south shore of the island. During the Civil War, Rock Island was chosen as a place to house Confederate prisoners of war. A plaque at Blunt and East Avenues marks the spot of the 12-acre site on the northern part of the island. Slightly more than 12,000 prisoners were held here from December 1863 to July 1865. Of the 12,000, almost 2,000 died, many of them during the camp's first winter, from diseases such as smallpox. That first year, the Army lacked supplies for all the prisoners and did not yet have a hospital. The cemetery is south of Rodman Avenue by Sylvan Island. Just east of the Confederate Cemetery is the **Rock Island**

LOCKS AND DAMS

The Mississippi is often called a working river. To get an idea about just how it works (or rather, has been engineered) to handle heavy-duty traffic of barges loaded with corn or coal, pay a visit to one of the many locks and dams along the Mississippi River or its tributary, the Illinois. Boating along the Mississippi River today, you'll discover, is a vastly different experience from when Meriwether Lewis and William Clark paddled through its waters 200 years ago.

As the river flows from its starting point in Minnesota to its endpoint in Louisiana and the Gulf of Mexico, it drops several hundred feet in elevation. The Army Corps of Engineers has installed dozens of dams along the river that control the flow of water southward. From St. Paul, Minnesota, to St. Louis, Missouri, for example, there are 29 dams. These dams create what the corps calls a stairway of water, with the top stairs being on the northern section of the river. Essentially they help keep the water deep enough for the boats that need

deep water to navigate. To go from one step or level of water to another, boats "lock through." It may sound baffling. But watch a barge or houseboat lock through and you should be able to grasp the gist of the process. Think of a lock as a water elevator. Say a boat is headed north; the driver steers it into the lock (which consists of gates in front of and behind the boat). The lock fills with water and slowly raises the boat to the level of the upper channel with the help of a series of valves and tunnels under the ground. The front gates open and the boat continues on its way north.

The Army Corps of Engineers has several visitors centers, locks, and dams where you can watch the barges or even scout for eagles: the **Illinois Waterway Visitor Center** (950 N. 27th Rd., Ottawa, 815/667-4054); the **Mississippi River Visitor Center** (Rock Island Arsenal, Lock and Dam 15, Rock Island, 309/794-5338); and the **National Great Rivers Museum** at the Melvin Price Lock and Dam 26 (Hwy. 143, East Alton, 618/462-6979).

Cemetery, where Army veterans and their families are buried.

Eventually the Army established an armory on the island, and by the end of the Spanish-American War in 1898, employees were churning out things such as guns and gun holsters. The armory's peak was during World War II when as many as 18,000 people worked there manufacturing tanks, machine guns, and other weapons and defense items. Hundreds of guns and other weapons produced by the armory are on display at the **Rock Island Arsenal Museum** (North Ave., Rock Island Arsenal, 309/782-5021, www.ria.army.mil, 10 A.M.–4 P.M. Tues.–Sun., free). It's loaded with long arms, machine guns, pistols, and various experimental firearms developed at Rock Island decades ago. You'll learn how the M-9 pistol was developed, view rifles from the 1870s used by Native American warriors during the Battle of Little Bighorn, and see sabers used by the U.S. military. Weapons themselves are no longer made here, but employees do assemble components such as armored doors for Humvees and tool kits.

From there, drive over to the **Army Corps of Engineers Mississippi River Visitor Center** (off the western tip of Rock Island Arsenal on Rodman Ave., 309/794-5338, 9 A.M.–5 P.M. daily, free). Climb to the observation deck and you can watch barges travel down the river. Staff and exhibits explain how locking works, and why there are locks in the first place. Other displays discuss boating safety and similar issues. The center also has restrooms, a water fountain, and an information center stocked with area maps and brochures. Arsenal Island is about three miles long and three quarters of a mile wide.

Quad City Botanical Center

A few blocks from the Mississippi Riverfront is the gorgeous Quad City Botanical Center (2525 4th Ave., Rock Island, 309/794-0991, www.qcgardens.com, 10 A.M.–5 P.M. Mon.–Sat., noon–5 P.M. Sun., $5), a complex of indoor and outdoor gardens. This is a must-see when you're traveling through the region in winter. Inside the main attraction is the center's "Sun Garden," a tropical garden with a nearly

15-foot-tall waterfall, little pools, and a variety of plants and flowers that thrive in the rainforest. Walk among huge palm trees, coconut trees, bird-of-paradise flowers, and orchids. Basically you can go any time of year, and you won't be disappointed. Outside you'll find a spring bulb garden, a perennial garden, a fall mum garden, a butterfly garden, and a conifer garden.

Niabi Zoo

Got kids? Haul them over to the Niabi Zoo (10908 Niabi Zoo Rd., Coal City, 309/799-3482, www.niabizoo.com, 9:30 A.M.–5 P.M. daily spring–Labor Day, 11 A.M.–4 P.M. Mon.–Fri., 9:30 A.M.–5 P.M. Sat.–Sun. Labor Day–end of Oct., 11 A.M.–4 P.M. Sat.–Sun. end of Oct.–Dec., $5). Have a seat on a car pulled by a miniature steam train ($1.50) and travel the 40-acre site. The zoo is home to about 1,000 animals, including elephants, elks, bison, camels, zebras, reptiles, and ostriches. In addition to the animal exhibits, the zoo has a playground, a carousel, and an education center. The center is focused on hands-on kid-friendly activities. It's got an aquarium stocked with fish and exhibits that explain what animals need to survive and thrive. The zoo is in Coal City, just south of I-280 and Moline, east of the Quad City International Airport.

ENTERTAINMENT

Every town needs an arts group like the one that runs the **Quad City Arts** (1715 2nd Ave., Rock Island, 309/793-1213, www.quadcityarts. com, 10 A.M.–6 P.M. Mon.–Sat., 10 A.M.–9 P.M. Fri., free). In addition to managing a gallery showcasing visual art (which may include photographs, paintings, sculpture, or mixed media), the group hosts regional, national, and internationally known visual and performing artists who read from their work, talk about their work, or perform. A recent guest was the playwright Edward Albee. If you're in town September–April, drop by for the free music concerts held 7–9 P.M. on Fridays.

The **Quad City Symphony Orchestra** (563/322-0931, www.qcsymphony.com) performs concerts throughout the year in venues around all the cities, including Augustana College in Rock Island.

Formerly known as the Mark, the **i Wireless Center** (1201 River Dr., Moline, 309/764-2054, www.iwirelesscenter.com) hosts visiting musical guests that have included Neil Diamond and Green Day, arena football events, Quad City Flames hockey games, and theater productions. It's just west of all the John Deere sites.

In a renovated 1921 movie house, **Circa 21 Dinner Playhouse** (1828 3rd Ave., Rock Island, 309/786-7733, www.circa21.com) presents American musicals, children's shows, and concerts. It has hosted the Lettermen and produced musicals such as *Pump Boys and Dinettes.* Tickets include a buffet dinner. Matinee and evening shows are scheduled throughout the year.

SPORTS AND RECREATION
Biking
The **Great River Trail** stretches for almost 63 miles from the Quad Cities to Savanna to the north. It's wide—about 10 feet—and primarily asphalt, so if you want to jog or in-line skate on it, you can. It starts at Sunset Park on the river south of downtown Rock Island, winds past the Quad City Botanical Center, the Rock Island Arsenal, several lock and dams, the John Deere headquarters, Campbell's Island in East Moline, and up to Port Byron, where the residents hold a tug-of-war contest every year with their neighbors across the river in Iowa. A four-mile trail around **Arsenal Island** takes riders past the island's major sights such as the Colonel Davenport house and the cemeteries. The Quad Cities Convention and Visitors Bureau rents bicycles and helmets at its office in the Moline Depot (2021 River Dr., Moline, 8:30 A.M.–4:30 P.M. Mon.–Fri., 10 A.M.–4 P.M. Sat. Memorial Day–end of Sept., $7 per hour, $28 for the day), as well as across the river in Davenport. You can rent regular bikes, tandems, and kid trailers.

Skiing
One of the few places in Illinois where you can downhill ski is on the southern outskirts of Rock Island and Moline. **Ski Snowstar**

riverboat gambling in the Quad Cities

GREAT RIVER VALLEYS

Winter Sports Park (9500 N. 126th St., Taylor Ridge, 309/798-2666 or 800/383-4002, 9 A.M.–9 P.M. daily winter, www.skisnowstar.com) is a 28-acre park atop a 790-foot hill. About half of the trails are labeled for advanced skiers, and the other half are for beginners or intermediates. All hills are open to skiers or snowboarders. In addition to the ski or boarding trails there's a fun tubing hill. You can rent skis and boards here. There's also a restaurant on-site. Lift tickets range $23–30 for adults. Tubing costs $9–19 to tube one hour or all day and includes the tube.

Gambling

Docked on the Mississippi River on Rock Island's riverfront is **Jumer's Rock Island Casino** (18th St. and the riverfront, Rock Island, 800/477-7447, www.jumerscri.com, 8 A.M.–3 A.M. daily), a genuine 200-foot paddlewheel boat. There are five stories of games and dining options here. Choose from around 700 slots (from penny to $25 machines) as well as table games such as roulette, stud poker, and craps. The **Effie Afton Towboat Restaurant** (11 A.M.–10 P.M. Mon.–Thurs., 11 A.M.–11 P.M. Fri.–Sat., 10 A.M.–10 P.M. Sun., $7–10), in a former towboat, serves buffets. Diners must be 21 years or older.

ACCOMMODATIONS
$50-100

In the Broadway Historic District of Rock Island, a residential neighborhood lined with Queen Anne and Italianate homes, the **Victorian Inn Bed and Breakfast** (702 20th St., Rock Island, 309/788-7068 or 800/728-7068, www.victorianinnbandb.com, $70–90) is a large brick home that dates to 1876. There are six rooms here with king, queen, full, and twin beds. All come with private baths and are furnished with family antiques and touches of white lace. The Victorian Inn bed-and-breakfast, like Top O' the Morning, is not too far from the botanical center.

Top O' the Morning Bed and Breakfast Inn (1505 19th Ave., Rock Island, 309/786-3513, rooms $70–90, suite $140) is a 1912 brick Prairie-style home across from Long View Park, a beautiful park that boasts several gardens and a greenhouse. There three rooms and a suite.

Because several interstates run through the Quad Cities, there's no shortage of national chain hotels along the exits. Here are a few. Contact the Quad Cities Convention and Visitors Bureau for a complete list. Near the airport you'll find **Comfort Inn** (2600 52nd Ave., Moline, 309/762-7000, $70–95), **Fairfield Inn** (2705 48th St., Moline, 309/762-9083, $90), and **La Quinta** (5450 27th St., Moline, 309/762-9008, $80).

Over $100

The 175-room **Holiday Inn** (226 17th St., Rock Island, 309/794-1212, $112–170) is in Rock Island's entertainment district. It has a mix of rooms and suites, an indoor pool, and a bar and grill restaurant.

Right on the riverfront in downtown Moline, the newer **Radisson on John Deere Commons** (1415 River Dr., Moline, 309/764-1000, $115–174) is within walking distance of all the Deere sites and the Mark of the Quad Cities, which hosts concerts and sporting events. The hotel has rooms and suites, an indoor swimming pool, an exercise room, and a restaurant.

FOOD
Coffee Shop

◖ **Dead Poets Espresso** (1525 3rd Ave., Moline, 309/736-7606, 7 A.M.–7 P.M. Mon.–Thurs., 7 A.M.–11 P.M. Fri., 7 A.M.–5 P.M. Sat., 8 A.M.–noon Sun., $6), within walking distance of Moline's riverfront, is a coffeehouse that serves healthy wraps, fruit smoothies, Italian sodas, pastries, and of course some pretty good coffee drinks. Wander over here after you've toured the John Deere Commons. It's got great outdoor seating in wide sunny alley.

Soda Fountains

◖ **Lagomarcino's Ice Cream Parlor and Confectionery** (1422 5th Ave., Moline, 309/764-1814, www.lagomarcinos.com,

9 A.M.–5 P.M. Mon.–Sat.) is an institution in the Quad Cities. Founded in 1908 by an immigrant from northern Italy, the shop and confectionery are now run by the fourth generation of Lagomarcinos. Slide into a walnut booth and order a phosphate or sundae topped with homemade fudge. Pick out a dozen or so homemade chocolates (the cream-filled ones are divine) for the ride home.

Mama Compton's (1706 3rd Ave., Rock Island, 309/786-6262, www.mamacomptons. com, 9 A.M.–4 P.M. Mon.–Fri., 10 A.M.–3 P.M. Sat., $5) is one of a kind. Part gourmet food and gift shop, part soda fountain, part deli, Mama Compton's is a friendly business in the District where you can buy a roast beef sandwich, a box of chocolates, a sundae, a pound of coffee, or a bottle of lotion. It's within a few blocks of the riverfront. After a day of biking along the riverfront, try a lemon shake-up.

Italian

In the District, **Huckleberry's** (223 18th St., Rock Island, 309/786-1122, 11 A.M.–3 P.M. Tues.–Fri., lunch buffet only Mon.) is best known for its cheesy pizza, of which there are many, many varieties beyond the tomato sauce, pepperoni, and mozzarella. Some come with pesto sauce, Gorgonzola cheese, cheddar, and barbecued beef (but not all together). Carnivores will like the Mississippi pizza, which has pepperoni, salami, sausage, ground beef, mushrooms, onions, green peppers, and cheese. Dine inside the casual spot or out on the sidewalk to take in the District's scene. Lunches can cost from $3 for a slice of pizza to $8 for a platter of Italian, Polish, and andouille sausages. Dinners range from $8 for gourmet salads to $14 for a chicken and pasta bake.

French

In Rock Island's entertainment district, **Le Figaro** (1708 2nd Ave., Rock Island, 309/786-4944, dinner Tues.–Sat.) serves classic French food, such as chateaubriand (beef tenderloin) and escargot (snails).

Bars and Grills

As the name implies, the house specialties at the 🍺 **Bier Stube** (415 15th St., Moline, 309/797-3049, www.bier-stube.com, 11 A.M.–2 A.M. Mon.–Sat., noon–midnight Sun., $6–13) are German (and meat-laden) dishes, such as sauerbraten and roulade. But the restaurant and bar also serve a variety of hamburgers and sandwiches. The Bier Stube is one of those places where you could spend an entire afternoon or evening swigging good beer and chatting with friends. Large windows, practically floor to ceiling, open onto the sidewalks, and inside are vintage tin ceilings and exposed masonry. It's just a cool (and popular) place in downtown Moline. The beer and wine lists are extensive and feature quite the array of German and European beverages.

River House Bar and Grill (1510 River Dr., Moline, 309/797-1234, 11 A.M. until bar closes daily, www.riverhouseqc.com, $10) is a casual bar and grill that cooks up everything from catfish dinners to meatloaf and lettuce wraps. For those not dieting, there's the appetizer called (no lie) "Hank's totally unique, unbelievable, unmatched, beer battered Rocky River oysters." That's a joke. It's a concoction with garlic mashed potatoes and pepper jack cheese rolled in beer batter. And it comes with ranch dressing. Local bands often play here on the weekends.

Live local bands also jam at **Rock Island Brewing Company** (1815 2nd Ave., Rock Island, 309/793-1999, www.ribco.com, 11 A.M.–3 A.M. Mon.–Fri., 5 P.M.–3 A.M. Sat., $7). This is a casual joint that serves quesadillas, chicken salads, grilled and fried chicken sandwiches, and fish and chips.

INFORMATION
Visitor Information

You can pick up brochures at the **Moline Depot** (2021 River Dr., Moline), at an information center on the north side of the terminal at **Quad City International Airport,** or at the **Mississippi Rapids Welcome Center,** just off the eastbound lane of I-80 in Rapids City, northeast of Moline just before you cross the Mississippi River into Iowa.

To view a barge locking through or on its way down the river, stop by the **Mississippi River Visitor Center** (off the western tip of Rock Island Arsenal on Rodman Ave., 309/794-5338). Staff and exhibits explain how locking works, and why there are locks in the first place (see the *Locks and Dams* sidebar), in addition to displays on boating safety and the like. The center also has restrooms, a water fountain, and an information center stocked with area maps and brochures.

Otherwise, you can contact the Illinois office of the **Quad Cities Convention and Visitors Bureau** (2021 River Dr., Moline, 800/747-7800, www.visitquadcities.com).

Media

The two daily newspapers are the *Rock Island Argus* (www.qconline.com) and the *Quad Cities Times* (www.qctimes.com). Both are available at most convenience stores and bookshops. The *River Cities Reader* (www.rcreader.com) is a free weekly with a blend of politics and entertainment. It's available at convenience stores plus dozens of cafés and restaurants around the Quad Cities.

Tours

The *Celebration Belle* (2501 River Dr., Moline, 309/764-1952 or 800/297-0034, www.celebrationbelle.com) offers lunch and dinner riverboat cruises aboard an 800-passenger excursion boat. Some cruises feature live music, such as brass bands; others are educational in focus and include commentaries on the history of the river and the surrounding region. Tours range in price from $12 for a 1.5-hour sightseeing cruise to $141 for an all-day 11-hour cruise.

GETTING THERE AND AROUND
Airport

The **Quad City International Airport** (2200 69th Ave., Moline, 309/764-9621, www.qcairport.com) is a few miles south of Moline and

Rock Island, south of I-280 and between U.S. 57 and U.S. 150. Several carriers serve the airport, including AirTran, American Eagle, Delta, Northwest Airlink, and United. Direct flights are available to and from Atlanta, Chicago, Dallas/Fort Worth, Denver, Detroit, Memphis, Minneapolis, and Orlando, Florida.

Car

Several rental car companies are at the airport. They include **Avis** (309/762-3605), **Enterprise** (309/764-9611), **Hertz** (309/762-9429), and **National/Alamo** (309/764-4696).

River Taxi

The Rock Island Metropolitan Mass Transit District operates the *Channel Cat* (309/788-3360, www.qcmetrolink.com), a 48-passenger open-air pontoon boat that shuttles people among the Quad Cities. You can board it at the John Deere Commons and *Celebration Belle* in downtown Moline and the riverfront in East Moline. It carries passengers to Leach Park in Bettendorf, Iowa, and East Davenport, Iowa. Bikes are allowed on board. The *Channel Cat* operates daily Memorial Day–Labor Day and on weekends only in September after Labor Day. As for the riverfront stop in East Moline, the shuttle stops there Wednesdays and Thursdays only. For updated hours and schedule, check the website. An all-day ticket on the *Cat* costs $6 per person.

VICINITY OF QUAD CITIES
Aledo

About 25 miles southwest of the Quad Cities is an unusual bed-and-breakfast. Once the Mercer County Jail, **The Slammer Bed and Breakfast** (309 S. College Ave., Aledo, 309/582-5359, www.theslammer.net, $65–85) is, well, a bed-and-breakfast. Rooms are simple, modern, clean, and not tucked into jail cells. You will eat breakfast, however, in cells on tables covered with black-and-white striped cloths. The three-story 1909 building has nine guest rooms with king and queen beds. On the third floor is a sauna and whirlpool baths for all guests.

Geneseo

Just north of I-80 and south of the Hennepin Canal, the quiet and picturesque town of Geneseo is known for its tree-lined streets and decorative Victorian homes. Downtown, **The Cellar** (137 S. State St., Geneseo, 309/944-2177, www.thecellar.info, 5–9 P.M. Tues.–Thurs., 5–10 P.M. Fri.–Sat., 4–9 P.M. Sun.) is in one of the many historic buildings lining State Street, in the basement of Geneseo House. Steaks, poultry, and seafood are cooked slowly over coals on the grill.

Recognizing the need for community theater, a creative bunch of area residents converted the top floor of a dairy barn into a performance space. The **Richmond Hill Players** (Robinson Dr., west of Oakwood Ave., Geneseo, 309/944-2244, www.rhplayers.com) now present six productions each year May–October. They tend to include a mix of comedies, dramas, and musicals, some well-known and others not.

Along the Hennepin Canal, just north of town, the **Geneseo Campground** (22978 Hwy. 82, Geneseo, 309/944-6465) rents canoes and kayaks for use on the canal. It also has dozens of RV sites and a handful of rustic cabins clustered close to each other.

Galesburg and Vicinity

A bustling town of about 32,000 people, Galesburg got its start as a railroad town, and to some extent it still is. Amtrak stops here and freight trains roll by often. The comprehensive Galesburg Railroad Museum near the Amtrak station has several cars you can tour and exhibits about the town's railroading past. Galesburg is also a college town. The small liberal arts school Knox College, founded by abolitionists, is just south of downtown. It is on that campus that Abraham Lincoln debated Stephen A. Douglas in 1858. Perhaps the best site of all is the Carl Sandburg State Historic Site, a three-room cottage and complex of buildings south and east of the railroad yard where Sandburg's father worked. Galesburg has quite the stock of beautiful historic buildings and homes. Its downtown along Main and Seminary Streets is filled with restaurants and shops.

It's easy to get to Galesburg. The town is just east of I-74 and south of U.S. 34. The north-south U.S. 150 runs through town, turning down Main Street for several blocks. The commercial district with hotels and shopping centers is along U.S. 150 and 34.

SIGHTS
Carl Sandburg State Historic Site

One of Illinois's (and the country's) most beloved writers, Carl Sandburg was born in a tiny cottage in Galesburg. The Carl Sandburg State Historic Site (313 E. 3rd St., Galesburg, 309/342-2367, 9 A.M.–5 P.M. Wed.–Sun., donation) offers tours of that cottage as well as exhibits in nearby buildings that shed light on the author and his work. At 20 by 22 feet, Sandburg's childhood home is no bigger than a two-car garage. Inside are a few furniture pieces that did belong to the family, such as a bureau and a few shelves. It's a quick visit. You'll spend more time in the main visitors building, where there are exhibits that chronicle his life, activities, and his writings.

Born in 1878 of Swedish immigrants, Sandburg spent the first few years of his life in a working-class neighborhood of Galesburg, not far from the railroad where his father worked repairing locomotives. As a young man, Sandburg enrolled in Lombard College in Galesburg, but he abandoned his studies to ride the rails and lead the life of a hobo. He traveled west through the Dakotas and on his return worked several jobs, including selling stereoscopes. He wrote for the *Galesburg*

© CHRISTINE DES GARENNES

Carl Sandburg's childhood home

Evening Mail and *System,* a business magazine. One of Sandburg's articles, called "Training Workers to Be Careful," is on view in the museum. He also worked for the *Chicago Daily News.*

It wasn't until 1914, when some of his poems were published in the Chicago-based journal *Poetry,* that Sandburg started to become better-known as a writer. The collection of verse called *Chicago Poems* was published in 1916, followed by *Cornhuskers,* which would build his reputation as an American poet. Influenced by Walt Whitman, Sandburg was a regular man's poet. When Edward R. Murrow asked him what was the worst word in the English language, Sandburg replied, "exclusive." In addition to poetry, Sandburg wrote children's stories and nonfiction. One part of the multivolume Lincoln biography, *Abraham Lincoln: The War Years,* won him the Pulitzer Prize for literature. Several of his books are on display for visitors. Also on view are items such as a photograph of his confirmation class at the Lutheran high school, a pocket knife that once belonged to him, his reporter's pass from

his days working for the *Chicago Daily News,* and clippings of his newspaper and magazine articles.

The building called "The Barn," which is behind the cottage and museum, contains more photos and displays on Sandburg, including several of him and Marilyn Monroe talking and practicing exercises together. Be sure to watch the 15-minute video; it shows Sandburg being interviewed by Edward R. Murrow and the author reading his poetry. Behind the tiny house is the Remembrance Rock, under which Sandburg's ashes were buried. Some of the stepping-stones that lead to the rock are engraved with lines of Sandburg's poetry, such as "Look at songs hidden in eggs" and "I am a brother of the cornhuskers."

Galesburg celebrates **Sandburg Days** in May with poetry readings, writing workshops, storytelling and music, antique car shows, and other exhibits.

Galesburg Railroad Museum

The Galesburg Railroad Museum (211 Seminary St., next to the Amtrak station,

Galesburg, 309/342-9400, www.galesburgrailroadmuseum.org, 10 A.M.–4 P.M. Tues.–Sat., noon–4 P.M. Sun. May–mid-Oct., noon–4 P.M. Sat.–Sun. mid-Apr.–May and mid-Oct.–mid-Nov., $4) is one of the finest attractions in the region. For just a few bucks you can tour several rail cars, a locomotive, plus a new depot that contains railroad history displays. The centerpiece of the collection is a hulking 1930 Baldwin locomotive, a shiny black engine with a coal bin attached to it.

Visitors also get to tour a rail car used by the Railway Mail Service, which was once a branch of the U.S. Postal Service. This car is set up as if it were still a working car, with letters ready to be delivered. The newly built depot and 1921 Pullman passenger car contain exhibits about railroading history and photographs of Galesburg depots from the past, plus old train schedules and telegraph equipment. The museum hosts the annual **Galesburg Railroad Days** at the end of June, a two-day festival with model train shows, a carnival, and other events.

Old Main and Abraham Lincoln

The fifth of seven Abraham Lincoln and Stephen Douglas debates was held on a platform erected just east of Old Main on the campus of Knox College (2 E. South St., Galesburg, 309/341-7000). The Gothic-style building, which dates to 1857, stands at the center of the college, with a lawn stretching out behind it. On October 8, 1857, Lincoln and Douglas met here. The building was renovated in the 1940s after it was designated a National Historic Landmark, and at the rededication ceremony Carl Sandburg read "Ode to Old Main," which he wrote for the occasion. At that time the college installed two bronze tablets of portraits of the speakers on the eastern wall of the building. In Lincoln's words, "He is blowing out the moral lights around us when he contends that whoever wants slaves has a right to hold them."

Across the street from Old Main is the **Arboretum** (Cedar and South Sts., Galesburg), where dozens of mature trees, such as elm and hickory, tower almost as high as Old Main.

© CHRISTINE DES GARENNES

Lincoln-Douglas debate site at Knox College

There's a gazebo in the center of the small park, and a few benches if you need to rest for a little bit.

Other Galesburg Sights

Within walking distance of the railroad museum is the **Discovery Depot Children's Museum** (128 S. Chambers St., Galesburg, 309/344-8876, www.discoverydepot.org, call for hours, $4.50).

While you're downtown, take a few minutes to walk by the gorgeous **Central Congregational Church** (on the central square, Main and Cedar Sts., Galesburg, 309/343-5145), a solid red sandstone church with huge rose stained-glass windows. It was built in 1898 and is now listed on the National Register of Historic Places.

Just off Main Street is the **Orpheum Theatre** (57 S. Kellogg St., Galesburg, 309/342-2299, www.theorpheum.org), a majestic theater (imagine theater boxes and a rich red curtain) boasting a melting pot of architectural styles, including Second Empire, Italian Renaissance, and French baroque. In the 1980s the community restored this 1916 vaudeville theater, and it now hosts concerts by the Knox-Galesburg Symphony and performances by other area arts groups.

SHOPPING

The main shopping district is along **Seminary Street** (383 E. Simmons St., Galesburg, 309/342-1000, www.seminarystreet.com). More than a dozen shops lie along Seminary and Main Streets. You'll find clothing, art, and antiques, plus gifts for grandma or baby. Some favorites are the **Galesburg Antique Mall** (349 E. Main St., Galesburg, 309/342-8571), **Toys and Teachers** (53 S. Seminary St., Galesburg, 309/344-5547), and **Cooks and Company** (93 S. Seminary St., Galesburg, 309/342-3433), a gourmet food and kitchen accessory shop and espresso bar.

ACCOMMODATIONS
$50-100

A stay at ❰ **The Barn Bed and Breakfast** (1690 Kenny St., Dahinda, 309/639-4408, $60–80) is to retreat to the country. Set on 200 acres, the newly constructed red barn (although you'd hardly know it; it looks quite rustic) contains a full kitchen, a hayloft where guests sleep, a bathroom with a claw-foot tub, exposed beams, dried flowers hanging from the ceilings, and plenty of rocking chairs. The barn sleeps 8–10 people, and guests have the entire barn to themselves. It's about 15 miles east of Galesburg.

Within the town of Galesburg there are plenty of chain hotels, including, for example, the **Best Western Prairie Inn** (I-74 at E. Main St., Galesburg, 309/343-7151, $69), a 109-room one-story hotel with an indoor pool and exercise room; **Super 8** (260 W. Main St., Galesburg, 309/342-5174, $90), a 48-room hotel that also has an indoor pool; and **Country Inn and Suites** (2284 Promenade Ct., Galesburg, 309/344-4444, $77–120), a 61-room hotel with indoor pool. For a complete list, contact the visitor bureau.

$100-150

Located along a tree-lined street in Galesburg's historic residential district, **The Fahnestock House** (591 N. Prairie St., Galesburg, 309/344-0270, $150) is somewhat of a unique bed-and-breakfast. Its two rooms are actually large suites. Both are quite impressive: The Victorian suite has a private balcony, and the Empire suite has a large bow window and a Chippendale four-poster canopy bed. The Queen Anne home, which features a three-story turret tower, is a few blocks from Knox College and Seminary Street.

FOOD
Bakeries and Food Shops

The apple fritters at ❰ **Swedough's Donuts and Deli** (1195 N. Broad St., 309/342-7517, 7 A.M.–5 P.M. daily) are fresh and fluffy, bigger than your hand, and less than $1. They don't have dozens of doughnut types or sandwiches to choose from, but those the employees do dish up (such as a turkey club) are fresh and so yummy. You can't go wrong by stopping here for a bite to eat.

Stock up on trail mix and other healthy goodies at **Cornucopia** (83 S. Seminary St., Galesburg, 309/342-6111, 7 A.M.–6 P.M. Mon.–Sat., 7 A.M.–4 P.M. Sun.), a health and natural food store. Adjacent to Cornucopia is **Uncle Billy's Bakery** (same contact information and hours), where you can indulge in warm fresh bread, thick rich brownies, and cookies.

American and Continental

Housed in a former meatpacking plant, the **Packinghouse Dining Co.** (441 Mulberry St., Galesburg, 309/342-6868, 11 A.M.–2 P.M., 5–9 P.M. Mon.–Thurs., 11 A.M.–2 P.M., 5–10 P.M. Fri.–Sat., noon–8 P.M. Sun.) is a popular spot during the lunch hour for its "Burger Bar." For about $7, it's all-you-can-eat burgers with French fries and unlimited toppings. But there's plenty more to this place than burgers. How about a rib-eye steak sandwich, catfish strips, or chicken walnut salad on a croissant? With an assortment of cheesecake desserts and hand-dipped ice cream, it's pretty much guaranteed you'll leave this place with a full stomach.

C **Chez Willy's and Willy's Wines** (41 S. Seminary St., Galesburg, 309/341-4141, 11 A.M.–2 P.M. Mon.–Fri., 4:30–9 P.M. Mon.–Sat., lunch $10, dinner $20) is an intimate storefront bistro with exposed brick walls that serves innovative and delicious food such as chicken with sherry mushroom sauce, coconut curried chicken, and vodka shrimp. Wines are available with dinner by the glass or bottle.

The **Landmark Café and Creperie** (62 Seminary St., Galesburg, 309/343-5376, 11 A.M.–9 P.M. Mon.–Thurs., 11 A.M.–10 P.M. Fri., 9 A.M.–10 P.M. Sat., 9 A.M.–9 P.M. Sun., $5–13), in the heart of the Seminary Street District, is a comfortable restaurant with a comprehensive menu, with breakfast perhaps offering the most tantalizing option: omelets, crepes, Belgian waffles, and strawberry pancakes. On to lunch and dinner and you'll choose from standards such as quiche and grilled sandwiches but also some unusual (for these parts, at least) offerings, such as roasted

duck quesadillas. In the summer, enjoy your meal on the patio.

INFORMATION

You can pick up brochures at the **Galesburg Area Convention and Visitors Center** (2163 E. Main St., Galesburg, 309/343-2485, www.visitgalesburg.com, 8:30 A.M.–5 P.M. Mon.–Fri.).

OQUAWKA REGION

North of Oquawka by about eight miles are two state parks near the Mississippi River offering hiking trails and bird-watching opportunities. Home to the oldest pine plantation in the state, the 2,900-acre **Big River State Forest** (East of County Rd. 1500E, between Keithsburg and Oquawka, 309/374-2496, www.dnr.state.il.us) has miles and miles of hiking or horseback riding trails on firebreaks (strips of land cleared to prevent the spread of fires). In the winter these trails are great for some snowshoeing and cross-country skiing, as you'll pass acres of stately red, white, and jack pines. The Riverview campground has about 50 sites for tents and RVs. Prime spots are those near the sandy beach. Camping costs $8–13 per day. South of Big River is **Delbar State Park** (follow signs from Hwy. 164 in Oquawka, 309/374-2496, www.dnr.state.il.us), an 89-acre park on the river. Trails about two miles long weave through the woods. The park also has boat launches and tent and RV camping. Anglers can also cast their lines in the 27-acre lake at nearby **Henderson County Conservation Area** (off U.S. 34, south of Gladstone, 309/374-2496), which has a boat ramp.

North of Gladstone on Highway 164 is a red covered bridge that dates to 1886. The bridge, about 100 feet long, is open to pedestrians only. Listed on the National Register of Historic Places, it has survived floods and two fires.

Love horses and horseback riding? Adjacent to the Big River State Forest, **Pine View Cabins** (County Rd. 2450N, four miles north of Hwy. 164, Keithsburg, 309/587-3217, cabins $75), with 3,000 acres and 70 miles of trails to explore nearby, is the place to go for serious horseback riding. Spend a day riding a Clydesdale, then retire to an A-frame pine cabin amid the pine trees. Unwind on the porch for a while, and then attend a bonfire. The log cabins have air-conditioning and heat. Horseback riding costs $20–25 per hour.

MONMOUTH

A quiet town of about 9,500 people, Monmouth has a scenic downtown square with historic eateries, shops, and an arts center.

Sights and Activities

A stagecoach driver, surveyor, and buffalo hunter, Wyatt Earp garnered fame as a skilled gunfighter and frontier lawman who attempted to bring order to towns such as Dodge City, Deadwood, and Tombstone in the 1870s. This legendary figure was born in Monmouth, west of Galesburg. The **Wyatt Earp Birthplace** (406 S. 3rd St., Monmouth) has been open by appointment for tours in recent years. As of this writing, it was for sale. If you're interested in visiting the inside, you might want to check its status with the **Monmouth Area Chamber of Commerce** (68 Public Sq., Monmouth, 309/734-3181, www.gomonmouth.com).

Just down the street from the Earp home near a lumberyard on 4th Avenue is a plaque marking the site of a **Lincoln-Douglas debate** that took place in Monmouth.

Buchanan Center for the Arts (64 Public Sq., Monmouth, 309/734-3033, 9 A.M.–5 P.M. Mon.–Fri., 10 A.M.–2 P.M. Sat., free) in downtown Monmouth hosts art shows spotlighting photography, sculpture, and you name it created by area artists.

On the north side of town is **Western Stoneware** (1201 N. Main St., Monmouth, 309/734-6809, www.westernstoneware.com), which has been in the region since the 1890s, when a group of family-owned potteries banded together to sell their wares. At their outlet store you can shop for crocks, mugs, plates, and other kitchenware made from clay mined south of Monmouth.

downtown Monmouth

© CHRISTINE DES GARENNES

Food

Before it was restored and converted to a soda fountain and lunch spot, **(Monmouth Soda Works** (112 S. 1st St., Monmouth, 309/734-3221, $5) was a Plymouth car showroom, a billiard hall, a millinery, and even a garage. Choose a booth along the wall, a stool at the bar, or even a seat out on the backyard patio and indulge in concoctions such as the huge banana-boat sundae. Follow the stairs and second-story walkway to check out an antique car collection. Typically it's open 10 A.M.–4 P.M. daily; however, sometimes during the week it closes at 3 P.M.

Maple City Candy Company (235 S. Main St., Monmouth, 309/734-3313, 6:30 A.M.–9 P.M. daily) has grown from a one-room candy shop to a three-story, five-building complex with a coffee shop, gift shop, and restaurant. It's pure bliss for anyone with a sweet tooth. Glass jars are filled to the brim with treats such as sweet tarts and licorice. Inside the complex is the colorful parrot-themed **(Coconuts** (69 Public Sq., 309/734-8999,

11 A.M.–3 P.M. Sun.–Mon., 11 A.M.–9 P.M. Tues.–Sat. summer, hours vary in winter, $6–12), a restaurant that serves such dishes as crab canapés, glazed apricot beef kebabs, and Cuban ham steak.

MACOMB

Home to Western Illinois University, Macomb is also county seat for McDonough County. Its courthouse square at Lafayette (U.S. 67) and East Jackson (U.S. 136) Streets is packed with craft and antiques shops, hometown cafés and diners, and bars. It's in the center of western Illinois, between the Illinois and Mississippi Rivers.

Events

Watching dozens of balloons coasting through the air is quite a sight. Even more fascinating is watching them glow in the evening. Macomb's annual **Balloon Rally** takes place in September and includes balloon flights during the day, live music, food, and a classic car rally.

Accommodations and Food

Built in 1901, the **Inselhaus Bed and Breakfast** (538 N. Randolph St., Macomb, 309/833-5400, www.inselhausbb.com, $90–145) is a large Victorian home with six bedrooms, all with private bathrooms. Macomb also has several chain hotels along U.S. 67 and other major roads. For a list, contact the visitor bureau.

If you're craving breakfast and it's 4 in the afternoon, head to **Cookie's Diner** (118 S. Lafayette St., Macomb, 309/837-1180, 6 A.M.–8 P.M. Mon.–Sat., 8 A.M.–3 P.M. Sun., $6). You can get Swedish pancakes, large omelets, and other morning plates all day long, if you desire. Otherwise, your options are similar to what you would find at a Denny's: patty melts, turkey clubs, and other sandwiches. The food and service are not exactly top-notch, but the atmosphere is homey and the food will fill you up.

The **Shoppes of the Taylor Block** (119–125 S. Randolph St., Macomb) is a group of businesses in a historic block near the courthouse square. They include **Sullivan Taylor Coffee Shop** (309/836-7064, 7 A.M.–5:30 P.M. Mon.–Fri., 8 A.M.–5 P.M. Sat.), which sells bagels, sandwiches, and soups in addition to coffees; **Your Wine Sellers** (309/836-9463), a gourmet food, wine, and beer shop; and **Jane's off Jackson** (309/836-2909), which sells kitchen supplies.

Information

For regional information, the place to call or visit is the **Western Illinois Tourism Development Office** (2900 E. Jackson St., Macomb, 309/837-7460, www.visitwestern illinois.info). Otherwise, the **Macomb Area Convention and Visitors Bureau** (201 S. Lafayette St., Macomb, 309/833-1315, www. makeitmacomb.com) can help you with any other questions about lodging, dining, or attractions in and around Macomb.

Argyle Lake State Park

Less than 10 miles west of Macomb, Argyle Lake State Park (640 Argyle Park Rd., Colchester, 309/776-3422, www.dnr.state. il.us) is a heavily wooded park with about five miles of rugged hiking trails. The artificial 93-acre lake is stocked with fish, and there's a concession stand where you can rent fishing boats.

GREAT RIVER VALLEYS

Peoria

Located on the west side of the Illinois River, the city of Peoria, which has a current population of about 113,000, grew up in the mid-1800s after meatpacking plants, distilleries, and machinery manufacturers set up shop here. A diverse workforce, comprising European immigrants and blacks from the South and Chicago, moved to Peoria to work in the factories. Then came the railroad boom in the 1850s, and Peoria became a major transportation hub for the Midwest. Because of its mix of so-called regular folk, Peoria became somewhat of a testing ground for the performing arts community and for politicians. The expression "Will it play in Peoria?" essentially meant, how will regular Americans respond to the play or the policy proposal?

Although Peoria developed its identity as a meatpacking center and manufacturing and transportation hub in the 1800s, Peoria's history actually goes back even further. French explorer La Salle built Fort Crèvecoeur on the east side of the river in 1680, making it the first European settlement in the state. A statue marks the spot in the present-day town of Creve Coeur, a middle-class city off Highway 116.

You'll spend most of your time in the city center, along the riverfront where there's a growing mix of restaurants and watering holes. It's also where the paddlewheel boat *Spirit of Peoria* is docked. To the north, the snakelike Grandview Drive offers some awe-inspiring views of the river valley. To the southeast is East Peoria, known for its riverboat casino.

SIGHTS
Riverfront
In recent years Peoria's riverfront has come alive with a 1.5-mile walkway lined with sculptures, a visitors center, an antiques mall, and restaurants. City officials and community groups, along with heavy-machinery equipment

view of the Illinois River from downtown Peoria

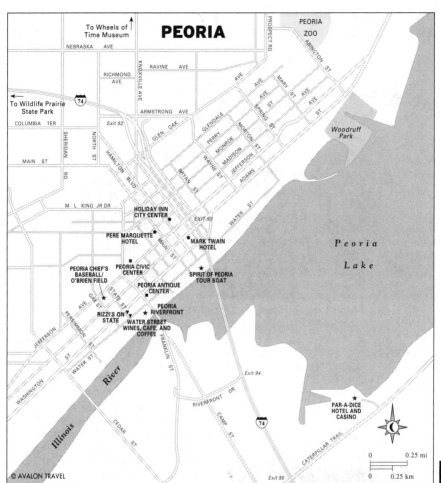

manufacturer Caterpillar (a major employer in the region), were planning to build a multi-million-dollar museum square that highlights the region's and Caterpillar's history. For now, though, the riverfront is home to a farmers market in the summer and a paddlewheel boat. On summer evenings the Peoria Park District hosts outdoor music concerts on the landing by the riverfront. For more information about the riverfront, contact the **Peoria RiverFront Association** (309/671-5555, www.peoriariverfront.com).

One of the major draws to the riverfront is the **Spirit of Peoria** (100 N.E. Water St., 309/636-6166 or 800/676-8988, www.spiritofpeoria.com), a paddlewheel boat docked at the landing. Choose from short sightseeing cruises during the day, dinner cruises, and overnight themed excursions. The overnight rides may include storytellers, ragtime jazz bands, Mark Twain impersonators, and food and drinks. Often you'll catch glimpses of soaring eagles, pass through locks and dams, and stop to visit historic sites, such as Père Marquette State Park

© CHRISTINE DES GARENNES

the *Spirit of Peoria*, docked in Peoria on the Illinois River

near Grafton or Starved Rock State Park near Utica. It also organizes fall foliage trips during October, when the ship cruises south to Dickson Mounds and Havana. Sightseeing cruises, which last about 1.25 hours, cost $14. Themed dinner cruises can cost around $40. Longer trips range $89–465.

Museums ✓

It's not a cavernous museum like the Art Institute of Chicago or the Field Museum, but **Lakeview Museum of Arts and Sciences** (Lakeview Park, 1125 W. Lake Ave., Peoria, www.lakeview-museum.org, 309/686-7000, 10 A.M.–4 P.M. Thurs.–Sat., 10 A.M.–8 P.M. Wed., noon–4 P.M. Sun., $6) is a nice little museum with a few rare finds. One of the museum's highlights is a copper plate called the Peoria falcon. The plate, no larger than 10 inches high, is believed to have once been part of a warrior's headdress. It dates back to sometime between A.D. 1300 and 1450 and probably belonged to a warrior or chief from a Middle Mississippian tribe. A Peoria banker reportedly found the plate in 1859

near Lake Peoria, but later it ended up in the hands of John Wesley Powell, an Illinois State University geologist who would later join the Smithsonian staff.

In addition to the Peoria falcon, the museum has a small but impressive gallery of Illinois folk art. There's an oil portrait by Olof Krans, Anna pottery, and a collection of Illinois River duck and goose decoys from the turn of the 20th century. The museum also contains a dozen or so art glass specimens called American Brilliant cut glass. There are cologne bottles, vases, bowls, and a cool boudoir type of lamp. Most of the pieces date from 1876 to 1916. Other finds include European lithographs, an armchair designed by Frank Lloyd Wright, and a chair designed by Frank Gehry. The museum also has a gallery for rotating exhibits, plus a planetarium and children's center. In coming years the Lakeview Museum of Arts and Sciences is slated to move to the Peoria Riverfront Museum in downtown Peoria.

On the northern edge of town is a fun detour called the **Wheels O' Time Museum**

(11923 N. Knoxville Ave., Peoria, 309/243-9020 or 309/243-5616, www.wheelsotime.org, noon–5 P.M. Wed.–Sun., May–Oct., $5.50). For a few bucks you could spend hours admiring the model airplanes and model trains, steam engines, music boxes, Packard automobiles, farm tractors and implements, and antique toys. Owned by dozens of collectors, this museum seems to get larger every year. As the name says, this place is all about things that go.

Parks

On the west side of the river, north of downtown, the **Peoria Zoo** (2218 N. Prospect Rd., Peoria, 309/686-3365, www.peoriaparks.org, 10 A.M.–5 P.M. daily, $6) has about 250 animals from around the world, including lions, sea lions, and zebras. There's also a petting zoo of farm animals. The zoo is undergoing an ambitious expansion project to triple its size and bring in more animals and exhibits, including one all about Africa.

Go north on Highway 29 or Galena Road along the west side of the Illinois River until you get to **Grandview Drive** and the park of the same name. Follow this narrow winding road up along the bluffs, past mansions and manicured lawns, for great views of the Illinois River valley below. After you've taken the drive, get ready for hiking some of these bluffs. Nearby, just off Prospect Road, a mile or two north of U.S. 150, is the **Forest Park Nature Center** (5809 Forest Park Dr., Peoria, 309/686-3360, www.peoriaparks.org, nature center 9 A.M.–5 P.M. Mon.–Sat., 1–5 P.M. Sun., trails dawn–dusk). The nature center is great for children, and the shop is great for naturalists—it's got everything from environmentally friendly cleaning products to wind chimes and greeting cards. But hikers, especially those in for a challenging hike, will salivate over the seven miles of rugged trails. The best time to go? Early morning just after the sun has started rising in the east, and you can look out over the valley through the trees.

For cheap summer entertainment head to the **George Luthy Memorial Botanical Gardens** (2218 N. Prospect Rd., Peoria, 309/686-3362, www.peoriaparks.org, grounds 8:30 A.M.–dusk daily, free, conservatory $2). Concerts are held on the grounds 5–7 P.M. on the second Sunday of the month May–August. The five-acre site is stocked with perennial and annual flowers, dwarf conifers, roses, poppies, and more. There's also a children's garden.

ENTERTAINMENT AND EVENTS
Performing Arts

Peoria has a vibrant arts community, with several dance, music, and theater companies staging productions throughout the year. The **Peoria Ballet** (8800 N. Industrial Rd., Peoria, 309/690-7990, www.peoriaballet.com) performs recitals and shows in Peoria's Scottish Rite Cathedral and the civic center. The **Illinois Ballet** (100 Walnut St., Peoria, 309/671-1222, www.illinoisballet.org) stages classic ballets, such as *Swan Lake* and *The Nutcracker* at locations throughout the region. The **Peoria Civic Center** (201 S.W. Jefferson St., Peoria, 309/673-8900, www.peoriaciviccenter.com) in downtown Peoria brings in comedians and touring musicians such as Nelly, and hosts Bradley University sports and other events. The **Peoria Symphony Orchestra** (203 Harrison St., Peoria, 309/637-2787, www.peoriasymphony.org) performs classical and pops music from around the world. Its shows are also in the civic center. For 50 years the **Corn Stock Theatre** (309/676-2196, www.cornstocktheatre.com) has been staging summertime shows outdoors in the Peoria area. It showcases musicals and comedies in a tent at Upper Bradley Park (Farmington Rd. at W. Main St. and Park Rd.).

Visual Arts

The **Peoria Contemporary Art Center** (305 S.W. Water St., Peoria, 309/674-6822, www.peoriacac.org, 11 A.M.–5 P.M. Tues.–Thurs. and Sat., 11 A.M.–8 P.M. Fri.), in a brick riverfront building, holds several local art exhibitions a year. Live local music concerts are held here Friday evenings.

GREAT RIVER VALLEYS

Events

Peoria is always partying, it seems. The River City Blues Society (www.rivercityblues.com) hosts a blues festival every summer on the riverfront. Tens of thousands of people flock to the Peoria Art Guild's **Fine Art Fair** at the end of September on the riverfront, where visual artists display their work for sale and musicians perform. **Jumbo Gumbo Mamba Combo** is a weekend of New Orleans jazz, zydeco, and salsa music. During East Peoria's **Festival of Lights** in December, decorated floats cruise downtown East Peoria followed by a fireworks show.

SHOPPING

If you like antiques, especially antique furniture, jewelry, and prints, you might just spend hours at the **Illinois Antique Center** (311 S.W. Water St., Peoria, 309/673-3354, 9 A.M.–5 P.M. Mon.–Sat., 11 A.M.–5 P.M. Sun.). In an old warehouse on Peoria's riverfront, the center has hundreds of booths containing antiques from the 1800s up to the 1970s and 1980s, and

Peoria's riverfront shopping and dining district

© CHRISTINE DES GARENNES

GREAT RIVER VALLEYS

styles from art deco to Victorian. Nearby are several other gift and home-decor shops.

Buy fruits and vegetables and local art at the outdoor **RiverFront Market** (309/671-5555, www.peoriariverfrontmarket.com, 8 A.M.–noon Sat. June–Sept.).

National chain stores like Banana Republic, Borders Books and Music, and Dick's Sporting Goods can be found at **Shoppes at Grand Prairie** (I-474 and War Memorial Dr., Peoria, www.theshoppesatgrandprairie.com), an open-air shopping center on Peoria's northwest side. There are restaurants like Flat Top Grill, a movie theater, and the CAT children's playland, which features tractors and trucks for the little ones.

SPORTS AND RECREATION

An indoor recreation center, **inPlay** (316 S.W. Washington St., Peoria, 309/676-1000, www.inplaypeoria.com, 3–9 P.M. Wed., 3–10 P.M. Thurs., 3–11 P.M. Fri., 11 A.M.–11 P.M. Sat., 11 A.M.–10 P.M. Sun.) is loaded with pool tables, basketball courts, a climbing wall, skee ball, and a bar and grill. It's a few blocks from the civic center near the riverfront.

Gambling

Par-A-Dice Hotel and Casino (21 E. Blackjack Blvd., East Peoria, 800/727-2342, www.par-a-dice.com, 9 A.M.–6 A.M. daily) is a permanently docked riverboat casino on the east side of the river. It's got countless slot machines here that are coinless—meaning that instead of cashing out coins, the machines print out tickets. The casino also has dozens of blackjack, roulette, craps, stud poker, and other table games. If you don't want to drop a lot of cash, there are the penny slots. A steakhouse, deli, and bar are on-site, and a hotel is adjacent to the casino.

Minor League Baseball

The **Peoria Chiefs** (O'Brien Field, 730 S.W. Jefferson St., 866/698-4253, www.peoriachiefs.com) are a Class A minor league affiliate of the Chicago Cubs; the season runs April–end of August.

ACCOMMODATIONS

The hotels listed here range widely in price, mostly because each hotel has standard rooms and luxury suites. Basically, in Peoria proper, you can expect to spend about $75 for a basic hotel room and up to $300 for a suite.

Listed on the National Register of Historic Places, the 🄲 **Hotel Père Marquette** (501 Main St., Peoria, 309/637-6500, www.hotel-peremarquette.com) was built in 1927. This downtown Peoria hotel is an old-style hotel with rich dark colors and attentive staff. It's usually the first choice of conventioneers and brides. There are 253 rooms here—some whirlpool-bath rooms, some suites, and some junior suites. Carnegie's is a classy dinner joint that serves items such as crab legs, grilled vegetables, veal, and duck.

In contrast to the old-school Père Marquette is the **Mark Twain Hotel** (225 N.E. Adams St., Peoria, 309/676-3600, www.marktwainhotels.com), a few blocks away and still within walking distance of the downtown riverfront district. This 110-room hotel, built in 1967, has deluxe rooms on the upper floors. Those have been renovated into tasteful rooms with DVD players, luxury bath products, and other nice touches. Some rooms have views of the river. A hot breakfast buffet is included, and a chain pizza parlor is in the building.

The 324-room **Holiday Inn City Center** (500 Hamilton Blvd., Peoria, 309/674-2500) in downtown Peoria is near the civic center and a short walk to the riverfront. The hotel features an indoor pool, whirlpool and sauna, game room, fitness center, and restaurant. It also has a mix of standard rooms and executive suites.

Stoney Creek Inn and Conference Center (101 Mariner's Wy., East Peoria, 309/694-1300, www.stoneycreekinn.com) is about a mile from Par-A-Dice Casino. It's got 165 rooms, all with standard features such as coffeemakers, high-speed Internet access, and hair dryers. The indoor pool is pretty large and is connected to another outdoor pool, so you can swim from one to the other.

The 168-room **Radisson Castle Hotel** (117 N. Western Ave., Peoria, 309/673-8040, $100–120) was once part of the Jumer's chain, which operated several English Tudor–style hotels in Illinois. Touches of the original Tudor can still be found (you can't miss the turret at the front), but it has been renovated in recent years and has the feel of most chain hotels. The main hotel features an indoor pool and exercise room. Rooms come with either a king bed, two queens, or two double beds. The restaurant, Flagstones (6 A.M.–10 P.M. daily), serves steak, seafood, and pasta dishes.

Adjacent to the casino, **Par-A-Dice Hotel** (21 E. Blackjack Blvd., East Peoria, 309/699-7711, www.par-a-dice.com) has 208 rooms and suites, all with wireless Internet access and other basic features such as coffeemakers in the rooms.

In Peoria's Randolph-Roanoke Historic District just west of I-74 and near Hamilton Boulevard, **Randolph Terrace Historic Bed and Breakfast** (201 W. Columbia Terr., Peoria, 309/688-7858 or 877/264-8266, www.randolphterrace.com) has four rooms, all with private bathrooms. They're furnished with antique beds and armoires and come with comfy robes for guests.

Accommodations are also available at **Wildlife Prairie State Park;** for more information, see *West of Peoria.*

FOOD
Cafés and Lunch Spots

Steamers, cappuccinos, Italian sodas: They've got it at **Water Street Wines, Cafe, and Coffees** (100 State St., Peoria, 309/966-4246, 6:30 A.M.–9 P.M. Mon.–Thurs., 6:30 A.M.–11 P.M. Fri., 8 A.M.–11 P.M. Sat.), a little stop on the Illinois River waterfront. In the evenings you can sip wine and nibble on small plate dishes such as prosciutto and melon or fondue.

The sunny **Emerald Tea Room** (132 McKinley St., East Peoria, 309/694-1972, 11 A.M.–2 P.M. Mon.–Sat.) in downtown East Peoria sells an array of sandwiches, soups, and teas from around the world.

American

As the name implies, **River Station** (212 S.W. Water St., Peoria, 309/671-7000, www.theriverstation.net, 11 A.M.–2 P.M. Mon.–Sat., 5–10 P.M. Mon.–Thurs., 5–11 P.M. Fri.–Sat., 10 A.M.–2 P.M. Sun.) is housed in an old railroad train station, listed on the National Register of Historic Places, on the riverfront. This is a good place to go if you're looking for fine dining along the riverfront (perhaps after a cruise on the *Spirit of Peoria*?). Chops, steak, seafood, pastas, and a combination thereof range in price about $13–28.

Kelleher's Irish Pub and Eatery (619 S.W. Water St., Peoria, 309/673-6000, www.kellehersirishpub.com, 11 A.M.–1 A.M. Mon.–Wed., 11 A.M.–2 A.M. Sat., $10) is a festive bar and restaurant in downtown Peoria's riverfront. It's especially festive on Thursday and Friday nights when local bands play for free. It serves a mix of Irish and American food, and the appetizer buffet on Thursdays always draws a crowd.

Italian

Rizzi's on State (112 State St., 309/673-2500, 11 A.M.–10 P.M. Mon.–Thurs., 11 A.M.–11 P.M. Fri., 4–11 P.M. Sat.) is probably one of the best places to eat Italian food in Peoria. The restaurant serves northern and southern Italian cuisine.

Nostalgic for the Rat Pack days? On the northwest side of town in the Shoppes at Grand Prairie shopping center, **Johnny's Italian Steakhouse** (5201 W. War Memorial Dr., Peoria, 309/692-3887, www.johnnysitaliansteakhouse.com, 11 A.M.–10 P.M. Mon.–Thurs., 11 A.M.–11 P.M. Sat., 11 A.M.–9 P.M. Sun., $12–29) evokes the time when guys and gals idolized Dean Martin and Frank Sinatra. Come here with an appetite. Appetizers include zucchini fries and big Caesar salads, and the steak and seafood dishes come with sides like bread, salad, mashed potatoes, veggies, rice, or potatoes. Nice touches, like cavatappi pasta and Maytag blue cheese, make the drive out here worth it.

Seafood

Jonah's Seafood and Oyster Bar (2601 N. Main St., East Peoria, 309/694-0946, www.jonahsseafood.com, 11 A.M.–10 P.M. Mon.–Sat., 4–10 P.M. Sun., $9–20) is another New Orleans–inspired restaurant. As you look out on the river, try some oysters on the half shell, a poor boy sandwich, or the place's pride and joy, crawfish étouffée. This is another restaurant with a well-stocked bar.

INFORMATION AND SERVICES
Visitor Information

Your first stop for attractions, dining, or lodging information should be the **Riverfront Visitors Center** (110 N.E. Water St., Peoria, 309/672-2860 or 866/896-6853, 9 A.M.–5 P.M. Mon.–Fri., 9 A.M.–4 P.M. Sat., 1–5 P.M. Sun. May–Sept.), just off I-74 and on the riverfront. It's run by the **Peoria Convention and Visitors Bureau** (www.peoria.org).

Media

The *Peoria Journal Star* (1 News Plaza, Peoria, 309/686-3000, www.pjstar.com) is published daily and sold throughout the region.

Tours

Carriage Classics (309/579-2833) offers horse-drawn carriage rides through downtown Peoria Friday and Saturday evenings April–October and Thursday–Saturday evenings mid-June–mid-August. It'll pick up riders at the Hotel Père Marquette and on the riverfront landing. The cost is $20 per couple.

The Peoria Historical Society and Citylink take visitors on a narrated two-hour **trolley tour** (309/688-5668, www.peoriahistoricalsociety.org) of the city on a renovated trolley. Tours run June–end of October, and the cost is $8 per person. Departure points vary by tour.

The paddlewheel boat **Spirit of Peoria** (100 N.E. Water St., 309/636-8000), docked on the riverfront, offers a variety of tours for visitors; for more information, see *Sights*.

GETTING THERE AND AROUND
Air

Several airlines serve the **Greater Peoria Regional Airport** (6100 W. Everett McKinley Dirksen Pkwy., Peoria, 309/697-8272, www.flypia.com). They include Allegiant Air to Las Vegas, Phoenix, and Ft. Lauderdale, Orlando, and Tampa/St. Petersburg, Florida; American Eagle to Chicago and Dallas/Fort Worth; Delta Connection to Atlanta; Northwest Airlink to Detroit and Minneapolis; and United Express to Chicago. Like other regional airports in the state, the cities and airlines serving the Peoria airport can change often. The airport is on the west side of town near I-474. Parking is free, except for the meters if you're dropping off or picking up passengers. You can rent a car at the airport, or you also can take Citylink, the public bus. The Route 7 or Garden bus goes to the airport Monday–Saturday.

Car and Bus

Try any of the following if you need to rent a car in town: **Enterprise** (at the Peoria Airport, 309/633-2200), **Avis Rent a Car** (500 Hamilton Blvd., 309/673-3081) and **Dollar Rent-A-Car** (200 N.E. Jefferson St., 309/674-2277).

For a taxicab, you can call **Peoria Yellow Checker Cab** (107 Cass St., Peoria, 309/676-0731).

Public transportation is provided by **Citylink** (309/676-4040, www.ridecitylink.org). A one-way bus ride costs $1; transfers are free.

NORTH OF PEORIA
Peoria Heights

At the tail end of Grandview Drive you'll come out onto Prospect Road and downtown Peoria Heights: a quiet, well-to-do suburb. Downtown, the main attraction is **Tower Park,** just off Prospect Road. A 170-foot-tall water tower has been outfitted as an observation tower. Take the elevator up to several decks and peek through the telescope for more views of Peoria and the Illinois River valley.

In a cottage just off the main drag, Prospect Road, **Leaves and Beans Roasting Co.** (4800 N. Prospect Rd., Peoria Heights, 309/688-7685, www.leavesnbeans.com, 7 A.M.–5 P.M. Mon.–Tues. and Fri., 7 A.M.–9 P.M. Wed.–Thurs., 7 A.M.–3 P.M. Sat., $7) is a welcoming café where the staff roasts their own beans. As a result, the coffee is just spectacularly fresh. Although you'll be quite pleased with a regular cup of coffee, Leaves and Beans also offers a ton of flavored and blended coffee drinks, plus milk shakes. A few sandwiches, such as smoked turkey panini and chicken salad, are also available.

Wine Country and French Toast (4600 N. Prospect Rd., Peoria Heights, 309/686-0234, www.winecountry-frenchtoast.com, 5–10 P.M. Tues.–Thurs., 5–11 P.M. Fri.–Sat., $15) is an upscale French restaurant and gourmet food and wine shop in downtown Peoria Heights. With its subdued lighting, white tablecloths, gourmet food, and impressive wine selection, the restaurant is the place to go to celebrate an event or if you like to treat yourself to fine French food, such as imported cheeses, rack of lamb, pork loin, and homemade ice cream.

Rock Island State Trail

One of many rails-to-trails projects in the state, the Rock Island State Trail follows the path of the former Peoria and Rock Island Railroad. From Alta in Peoria County to Toulon in Stark County, the trail etches a path through prairie and woods for 26 miles. Pedal along past creeks, over the Spoon River, and through small towns such as Wyoming, Princeville, and Dunlap, where you'll come upon Green View Nursery, an extensive plant nursery. North of Alta off Fox Road is the Kickapoo Creek Recreation Area, home to a restored prairie. The trail is accessible in several places, including near the Williams Street Depot in Wyoming off Highway 17, by Parks School Road in Dunlap, and at the Peoria-Stark county line at North Cedar Bluff Road. The trail headquarters is at 311 East Williams Street, Wyoming, 309/695-2228, www.dnr.state.il.us.

Chillicothe

About 10 miles north of Peoria is the small riverfront town of Chillicothe. **Three Sisters Park** (17189 Hwy. 29, south side of Chillicothe, across from the Illinois River, 866/278-8837) is a 400-acre park donated to the city by three sisters. The site includes a white vintage farmhouse, a big red barn made to resemble barns built in the early 1900s, a butterfly garden with a gazebo, and a handful of fruit trees. The park hosts a bluegrass festival in early June.

EAST OF PEORIA
Morton

At the hilarious **Punkin Chuckin'** in Morton at the end of October, participants see how far they can shoot pumpkins using slingshot-type contraptions and heavy-duty air cannons. Their targets? Stuff rescued from junkyards: beat-up cars, old refrigerators. All the while visitors dine on pumpkin doughnuts and pumpkin pie. There's usually an admission fee of a few bucks per car. Morton, by the way, calls itself the pumpkin capital of the world because

85 percent of the world's pumpkins are processed here. The town also holds a more traditional pumpkin festival in September with food tents, carnival rides, a parade, and other activities. For more information about the festival or Punkin Chuckin', contact the Morton Chamber of Commerce (888/765-6588, www.pumpkincapital.com).

WEST OF PEORIA
Wildlife Prairie State Park

Wildlife Prairie State Park (3826 N. Taylor Rd., Peoria, 309/676-0998, www.wildlife-prairiestatepark.org, $5.50, Tues. $2, Mar. and Nov.–Dec. $3.50) is a 2,000-acre park modeled after what Illinois may have looked like when the first wave of pioneers came through here. The park is home to animals that were native to Illinois, such as timber wolves, bison, black bears, elks, and deer, plus birds of prey. In one area staff have assembled a replica of a pioneer homestead and added some farm animals there. You can tour the park by riding a miniature train ($2), but at least spend some

bison in the distance at Wildlife Prairie State Park near Peoria

time walking along the many trails. Climb a hill filled with wildflowers, pass a butterfly garden and several lakes, and stop at one of the viewing decks to look for wildlife and listen to songbirds. Pick up a map at the visitors center and staff will be able to tell you what animals you'll be able to see on certain trails that day. The park's schedule varies year to year, but generally it's open 9 A.M.–4:30 P.M. daily end of March–end of April and October–mid-December, and 9 A.M.–6:30 P.M. throughout May and September, 8 A.M.–6:30 P.M. June–early September.

One of the park's best-kept secrets is its original lodging options. You can stay overnight in a caboose, stable, cottage, or cabin for $70–125. The cabin is a genuine one-room cabin with a queen and two double beds, a kitchenette, and a front porch complete with a porch swing. The cottages, which are along a lake, can sleep 3–8 people. They also come with small kitchenettes, heat, and air-conditioning. The Prairie Stables building, which looks like a horse stable, is actually quite a modern building with two bedrooms. Some lodgings are available year-round; others are open only spring through summer. Staying in the cabins or cottages includes park admission.

Canton
Once home to plow manufacturers, a cigar factory, and coal mines, the Canton area is now a comfortable suburb of Peoria, about 30 miles southwest of the city. Make the trip out here to visit the Palm Café.

The **Landmark Inn** (1060 N. Main St., Canton, www.landmarkinnofcanton.com, $72–89), a bed-and-breakfast on the north end of Canton, has four rooms available, each decorated with a different theme, from the seashore-themed Cape Cod and Florida rooms to the Southwest room. Two have private baths; the other two share a bathroom.

The **C Palm Café** (101 E. Elm St., Canton, 309/647-2233, dinner from 5 P.M. Wed.–Sat., $15) is one of those places that makes you willing to travel great distances to enjoy a meal there. Transplants from the West Coast, chef Heidi Wilner and her husband, Gary Leese, the host, opened this intimate restaurant in the late 1990s within the restored Canton House Hotel. With its slate floors, windows looking out on the Canton street scene (not much, but mood-setting nonetheless), and subdued lighting, it's a beautiful restaurant with great food. The menu changes often, but you can expect such entrées as pan-seared duck breast with apricot sauce or grilled pork chops with bourbon mustard glaze. Don't skip dessert. Previously served dishes have included the jaw-dropping mocha pot and apple bread pudding with rum butter sauce.

The casual, family-friendly **Geppetto's** (47 S. Main St., Canton, 309/649-0240, 11 A.M.–2 P.M. daily, 4–9 P.M. Sun.–Thurs., 4–10 P.M. Fri.–Sat., $7) serves toasty meatball sandwiches, thin and pan pizza, plus the usual Italian pasta fare such as linguine with clam sauce and tortellini. The food is good and prices are reasonable, plus it features imported Italian beer.

Winery
Just west of Peoria the **Kickapoo Creek Winery** (6605 N. Smith Rd., Edwards, 309/495-9463, www.kickapoocreekwinery.com) hosts fun events like a grape stomp at the end of August. Here you can sample dry, semidry, sweet, and semisweet wines.

The Imperial Valley and Vicinity

With the Spoon River to the northwest, the Sangamon River to the east, and the Illinois River in between, the Imperial Valley region, as it is often referred to, is home to many fruit and vegetable farms where crops such as pumpkins and watermelon are grown. The towns along this stretch of the Illinois River are small, quiet, and rural. And in between are large, primarily rustic local, state, and national wildlife areas, home to eagles, herons, waterfowl, and other animals. The roads that run through here are wandering, two-lane highways. Highway 100 and U.S. 24 follow the west side of the river connecting Beardstown to Havana. On the east side is Highway 78.

LEWISTOWN AND HAVANA
Dickson Mounds
On a bluff overlooking the Illinois River, Dickson Mounds (10956 N. Dickson Mounds Rd., Lewistown, 309/547-3721, www.museum. state.il.us, 8:30 A.M.–5 P.M. daily, free) is a 230-acre site where a Native American mound-building culture lived about 1,500 years ago. Unlike the Cahokia Mounds near Collinsville and East St. Louis, these mounds are in a more rural area. They were discovered in 1927 when the area was a farm. Landowner Don Dickson removed the dirt of the mounds, left the bones there, covered the area with a tent (and later a building), and then charged people admission to visit the archaeological site. Eventually he sold the land to the state of Illinois, which later added more buildings and a museum. The museum has several floors of exhibits about the Illinois River valley geography and its history going back thousands of years. There are extensive displays about the Native Americans who lived in the Illinois River valley and the Mississippi River mounds culture. Don't forget to walk out onto the third-floor observation deck. From there you can see the Larson site, the site of another mound village that's now a picnic area. The Eveland Village site, also on the grounds, shows the excavated remains of a village. And the Ogden-Fettie site, on the south end of the park, has more mounds.

Another Native American historical site, the **Rockwell Mound** (N. Orange and Franklin Sts., Havana, 309/543-6240) is near the town of Havana. At about 14 feet high and two acres in size, it's one of the largest in the area. The Rockwell Mound dates to about A.D. 200.

Chautauqua National Wildlife Refuge
Eight miles north of Havana on the Illinois River is the beautiful Chautauqua National Wildlife Refuge (19031 E. County Rd. 2110N, Havana, 309/535-2290, free), home to about 250,000 waterfowl and 10,000 shorebirds. With that said, it's a great, great spot for bird-watching. It's in the middle of the Mississippi River Flyway, and migratory birds such as Canada geese and trumpeter swans drop by often for a visit, especially in the backwater lakes. Bald eagles nest here from late fall to early spring. What else can you see? Great blue herons, egrets, and wood ducks. The entire site is about 6,200 acres with backwater lakes, wetlands, and bottomland forest. If you want to take a boat out onto one of the backwater lakes, you can launch it from the ramps at Eagle Bluff Access Area. You can also park your car there and explore 12 miles of levee roads on the back of your bike. Otherwise, the refuge headquarters (on County Rd. 2110N) has a short wheelchair-accessible nature trail, where you may also see more wildlife.

Nearby, just east of Highway 78 and north of Havana, is **Emiquon** and the Merwin Preserve at **Spunky Bottoms,** sites owned and managed by The Nature Conservancy along with the Illinois Department of Natural Resources and other agencies. Most of Emiquon is farmland, created by draining wetlands and clearing woodlands. However, the conservancy along with governmental agencies is working to restore the area to wetlands and to build a diverse habitat.

© CHRISTINE DES GARENNES

Chautauqua National Wildlife Refuge

Sand Ridge State Forest

North of Chautauqua is Sand Ridge State Forest (accessible from County Rds. 2300N or 2500N, Forest City, 309/597-2212), another huge park on the east side of the river. The 7,200-acre park is full of sandy prairies and native oak-hickory forest and pine plantations. The pines were planted by members of the Civilian Conservation Corps to control erosion. This is a working forest; pine trees are still felled here. In the sand prairie areas you'll come across plants normally found in the American Southwest such as prickly pear cactus. (Yes, cacti grow in Illinois.) The sandy areas were created thousand of years ago when the Kankakee torrent flooded the region as a glacier melted. The flood was followed by a long dry and windy period when 100-foot-high dunes formed at the base of ridges in the park.

The park has a staggering 44 miles of hiking trails, each trail ranging about 1.5–17 miles. There are also numerous fire lanes, which are rustic roads that you can drive or bike along. Pine Campground has 27 sites with pit toilets.

Plus there are 12 sites scattered throughout the park near the hiking trails for people interested in backpack campsites. You'll need a permit to camp in the primitive sites. Also, there's a huge fish hatchery on the north side of the forest. It stocks many of the lakes in the state.

Downtown Havana and Lewistown

While you're in the area, take a few minutes to stroll downtown Havana and Lewistown, small river towns with a few craft stores, antiques shops, and bar-and-grills.

Information

The **Fulton County Tourism Council** (700 E. Oak St., Canton, 309/647-6074, www.fultoncountytourism.org) publishes a brochure listing annual events and lodging and dining options.

Camp Ellis

After the Japanese attacked Pearl Harbor on December 7, 1941, and the United States entered World War II, the Army bought 17,500

GREAT RIVER VALLEYS

acres in southwestern Fulton County to build a Army service unit training camp. The Army demolished farm buildings and built a railroad, landing strip, and dozens of buildings. Before closing in 1945, about 125,000 Army personnel trained at Camp Ellis. It also held prisoners of war. This is a place in Illinois you don't hear about often. The buildings are now piles of bricks and concrete blocks, and most of the area has been returned to farmland. But it may interest historians, particularly World War II buffs. The area is north of U.S. 136 near the tiny towns of Ipava and Table Grove. Along the route you'll see Dobbins Cemetery, where some German prisoners were buried, and old baseball diamonds. More information is available from the Dickson Mounds Museum or Fulton County Tourism Council.

CHANDLERVILLE
Sanganois Conservation Area
The Illinois River floodplain between Peoria and Beardstown is marshy, with a lot of sloughs and bottomland forests. North of Beardstown, the Sanganois Conservation Area (3594 County Rd. 200 N., Chandlerville, 309/546-2628, www.dnr.state.il.us, free), on the east side of the Illinois River and west of the Sangamon River, is a huge 11,000-acre site. Like Chautauqua National Wildlife Area, this area is rustic and loaded with hiking and birdwatching opportunities. Walk, bike, or drive along the 18.5 miles of levee roads, past willow and black walnut trees, and creatures such as ducks, beavers, turtles, osprey, and bald eagles. Once a private duck-hunting club, the Sanganois Conservation Area is still often visited by waterfowl hunters. It's also prone to flooding. If you visit in the winter or spring, call to check if any access roads are closed because of flooding.

Jim Edgar Panther Creek State Fish and Wildlife Area
The parks in the Illinois River valley just seem to get bigger and bigger. At 16,500 acres and 26 square miles, Jim Edgar Panther Creek State Fish and Wildlife Area (10149 County Hwy. 11, Chandlerville, 217/452-7741, www.dnr.state.il.us, free) is one of the largest in the state. Formerly called Site M (in reference to utility company and former landowner Commonwealth Edison's name for it), the area was once targeted to be the location of a coal power plant. That never happened, and the state eventually bought the land. The site has all kinds of landscapes, from farms to meadows to forests. Deer and pheasant are common sights. The park is also home to hawks, bluebirds, frogs, and turtles. The lady's slipper orchid, an Illinois endangered species, has been found here. Because the park was purchased and developed in the 1990s, buildings and trails are fairly new. About 24 miles of rough trails carve paths through woody ravines, hilly prairie, and past sunflower and wheat fields. There are three main hiking loops. The northernmost Governor's Trail and the Yellow Trail, in the middle, have several scenic overlooks above Panther Creek. You can get to either the Red or Yellow Trails at the South Trailhead off South Reed Road. A three-mile hiking, walking, or jogging trail winds around Gridley Lake. There are three lakes—Gridley Lake, Prairie Lake, and Drake Lake—where you can launch a fishing boat, canoe, or sailboat. Prairie Lake is the largest at 210 acres.

If you dig quiet rustic campsites, the park has walk-in sites about 0.25 mile from a parking lot. Dozens of other sites with modern shower facilities and electrical hookups are also available. If you didn't pack along any camping gear, you can rent a tent for $8–12. The rent-a-tent package actually includes much more than a tent: a camp light, broom and dust pan, and fire extinguisher. The tent fee is in addition to a $5 utility fee. The park also has nine cabins available for rent for $40 per night. Accommodations are rustic (no bathroom or air-conditioning), with two bunk beds and a full bed. But they do have ceiling fans and an electric heater for chilly nights. Outside are decks and picnic tables. You will need to make reservations for the tents and cabins.

MEREDOSIA

On the banks of the Illinois River, the quiet river town of Meredosia is a good spot for eagle scouting in the winter. The town hosts an eagle-watching festival in mid-January. During the event you can watch a live raptor show in the local high school, attend a workshop about eagles, tour the river museum, and of course scout for eagles.

One of the best spots to look for eagles is in or near the **Meredosia National Fish and Wildlife Refuge** (309/535-2290), a 3,000-acre-plus refuge north of town along the river and Lake Meredosia. In and around Meredosia, you'll notice that the Illinois is a working river. There are grain elevators and shipping points, and coal- and oil-fired power stations. But this refuge offers relief from that scene. Just north of the town is an observation platform off Beach Road, where you can look for eagles. A short trail through some pine trees leads you to a wooden deck tucked into the bottomland forests of the river and Lake Meredosia. Follow signs to the trail and viewing platform from Highway 104 from downtown Meredosia.

While you're in town, stop by the small **Meredosia River Museum** (305 Main St., Meredosia, 217/584-1356, 1–4 P.M. Fri. summer, noon–4 P.M. Sat. winter, donations), which has a few display cases of arrowheads and videos and books about eagles, plus a tiny but eye-opening display about the fur-trading business, including traps and stretch boards for furs.

Meredosia saved its old 1882 train depot from demolition, and you can drive by to take a look at it. It's on the south side of the river off Montgomery Street.

Jacksonville and Vicinity

Jacksonville is a town for history and architecture buffs. It's not a booming metropolis now, but it once was, and it has a number of surprises, such as the Three-Legged Dog Café and the restaurant Mugsy's. If you love big old homes, brick streets, and towering oak and elm trees, take a drive through the historic neighborhoods in Jacksonville. Meander down State Street and East College Avenue.

You'll notice this is a town focused on education. Illinois College was established in 1829 in part by Harriet Beecher Stowe's brother, Edward Beecher, who was the college's first president. (The college was considered a center for abolitionism.) On the east side of town is MacMurray College, founded in 1846 as the Illinois Conference Female Academy. But wait, there's more: The Illinois School for the Deaf, Illinois School for the Visually Impaired, and Jacksonville Mental Health and Developmental Center were all built here. During the Civil War, Ulysses S. Grant and his Illinois division of troops camped in an area of Jacksonville that is now part of the Morgan County Fairgrounds. And William Jennings Bryan and Stephen Douglas practiced law here.

SIGHTS
Underground Railroad

The town of Jacksonville was a stop along the Underground Railroad for many blacks escaping from the South. Several families in the area provided shelter, food, and other necessities for escaped slaves as they made their way north from the 1830s through the Civil War. You can drive by or tour the inside of some of these homes. Perhaps the best Underground Railroad site is the Woodlawn Farm, east of town, recently purchased by the Morgan County Historical Society. It plans to convert it to a living-history museum and now hosts tours and events throughout the year. You can also drive by other homes in the area said to have been stops along the railroad, including the Talcott Home (859 Grove St., Jacksonville); the Gillett Home (1005 Grove St., Jacksonville); and the Clay

Home (1019 W. State St., Jacksonville). For a tour, contact the Morgan County Historical Society's Underground Railroad Committee (217/243-3755, www.woodlawnfarm.com) or the Jacksonville Area Convention and Visitors Bureau (see *Information*).

Community Park
In the northeast corner of Jacksonville's Community Park (U.S. 67/Main St. and Morton Ave.) is Big Eli No. 17, the 17th Ferris wheel built by the Eli Bridge Company, in 1907. The company is credited with building the first portable Ferris wheel in 1900, which made its debut in Jacksonville. The original Ferris wheel, introduced to the world at the World's Fair in Chicago in 1893, was much, much larger, at 264 feet tall; W. E. Sullivan wanted to scale it down. Townspeople moved the wheel to the park in the late 1950s. Eli Bridge is still in the business of building wheels and other carnival rides. Ever taken a spin on the Scrambler? That's an Eli Bridge Company invention.

In addition to the wheel, in the middle of the park you'll find two ornate Victorian-style bandstands that are more than 130 years old. Nearby are a few picnic benches if you want to take a break.

Art Gallery
Donated to the city's arts association, this stately brick mansion houses the **David Strawn Art Gallery** (331 W. College Ave., Jacksonville, 217/243-9390, www.strawnartgallery.org, Sept.–May). It showcases local and nationally known artists, plus a permanent collection of antique dolls and Native American pottery.

ACCOMMODATIONS
Basically, if you're going to stay in Jacksonville, you're going to stay in a chain hotel near I-72 and U.S. 67. Your best bet is the 72-room **Comfort Inn** (200 Comfort Dr., South Jacksonville, 217/245-8372, $90–150) or the 41-room **Super 8** (1003 W. Morton Ave., Jacksonville, 217/479-0303, $56), which is on the west side of town.

© CHRISTINE DES GARENNES

Big Eli No. 17, a Ferris wheel built in 1907, in Jacksonville's Community Park

FOOD
American
Imagine an antique unicycle hanging on a brick wall, a vintage model airplane dangling from the ceiling, and photos of Elvis Presley. Throw in a few local ladies celebrating a birthday in the back and a couple of guys watching an Illini basketball game at the bar. That's the scene at (**Mugsy's** (230 Mauvaisterre, Jacksonville, 217/245-0641, 11 A.M.–9 P.M. Tues.–Thurs., 11 A.M.–10 P.M. Fri.–Sat.), a cozy restaurant just off Jacksonville's town square. From outside, the place looks a little fancy, but inside it's casual and upbeat. The food is comforting, with beer cheese soup, pub pickles (breaded and fried pickle spears), and entrées such as blackened chicken, catfish fillet, and the favorite horseshoe sandwich. Prices range from about $7 for sandwiches to $10–20 for entrées. Mugsy's has a little patio out back.

Quick Bites
At the **Classic Diner** (100 Comfort Dr., South Jacksonville, 217/243-9962, 6 A.M.–10 P.M.

daily) you can fill up on steak and egg combos, omelets, biscuits and gravy, and pigs in a blanket (sausage links rolled up in pancakes). Mmm. The restaurant is right on U.S. 67, just north of I-72. It's not a bona fide diner, but it certainly looks like one with shiny red, white, and black decor and images from *Life* magazine circa 1950. It also serves lunch and dinner.

Popular among truckers, **CR's Drive In** (403 E. Morton Ave., Jacksonville, 217/243-2100, call for hours, $5) has burgers for about $3, horseshoe sandwiches, chili dogs, and apple pie. Walk up or drive up to place your order.

Café

The **Three-Legged Dog Café** (27 S. Central Park Plaza, Jacksonville, 217/243-4769, 7:30 A.M.–7 P.M. Mon.–Tues., 7:30 A.M.–9 P.M. Wed.–Thurs. and Sat., 7:30 A.M.–10 P.M. Fri., 8 A.M.–1 P.M. Sun., $3–7) on Jacksonville's square is housed in a two-story building filled with vintage wooden booths, tables, and an ornate wooden bar salvaged from an old confectionery. Espresso drinks plus teas, beer, and wine are available here along with a small selection of sandwiches and salads.

INFORMATION

The **Jacksonville Area Convention and Visitors Bureau** (155 W. Morton St., Jacksonville, 217/243-5678 or 800/593-5678, www.jacksonvilleil.org) is in Community Park. It's open Monday–Friday, but if you visit on a weekend, a sign outside has a map of Jacksonville with all the major sights highlighted on it.

PITTSFIELD
Accommodations and Food

Red Dome Inn and Wine Nook (109 N. Madison St., Pittsfield, 217/285-6502) is in a renovated former department store building that dates to the 1880s. With restored tin ceilings and gleaming original woodwork, it's a beautiful place to dine, something you would expect to see in Springfield, not Pittsfield, a town of about 4,500. Food is primarily American and varies from the inexpensive $3 roast beef sandwich to

a $17 prime rib dinner. The Domeburger special consists of two four-ounce hamburger patties on a bun with potatoes. Try the onion rings; they're hand-cut and batter-fried. Adjacent to the restaurant is the Wine Nook, which stocks about 70 different kinds of wine, from Illinois wines (such as Collver Winery in Barry) to those from Chile and France.

Typically, small towns in Illinois have two lodging options for travelers: little bed-and-breakfasts in homes, or older motel rooms off Main Street. Open since 2004, **Monroe Street Suites** (221 S. Monroe St., Pittsfield, 217/285-6129, $50–60) is a real find. Rooms are immaculate and originally designed (each is different), similar to those in a bed-and-breakfast. However, the six rooms are in a renovated engraving building a few blocks from the courthouse square. It's not exactly a motel and not exactly a bed-and-breakfast (there is no breakfast). But the rooms are comfortable and decorated in a lightly African theme with muted browns, maroons, tans, and yellows. Guests have use of lockers outside in the rear of the building if they come bearing fishing or hunting gear.

Harpole's Heartland Lodge

Harpole's Heartland Lodge (rural Nebo, 217/734-2526 or 800/717-4868, www.heartlandlodge.com, Jan.–Sept.), south of Pittsfield, is, if you can imagine it, a bed-and-breakfast, hunting lodge, horseback-riding farm, and all-around country retreat. The whole place has an Up North atmosphere and attitude. It's laid-back, and people are friendly and ruddy—probably because everyone here is busy enjoying the outdoors, whether it's setting off on a guided trip to hunt for waterfowl, upland game, or deer; horseback riding; riding all-terrain vehicles; mountain biking; or in the winter, cross-country skiing. You don't have to stay at the lodge to take a horseback ride here. Rent a horse by the hour and take off on some of the trails (there are about 40 miles of horseback-riding trails to explore). But do think about staying here. The main lodge has several rooms with twin beds and bathrooms, plus several more luxury suites tailored to couples. These come with things such as fireplaces, decks, whirlpool tubs, and four-poster beds made of rustic pine. An overnight package typically includes dinner, a hayride, bonfire, and brunch.

Room rates range $130–260 with meals, $65–168 without meals. If you stay Sunday–Thursday, deduct $10 per night. Mountain bikes rent for $7 per hour; ATVs are $35 per hour; and horseback rides are $25 per hour. Hayrides are free. Fishing and hunting fees vary. If you have your own horse, you can board it here.

GRIGGSVILLE

In the center of Griggsville, a small town just off I-72, towers the 40-foot-tall "Empire State Building of the Bird World," a complex of about 600 different compartments that house up to 1,200 purple martins. Residents of Griggsville, the Purple Martin Capital of the World, just love these mosquito-eating birds. They've erected birdhouses all along Quincy Street (otherwise known as Purple Martin Boulevard), and just about everyone has a purple martin house in the front or back yard. Visit Griggsville April–August and you're bound to see these little birds all over the place.

Back in the 1960s, the purple martin, a member of the swallow family, was nearing the endangered species list. Birders got together and started building and buying shelters for

purple martin sanctuary, Griggsville

© CHRISTINE DES GARENNES

these little guys. (The males are deep blue and black with forked tails, and their heads and the tops of their wings have a purple iridescence to them. The females are light-bellied.) One of the largest manufacturers of purple martin homes is in Griggsville. At the **Nature House Showroom and Store** (Hwy. 107, Griggsville, 217/833-2323, 8 A.M.–5 P.M. Mon.–Fri.) you can buy your very own purple martin house.

Nauvoo

Standing near the gardens in front of the re-built Mormon Temple, you'll soon realize why Joseph Smith and his Mormon followers chose this area as their home in 1839. At a bend on the east bank of the Mississippi River, the historic town of Nauvoo sits on a bluff looking out over the river and the valley. It's a beautiful sight, and perhaps that's why Smith christened the town Nauvoo, which may or may not mean beautiful place in Hebrew (the topic is

subject to debate). The Joseph Smith Historic Site, where Smith's home along with a dozen or so other historic homes are situated, is in the lower part of the town, closer to the river. The downtown commercial area with shops, restaurants, and lodging options is up on the hill near the temple. Although it's certainly rich in Mormon history, Nauvoo also has a past linked to wine-making and cheese-making. After you visit the Mormon temple and other sights, be sure to drive east of town to Baxter's Vineyards and Winery. One way to see Nauvoo is to take a horse-drawn carriage ride.

HISTORY

Nauvoo was actually a Native American village before Joseph Smith and his family and followers arrived in 1839. Between 1839 and 1846 the Mormons built more than 2,000 homes here, and Nauvoo became the center for the church. They started building a temple in 1841 and established the Nauvoo Legion, a state militia. Nauvoo grew into quite a thriving town, eventually attracting the attention of other Illinois towns as well as politicians. At the helm of this prosperous city was Smith, who acted as mayor, lieutenant general of the legion, justice of the peace, and several other local leadership positions.

Eventually some members grew dissatisfied, and they started publishing a newspaper that was critical of Smith. The city council, under the direction of Smith, of course, called the publication a nuisance and ordered the press be demolished. Not surprisingly, the publishers filed a complaint against Smith and other members of the city council, including Smith's brother Hyrum. Smith and the others traveled to Carthage, the county seat several miles east of Nauvoo, to respond to the claims filed against them in which the publishers stated Smith violated their Constitutional right of freedom of the press. Some of the accused posted bail and simply went home. Smith stayed at the jail to wait and talk to the governor about the situation. Later he and the others were charged with treason and inciting a riot. On June 27, 1844, a group of men came to the jail and shot and killed Smith and his brother Hyrum. With their leader dead, many Mormons eventually left in the year or two that followed. Most went to Utah; some headed to Texas and Michigan. A few stayed.

Hearing that the town was nearly empty, a Frenchman named Etienne Cabet decided to establish his own colony here. He and his followers, called Icarians, settled here in 1849. The colonists, mostly French and German immigrants, found the sunny hills were well suited to grape-growing, and they introduced wine-making into the region. But communal living didn't suit the residents, and the colony disbanded a few years after they arrived. Several decades after that, residents discovered the cellars that used to store wine bottles could also be used to age cheese, and Nauvoo became somewhat of a center for cheese-making.

SIGHTS
◖ Joseph Smith Historic Site

A good way to begin your visit in Nauvoo is by dropping by the Historic Nauvoo Visitors Center on the grounds of the Joseph Smith Historic Site (149 Water St., Nauvoo, 217/453-2246). Here staff will be able to tell you when the next guided walking tour of the sites begins. And while waiting for the next tour to start, you can view a few exhibits about the history of Nauvoo and the Mormons. The center has a 20-minute video that provides a good overview of the site, plus a few original Smith family pieces, including a washstand and a Nauvoo temple chair. Feel free to walk around the historic site yourself, but the walking tours are wonderfully narrated by members. They know their stuff and can talk endlessly about Smith and Nauvoo. On your walking tour, you'll visit the **Joseph Smith Homestead** and the mansion house he and his family moved into after the town began to prosper. The **mansion house** has its original pillars and stoop. The bedroom of Joseph and his wife, Emma, contains a bureau and mirror that belonged to them, plus a trunk with a secret compartment where Emma stored Joseph's translation of the Bible. After Joseph and his brother were killed in Carthage, their bodies were put on display in the mansion, and about 10,000 people came through to view them.

Next to the homestead is the **Smith Family Cemetery.** After the funeral the coffins were actually emptied, and the empty coffins were buried in a tomb near the temple. The bodies were secretly buried near the Nauvoo House, then reburied under a small building by the homestead house. Later, the construction on the **Nauvoo House** forced them to move the bodies. In 1928 the grandson of the Smiths hired a surveyor to find the graves, and they then moved the bodies a few feet and also buried Joseph's parents in the cemetery. They're expected to stay put near the homestead house.

Throughout the site are several other beautifully restored original brick buildings where the Mormons lived and worked: **Scovil Bakery, Lyon Drug Store, Stoddard Tin Shop,** the post office and dry goods store, a boot shop, and a gun shop. Inside these shops church members, dressed in period costumes, talk about the proprietors of the shops and explain how people used to make tin pans and candleholders, how boots were made, and so on. These stops are quite revealing not only about the early Mormons but about pioneer life in general. For example, people would write lengthwise and widthwise on the same side of a piece of paper to save money. The **Red Brick Store** is the only building that is a reconstruction of the original. You can barely tell. Here

you can buy journals, pens, candy, and other items. It's organized just as it was more than 150 years ago, based on an old ledger that detailed what was bought and sold here.

The sites are open 9 A.M.–5 P.M. Monday–Saturday, 1–5 P.M. Sunday May–October; 10 A.M.–4 P.M. Monday–Saturday November–December; 10 A.M.–4 P.M. Friday–Saturday January–February; 10 A.M.–4 P.M. Monday–Saturday, 1–4 P.M. Sunday March–April. Admission to the visitors center and the Red Brick Store is free; a guided tour costs $2.

Nauvoo Illinois Temple

In 1848, after the Mormons left town and had sold the temple, someone set the building on fire, and eventually it crumbled to the ground. About 150 years later the church decided to rebuild it, and the Nauvoo Illinois Temple (Mulholland and Wells Sts., Nauvoo, 217/453-6252, visitors center 9 A.M.–6 P.M. Mon.–Sat., 11 A.M.–5 P.M. Sun. May–Aug., 9 A.M.–5 P.M. Mon.–Sat., 12:30–5 P.M. Sun. Sept.–Apr., free) was dedicated in June 2002. This huge

Joseph Smith Historic Site

54,000-square-foot limestone building stands on the western edge of downtown Nauvoo looking west. On the site of the former temple, this temple is a working one. The church performs baptisms here and holds other church-related activities. You won't be able to tour the inside of the temple, but you can view a video and pictures of it in the visitors center. Only members of the church who receive a recommendation to visit can see the inner sanctum.

Nauvoo State Park

East of the Joseph Smith Historic Site and south of the downtown is the 150-acre Nauvoo State Park (Hwy. 96 and Parley St., Nauvoo, 217/453-2512, www.dnr.state.il.us). In the center is a brick home built by a Mormon family in the 1840s, later occupied by a French Icarian family. This building now houses the **Nauvoo State Park Museum,** which has exhibits about the area's wine-making past. In 1880 there were about 40 wine cellars and 600 acres of grapevines in the area. The oldest vine still around (it's a Concord grapevine) was planted in 1851, and it is just behind the house. It's still producing grapes. A tour of the house and environs includes a visit to a room where the Icarians pressed grapes and a cellar where wine was stored. You can see the exhibits and tour the home, including the wine cellar, 1–5 P.M. daily May–mid-October.

There is one trail about 1.5 miles in length through the park. Most of it follows the shoreline of Lake Horton, a 13-acre artificial lake. It's a quiet lake; only boats with electric trolling motors are allowed. You can fish from the shore for catfish, bass, and bluegill. The park also has a campground.

Held during Labor Day weekend, when the grapes are ripening, the **Nauvoo Grape Festival** (Nauvoo State Park, 217/453-6648, www.nauvoograpefestival.com) is a three-day event celebrating the region's wine heritage. The festival's main event is called the "Wedding of the Wine and Cheese," modeled after a traditional French pageant. As expected, there are wine tastings, a grape stomp, and plenty of food tents. Other activities include

Nauvoo Illinois Temple

© CHRISTINE DES GARENNES

a car show, a carnival, an arts and craft show, and the tradition of almost every Midwestern festival: pancake breakfasts.

Baxter's Vineyards and Winery

Less than a mile east of the state park on a bucolic country road are more vineyards. Baxter's Vineyards and Winery (2010 E. Parley St., Nauvoo, 217/453-2528 or 800/854-1396, www.nauvoowinery.com, 9 A.M.–5 P.M. Mon.–Sat., 10 A.M.–5 P.M. Sun.) is the oldest winery in Illinois. It was founded by Emile Baxter, who was part of the Icarian colony. He and his family remained in the area after the colony disbanded. Eventually his sons joined him in the wine-making business, and his descendents are still involved in the venture. Here they make wine and juice from Concord grapes, plus wines from several other grape varieties. They offer free tours and wine tastings and sell accessories such as wine racks, wine glasses, and wine-making supplies for people interested in starting a new hobby. They also sell homemade pies and other baked goods in the main winery building.

Weld House

To research archives about early Nauvoo, visit the **Weld House** (1380 Mulholland St., Nauvoo, 1–4 P.M. daily May–Oct.) run by the local historical society. Here you'll also find exhibits about Nauvoo in the 1800s and life along the Mississippi River.

ACCOMMODATIONS

In addition to the listings here, there are several homes in the area available for rent. To gather information on these, contact the Nauvoo Tourism Office (see *Information and Services*).

C Ellis Sanders (1285 Sidney St., Nauvoo, 888/253-2444, www.ellissandershouse.com, suites $139) is a circa-1844 red brick Federalist home on a hill above Nauvoo State Park and the Joseph Smith Historic Site. One of the owners' great-grandfathers was a Mormon who lived in Nauvoo before moving out West. The owners offer evening dessert served by candlelight and serve a four-course breakfast at 9 A.M., but you can have a continental breakfast earlier if you request it. Drinking alcohol is not permitted. There are two bedrooms available.

As the name implies, **Nauvoo Family Inn and Suites** (1875 Mulholland St./Hwy. 96, Nauvoo, 217/453-6527 or 800/416-4470, www.nauvoonet.com) is geared toward large families that travel, and you'll find plenty of extended families staying here while touring through Nauvoo. (If you want to avoid children, this is not the place to go.) It's a newer hotel with a faux historic facade that fits well with the brick Federalist-style architecture common in the area. The 136-room hotel has family suites that contain one, two, or three bedrooms. Rooms are big, and some contain extras such as minifridges and microwaves. The extralarge "Family 7" and "Family 12" units come with full-size refrigerators and kitchenettes if you're planning to stay in town for a long time or are with a group of seven or 12 people. During the summer rates can range from $70 for a room with a full bed to $170 for a three-bedroom, two-bathroom suite.

Built in 1841, the slate-blue **C Hotel Nauvoo** (1290 Mulholland St., Nauvoo, 217/453-2211, www.hotelnauvoo.com, $65–125) is considered a Mormon Prairie-style building. The front porch and second-story balcony overlook Nauvoo's main drag, Mulholland Street. The hotel has eight rooms, most of them with one queen bed. All come with private baths and are decorated with country touches such as quilts. The hotel is attached to a restaurant. A cottage on the site is also available for rent.

Just down the street is the **Motel Nauvoo** (1610 Mulholland St., Nauvoo, 217/453-2219), which has similar but cheaper accommodations on the lower end of this price category. It also has a mix of room styles, including one queen and two queens.

A few miles south of Nauvoo, the folks at **Sonora Farmstead Properties** (County Rd. 2100, Nauvoo, 309/221-7286, www.sonoragardens.com, from $89) have several different lodging options for guests. The Sonora Gardens Bed and Breakfast has rooms in a farmhouse (this is a real grain farm); the Town Hall is a separate restored building on the farmstead with a sleeping area, living area, and bathroom; and finally the Red Barn offers the most space for guests: In addition to the bedroom and living room, there's a full kitchen and laundry room. It's ideal for longer stays.

Camping

Nauvoo State Park has 150 sites for tent and RV camping. The best sites are those near the shore of Lake Horton. There's a small boat launch, picnic areas, playgrounds, and a 1.5-mile walking trail. Fees are $13–15 per night.

FOOD

There are several rooms where diners can eat at the **Hotel Nauvoo** (1290 Mulholland St., Nauvoo, 217/453-2211, www.hotelnauvoo.com, dinner Mon.–Sat., brunch Sun., $12), which is much like a big historic home. The dinner buffet, a popular option, features carved roast beef, catfish, steamed vegetables, muffins, and homemade bread. The buffet runs about $12 per person. Other options include sugar-glazed ham and fried shrimp. There is a small bar that serves wine, beer, and mixed drinks. Spirited hot and cold drinks are also a good way to finish a meal. The staff can whip up grasshoppers (crème de menthe and crème de cacao) or Irish coffees. The restaurant is closed in the winter.

Downtown Nauvoo is lined with several casual restaurants. Each serves standard American sandwiches such as turkey clubs and hamburger-and-french-fry meals for under $10. You can't go wrong with any of these for lunch spots: **Nauvoo Mill and Bakery** (1530 Mulholland St., Nauvoo, 217/453-6734, 8 A.M.–7 P.M. Mon.–Sat., 11 A.M.–5 P.M. Sun.); **Past Times** (1390 Mulholland St., 217/453-2050, 11 A.M.–9:30 P.M. daily); and **Grandpa John's Café** (1255 Mulholland St., Nauvoo, 217/453-2310 breakfast, lunch, dinner Mon.–Sat., brunch Sun.).

INFORMATION AND SERVICES
Visitor Information
The **Historic Nauvoo Visitor Center** on the grounds of the Joseph Smith Historic Site (Young and Hubbard Sts., Nauvoo, 888/453-6434, www.historicnauvoo.net, 9 A.M.–7 P.M. Mon.–Sat., 9:30 A.M.–6 P.M. Sun. mid-May–Aug., 9 A.M.–5 P.M. Mon.–Sat., 9:30 A.M.–5 P.M. Sun. Sept.–Apr.) is run by the Community of Christ, an offshoot of the Church of Jesus Christ of Latter-day Saints.

The **Nauvoo Temple Visitors Center** (on Wells St., between Mulholland and Young Sts., Nauvoo, 217/453-6844, 9 A.M.–6 P.M. Mon.–Sat., 10:30 A.M.–6 P.M. Sun. May–Aug., 9 A.M.–5 P.M. Mon.–Sat., 12:30–5 P.M. Sun. Sept.–Apr.) is run by the Church of Jesus Christ of Latter-day Saints.

In addition, the **Nauvoo Tourism Office** (1295 Mulholland St., Nauvoo, 877/628-8661, www.beautifulnauvoo.com) has comprehensive information about attractions, lodging, dining, and events.

Tours
When your feet get tired of walking through Old Nauvoo, take your pick from several guided tours. The oxen and wagon rides mimic the experience of following the Mormon Trail. They leave from the Main Street Historic Complex. The horse-drawn covered wagon rides, which leave from the Historic Nauvoo Visitors Center, take you past all the major sites in Old Nauvoo, including the Joseph Smith Homestead, the mansion, and all the little shops. Both wagon rides operate 9:30 A.M.–4:30 P.M. Monday–Saturday May–August and 10 A.M.–3 P.M. Monday–Saturday September–April. Carriage rides to Inspiration Point, which overlooks the Mississippi River, are also available from the visitors center. For more information about any of the tours, contact the Nauvoo Tourism Office (see *Information and Services*).

CARTHAGE
About 25 miles southeast of Nauvoo is the town of Carthage, a plain small town off U.S. 136. Visitors interested in learning more about the murder of Mormon founder Joseph Smith and his brother Hyrum can tour the **Carthage Jail** (Marion and Walnut Sts., Carthage, 217/357-2989, 9 A.M.–9 P.M. Mon.–Sat., 11 A.M.–6 P.M. Sun. summer, 9 A.M.–5 P.M. Mon.–Sat., 12:30–5 P.M. Sun. winter, free), where, after being charged with treason, they were gunned down by a group of men on June 27, 1844. A tour of the restored jail includes a visit to the room where Joseph was killed and a look at the bed, writing desk, and rocking chair that Joseph used during his stay in the jail. Outside the jail is a garden with a statue of the two brothers.

Quincy and Vicinity

Perched on bluffs above the Mississippi River, Quincy is a quintessential river town with a historic downtown and city square surrounded by tall brick and sandstone buildings and tree-lined residential neighborhoods with brick-lined streets. Originally a Sauk Indian village, Quincy was a boomtown in the 19th century after it became a decent-size port on the river. It attracted European immigrants and Americans from the Northeast, including abolitionists. In 1858 Lincoln and Douglas met in Quincy to debate the subject of slavery—quite the controversial topic because just on the other side of the river was Missouri, which allowed slavery. Today Quincy is a midsized town of about 40,000 people, a small liberal arts school, Quincy University, and a number of architecturally interesting sites, including a Moorish villa and grand Romanesque home, and a museum entirely devoted to river-town architecture.

SIGHTS
Museums

The **Gardner Museum of Architecture and Design** (332 Maine St., Quincy, 217/224-6873, www.gardnermuseumarchitecture.org) has been open since 1977, but the building itself, an awesome limestone Richardson Romanesque building, was built 1888–1889 and was home to the Quincy Public Library. The museum's focus is on the architecture and design characteristics of Mississippi River towns such as Quincy. Permanent exhibits highlight historic buildings that once stood or are still standing in Quincy, and there are useful displays that explain to novices the different types of building materials and styles. The library's former reading room is a must-see: The room, which has a vaulted ceiling more than 20 feet high, has a beautiful stained-glass exhibit showcasing glass pieces salvaged from churches long gone. Galleries are open 1–4 P.M.

view of the Mississippi River from Quincy

Wednesday–Sunday, and the store and library are open 9 A.M.–5 P.M. Monday–Friday.

Illinois Veterans Home and All Wars Museum (1701 N. 12th St., Quincy, 9 A.M.–noon, 1–4 P.M. Tues.–Sat., 1–4 P.M. Sun., donation) has thousands of military artifacts, including uniforms, medals, patches, and some artillery from as far back as the Civil War up to the current war in Iraq.

In a huge 1891 Romanesque stone mansion, the **Quincy Museum** (1601 Maine St., Quincy, 217/224-7669, www.thequincymuseum.com, 1–5 P.M. Tues.–Sun., $3) has several floors of local-history displays and exhibits for children, including a *Tyrannosaurus rex* and other dinosaur replicas and an Indian village. You'll also be able to tour some of the mansion's grand rooms, including the den and parlor, where you'll be able to glimpse some of the intricate woodwork and other details.

The Jesus Tree

You know how sometimes oak trees have protruding growths from their trunks? And they look like humps or giant tree warts? Well, a big old oak tree in the middle of a Quincy cemetery happens to have one of those growths, along with some discolored bark. It's known as the Jesus Tree or Apparition Tree (Calvary Cemetery, 1730 N. 18th St., Quincy, free). Some believe the image of Jesus Christ appears on the tree. If you step back and turn your head just so, and squint your eyes, it does look a little like a man with a beard in a robe. Unfortunately, as the years go by, the hump continues to grow, and as one resident put it, "It doesn't look so much so anymore since the growth has gotten bigger." The tree is in the middle of the cemetery; it's one of the biggest ones.

Parks

While they were both campaigning for the U.S. Senate, Abraham Lincoln and Stephen A. Douglas met in Quincy's **Washington Park** (bordered by 4th, 5th, Main, and Hampshire Sts.) on October 13, 1858, to debate slavery, among many other topics. A Lorado Taft sculpture marks the site.

An image of Jesus or a bump in an old tree?

© CHRISTINE DES GARENNES

Looking for a place to picnic? North of downtown Quincy in the Mississippi River is **Quinsippi Island** (Front and Cedar Streets). To get there you'll have to cross a one-lane plank bridge. The island has several picnic areas, a playground, and log cabins moved here from around Adams County.

Historic Homes

Villa Katherine (532 Gardner Expwy./3rd St., Quincy, 217/224-3688, by appointment) looks as if it would fit in Morocco, not Quincy. This majestic-looking estate is on a bluff overlooking the Mississippi. Quincy native George Metz built it in 1900 and based the design on places he had visited around the world.

The **John Wood Mansion** (425 S. 12th St., Quincy, 217/222-1835, 10 A.M.–2 P.M. Tues.–Sat. Apr.–Oct., $3) is a good example of a Greek-revival mansion, painted white and featuring several tall columns and a second-story balcony in the front. It was built for Quincy's founder, John Wood, who served several terms as the city's mayor.

While he was lieutenant governor, the governor died, and Wood acted as governor for 10 months in 1860. Wood did not seek the governorship after the term ran out; he chose to stay in Quincy. Also on the mansion grounds are an 1835 log cabin and a parsonage containing local-history exhibits.

ACCOMMODATIONS

The **C Althoff Motel** (3511 N. 24th St., Quincy, 217/228-2460, $45) is a medium-size brick motel in a suburban area north of town. It has an indoor pool and hot tub and offers continental breakfasts.

The location may not be so great (it's in a nondescript commercial corridor east of downtown), but the **C Stoney Creek Inn** (217/223-2255 or 800/659-2220, www.stoneycreekinn.com, $89 and up) has outstanding accommodations. With fieldstone and pine log accents throughout the building, the decor here is lodge style. The regional chain hotel has a variety of rooms, from the basic double to corporate suites with whirlpool tubs and family-style suites with bunk beds. The building has an exercise room and pool.

The **Days Inn** (200 Maine St., Quincy, 217/223-6610), a motor lodge, and the **Hampton Inn** (4th and York Sts., Quincy, 217/224-8378) are within walking distance of downtown Quincy and its shops and restaurants. Both overlook the Mississippi River. Rates vary but average around $85.

Several other bed-and-breakfasts and chain hotels are in and around Quincy. For a complete list, contact the Quincy Convention and Visitors Bureau (see *Information*).

FOOD
Quick Bites

The regional fast-food chain called **Maid Rite** (507 N. 12th St., Quincy, 217/222-9767, 11 A.M.–7:30 P.M. daily, $3) got its start in Quincy in 1928. A visit here is a bit like stepping back into the past. Employees still don hairnets and white paper hats, and the decor looks as if it hasn't been updated in a few decades. That's the, um, charm of this place, along with the ground-beef sandwiches and slew of cheap food options such as the fried-egg sandwich and the hot ham and cheese sandwich. Maid Rite is reportedly the country's second-oldest franchise.

Italian

The divine **C Tiramisu** (137 N. 3rd St., Quincy, 217/222-9560, www.tiramisuquincy.com, 11 A.M.–2 P.M. Mon.–Fri., 4:30–9:30 P.M. Mon.–Sat., $12), a white-tablecloth Italian restaurant, is in a vintage building near the riverfront. The staff do everything well here, from simple sautéed spinach salad to the pastas and entrées, such as the surprisingly fresh *spaghetti arlecchino,* which is spaghetti topped with shrimp, calamari, sea scallops, mussels, and clams and tossed with olive oil, garlic, and cherry tomatoes. Individual pizzas are available at lunchtime.

Mexican

In a small strip mall behind an auto parts store, **El Rancherito** (307 N. 36th St., Quincy, 217/228-2182, $8) may not be in a choice location, but that doesn't keep the locals from coming. The food here is billed as authentic Mexican, and it is delicious and served in hefty portions. Take your pick from fajitas, enchiladas, or burritos accompanied by fresh chips and salsa and "monster margaritas." Finally, top off the meal with a dish of deep-fried ice cream.

Chinese

The lunch and dinner buffets are popular choices at **China Palace** (1139 Broadway, Quincy, 217/224-5501, 11 A.M.–9 P.M. Sun.–Thurs., 11 A.M.–10 P.M. Fri.–Sat., $8), a semi-casual restaurant on the main strip leading to downtown Quincy. Chicken, pork, beef, and tofu dishes are available, including traditional meals such as General Tso's Chicken (chicken coated with water-chestnut flour and served with hot ginger sauce), pot stickers, and wontons.

INFORMATION

The **Quincy Convention and Visitors Bureau** (300 Civic Center Plaza, Quincy, 217/223-1000 or 800/987-4748, www.quincy-cvb.org) can help with any questions you have about lodging, dining, or recreational opportunities in and around Quincy.

Villa Katherine (532 Gardner Expwy./3rd St., Quincy) also serves as a **tourist information center.** You can pick up brochures and maps when the mansion is open. During all other times, you can park in the lot and walk to view the river from the bluff. There's a Great River Road way-finder sign with a map of the routes along the river.

The daily **Quincy Herald-Whig** newspaper (130 S. 5th St., Quincy, 217/223-5100 or 800/373-9444, www.whig.com) is available at most gas stations and grocery stores.

GETTING THERE AND AROUND
Air

Quincy Regional Airport (1645 Hwy. 104, Quincy, 217/885-3241, www.quincyregionalairport.com) has daily round-trip flights aboard Great Lakes Airlines to St. Louis Lambert International Airport.

Car

You can rent a car or truck from **Hertz** (217/885-3994) or **Budget** (217/224-7253) while in the Quincy region.

Train

The **Amtrak** Illinois Zephyr and Carl Sandburg trains travel between Quincy and Chicago daily. The station is at 30th Street and Wismann Lane in Quincy (800/872-7245, www.amtrak.com).

GOLDEN

Settled mainly by German immigrants, the rural town of Golden, about 30 miles northeast of Quincy, is home to an 1873 windmill once used by the town's residents to grind corn. At one time there were several mills operating in the area, but the **Prairie Mills Windmill** (902 Prairie Mills Rd., Golden, www.goldenwindmill.org, 1–4 P.M. Sat.–Sun. May–Oct., $3) is the only one that remains. It was operational until the 1920s. Inside is a local-history museum that contains information about the windmill, farm tools, and a gift shop.

BARRY

Near a cement factory and just off I-72, the **Collver Family Winery** (2 Rooster Wy., just off Hwy. 106, Barry, 217/335-3279, 10 A.M.–5 P.M. Mon.–Wed., noon–5:30 P.M. Sun.) may not be in the most scenic of spots, but the wine is pretty good. It's known for its sweet wines, such as the Red Rooster, which has hints of plum in it. It also makes a dry red, Ramaja, which has a black-cherry flavor. There's a shop with accessories such as glasses and wine-chilling bags, plus books on wine and cookbooks.

Alton, Grafton, and Vicinity

To be honest, the East St. Louis area is not very charming. Refineries, factories, and other industrial sites line the Mississippi River and most major highways. But hang in there; head northwest toward Alton, and beyond that Grafton, and you'll be pleasantly surprised. Along the towns' main streets (often lined with Victorian and Federalist architecture), you'll discover an ice cream shop here and an antiques shop there, followed by a historic hotel and small-scale wineries. The two-lane scenic Highway 100 connects Alton and Grafton with the Mississippi on one side and sandstone bluffs on the other. This is where the Mississippi River takes a turn to the east before going south again. And it's also where the Illinois River meets the Big Muddy.

Alton and Grafton are old river towns with colorful histories. French explorers Marquette and Jolliet landed here while exploring the region in the late 1600s. Lewis and Clark spent the winter of 1803–1804 south of Alton near Hartford before setting off on their journey westward. Their populations grew because of the steamboat traffic coming through here and as steel mills, glassmaking factories, and quarries kick-started their operations. In the years leading up to the Civil War, Alton drew national attention after an abolitionist was killed. Just across the river from the slave state of Missouri, Alton became a common stop on the Underground Railroad for slaves escaping to the North. In 1837 Elijah Lovejoy, publisher of an antislavery newspaper in Alton, was killed defending his press from a mob that had destroyed several other presses. Later, Lincoln and Douglas squared off in a debate about slavery in the town in 1858. And during the Civil War, Alton housed thousands of Confederate prisoners of war.

Alton is the larger of the two towns, with

downtown Alton

about 30,000 people. Grafton, which is lower and closer to the river, is the more touristy of the two. Motorcyclists and RVers often stop by for a fish sandwich and ice-cream cone, and then drive or walk through nearby Père Marquette State Park. The park, high in the hills above the river, is just north of Grafton. Book a room or campsite at this park, or at least visit for the Sunday brunch.

ORIENTATION

The main road through this region is Highway 100. It's part of the Great River Road, although this leg has been dubbed the Meeting of the Great Rivers Road because the Mississippi, Illinois, and Missouri converge near here. It's about 15 miles between Père Marquette and Alton, and you can travel between the two by way of Highway 100 or the Sam Vadalabene bike trail, which follows the Mississippi. Another option is to take Highway 3 north of Grafton to Godfrey and then enter Alton from the north. Around the Grafton area there are several ferries that shuttle cars and passengers between Illinois and Missouri. They include the **Grafton Ferry Company** (636/250-3103, www.graftonferry. com), which goes between Grafton and the St. Charles County Airport in Missouri; the **Winfield and Golden Eagle Ferries** (618/396-2447 or 618/396-2535, www.calhounferrycompany.com), which go to St. Charles County, Missouri; and the **Brussels Ferry** (618/786-3636), which connects Highway 100 between the Grafton and Père Marquette State Park area with the town of Brussels. St. Louis is just across the Mississippi and Missouri Rivers from Alton. That huge cable-stay bridge (part of U.S. 67) in Alton is called the Clark Bridge, and it's 4,000 feet long.

ALTON
Sights
LEWIS AND CLARK INTERPRETIVE CENTER

Before they launched their historic exploration of the West, Meriwether Lewis and William Clark camped out near the confluence of the Illinois and Missouri rivers, called Camp

Lewis and Clark Interpretive Center, near Alton

COURTESY OF THE TOURISM BUREAU OF SOUTHWEST ILLINOIS

River DuBois, to gather supplies, train men, and basically prepare for the trip. Before the bicentennial celebration of their journey got under way across the country, the state opened the Lewis and Clark Interpretive Center (New Poag Rd., just off Hwy. 3, Hartford, www. campdubois.com, 9 A.M.–5 P.M. Wed.–Sun., free), a few miles south of Alton. It's an impressive 14,000-square-foot center with museum exhibits and a reproduction of the camp, complete with a wooden stockade. The most impressive item in the museum is a 55-foot keelboat replica, designed to resemble the original one used on the trip. Other exhibits explain what the men and their team did while in Illinois, plus highlights from the trip. Reproductions of their journals and the drawings in them are included throughout the museum as well as highlights about the tools they used and the maps they brought with them. The exhibits don't just discuss what they saw and did; they discuss the significance of the West and what it meant to the country that Lewis and Clark went to check it all out. In addition to the museum, gift shop, bookstore, and stockade, the site has some walking trails through woods and prairie.

NATIONAL GREAT RIVERS MUSEUM

What's the story behind the Mississippi River? How did it evolve into one of the most important rivers, if not the most important river, in the country? At the National Great Rivers Museum (at the Melvin Price Lock and Dam 26 off Hwy. 143, East Alton, 877/462-6979, 9 A.M.–5 P.M. daily, free), run by the Army Corps of Engineers, visitors learn about the river's natural history and the river's connection to the development of the country. The new 12,000-square-foot museum and Illinois Esplanade, an adjacent park, are right on the river and offer great barge-watching opportunities. It's also got some hands-on kid-friendly exhibits, such as the simulation of driving a boat through the locks. Tours of the lock and dam are given at 10 A.M., 1 P.M., and 3 P.M. daily.

MONUMENTS AND HISTORICAL MARKERS

A monument to newspaper publisher **Elijah Lovejoy** is on Monument Avenue in the Alton Cemetery, north of Broadway. One of the presses dug up from the river is on display at the offices of *The Telegraph*, 111 East Broadway, Alton.

In October 1858, while campaigning for the U.S. Senate, politicians and orators Lincoln and Douglas met in front of Alton's city hall (no longer standing) to debate current issues, including slavery. Two bronze statues of the men are at what is now called **Lincoln-Douglas Square** at Broadway and Market Street in Alton.

During the Civil War a closed prison in Alton was reopened to house prisoners of war from the Confederacy. During the war years about 11,000 soldiers passed through the prison. More than 1,000 of them died because of a smallpox outbreak, malnutrition, and other diseases. The long-gone Confederate prison near the riverfront was at Broadway and Williams Street in Alton, and a monument stands on Rozier Street where prisoners were buried (go north from town on State Street; it's south of Highway 3).

When Alton native **Robert Wadlow** died in 1940 at age 22, he measured eight feet 11.1 inches tall. Wadlow, who earned the nickname "the gentle giant" for his demeanor, was the tallest man in the world. A life-size statue of him is on College Avenue (Highway 140) above the river.

With a painted human face, long sharp teeth, scales like a fish, and horns like a deer, the mythical **Piasa Bird** was a mysterious creature from Native American lore. Hundreds and hundreds of years ago the image of this frightening-looking bird-man-animal was carved high on the side of a cliff. Jolliet and Marquette wrote about it during their journey down the river in the 1670s. A re-creation of that image has been painted on a rock face, closer to drivers' eye level, between Alton and Grafton. It's on the east side of Great River Road (Highway 100) at Piasa Park.

Biking

Piasa Park is a good spot to park your car if you're planning on biking along the Great River Road. The 15-mile-long **Sam Vadalabene Bicycle Trail** connects Alton and the gorgeous Père Marquette State Park in Grafton to the north. It's just about as close to the Mississippi River as you can get. The park is just north of State Street in Alton, east of Highway 100.

Gambling

Argosy's Alton Belle Casino (Alton riverfront, 800/711-4263, www.argosy.com, 8 A.M.–6 A.M. daily) is a gambling and restaurant complex near the Clark Bridge on Alton's riverfront. Inside are a variety of table games and about 1,000 slot machines, several restaurants, and a stage where national touring musical acts often perform.

Accommodations

The ◖ **Beall Mansion** (407 E. 12th St., Alton, 866/843-2325, www.beallmansion.com, $119–269) is a renovated 1903 home in one of Alton's historic turn-of-the-20th-century residential neighborhoods. There are five guest rooms (four rooms, one suite) available, each outfitted with private bathrooms, feather beds, and other comforts. The mansion offers a lot of extras here, such as in-room massages, robes, and nightly turn-down service. Choose to have breakfast in bed or in the dining room.

Other options in town include the **Comfort Inn** (11 Cross Roads Ct., Alton, 618/465-9999, $95–120); **Holiday Inn** (3800 Homer M. Adams Pkwy., Alton, 618/462-1220, $95–145); and **Super 8** (1800 Homer M. Adams Pkwy., Alton, 618/465-8858, $56).

Food

The menu changes often at **The Cane Bottom/ My Just Desserts** (31 E. Broadway, Alton, 618/462-5881, 11 A.M.–3 P.M. daily, $6), a popular lunch and dessert place in downtown Alton, but basically you can expect sandwiches such as chicken salad and roast beef and an array of desserts. Don't even think about leaving without slicing your fork into a divine piece of pie or buying one whole and taking it home for later. Two favorites: blackberry cobbler and caramel apple.

The friendly **Italia Bakehouse** (104 W. 3rd St., Alton, 618/462-8384, lunch Mon.–Sat., $7) serves hearty sandwiches with sides such as slaw, chips, or pasta. Options include meatball sandwiches, hot ham and cheese, or hand-breaded grouper fillets. You can also get pizza here.

Fried tacos are the specialty at **Morales Tacos** (121 W. 3rd St., Alton, 618/465-6033, lunch and dinner daily, $8), a sit-down Mexican restaurant that also serves heaping plates full of nachos, tostadas, and giant burritos.

MARKET

Local vendors pitch tents and tables to sell fruit, vegetables, and arts and crafts at Alton's **Farmers and Artisans Market** held 8 A.M.–noon Saturdays June–October in the parking lot off 3rd Street in downtown Alton.

Information and Services
VISITOR INFORMATION

The Tourism Bureau Southwest Illinois (10950 Lincoln Tr., Fairview Heights, 618/397-1488, www.thetourismbureau.org) publishes brochures on attractions, lodging, and dining information for the Metro East Louis region.

Alton Regional Convention and Visitors Bureau (618/465-6676 or 800/258-6645, www.visitalton.com, 8:30 A.M.–5 P.M. Mon.–Fri., 9 A.M.–3 P.M. Sat.–Sun.) operates a visitors center at 200 Piasa Street, between downtown and the riverfront.

TOURS

The site of a former Confederate prison, a stop along the Underground Railroad, and an all-around old river town, perhaps it's not surprising that Alton has been called one of the most haunted small cities in the country. Two groups have organized evening tours of the city's more notoriously haunted places, such as a church and a cemetery. Choose from **Antoinette's Alton Haunted History Tours** (618/462-4009, www.haunteddalton.com) or **History and Hauntings Tours of Alton** (618/465-1086, www.altonhauntings.com).

Getting There and Around
AIRPORT

St. Louis Lambert International Airport (1071 Lambert International Blvd., St. Louis, Missouri, www.lambert-st.louis.com) is just across the river from Alton. Just follow U.S. 67 south to I-270. All the major airlines fly in and out of Lambert.

TRAIN

Several **Amtrak** (3400 College Ave., Alton, 618/462-1879 or 800/872-7245, www.amtrak.com) train lines stop in Alton daily, including the Texas Eagle, which goes to San Antonio, Texas, and Los Angeles; the Lincoln Service between St. Louis and Chicago; and the Ann Rutledge between Chicago and Kansas City.

Metrolink (618/271-2345, www.metrostlouis.org) is the St. Louis regional light-rail line that stops daily in some Illinois towns, such as East St. Louis, Fairview Heights, and Belleville.

CAR

You can rent a car from **Enterprise** (590 Lewis and Clark Blvd., East Alton, 618/254-0638) or **Premier Auto Rental** (18 Terminal Dr., East Alton, 618/259-3230).

GRAFTON

With a string of antiques shops on Main Street, two wineries, a kitschy fish restaurant, and a magnificent state park, Grafton has become quite the weekend destination for area residents and people driving along the Great River Road.

Père Marquette State Park

Next to Starved Rock, Père Marquette State Park (Hwy. 100, Grafton, 618/786-3323, www.dnr.state.il.us) is one of the most popular parks in Illinois. You can't get a better location. The 8,000-acre park is on a bluff overlooking the Illinois and Mississippi Rivers just north of the Great River Road. It's hard to pinpoint the park's best feature. It could be the 12 miles of hiking trails, many of which offer awesome views of the river valley. Or is it the scenic drive through the park's wooded hills and even more scenic overlooks, which are perfect for watching eagles swoop to catch fish? Instead of hiking, you can explore the park by horseback. Rides are offered April–October and by appointment November–April. For more information contact Père Marquette Riding Stables at 618/786-2156.

One of the stars of the park is the stone- and slate-colored timber lodge built by the Civilian Conservation Corps in the 1930s. Inside are a 50-foot-high stone fireplace and 50 guest rooms. Nearby are 22 stone cabins. Before you hit the trails or head to the lodge, stop by the park's visitors center, which contains a 300-gallon aquarium. Here you can pick up trail maps, learn about the park's natural history, and take a look at the calendar of events. A popular spot for watching bald eagles, Père Marquette hosts **Bald Eagle Days** in December and January, when park interpreters lead people on eagle-watching expeditions. Père Marquette's campground has sites for tents and electric hookup

sites for RVers. You can rent tents and tent equipment at the park.

Biking, Canoeing, and Birding

You've seen the Illinois and Mississippi rivers from the car window. Now park that car and get a little closer to the waterways. **Grafton Canoe and Kayak Rentals** (618/786-2192 or 618/786-3632, www.graftonoutdooractivities.com, sunrise–sunset daily) rents personal watercraft, water-skiing boats, pontoon boats, kayaks, and bicycles. Take your pick. You can also rent canoes, kayaks, and bicycles from **Riverside Recreation** (618/786-2455). If you plan to bicycle, one popular route is the approximately 15-mile-long **Sam Vadalabene Bicycle Trail** between Père Marquette State Park and Alton. As far as kayaking goes, just north of Grafton is where the two rivers meet, and there are several backwater lakes.

If you're looking for solitude, continue west on the Great River Road, Highway 100, and take the Brussels ferry across the Illinois River. From there follow the signs to the **Two Rivers National Wildlife Refuge** (618/883-2524, www.fws.gov/midwest/tworivers). Within the refuges are thousands of acres of wetlands, home to bald eagles, ducks, geese, shorebirds, and other birds migrating along the Mississippi River Flyway. A good time to see migrating birds here is either October–November or March–April. You can pick up maps at the refuge headquarters.

Water Park

Since water in the Mississippi and Illinois Rivers is not exactly crystal clear, a good place to cool off and wash off that road-trip grime is the newer **Raging Rivers** (100 Palisades Pkwy., just off the Great River Road, Grafton, 618/786-2345, www.ragingrivers.com, call for hours, Memorial Day–Labor Day, $19.50). The water park has a wave pool, lazy river, body slides, and other devices to cool you off in the summer.

Wineries and Farm Visit

At the **Piasa Winery** (211 W. Main St.,

THE RETURN OF THE BALD EAGLE

Illinois is somewhat of a magnet for bird-watchers, particularly people who enjoy watching birds of prey in action. Why? The Mississippi River borders the western part of the state, meaning Illinois is part of the Mississippi River Flyway. It's like I-95 on the Eastern Seaboard when residents of New York, Pennsylvania, and elsewhere head south to Florida for the winter and return in the spring. Well, eagles, ducks, snow geese, and many other birds travel along the Mississippi River during the fall and spring migrations. Some of the birds are headed south to the Gulf of Mexico or beyond. Others, such as the eagles, come down from the north and settle in Illinois for several months before heading back north when the weather warms.

For decades, bald-eagle sightings along the Mississippi River and its tributaries such as the Illinois River were rare. Thanks to hunting, pesticides such as DDT, and other chemicals, populations took a nosedive. Bald eagles were placed on the endangered species list, but they're making a comeback. Today you can visit parks such as Père Marquette State Park in Grafton in the winter, stake out a

spot with a view of the river, and chances are you won't have to sit long before seeing an eagle. Bald eagles tend to show up in Illinois beginning in November and will stay through late March. The peak eagle-watching time is January and February. They roost in groups, with giant nests (as big as 10 feet in diameter) high in trees. Eagles, which can weigh up to 14 pounds, have wingspans of up to almost eight feet. They're birds of prey. They hunt fish, which is why they stick to the river shores, although they will pluck up small animals to eat too.

A few choice eagle-watching spots are the Chautauqua and Meredosia national wildlife refuges south of Peoria on the Illinois River, Mississippi Palisades State Park in Savanna, Starved Rock State Park in Utica, and Père Marquette State Park in Grafton. Several towns and state parks host bald eagle-watching events in January in February, including Meredosia, Père Marquette, and Starved Rock. If you don't spot an eagle on your visit, maybe you'll be able to see other birds that frequent the river and its backwaters, such as the great blue heron.

Grafton, 618/786-9463, www.piasawinery.com, 11 A.M.–6 P.M. Mon.–Thurs., 11 A.M.–9 P.M. Fri.–Sat., noon–7 P.M. Sun.) you can sip wine while sitting at a table outdoors with the Mississippi River in front of you. The winery, housed in a stone cottage along the Great River Road, features sweet whites to dry reds, sausages, cheese, other goodies, and wine accessories. The newest addition to the winery is the adjacent Piasa Pub, an English-style pub with imported beers and sandwiches.

Up the hill from the Piasa Winery is the newer **Aerie's Riverview Winery** (Grafton, 618/786-8439, www.aerieswinery.com, 1–9 P.M. Mon.–Thurs., noon–midnight Fri.–Sat., noon–9 P.M. Sun.), another scenic spot to drink Illinois wines. Munch on cheese and crackers and order a glass while sitting on a deck above the river. To get to the winery

follow Mulberry Street north from Main Street in Grafton.

Traveling with kids? They'll love **Eckert's Farm** (20995 Eckert Orchard Rd., Grafton, 618/786-3445, 9 A.M.–6 P.M. daily July–Oct.). The Eckerts grow and sell peaches, apples, and pumpkins, but in recent years the place has become much more than a farm and evolved into a place where you can spend hours letting the kids run around. There are a petting zoo, a miniature golf course, and an outdoor concert venue. They've even added a few inflatable rides for the kids. To get to the farm, from Grafton drive north of Highway 3 and then west on Otterville Road and look for the signs.

Accommodations

If you want to be within walking distance of the river, Grafton's antiques markets, and the handful of restaurants on Main Street, book a room at the (**Ruebel Hotel** (Main St., Grafton, 618/786-2315, www.ruebelhotel .com, $60–200), a historic 22-room hotel. The original 1884 hotel and restaurant, which served steamboat traffic, was damaged by a fire. It was later rebuilt after the turn of the 20th century and then remodeled in the late 1990s by the current set of owners. Accommodations include 22 standard hotel rooms above the restaurant, plus cottages and lodge rooms on a hillside above town. The bar and restaurant, or "saloon" as the owners call it, also serves walleye, catfish, and buffalo-fish platters. Food is available 11–9 P.M. daily, although the bar is open later. In front of the hotel you can catch a 15-minute horse-drawn stagecoach ride through Grafton. The cost is $4 per person.

For awesome views of the Mississippi and Illinois Rivers, consider staying at **Tara Point Inn** (Tara Point Dr., Grafton, 618/786-3555, www.tarapoint.com, $168–216), located among the bluffs above Grafton. You can stay in one of the rooms in the main house, but if you're looking for more of a private getaway, stay in one of the cottages also on the property. Each one has a private deck looking out across the river valley, and they all come with a bedroom, bathroom, and living room.

The (**Père Marquette State Park Lodge** (618/786-2331, $88–113 including tax), also located among the bluffs, has 50 guest rooms plus an indoor pool and dining room. The park also rents 22 stone cottages. Advice: book way in advance. The cottages and lodge rooms go fast, especially during the winter Bald Eagle Days and during the summer months. Camping is also available here.

Food and Drink

Fish, fish, and more fish. The **Fin Inn** (100 W. Main St., Grafton, 618/786-2030, www. fininn.com, 11 A.M.–9 P.M. daily summer, 11 A.M.–8 P.M. daily winter, $7) batters and fries up catfish, buffalo fish, grouper, and other kinds of fish in a kitschy restaurant and gift shop north of the Great River Road. The decor

may be dated, but it's a fun place. Two dozen booths have aquariums right next to them in the wall. The aquariums, which contain a total of about 8,000 gallons of water, are stocked with common Mississippi River fish, turtles, and other critters. The menu also lists items such as hamburgers, hot dogs, shrimp, and frogs' legs.

If you want a fish sandwich to go, drop by **O'Jan's Fish Stand** (101 W. Main St., Grafton, 618/786-2229).

Another quick spot is **Grafton Ice Cream Company** (224 E. Main St., Grafton, 618/786-2663) where you can order a hand-dipped ice cream cone.

Beyond the Bubble (301 E. Main St., Grafton, 618/786-2758, Thurs.–Sun.) has iced coffee and tea drinks, plus salads, muffins, and other yummy light bites.

Tours

Peer up at the bluffs or out across the great Mississippi River onboard the Heron, run by **Great Rivers Tour Boat Company** (Grafton Marina, 215 W. Water St., Grafton, 618/786-1855 or 866/976-2628, www.greatrivers tourboat.com). The company runs 1.5-hour sightseeing cruises, evening cruises with appetizers, and sunset cruises. Some are narrated, others are not. All routes are along the Illinois and Mississippi Rivers. Cruises cost $25–35 and run Memorial Day–October.

KAMPSVILLE

This region's history goes way back beyond the French traders and the pioneers, and there's an excellent center where you can learn about that history.

The **Center for American Archeology** (in the Kamp General Store building, Hwy. 100, downtown Kampsville, 618/653-4316, www. caa-archeology.org, 10 A.M.–5 P.M. Tues.–Fri., 10 A.M.–4 P.M. Sat., noon–4 P.M. Sun., free) may be a bit off the beaten track (it's about an hour's drive from any interstate highway), but it is a gem and well worth the ride for students of history. The center dates to the 1950s. Since then, archaeology students from the University of New Mexico and Northwestern University have spent their summers digging, researching, and learning about the people who lived in this part of the state several thousand years ago.

Inside a former general store (a building listed on the National Register of Historic Places and beautifully renovated), the center consists of a museum about Native American culture, a museum store, and a clearinghouse of sorts for several archaeology workshops. Staff conduct a variety of workshops, from one-day to four-week programs, such as a "Family Dig It Weekend," when parents and children visit excavation sites and learn about prehistoric culture, crafts, and more. If you don't participate in a dig, a visit to the museum is still worth it. Exhibits illustrate the history of this region (where the Illinois and Mississippi Rivers meet), which the center refers to as "the Nile of North America," as well as the people who inhabited this land thousands of years ago.

Need a ride across the Illinois River? The free **Kampsville Ferry,** which operates 24 hours a day, weather permitting, shuttles cars to and from Highway 108 in Calhoun County on the east side of the river with Highway 96/100 at Kampsville on the west side.

American Bottoms: Cahokia to Chester

You never know what you'll stumble upon in the region east and south of East St. Louis. At one intersection you may see a sign advertising a winery. On another corner you'll see a sign pointing to the local taxidermy shop. It's a diverse area, rural and industrial, home to the historic Cahokia Mounds, an ancient Native American Indian village, a French-Catholic church built by missionaries in 1699, and iconic roadside architecture such as the Brooks Catsup Bottle. Towns close to St. Louis such as Collinsville, which is about 14 miles from the city, are busy commercial towns with middle-class residents. South of Belleville, the countryside is dotted with horse stables and livestock farms.

This is where Illinois began: in settlements along the low-lying Mississippi River floodplains. Called the American Bottoms, this region has rich, rich soil and a past that goes back thousands of years. Before the industrialists opened refineries and factories, before the American colonists took control of the area from the British, before the French fur traders and missionaries established outposts, and even before a mound-building culture built a great city near present-day Collinsville, this area attracted travelers. On a quiet highway south of Prairie du Rocher is an indentation of sorts in the side of a rock cliff. It's called the Modoc Shelter, and archaeologists have determined that humans sought shelter there as far back as 9,000 years ago. Perhaps the people were on a hunt and following the buffalo. Perhaps they were merely stopping by on a journey elsewhere.

COLLINSVILLE AND CAHOKIA
(Cahokia Mounds
Even if it's a hot summer day, tough it out. Grab a water bottle and climb to the top of Monks Mound, a 100-foot-tall earthen mound east of the Mississippi River. Atop the mound you'll be able to see dozens of mounds rising from the land and imagine a Native American village that thrived about A.D. 700–1400. The Cahokia Mounds (Collinsville Rd. and Ramey St., Collinsville, 618/346-5160, www.cahokiamounds.com, donation), are an impressive sight. As you can imagine, the landscape has changed drastically since Cahokia was inhabited by Native American tribes. You can still find cornfields in this fertile area, but the residential and commercial districts directly surrounding the mounds are not exactly picturesque. It's not uncommon to drive past pawn shops and empty storefronts. Nevertheless, this is one of the rarest finds in North America, and

© CHRISTINE DES GARENNES

Monks Mound in Cahokia, home to a thriving city in A.D. 1100

well worth a visit. You might want to start your visit at the visitors center, on the south side of Collinsville Road. Monks Mound is on the north side of the road, across from the center. Woodhenge, a calendar made of wooden posts thought to have been built between A.D. 900 and 1100, is just west of Monks Mound, also on the north side of the road. Walking trails are accessible from the visitors center and wind past several smaller mounds and borrow pits.

The area is called Cahokia (after an Illinois Indian tribe that lived in the same region in the 1600s), but we don't know the real name of the Indians who lived there when it was a bustling city. When it was a city Cahokia stretched six square miles, and 10,000–20,000 people lived there from A.D. 700 to 1400. First came the Woodland Indians and then the Mississippian Indians. Peak prosperity was probably around A.D. 1100. Originally there were about 120 mounds of various sizes. Today 69 mounds have been documented within the park (it's a 2,200-acre site). The other mounds were plowed over decades ago through development or farming. The tribes built the mounds

with dirt dug from nearby pits called borrow pits. Some of these empty holes would become dumping grounds. Others would fill with water and become ponds. Some mounds were used to bury important people in the city; others were used as sites for religious ceremonies, and some mounds were reserved for rulers and priests.

As you walk through the grounds, you can see parts of a reconstructed wall made of timber. Residents erected this wall around the city's center three times, requiring 15,000 logs each time. Historians do not know the true purpose of the wall but have theorized that it was built for defense or to separate residents from the outside world. No one is quite sure what happened to the city after about A.D. 1200 or 1400, but many believe the city may have deteriorated or been abandoned because of overpopulation, overuse of the area's natural resources, disease, or war.

You can easily spend several hours at Cahokia, visiting the center, walking the grounds, climbing Monks Mound, and checking out Woodhenge, a calendar made of wooden posts (it's next to a cement factory and along the busy Collinsville Road). The center has numerous exhibits about the Native Americans who lived there, what they ate (corn, berries, fish, and deer), how they lived (in grass huts), rituals, and what they made. Researchers believe Cahokia was a trade center. In their excavations they've found objects such as sea shells, which are not native to this area.

The grandest mound is Monks Mound. With a base of 14 acres and a height of 100 feet, it is the largest Indian mound north of Mexico. This is where the ruler lived and some ceremonies were conducted. You will have to climb 154 steps to get to the top of Monks Mound, but it's worth it. You can get a better sense of the city from above as you watch tourists strolling about. Monks Mound was named after the French monks who lived in the area at the turn of the 17th century. They did not live on the mound.

The grounds are open 8 A.M.–dusk; the interpretive center is open 9 A.M.–5 P.M. Wednesday–Sunday. You can get a free self-guided taped tour from the visitors center, which describes the mounds you see along three hiking trails. The tour takes about 30–45 minutes, depending on your pace. Free guided tours are held at 10:30 A.M. and 1:30 P.M. Wednesday–Saturday, and at 12:30 and 2:30 P.M. on Sunday in June, July, and August. Tours are at 1:30 P.M. Saturday and Sunday in April, May, and September. Cahokia Mounds is a state and National Historic Landmark as well as a United Nations Educational, Scientific, and Cultural Organization World Heritage Site.

Brooks Catsup Bottle

The iconic Brooks Catsup Bottle (800 S. Morrison Ave./Hwy. 159, Collinsville, 618/345-5598, catsupbottle.com) stands 170 feet tall off the National Road in Collinsville. Built in 1949, the tower stored water for the city and the catsup factory. Eventually the factory closed, and the tower fell into disrepair. In the 1990s a local resident noticed its sorry state and rallied the troops, and they saved it from demolition. The restored tower is now a beloved symbol of revitalized roadside architecture.

Town of Cahokia Sights

Sometimes Illinoisans forget that the first explorers and settlers to Illinois were the French. Perhaps it is because a lot of them chose to leave when the British took over the territory, leaving few buildings behind. However, the town of Cahokia, just south of East St. Louis, has two buildings built by the state's first white residents. More than three centuries ago French missionaries founded the Holy Family Parish. They built the **Holy Family Church** (1st and Church Sts., Cahokia, 618/337-4548, call for a tour, free) in 1799. It's believed to be the oldest church west of the Allegheny Mountains. Like the nearby Cahokia Courthouse, it was built in typical French outpost style: hewn logs placed upright with the spaces filled in with mortar and stone. Part of the Belleville Diocese, it's still a functioning church. Masses are held there on Saturday evenings and Sunday mornings. Call the parish to make an appointment to tour the church.

About two blocks from the church is another building from the same period. The **Cahokia Courthouse** (1st and Elm Sts., Cahokia, 618/332-1782, 9 A.M.–5 P.M. Wed.–Sun., free), a state historic site, was built in 1740. Back then only about a dozen Frenchmen lived in the area, and they got along well with the Indian tribes nearby. Within a few years the area became a trading post, and more people moved into the area. When Illinois became a state, Cahokia was chosen as the county seat for St. Clair. However, because it was near the river, the town was often flooded, and the county seat was moved to Belleville. The courthouse was dismantled and shown in the St. Louis World's Fair in 1904, and later dismantled again and moved to Jackson Park in Chicago. It wasn't until 1939 that it was returned to Cahokia. Today the four-room building contains a courtroom, schoolroom, and offices.

Events

Collinsville is not only home to the world's largest catsup bottle, it's the Horseradish Capital of the World: About 65 percent of the world's horseradish is grown in the region. The much-loved root is honored annually at the

International Horseradish Festival (www. horseradishfestival.com) held the first weekend in June in Collinsville's Woodland Park. Events include cooking contests, root tosses, and food vendors selling dishes made with horseradish.

Cahokia Mounds hosts several solstice and equinox events throughout the year. In addition, Cahokia often sponsors artisan workshops and performing arts concerts on the grounds. You can listen to flutists, learn how Native Americans stored food to keep it from spoiling, how to make moccasins, and how to carve gourds.

Accommodations

If you want to stay in or around Collinsville, chances are you're going to stay in a hotel room off I-55. About a dozen midsize and midpriced hotels ($50–100) are here, including the 73-room **Hampton Inn** (7 Commerce Dr., Collinsville, 618/346-4400), which has an indoor pool and exercise room; the **Drury Inn** (602 N. Bluff Rd., Collinsville, 618/345-7700), which has an indoor pool and allows pets; and **Howard Johnson's Express Inn** (301 N. Bluff Rd., Collinsville, 618/345-1530), which has an outdoor pool and lounge.

Information

More info on lodging, dining, or attractions is available from the **Collinsville Convention and Visitors Bureau** (1 Gateway Dr., Collinsville, 800/289-2388, www.discover-collinsville.com).

THE OLD FRENCH FORTS: KASKASKIA AND FORT DE CHARTRES
Fort Kaskaskia State Historic Site

You'd hardly know it today, but the area in and around the Fort Kaskaskia State Historic Site was one of the more important forts and towns in Illinois's early years. The state historic site itself is a small park of about 200 acres high above the river. It was here that Fort Kaskaskia once stood. It was originally a French fort, but the British took over after 1763. And a

few years after that, Virginian George Rogers Clark secured the fort for the American colonists during the Revolutionary War. There's not much left of the fort, except for some earthen mounds at the top of the bluffs. What else is long gone? The town of Kaskaskia, the second European settlement in the state and the first capital. Established near the confluence of the Kaskaskia and Mississippi rivers, the town was often flooded. Drive through the park to the scenic overlook of the valley. Nearby, at the shelter, there's a poignant photograph of a house barely standing after one of the many floods. Also nearby is the remarkable Garrison Hill Cemetery on a steep hill overlooking the river. These are the graves of people who had been buried in Kaskaskia, but because of the floods they had to be moved in 1881. In the spring, locals reenact Revolutionary War camp life in the park. And there is a small campground on-site.

Across the river from the old fort is the **Kaskaskia Bell** (4372 Park Rd., Ellis Grove). It's on a 14,000-acre island on the western side of the Mississippi River, and it's quite the drive to get there. The area is remote and barely inhabited. After George Rogers Clark claimed Kaskaskia for the Americans in 1778, France's King Louis XV presented this bell to the residents.

Fort de Chartres

A remote and sometimes overlooked site in southwest Illinois is Fort de Chartres (Prairie du Rocher, 618/284-7230, 9 A.M.–5 P.M. Wed.–Sun., www.ftdechartres.com), a partially rebuilt French fort near the Mississippi River. Far from any major town, the fort is situated in the river's floodplain. And that's one of the reasons why the fort was eventually abandoned: It flooded a lot. The remarkable feature of the fort is its sheer size. It's not just a wall of logs. The stone fort had walls 15 feet high and several feet thick. There are musket ports, a powder magazine, a barracks, a chapel, and other rooms and buildings. What visitors see today is actually based on the third fort that stood on this site. The first one was made of logs and assembled rather hastily; it didn't last

COURTESY OF THE TOURISM BUREAU OF SOUTHWEST ILLINOIS

a reenactment at Fort de Chartres, Prairie du Rocher

long. A second one was built in 1725. It was larger, and builders added the powder magazine, prison, and other components. The third and final fort was the largest and most expensive to build. It served as a fort in the French territory roughly 1753–1763, when the French ceded the Illinois Territory to the British as a result of losing the French and Indian War. After the Brits took possession of the fort, they called it Fort Cavendish. But they didn't stick around for long and ordered it closed in 1771.

Through time the stone walls started to crumble, and people hauled away the stones. The only structure to survive was the powder magazine. The rest has been rebuilt. But you'd hardly know the difference; it looks pretty authentic. Feel free to stroll around the grounds and through the rooms (the chapel, the priest's room, and a grain-storage area). Be sure to tour the museum inside the storehouse building. It has several items on display, such as weapons, that date to when Illinois was part of France. If you're wondering when to visit, think about June. The fort hosts a popular two-day rendezvous then when people dress up in French

military uniforms and fur-trader outfits and dance, cook out, and compete in shooting contests. To get to the fort, follow signs from Highway 155 near Prairie du Rocher.

Modoc Rock Shelter

Beginning around 9,000 years ago Native American people used the Modoc Rock Shelter (County Rd. 7, two miles south of Prairie du Rocher) to seek shelter from storms or to camp while passing through the area in search of animals to hunt. Because of changes in topography during the last several thousand years, the shelter gradually filled with sediment. Today, driving by it, you'll see that it's a small indentation on the side of a rock cliff. The site is listed on the National Register of Historic Places.

Pierre Menard State Historic Site

Tucked into the side of a hill in a beautiful remote part of the county a few miles south of the Fort Kaskaskia State Historic Site is an old French colonial home built for Pierre Menard, a French-Canadian who was a successful fur trader in the area and later went on

© CHRISTINE DES GARENNES

Pierre Menard home, an example of French influence in early Illinois, Ellis Grove

to become lieutenant governor of Illinois in 1818. The Pierre Menard State Historic Site (Fort Kaskaskia Rd., Ellis Grove, 9 A.M.–5 P.M. Wed.–Sun. Mar.–Oct., 9 A.M.–4 P.M. Wed.–Sun. Nov.–Feb., free) comprises the 1802 home, with its long front porch that faces the Mississippi River, and a few outbuildings, such as Menard's smokehouse, plus an herb garden.

Wineries

This region is home to a handful of boutique wineries. Both of these offer free tastings and tours: **Lau-Nae Winery** (1522 Hwy. 3, Red Bud, 618/282-9463, www.lau-naewinery.com, 11 A.M.–7 P.M. Wed., 11 A.M.–10 P.M. Thurs.–Fri., 11 A.M.–5 P.M. Sat.–Sun.) crafts wine from French hybrid grapes, Concord grapes, and other fruit grown on-site. You can drink the wines while sitting on the front porch or inside by the fireplace. **Waterloo Winery** (725 N. Market St., Waterloo, 618/939-5743, noon–5 P.M. Wed.–Sun.) is on an 18th-century farmstead where the wines are aged in caves under the home. Unwind with a glass while sitting on the patio overlooking the vineyard.

CHESTER AND RED BUD
Sights and Activities

Popeye creator Elzie Segar was born in Chester, a quiet river town south of Fort de Chartres and the Pierre Menard home. To honor his memory, the town erected a Popeye statue at **Elzie Segar Memorial Park,** a small park on Highway 3, just before you cross the Chester Bridge to go to Missouri. Other residents have paid tribute by amassing hundreds of pieces of Popeye memorabilia. At the **Spinach Can Collectibles** (1001 State St., Chester, 618/826-4567, www.popeyethesailor.com, 9:30 A.M.–4:30 P.M. Mon.–Fri., 9 A.M.–4 P.M. Sat., free), vintage figurines, lunch boxes, toys, and other Popeye paraphernalia are for show and some are for sale. The museum is in the back of the store.

If you're in the mood for a scenic country drive, follow Highway 150 northwest of Chester to see the **Mary's River Covered Bridge,** an 1854 oak timber bridge. Once part of a regional toll road, the bridge was used by car travelers up until 1930. Visitors can walk across it.

Accommodations

Red Bud is a picturesque little town with brick sidewalks and old-fashioned lamp posts just off Highway 3, a rolling two-lane highway near the Mississippi River. Along Main Street is ◖ **Magnolia Place Bed and Breakfast** (317 S. Main St., Red Bud, 618/282-4141, www.magnolia-place.com, $75–160), a brick Victorian mansion with three rooms. One of the best features of this bed-and-breakfast is its garden, where couples often wed in the gazebo surrounded by flowerbeds. Unlike some bed-and-breakfasts in Victorian homes, you're not expected to forgo modern devices such as televisions in your room. Also, you pick the time of your breakfast in the morning.

Two other options where rooms are under $100 are **Red Bud Country Inn** (1617 S. Main St., Red Bud, 618/282-4444), a newer 12-room motel just off Red Bud's Main Street, where continental breakfast is included; or **Reid's Best Western Inn** (2150 State St., Chester, 618/826-3034), a 46-room motel with an outdoor pool.

Also, **Fort Kaskaskia State Historic Site** has 23 electrical hookups for RV campers.

◖ ILLINOIS CAVERNS STATE NATURAL AREA

What's awesome (and to some, terrifying) about Illinois Caverns State Natural Area (south of Waterloo near Redbud, 618/458-6699 or 618/785-2555, www.dnr.state.il.us, free) is the darkness. You will not explore the cave while sitting on a tram or following a group of 30 people along a lighted passage. Instead you explore the miles of passages guided by the light of your waterproof flashlight. The only cave open to the public in the state, Illinois Caverns is owned and managed by the Illinois Department of Natural Resources. Although this is the state's only cave open to the public, Illinois has several hundred caves. They're found in the driftless area in the northwest, throughout the Shawnee Hills, and along much of the Mississippi River in Illinois in what geologists call karst areas, which are marked by sinkholes and shallow depressions in the land. Hundreds of millions of years ago shallow seas covered much of Illinois. The seas deposited organic and carbonate sediment, which would become limestone and dolomite bedrock. Through time rainwater and groundwater dripped through the cracks of these rocks, causing a chemical reaction, and the rocks gradually dissolved. Streams meandered through the rock and formed caverns.

The experience here is, as the brochure bills it, wild. Lace up your boots, then pick up a map of the cave from the entrance. There are a total of about six miles of paths to explore, and about three of those miles where you can stand up. You will come upon areas called Cascade Canyon (a pleasant sight) and Marvin's Misery, where you'll crouch and crawl through slippery mud-like material (not as pleasant). Along the way you may see bats, salamanders, and the endangered amphipod, a tiny shrimp-like creature. You'll also see stalagmites and stalactites (when mineral-rich water drips down, the minerals—calcium carbonate—pile up).

The cave is on a 120-acre preserve on a former farm. The whole site is pretty rustic; there's no running water. But there is a half-mile walking trail through a meadow prairie if you want to take a walk above ground. Before you go, a few things to know: Visitors must explore the cave in groups of four or more, wear boots and a hard hat, and carry three sources of light per person (waterproof flashlights, lanterns, etc.). To get to the cave follow Highway 3; a few miles south of Waterloo, go right on Kaskaskia Road, left on County KK, and then right on County G. It's open 8 A.M.–3:30 P.M. Wednesday–Sunday April 15–September 15, 8 A.M.–3:30 P.M. Thursday–Saturday September 16–April 14. No one is allowed to enter the cave after 2:30 P.M.

INFORMATION

Staff at **The Tourism Bureau of Southwest Illinois** (10950 Lincoln Tr., Fairview Heights, 618/397-1488 or 800/442-1488, www.thetourismbureau.org) will be able to help you plan your itinerary through this region.

GREAT RIVER VALLEYS

THE GRAND PRAIRIE

Back in Illinois's early days as a state, settlers initially avoided the central region, which back then was covered by a vast prairie. Smoothed by ancient glaciers, the Grand Prairie was flat, muddy, and chock-full of insects. Trees were few and far between (except along the rivers), and the winters were long and bitter, especially when the winds rushed in from the northwest. But under the tall prairie grasses was black soil loaded with nutrients. After Grand Detour blacksmith John Deere invented a plow that could cut through the thick soil, settlement took off. Immigrants carved out homesteads along rail lines and near towns, most of which were near wooded areas along the rivers. Agriculture dominated the region in the 1800s, and it still is an economic driver. In the summer you don't have to drive far to find grain elevators dotting the landscape or a white farmhouse and red barn surrounded by fields of tall corn stalks.

Much of what you see out your windshield while driving through the region is grain farms. But the landscape also features several rivers. The Sangamon River weaves a diagonal path through the central part of the state, from northwest of Champaign toward the southwest and eventually the Illinois River. The Middle Fork National Scenic River snakes past sandstone outcroppings on the eastern side of the state. And the headwaters region of Champaign County is where six rivers, including the Sangamon, Kaskaskia, and Embarras (pronounced "EM-braw"), begin their journeys.

Central Illinois is very much Lincoln land. During the quarter of a century that he lived

HIGHLIGHTS

LOOK FOR ◖ TO FIND RECOMMENDED SIGHTS, ACTIVITIES, DINING, AND LODGING.

◖ **Lincoln Home National Historic Site:** Before the 16th American president moved to Washington, D.C., Abraham Lincoln lived in a two-story home with his family in Springfield. The home and visitors center are surrounded by other historic homes near downtown (page 270).

◖ **Abraham Lincoln Presidential Library and Museum:** The Lincoln Museum takes a comprehensive look at Lincoln by displaying artifacts and presenting several multimedia shows. You won't catch yourself yawning here (page 272).

◖ **Lincoln's New Salem:** In 1831 Lincoln moved to the village of New Salem as a 22-year-old man and spent several years working here. The pioneer town, once long gone, has been recreated as a state historic site with log cabins and volunteers who demonstrate milling, weaving, and other chores (page 286).

◖ **Robert Allerton Park:** The early-20th-century former estate of a grain baron, with its sunken garden, wooded trails, and reflection pond, is a jewel of the Illinois prairie. The mansion and surrounding gardens, part of the University of Illinois, are in Monticello (page 305).

◖ **Amish Country Farm Visits:** Surrounded by vast corn and soybean farms, the little towns of Arthur and Arcola, just off I-57, are home to thousands of enterprising Amish and non-Amish farmers. The Great Pumpkin Patch is a must-see in the fall; in the springtime, the Amish greenhouses dotting the countryside brim with flowers and early tomatoes. For a real taste of farm life, visitors can arrange for a home-cooked meal on an Amish farm (page 311).

◖ **Kickapoo State Park and Middle Fork State Fish and Wildlife Area:** Paddle down the Middle Fork, a National Scenic River that weaves through Vermilion County's former coal-mining region past sandstone bluffs and hardwood forests. Along the river's shores are two great state parks with miles and miles of rugged trails for hiking and mountain biking (page 331).

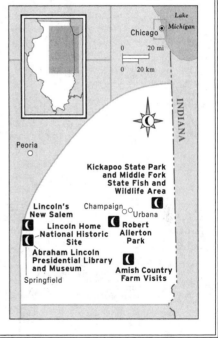

in Illinois, Abraham Lincoln traveled much of the state practicing law, serving as a captain in the Black Hawk War, and working on a steamboat. But it was in New Salem where Lincoln developed his business skills as a general store clerk. And it was in Springfield he matured as a politician and orator. He was fond of the region and its people. Before leaving Springfield for Washington, D.C., Lincoln told a crowd gathered at the train station, "To this place, and the kindness of its people, I owe everything." Central Illinois towns, even the bigger ones such as the capital, Springfield, still manage to give off good Midwestern vibes. They are Main Street kind of towns, with coffee shops frequented by regular groups of farmers, drive-ins where teens meet on Friday nights, and VFW halls where pancake breakfasts are served.

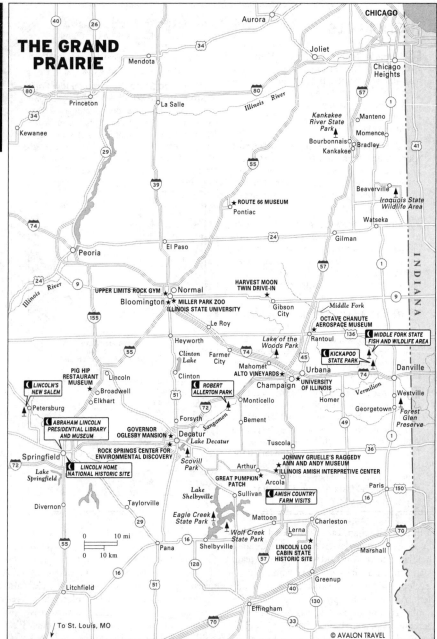

THE GRAND PRAIRIE

CHICAGO

Aurora
Joliet
Mendota
Chicago Heights

Princeton
La Salle
Illinois River
Kewanee

Manteno
Momence
Kankakee River State Park
Bourbonnais
Bradley
Kankakee

Beaverville
Iroquois State Wildlife Area

★ ROUTE 66 MUSEUM
Pontiac

Watseka

Peoria
El Paso
Gilman

INDIANA

UPPER LIMITS ROCK GYM ★
Normal
HARVEST MOON TWIN DRIVE-IN
★

Bloomington ★★ MILLER PARK ZOO
ILLINOIS STATE UNIVERSITY
Gibson City
Middle Fork

Illinois River
OCTAVE CHANUTE AEROSPACE MUSEUM

Heyworth
Lake of the Woods Park
Rantoul
☾ MIDDLE FORK STATE FISH AND WILDLIFE AREA

Clinton Lake
Farmer City
☾ KICKAPOO STATE PARK

PIG HIP RESTAURANT MUSEUM
Mahomet
ALTO VINEYARDS ★
Urbana
Danville

☾ LINCOLN'S NEW SALEM
Lincoln
Clinton
Champaign
UNIVERSITY OF ILLINOIS
Vermilion

Broadwell
☾ ROBERT ALLERTON PARK
Homer
Westville

Petersburg
Elkhart
Monticello
Georgetown
Forest Glen Preserve

☾ ABRAHAM LINCOLN PRESIDENTIAL LIBRARY AND MUSEUM
Forsyth
Sangamon
Bement

GOVERNOR OGLESBY MANSION ★
Decatur
Lake Decatur
Tuscola

Springfield
ROCK SPRINGS CENTER FOR ENVIRONMENTAL DISCOVERY
Scovill Park
JOHNNY GRUELLE'S RAGGEDY ANN AND ANDY MUSEUM ★
ILLINOIS AMISH INTERPRETIVE CENTER ★

☾ LINCOLN HOME NATIONAL HISTORIC SITE
Arthur
Lake Springfield
GREAT PUMPKIN PATCH ★
Arcola
Paris

Divernon
Taylorville
Lake Shelbyville
Sullivan
☾ AMISH COUNTRY FARM VISITS
Mattoon
Charleston

Eagle Creek State Park
Lerna

0   10 mi
0   10 km
Wolf Creek State Park
LINCOLN LOG CABIN STATE HISTORIC SITE ★
Marshall

Litchfield
Pana
Shelbyville
Greenup

Effingham

To St. Louis, MO

© AVALON TRAVEL

PLANNING YOUR TIME

While planning your itinerary through the Grand Prairie, ask yourself this question: How much do you love Abraham Lincoln? This being Abe land, you could easily spend several days traveling from one Lincoln sight to another, such as the **Abraham Lincoln Presidential Library and Museum** in Springfield or his old stomping grounds at **New Salem State Historic Site.** A week will allow you time to hit the main Lincoln sights in Springfield, the **University of Illinois** campus in Champaign and Urbana, put in some hiking time at **Kickapoo State Park** by Danville, go antiquing in the town of **Lincoln,** or go camping near **Lake Shelbyville.** Because the region is connected to Chicago by I-57 and I-55, it's easy to take off on a two- or three-day weekend jaunt to Grand Prairie towns from Chicago. If you're in the mood for small towns, drive **Route 66** from Chicago toward Springfield. Or visit an **Amish family farm** near Arthur and Arcola and browse for handmade furniture or visit a pumpkin patch. All major metropolitan areas in the Grand Prairie region (Springfield, Bloomington-Normal, Champaign-Urbana, Decatur, Danville) are connected by interstates, making it easy to get to one from another.

an iconic Route 66 sign

© JOHN RODRIGUEZ/ISTOCK.COM

Access

Aside from the occasional road-construction project, driving through central Illinois is usually free of any major hassles. Traffic jams are few and far between. The interstates and highways are in good shape and most of the cars and trucks clip along at a speedy pace. The main arteries through the Grand Prairie are Interstates 55, 57, and 72, and 74. I-55, the major northeast-to-southwest highway in the state, is the quickest route from Chicago to St. Louis, with stops around Bloomington-Normal and Springfield and other midsize towns along the way, such as Lincoln and Dwight. I-55 follows much of Historic Route 66, a good two-lane option if you need a break from interstate driving for a while. I-57 is a north-south highway primarily through the eastern part of the state, from Chicago and down to the south. U.S. 45 runs along most of I-57 through the central part of the state.

There are plenty of scenic two-lane options: Highway 10 from Champaign to Lincoln, Highway 133 through the Amish towns of Arcola and Arthur, and Illinois 1. Also known as the Dixie Highway, Illinois 1 was once the main route into Chicago from the south. It's a straight line along the eastern part of the state from Chicago to Danville, through Watseka, Momence, and more.

Resources

Most towns in central Illinois have convention and visitors bureaus or chambers of commerce with helpful, friendly residents working there. For information on the entire region, check with the **Central Illinois Tourism Development Office** (Upper Mezzanine Level, Hilton Hotel, 700 E. Adams St., Springfield, 217/525-7980, www.visitcentralillinois.com). Its territory covers much of the Grand Prairie region.

Springfield

I hope you like Abraham Lincoln because Springfield is a virtual Lincoln-o-rama. It's impossible to tour the town without seeing his likeness (the stovepipe hat, the tall bony frame) or seeing his words, usually excerpts from speeches, engraved or printed on plaques outside of buildings. As you'll see, many places you visit or walk by in Springfield play up a connection to Abraham Lincoln, who lived in this town 1831–1861. Sure, you can see his home and tomb, but also on display are his bank ledger and a target board he used during shooting practice.

Springfield, especially the downtown and the Old Aristocracy Hill District surrounding it, has a historic feel to it. Some of the streets are brick-lined and the homes restored Victorians. With a population of about 116,000, Springfield is home to state bureaucrats, lobbyists, agribusiness employees, and people working in the service industry. It's a fairly quiet town compared with some other capital cities in other Midwestern states, such as Madison, Wisconsin, or Des Moines, Iowa. The skyline comprises mostly the Hilton hotel tower and the capitol building. Most shops and restaurants downtown are closed on Sundays. But it's a fun town, full of friendly people who like to eat (the hearty horseshoe sandwich was invented here) and who are proud of the city's history, whether because of the famous son Lincoln or its connection to Route 66, which slices through the center of the city.

ORIENTATION

Navigating through Springfield is fairly easy. The downtown streets that run north and south are numbered from 1st Street on up, getting higher as you head east. Madison, Jefferson, and Washington streets are all downtown, and Capitol Avenue, not surprisingly, leads to the capitol. You'll find plenty of street signs throughout the city (not just downtown) that point visitors to Lincoln sights. The major Lincoln attractions, such as the Lincoln home, library, state museum, and capitol buildings are all within about a 10- to 15-minute walk of each other. You could stay downtown and not have to drive to any sights except the Lincoln tomb, state fairgrounds, and some parks, which are generally on the north and northeast side of the city. I-72 runs east-west through town, and I-55 runs north-south, circumventing the city on the east to southeast. Route 66, or Business 55, cuts through the center of town from the northeast.

SIGHTS
◖ Lincoln Home National Historic Site

The best place to start your visit is at Abraham Lincoln's former home (426 S. 7th St., Springfield, 217/492-4241, www.nps.gov/liho, 8:30 A.M.–5 P.M. daily, free). The tours are free, but you need to get a ticket at the visitors center (it limits the number of folks going through the home at a given time). You might want to take a preview tour by watching the free film in the visitors center called *At Home with Mr. Lincoln*. It shows the inside of the rooms and shares a little history of how the house was built (in stages). You'll join a group of folks and listen to an interpreter share a little background on Lincoln's life and his activities in Springfield, where he worked as a lawyer and state legislator before being elected as the 16th president of the United States. Your trip through the house may last about 20 minutes. It goes by quickly, especially in the summer when tours seem to run every five minutes. The home is not especially grand compared with some of the ornate Victorian homes south of the neighborhood. In fact, some of the furnishings are particularly dark. Some of the furniture, such as a first-floor couch, is literally black. That's the way it was when Lincoln lived there.

What makes a visit to the Lincoln home so cool is the historic district that immediately surrounds it. You can amble down the street on plank sidewalks just like Abe used

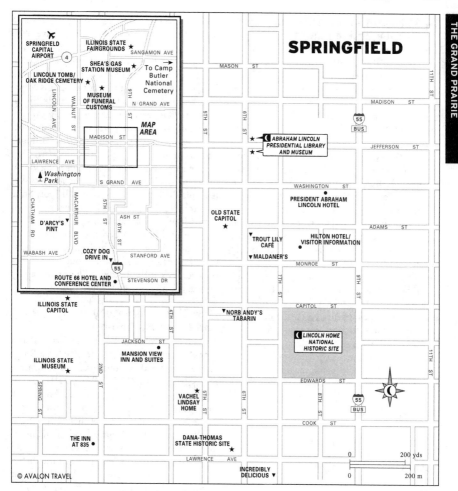

SPRINGFIELD

to do. (The planks are not original, however. Because of the volume of visitors who come here every year they actually have to be replaced about every 10 years. And the gravel road was dirt when Lincoln lived here.) Several homes have been restored to their mid-1800s appearance. Some of them now contain the offices of Illinois senators, some are being renovated, and others are open to the public. The Arnold House, across the street from the Lincoln home, has an excellent exhibit (preservationists will definitely want to see this)

called *If These Walls Could Talk: Saving an Old House.* It has photographs of the district's homes through the decades, before and after restoration, and explains the restoration processes used on the homes. There are also photographs and stories about Lincoln's neighbors. The Dean House, catercorner to the Lincoln home, has an exhibit called *What a Pleasant Home Abe Lincoln Has,* which provides background on the home's construction and the Lincoln family. From there, you can walk to other Lincoln sights.

Abraham Lincoln Presidential Library and Museum

The newest and grandest of them all is the multimillion dollar Abraham Lincoln Presidential Library and Museum (212 N. 6th St., Springfield, 217/558-8844, www.alplm. org, 9 A.M.–5 P.M. daily, $7.50). The complex, which encompasses several city blocks and almost 100,000 square feet, contains exhibits that chronicle Lincoln's life, his politics, and the state of the nation while he was president. After it opened to much fanfare (President George W. Bush dropped by for the grand opening), some scholars and visitors criticized the design (and price tag) because the place has too many bells and whistles. One exhibit that has raised the ire of some people is the election section, where faux news anchors talk about Lincoln's chances of winning the 1860 presidential election and commercials for the candidates are aired. It is a bit odd, but it certainly is a refreshing take on a presidential museum. While the museum certainly has its fair share of artifacts, such as Lincoln's shaving kit,

the place seems to be less about objects and more about exploring what might have been going on in his mind while he was drafting the Emancipation Proclamation. Visitors walk through a replica of a log cabin to learn about Lincoln's early years, and learn about his courtship with Mary Todd and their early life in Springfield together. The "whispering gallery" highlights all the cruel cartoons and comments made about Lincoln, poking fun at his looks and his politics, among other things. An eerie exhibit shows one of Lincoln's sons lying in bed ill during the inaugural ball. And later a casket is displayed in a mockup of the Illinois State Capitol after Lincoln is brought back to town after his assassination. Especially helpful are the "Learn More" placards, which are placed near the exhibits and which provide suggestions for reading and finding out more about the country's 16th president. There's also a play area in the museum for children.

Oak Ridge Cemetery and Lincoln's Tomb

As far as tombs and monuments go, the **Lincoln Tomb State Historic Site** (Oak Ridge Cemetery, North Grand Ave. to Monument Ave., Springfield, 217/782-2717, 9 A.M.–5 P.M. daily, free) is pretty magnificent. An obelisk towers above the cemetery's graves (the height of the entire tomb and monument is 117 feet). At the entrance is a bronze head of the president, with his nose showing some wear and tear; visitors rub it for good luck. Lincoln actually wasn't buried here immediately after his death. He was placed in vault in a nearby hillside. It wasn't until fans raised enough money that they built the huge granite monument. Completed in 1874, the tomb also would eventually contain Lincoln's wife, Mary Todd, and three of their sons. (Robert Todd, the only one to survive through to adulthood, is buried in Arlington National Cemetery.)

The 365-acre cemetery on the north side of town is the largest in the state. Several governors are buried here, as well as poet Vachel Lindsay. Oak Ridge also contains an Illinois Vietnam Veteran's Memorial.

© CHRISTINE DES GARENNES

Lincoln's tomb in Oak Ridge Cemetery

In a mausoleum-like building near the entrance of the cemetery, the **Museum of Funeral Customs** (Oak Ridge Cemetery, 1440 Monument Ave., Springfield, 217/544-3480, www.funeralmuseum.org, 10 A.M.–4 P.M. Tues.–Sat., 1–4 P.M. Sun., $4) takes a serious and artistic look at how caring for the dead has evolved throughout the decades. There are a re-creation of an embalming room (with an explanation of how embalming works), a scale model of Lincoln's tomb, and a variety of caskets. One of the neatest exhibits, which looks as if it is straight out of a Victorian novel, is a black horse-drawn hearse.

More Lincoln Sights

A few blocks north of the Lincoln home and just across the street from the Old State Capitol is the **Lincoln-Herndon Law Offices State Historic Site** (6th and Adams Sts., Springfield, 217/785-7960 or 217/785-7289, typically 9 A.M.–5 P.M. Tues.–Sat. Mar.–Oct., 9 A.M.–4 P.M. Tues.–Sat. Nov.–Feb., but call ahead for hours, donation). Lincoln and his partner, William Herndon, practiced law on the third floor from 1843 to 1852. Staff from the state historic preservation agency have recreated his office, complete with long tables, candlesticks, quill pens, and a portrait of George Washington hanging on the wall. Their office was nothing fancy. Exhibits explain the building's history; it was also used as a courtroom and judge's chamber.

Like most well-to-do families in town, the Lincolns had a pew reserved for them at the **First Presbyterian Church** (321 S. 7th St., Springfield, 217/528-4311, www.first-pres-church.org, 10 A.M.–4 P.M. Mon.–Fri. June–Sept.). The church in which the pew is now housed was actually built after Lincoln died. The old church is long gone. You can view the pew, but don't try to sit in it. Its seat is cordoned off by a rope. Call ahead and let staff know you're coming if you want a more personal visit. A docent can guide you through the church and tell you about the family's connection to the church during those hours. The Illinois Symphony Orchestra holds some concerts here.

the Lincoln-Herndon Law Offices

Chase Bank has on view in its lobby the **Lincoln Ledger** (Washington and 6th Sts., Springfield, 217/527-3860, 8 A.M.–6 P.M. Mon.–Fri., 8 A.M.–noon Sat., free), the family's balance sheet managed by the Springfield Marine and Fire Insurance Company, where the Lincolns deposited their money.

When Abraham Lincoln left Springfield on February 11, 1861, for his inaugural trip to Washington, D.C., he said, "I now leave, not knowing when, or whether ever, I may return." You can visit the train depot where he addressed his supporters and spoke those words. It is now called the **Lincoln Depot** (10th and Monroe Sts., Springfield, 217/544-8695 or 217/788-1356, 10 A.M.–4 P.M., free). Fire damaged most of the building in the 1960s, but there are some things still intact, such as the stairs Lincoln walked up to visit the depot manager's office. National Park Service history interpreters are on hand to recount Lincoln's last day in Springfield. Inside the building the depot's waiting room has been re-created, a video recounts Lincoln's train trip to D.C., and photographs show how the depot has changed structurally throughout the years.

© CHRISTINE DES GARENNES

Old State Capitol, where Lincoln delivered his "House Divided" speech

State Capitol Buildings

A lot of state bills were debated and laws passed at the **Old State Capitol** (between 5th and 6th Sts., just south of Washington St. and north of the pedestrian walkway, 217/785-7961, 9 A.M.–5 P.M. Tues.–Sat. Mar.–Oct., 9 A.M.–4 P.M. Tues.–Sat. Nov.–Feb., donation), but this government building is probably most famous for Lincoln's "House Divided" speech, when he told his fellow state representatives that a house divided against itself cannot stand. You can visit the meeting room where he delivered this speech, the library, the Illinois State Supreme Court room, and wander through the hallways. The building's exterior, designed in a Greek-revival style, is rather simple, but inside you'll find a grand stairway, Grecian columns, and ornate rooms for the legislators and judges. Most of the furniture pieces you will see inside the building are reproductions. However, a few, such as a senate desk, are original. Interpreters present a "living history program" 10 A.M.–noon and 2–4 P.M. Friday and Saturday January–April and June–December. Costumed volunteers hang out in

different rooms in the capitol and assume the roles of clerks or businessmen. They tell stories about the building's history and the people who once walked its halls. Guided tours of the building are organized on a rolling basis throughout the day.

Because of Illinois's robust growth during its early days of statehood, politicians, judges, and bureaucrats soon ran out of space in the Old State Capitol. In response they built the second capitol building, now called the **Illinois State Capitol** (2nd St. and Capitol Ave., Springfield, 217/782-2099, www.illinois.gov, 8 A.M.–4 P.M. Mon.–Fri., 9 A.M.–3 P.M. Sat.–Sun., free), which is still in use today. This is where the governor, lieutenant governor, secretary of state, attorney general, and others keep offices (in addition to their Chicago offices). The most stunning feature of the capitol is the 400-foot-tall dome, which seems to glitter on sunny days. Built 1868–1888 and listed on the National Register of Historic Places, this capitol was designed in Renaissance-revival and Second Empire styles. When the legislature is in session, you can watch the representatives and senators debate, table, and vote on bills from the gallery above.

Illinois State Museum

The newest permanent exhibit at the Illinois State Museum (502 S. Spring St., Springfield, 217/782-7386, www.museum.state.il.us, 8:30 A.M.–5 P.M. Mon.–Sat., noon–5 P.M. Sun., free) is called *Changes: Dynamic Illinois Environments.* Most history or geography exhibits typically begin the story with the last ice age, which dates to roughly 24,000 years ago. But the Illinois State Museum exhibit starts history way, way back in time—500 million years ago. The exhibit, which extends through several rooms on the first floor, is interactive without being too geared toward children.

Visitors learn about creatures that lived in the oceans millions of years ago, about Illinois's diverse environments and how they came to be, about floodplains along rivers, and more. On the second floor of the museum, exhibits called *Peoples of the Past* and *At Home in the Heartland* depict scenes from everyday life from the 1700s to the 1980s. (The 1980s exhibit is a re-creation of a teenager's bedroom. Note the vintage U2 poster.) Visiting and rotating exhibits are also on the second floor. On the lower level is a hands-on discovery area for kids, plus a room full of stuffed birds that are native to Illinois. The museum also has rotating exhibits throughout the year. And a museum store has a decent collection of artwork by Illinois residents, including pottery and jewelry, books, and the standard souvenirs such as postcards and key chains.

More Museums

On the lighter side of things, **Shea's Gas Station Museum** (2075 Peoria Rd., Springfield, 217/522-0475, 7 A.M.–4 P.M. Tues.–Fri., 7 A.M.–noon Sat., donation) is an entertaining and nostalgic stop along Route 66. Bill Shea, the genial proprietor, pumped gas at this Marathon gas station for decades before closing shop in the early 1980s. He will personally take you through the museum and share with you his memories of what it was

like to run a station on 66. The museum consists of two former gas station buildings, one that dates to the 1920s and another from the late 1940s. Both buildings are jam-packed with Shea's mementos from throughout the years, including many photographs and newspapers, vintage toys and tools, you name it. The old gas pumps, which have been restored and are shiny, always seem to draw the most attention from visitors, as do the photographs of Route 66 during its heyday.

Perhaps one of the more unusual museum collections in the state is at the **Illinois State Military Museum** (Camp Lincoln, 1301 N. MacArthur Blvd., Springfield, 1 P.M.–4:30 P.M. Tues.–Sat., free), which has on view the artificial leg of Mexican general Santa Anna. The museum, which focuses its exhibits on the National Guard's history, also has a target board once used by Abraham Lincoln.

More military memorabilia is on view at the **Grand Army of the Republic Memorial Museum** (629 S. 7th St., Springfield, 217/522-4373, 10 A.M.–4 P.M. Tues.–Sat., Jan.–Nov.),

© CHRISTINE DES GARENNES

Shea's Gas Station Museum, along Route 66

SPRINGFIELD AND THE NAACP

Despite being the former hometown of Abraham Lincoln, the "Great Emancipator," Springfield in its early years was not exactly a town where whites and blacks lived in harmony. After the turn of the 20th century, Springfield, like many growing industrial cities in Illinois, attracted European immigrants and Southern blacks. They moved to Springfield in hopes of landing jobs in the factories or starting businesses that would cater to the booming population. Eventually tensions began to build between the two communities, which were in separate areas of town.

In the summer of 1908, a white man named Clergy Ballard was murdered after chasing down an intruder to his house. Before he died, Ballard fingered a black man for the attack and reportedly said he had seen the intruder at his daughter's bedside. Not too long after that, a white woman named Mabel Hallam claimed she had been raped by a local black man. On August 14, while both black suspects were being held in jail, a mob of white residents gathered at the jail where the accused were being held. Fearing for the suspects' safety, the police transported them to another jail, which prompted the crowd to grow even angrier.

The mob then went on a violent rampage that lasted several days. People trashed a restaurant and car that belonged to a businessman whom they believed helped transport the suspects away from the jail. They smashed windows and set fire to homes and businesses that belonged to the city's black residents and threatened more violence if blacks didn't leave town. Eventually the mob killed a prominent black businessman named William Donovan, who was said to have been Abraham Lincoln's cobbler. After the National Guard swooped into Springfield and the dust cleared, about $200,000 worth of property had been damaged, and several blacks and whites were dead. Later, Mabel Hallam confessed she had never been raped.

Stunned at the violent outbreak, a group of white and black activists called for a meeting in New York City to discuss race and violence against blacks. Among those who came to the meeting: W. E. B. Du Bois and Ida Wells-Barnett. This group, initially called the National Negro Committee, would become the National Association for the Advancement of Colored People.

Several historical markers about the riots have been placed throughout downtown Springfield. The self-guided tour starts at 7th and Jefferson Streets. More information is available from the Springfield Convention and Visitors Bureau.

---

where the focus is on Union artifacts and photographs from that era. The museum has a flag that hung in the Ford Theatre in Washington, D.C., where Lincoln was assassinated.

Historic Homes

Unlike the other major homes in Illinois designed by Frank Lloyd Wright, the **Dana-Thomas State Historic Site** (301 E. Lawrence Ave., Springfield, 217/782-6776, www.dana-thomas.org, typically 9 A.M.–4 P.M. Wed.–Sun. but call ahead for hours, $3 suggested donation) is inexpensive to visit. (Others, such as his home and studio and the Robie house in the Chicago region, charge at least $10 per person.) Situated within the Old Aristocracy Hill Historic District in Springfield, less than a mile from Lincoln's home and a few blocks from the governor's mansion, this house is one of a few Prairie-style homes in the neighborhood (many are Victorian and Italianate). The primarily beige home was built 1902–1904 and features typical Wright characteristics such as low-pitched roofs, an open floor plan, and art glass (dozens of frames surround the house). It is a house that flows horizontally. Note the entranceway on Lawrence Avenue with bricks lying horizontally and fanning out around the archway. Other than the state of Illinois (which now owns the home), there have been only two owners: the Dana family, who originally commissioned the house and who lived here until 1928; and the Thomases, who used the house as a business office. The inside has not been tampered with and is in great shape. It's one thing to admire a Wright home from the sidewalk, another to wander through the hallways and rooms. What makes a trip through here worth it is that the house is filled with authentic Wright-designed furniture, most notably dozens of white-oak pieces. Walking tours take about an hour. For souvenirs, drop by the house's Sumac Shop, 217/744-3598, www.sumacshop.com, which is stocked with Wright-inspired Prairie-style jewelry and other items.

Just north of the Dana-Thomas home is another grand home, designed with an entirely different point of view. The **Governor's Executive Mansion** (410 E. Jackson St., Springfield, 217/782-6450, free) has a Georgian exterior and Greek-revival interior. Built 1853–1855, it is situated on a hill surrounded by lush gardens. On the tour you can see several parlors, the dining room, ballroom, and several bedrooms. The executive mansion is open for tours Tuesday, Thursday, and Saturday; call for hours.

Across the street from the governor's mansion is the **Vachel Lindsay Home** (603 S. 5th St., Springfield, 217/524-0901, noon–4 P.M. Tues.–Sat., free). The frequent contributor to Chicago-based *Poetry* magazine was a well-known American poet at the turn of the 20th century. It was in this house that he was born in 1879 and where he would eventually return and commit suicide in 1931. In recent years the state spent $1 million restoring this quaint gray house. Built in the 1840s, it was once home to Mary Todd Lincoln's sister and her family. Lincoln was reportedly a frequent guest in the home.

Parks

Designed by landscape architect Jens Jensen, **Lincoln Memorial Garden and Nature Center** (2301 E. Lake Shore Dr., Springfield, 217/529-1111, www.lmgnc.org, free) has five miles of trails through prairie and woodlands along Lake Springfield (southeast of downtown

Springfield, east of I-55 and Exit 88). Developed in the 1930s as a memorial to Lincoln, the 100-acre site is one of the best places to go for a walk in central Illinois. Along the trails are wildlife-observation areas, benches, and bridges that stretch over ponds and streams. Throughout the park there are also council rings, circular stone benches where community groups meet and events are held. The trees planted throughout the park—such as oaks and hickories—are native to the Midwestern states where Lincoln lived, including Illinois, Indiana, and Kentucky. The park is open sunrise–sunset daily. The nature center is open 10 A.M.–4 P.M. Tuesday–Saturday, 1–4 P.M. Sunday. The garden is open sunrise–sunset.

If you're in Springfield and need a quick relief from touring, **Adams Wildlife Sanctuary** (2315 E. Clear Lake Ave., Springfield, 217/544-5781, sunrise–sunset daily, free) is a good spot to take a break and stretch your legs by going for a short walk or sitting on a bench and watching for birds. The 30-acre site contains a restored prairie and an old fruit orchard. It's a few miles northeast of Lincoln's home.

Washington Park (1740 W. Fayette Ave., Springfield, 217/753-6228, www.springfield-parks.org, free) has a botanical garden and impressive 132-foot-tall carillon bell tower. The domed conservatory contains tropical plants and flowers such as orchids. Throughout the year the conservatory hosts several flower and plant shows. Outside the dome are several gardens stocked with roses, irises, and cacti. The botanic garden is open noon–4 P.M. Monday–Friday, noon–5 P.M. Saturday–Sunday.

Also in Washington Park is the **Thomas Rees Memorial Carillon** (217/753-6219, www.carillon-rees.org), reportedly the third-largest bell tower in the world. You can climb up the tower (there are three different levels where you can stop and take in the view) or ride the elevator to the top. This is a good cheap way to see Springfield from above. The carillon has 67 bronze bells. To give you an idea of how huge it is, and how impressive it is when you hear the music, the bells range from 22 pounds to a 7.5-ton G-flat. It was installed in the park in 1962.

Camp Butler National Cemetery

© CHRISTINE DES GARENNES

You can listen to the bells on Sunday afternoons throughout the year and on Wednesday evenings in the summer. Tours of the tower tend to be available to visitors Wednesday–Sunday Memorial Day–Labor Day and occasionally in September; call for hours.

The local zoo, **Henson Robinson Zoo** (1100 E. Lake Dr., Springfield, 217/753-6217, www.hensononrobinsonzoo.com, 10 A.M.–5 P.M. Mon.–Fri., 10 A.M.–6 P.M. Sat.–Sun. Mar.–Oct., 10 A.M.–4 P.M. daily Nov.–Feb., $3.75), has 300 animals from around the world, including cheetahs, monkeys, and bears. In addition there is a barn with farm animals and a butterfly garden. It's on the south side of Lake Springfield.

Camp Butler National Cemetery (5063 Camp Butler Rd., Springfield, 217/492-4070, open during daylight hours daily, free), northeast of town, is a veteran's cemetery where Union and Confederate soldiers are buried, as are soldiers who died during the world wars and other conflicts throughout the decades. Before it was made a cemetery, the site held a Union training camp during the Civil War. Later in the war a prison was established to house Confederate soldiers, and 700 people died of a smallpox epidemic during the summer of 1862.

ENTERTAINMENT AND EVENTS
Arts

The restored **Route 66 Drive-In** (Knight's Action Park, 1700 Recreation Dr., Springfield, movie info 217/698-0066, park 217/546-8881, $5) is a twin drive-in adjacent to the adventure park. Movies are shown nightly Memorial Day–Labor Day, then on weekends only through October. The concessionaire sells corn dogs, cotton candy, ice cream, and other snacks.

The Springfield Hoogland Center for the Arts (420 S. 6th St., Springfield, 217/523-2787, www.scfta.org) is a community gathering place for visual artists, actors, musicians, and other performing artists. The 80,000-square-foot building (formerly a Masonic temple) houses three theaters, a gallery, and other reception areas. Something's cooking there every weekend, whether it's a local community theater production, a gospel concert, or photography exhibit reception.

The **Illinois Symphony Orchestra** (524½ E. Capital Ave., Springfield, 217/522-2838, www.ilsymphony.org) plays classics (Mozart, Rachmaninoff), pops concerts, matinees for children, chamber concerts, holiday shows, and more. Musicians perform at First Presbyterian Church in Springfield (321 S. 7th St.) and Sangamon Auditorium at the University of Illinois at Springfield campus (entrance off Shepherd Rd., south of I-72 and east of I-55).

Events

For more than 150 years, Illinois residents have been bringing their prized hogs, goats, and cattle to the **Illinois State Fair** (State Fairgrounds, Sangamon Ave. and Business 55, Springfield, 217/782-6661, 7 A.M.–midnight fair days, admission $3, parking $7). While livestock shows are definitely a part of the fair, people do go for more than the animals. Homemade pies, jams, and wines are judged here. There are carnival rides, numerous food and drink vendors, and lots of bands performing country, classic rock, and some pop music. Inside the state fairgrounds is the Illinois Fire Museum (in Building 7) which houses antique fire equipment, photos, and patches. The fair runs for 10 days mid to late August every year. The 366-acre site is on the north side of town.

About 60,000 people make tracks to the **International Route 66 Mother Road Festival** (217/422-3733 or 866/783-6645, www.rte66fest.com) held in downtown Springfield every year in mid-September. Walk past hundreds of shiny vintage cars, jitterbug in the street to a live band, and watch a parade go by. This festival, which started in 2001, expands every year.

Well over 100 artists from Illinois and surrounding states gather on the grounds of the Old State Capitol for the annual **Old Capitol Art Fair** (www.socaf.org), held on a weekend in mid to late May. Shop for original pottery, jewelry, glassware, paintings, photographs, and more. This favorite spring event features free music, children's activities, and plenty of food. The Old State Capitol is located between Fifth and Sixth Streets, north of Monroe Street.

SHOPPING

The main shopping areas in town are **Parkway Pointe** (Freedom Dr. and Veterans Pkwy.) where you can find big discount retailers such as Target and Wal-Mart; and the **Simon White Oaks Mall** (Veterans Pkwy. and Wabash Ave.), an enclosed mall with 115 stores, including the department store Famous Barr, Gap, and others. Near downtown **The Weber House** (925 S. 7th St., Springfield) is home to several boutiques, such as the gift shop Lily's, gourmet kitchen shop Thyme to Cook, and Incredibly Delicious, a bakery.

While you're downtown, satisfy your sweet tooth by dropping into **Del's Popcorn Shop** (213 S. 6th St., Springfield, 217/544-0037), which sells kettle corn, roasted nuts, ice cream, and candy.

Pease's (6th and Washington Sts., plus other locations in Springfield, 217/523-3721 or 888/373-2737, www.peasescandy.com) is a local candy-making company with roots that go back several generations. They whip up goodies like caramel apples, fudge, and various crème-filled and nut-covered chocolates. Try the mint melt-a-ways.

Also downtown, collectors will enjoy a walk through **Prairie Archives** (522 E. Adams St., Springfield, 217/522-9742), which specializes in antique books, rare books, and used books. Literary types can easily while away the afternoon here browsing through history books and literature. It also has a good collection of vintage children's and hobby books. Nearby **Recycled Records** (625 E. Adams St., Springfield, 217/522-5122) sells used CDs, records, and tapes.

RECREATION
Amusement and Water Park

Bumper boats, go-karts, volleyball—what'll you have? On the south side of Springfield, **Knight's Action Park** (1700 Recreation Dr., Springfield, 217/546-8881, www.knightsactionpark.com) is a combo amusement park and water park with water slides, miniature golf, batting cages, a driving range, an arcade area, and a Ferris wheel. Water park admission is $24 per person, $18 for kids under 48 inches and adults over 55 years. But admission into the regular amusement park is free: You just pay for the rides and the activities as you choose them. Fees vary, such as $3–5 for activities such as miniature golf and hitting buckets of balls. The amusement park is open 9 A.M.–10 P.M. daily in the spring and until 11 P.M. mid-May–Labor Day weekend. The water park is open 10 A.M.–7 P.M. daily mid-May–Labor Day weekend. However, the water park is closed the Monday–Friday before Labor Day weekend. Discounts are available for some afternoon admissions. Next door to Knight's Action Park is the **Route 66 Drive-In** (for more information, see *Entertainment and Events*).

ACCOMMODATIONS
Hotels
$50-100

The affordable **Carpenter Street Hotel** (525 N. 6th St., Springfield, 217/789-9100 or 888/779-9100, www.carpenterstreethotel.com, $70) is north of downtown tourist sights, on the way to the state fairgrounds. Rooms in this newer building are sparse but clean. The building has a coin-operated laundry and staff set up a continental breakfast in the morning. The entire building is smoke-free.

On the outskirts of southwest Springfield you'll find the economical, clean **Sleep Inn** (3470 Freedom Dr., Springfield, 217/787-6200 or 800/221-2222, www.sleepinn.com, $89–95). Hotel rooms come with one queen or two full-size beds, plus a few extra amenities such as in-room irons and ironing boards.

On the south side of town, along Route 66 and not far from the Cozy Dog Drive-In, is the **◖ Route 66 Hotel and Conference Center** (615 E. St. Joseph St., Springfield, 217/529-6626 or 888/707-8366, www.rt66hotel.com, $70–150). This hotel has 108 rooms and six suites. Its slogan is "the museum you

can sleep in" because it has several antique cars and motorcycles on display in the lobby. The rooms resemble those found in most national chain motels, with big beds, televisions, tables, and coffeemakers. The hotel has RV parking available. Within the hotel is a casual Route 66–themed restaurant called the Filling Station Bar and Grill. It serves regional and American food (such as horseshoe sandwiches) on red-and-white checkered tables.

Consider the **◖ Mansion View Inn and Suites** (529 S. 4th St., Springfield, 217/544-7411, www.mansionview.com, $80–130), an upscale motor lodge. There are 93 rooms, some of them two-room suites and some with exterior entrances. The brick building fits in nicely with the historic downtown district surrounding it. You can walk to the Lincoln home, capitol buildings, and downtown restaurants and shops, and it's across the street from the governor's mansion.

OVER $100

Just down the block from the Lincoln home, within walking distance to the Old State Capitol and downtown restaurants, is the **President Abraham Lincoln Hotel** (701 E. Adams St., Springfield, 217/544-8800, www.presidentabrahamlincolnhotel.com, $119), a popular spot for people in town doing business with the government. There are 316 rooms here, and the building contains an indoor swimming pool, tavern, and fine-dining restaurant.

For a more pampered experience, try **◖ The Inn at 835** (835 S. 2nd St., Springfield, 217/523-4466, www.innat835.com, $110–200), where you can lounge in a four-poster or sleigh bed, order a bottle of wine or scotch to your room, and draw a bath in a claw-foot tub. The inn has a combination of rooms and several suites in the main building, a former luxury apartment building built at the turn of the 20th century and now listed on the National Register of Historic Places. The best rooms are those with large brick private balconies facing south—excellent spots to enjoy a morning cup of coffee or evening glass of wine. The building has high-speed Internet access, an elevator, and is wheelchair accessible. The bungalow behind the inn contains two more suites. Extended-stay corporate suites area also available.

Formerly an apartment home, the 1896 **Pasfield House Inn** (525 S. Pasfield St., Springfield, 217/525-3663, www.pasfieldhouse.com, $125–150) is a stately white house in downtown Springfield, several blocks west of the Lincoln sites. The recently remodeled, spacious Georgian has six suites with private baths. Have a glass of wine on the patio out back or browse the DVD library and retreat to your room. Rooms have sitting areas and work areas or both, flat screen TVs, and kitchenettes with mini-fridges stocked with breakfast items for the guest in advance. The inn also holds evening cheese and wine hours, and cooking classes are sometimes held in the Chef's Table, the inn's kitchen and dining room.

On the south side of Springfield, just off I-55, the 228-room and 14-suite **Crowne Plaza** (3000 S. Dirksen Pkwy., Springfield, 217/529-7777, www.cpsspringfield.crowneplaza.com, $120–175) has an indoor pool, fitness center, sundeck on the 14th floor, and restaurant. This is popular place for conventions and meetings.

Bed-and-Breakfasts

Perhaps the closest place you can get to Lincoln is by staying overnight at **The Henry Mischler House** (802 E. Edwards St., Springfield, 217/525-2660, www.mischlerhouse.com, $95–125), a bed-and-breakfast just down the street from the Lincoln home and across the street from the Lincoln historic district. The Queen Anne home, built in 1897, has five guest rooms, some with private bathrooms in the room and others down the hall from the room. (Those with bathrooms down the hall receive bathrobes.) You can see the Lincoln home from a window in the Henry and Louise Suite. When you need a little R&R, there's a back patio with a garden and chairs. Wine and cheese is served in the evenings, and a full breakfast is served in the morning.

If you're looking to stay in a more residential area, try **The Hidden Cottage** (2209 E. Reservoir St., Springfield, 217/789-6018, www.

hiddencottagespringfield.com, $135) northeast of downtown Springfield. The little cottage has a kitchen (stocked with continental breakfast items) and three queen-size beds (one in a loft), plus a sunroom with a Jacuzzi tub.

Also on the north side of town is the bed-and-breakfast **The Rippon Kinsella House** (1317 N. 3rd St., Springfield, 217/241-3367, www.ripponkinsella.com, $95–125), near the Oak Ridge Cemetery, where Lincoln is buried. This 1871 brick home has three guest rooms, all tastefully decorated in warm red, peach, and cream colors, and antique bedroom furniture. Spend some time on the expansive porch or on the nicely landscaped lawn after a day of visiting the historic sites or driving on Route 66. The inn has bikes for guests and also offers pickups from the airport or Amtrak station.

FOOD
Cafés

What's the weather in Paris today? Drop by **Incredibly Delicious** (925 S. 7th St., Springfield, 217/528-8548, www.incrediblydelicious.com, 7:30 A.M.–4 P.M. Mon., 7:30 A.M.–5 P.M. Tues.–Fri., 7:30 A.M.–3 P.M. Sat.), a boulangerie, patisserie, and café all rolled into one, to find out. (They post the weather there for those who miss or long to be in France.) At Incredibly Delicious, located in the Weber House, you can buy freshly baked breads such as a baguette, a croissant (plain, chocolate, raspberry, or other flavors), or truly scrumptious treats like fruit tarts, brioches, and cookies (including the "chocolate avalanche," which left a very pregnant traveler more than satisfied). Have a seat at one of the many tables scattered throughout the house and try some of the quiche or chicken salad. Or, finally, you can walk through the pleasant little garden and admire the arbor.

Andiamoi (204 S. 6th St., Springfield, 217/523-3262, 7 A.M.–4 P.M. Mon.–Tues., 7 A.M.–8 P.M. Wed., 7 A.M.–midnight Thurs.–Fri., 8 A.M.–2 P.M. Sat., $6) has a little bit of everything—café au lait, bagels, and muffins for breakfast, salads and sandwiches for lunch and dinner, plus wine for the evening. All are served in a small storefront space with about 10 tables.

Just down the street is the cheery ◖ **Trout Lily Café** (218 S. 6th St., Springfield, 217/391-0101, www.troutlilycafe.com, 7 A.M.–4:30 P.M. Mon.–Fri., 9 A.M.–3 P.M. Sat., 9:30 A.M.–2 P.M. Sun., $6), which specializes in preparing quiche and gourmet coffee and tea drinks. It also has sandwiches such as ham and cheese and turkey. This is a good spot to sit at a table inside or on the sidewalk and strike up a conversation with the owner or the regulars about political or cultural activities in town.

American

A local favorite, the **Feed Store** (516 E. Adams St., Springfield, 217-528-3355, 11 A.M.–3 P.M. Mon.–Sat., $7) is popular among government employees for its homey inexpensive food such as roast beef sandwiches, the veggie hero, and apple cake.

On the lower level of one of Springfield's oldest buildings downtown, ◖ **Norb Andy's**

Tabarin (518 E. Capitol Ave., Springfield, 217/523-7777, 11 A.M.–2 A.M. Tues.–Sat., $5–15) serves a mean horseshoe sandwich accompanied by live music. Norb Andy's also serves hamburgers and other filling pub fare.

Springfield is a long way from any ocean, but you'll be able to find some quality seafood at **Augie's** (2 W. Old State Capitol Plaza, Springfield, 217/544-6974, lunch 11 A.M.–4 P.M. Mon.–Fri., dinner 5–10 P.M. Mon.–Sat., $15). Dishes may include an Asian-pesto red snapper or grouper. The restaurant also serves meat entrées such as roast duck.

People flock to **D'Arcy's Pint** (2413 S. MacArthur Blvd., Springfield, 217/492-8800, 11 A.M.–10 P.M. Mon.–Thurs., 11 A.M.–11 P.M. Fri.–Sat., $5–15) for its horseshoe sandwiches, which consist of toast, meat, French fries, and melted white American cheese on top.

Maldaner's (222 S. 6th St., Springfield, 217/522-4313, www.maldaners.com, 11 A.M.–2:30 P.M. Mon.–Fri., 5–9:30 P.M. Tues.–Sat.) has been around a long time—since 1884, to be exact. Look for the flower pots and potted

Maldaner's restaurant, a downtown Springfield landmark

© CHRISTINE DES GARENNES

trees outside its entrance in the historic district within walking distance of the Lincoln museum and the state capitol. With its dark wood trim, white tablecloths, deep green booths, and private dining rooms, Maldaner's has a bit of a clubby atmosphere, as if a lot of government deal-making occurs in the restaurant's booths. A few pasta dishes grace the menu, but this is mostly a joint for carnivores. The restaurant, which sometimes features ingredients from local farms, has menu items like smoked trout with horseradish sauce and rye bread, quail stuffed with sausage, and traditional rib eye and prime ribs. Desserts are created in-house, so save some room for bread pudding, a popular choice among locals. The bar also serves up cocktails and cordials.

At the sunny **Garden of Eatin'** (115 N. 6th St., Springfield, 217/544-5446, 11 A.M.–3 P.M. Mon.–Fri., noon–3 P.M. Sat.), located a stone's throw from the Lincoln Museum, cheery staff can fix you a variety of salads, soups, and sandwiches for about $5.

Drive-In, Walk-In, Drive-Ups

A Route 66 institution, the 🅒 **Cozy Dog Drive In** (2935 S. 6th St., Springfield, 217/525-1992, www.cozydogdrivein.com, 8 A.M.–8 P.M. Mon.–Sat., $5) is most famous for creating the Cozy Dog, otherwise known as the corn dog. After you've scarfed down one or two of the signature dogs, take some time to look at photos of the highway and Springfield from decades ago. The restaurant has tons of Route 66 memorabilia plastered on the walls and on shelves and tables. There are some cool vintage road maps of Route 66 and the states it slices through.

Asian

Magic Kitchen (115 N. Lewis St., Springfield, 217/525-6975; 4112 N. Peoria Rd., Springfield, 217/525-2230) often wins accolades annually from the local press and Springfield residents. The popular spot is friendly, casual, and affordable. The food is also delicious. Here you can order yummy Thai favorites like spring rolls and pad thai (you choose the level of

THE HORSESHOE

Dieters, cardiologists, and nutritionists beware: The horseshoe sandwich, for which Springfield is famous, is not only loaded with fat and calories, it is also so tasty, especially after a packed day of touring or partying.

The sandwich is believed to have been invented by a chef or chefs at the Leland Hotel in Springfield (now long gone). Each horseshoe is different, but essentially the open-faced sandwich begins with two, maybe three pieces of toast, followed by your choice of meat (hamburger, ham steak, turkey, corned beef, you name it), French fries, and then a melted-cheese concoction. Sometimes the order of the cheese and the fries is reversed. Every sandwich is different, usually because everyone has a different recipe for the cheese sauce. Some make it with a cheddar and beer blend, with a touch of Worcestershire sauce. Others use white American cheese or Colby cheese with a dash of mustard. A lighter version of the horseshoe is the pony shoe, which (depending on the restaurant) will have one slice of toast, a smaller amount of meat, and fewer fries. It was dubbed the horseshoe because it resembled one: The ham represents the shoe and the fries are like nails.

spiciness desired) and, oddly enough, a slice of an American pie on the menu: Homemade apple pie, anyone? Dishes, which include noodles, rice, and curries, go for about $8. Magic Kitchen has a location in downtown Springfield on Lewis Street (a few blocks north and west of the capitol building) and another restaurant on the far northeast end of town on Peoria Road (Business 55).

Italian

Another Springfield institution is **Saputo's** (801 E. Monroe Ave., Springfield, 217/544-2523, www.saputos.com, 10:30 A.M.–10:30 P.M. Mon.–Fri., 5–10:30 P.M. Sat., 5–9:30 P.M.

Sun.). The casual Italian restaurant has been on the same street corner in downtown Springfield for over 60 years. (You can't miss its neon sign.) This is old-school Italian: baked pasta dishes, veal, chicken, and steak options, plus sandwiches such as the hefty meatball sandwich and entrées like eggplant parmigiano. Lunches are about $6, dinners about $15, more for steak or seafood.

Middle Eastern

Greek and Lebanese food is served at the **Holy Land Diner** (518 E. Adams St., Springfield, 217/544-5786, 11 A.M.–2 P.M. Mon.–Fri., 11 A.M.–9 P.M. Fri.–Sat., $10). You can try gyros, kebabs, and falafel sandwiches here.

INFORMATION AND SERVICES
Visitor Information

Springfield Convention and Visitors Bureau (109 N. 7th St., Springfield, 217/789-2360 or 800/545-7300, www.visit-springfieldillinois.com) has lots of brochures and helpful detailed maps of the city with the major points of interest, hotels, and restaurants marked on them. Unfortunately it is not open on the weekends: Hours are 8 A.M.–5 P.M. Monday–Friday. You can pick up regional maps and brochures at the **Central Illinois Tourism Development Office** (Hilton Hotel, 700 E. Adams St., Springfield, 217/525-7980, www.visitcentralillinois.com, 8:30 A.M.–5 P.M. Mon.–Fri.). It also has a collection of some state attractions, plus visitor magazines. The **Capitol Complex Visitors Center** (425 S. College St., Springfield, 217/524-6620, 9 A.M.–3:30 P.M. Mon., 8 A.M.–4:30 P.M. Tues.–Fri., 9 A.M.–4 P.M. Sat.) has brochures, informational videos, and exhibits about the capitol.

Tours

Guides with the newer **Springfield Walks** tour company (tickets at Tinsley Dry Goods store, 209 S. 6th St., Springfield, 217/525-1825, www.springfieldwalks.com, $12) often dress up in period costumes, carry lanterns, and take visitors along on walks past Springfield's historic sites. They offer tours of Lincoln's Springfield, a ghost tour, and one that focuses on the 1908 race riots. Tour times and dates vary, so call or check the website for detailed information. The tours are wheelchair accessible.

Feet tired? Climb aboard a pedicab with **Capital City Cycle Tours** (7th and Adams Sts., 217/971-5752, adults $6, children $4). See the downtown sites during a half-hour bike tour or hire the company to shuttle you from one attraction to a restaurant or hotel. Rides are available March–October.

Springfield Trolley (522 E. Monroe St., Springfield, 217/528-4100) stops at most of the city's tourist attractions, including the Lincoln home.

The Springfield Mass Transit District (217/522-5531, www.smtd.org) offers a **historic sites bus route** that runs every 30 minutes April–October. You'll pass by sites such as the Lincoln home, Lincoln tomb, and Dana Thomas house. The buses run from around 8:15 A.M.–5:45 P.M. Mon.–Sat. The fare is $1 per trip, and a day pass is $3.

Hospitals

If you sprained an ankle or are feeling under the weather, you can visit one of the walk-in clinics in town, such as **Springfield Urgent Care Center** (1836 S. MacArthur Ave., Springfield, 217/789-1403) or **Prompt Care** (1025 S. 7th St., Springfield, 217/753-2273). For more serious matters, there is **St. John's Hospital** (800 E. Carpenter St., Springfield, 217/544-6464, www.st-johns.org).

Post Offices

Downtown there are two U.S. post offices. The downtown station is at 411 East Monroe Street, 217/753-3432, open 7:30 A.M.–5 P.M. Monday–Friday. The capital station is at 211 South Spring Street, 217/753-3543, open 9 A.M.–5 P.M. Monday–Friday.

GETTING THERE AND AROUND
Airport

Several airlines offer flights to and from

THE MOTHER ROAD: ROUTE 66

If you really want to get a feel for Illinois, get off the interstate and take a drive down one of the historic two-lane highways that crisscross the state. The mother of all these is the legendary Route 66, which begins (or concludes) in Chicago.

Route 66 has been called the "Main Street Through America," and as you drive through the Illinois section, you'll see why that name fits. Aside from the Chicago and East St. Louis legs, a trip down Route 66 is largely rural in nature, past countless corn- and soybean fields and small towns home to grain elevators or former coal mines. Some of these towns have lively downtown districts complete with cozy luncheonettes and antiques shops, while others have empty storefronts and crumbling motels. Scattered along the way are signs of the old Route 66: vintage gas stations and Googie-style neon signs outside of businesses. This space-age type of design, with accents such as boomerangs and starbursts, can still be found in some sections along the historic highway.

The entire highway is about 2,400 miles long, with the Illinois section comprising about 300 miles. Construction started in the 1920s, although there were some noncontiguous roads along the route. For decades it was the main thoroughfare between Chicago and St. Louis and the way to go West. For the most part, the road follows I-55 on a northeast to southwest path. There are a few alternate routes through or around some cities such as Springfield. After I-55 was built in the 1970s, Route 66 essentially became a frontage road.

The highway begins at Jackson Boulevard and Lake Shore Drive along Chicago's lakefront. The route through Chicago and the suburbs can be nerve-wracking, time-consuming, and, in this traveler's opinion, not worth it if you specifically are out to drive the road. Neighborhoods and commercial districts along this section of the route have been so developed and redeveloped that it's often hard to imagine what it would have been like to drive the leg during the road's heyday. To avoid traffic headaches, you might want to start the journey near Joliet, which is about an hour or so southwest of the city. You'll pass through Wilmington, home to the Launching Pad Drive-In and several antiques shops; Pontiac and its Route 66 museum; Lincoln, with its courthouse square that's home to more antiques shops and a few cafés. In Springfield, the top Route 66 attractions are Bill Shea's Gas Station Museum and the Cozy Dog Drive-In, followed by the Sky View Drive-In Theatre, which has been showing films since 1951 in nearby Litchfield. Finally, the iconic Brooks Catsup Bottle in Collinsville is a must-see for fans of roadside architecture.

Like to party with like-minded road warriors? Springfield hosts the **International Route 66 Mother Road Festival** (217/422-3733 or 866/783-6645, www.route66fest.com) every year in mid to late September in downtown Springfield.

Springfield's **Abraham Lincoln Capital Airport** (1200 Capitol Airport Dr., west of J. David Jones Pkwy., Springfield, 217/788-1060, www.flyspi.com), north of the city. American's commuter service, American Connection, flies to and from St. Louis. United Express flies to Chicago O'Hare and Washington, D.C.'s Dulles Airport. Parking at SPI is free. Avis (217/522-7728), Budget (217/523-9215), and Hertz (217/525-8820) have rental-car agencies at the airport. You can also hail a cab at the airport.

Train

Amtrak has several trains that make stops at Springfield's station (Washington and 3rd Sts., Springfield, 800/872-7245, www.amtrak.com). The Texas Eagle runs between Chicago and San Antonio, Texas, and on to Los Angeles, stopping in the Illinois towns of Joliet, Pontiac, Bloomington, Springfield, Lincoln, and Alton. The Lincoln line operates daily between Chicago and St. Louis, with stops in Summit, Dwight, Joliet, Pontiac, Bloomington, Lincoln, Springfield,

Carlinville, and Alton. The Ann Rutledge serves Chicago, St. Louis, Kansas City, and some towns in between, including Springfield. It's about a 3.75-hour train ride from Chicago to Springfield, and a little over 2 hours between Springfield and St. Louis. A one-way ticket between Chicago and Springfield will cost about $40, and about $25 to or from St. Louis. The Springfield train station is staffed 6 A.M.–10:30 P.M. daily.

Bus
Springfield Mass Transit (217/522-5531, www.smtd.org) buses run roughly 6 A.M.–6 P.M. Monday–Saturday. There are 12 different lines through the city. A one-way fare will cost $1. Routes 1 and 2 take you to and from the fairgrounds. You can pick up a map and schedule at the convention and visitors bureau.

The **Greyhound** station is at 2351 South Dirksen Parkway in Springfield. You can contact the station at 217/544-8466.

Taxi
Several taxicab companies operate in Springfield, including **Checker Radio Cab** (217/525-1630), **Lincoln Yellow Cab** (217/523-4545), and **United Taxi Cab** (217/585-8577).

SOUTH OF SPRINGFIELD
Litchfield
A must-do for Route 66 travelers, the **Sky View Drive-In Theatre** (Route 66, Litchfield, 217/324-4451, www.litchfieldskyview.com, $2) has been alive and kicking as a drive-in along the historic road since 1951. New movies and classics are shown here. Pizza, chili dogs, popcorn, and drinks are sold at the concession stand. It's open the first or second weekend in April–late October, depending on the weather. Movies are shown daily except after Labor Day and before Memorial Day, when they're shown Friday, Saturday, and Sunday only. It's 0.5 mile north of Highway 16 on Route 66.

Another Route 66 landmark is the **Ariston Cafe** (S. Old Route 66, Litchfield, 217/324-2023, www.ariston-cafe.com, 11 A.M.–9 P.M. Tues.–Thurs., 11 A.M.–10 P.M. Fri., 4–10 P.M. Sat., 11 A.M.–8 P.M. Sun.) The restaurant, which first opened in Carlinville in 1924, has been in its present location on the historic highway since 1935. Run by descendants of the original Greek owners, the Ariston has a little bit of everything: Italian dishes like manicotti, steaks, burritos, tamales, coconut shrimp, catfish fillets, and the central Illinois favorite, the horseshoe sandwich with loads of beef, fries, and cheese. Plus the café always has fresh baklava on hand.

New Salem and Vicinity

◀ LINCOLN'S NEW SALEM
In 1831, when Abraham Lincoln was 22 years old, he left home to make a living for himself in New Salem, a pioneer town near the Sangamon River. The Illinois Historical Preservation Agency has re-created the town with a state historic site called Lincoln's New Salem (Hwy. 97, two miles south of Petersburg, 217/632-4000, www.lincolnsnewsalem.com, typically 9 A.M.–5 P.M. Wed.–Sun. Mar.–mid-Apr. and Labor Day–late Oct., 9 A.M.–5 P.M. daily mid-Apr.–Labor Day, 8 A.M.–4 P.M. Wed.–Sun. Nov.–Feb., donation). Lincoln lived here for six years, although he left briefly to fight with a militia in the Black Hawk War. New Salem, historians say, is where Lincoln came of age, working as a store clerk, surveyor, and postmaster. He was a jack-of-all-trades here. During this time he began reading voraciously and learning about business, literature, and politics. This is also where Lincoln allegedly met Ann Rutledge, who, according to some folks, was the love of his life. While in New Salem, Lincoln was elected to serve as a state representative. He reported for duty in Vandalia, then the state capital, in 1834.

The town of New Salem has been reconstructed to appear as it did back in Lincoln's day. Staff achieved this by studying plat maps,

© CHRISTINE DES GARENNES

Lincoln's New Salem

surveys, and reading diaries. It's an impressive place, and except for the T-shirted tourists with cameras, it looks like a pioneer village with a dozen or so buildings lining the roads. Women sit in log cabins sewing, and men fiddle with the gristmill. The tour is a self-guided walking tour, so you can take in the village at your own pace. There are 700 acres here and several miles of trails through the woods.

Also on the historic site is an outdoor amphitheater called **Theatre in the Park,** where locals dress in period clothing and share stores about pioneer life in Illinois or stage shows such as Mark Twain musicals. Productions are held Friday–Sunday evenings June–August.

Want to pick up some more Lincoln vibes? Camp overnight in the **Lincoln's New Salem Campground** (Hwy. 97, two miles south of Petersburg, www.lincolnsnewsalem.com, $10–15 per night), which has 200 campsites. Half of those come with electricity. All of the sites are available on a first-come, first-served basis. It is open year-round; however, the water in the two shower buildings is not turned on December 1–March 15.

NEARBY SIGHTS

Continuing north from Lincoln's New Salem on Highway 97 is a newer winery to the region. **Hill Prairie Winery** (just south of Oakford off Hwy. 97, Oakford, 217/635-9900, 11 A.M.–5 P.M. Mon.–Sat., noon–5 P.M. Sun. June–Dec., 11 A.M.–5 P.M. Wed.–Sat., noon–5 P.M. Sun. Jan.–May) bottles everything from sweet to dry white, red, and blush wines. Many come with Illinois-appropriate names like prairie sunshine (a sweet white) and crimson moon (described as a port-style wine). They often host local music shows and the occasional murder mystery dinner.

While he was living and working in New Salem, Lincoln reportedly often stopped by the nearby town of Athens, about six miles to the east. He'd visit the post office and general store there and visit with the owner, Colonel Matthew Rogers. After he was elected to the state legislature, Lincoln along with eight other men lobbied for the state capital to be moved from Vandalia to Springfield. After their colleagues approved the move, the "long nine" (they were all over six feet tall) celebrated at a dinner in a banquet room above the post office and general store. That building, which still very much looks like a general store and post office from the outside, is now the **Long Nine Museum** (200 S. Main St., Athens, 217/636-8755, 1–5 P.M. Tues.–Sat. June 1–Sept. 1, or by appointment, $2). Inside, the first floor has a hodgepodge collection of vintage items (dolls, pottery, etc.) and the second floor, where the dinner took place, has some dioramas about Lincoln's life, including a scene of him surveying in Athens.

Growing up in the small rural towns of Petersburg and Lewistown in the 1880s, Edgar Lee Masters would encounter dozens of residents, from not-so-chaste ladies to bitter old men. Later on in his life, far away from these towns and their characters, Masters would be inspired to write honest collections of poems about small-town life. The result was the celebrated *Spoon River Anthology*. This book of poetry, along with other Masters works, are on view at his boyhood home in Petersburg, the **Edgar Lee Masters Home** (Jackson and 8th Sts., Petersburg, 10 A.M.–noon, 1–3 P.M. Tues. and Thurs.–Sat. Memorial Day–Labor Day, free). For more information about the house or if you want to arrange a tour, call the Petersburg Chamber of Commerce at 217/632-7363. Masters is buried in Oakland Cemetery, west of Oakland Avenue on the southwest side of town.

RECREATION
The folks with **New Salem Canoe** (217/494-3957 or 217/632-2585, www.newsalemcanoe.com, $25–45) will drop off canoes or kayaks for you to use on the Sangamon River near Petersburg or on an area lake. Choose from 3- to 20-mile-long paddling trips, canoes or kayaks, half-day or full-day trips.

ACCOMMODATIONS
Petersburg has two fine Italianate-style bed-and-breakfasts, both up on the hills overlooking Petersburg. **The Oaks** (510 W. Sheridan, Petersburg, 217/632-5444 or 888/724-6257, www.theoaksbandb.com) is a grand brick home on a 5.5-acre estate. The 1875 mansion once belonged to a state senator. There are five rooms available here, including the "maid's quarters," a gorgeous room with a private screened-in porch. Rates are from $75 for a room with a queen bed, fireplace, and private bath down the hall to $145 for a two-room suite with two fireplaces. Breakfast and afternoon wine and cheese are included. The Oaks also offers lunch to the public 11 A.M.–2 P.M. Wednesday–Saturday and dinner by reservation for bed-and-breakfast guests.

A few blocks away in a historic neighborhood is the newer **Maple Crest** (319 S. 9th Ave., Petersburg, 217/632-0128 or 800/653-8012, www.maplecrest.us, $70–110), an 1865 formal home with four rooms available, two of which come with private bathrooms.

The **Branson House B&B** (324 W. Jackson St., Petersburg, 866/562-5095, www.bransonhousebnb.com, $85–95) is a striking Victorian bed-and-breakfast on a hill. There are four rooms available here; two come with private bathrooms in the rooms and the other two have private baths down the hallway.

If you prefer the hotel experience, try **RiverBank Lodge** (522 S. 6th St., Petersburg, 217/632-0202, www.riverbanklodge.com, $75–140), a 24-room motel on the Sangamon River southeast of Petersburg and near Lincoln's New Salem. The rooms feature decent modern accommodations such as flat-screen TVs and wireless Internet access. Some rooms have views of the river. Continental breakfast is also included.

FOOD
In a neat old building across the street from the Long Nine Museum is the **Starlight Café** (201 S. Main St., Athens, 217/636-8511, breakfast and lunch daily, dinner Tues.–Sat., $5), a place where, amid the sound of clinking china, teens hang out, Rotarians hold meetings, and families come to eat. The menu is several pages long, with numerous sandwich options, most of them traditional, such as horseshoes, BLTs, and on Fridays, walleye or catfish sandwiches.

Lots of the dishes, particularly those served during breakfast, bear old-school celebrity names: the Roy Rogers Western omelet, the Cyd Charisse French toast. Breakfast is served until 2 P.M. The Starlight also has lunch and dinner buffets.

INFORMATION

Several local groups have assembled a website for the New Salem region. On www.visitmenardcounty.com you can find a listing of restaurants, lodging options, and the occasional tours.

I-55: Lincoln to Williamsville

If you dig road trips, small historic downtowns, and vintage roadside attractions, one of the best legs along Route 66 in central Illinois is between Bloomington and Springfield. Drive the approximately 20-mile strip from Lincoln to Williamsville and you'll come upon Elkhart, a small town with a pioneer cemetery, antiques shop, and bakery. There's also no shortage of tributes to Abraham Lincoln. When he was a lawyer traveling on the Eighth Judicial Circuit, Lincoln tried cases at the Postville and Mount Pulaski courthouses. He also christened the town of Lincoln in 1853 by slicing open a watermelon.

LINCOLN
Downtown Lincoln

Park the car and take about an hour or so to walk around Lincoln's downtown and the courthouse square at Broadway, McLean, Pulaski, and Kickapoo Streets. Not far from the train tracks is a plaque that marks the probable spot where Lincoln broke open a watermelon, christening the town named after him (it's at Broadway and Chicago streets). From there you can check out some colorful murals that have been painted on its buildings downtown around the courthouse. Not surprisingly, many feature a young Abe Lincoln. Throughout downtown are several antiques shops, including the multistory **Lincoln Antiques and Furniture Center** (112 S. McLean St., Lincoln, 217/732-2000) and some specialty shops, such as **Beans and Such** (115 S. Kickapoo St., Lincoln, 217/735-5520), where you can buy coffee beans by the pound and shop for dishware and other kitchen stuff.

Drop by the J&S Auto Center (Woodlawn Road and Route 66) to see the world's largest covered wagon (at least, so says the *Guinness Book of World Records*). Formerly located in the little town of Divernon, south of Springfield, **"The Railsplitter" covered wagon** moved to Lincoln in 2007. At the front of the 40-foot-long wagon sits a 12-foot-tall Abe Lincoln dressed in a black suit and stovepipe hat reading a book titled *Law.*

Postville Courthouse State Historic Site

On the west side of town is a replica of the Postville Courthouse (5th St./Rte. 66, between Madison and Union Sts., Lincoln, typically noon–5 P.M. Tues.–Sat. Mar.–Oct., noon–4 P.M. Nov.–Feb. but call ahead for hours, $2 donation), where Abraham Lincoln once tried cases back in the 1840s. The real one is in Dearborn, Michigan, where Henry Ford (yes, the car guy) moved it in 1929 after buying the building and the block on which it stood. (He had it dismantled and rebuilt in Greenfield Park.) The timber courthouse that visitors see today was rebuilt in the 1950s, although it was modeled after how it may have looked in 1840. Back then the area was called Postville, and it was the county seat of Logan before the seat was switched to Mount Pulaski to the south in 1848, and a few years after that to Lincoln, a few miles to the east. (Eventually Postville disappeared as a town and Lincoln expanded its boundaries.) When he was a lawyer on the circuit court in the 1840s, Abraham Lincoln, like many other lawyers and judges, traveled through the county and set up shop a few days before holding trials and taking care of business transactions. They'd come a few times a year. The courthouse, like many of its kind during that time, held offices for the county clerk, surveyor, sheriff, and others. And the replica is furnished much as it probably was back in the 1840s, with separate offices and a meeting space. Across the street from the courthouse is a VFW post on the site of Dekins Tavern, where lawyers such as Lincoln would stay while in town.

Edward R. Madigan State Park

Need a break from driving? Pull into Edward R. Madigan State Park (1366 1010th Ave., Lincoln, 217/735-2424, www.dnr.state. il.us) on the south side of Lincoln and just off Route 66. The 723-acre park along Salt Creek is divided into a north and south side. The north side, near the state correctional facility, has nature trails through meadows, and the south side has a canoe launch on the creek. It's not the largest or most popular park in the state, but it certainly has a peaceful atmosphere; there are no crowds, no lines of RVs.

Railsplitting Festival

Brush off your bonnets, tomahawks, and other pioneer gear for the annual **Abraham Lincoln National Railsplitting Contest and Craft Fair** held on the Logan County Fairgrounds in mid-September. As a nod to the 16th president (and one of the many jobs Lincoln held down before studying law, becoming a lawyer, and entering politics), this fun event pits novice and professional railsplitters against each other to see how fast and how well they can split logs into rails. But there's so much more: vintage baseball games, period dancing, tomahawk throwing contests, tug-of-war events, log-rolling contests, food, music, you name it. More information is available from the Logan County visitors bureau or www.railsplitting.com.

"The Railsplitter" covered wagon in its new home, Lincoln

© CHRISTINE DES GARENNES

Accommodations

Most of the hotels and motels in Lincoln are at I-55 and Highway 10. Rates start at $40–50 per night and go up to $130 per night for suites at the chain hotels. Here's a list: **Lincoln Inn** (1730 5th St., Lincoln, 217/732-9641); **Super 8** (2800 Woodlawn Rd./Hwy. 10, Lincoln, 217/732-8886); **Comfort Inn of Lincoln** (2811 Woodlawn Rd./Hwy. 10, Lincoln, 217/735-3960); and **Holiday Inn Express** (130 Olson Dr., Lincoln, 217/735-5800).

Food

The **Blue Dog Inn** (111 S. Sangamon St., Lincoln, 217/735-1743, www.bluedoginn.com, 11 A.M.–2 P.M. Mon., 11 A.M.–10 P.M. Tues.–Thurs., 11 A.M.–11 P.M. Fri.–Sat., $5–18) is an amusing dog-friendly pub and restaurant. There's no shortage of photographs and paintings of dogs hanging on the walls. And some of the sandwiches, such as "the rare breed" (roast beef with cream cheese), have been named after dogs. Dinners include boneless pork loin and fried shrimp. Save room for a slice of chocolate or lemon cream pie.

Brandt's Arcade Café (513 Pulaski St., Lincoln, 217/735-1443, 6 A.M.–2 P.M. Mon.–Sat., $5) is a meat-and-potatoes kind of place. The breakfast and lunch spot, with its vintage counter and handful of tables, serves inexpensive comfort food, such as scalloped potatoes. It seems to be popular among the white-haired set.

Information

For information, contact the **Abraham Lincoln Tourism Bureau of Logan County** (1555 5th St., Lincoln, 217/732-8687, www.logancountytourism.org or www.abe66.com).

Getting There

Several **Amtrak** (800/872-7245, www.amtrak.com) trains stop at Lincoln's downtown train station, at Broadway and North Chicago Streets. The Texas Eagle, from Chicago to San Antonio, Texas, comes through three times a week; the Ann Rutledge, between Chicago and St. Louis, stops in Lincoln daily, as does the Lincoln Line between Chicago and Springfield.

BROADWELL

To get a sense of what traveling along Route 66 might have been like in the 1950s, drive to Broadwell, population 200. Here you'll come across a long-shuttered roadside motel, garage, and restaurant, which was once a museum that venerated Route 66, the restaurant's past, and, yes, pigs. The Pig Hip Restaurant Museum (Oak St. and Frontage Rd., Broadwell) closed in 2007 after a fire, but you can still drive by and visit the memorial. The Pig Hip Restaurant was famous for its pig-hip sandwiches, and over the years Route 66 travelers would stop by not just for the sandwiches but to chat with local residents Ernie and Frances Edwards, who ran the restaurant for more than 50 years, from 1937 to 1991.

ELKHART

Many of the early settlers to Illinois and those who would continue west to St. Louis and beyond passed through the Elkhart area, which used to be called Sangamo. They followed a trail known as Edwards' Trace, which weaved through Elkhart and connected the French towns to the south, near St. Louis, with those in the north by Lake Peoria.

Sights and Activities

East of town, overlooking the village and the region, is Elkhart Hill, one of the highest places in central Illinois (although you'd hardly know it; it tops out at 711 feet above sea level). The hill belonged to rancher John Dean Gillett, and his descendants still own land there. Richard Oglesby, governor from the mid-1860s through the mid-1880s, married Gillett's daughter and is buried in the cemetery at the top of the hill. The **pioneer cemetery** is quite a sight. You enter through grand iron gates, and in the center is St. John the Baptist, a little Gothic church made of limestone with Tiffany stained-glass windows. To get to the cemetery follow Highway 10/Chapel Road north of downtown Elkhart.

It's still a private residence, but the **Old Gillett Farm** (entrance off Gillett St., north of downtown by Hwy. 10, 217/947-2346, www.oldgillettfarm.org) is open occasionally (with notice) to visitors who are interested in hearing about the family and the estate's history. The chapel and 33-room main house are lovely spots for weddings or other formal events. Nearby is the 65-acre Elkhart Grove Forest Preserve, which has native trees and little bluebell flowers along its paths. You'll need permission from the house to walk the trails through here. If you're traveling with a group and you like to travel in style, you can stay at the farm's guesthouse, a three-bedroom 2.5-bath brick house. It's called a guesthouse, but it's just like renting an entire house (unless you normally live in a 33-room mansion). The guesthouse is beautifully restored and decorated with a mix of modern furniture and antiques. There's a full kitchen, formal dining room, and a pavilion and gardens outside.

Food

Bluestem Bake Shop (8 A.M.–4 P.M. Tues.–Sat., 8 A.M.–2 P.M. Sun., $5) sells gourmet coffees and teas, sandwiches such as turkey clubs, and salads. Fresh bread, fresh lettuce, fresh tomatoes—it doesn't get any better. On Sundays it serves warm quiche.

WILLIAMSVILLE

Farther along Route 66 is another quiet rural town called Williamsville, where older men sit on stoops and front porches and kids roll down the sidewalks on tricycles ringing their bells. The highlight of this Mayberry-like town is **Die Cast Auto Sales** (117 N. Elm St., Williamsville, 217/566-3898), a 1930s-era service station along Route 66 that now displays an impressive collection of automobile and Route 66 memorabilia, including scale-model cars and gas pumps. The owner has not only amassed model cars and trucks but also a wide variety of toys—windup toys, vintage soda machines, and action figures from any given decade. Hours tend to vary, so it's best to call ahead.

The Williamsville Historical Society has stocked a boxcar full of local-history items such as farming tools, high school yearbooks, and old photographs of the town from decades ago. The result is the **Boxcar Museum** (Old Rte. 66/Elm St., just west of the train tracks, Williamsville, 217/566-2470, 10 A.M.–2 P.M. Wed., free).

Champaign-Urbana and Vicinity

Champaign-Urbana may lack the scenic overlooks common in hillier regions to the south and northwest, but the area is chock-full of recreational and cultural opportunities. This is in large part due to the presence of the University of Illinois, whose campus sits partly in Champaign and partly in Urbana. Known primarily for its engineering, physics, and computer science departments (the campus is home to the National Center for Supercomputing Applications), the UI attracts students from all across the state and the world. Its Krannert Center for the Performing Arts brings in top-notch musicians and shows, such as Ravi Shankar and the Juilliard Quartet. And fans from all around come to cheer on the Fighting Illini at basketball and football games. The cities, which have a combined population of about 100,000, are home to a vibrant mix of musicians, actors, scientists, historic preservationists, and more. There are a decent stock of Victorian and Craftsman-style homes, cobblestone streets in historic residential districts, plus revitalized downtown districts with a growing number of restaurants, coffee shops, and drinking spots.

Although designated a county in 1833, it wasn't until the 1850s that Champaign County started attracting settlers and began to prosper. That was when the Illinois Central Railroad

CHAMPAIGN-URBANA

© AVALON TRAVEL

decided to lay tracks in the area and build a depot in Champaign County. The town of Urbana came first, and people established homesteads around Boneyard Creek (now largely a drainage ditch through the towns). The county courthouse was built in Urbana in 1848, with the soon-to-be-famous Abraham Lincoln occasionally arguing a few cases there. Most of the industry around Champaign and Urbana is still farm-related. You'll notice quite a few grain-processing plants and elevators on the outskirts of town, plus farm machinery retail stores. Of course, the University of Illinois, initially the Illinois Industrial University when it was established in 1867, is a huge employer, as is Kraft Foods. When the wind is right, you can smell salad dressings and cheese powder brewing in the west Champaign plant.

SIGHTS
The University of Illinois
Established in 1867, the University of Illinois was and is a focal point of culture and events in the two towns, and it sits right between the two. The campus extends from First Street to the west and Lincoln Avenue to the east, University Avenue to the north and Windsor Road to the south. Take a stroll through the quad and the Illini Union, where you can grab a cup of coffee, view artwork by students, or go bowling. From the union, you can visit fine museums, among them the Krannert Art Museum and the Spurlock Museum, parks such as the arboretum, and unique buildings such as the Assembly Hall, all within about a 15-minute walk.

The Krannert Art Museum (500 E. Peabody Dr., Champaign, 217/333-1860, www.kam.uiuc.edu, 9 A.M.–5 P.M. Tues.–Wed. and Fri.–Sat., 9 A.M.–9 P.M. Thurs., 2–5 P.M. Sun., donation) showcases a wide variety of artwork, including Latin American textiles, French lithographs, and contemporary American drawings. The museum also shows artwork by UI graduate students and faculty. Each gallery in the **Spurlock Museum** (600 S. Gregory Dr., Urbana, 217/333-2360, www.spurlock.uiuc.edu, noon–5 P.M. Tues., 9 A.M.–5 P.M.

Wed.–Fri., 10 A.M.–4 P.M. Sat., noon–4 P.M. Sun., donation) focuses on different world cultures, including those of Asia, Africa, the Middle East, Oceania, Europe, as well as Native American and ancient Mediterranean cultures. You'll see items such as brass engravings from 12th-century Europe, a Roman iron spearhead and sling bullets from 1000 B.C., gongs from Ecuador, a replica of a Confucian home, Egyptian funerary masks from 1000 B.C., and more.

Touted as the largest public university library in the world, the **University of Illinois Library** (1408 Gregory Dr., Urbana, 217/333-2290, 8 A.M.–midnight Mon.–Thurs., 8 A.M.–6 P.M. Fri., 9 A.M.–6 P.M. Sat., 1 P.M.–midnight Sun., hours vary during summer and school holidays, free) is a massive and impressive building for book lovers, with special and rare books collections that boast a first edition of John James Audubon's *Birds of America* and personal letters of Carl Sandburg, John Milton, and other notable authors. Free tours of the undergraduate library (built totally underground) and the main library are allowed. Pick up an audiocassette at the information desk.

That massive white spaceship-looking building on the southwest side of campus is **The Assembly Hall** (1800 S. 1st St., Champaign, 217/333-5000, www.uofiassemblyhall.com), an indoor arena where the Illini basketball teams play, where big-name musicians play, and where Broadway touring companies perform when in town.

The University of Illinois Arboretum (Lincoln Ave., between Florida Ave. and St. Mary's Rd., Urbana, 217/244-9934, free) is a fine spot to take a walk or pick up gardening ideas. The arboretum has rows of trees such as cypress and gardens of flowering plants, vegetables, and roses.

Museums
After years of fund-raising, soliciting artifacts, and extensive restoration efforts, the Champaign County Historical Society in 2001 opened the **Cattle Bank Museum** (102 E. University Ave., Champaign, 217/356-1010,

Cattle Bank Museum, Champaign

www.champaignmuseum.org, noon–4:30 P.M. Wed.–Thurs., noon–4 P.M. Sat., free). Believed to be the oldest known commercial building in the Champaign-Urbana area, the Cattle Bank is an Italianate-style building that began life in 1857 as an actual cattle bank. For most of the years that the building was open and operating, it was a grocery and drug store. Here you'll find exhibits on businesses that operated in town for decades, such as a shoe cobbler, displays of vintage clothing and accessories, and many photos of the towns. The front room has been re-created into a grocery store circa the turn of the 19th century, complete with an antique counting machine, paper dispenser, and twine ball.

The **Orpheum Children's Science Museum** (346 N. Neil St., Champaign, 217/352-5895, 10 A.M.–4 P.M. Tues.–Fri., 1–5 P.M. Sat.–Sun., $3, ages 2–18 $2) is technically a hands-on children's museum, but because it is inside a former vaudeville theater built in 1916, architecture buffs and preservationists might want to stop by to take a look at the building's architectural features and check out the small

exhibit on vaudeville theater. The building is a one-third-scale model of La Salle de Spectacle, the opera house at Versailles, with French Renaissance and baroque friezes, among other intriguing accents. Children can engage in water play, learn about levers and pulleys, and more.

ENTERTAINMENT AND EVENTS
Live Music

Because Champaign-Urbana is home to thousands of undergraduate and graduate college students, it's no surprise that the towns have a thriving live music scene. Being not too far from Chicago, Champaign-Urbana is often a stop for bands coming or going to the Windy City, from blues musicians to popular bands. Venues range from the expansive Assembly Hall to the pub Mike 'n' Molly's.

Mike 'n' Molly's (105 N. Market St., Champaign, 217/355-1236) is a small bar with a large, always hopping beer garden. Beer connoisseurs, prepare to salivate over the number of beers from around the world on tap and available in the bottle. In the mood for a specialty imported beer such as a Lindeman's Frambois? Chances are, Mike 'n' Molly's will have it. The pub hosts everything from spoken-word performances to comedy contests to the Prairie Jam music festival held there annually during Labor Day weekend.

On any given night, **The Highdive** (51 W. Main St., Champaign, 217/359-4444) could feature a Cajun band from Louisiana, DJs spinning club or hip-hop music, or even a country swing band. The Highdive serves imported and domestic beers, plus specialty drinks such as martinis. With two bars and plenty of bartenders, you don't have to wait long for a drink. Stop by for the popular jazz happy hour on weekday evenings.

Inside a former movie theater, **The Canopy** (708 S. Goodwin Ave., Urbana, 217/344-2263) is an intimate live music venue, with 1,000 seats and rainforest murals painted on the walls. The club, near the U of I campus, tends to attract the college crowd. Expect bands such as Frank Black and the Catholics or the String Cheese Experiment. The club also hosts the occasional Grateful Dead night or open mic night.

Bars

The beautiful **Boltini's** (211 N. Neil St., Champaign, 217/378-8001), in a renovated turn-of-the-20th-century storefront, has cool architectural features such as a silver-painted tin ceiling, intimate booths, and subdued lighting. You can order all kinds of specialty cocktails and imported and domestic beer here, as well as delectable munchies such as bruschetta. There's a small deck outside for summer evenings.

Farren's (308 N. Randolph St., Champaign, 217/359-6977, http://farrenspub.com) is part pub and part sandwich spot. Situated in a sunken room in a building accessible via an alley in downtown Champaign, Farren's features delicious but inexpensive drinks and sandwiches. Yes, you can get a basic burger here, but Farren's also serves a decent green chili burger and has quite a few veggie sand-wiches, such as the spinach panini. Sandwiches start at $3.50.

Jupiter's Pizzeria and Pool (39 Main St., Champaign, 217/398-5988, www.jupiterspizza.com) is a pool hall that serves beer on tap and by the bottle, including Bell's Amber and Pabst Blue Ribbon. The kitchen serves thin-crust piz-zas, such as pizza margherita and pizza pesto. A popular spot any time of the day, Jupiter's is in a turn-of-the-20th-century building with features such as high ceilings and hardwood floors.

The Office (214 W. Main St., Urbana, 217/344-7608), housed in a vintage building in downtown Urbana, is a good place to chat with friends over a pint. It's not a full-blown sports bar with hundreds of TVs, but not yet a nightclub. With its many wooden booths, it's a place you can hang out for a while. You can order bar food such as nachos and burgers, and play a round of pool or a game of darts.

Theater and Film

You can see just about any kind of show at the **Virginia Theatre** (203 W. Park Ave., Champaign, 217/356-9053 or 217/356-9063), from films during the Roger Ebert Overlooked Film Festival to the local theater company's rendition of *The Sound of Music*. A former vaudeville playhouse and movie theater, the Virginia is an Italian Renaissance building on the exterior with Spanish Renaissance features inside, including paintings of Spanish explorers.

The Champaign-Urbana Theater Company (203 W. Park Ave., Champaign, 217/356-9053) stages about three musical comedies per year in the Virginia Theatre.

The Celebration Company, a community theater group, produces original and traditional musicals such as *The Mikado* and dramas like *Orpheus Descending* in the intimate Station Theatre (223 N. Broadway Ave., Urbana, 217/384-4000, www.stationtheatre.com), a 1923 train station.

Built in 1913 as the Park Theatre, a poor man's version of the more ornately decorated Virginia Theatre and Orpheum, **Boardman's**

© CHRISTINE DES GARENNES

Champaign's Virginia Theatre, home to Roger Ebert's Overlooked Film Festival

New Art Theatre (126 W. Church St., Champaign, 217/355-0068, www.boardman-sarttheatre.com) presents foreign and art films, including Inuit movies and midnight showings of *The Rocky Horror Picture Show.*

The Krannert Center for the Performing Arts (500 S. Goodwin Ave., Urbana, 217/333-6280, www.krannertcenter.com) brings in professional touring opera companies, renowned musicians such as Ravi Shankar, and University of Illinois string quartets.

Events

Roger Ebert's Overlooked Film Festival in April keeps getting bigger every year. Films missed by most critics and audiences are shown in the classic Virginia Theatre. Another April favorite is the **Boneyard Arts Festival** when galleries, restaurants, and area businesses host art shows, sales, tours, concerts, and more. Area restaurants and artists set up booths at the **Taste of Champaign-Urbana** in West Side Park in Champaign in June. Corn is golden at Urbana's **Sweet Corn Festival** every August.

SHOPPING

Although a bit of a renaissance is occurring in downtown Champaign, with a few more boutiques opening here and there, the region remains mall-focused. **The Market Place Mall,** on Market Street north of I-74, is anchored by the department store Famous Barr and contains national chains such as Gap and Eddie Bauer. The mall is surrounded by numerous shopping centers that contain chain bookstores and home improvement stores.

You will find a few independently owned stores scattered throughout both towns. At **Champaign Surplus** (303 S. Neil St., Champaign, 217/356-4703) you can load up on camping supplies or field gear for your next bird walk or hiking trip.

Walnut Street Tea Company (115 S. Walnut St., Champaign, 217/351-6975) specializes in all kinds of imported teas and accessories.

It is possible to spend an afternoon exploring the three floors of **Jane Addams Book Shop** (208 N. Neil St., Champaign, 217/356-2555). This antiquarian shop specializes in out-of-print books and has quite the collection of cooking and art books.

Every Friday and Saturday, **The Corkscrew** (203 N. Vine St., Urbana, 217/337-7704, www.thecorkscrew.com) offers wine and beer samples at moderate prices (from $3 a person). In one afternoon you can try about 8–10 different wines of the Rhône region in France, and another day you can sample stout beers. Most of the wine bottles for sale have been reviewed (and extensively described) by savvy staff members.

RECREATION

Meadowbrook Park, at Windsor Road and Race Street in Urbana, is a stunning park on the southeast edge of town. The park contains organic gardens tended by area residents, a paved path for inline skating and bicycling, a hiking trail along a creek and through a meadow, plus 80 outdoor sculptures throughout the park.

The newer **Sholem Aquatic Center** (2200 W. Sangamon Dr., Champaign, 217/398-2581, www.champaignparkdistrict.com, hours vary by season, Memorial Day–Labor Day, $4.50–9) is a great spot to cool off if you're traveling through Champaign-Urbana during the summer (especially if you've got a crew of kids along). The pool has a lazy river, inner-tube slide, tunnel slide, zero-depth pool with play areas for children, and a toddler pool. Swing by for some lap swimming or diving.

ACCOMMODATIONS

The vast majority of hotels and motels are north of I-74 by the Market Place Mall, between Prospect and Lincoln Avenues. Here you'll find all the chain hotels and motels.

$50-100

Most chains are well-represented, including, for example, **La Quinta** (1900 Center Dr., Champaign, 217/356-4000, www.lq.com), **Country Inn & Suites** (602 W. Marketview Dr., Champaign, www.countryinns.com), and the **Baymont Inn** (320 Anthony Dr., Champaign, 217/356-8900). The clean

Hampton Inn (1200 W. University Ave., Urbana, 217/337-1100, www.hamptoninn.com) does not overlook I-74 and instead is located within town near the north side of campus and a short drive to downtown Champaign. They serve hot continental breakfasts.

Over $100

Sylvia's Irish Inn (312 W. Green St., Urbana, 217/384-4800, $125–250) is a Queen Anne house (complete with turrets and gables) in a historic district and within a short walk of downtown Urbana. The inn has three rooms with queen-size beds, a third-floor suite with a king-size bed, plus a carriage house with a kitchenette.

Akademika Bed and Breakfast (714 W. Michigan Ave., Urbana, $100–170) is within walking distance of campus and Urbana parks. This brick home, on one of Urbana's "state streets," a tree-lined cobblestone street, has four rooms (some with shared bathrooms). The rainbow suite on the third floor is a 700-square-foot room with a king bed and private bathroom. The house comes with features like wireless access and a sun room.

You'll find ◖ **The Illini Union Guest Rooms** (1401 W. Green St., Urbana, 217/333-3030, $94–170) in the center of the campus. The 72 rooms are above the union, and all have private bathrooms. You don't need to be an alumnus or visiting scholar to stay here.

The **Hilton Garden Inn** (1501 S. Neil St., Champaign, 217/352-9970, www.hiltongardeninn.com, $123) is within walking distance of Memorial Stadium and the Assembly Hall. This new hotel has spacious beautiful rooms, although the hotel can be loud on the weekends.

A good bet in the moderate to high-end price range is **The Drury Inn** (905 W. Anthony Dr., Champaign, 217/398-0030 or 800/378-7946, www.druryhotels.com, $105–155). Two great things about staying at the Drury Inn are the free evening cocktail hours during the week and the extensive continental breakfast, including fare such as steaming waffles and sausages.

The hotel has 133 rooms, an indoor pool, fitness center, and high-speed Internet access in rooms.

FOOD
Cafés
◖ **Café Kopi** (109 N. Walnut St., Champaign, 217/359-4266, 7 A.M.–midnight daily, $6), a thriving coffee shop in downtown Champaign, not only serves a gripping espresso, but also wholesome sandwiches and salads such as hummus plates, crab salad sandwiches, and spring greens. Expect the usual coffee-shop atmosphere: provocative art on the walls, newspapers scattered about on tables, and the freedom to lounge around for a while.

Caffé Paradiso (801 S. Lincoln Ave., Urbana, 217/384-6066) tends to attract more college students than Café Kopi does, since it is near the University of Illinois campus. The coffee menu is quite extensive, plus it has a variety of cookies, pastries, and sandwiches. Unlike other coffee shops in town, you are allowed to smoke here. A few tables are set up for chess or backgammon.

Casual
Jerusalem Restaurant (601 S. Wright St., Champaign, 11 A.M.–9 P.M. daily, $4) is right in the middle of fast-food central, surrounded by burger and pizza joints. But at the Jerusalem Restaurant you can get items such as cucumber yogurt salad, falafel, and kebabs for the same price as a burger from a national chain, and served in just about the same amount of time. Try the Arabian tea.

Li'l Porgy's (1917 W. Springfield Ave., Champaign, 217/398-8575; 101 W. University Ave., Urbana, 217/367-1018, lunch and dinner daily, $6) serves the best 'cue in town (though Famous Dave's might dispute that) with all the fixings: corn on the cob, collard greens, and corn bread. It also has great pork sandwiches, ribs, and charbroiled chicken.

Open 24 hours, **Merry Ann's Diner** (1510 S. Neil St., Champaign, 217/352-5399; 15 E. Main St., Champaign, 217/531-1160) attracts townies, farmers, and college students. There's a reason the place is always packed. Speedy, adept, and friendly cooks and waitresses serve diner fare: eggs, pancakes, and sit-in-your-stomach biscuits and gravy. Try the genuine hot chocolate on a chilly day.

American
Inside a former lumber mill, ◖ **Silver Creek** (402 N. Race St., Urbana, 217/328-3402, 11 A.M.–10 P.M. Mon.–Thurs., 11 A.M.–11 P.M. Fri.–Sat., 10 A.M.–2:30 P.M. and 4–10 P.M. Sun.) is just a neat place to go eat. One of its dining rooms is in an enclosed greenhouse. With dishes such as London broil and veal cutlet, candles flickering on the tables, and soft music playing in the background, Silver Creek tends to attract couples and older crowds. Lunch dishes are around $6; dinner entrées run $12–22.

Another unique setting for a restaurant is the ◖ **Courier Café** (111 N. Race St., Urbana, 217/328-1811, 7 A.M.–11 P.M. Sun.–Thurs., 7 A.M.–midnight Fri.–Sat., $6) which is in a former newspaper office building and on the site of a cabin of an early settler from the mid-1800s. Antiques are placed throughout the restaurant: light fixtures in every booth, a massive gold-painted cash register, and stained glass windows. Food is basic and homey, such as BLTs and blueberry pancakes. The Courier serves breakfast, lunch, and dinner.

Asian
Savor fresh curries and rice and noodle dishes at friendly **Siam Terrace** (212 W. Main St., Urbana, 217/367-8424, www.siamterrace. com, 11 A.M.–3 P.M., 5–10 P.M. Mon.–Fri., 11 A.M.–10 P.M. Sat., noon–9 P.M. Sun., $9–14) in downtown Urbana. The menu features fun appetizers like dragon shrimp (tiger shrimp wrapped in crispy noodles, fried, and served on a stick) and an array of entrées such as Bangkok duck with ginger sauce, carrots, broccoli, and sesame seeds. For a dish with kick try the jungle curry with coconut milk, bamboo shoots, baby corn, green beans, eggplant, carrots, mushrooms, and finally, basil. The food here is not oily or greasy, and the veggies are

beautiful: The broccoli is bright green and the carrots a shiny orange.

Eclectic

Fusing South American, Latin American, European, and African influences, **(Radio Maria** (119 N. Walnut St., Champaign, 217/398-7729, lunch 11 A.M.–2:30 P.M. Tues.–Fri., dinner 5–10 P.M. Tues.–Sat., brunch 11 A.M.–2:30 P.M. Sun.), serves dinner dishes such as Caribbean jerk chicken, polenta, and other meals made with ingredients such as mangoes and bananas. Like the meals, the setting is aesthetically pleasing, with oil paintings by local artists hanging on the walls, tabletops designed with scenes from vintage postcards, and red velvety curtains. Dinners are about $11. Also check out the impressive Sunday brunches from about $7. New to the menu are tapas.

The dark, modern **Ko Fusion** (1 E. Main St., Champaign, 217/531-1166, www.kofusion. com, 5–11 P.M. Mon., 11 A.M.–2 P.M., 5–11 P.M. Tues.–Fri., 3–11 P.M. Sat., 4–11 P.M. Sun., bar open later), with its neon light accents and fish tanks, is a new local favorite. They've got everything from sushi to fish entrées, steaks, and pizza. In addition to the maki rolls, nigiri, and sushi combination plates, here's a sampling of some entrées from a recent menu: grilled lamb T-bone with three-chili wild boar sausages and citrus couscous, tomato chutney, and mint oil; or spice-brined organic chicken with baby gem lettuce, red chard, parmesan, and Israeli couscous. If you've already eaten elsewhere, drop by Ko Fusion for sake, schnapps, and live music on the weekends. The outdoor patio is hopping on weekends in summer and fall when students return to the university. On Mondays the restaurant offers discounts on its sushi.

Sweets

Chocolate aficionados need to head to **Moonstruck** (709 S. Wright St., Champaign, 217/367-7402, 7 A.M.–1 A.M. Mon.–Fri., 9 A.M.–1 A.M. Sat., 10 A.M.–midnight Sun.), a chocolate bar where everything on the menu has chocolate as an ingredient. Choose from truffles, German chocolate cake slices, mocha

lattes, and more. The atmosphere is soothing and relaxing with overstuffed chairs and occasional jazz musicians; you'll want to hang out for a while.

(Mirabelle's (124 W. Main St., Urbana, 217/384-6460, 8:30 A.M.–6 P.M. Tues.–Fri., 8 A.M.–3 P.M. Sat., $3) has such a fine reputation for its fine pastries and breads that many people are willing to stand in line first thing on a Saturday morning to get their pick of fresh-baked brioche, baguettes, or fruit tarts. The line often stretches outside the shop and onto the sidewalk.

What's summer without a cup or cone of creamy, creamy custard? **Jarling's Custard Cup** (309 W. Kirby Ave., Champaign, 217/352-2273, noon–10 P.M. Mon.–Sat., 1–10 P.M. Sun. Mar.–Nov.) is a local favorite. Their version of the "blizzard" is a snowstorm, and you can get yours with a slew of different sweets. Brownie or berry sundaes, phosphates, milkshakes—you name it, the Custard Cup's got it. Sit outside at a picnic table or on one of the benches inside.

Markets

Being surrounded by farms definitely has its advantages. May–October, area farmers, including the Amish, set up booths in Champaign and Urbana. You can find everything from kohlrabi to zucchini, granola to free-range turkey at the area's **farmers markets.** In Urbana they sell goods on Saturdays 7 A.M.–noon in the Lincoln Square parking lot at the corner of Vine and Illinois Streets. In Champaign they sell on Wednesdays 7 A.M.–1 P.M. in the Country Fair Shopping Center parking lot, by Springfield and Mattis Avenues.

INFORMATION AND SERVICES
Visitor Information

For more information about Champaign-Urbana, contact **The Champaign County Convention and Tourism Bureau** (1817 S. Neil St., Champaign, 217/351-4133 or 800/369-6151, www.visitchampaigncounty. org). It stocks an information center in Market Square Mall on North Prospect Avenue.

© CHRISTINE DES GARENNES

farmers market at Lincoln Square, Urbana

Media

The News-Gazette (www.news-gazette.com), the daily newspaper, serves both towns and the surrounding area. You can find it at gas stations and convenience stores, bookstores, and libraries.

Internet Access

Most cafés in downtown Champaign and Urbana offer free wireless access. You can also go online for a fee at **FedEx Kinko's Copies** (506 S. Mattis Ave., Champaign, 217/355-3400; 613 S. Wright St., Champaign, 217/398-0003). Or you can log on for free at one of the public libraries: **The Champaign Public Library** (505 S. Randolph St., Champaign, 217/356-3980) or **The Urbana Free Library** (210 W. Green St., Urbana, 217/367-4069).

The two main hospitals are **Carle Foundation Hospital** (210 E. University Ave., Champaign, 217/337-3911) and **Provena Covenant Medical Center** (1400 W. Park Ave., Urbana, 217/337-2131).

The downtown **Champaign Post Office** is at 600 North Neil Street. The **Urbana Post Office** main office is at 3104 East Tatman Court.

GETTING THERE
Air

University of Illinois Willard Airport (U.S. 45 and Monticello Rd., Savoy, 217/244-8604, www.flycmi.com), about four miles south of Champaign, is served by two airlines, American and Northwest, with flights to cities such as Chicago, Detroit, and Dallas/Fort Worth.

Train

The **Amtrak** City of New Orleans train, which runs between Chicago and New Orleans, and the **Illini** and **Saluki** trains stop daily at Champaign's Illinois Terminal. Round-trip fares from Chicago to Champaign range roughly $32–64, depending on how far in advance you book your seat. The Amtrak ticket office is in the Illinois Terminal (45 E. University Ave., Champaign, 217/352-5905 or 800/872-7245).

Bus

Greyhound (Illini Terminal, 45 E. University Ave., Champaign, 217/352-4150 or 800/231-2222) has five buses that run between Chicago and Champaign every day. Four buses per day travel between Champaign and St. Louis. And two buses go to and from Indianapolis and Carbondale.

LEX-Lincolnland Express (217/352-6682, www.lincolnlandexpress.com) offers van rides to various spots in Chicago as well as the Indianapolis airport. In Champaign-Urbana, buses pick up and drop off passengers from the Illini Terminal downtown and the University of Illinois campus. **Megabus** (877/462-6342, www.megabus.com) takes passengers to Chicago and Memphis. Their stop is near the Illini Terminal at Market and Locusts Streets in Champaign.

GETTING AROUND
Bus

Champaign-Urbana Mass Transit District (217/384-8188, www.cumtd.com) runs routes seven days a week throughout both towns and to the southern suburb of Savoy, generally 6 A.M.–midnight. Buses depart every 10 minutes during peak hours and every hour on Sundays. Some routes around campus run until about 2:30 A.M. on the weekends. Buses do not run on major holidays: New Year's Day, Easter Sunday, Memorial Day, Fourth of July, Labor Day, and Christmas. Each ride costs $1; transfers are free. Exact change is required after 7 P.M. All routes are served by buses that are wheelchair-accessible, and all buses are equipped with bike racks. Pick up a map and schedule at the Illini Terminal (45 E. University Ave., Champaign).

Car

Most car-rental companies are at Willard Airport or within a few miles of the airport. **Avis** (407 S. Neil St., Champaign, 217/359-5441) can be found at Willard. **Enterprise** (1804 S. Neil St., Champaign, 217/351-1400 or 217/355-1300) is just south of the airport.

Taxi

You can catch a cab at the airport or Illini Terminal, but good luck trying to flag one down on a street corner or asking one to pick you up at a restaurant and take you to a bar. The towns' taxi companies stick to picking up and dropping off people at the airport. If you're coming into town at a late or early hour, you might want to call first to arrange a pickup. Try **Checker Cab** (217/355-0200), **Yellow Cab** (217/351-0971), **Orange Taxi** (217/363-1500), or **Illini Taxi** (217/384-5892).

MAHOMET
Sights and Activities

The 900-acre **Lake of the Woods Park** (109 S. Lake of the Woods Rd., Mahomet, 217/586-3360, www.ccfpd.org, free), run by the Champaign County Forest Preserve District, could be described as a suburban-style park. It's not right in town, but it's not exactly in the wilderness either. (It's difficult to get lost here. You're never too far from a golf course, trailhead, or road.) There's a little bit for everyone here: a lake for bank fishing, a 3.3-mile multiuse trail along the Sangamon River, botanical gardens, an 18-hole golf course, a par-3 nine-hole golf course, a covered bridge, and a bell carillon for your listening pleasure.

There's lots of walking to be done in Lake of the Woods. A paved multipurpose trail follows the Sangamon River through the length of the park and extends west of Highway 47 for a little more than three miles. You can continue on the asphalt path or alongside on the gravel path. Throughout the 266 acres are mowed trails that weave up and down hills and near the river. Near the botanical gardens is a woodsy winding nature trail in a section of the park called **Rayburn-Purnell Woods.** Finally, one of the nicest spots is the botanical gardens and the Miriam Davies Enabling Garden. This area was designed specifically for children and adults with disabilities, and it features raised beds (so people in wheelchairs can smell the flowers) and plenty of patio space for relaxing by the little waterfall.

During the summer you can rent canoes,

© CHRISTINE DES GARENNES

Lake of the Woods Park, Mahomet

kayaks, rowboats, and paddleboats at Lake of the Woods Park (1–5 P.M. Sun., $3). The park is open 7 A.M.–10 P.M. daily. The gardens are open dawn–dusk.

Within Lake of the Woods park is the **Early American Museum** (600 N. Lombard St./ Hwy. 47, Mahomet, 217/586-2612, www.earlyamericanmuseum.org, 10 A.M.–5 P.M. Mon.–Sat., 1–5 P.M. Sun. summer, 1–5 P.M. daily Mar.–May and Sept.–Dec., free), a first-rate local museum. Volunteers put together excellent rotating exhibits throughout the year. One recent exhibit highlighted how the Depression affected the region. In addition to the rotating shows, the museum's permanent collection tells the story of how the region was settled and what early pioneer life was like on the prairie. Displays include agricultural equipment and a re-created blacksmith shop. On occasional Sundays, an artisan sets up shop in or outside the museum to demonstrate his or her art, such as woodcarving or quilting.

Farmers Markets
The Asbill family's farm ◖ **First Fruits** runs a small welcoming store and restaurant (101 N. Lombard St., Mahomet, 217/586-1333, www.firstfruitsproduce.com, 10 A.M.–6 P.M. Tues.–Fri., 10 A.M.–4 P.M. Sat.) in downtown Mahomet. It features bath and beauty items, items like honey, jams, and produce, and meals made with, for example, chickens and produce grown on their farm. The farm, just off Highway 47 north of town, is constantly expanding, it seems, and there's always a variety of fruits and vegetables. Throughout the spring there are asparagus and salad greens, and into the summer, strawberries, carrots, potatoes, and huge garlic bulbs.

NORTH OF CHAMPAIGN
Rantoul
When the Air Force closed Chanute Air Force Base in 1993, Rantoul was left with a huge site on the east side of town with warehouses, barracks, and offices. One of the best things to happen to the space was the creation of the **Octave Chanute Aerospace Museum** (1011 Pacesetter Dr., Rantoul, 217/893-1613, www.aeromuseum.org, 10 A.M.–5 P.M. Mon.–Sat.,

noon–5 P.M. Sun., $7), which not only has extensive exhibits about the history of the base and life there (including an old food line), but the museum also has an amazing collection of airplanes. We're talking fighter jets and bombers, plus missiles. The museum also has exhibits on Rantoul area history. The former Chanute Air Force Base is east of U.S. 45 in Rantoul, south of U.S. 136.

Gordyville USA

West of Rantoul about 10 minutes is Gordyville USA (U.S. 136, Gifford, 217/568-7117, www.gordyvilleusa.com, free), a vast complex in the middle of corn and soybean country where Amish farmers buy and sell horses and antique dealers sell everything you can imagine: books to tea kettles, china to farm equipment. Gordyville, by the way, is not an actual town but is the name of the complex, named after the owner, longtime auctioneer Gordon Hannagan. Flea markets and auctions tend to be held on the second weekend of each month, 4–9 P.M. Friday, 9 A.M.–6 P.M. Saturday, 9 A.M.–4 P.M. Sunday.

Gibson City

One of the best ways to spend a summer evening is catching a movie at the drive-in. **Harvest Moon Twin Drive-In** (Hwy. 47, Gibson City, 217/784-8770 or 877/546-6843, www.harvestmoondrivein.com, weekends Apr.–May and Sept., daily June–Aug., $6) is one of the few places in the state and the Midwest where you can see a flick under the stars (that is, if you choose to watch from the hood of your car or if you've got a sunroof or convertible). After opening in 1955, it had to be rebuilt a decade later after a tornado tore down the screen. Like many drive-in theaters, it closed when big movie theaters started cropping up and becoming more popular. It was closed for much of the 1980s before being reopened by a local drive-in devotee. Here the movies are shown even in the rain. All you need is an FM dial on your car radio and you can listen to the movie. Harvest Moon has two movie screens, picnic grounds, a concession stand, and it hosts events throughout the season, such as car shows and fireworks on the Fourth of July. The grounds open one hour before movies, which usually start around 7 P.M.

ACCOMMODATIONS AND FOOD

Run by Berlin natives, the **Bayern Stube** (209 N. Sangamon Ave., Gibson City, 217/784-8304, www.bayernstube.com, 4:30–9 P.M. Tues.–Sat., 11:30 A.M.–8 P.M. Sun., lunch 11 A.M.–2 P.M. Thurs.) is a restaurant and bed-and-breakfast that since opening in 1991 has developed a cultlike following among central Illinoisans who love German beer and German food. The restaurant is decorated somewhat like a lodge, with no shortage of beer steins and taxidermy on the walls. And the food is oh-so-hearty, with plenty of sausage, sausage, sausage. And if sausage is not your thing, there's beef tenderloin with portobello mushrooms and gorgonzola cheese, potato pancakes, frogs' legs, and pickled herring, followed with some old-fashioned homemade strudel. Or maybe you're not hungry enough for a meal. At least drop by for a pint of German beer and a stuffed pretzel. Throughout the year the owners organize food and drink fests, such as Oktoberfest in late September and early October, a hunters' feast in mid to late February, and May Fest in early to mid-May. There are two bed-and-breakfast rooms that come with kitchenettes (microwave, sink), whirlpool baths, and continental breakfast when you want it. Room rates are $85–98 per night.

INFORMATION

Feel free to call the **Gibson City Area Chamber of Commerce** (126 N. Sangamon Ave., Gibson City, 217/784-5217) if you have any questions about the town or navigating through the area.

HOMER LAKE

Large bodies of water are hard to come by in east-central Illinois. Most of the water you'll find is in drainage ditches or retention ponds. If you're in the area and just itching to take a canoe ride or have a picnic by the edge of a lake, take a 30-minute drive east of Champaign-Urbana. The centerpiece of the **Homer Lake Forest Preserve** (2573 S. Homer Lake Rd., Homer, 217/896-2455, www.ccfpd.org), is the approximately 80-acre Homer Lake, created by damming the Salt Fork River. It's not a big blue expanse, but this little lake and the preserve that surrounds it (about 800 acres in total) is quite the little gem in the middle of corn and soybean country. There are plenty of walking trails through woods and prairie, benches along the lake, and fishing spots for catching bass and other fish. The environmental education center, with its animal exhibits, is a hit with kids. There's even a bird-feeding area outside the center and a little area inside where you can spot cardinals and other birds. The education center is open 8:30 A.M.–5 P.M. Monday–Friday and 10 A.M.–4 P.M. Saturday April–October; 8:30 A.M.–5 P.M. Monday–Friday November–March. It can be a little tricky finding Homer Lake. From St. Joseph,

which is about 10 minutes east of Urbana, keep driving east on Highway 49, then follow the signs south and east for about 2 miles to the park.

SADORUS

So the ocean is hundreds and hundreds of miles away, but that doesn't mean little Sadorus, Illinois, can't have a **National Museum of Ship Models and Sea History** (201 S. Market St., Sadorus, 217/352-1672, 10 A.M.–4:30 P.M. Sat. and by appointment, $5). About 15 miles southwest of Champaign in downtown Sadorus, a small farming community, is the rare and impressive museum. Housed in a beautifully restored storefront space (formerly a general store), the museum's collection includes ship models used in Hollywood films, paddle wheels, ocean liners, and more. The boats are on two floors, and there are nautical photographs and paintings hung around the building.

Monticello and Piatt County

Back in the 1890s the town of Monticello, about 20 miles southwest of Champaign, was quite well known throughout the state thanks to Dr. W. B. Caldwell. He invented a laxative that would bring him and his local business partners at the Pepsin Syrup Company (now demolished) loads of money. Mansions that once belonged to these medicine barons can be seen by taking a stroll or drive along North State Street, dubbed Millionaires' Row. A self-guided walking tour pamphlet, available from the Wabash Depot (see *Information*), highlights some of the most magnificent homes and points out their neoclassical, Victorian, and Gothic-revival architectural features.

Monticello is now a growing community that keeps getting more intriguing every year, as artisans such as weavers, glassblowers, and potters move into town and open galleries. Because it is within a 30-minute drive of Champaign-Urbana to the east and Decatur to

the west, it has become somewhat more metropolitan than in years past, with more professionals commuting to the cities and quite a few subdivisions popping up on the outskirts of town.

SIGHTS
◖ Robert Allerton Park

Situated among silver maple and sycamore woods, sprawling lawns, manicured gardens, and a reflection pond, Robert Allerton Park (515 Old Timber Rd., Monticello, 217/762-2721, www.allerton.uiuc.edu, 8 A.M.–sunset daily) evokes the feel of a 19th-century European estate. Once a second home to Allerton, a Chicago banker, philanthropist, and art collector, the house, along with its gardens and farm fields, was deeded to the University of Illinois on his death in 1946. The main house tends to be closed to the public, unless you are attending a special event or conference sponsored by the university. But you can certainly explore the nearly 20 miles of trails and acres of gardens. (Go ahead and peek through the windows for a good look at the impressive library.) Favorite spots include the Fu Dog Garden, where lapis lazuli ceramic *Fu Dogs* hold court; the sunken garden, a local favorite spot for weddings; and the southwest field, where the bronze *Sun Singer* raises his arms toward the sky. Allerton Park hosts several great events during the year, such as concerts in a restored barn, concerts in the English walled garden, food tastings, and children's educational activities. The visitors center is open 9 A.M.–5 P.M. daily during the summer, and 8:30 A.M.–4:30 P.M. during the winter.

Museums

At the **Monticello Railroad Museum** (Iron Horse Pl., Monticello, 217/762-9011, rides on weekends May–late Oct., $6), you can catch a short train ride through the town, past the surrounding farms, and along the Sangamon River valley. Illinois is home to a lot of railroad museums; the Monticello museum is one of the best because of the sheer number of cars and equipment it has on display. At the museum's railroad park, check out a variety of vintage diesel and steam locomotives, as well as freight and Pullman passenger train cars. The museum also offers special train rides geared toward kids, such as the Ghost Train and Haunted Box Car rides around Halloween and a Santa Train ride during the holiday season. The museum is off Iron Horse Place, a frontage road along I-72, off Monticello's Market Street exit. You can board the train there or at the Wabash Depot, at Center and State Streets in downtown Monticello.

Like the Cattle Bank Museum in Champaign, the **Piatt County Museum** (315 W. Main St. and 315 W. Washington Ave., Monticello, 217/762-4731, www.piatt museum.org, open by appointment, donations) is stocked with local artifacts, many of them related to farming. You'll also find photos taken of the town in the 19th and early 20th centuries. The museum is restoring a University of

Allerton Park's sunken garden, Monticello

© CHRISTINE DES GARENNES

Illinois beef barn located on the railway museum grounds and plans to move into the barn when it's finished.

A few miles south of Monticello the rural community of Bement lays claim to the fact that it was here (or at least, on a road outside of town) that U.S. Senate candidates Abraham Lincoln and Stephen A. Douglas decided to hold a series of debates, which would later catapult Lincoln into the national spotlight. The story goes that Lincoln and Douglas passed each other on the road between Monticello and Bement in 1859. They later met at the home of Francis Bryant, now called the **Bryant Cottage State Historic Site** (146 E. Wilson St., Bement, 217/678-8184, 9 A.M.–5 P.M. Thurs.–Sun. Mar.–Oct., 9 A.M.–4 P.M. Thurs.–Sun. Nov.–Feb., donation). Douglas was staying with Bryant, who had been a state legislator with Douglas in the 1850s. At the home (a little white cottage with green shutters and cedar shingles) Lincoln and Douglas forged plans for the debate. Today the home is being restored, and it is adjacent to a city park with picnic tables, a playground, and a veteran's memorial. Hours can change; call ahead.

ENTERTAINMENT

For a look at local color, visit **Bement Country Opry** (117 S. Macon St./Hwy. 105, Bement, 217/877-6499, www.bementcountryopry.com), where you can put on your cowboy hat and boots for live country music and dancing every Friday at 8 P.M.

SHOPPING

Monticello has quite a few galleries and artisans' shops, mostly clustered around the courthouse square. In the Old Levee Street Shoppes, you'll find, for example, **Prairie Fire Glass** (217 W. Washington St., Monticello, 217/762-3332), which sells hand-blown glass and custom stained glass, and offers workshops. **WackyNackies Gifts & Café** (206 W. Washington St., Monticello, 217/762-2022) is a coffee shop that also sells bath and beauty items, jewelry, purses and bags, chocolates, jams, Webkinz, you name

it. **Bee Active Toys** (204 W. Washington St., Monticello, 217/762-4386, www.beeactivetoys.com) sells board games, action figures (knights, pirates, army guys), plus kid craft and painting sets. Nearby is **Out of the Blue** (116 E. Main St., Monticello, 217/762-7173), which specializes in imported Polish pottery and other collectibles. Browse the **Steeple Gallery and Coffee House** (102 E. Lafayette St., Monticello, 217/762-2924, www.steeplegallery.com) for framed prints of pastoral scenes of American life, such as the red barn and town square.

RECREATION

Valentine Park, run by the Forest Preserve District of Piatt County, is a secluded little park on the outskirts of Monticello (on Cemetery Rd. east of Market St.). It's a great spot for a short walk or picnic; it's never crowded. In contrast to the open prairie nearby, Valentine Park sits among a dense grove of trees. The half-mile tree-identification walk takes you past hickory, black walnut, maple, and sycamore trees.

downtown Monticello

Bird-lovers should bring their binoculars for a visit to the bird-viewing area.

Lodge Park, about 1.5 miles north of town off County Highway 105, is a 500-acre park along the Sangamon River. You'll find several picnic tables, a playground, and some campsites.

ACCOMMODATIONS

If you stay overnight in Monticello, check into the **Best Western Gateway Inn** (805 Iron Horse Pl., 217/762-9436, from $60). Rooms are clean and comfy in this new building. The hotel features an indoor heated pool and continental breakfast of bagels and juice.

FOOD

You can't go wrong with any of the restaurants on the square. Two top picks are The Brown Bag Deli and Restaurant for casual food and Montgomery's on the Square for fine dining. For fresh healthy snacks, browse the Monticello farmers market held on the square Thursday afternoons spring through fall.

The Brown Bag Deli and Restaurant (212 W. Washington St., Monticello, 217/762-9221, call for hours, $5) lunch counter and coffee shop serves homemade soups such as cream of asparagus and minestrone and a variety of deli sandwiches. The restaurant is well-known for its pies, such as coconut cream and key lime.

Montgomery's on the Square (108 S. Charter St., Monticello, 217/762-3833, www.montgomerysonthesquare.com, 5–9 P.M. Thurs., 5–10 P.M. Sat.–Sun.) is the white-tablecloth dinner spot that features menu items featuring free-range poultry and grass-fed beef, plus some more definitely not local items like sea scallops and roasted wild boar (with cherries and fennel!). The menus change seasonally, plus there's a decent wine and dessert selection.

Down the street from the Opry in Bement is **Sweet Dreams** (201 S. Macon St./Hwy. 105, Bement, 217/678-2663, 11 A.M.–9 P.M. Mon.–Sat., 1–9:30 P.M. Sun.), a locally owned frozen custard joint with tables outside for eating the custard and watching the cars go by.

INFORMATION

Stock up on travel brochures at the **Wabash Depot** (Center and State Sts.), an old railroad station that houses a visitors center and offices of the **Monticello Chamber of Commerce** (217/762-7921 or 800/952-3396, www.monticellochamber.org).

Amish Country: Arthur and Arcola

Wide blue skies, long country roads, and the occasional horse-drawn black buggy and bicyclist—the area south of Champaign-Urbana and southeast of Decatur, where Coles, Moultrie, and Douglas Counties come together, is Illinois Amish country. This bucolic region is home to several thousand Amish who make their livings on diversified farms, greenhouse operations, and carpentry shops. Drive through here and you may see an Amish farmer driving a set of Belgian horses through a field to cut hay or an Amish woman washing clothes with a wringer washer and then hanging the clothes out to dry. The main hubs are Arcola, just west of I-57, and Arthur, about 10 miles west of Arcola along Highway 133. Both are picturesque towns with small residential districts with brick-lined streets and well-cared-for homes and downtowns full of antiques, gift shops, and casual American restaurants.

The Amish started settling in this area beginning in 1865 from places such as Indiana and Pennsylvania. Like others, they were seeking affordable land in a less-crowded part of the country. The Amish work and socialize within their community; however, many of the children do attend public school with other area children, and the people are quite receptive to polite, curious visitors. Some are willing to invite you into their homes to show

© CHRISTINE DES GARENNES

a horse-drawn buggy in downtown Arthur

you how they live (without electricity) and to talk about their customs. Not everyone in town is Amish. After the first farmers drained the ground in the late 1800s and discovered how rich the soil was, more pioneers from the south and east established homesteads next to the Amish. Today the region also has many large-scale corn and soybean farmers and businesses that cater to them.

ORIENTATION

If your main objective in the Arthur and Arcola area is to shop, it's a good idea to pick up a regional map from the Arthur visitors bureau. There are plenty of shops in downtown Arthur and Arcola; however, some of the best furniture stores and greenhouses are on the back roads. Many business owners have placed directional signs at intersections, making it easier to find their homesteads than if you were to drive around randomly. Still, if you're not familiar with the county road system, it can be a little confusing. (As you go north the road numbers increase. For example, you'll pass 1500N, then 1600N, 1700N, and

so on. Sometimes you'll come upon a 1525N or 1650N, but not always, and this is when it can get tricky.) At any rate, if you're ever lost, there's no shortage of friendly people around to help get you back on track. This is a close-knit community, and everyone knows where everyone lives and the best route to get there. Because the Amish are religious and hold lengthy church services on Sundays, just about everything shuts down then. Shop and farm hours are generally 8 A.M.–4 P.M. Monday–Saturday. Some Amish businesses have phone numbers that connect callers with an answering service or answering machine. And some Amish carry cell phones (which run on batteries, after all, not electricity).

This is beautiful country, and a great way to explore it, as well as to meet some Amish folks as you pedal along the back roads, is by bicycling. Try to bring a bicycle along on this trip.

While visiting the area, remember that the Amish do not like to be photographed, although feel free to photograph an empty buggy or their horses. The back roads do have wide shoulders to accommodate the Amish buggies,

BEYOND THE BUGGIES: ILLINOIS'S AMISH

With their plain dress, horse-drawn buggies, and religious lifestyle, the Amish are an intriguing bunch, especially to visitors. The central Illinois Amish community, about 4,000 members strong, lives mostly in and around the towns of Arcola and Arthur, towns that are also home to non-Amish people, including Mexican immigrants and people of other nationalities.

Illinois has been home to the Amish since the mid-1800s. Their roots are in the Anabaptist movement in Switzerland. In the late 1500s, a group of Protestants, led by a Dutchman named Menno Simons, believed people should be baptized as adults. About 100 years later a splinter group formed, named the Amish after their leader Jacob Amman. Fleeing harassment in Europe, the Amish immigrated to the United States throughout the 1700s, focusing mainly around Pennsylvania. In 1865 several families from Pennsylvania moved to present-day Arcola.

The Amish live simply. Essentially their lifestyles resemble those of families in American rural communities before electricity arrived. Their homesteads, about 80 acres in size, are comprised of hay fields, vegetable gardens, fruit trees, horses, and a mix of livestock such as cattle, hogs, and chickens. There are the main house, several outbuildings, and usually a home for the grandparents. Inside the homes, refrigerators and stoves run on propane. Some appliances, such as sewing machines, are pedal and air-powered. You won't find any paintings or photographs on the walls. The Amish emphasize humility and don't believe in images (because preserving and showing off images could promote pride). That means they prefer not to have their photographs taken.

The Illinois Amish speak German among themselves and hold religious services in their homes on Sundays. Children attend school until they're in eighth grade and are baptized in their late teens and early 20s, before they're married. The Amish wear handmade clothes; women don dresses or skirts with white prayer caps, and you'll often see men in suspenders. Women wear their hair long and pin it up in buns. Men wear helmet or bobbed styles. After men marry, they grow beards.

While they certainly do live much more simply than most people, the Amish are inventive, successful businesspeople. They read newspapers and follow local and world events. Some have cell phones. And as land prices continue to rise and it becomes more of a challenge for them to expand farmsteads, many Amish have increased their carpentry businesses, built greenhouses for growing plants, fruits, and vegetables, and launched other businesses.

but use caution when passing them in your car. Slow down. You'll notice while traveling through the area that the Amish speak German among themselves. The men grow beards (even in the summer) and the women wear little white prayer caps over their buns.

SIGHTS

To learn more about the Amish and Mennonite communities, stop by **The Illinois Amish Interpretive Center** (111 S. Locust St., Arcola, 888/452-6474, www.amishcenter. com, 9 A.M.–5 P.M. Mon.–Sat. Mar.–Nov., by appointment Dec.–Mar., $5). The center contains a lot of helpful historical information about how the Amish settled in this region.

Inside, visitors can see a vintage buggy, quilts, bibles, and a bedroom set displayed as if it were in an actual home. Here you'll be briefed about polite and not-so-polite behavior around the Amish. The center also organizes tours of the region.

Raggedy Ann and Andy creator Johnny Gruelle spent the first two years of his life in this region before moving to Indiana and the East Coast. Inspired by the quaint atmosphere of Arcola, his granddaughter Joni Gruelle Wannamaker decided to open the **Johnny Gruelle's Raggedy Ann and Andy Museum** (110 E. Main St., Arcola, 217/268-4908, www. raggedyann-museum.org, 10 A.M.–4:30 P.M. Tues.–Sat. Mar.–Dec., by appointment

Jan. 1–Mar. 15, donation) here. This excellent little museum (which may impress people other than doll collectors) has a recreation of Gruelle's drawing studio, books, tea sets, and other toys inspired by the Raggedy dolls. And of course, there are plenty of Raggedy Ann and Andy dolls, with their button eyes, striped stockings, red hair, and freckles. In addition to showcasing the various styles of dolls through the years, the exhibits explore the path he took to creating the dolls and his other ventures, including creating the newspaper proverb series "Love is . . ." and painting murals. The story behind the dolls is that he found an old doll in an attic, painted a new face on it, and gave it to his daughter Marcella, who later died from a smallpox vaccination. (In the book series, the girl who cares for the dolls is named Marcella.) Gruelle patented the Raggedy Ann doll in 1915, and he started writing the books in 1918.

Between Arcola and Arthur, **Rockome Gardens** (125 N. County Rd. 125E, Arcola, 217/268-4106, www.rockome.com, call for hours, Apr.–Oct., $8, plus more for buggy and train rides) is somewhat of an Amish theme park for children and grandmas. On the grounds are several shops, including a furniture shop, doll shop, and general store that sells things such as homemade apple butter, honey, and noodles. For the kids there's a petting zoo, train rides, buggy rides, a one-room schoolhouse, and other buildings. Several music shows are held here throughout the summer and early fall, including bluegrass and fiddling contests. A restaurant, open 11 A.M.–7 P.M. when the gardens are open, serves family-style meals such as fried chicken and homemade rolls.

Farm Visits

Sure, **The Great Pumpkin Patch** (Springfield Rd., west of County Rd. 1800E, southwest of Arthur, www.thegreatpumpkinpatch.biz, 9 A.M.–6 P.M. daily mid-Sept.–end of Oct.) has acres and acres of pumpkins, but it also sells hundreds of heirloom and rare squashes— we're talking delicious, edible squashes from around the world. Pick your own or choose from among those already picked. The owners,

© CHRISTINE DES GARENNES

The Great Pumpkin Patch, southwest of Arthur

the Condill family, also sell mums, Indian corn, and other fall goodies.

On the outskirts of Arthur, the friendly Graber family grows big beautiful vine-ripened tomatoes at **Graber's Greenhouse** (Cadwell Rd./County Rd. 1500E, south of Hwy. 133, Cadwell, 217/543-5140). In addition to produce such as juicy cantaloupes, the Grabers, an Amish family, sell seeds and a variety of flowers, such as annual hanging baskets. Call the answering service for hours and to find out what's in season.

Visitors can arrange for an Amish farm tour or a home-cooked meal on an Amish farm through the interpretive center in Arcola (111 S. Locust St., Arcola, 888/452-6474).

ENTERTAINMENT AND EVENTS

The annual **Raggedy Ann and Andy Festival** in downtown Arcola features look-alike contests, doll shows, storytelling, a parade, music, and food. It's held in June, and more information is available from the Arcola Chamber of Commerce. Downtown Arcola is also host to the popular **Broomcorn Festival,** which celebrates the area's history as a broom-making capital. It's held annually in September. Over in Arthur, folks line up early for free cheese at the always well-attended **Arthur Cheese Festival** (www.arthurcheesefestival.com) held every year during Labor Day weekend. In addition to the free-cheese tent (hundreds of pounds of cheese are given away for free each year), there are tractor pulls, pancake breakfasts, live music, and a fun run.

SHOPPING

Downtown Arthur and Arcola are lined with Amish furniture and food shops. In addition, dozens of wood shops, spice shops, and produce farms are scattered throughout the countryside. For a map of business locations, call or visit the area visitors bureaus. Most stores are closed Sunday.

ACCOMMODATIONS

The **Arcola Inn** (238 S. Jacques St., Arcola, 217/268-4971, around $50) is a one-story brick

motel with full, queen, and king beds. It's just off I-57. The **Arthur Country Inn** (785 E. Columbia St., Arthur, 217/543-3321, around $50) is also a one-story brick motel with entrances from the outside. It's on Highway 133 as you enter Arthur from the east.

One of the best features of the **Heart and Home** (210 E. Illinois St., Arthur, 217/543-2910, $80), a bed-and-breakfast within walking distance of downtown Arthur, is the big wraparound porch. You could sit here for hours. Heart and Home has three rooms available, all with private bathrooms and decorated with antiques.

If you prefer to stay in a newer home, **Marsha's Vineyard** (212 Chaise Ln., Arthur, 217/543-4001, $93) is a bed-and-breakfast in a recently built saltbox-style home. There are two suites to choose from: The first-floor "garden room" comes with a queen and a twin-size bed and has direct access to the patio outside, and the loft room upstairs has a king and a full-size bed.

As the name suggests, the **Flower Patch B&B** (225 E. Jefferson St., Arcola, 217/268-4876, www.arcolaflowerpatch.com, $86–298) is surrounded by lots of colorful gardens and a charming little gazebo and front porch. The pale-pink house has five sunny rooms, three of them with private baths. The owner, a gardener, sells herbs and perennials.

The newer two-story **Comfort Inn** (610 S. Ridge St., Arcola, 217/268-4000, $60–90), just off I-57, has an outdoor pool and continental breakfast.

FOOD

Arthur and Arcola have several Amish families who open their homes to visitors and invite them to share a meal (for a fee), tour the home, and perhaps even go for a buggy ride. To arrange a dinner, call the visitors bureaus for more information. Otherwise, there are several other restaurants in the area that feature country-style cooking. And by that I mean freshly baked bread, meats from locally raised livestock, sweet corn grown in area fields, and more. Here's a sampling.

Dutch Kitchen (127 E. Main St., Arcola, 217/268-3518, 7:30 A.M.–7 P.M. daily, $8) in downtown Arcola serves meals such as fried chicken, Amish sausage, a variety of sandwiches, and homemade breads. It also has a salad bar.

If you're in the mood to eat, stake out a table at **Yoder's Kitchen** (1195 E. Columbia St./Hwy. 133, Arthur, 217/543-2714, www.yoderskitchen.com, 7 A.M.–8 P.M. Mon.–Sat., lunch $5, dinner $10), where the all-you-can-eat buffet features heaps of mashed potatoes, pork chops, bread, and real, creamy butter. If buffets aren't your thing, try a broasted chicken dinner, ham steak, or patty melt sandwich, followed by a slice of apple pie.

(**Dick's Pharmacy** (118 S. Vine St., Arthur, 217/543-2913, 8 A.M.–6 P.M. Mon.–Fri., 8 A.M.–5:30 P.M. Sat.) is a genuine soda fountain shop and pharmacy serving phosphates, ice cream sodas, and sundaes.

Food Markets

Clear out the cooler or run to the gas station and buy another one. **Dutch Valley Meats** (376 E. Hwy. 133, Arthur, 217/543-3354) is a great place to stock up on smoked sausages, homemade sausages, and butterfly pork chops. The folks here sell fresh and frozen meats, plus some items such as homemade noodles.

Garlic, basil, and other bulk herbs and spices are sold at bargain prices at the **Country Spice Shoppe** (661 N. County Rd. 100E, Arthur, 217/543-3664).

INFORMATION

Not only can you get tips on what to see and where to stay, the **Arcola Depot Welcome Center** (135 N. Oak St., Arcola, 217/268-4530 or 800/336-5456, www.arcola-il.org) contains an impressive collection of antique brooms and brushes manufactured in the area. You can pick up maps and brochures and use public restrooms at the **Arthur-Amish Country Visitors Center** (106 E. Progress St., Arthur, 217/543-2242 or 800/722-6474, www.illinoisamishcountry.com). It's in a little hut in downtown Arthur.

Staff with the interpretive center in Arcola can arrange **Amish Country Tours** (111 S. Locust St., Arcola, 888/452-6474) for you while you're in the area. Choose from a farm tour, dinner in an Amish family home (prepared by Amish housewives), or a tour of a furniture and woodworking shop.

TUSCOLA AND ATWOOD

North of Arcola and Arthur by about six miles is Tuscola, another town with agricultural roots (a large grain-storage operation is here). But unlike the towns to the south, Tuscola is not home to nearly as many Amish. It's perhaps best-known by travelers for its shopping opportunities, both at the outlet shops just off I-57 and downtown.

Sights and Activities

The **Tanger Outlet Center** (Tuscola Blvd., U.S. 36 and I-57, 217/253-2282, www.tangeroutlet.com, 10 A.M.–9 P.M. Mon.–Sat., 11 A.M.–6 P.M. Sun. Mar. 1–Dec. 31, 10 A.M.–6 P.M. Mon.–Thurs., 10 A.M.–9 P.M. Fri.–Sat., 11 A.M.–6 P.M. Sun. Jan. 1–Feb. 28, extended hours around Christmas) has around 45 stores, including Gap, Harry and David, and Rockport Shoes. Next to the outlet mall is **Amishland Red Barn** (1304 Tuscola Blvd., Tuscola, 217/253-9022, www.amishland.com, 11 A.M.–8 P.M. Mon.–Fri., 10 A.M.–9 P.M. Sat., 10 A.M.–8 P.M. Sun.) with several shops inside, including Amish furniture, antiques, and a casual buffet restaurant that serves country-style meals (i.e. meat, potatoes, and rolls).

Drive west to downtown Tuscola and you'll come upon a handful of antiques and collectibles stores in the **Sale Street District,** including **Prairie Sisters Antique Mall** (102 W. Sale St., Tuscola, 217/253-5211). On the town's main drag west of town is **Route 36 Antiques** (101 E. Southline Rd., Tuscola, 217/253-9110).

If shopping is not your thing, **Ironhorse Golf Club** (2000 Ironhorse Dr., off Prairie St., Tuscola, 217/253-6644, www.ironhorsegc.com) is an 18-hole public course north of town.

A few miles farther west of Tuscola is

© CHRISTINE DES GARENNES

Flesor's Candy Kitchen, Tuscola

Atwood, a picturesque town of 1,000 people or so. Here you'll find the **Village Craftsman** (102 N. Main St., Atwood, 217/578-3834), where you can shop for finished handmade Amish furniture or special-order a table, rocking chair, or other piece of furniture. If you're in the area in mid-August, you must spend some time in downtown Atwood at the **Atwood Apple Dumpling Festival** to gobble some of the richest apple dumplings (topped with ice cream) you'll ever taste. Other typical fair food, such as kettle corn and pork sandwiches, are also sold at this food-laden festival.

Accommodations

Simple Pleasures B&B (600 N. State St./ Hwy. 130, Tuscola, 217/253-3319, www.simplepleasuresbnb.com, $100–115) is an 1870 robin's egg–blue home set on 11 acres, some of it wooded (yes, there are trees in the Grand Prairie region). The house has five decorative bedrooms available as well as several common areas that are quite unusual for a bed-and-breakfast in these parts, such as the whirlpool tub in the glass conservatory and the pool table in the house.

If you're intrigued with the idea of a stay in the country, another option is **Riverbend Retreat** (835 N. County Rd. 1500E, Tuscola, 217/253-3555, www.callriverbend.com). One local family beautifully renovated a 1919 bungalow near the Embarras River. The two-story house has two bedrooms on each floor, plus two kitchens (with new appliances), and a living room. Other pluses: a washer and dryer for guests and picnic tables outside the house. You'll find the cottage east of I-57 on Route 36. Rates are $60–225 depending on whether or not you stay one night in a king room or rent the entire bungalow.

Several national chain hotels sit off I-57 at the Tuscola U.S. 36 exit. Rates are generally $60–90. Two good options are the **Holiday Inn Express** (1201 Tuscola Blvd., Tuscola, 217/253-6363), an 82-room hotel with an indoor pool, a decent-size breakfast bar, in-room coffeemakers, and free wireless Internet. The 59-room **Baymont Inn** (1006 Southline Rd., Tuscola, 217/253-3500) also offers guests continental breakfast and an indoor pool, and it has two whirlpool suites.

Food
Does it get any better than a plate with a hamburger and fries and a milkshake on the side? **Flesor's Candy Kitchen** (101 W. Sale St., Tuscola, 217/253-3753, www.flesorscandy.com, 9 A.M.–6 P.M. Mon.–Sat., 11:30 A.M.–5 P.M. Sun., $6) is one of those places you want in every hometown. Genuinely friendly owners and wait staff, beautifully old but restored downtown building, truly made by hand chocolates and candies, and traditional American diner food like ham and cheese or Reuben sandwiches: a real find.

Information
Both Atwood and Tuscola have visitors centers staffed with local residents who can help you with navigating through the area or let you know about any new restaurants or hotels. They are the **Tuscola Tourism and Visitors Center** (122 W. North Central Ave., Tuscola, 217/253-6240 or 800/441-9111, www.tuscola. org) and **Atwood Tourist and Information Center** (112½ S. Main St., Atwood, 217/578-2734).

Decatur

As you drive toward Decatur from virtually any direction, you can't miss seeing the smokestacks and grain elevators. Decatur is, for the most part, a blue-collar town, home to agricultural processing plants and foundries. Many rail lines pass through here. The city has seen better days and seems to grab national attention only when something bad happens here, such as the closing of the Firestone tire plant or the racial clashes between black and white high-school students. But Decatur does have some great parks and gardens, and the people are welcoming. And there is something cool about being able to see industry up close. Corn and soybean processors Archer Daniels Midland and A. E. Staley are right there on Eldorado Street, crushing beans and shipping them across the world.

SIGHTS
Scovill Park
Every community should have a Scovill Park. Overlooking Lake Decatur, Scovill is a conglomeration of several museums, a zoo, and gardens. If you are traveling with children, this is a place you could spend the entire day. Start with **Scovill Zoo** (71 S. Country Club Rd., Decatur, 217/421-7435, www.decatur-parks. org, 10 A.M.–4 P.M. Mon.–Fri., 10 A.M.–6 P.M.

Sat.–Sun. Apr.–end of May and end of Aug.–Oct., 10 A.M.–7 P.M. daily end of May–end of Aug., $4.50), which has birds, reptiles, and mostly small animals housed on 10 acres. There are lots of winding sidewalks past the exhibits; some animals are in cages, some are in fenced-in areas. You'll pass by bald eagles, toucans, and flamingos. You can walk on a deck above the cheetah's playing ground or walk through a bird aviary where tropical birds preen themselves. Exhibits also include lemurs and prairie dogs. For a quick and easy visit, tour the zoo while riding a small train through the park. There's also a carousel near the entrance and exit featuring endangered animals.

Adjacent to the zoo are the **Oriental Gardens** (10 A.M.–dusk daily, free), an excellent space with shady areas, a waterfall, and Chinese Fu dog statues. Much of the gardens is wheelchair-accessible. Nearby is a large gazebo surrounded by colorful flowers such as salvia.

Inside the **Children's Museum** (55 S. Country Club Rd., Decatur, 217/423-5437, www.cmofil.com, 9:30 A.M.–4:30 P.M. Tues.–Fri., 10 A.M.–5 P.M. Sat., 1–5 P.M. Sun., $4) children are squealing and clapping, and light-bulbs are going off in their heads. As with most children's museums, this place is hands-on and educational. Kids can shop in a make-believe

© CHRISTINE DES GARENNES

Scovill Zoo

grocery store, blow giant bubbles, play with model trains, climb into a plane cockpit, or race boats. There's a picnic area outside with "whisper disks"—one person whispers into a parabolic dish and the other person across the lawn can hear what he or she says.

Public engineers and contractors will probably best enjoy a trip through the **Hieronymus Mueller Museum** (61 S. Country Club Rd., Decatur, 217/423-6161, 1–4 P.M. Thurs.–Sat., $1). Mueller was an inventor of sorts and in one way or another influenced the designs of drinking-water fountains, fire hydrants, and roller skates.

Millikin University

West of downtown Decatur on West Main Street, Millikin University is a small liberal arts college where students study to be anything from musicians to medical technicians. It was founded in 1901 by local banker James Millikin, whose house, near the picturesque campus, is open to the public. It is home to two fine museums.

Birks Museum (Gorin Hall, 1184 W. Main St., Decatur, 217/424-6337, www.millikin.edu, 1–4 P.M. daily during the school year, free) is known mostly for its decorative arts collection containing objects from around the world, including several objects from Asia. You will find Tiffany art glass, china vases, and handcrafted furniture on display here.

Kirkland Fine Arts Center and the Kirkland Galleries (1184 W. Main St., Decatur, 217/424-6318, www.millikin.edu, 8 A.M.–5 P.M. Mon.–Fri., 10 A.M.–1 P.M. Sat., free) feature excellent work from established and up-and-coming regional and national artists and students. Stop by the studio gallery, where the photography exhibits tend to be held. The center hosts music concerts and theatrical performances.

The **Millikin Homestead** (125 N. Pine St., Decatur, 217/422-9003, 2–4 P.M. last Sun. of the month, Apr.–Oct., $2) was built in 1876 for the founder of Millikin University, James Millikin, who was quite an interesting figure in Decatur. He owned a lot of farmland and rented the land to livestock farmers, then got into real-estate buildings and banking, and eventually became a city alderman. It's a gorgeous house that has been well-maintained. The Italianate-style brick mansion features stained-glass windows, fancy moldings, paintings on the walls, and period furniture throughout. It's decorated as though the Millikins were still living there in the 1880s.

Historic Sights

Arguably Decatur's most famous resident, Richard J. Oglesby was a renaissance man. Among Illinois residents he is perhaps best-known as being a three-term governor in the 1870s and 1880s. But the man also was a gold miner in California, a real-estate developer, state senator, U.S. senator, and a Civil War general. A friend to Ulysses S. Grant and Abraham Lincoln, he reportedly dubbed Lincoln "the rail-splitter" candidate because of his days chopping wood in New Salem, Illinois. Oglesby helped raise money for the construction of Lincoln's tomb in Springfield. You can learn all about one of Decatur's favorite sons by touring the **Governor Oglesby Mansion** (421 W. William St., Decatur, 217/429-9422, 2–4 P.M. last Sun. of the month Mar.–Nov., free). Like the Millikin mansion, the seven-room, two-story house, built in 1874, is Italianate. The original plans were drafted by architect William Le Baron Jenney, who is often called the father of the skyscraper. The mansion is not open often, but if you are in town when it is open for tours, it's worth a look. You won't be disappointed. It's a grand house with high ceilings, French doors, and several fireplaces with elaborate mantels. One of the mansion's finest rooms is the library, which is made of rich black walnut and features glass bookcases and a parquet floor.

The **Macon County Historical Museum Complex** (5580 N. Fork Rd., Decatur, 217/422-4919, www.mchsdecatur.org, 1–4 P.M. Tues.–Sat. and every fourth Sun., $2) is a mock village where several rescued historical buildings are arranged in a parklike setting. Prairie Village, as it is called, contains a gun and tackle shop, train depot, one-room schoolhouse, and log cabin, plus various modes of transportation from the past, including wagons, sleds, and a caboose. The log cabin was actually a courthouse in the 1830s, and Abraham Lincoln practiced there while he was a young lawyer.

Farm Visit

Maribeth King, the late owner of **Mari-Mann Herbs** (1405 Marimann Ln., St. Louis Bridge Rd. at Hwy. 48, Decatur, 217/429-1404 or 800/779-4372, www.marimann.com, 9 A.M.–5 P.M. Mon.–Sat., noon–5 P.M. Sun.) credited homeopathic remedies and herbs for helping her beat cancer. Her herb farm and shop provide visitors with a little oasis on the outskirts of Decatur. You can stroll through rows of chamomile and echinacea and then browse through her shop packed with everything from gourmet salsa to Saint-John's-wort. There are vitamins, candles, books, jellies, and dried herbs. Herb Fest, a well-attended local event, is held during Labor Day weekend.

Mari-Mann herb farm

ENTERTAINMENT AND EVENTS
Theater

Built in 1916, the **Lincoln Square Theatre** (141 N. Main St., Decatur, 217/442-1711, www.lincolnsquaretheatre.com) is a beaux arts theater downtown that plays host to various music concerts and movie screenings.

Millikin University's **Kirkland Fine Arts Center** (1184 W. Main St., Decatur, 217/424-6318, www.millikin.edu) hosts dozens of dramas and comedy theater productions, classical and modern music concerts, and lectures. Performances are by visiting artists, faculty, and students. A recent season included visits by the Smothers Brothers and the Vienna Boys Choir.

Events

Naturalists will want to stop by Rock Springs in September for the annual **Prairie Celebration** (Brozio Ln. and Rock Springs Rd., Decatur, 217/423-7708, www.maconcountyconservation.org, free). You can go birding with other fellow amateur ornithologists, watch locals re-enact scenes from history at the center's homestead museum, or take in the sights of the park aboard a wagon. The **Decatur Celebration** is a giant street festival in early August. Music acts (former big names like War and Styx), carnival rides, foods, and arts and crafts are featured. In odd-numbered years at the end of August, Richland Community College in Decatur hosts the so-called Super Bowl of Agriculture, the **Farm Progress Show.** Tens of thousands of people each day, for three days, come to check out the latest in farm equipment and related merchandise. Food, music, and comedy acts are also on hand.

SHOPPING

Forget about shopping at the mall off the interstate. **The Wabash Depot Antique Center** (780 E. Cerro Gordo St., Decatur, 217/233-0800, 10 A.M.–5 P.M. Mon.–Sat., noon–5 P.M. Sun.) is an indoor antiques center housed in a former train depot that dates back more than a century. Vendors sell vintage toys, out-of-print books, pottery pieces such as bowls and pitchers, and salvaged architectural items.

SPORTS AND RECREATION
Rock Springs

At 1,300 acres, **Rock Springs Center for Environmental Discovery** (Brozio Ln. and Rock Springs Rd., Decatur, 217/423-7708, www.maconcountyconservation.org, free) is one of the largest parks in the region, an excellent place for quiet hikes in the summer and cross-country skiing trips in the winter. This sprawling park has about six miles of well-groomed trails through varied but easy-to-navigate terrain such as rolling hills, flat prairie, and woodlands. The River Trail takes you past ponds (look for the turtles), through woods, and by the former site of a bottling plant for Rock Springs Water (a company used to sell water from the springs here). The park's other trails, such as the Big Oak Trail and Prairie Path, take you through quiet prairies and woods. The Lookout Trail, as the name implies, leads to a lookout tower over the river and prairie, past wildflowers and hopping bunny rabbits.

A short walk (less than five minutes) from the visitors center parking lot is the **Homestead Prairie Farm,** also known as the Trobaugh-Good Home. Listed on the National Register of Historic Places, it was initially built as a one-room log home in 1850. Eventually other rooms were added (although it is still tiny by today's standards). The pale yellow house contains furniture and items that date to the 1860s, such as a stove and dish cupboard.

Back at the visitors center you'll find several rooms with displays on Illinois geology, the prairie, wetlands, and wildlife. A large picture window in one room allows you to watch for birds such as downy woodpeckers and cardinals. You can shop for stuffed animals and items such as maple syrup made from the sap collected from trees at Sand Creek Recreation Area south of Decatur.

Another attraction in Rock Springs is the vintage baseball field at the northern part of the park. Throughout the year a group of locals plays on this grass field.

The Rock Spring visitors center is open 8 A.M.–5 P.M. Monday–Friday, 9 A.M.–4:30 P.M. Saturday, and 1–4 P.M. Sunday. The trails are open 7 A.M.–dusk daily. The Homestead Prairie Farm is open 1–4 P.M. weekends June–October and by appointment. During the winter, you can rent cross-country skiing equipment 9 A.M.–2 P.M. for $6; trails are open 8 A.M.–sunset, weather permitting, and are free.

The Rock Springs/Fairview Bikeway (217/423-7708) is an easy, scenic 2.5-mile paved trail between Fairview and Kiwanis Parks and Rock Springs. A good access point is at Rock Springs, where there is plenty of parking near the visitors center. The well-maintained trail jogs along Stevens Creek and over the Sangamon River.

Other Parks

About 10 miles southeast of Decatur, **Fort Daniel Conservation Area** (Fort Daniel Rd. and County Rd. 57, Mount Zion, 217/423-7708, free) has an intriguing history. It is named after area resident Rev. Daniel Traughber, who reportedly was a Southern sympathizer during the Civil War. He and his followers would ride on horseback through the night threatening pro-Union farmers. The area within and surrounding the park was first known as Whistleville, and it was a community comprised mainly of settlers from Kentucky who built log homes there. The 200-acre park has 4.5 miles of trails that follow the rambling Big Creek, past an old well and through restored prairie.

On the west side of town by Millikin University, **Fairview Park** (U.S. 36 and Hwy. 48, Eldorado and Fairview Sts., Decatur, 217/422-5911, www.decatur-parks.org) has quite a few spots alongside ponds and under trees that are good for picnicking. On the southeast side of town on Lake Decatur you can rent regattas for $1 per day at **Nelson Park** (Decatur Park District, just south of U.S. 36, 217/424-2837) on Saturdays mid-July to late August. Nelson Park also has boat ramps for visitors interested in exploring Lake Decatur and the Sangamon River.

Horseback Riding

One of the best places to bring your horse for a ride in the Decatur area is **Sand Creek Recreation Area** (S. Franklin St., Decatur, 217/423-7708, 8 A.M.–dusk, access to horseback trails $2). Part of the old Paris-Springfield Road runs through Sand Creek. A common thoroughfare from about the 1820s to the 1850s, it was this road many homesteaders followed to find land. They included Abraham Lincoln and his family, who migrated to Illinois in 1830. South of Decatur on the Sangamon River, Sand Creek has 755 acres and 7.6 miles of trails for horseback riding or hiking. The park is quite accommodating to horses and their owners. There are hitch racks for horses at the entrances to trails and gravel picnic areas. Trails through oak and hickory woodlands and maple trees and along the creek are especially scenic.

Try to swing by in the early springtime, such as in March. This is when park staff tap the maple trees and catch the sap in buckets to produce maple syrup. (You can buy some syrup at the Rock Spring store.) Staff also have installed several bluebird houses throughout the park, and it is not uncommon to spot these birds during a walk or ride. Because the park is in a floodplain, it can experience flooding in the springtime and does close some of its trails when this happens. If you plan to visit during a rainy spring, call first to inquire about the state of the trails.

ACCOMMODATIONS

Staying overnight in Decatur will cost $70–100, with some select suites at the Decatur Conference Center and hotel costing more. There is a string of small motels near the grain processing plants on Decatur's east side that go for less than $70 per night, but they're not exactly in desirable locations.

Here's a sampling of national chain hotels. Near I-72 and U.S. 51 are **Holiday Inn**

Express (5170 Wingate Dr., Decatur, 217/875-5500) and **Country Inn and Suites Hotel** (5150 Hickory Point Frontage Rd., Decatur, 217/872-2402), both of which offer indoor pools, exercise rooms, and continental breakfast for guests. There's also the **Hampton Inn** (1429 Hickory Point Dr., Decatur, 217/877-5577) and the 370-room **Decatur Conference Center and Hotel** (U.S. 36 and Wyckles Rd., 217/422-8800, www.hoteldecatur.com), which has a restaurant and lounge on-site.

There are two bed-and-breakfasts in town. Both are on the west side in historic districts. The **Younker House Bed and Breakfast** (500 W. Main St., Decatur, 217/429-9718), a large brick home on a brick street, has three bedrooms, a screened-in porch, and a fenced-in backyard with gardens. Just down the street you'll find four rooms at **Victoriana** (640 W. Main St., Decatur, 217/428-0637) by Millikin University. The front porch looks out onto Main Street.

FOOD

Close to Millikin's campus, **Lock Stock and Barrel** (129 S. Oakland Ave., Decatur, 217/429-7411, www.lsb1.com, 11 A.M.–1 A.M. Mon.–Wed., 11 A.M.–2 A.M. Thurs.–Sat., 10 A.M.–10 P.M. Sun., $7) tends to attract the college crowd, especially on Sundays for the all-you-can-eat brunches. Food varies from healthy salads to the not-so-healthy horseshoe sandwiches. It has lots of hot and cold sandwiches plus sides such as twice-baked potatoes. Drop by for dinner on a Friday or Saturday and then stick around to hear a local rock or jazz band play.

Located in Nelson Park's former bathhouse, **Beach House** (2301 E. Lake Shore Dr., Decatur, 217/422-7202, www.decaturbeachhouse.com, 11 A.M.–10 P.M. Mon.–Fri., 4–10 P.M. Sat., bar open later Fri.–Sat., $7–25) offers views of Lake Decatur (yeah, it's not Lake Tahoe, but we'll take what we can get) and classic American eats: mushroom and Swiss burgers, walleye fish sandwiches, pizza, and some higher-end entrées like New York strip steak.

Classic road food like burgers and shakes are the specialty at **Krekel's** (801 E. Wood; 1355 N. Route 48; 2320 E. Main St.; 3727 N. Woodford St., Decatur, 217/429-1122), a regional chain with several locations in Decatur and Springfield. Mmm, hot fudge sundaes.

As the name implies, **Circa 1860** (411 W. Main St., Decatur, 217/423-1860, www.circa1860.com, 11 A.M.–4 P.M. Mon.–Sat., 5–9 P.M. Sat.–Sun.) is in a renovated Victorian home that the owners saved from demolition. Guests will dine in the former parlor rooms surrounded by stained glass windows, walnut trim, and other historical touches. Meals are on the lighter side, such as egg salad or tuna salad sandwiches and mixed greens. A three-course tea (reservations required) for about $15 is offered in the afternoon.

French dining in Illinois is not just limited to Chicago. **Bizou** (259 N. Main St., Decatur, 217/422-7000) is a high-end restaurant in downtown Decatur that serves French and other Continental food and features a few other dishes, like sushi, sometimes. Entrées can include pecan-encrusted rainbow trout, stuffed chicken breast, or lobster. Entrée prices range from $14 for a chef's salad to $65 for a fillet and seafood pairing. *Bizou,* by the way, are those little pecks on the cheeks the French greet each other with.

INFORMATION AND SERVICES
Visitor Information

The **Decatur Area Convention and Visitors Bureau** (202 E. North St., Decatur, 217/423-7000 or 800/331-4479, www.decaturcvb.com) publishes brochures and events information annually and maintains a listing of area lodging and dining options. You can pick up information there or at the airport, where the CVB manages an information desk.

Media

The Decatur Herald and Review is published daily and is available at all convenience stores, gas stations, and the library. Buy a copy of the bimonthly *Decatur*

Magazine (www.decaturmagazine.com) at area grocery stores to get the scoop on any new restaurants, theater productions, or to read profiles about local residents. It costs $3.95 per issue.

Tours

For an entertaining look at Decatur's ghostly past and present, join one of the evening **Haunted Decatur** tours (228 W. Main St., Decatur, 888/446-7859, www.illinoishauntings.com, Apr.–Oct.). Get your tickets at the Prairie Fire bookshop downtown. The company also offers tours in several other Illinois cities.

Hospitals

There are two hospitals in town: **Decatur Memorial Hospital** (2300 N. Edward St., Decatur, 217/876-8121, www.dmhhs.com) and **St. Mary's Hospital** (1800 E. Lake Shore Dr., Decatur, 217/464-2966, www.stmarys-hospital.com).

Post Office and Library

You'll find the main **Decatur Post Office** downtown at 200 North Franklin Street (217/428-4471). Nearby is the **Decatur Public Library** (130 N. Franklin St., Decatur, 217/424-2900).

GETTING THERE AND AROUND
Air and Bus

Regional carrier Great Lakes Airlines offers daily flights between the **Decatur Airport** (910 S. Airport Rd., Decatur, 217/428-2423, www.flydecatur.com) and St. Louis Lambert International Airport. Parking at the airport is free.

    Greyhound buses stop at Sandy's Motel (1675 E. Pershing Rd., Decatur, 217/877-6262).

Public Transportation

The **Decatur Public Transit System** (55 E. Wood St., Decatur, 217/424-2800, www.ci.decatur.il.us) runs 13 bus lines through

town from about 5:30 A.M. to 7 P.M. Monday–Thursday and 5:30 A.M.–9 P.M. Friday–Saturday. Each ride costs $0.75. On Saturdays you can buy an all-day pass to ride the buses for $1.50. The transit system also operates **free trolleys** Monday–Saturday through downtown Decatur and around the Millikin University campus.

VICINITY OF DECATUR
Lincoln Homestead Site

Diehard fans of Lincoln will want to trek it on over to the **Lincoln Trail Homestead State Memorial and Lincoln Trail Homestead State Park** (705 Spitler Park Dr., Mount Zion, 217/864-3121, www.dnr.state.il.us). After arriving in Illinois, Lincoln and his father and stepmother chose a spot along the Sangamon River to build their first home. Lincoln lived there before moving on to New Salem. The actual log cabin is long gone; the state has placed a stone and plaque there.

Illiopolis

If you ever wanted to go country-western dancing, here's your chance. The **Prairie Land Dance Club** (650 Matilda St., Illiopolis, 217/428-1560, www.pldc.org) devotes several evenings a week to line dancing, square dancing, and other country moves. Plus, throughout the year it holds workshops on salsa dancing, the merengue, and more. The club is open for dancing 7–10 P.M. Wednesday, Friday, and Saturday nights. Admission is $5 for nonmembers.

COAL COUNTRY: PANA AND VICINITY

The town of Pana is in the heart of coal country, or at least it was during the peak coal-mining years during the first half of the 20th century. At one time there were five mines operating in the area and several railroad lines running through town. Throughout downtown Pana are murals that offer glimpses at what life was like back then, with images of a marching band and people waiting to catch a train. You can also get a sense of the town's glory days by driving along Spruce, Locust, 2nd, and 3rd Streets. You'll pass once-grand old homes where the coal barons used to live. Pana is also called the city of roses. At the turn of the 20th century there were hundreds of greenhouses in the area, and every year millions of roses grew inside them. You'll notice several homes are bedecked with rose gardens in the summer.

Sights and Activities

Managed by the local high school, **Anderson Prairie Park** (Chestnut St., just south of 9th St., Pana, 217/562-4240, www.andersonprairie.org, sunrise–sunset daily, free) is a quiet natural park along an old railroad line. At the southern entrance off Chestnut Street you'll find an observation tower and a few benches. These are good spots to watch birds, such as cedar waxwings and indigo buntings, plus wild turkeys, owls, and a variety of butterflies. From there you can follow a narrow walking trail on a boardwalk past wildflowers. The north side of the park is a bit more wooded and easy to walk, as the main trail is wide and is made of gravel and dirt. It's good for hiking, biking, or jogging.

For a longer trip take to the **Lincoln Prairie Trail,** an asphalt trail that stretches for about 15 miles between Pana and Taylorville, to the northwest. It's a fairly level trail through woods, meadows, and farm fields and over creeks. The trail, which follows a former railroad bed and runs for the most part alongside Highway 29, opened in 2001 and is one of the state's newer rails-to-trails projects. You can reach it from Bear Creek Road in Pana.

Four genuine log cabins are open to the public at **Coal Creek Pioneer Village** (Pana Tri-County Fairgrounds, Pana, 217/562-4240, call for hours, free). The one-story cabins, built from the 1840s to the 1870s, hail from throughout Illinois.

On the south side of town is **Kitchell Park** (U.S. 51 and 8th St., Pana, 6 A.M.–11 P.M. daily, free), a city park with an outdoor auditorium for band concerts, plus picnic tables, playgrounds, a little pond with a fountain,

baseball diamonds, and a public swimming pool. The park was named after John Kitchell, a local resident who was a Civil War captain for Lincoln.

Accommodations

The **Lake Lawn Inn** (Hwy. 16 and U.S. 51, Pana, 217/562-2123, about $45) is a clean motor lodge on the outskirts of town. It's got an outdoor swimming pool and a casual restaurant on-site.

The **Oak Terrace Resort** (100 Beyers Lake Rd., Pana, 217/539-4477 or 800/577-7598, www.oakterraceresort.com, about $95) has a 37-room hotel with some rooms overlooking golf holes. In addition to the hotel and 18-hole golf course, the casual resort has an indoor pool, small exercise room, and a private lake for fishing or taking a pontoon boat out for a ride. It also has a spa area where you can unwind with a massage or pedicure. Mulligans, a casual American restaurant, serves breakfast, lunch, and dinner daily.

Information

The **Pana Chamber of Commerce** operates a visitors center in Karla's Kollectibles Antique Mall (Hwy. 16 and U.S. 51, Pana). For more information call the chamber at 217/562-4240 or visit www.panaillinois.com.

Moweaqua

The quiet mining town of Moweaqua was struck with tragedy on December 24, 1932, when methane gas in its coal mine exploded when the gas was exposed to carbide lights carried by the miners. As a result, 54 miners were killed. Two years later the mine closed. As a tribute to those who died in the accident and to educate folks about what it was like to be a coal miner in Illinois, local residents organized the **Moweaqua Coal Mine Museum** (129 S. Main St., Moweaqua, 217/768-3019, by appointment, free), a small museum on tiny Main Street where you can read newspaper clippings about the disaster, view photographs of the mine and the town, and see some mining artifacts and tools.

Taylorville

Taylorville is the self-proclaimed Christmas Capital of Illinois. And if you like twinkling light shows, this is one you've got to see. During the winter holiday season the town hosts a tour of homes, a Santa parade, cookie-baking events, and the festival of trees and "flight of angels," which are wire and light sculptures hanging in trees around the court-house square. For information on Taylorville, contact the **Taylorville Tourism Council** at 217/824-2194 or the **Taylorville Chamber of Commerce** at 217/824-4919.

Nokomis

The town of Nokomis, population 2,300, has produced three national Hall of Fame baseball players (as well as several others who went on to play great baseball!). And boy, are the Nokomis residents proud of their connection to the sport. The **B-R-S Baseball Museum** (121 W. State St., Nokomis, 217/563-2516, 9–11 A.M. Mon.–Sat., free) in downtown Nokomis highlights the careers of "Sunny" Jim Bottomly, a first baseman for the St. Louis Cardinals, Cincinnati Reds, and St. Louis Browns in the 1920s; Charles "Red" Ruffing, who, despite losing four toes in a mining accident as a child, went on to become a pitcher in the 1930s for the Boston Red Sox, New York Yankees, and Chicago White Sox; and Ray Schalk, a catcher for the New York Giants and Chicago White Sox in the 1910s known for his talent of stealing bases.

Lake Shelbyville Region

After Congress passed the Flood Control Act of 1958, which authorized the Army Corps of Engineers to create Lake Shelbyville, central Illinois would never be the same. Water, water everywhere! People could buy boats—big boats—and they could lounge for hours on sandy beaches. The massive (in size and cost) dam project involved filling old mines, rerouting gas pipelines, moving graves and cemeteries, and building a 100-foot-tall, 3,000-foot-long dam on the Kaskaskia River. The result was an 11,000-acre lake with 250 miles of shoreline. The whole purpose was to control flooding, establish a water supply for area towns, and spark development of the area as a recreation destination. Well, it's not Lake Powell, but for water-starved central Illinoisans it's an oasis. Two state parks are on its shores, one of them, Eagle Creek, with a resort and golf course. The town of Shelbyville on the south end of the lake has several restaurants and shops in its downtown, and there are countless modern campsites around the lake, making the area quite a gathering place for RVers.

ORIENTATION

The largest town in the area, Shelbyville is off Highway 16, just west of the dam and three of the Army Corps of Engineers recreation areas. Shelbyville is where you'll find the bulk of the dining and lodging options. Other area towns include Sullivan and Kirksville on the north end, Findlay on the west coast, and Windsor on the east. Wolf Creek and Eagle Creek state parks are opposite each other on the lake (Wolf is on the east side, Eagle is on the west). It's rather difficult and time-consuming to drive around the lake. Lake Shelbyville is not shaped like a circle and there is no one road that follows the shoreline. There are dozens of parking areas and boat launches scattered around the lake.

SIGHTS
The Spillway and Dam East and West Recreation Areas

For a good overview of the lake, drop by the **Army Corps of Engineers Lake Shelbyville Visitors Center** (217/774-3951) one mile east of Shelbyville, just east of the dam from

Highway 16. There you can pick up some maps and read about the history of the dam project. Visitors can walk along the spillway and through the picnic areas above the lake. Or you can take a tour of the dam with Army Corps staff at 11 A.M. Saturdays and 3 P.M. Sundays Memorial Day–Labor Day. On the other side of the lake from the visitors center, just off Highway 16, is **Dam West Recreation Area,** with a sand beach and boat ramp. The beach is open 8 A.M.–sunset late May–mid-September. Beach access costs $1 per person. There are also boat-launching fees.

Eagle Creek State Recreation Area

One of the best places along the shores of Lake Shelbyville is Eagle Creek (south of the Bruce-Findlay Rd., east of Hwy. 128, Findlay, 217/756-8260, www.dnr.state. il.us), technically a state park, but probably more known for the resort there by the same name (800/876-3245, www.eaglecreekresort. com). Its main attraction is the 6,900-yard **golf course** designed by Ken Killian. But the resort also has a slew of other stuff to do: Rent bikes and explore the park and the nearby country roads; rent a paddleboat or pontoon boat and discover some of the lake's inlets; take a dip in the outdoor swimming pool; take in a round of miniature golf; or play tennis. In addition, the park has a great 12-mile **hiking trail** that weaves along the woods and shoreline. If the area receives enough snow in the winter, you can cross-country ski on groomed trails in the park. Eagle Creek also has tent and RV campsites available (for more information, see *Accommodations*).

Wolf Creek State Park

Opposite Eagle Creek on the east side of the lake is Wolf Creek State Park (west of Hwy. 32, eight miles north of Windsor, 217/459-2831, www.dnr.state.il.us), a popular weekend getaway for families as well as horse owners. There are nearly 300 tent and RV campsites here, plus a swimming beach at the southwest part of the park, a boat ramp, playground, and picnic areas. A 12-mile horseback-riding trail (which you can also hike along) winds through the park.

More Trails

Bird-watchers will want to make tracks to the 1.2-mile **Okaw Bluff Trail** at Okaw Bluff Group Camp, on the east side of the lake north of the town of Bruce, off the Bruce-Findlay Road and east of Highway 32. Hike atop a bluff overlooking the lake and then past a 100-acre wetland area, stopping at the wildlife-viewing stands to look for herons and other waterfowl.

You can find the 11-mile **Chief Illini Trail** between Shelbyville and Eagle Creek Recreation Area at the Lone Point campground. Follow this invigorating trail up along the bluffs and down near the water and you'll be able to get a good sense of the Lake Shelbyville environment as you pass wildflowers and perhaps see fish jumping or catch a glimpse of a doe and her fawn walking through the woods or crossing a meadow. The shorter version of this trail, the **Little Chief Illini Trail,** is about two miles long and also accessible from the Lone Point campground. A four-mile bicycle trail, the first section of the General Dacey Bike Trail, is accessible from the Dam West Recreation Area. Eventually the goal is for the Dacey Trail to be part of a 170-mile trail system through Shelby and Moultrie Counties.

Boating and Fishing

Lake Shelbyville has three marinas where visitors can rent boats, launch their own boats, stock up on snacks and drinks, bait, and lures, and find out where the fish are biting. **Lithia Springs Marina** (217/744-4121 or 800/447-4121) is on the southeast side of the lake where Lithia Springs Creek enters the lake. The marina rents out houseboats and fishing boats. To get to Lithia Springs, follow County Road 2200E north from Highway 16, east of Shelbyville. East of Findlay, north of Eagle Creek and

© CHRISTINE DES GARENNES

a popular spot for fishing, Lake Shelbyville

the Bruce-Findlay Road, is the **Findlay Marina** (217/756-8595) and to the northeast is **Sullivan Marina and Campground** (217/728-7338), just east of Highway 32. Several anglers in the area offer their expertise to visitors. For a complete list of fishing guides call or visit the Shelby County Office of Tourism (see *Information*).

Orchard

Bite into a crisp Granny Smith or take home an apple pie at **Okaw Valley Orchard** (rural Sullivan, 866/277-5371, www.okawvalleyorchard.com, approximately mid-July–late Oct.), an orchard located between the towns of Sullivan and Lovington. Here they grow a variety of apples (and make cider using a genuine press) plus other fruit such as peaches and raspberries. Treats like doughnuts and their famous cider are also for sale. To get to the orchard from Sullivan, follow Route 32 north for several miles, then follow signs to County Road 1725 North for a couple of more miles. The owners also run a B&B, the Okaw Valley Orchard Inn; see *Accommodations*.

ENTERTAINMENT AND EVENTS

The pet project of the local chamber of commerce and area automobile dealer Bob Boarman (his auto shop is just down the street), the **Roxy Theatre** (147 E. Main St., Shelbyville, 217/774-7699, www.boarmansroxytheatre.com, $3) is a cool vintage movie theater in downtown Shelbyville. Classic, current, and kids' flicks are shown here.

Within Shelbyville's Forest Park is the **Chautauqua Auditorium** (N. 9th St., Forest Park, Shelbyville, 217/774-5531), a historic round building that dates to 1903. Billy Sunday preached here. The John Philip Sousa Band performed here. Local and visiting musicians perform here throughout the summer. Contact the tourism office for a calendar of events.

The Little Theatre on the Square (16 E. Harrison St., Sullivan, 217/728-7375 or 888/261-9675, www.thelittletheatre.org) in downtown Sullivan is a professional theater that presents about six musicals and plays throughout the year. It tends to produce classic Broadway shows such as *42nd Street, Fiddler* *on the Roof,* and children's shows such as *The Jungle Book.* Sullivan is on the north end of Lake Shelbyville.

Go treasure hunting at the annual **Spores 'n' More** festival held in April in towns in Shelby County. Morel mushroom hunters pack into a bus and are driven to a secret location to find the rare fungi. Later in the afternoon the goods are auctioned off. Complete with sausage sandwiches, a rummage sale, and a plant sale, the Spores 'n' More fest is a great way to spend a spring day.

SHOPPING

Downtown Shelbyville has a few antiques and gift shops, including **The Wishing Well** (135 E. Main St., Shelbyville, 217/774-1321, 10 A.M.–5 P.M. Tues.–Sat., 1–5 P.M. Sun. summer, call for winter hours), which has a variety of vintage collectibles, antique furniture, and other items.

On the outskirts of town is **Jake's Antiques and the Amish Warehouse** (W. Rte. 16, Shelbyville, 217/774-4223, 9 A.M.–5 P.M. Mon.–Fri., 10 A.M.–2 P.M. Sat.), which is chock-full of handmade oak furniture and furniture from the past. You'll find Victorian, art nouveau, mission, and other styles.

ACCOMMODATIONS

Folks on a budget can stay at the 21-room **Spillway Motel** (Hwy. 16, by the dam, east of Shelbyville, 800/845-0414, $50–54) for no-frills accommodations. It caters to boaters here with the large parking area, bait shop, and electrical hookups for recharging those boat batteries. Billed as a Victorian Inn, **The Shelby Inn** (816 W. Main St., Shelbyville, 800/342-9978, www.theshelbyinn.com, $65–85) is actually a newer-construction inn with buildings that feature several porches. (Room registration is in the Tallman House, a restored 1905 home listed on the National Register of Historic Places.) The 51 rooms come with double or king-size beds. The hotel is close to downtown and the lake.

■€ **Eagle Creek Resort** (217/756-3456 or 800/876-3245, www.eaglecreekresort.com,

$99–145) has 138 guest rooms and 10 suites, decorated slightly different from your run-of-the-mill lakeshore resort, such as with Amish-made furniture. Rooms are nice and clean, but the main reason to stay here is the slew of activities available outdoors: swimming in the pool, playing tennis, playing golf or minigolf, hiking, boating, and fishing. There is a restaurant on-site. The resort has a two-night minimum on weekends in the summer.

For a romantic getaway, stay at the **Okaw Valley Orchard Inn** (rural Sullivan, 217/728-4093, www.okawvalleyorchardinn.com, $89–115) during late spring when acres and acres of apple trees are blooming. The remodeled barnlike B&B has three rooms, all with private baths. (The building was not actually a barn but a former house for the owners.) To get to the orchard from Sullivan, follow Route 32 north for several miles, then follow signs to County Road 1725 North for a couple more miles.

Lithia Resort (County Rd. 1500N, Shelbyville, 217/774-2882, www.lithiaresort.com) has two lodging options: 12 basic rooms in a motor lodge–type of building or newer log cabins. Several different layouts are available, but basically all include a kitchen. The resort has fishing ponds for bank fishing. Rates vary according to the season, but are generally $58–136.

For weekly accommodations, consider renting a single-family cottage or cabin in the area. For a list of these options, contact the Shelby County Office of Tourism; see *Information.*

Camping

Lake Shelbyville is a popular spot for visitors traveling with recreational vehicles. Wolf Creek State Park and Eagle Creek State Recreation Area both have campgrounds with tent and RV sites, but the Army Corps of Engineers has several campgrounds, and there are a handful of private campgrounds situated around the lake. Here's a rundown on your options, in addition to the state parks.

The Army Corps of Engineers manages six campgrounds around the lake, including the 79-site **Forrest W. Bo Wood Recreation Area** (south of Sullivan on Hwy. 32); the 209-site **Coon Creek Recreation Area** (south of Findlay east of Hwy. 128 and south of County Rd. 1800N); the 114-site **Lithia Springs Recreation Area** (east of Shelbyville on Hwy. 16); the 98-site **Lone Point Recreation Area** (also south of County Rd. 1800N); the 79-site **Opossum Creek Recreation Area** (north of Shelbyville off Hwy. 128); and the 81-site **Whitely Creek Recreation Area** (east of Hwy. 32 and north of the Bruce-Findlay Rd.). Campgrounds are open April or May to September or October, depending on the site. Fees are $12–20 per night. To make a reservation for any of these campgrounds you'll have to go through the **National Recreation Reservation Service** (877/444-6777, www.reserveusa.com). Reserve anytime from 240 to four days in advance.

With about 200 campsites, most of them wooded, **Robin Hood Woods** (Hwy. 16, about three miles east of Shelbyville, 217/774-4222, www.robinhoodwoods.com, campsites $20–28, cabins $80–140) is one of the largest campgrounds in the area. It's popular among young families and the senior crowd because of its fishing pond, in-ground pool, horseshoe pits, and game room. Robin Hood Woods also has one-room cabins and two-bedroom cabins with air-conditioning and heating. There's a camp store on-site. For a comprehensive list of private campgrounds, contact the Shelby County Office of Tourism (see *Information*).

FOOD

You'll find many fast-food chain restaurants in and around Shelbyville, but you'll also find a few surprises in the family-owned restaurants in downtown Shelbyville. Your best option is to walk down Main Street, just west of the dam and by the Shelby County Courthouse.

When we say a dish is "just like Grandma used to make," we're not talking about baked potatoes with low-fat cheese, or salads that hold the dressing; we're talking about dishes rich in butter and other good things. **Just Like Grandma's** (124 E. Main St., Shelbyville,

217/774-1721, 7 A.M.–1:30 P.M. Tues.–Wed. and Fri.–Sat., 11 A.M.–2 P.M. Sun., $5) is a homey place with antique kitchen utensils hanging on the walls and a menu that lives up to its claim, such as "chicken-fried chicken," i.e. breaded and fried chicken. It ain't fancy, but it's clean and you certainly won't leave hungry.

After you've worked up an appetite hiking or spent the day boating, head to the casual pizza joint in town, **Joe's Pizza** (114 E. Main St., Shelbyville, 217/774-3535, 11 A.M.–1 P.M. Tues.–Fri., 4–10 P.M. Thurs. and Sun., 4–11 P.M. Fri.–Sat., $9), which has everything from standard pepperoni to Hawaiian and taco-style pizzas.

Chicken, steaks, and pasta are the fare at **Longbranch Grill** (203 E. Main St., Shelbyville, 217/774-1700, 11 A.M.–2 P.M. Mon.–Fri., 4–10 P.M. Mon.–Sat., $12), an American bar and grill in downtown Shelbyville.

INFORMATION

The **Army Corps of Engineers Lake Shelbyville Visitors Center** (217/774-3951) is one mile east of Shelbyville, just east of the dam. Follow signs from Highway 16. The center is open noon–4 P.M. Saturday and Sunday early September–mid-October and early to mid-May. Starting in mid-May it's open 10 A.M.–4 P.M. daily through early September. More information is also available on the Corps's website, www.mvs.usace.army.mil.

The **Shelby County Office of Tourism** (315 E. Main St., Shelbyville, 217/774-2244 or 800/874-3529, www.lakeshelbyville.com) has comprehensive hotel, camping, and dining info. During the summers the office is staffed on the weekends 10 A.M.–3 P.M.

VICINITY OF SHELBYVILLE
Covered Bridge

Well, it's not as picturesque as some of the barns featured in the film *The Bridges of Madison County* (declarations such as "LSD is for me" and "I love Carla" are carved and painted on the walls), but the **Thompson Mill Covered Bridge** is one of a handful of original covered bridges left in the state. Built in the late

1880s, the cedar-shingled bridge stretches over the Kaskaskia River south of Shelbyville and east of the little town of Cowden. You cannot drive on the bridge, but you can walk through it. To get to the bridge take Highway 128 into Cowden, and then follow signs to the covered bridge, about four miles to the east.

Vahling Vineyards
Tired of raising hogs full-time for a living, the Vahling family decided to give grape-growing a shot on their livestock and grain farm. After several years of testing different grape varieties, they developed several varieties that grew well on the relatively flat land in the Grand Prairie. Vahling Vineyards (County Rd. 400N, 0.25 mile west of Hwy. 32, Stewardson, 217/682-5409, www.vahlingvineyards.com, 10 A.M.–5 P.M. Tues.–Thurs., 10 A.M.–8 P.M. Fri.–Sat. June–Aug., 1–5 P.M. Sun.) sells sweet and semisweet wines, such as Prairie White, a semidry from the American hybrid Cayuga grapes, and Country Red, made with Fredonia grapes. Feel free to visit the unpretentious wine-making operation south of Shelbyville.

Coles and Edgar Counties

A quiet part of the state, Coles and Edgar Counties are, like the neighboring counties, rural in nature. The terrain starts to change here, though, as there are more rolling hills and wooded areas. The scenic Embarras River curls through the eastern part of Coles County and several creeks meander through Edgar to the east. The largest towns in the region are Charleston in Coles County and Paris in Edgar. Both are courthouse-square towns and railroad towns. This is also Lincoln country. His father, Thomas, and his stepmother, Sarah, lived on a farm south of Charleston, and he reportedly did visit with them there. Also, as a circuit lawyer he passed through the towns offering legal services to residents several times a year. Highway 16 is the main east-west thoroughfare, and Highway 1, otherwise known as the Dixie Highway, runs north and south on the eastern edge of the state.

COLES COUNTY
Lincoln Log Cabin State Historic Site
Living-history villages are a dime a dozen in the Midwest, but the Lincoln Log Cabin State Historic Site (County Rd. 1420E, Lerna, 217/345-1845, www.lincolnlogcabin.org, 8:30 A.M.–dusk daily, donation) is one of the best and perhaps one of the most underrated.

It's not particularly easy to get to; it's not off an interstate, and it's about a 15-minute drive south of Charleston in a rural area. Essentially the 86-acre site consists of the reconstructed homestead, several outbuildings, plus vegetable and fruit gardens and farm animals. This is the farmstead where Abe Lincoln's father, Thomas, lived with his wife (and Abe's stepmother) Sarah. Abe did not live at the site, but he did visit. Sarah and Thomas Lincoln moved to the area in 1840 and Sarah, who outlived her husband, lived here until she died in 1869. Her grandson lived in the cabin until it was moved to the Chicago World's Fair in 1892 for display. What happened to the cabin after the show is a mystery.

Walking through the farm, you'd swear you were walking through an 1840s farm (minus the gravel walkways). Volunteers dressed in 1840s clothing are out and about hanging herbs to dry, dying or spinning wool, gathering peppers from the garden, and cooking over the cabin's hearth. A handful of horses, pigs, sheep, and chickens mill around in their fenced-in pens. Cucumber vines twist around twig contraptions. A wagon is off to the side as if someone had just pulled in for a visit, and piles of logs are common throughout the grounds. Throughout the year the park holds events to show visitors what life was like more than 150 years ago. It's had demonstrations on flax processing, gunsmithing, and cheese-making, and has even re-created weddings. The Harvest Frolic and Agricultural Fair, held in early October, includes activities such as music, a barn dance, and candlelight tours of the two farms.

Adjacent to the Lincoln farm is the Sargent Farm. A trail connects the two. Originally situated a few miles east of the Lincoln homestead, the Sargent Farm was larger—it had about 400 acres of cropland and 600 animals. The original buildings, including the white frame house (which is quite a bit larger than the Lincoln log cabin), were moved to the site.

The visitors center has exhibits on the Lincoln family's migration, going back all the way to Samuel Lincoln, who was born in England in 1637. Displays include images of the cabin, including one taken in 1891; a chest said to have been made by Thomas Lincoln and a man named Reuben Moor; and other tools, dishes, and items from the 1840s. One revealing tidbit is information gathered about the Lincoln farm from the 1850 census. The Lincolns had 16 sheep, two cows, and 20 swine. There's also a 15-minute video about the site and the Lincoln family. The site has shelters and picnic areas for visitors. To get to the park, follow signs south from University Drive in Charleston for about seven miles.

Fox Ridge State Park

On a glacial moraine above the Embarras River, Fox Ridge State Park (seven miles south of Charleston, east off Hwy. 130, 217/345-6416, www.dnr.state.il.us) is a rustic park with a mix of wooded hills and some lowland grassy areas with shrubs and small trees. There are six miles of hiking trails through the park, most of them moderately easy to rugged and varying from 0.75 mile long to 1.5 miles long. The No Name Trail (that's actually the name) follows a section of the Embarras near the South Point canoe-launch area. There you can launch your canoe into the Embarras River for a peaceful ride. Chances are you'll see more turtles, birds, and fish than people. The Natural

History Survey operates a research station here. Fishing is allowed, but you'll need permission from the survey.

Entertainment

Eastern Illinois University's **Tarble Arts Center** (S. 9th St., Charleston, 217/581-2787, 10 A.M.–5 P.M. Tues.–Fri., 10 A.M.–4 P.M. Sat., 1–4 P.M. Sun. during the school year, call for summer hours) hosts art shows, music concerts, and lectures throughout the year.

Just west of the courthouse square, **Charleston Alley Theatre** (718 Monroe Ave., Charleston, 217/345-2287, www.charlestonalleytheatre.com) is a small community theater that presents classic comedies, dramas, and musicals.

Accommodations and Food

There are two main hotels in Charleston, both with rates around $50–70, depending on the day of the week and time of year. Both are near one another on the main drag through town, Lincoln Avenue, or Highway 16. The **Best Western Worthington Inn** (920 W. Lincoln Ave., Charleston, 217/348-8161) has 67 rooms, some with refrigerators and microwaves. The hotel has an outdoor pool and restaurant on-site. The 52-room **Days Inn** (810 W. Lincoln Ave., Charleston, 217/345-7689) is a newer hotel that also has some rooms that come with refrigerators and microwaves. Like the Best Western, standard rooms come with in-room coffeemakers. Continental breakfast is included.

How often do you get to stay in a genuine Civil War–era cabin? Set on a 50-acre country spread just west of Charleston, the ◖ **Osage Inn** (1344E County Rd. 720N, Charleston, 217/345-2622, closed Jan., $85–95) is a restored hewn-log house that's more than 150 years old. There's a bedroom with a queen bed on the first floor and a full and twin in the bedroom on the second floor. Outside is a porch with rocking chairs, an arbor where you can eat breakfast or drink some wine, and a meadow for lounging or playing catch (kids are welcome here).

Fox Ridge State Park (seven miles south of Charleston, just east off Hwy. 130, 217/345-6416, www.dnr.state.il.us, $6–12) has tent and trailer camping available. Plus, it offers a cabin that can sleep six people, with bunk beds, a table, deck, electricity, drinking water, showers, and dumping station.

Marianne's (615 Monroe, Charleston, 217/348-7733, breakfast and lunch, $6) is a casual café with local art on the wall, magazines and newspapers scattered about, and a variety of sandwiches and desserts on the menu. Food is called "European" and there's no shortage of German-type fare, such as the grilled brat topped with sauerkraut on rye bread, or a lighter option, "Willems," a veggie sandwich on chewy multigrain bread. The best part about Marianne's is the desserts: the Black Forest cake slices, apple kuchen, or thick cheesecake (there's a vegan option made with tofu).

Information

The **Charleston Tourism Office** (520 Jackson Ave., Charleston, 217/348-0430, www.charlestontourism.org) publishes a visitors guide that you can order on the website or by calling the office during the week.

EDGAR COUNTY
Paris

The area in and around Paris is home to several small innovative farms. Not everyone grows corn and soybeans. Explore the countryside and you'll find everything from strawberries to ostriches. The farms, while open to tourists, don't have set hours; just call ahead. Most owners, you'll find, are willing to take you around. **Barkley Farms** (1300th Rd., Paris, 217/463-7003) specializes in perennials. **Indian Boundary Farm** (16132 E. 1950th St., Bloomfield, 217/269-2445) has a pick-your-own strawberry patch in the late spring and sweet corn and other veggies later in the summer. Fall is peak time for **Pumpkin Works** (21788 E. Terra Haute Rd., Elbridge, 217/275-3327), where owners sculpt several intricate corn mazes every year. They also offer hayrides and open their barn, where they sell pumpkins, corn, gourds, and other fall items. To the west is a similar operation, **Country Bumpkin Pumpkin Path** (5556 E. 150th Rd., Grandview, 217/273-4099), which also boasts a corn maze, wagon rides, and pumpkins.

Abraham Lincoln devotees can visit the **Edgar County Historical Society Complex** (408–414 N. Main St., Paris, 217/463-5305, call for hours, free) to view a desk and chair once used by Lincoln when he stopped by Paris to try cases. The museum also has exhibits on local history.

Andrew's at the Westbrook Farm (7397 N. 1200th St., Paris, 217/465-2003, www.andrewsatwestbrook.com, 5:30 P.M.–10 P.M. Thurs.–Sat.) serves seasonal cuisine and wine in a mid-19th-century farmhouse west of Paris.

For more information about the area, contact the **Paris Area Chamber of Commerce** (105 N. Central Ave., Paris, 217/465-4179).

Danville and Vicinity

On the eastern end of the state, Vermilion County stands out among other counties in the Grand Prairie. For one thing, it's hilly, and the topography resembles more the eastern forests common in states such as Ohio than the flat, rich farmland and prairie to the west. And there's water: scenic rambling rivers such as the Vermilion, the Little Vermilion, and the Middle Fork, a National Scenic River.

Its history too is not so deeply tied to agriculture as other towns in the central part of the state (although it is definitely a major industry here).

Founded in 1765, Danville was first known for its saltworks. For hundreds of years Native American Indian tribes would live and hunt through the region, following the tracks of animals, such as buffalo and deer, as they made their way to the salt springs along the Salt Fork River. Settlers discovered these springs and set up a saltworks where the brine was boiled in giant kettles. Eventually the supply diminished and the salt industry was eclipsed by another: coal mining. Coal was king in the latter half of the 19th century and the first half of the 20th century. Strip-mining was a common practice in Vermilion County. Kickapoo State Park north of Oakwood was once all strip-mining land. Eventually coal production also dwindled. Today Danville is, you might say, in a transition phase. After the town lost its major employer (General Motors) in the 1990s, residents and businesses packed up and left town. It's still a manufacturing center with grain-processing and distribution companies set up in town, but the Danville of today is much different from the one 50 years ago when famous former residents such as Jerry and Dick Van Dyke and the late singer Bobby Short were growing up here. Downtown Danville is recovering. Residents are working to restore a historic downtown opera house. Welcoming businesses are setting up shop, such as the Java Hut. But the real reason to visit Vermilion County is to spend time hiking, biking through the parks, or canoeing down the Middle Fork.

The Danville area is home to several gorgeous parks. First is Kickapoo State Park on the Middle Fork River, and north of there are the Middle Fork State Fish and Wildlife Area and Kennekuk County Park. All of these are on the river and offer wooded, hilly hiking and biking trails. The state recently acquired more land between Kickapoo and Middle Fork, and one day these two state parks may merge. Finally, there's Forest Glen, south of Danville, with its stunning tallgrass prairie and pioneer homestead.

ORIENTATION

The major metropolitan area in the county is Danville, which has about 33,000 residents. It's just north of I-74, west of the Illinois-Indiana border. Navigating Danville can be tricky. The major state and U.S. highways don't stick to straight north-south or east-west routes in

town. For example, Highway 150 runs north into Danville from south of I-74 and then shoots west through town. It's a good idea to review your map before driving through the area. The major parks are all west of town and north of I-74.

SIGHTS AND ACTIVITIES
◖ Kickapoo State Park and Middle Fork State Fish and Wildlife Area

Once strip-mine land, **Kickapoo State Park** (10906 Kickapoo Rd., Oakwood, 217/442-4915, www.dnr.state.il.us) is now one of the best parks in central Illinois. The 2,800-acre park, which borders the east and west side of the Middle Fork River, has challenging hiking and jogging trails, mountain-biking trails, horseback-riding trails, and canoeing, kayaking, and tubing opportunities. What more could you ask for?

First off, the water adventures: **Kickapoo Landing** (217/446-8399, www.kickapoo landing.com, 7 A.M.–7 P.M. Sun.–Thurs., 7 A.M.–9 P.M. Fri.–Sat.) inside the park organizes canoeing, kayaking, and tubing trips down the river. Float or paddle past bluffs, sandbars, and bottomland forests. The tubing loop is about two miles long and takes about an hour. Choose from eight-mile and 13-mile canoe or kayak trips, which can take 3–8 hours. Or you can rent by the hour and paddle around Clear Lake, a nearby inlet. Rates vary according to the day of the week you visit (prices are slightly higher on the weekends). Tubing costs $4–5. Canoeing and kayaking is $15–35. Kickapoo Landing also serves food.

Next up, the trails: Kickapoo is one of the few places in the state where there are designated **mountain-biking trails.** And they're pretty fine. You've got about 12 miles of single-track trails along the river, up the hills, and through the woods. Then there's the 7.6-mile "out and back" trail for hiking or jogging. This narrow pathway also leads you through varied terrain, including some level areas along the river and up steep hills. For a bit less physically stressful tour of the park, you can go **horseback riding** by renting horses at the park's stables (217/446-8575). Guided trail rides, which last 1–2 hours, are offered April–October.

Kickapoo State Park also has two campgrounds with a total of 184 electric, tent, and primitive sites.

A few miles upriver from Kickapoo State Park is the **Middle Fork State Fish and Wildlife Area** (same contact information as Kickapoo), a 2,700-acre site just loaded with trails for horseback riding and hiking. In total there are 35 miles of trails through this park. If you brought your own canoe or kayak, you can launch it here. Middle Fork State Fish and Wildlife Area also has electric, tent, and backpack campsites.

Kennekuk County Park

East of the Middle Fork State Fish and Wildlife Area is Kennekuk County Park (22296 Henning Rd., Danville, 217/442-1691, www.vccd.org) and Lake Mingo, a deep pond created by strip-mining. Start your visit with a hike

around some of the lake (it's 7.5 miles long), and then camp out on the beach and doze in the sun. Before you leave, tour the **Bunker Hill Historic Area,** a living history village with a pioneer chapel, school, train depot, and other buildings.

Forest Glen Preserve

Kickapoo and the other parks along the Middle Fork north of I-74 are certainly scenic, with their countless trails along rugged wooded bluffs and rambling rivers, but there's another great park to the south. Set aside some time to explore the Forest Glen Preserve (2031 E. 900 Rd., Westville, 217/662-2142, www.vccd.org). Begin with a climb up the 72-foot-tall observation tower overlooking the Vermilion River Valley. Then choose your trail. As in the parks to the north, there's no shortage of trails here. About 25 miles of trails offer visitors views of tallgrass prairie, wetlands, and woods. Within the park is the **Duffin Nature Preserve and Forest Glen Seep Nature Preserve,** which protects a rare plant, the twayblade orchid, that

tubing on the Vermilion River

© CHRISTINE DES GARENNES

grows in bogs. Forest Glen also has an arboretum with more than 600 varieties of trees, with an emphasis on native Illinois trees. You'd be surprised to learn just how many varieties of oaks there are in the state. Finally, if you have your own canoe, you can launch it here for a quiet ride on the Vermilion River.

Museums

Veterans and historians will be impressed with the wide-ranging collections in the **Vermilion County War Museum** (307 N. Vermilion St., Danville, 217/431-0034 or 800/383-4386, www.vcwm.org, noon–3 P.M. Tues.–Fri., 10 A.M.–4 P.M. Sat., 1–4 P.M. Sun., donation). Museum staff has filled two floors and almost 13,000 square feet of exhibit space with items from more than 200 years of American war history, including the Spanish-American War and Desert Storm. Mannequins are dressed in uniforms from different branches of service, medals from several wars are displayed in glass cases, and there's an array of newspaper clippings announcing deployments and major battles, flags, and more.

Here's another stop for travelers who are on quests to visit all the Lincoln sites in the state. The **Vermilion County Museum and Fithian Home** (116 N. Gilbert St., Danville, 217/442-2922, www.vermilioncountymuseum.org, 10 A.M.–5 P.M. Tues.–Sat., $2.50–4) consists of two main buildings: One is the Vermilion County Museum, which is a replica of the old courthouse where Lincoln once practiced law. This building contains displays about the county's coal-mining history, its connection to the Dixie Highway, and a re-creation of what Lincoln's law office may have looked like in Danville. However, the must-see for Lincoln buffs is the Fithian Home, which is near the museum. Inside this brick 1855 home is a bed where Lincoln reportedly slept while visiting his friend, homeowner William Fithian.

Vineyard

One of the newer vineyards in Illinois is **Sleepy Creek Vineyard** (8254 E. 1425 N. Rd., Fairmount, 217/733-0330, www.

sleepycreekvineyards.com), found among the slightly rolling hills south of Oakwood and Kickapoo State Park. They use grapes grown right outside the barn door to make dry, semidry, and sweet white and red wines. The vineyard has a tasting room and art gallery, and occasionally holds live music concerts and other events.

ENTERTAINMENT AND EVENTS
Performing Arts

The **Danville Symphony Orchestra** (office 2917 N. Vermilion St., Danville, 217/443-5300, www.danvillesymphony.org, box office 10 A.M.–4 P.M. Mon.–Fri.) performs four concerts a year, plus a children's show and performance during Danville's Art in the Park festival in June. Concerts are held in Danville High School (202 E. Fairchild St., Danville). Tickets are available from the office or 90 minutes before the show.

Performers with the **Danville Light Opera** (217/431-1660, www.danvillelightopera.com) present such musicals as *Chicago* throughout the year. They also stage productions in the high school.

Events

Taking a cue from a *WKRP in Cincinnati* episode, members of the Balloon Association of Greater Illinois lift off from Turtle Run Golf Course (332 E. Liberty Ln., Danville, 217/442-3320) and drop rubber chickens from their balloons on the morning of Thanksgiving. Relax; they're not real. It's called the **Les Nessman Turkey Drop.**

Every June regional visual and performing artists participate in **Arts in the Park,** held in Danville's Lincoln Park on North Gilbert Street.

Hoopeston, which has declared itself the sweet-corn capital of the world, holds a **Sweetcorn Festival** every September, usually on Labor Day weekend. There's a parade and a sweet-corn sweetheart pageant, plus carnival rides, a demolition derby, a beer tent, you name it. Oh, and bushels and bushels of free sweet corn for festival attendees. For more information contact the Danville Area Convention and Visitors Bureau (see *Information and Services*).

SPORTS

The real Babe Ruth didn't play baseball at **Danville Stadium** (Highland Blvd., east of Hwy. 150/Gilbert St., Danville, 217/431-2260), but the stadium was used as an on-site film location for *The Babe*, a movie about him. The stadium is somewhat of a historic site and reminiscent of what ballparks used to look like more than 50 years ago. Built in 1946, the 5,000-seat stadium was once a part of the farm team system for the Brooklyn Dodgers. Back then many of the players would go on to join the major leagues. Now the team, the Danville Dans, is part of the Central Illinois Collegiate League.

ACCOMMODATIONS

Your lodging options in Danville are limited to chain hotels just off the interstate. Rates vary $50–100 depending on the type of room you choose and the day of the week you visit.

On the lower end of that range are **Super 8** (377 Lynch Dr., Danville, 217/443-4499), which has the standard free continental breakfast and choice of double or king beds; and just down the street is the **Comfort Inn** (383 Lynch Dr., Danville, 217/443-8004), which has an indoor heated pool and some suites with microwaves and fridges. Slightly more upscale accommodations (meaning there are usually coffeemakers, hair dryers, and other amenities in the rooms) include the **Fairfield Inn** (389 Lynch Dr., Danville, 217/443-3388), which has continental breakfast, indoor pool, and some suites with microwaves and fridges; **Sleep Inn and Suites** (361 Lynch Dr., Danville, 217/442-6600), which has an indoor pool and exercise room; and **Holiday Inn Express and Suites** (310 E. Gate Dr., Danville, 217/442-2500), another newer hotel with an indoor pool, exercise room, and high-speed Internet access.

If you prefer the bed-and-breakfast route, there's the **Lamp Post Inn** (420 N. Gilbert St., Danville, 217/446-9458) in a historical section of town. The Lamp Post is part of the Corner Victorian Shops, a group of home-decor shops and a tea room. There are five guest rooms here, two with private bathrooms.

FOOD
Casual

The **Java Hut** (13 N. Vermilion St., Danville, 217/443-6808, 6:30 A.M.–5 P.M. Mon.–Fri., 7:30 A.M.–1 P.M. Sat., $5) is a lively local coffee shop and sandwich place where you'll find it's easy to pass the afternoon reading a book while sipping a cappuccino. It's a community gathering place of sorts, a lively place in downtown. The Java Hut serves bagel sandwiches, quiches, pastries, and sandwiches such as turkey clubs and Italian beef. Local artwork hangs on the walls.

So the name may not be that appetizing, but **Gross's Burgers** (25 Henderson St., Danville, 217/442-8848, 11 A.M.–8 P.M. Mon.–Sat., $3) has developed a loyal fan base of diners around town and the country for its burgers, which Gross's has been selling in Danville for two decades. Got an appetite? Order the triple cheeseburger. The fast-food restaurant is named after the family's surname, by the way.

After a long hot day tubing or paddling in Kickapoo State Park, make tracks to **Custard Cup** (2507 N. Vermilion St., Danville, 217/443-0221) for their locally famous concoctions. Their "snowstorms" are similar to Dairy Queen's "blizzards." The shakes are superthick, and the phosphates are also worth a try.

Fine Dining

Chops, seafood, and ribs are the fare at the **Possum Trot** (2918 Batestown Rd., Oakwood, 217/442-6066, 4–9 P.M. Mon.–Thurs., 4–10 P.M. Fri.–Sat., 11 A.M.–8 P.M. Sun., $17), a supper club west of Danville and south of Kickapoo State Park. Here you can watch the chef cook your steak on the giant grill, listen to a pianist perform, and sip some red wine or a glass of whiskey. If you're not in the mood for filet mignon or strip steak, choose from entrées such as fried grouper, baby back ribs, or grilled chicken.

In a historic renovated storefront in downtown Danville, **The Heron** (34 N. Vermilion St., Danville, 217/446-8330, www.danville-heron.com, 5:30–9:30 P.M. Wed.–Sat.) is a classy joint where you dine on tuna steaks or herbed chicken, followed by a slice of smooth tiramisu, and all the while a jazz musician sings in the background. Entrées are around $20.

INFORMATION AND SERVICES

At some point during your trip, make a point to stop by the I-74 travel plaza just west of Danville. The **Salt Kettle Welcome Center** (at Exit 206) not only has a dozens of brochures for the taking, but also an educational display about the region's history, including information about the salt springs and coal-mining industry. For more information on the area, contact the **Danville Area Convention and Visitors Bureau** (100 W. Main St., Ste. 146, Danville, 217/442-2096 or 800/383-4386, www.danvillecvb.com), which publishes a guide listing area attractions, hotels, and restaurants.

The main hospital in the area is **Provena United Samaritans Medical Center** (812 N. Logan Ave., Danville, 217/443-5000, www.provenausmc.com) on the west side of town. The **U.S. post office** in Danville is at 303 North Hazel Street, Danville, 217/446-9440. It's north of Main Street and east of Gilbert Street.

Kankakee and Iroquois River Valleys

Before the white settlers arrived beginning in the mid-1830s, the land along the Kankakee River was used by the Miami and Potawatomi Indians for hunting and fishing. Unlike parts of the prairie to the south, the land near the river was lush and full of native black walnut trees and oak and hickory forests. Because the area was teeming with game, eventually the French fur traders took notice and moved into the area also. The French founded the town of Bourbonnais (it actually came first, before Kankakee, which is now the larger of the two cities). And after the Illinois Central Railroad in 1855 established a stop in the area, along came settlers from the East Coast. In addition to the new white Yankees were African-Americans who settled east of Kankakee in the Pembroke area. The historically black area and the city of Hopkins Park celebrate their heritage every year with Pembroke Days in August as well as the Thyrl Latting Rodeo Spectacular during Memorial Day weekend, which spotlights African-American achievements in the American West.

Kankakee and Iroquois Counties were back then, as they are now, heavily into agriculture (including large- and small-scale farmers) and companies such as fertilizer and chemical manufacturers. Kankakee also prides itself on its connection to the Dairy Queen ice cream chain. In 1938 a man named Sherb Noble, who ran Sherb's, an ice-cream shop in Kankakee, offered customers soft-serve ice cream for the first time. He had recently partnered with an Iowan who had developed a new way of serving ice cream: soft. Later Noble would open the first Dairy Queen franchise in Joliet.

ORIENTATION

Kankakee is the largest city in the region, with about 26,000 people. Immediately adjacent to the city's borders are Bourbonnais to the northwest and Bradley directly to the north. The entire county of Kankakee has about 100,000 people. Iroquois County to the south and east is a rural county with only about 30,000 people. The largest town there is Watseka, about 12 miles east of I-57, with about 5,000 people. I-57 runs north-south through the region, skirting the west side of Kankakee. U.S. 45/52 slices through most of the east and center part of Bradley and Kankakee. The highlight of the region is Kankakee River State Park with its limestone bluffs, hiking trails, and campground, northwest of the city of Kankakee.

KANKAKEE COUNTY
Kankakee River State Park

Stretching for 11 miles along the north and south sides of the river, the Kankakee River State Park (513 W. Hwy. 102, Bourbonnais, 815/933-1382, www.dnr.state.il.us) is a refreshing spot, topographically speaking, in an area dominated by corn and soybean fields. The park is about 4,000 acres with spots for fishing, sitting on a rock and writing or reading, trails for walking, bicycling, cross-country skiing, or horseback riding. It's about six miles east of I-57, and if you've been on the road for a while, this is a good spot to stretch your legs. A good place to begin is the visitors center, where you can pick up trail maps and walk through the wildflower identification gardens outside or the prairie restoration area.

There's lots to do here. You can park your car at the Davis Creek Area on the far south end of the park (where the group campground is) and then hop on your bike and ride the 10.5-mile biking trail along the north side of the river. Or you can explore the south side of the river by meandering along the 12-mile equestrian trail. (Until 2006 you could rent a horse at the park's stables, but as of this writing the park had closed the stables. You can still bring your own horse to the park, however.) In the winter you can go cross-country skiing on these trails. You can stroll along the bicycle trail, but there are several other nature trails and hiking trails, such as the two-mile Rock Creek Canyon trail near Rock Creek, which empties into the Kankakee. Here you can get a good look at the limestone canyons for which the park is famous. Walk along the Shaw-waw-nas-see nature trail north of the main entrance (off Deselm Road near the horse stables) and you can glimpse a waterfall. Or walk across the river on a suspension bridge to explore the south side of the park, keeping an eye out for red-tailed hawks and wildflowers. The islands in the middle of the river are nature preserves where the Kankakee mallow, an endangered flower, grows.

There are two campgrounds here: Chippewa Campground to the north and Potawatomi to the south. Both have sites near the river. Hunting is allowed in the park in the fall, so use caution when hiking or horseback riding through the area during that time of the year. There is no swimming allowed in the river. The Kankakee River is notorious for its strong currents, and people have drowned off the river's shores.

Scuba Diving

For about $20, you can explore a spring-fed quarry north of Highway 17, west of Bradley and Kankakee. **Haigh's Scuba Diving Quarry** (2738 E. 2000 N. Rd., Kankakee, 815/932-7797, www.haighquarry.com, hours vary by season, call ahead or check website before going) has observation platforms at different levels of the quarry down to 70 feet. Haigh's has sunk stuff like a dump truck and a boat for you to explore. It costs $20 to dive for the day, more if you rent any equipment ($60 for a complete set with tank, suit, etc.). A concession stand sells burgers, fries, sodas, and such. And you can also fish for bluegill, bass, and others.

Perry Farm Park and Exploration Station

One of the first farmsteads in the area, established in the 1830s, the Perry family farm has been transformed into the Perry Farm Park (456 N. Kennedy Dr., Bourbonnais, 815/933-9905, www.btpd.org), a 170-acre complex with farm buildings, a petting zoo, a children's museum, and four miles of walking trails that lead along Bourbonnais Creek and to some caves. A popular spot for school groups, the park also has a pavilion where local musicians play on Tuesday nights in the summer, a rose garden, and an orchard. At Exploration Station, the children's museum, visitors learn about arts and science through hands-on exhibits. The park and trails are free and open sunrise–sunset daily. Exploration Station is open 10 A.M.–5 P.M. Monday–Saturday, 1–5 P.M. Sunday. Admission is $5 for adults, $4 for children age 1–17. On Tuesdays admission is a suggested $1 donation.

Museums

At the **Kankakee County Museum** (801 S. 8th Ave., Kankakee, 815/932-5279, www.kankakeecountymuseum.com, 10 A.M.–4 P.M. Tues.–Fri., 1–4 P.M. Sat.–Sun., closed Sat. Oct.–Mar., $3, Fri. free) you can view permanent and rotating exhibits about the first 100 years of the county, 1853–1953. There are also exhibits on the area's Native American history and displays about the three Illinois governors who hailed from the county (including most recently George Ryan, who was in office 1999–2003). Temporary exhibits have focused on the French influence in the United States and art deco buildings in the region. In addition to the main museum building, the grounds contain the boyhood home of Len Small, who was governor in the 1920s, and a one-room schoolhouse. For more glimpses of Kankakee's past, visit the **Kankakee Railroad Museum** (197 S. East Ave., Kankakee, 815/929-9320, www.kankakeerrmuseum.com, 11 A.M.–4 P.M. Tues.–Sat., noon–4 P.M. Sun., donation) housed in a grand old train depot in downtown Kankakee. The local model-railroading club has several model-train displays on view that depict scenes from Kankakee's past. Outside there's a Pullman coach from the 1940s and a Union Pacific caboose. The museum is closed every fourth weekend of the month.

Events

Every Memorial Day weekend in Hopkins Park, a historically black community west of Kankakee, folks come out and celebrate African-Americans in the American West with the **Thyrl Latting Rodeo Spectacular,** complete with lassoing and other roping and riding demonstrations. The town also honors its heritage with **Pembroke Days** in August by showcasing blues, gospel, and jazz music. The Kankakee municipal band plays free at 7:30 P.M. Thursday nights at the riverside Bird Park the first week of June through the first week of August.

Free concerts are also held at the gazebo on the Perry farm Tuesday evenings in July and August, 7–8:30 P.M.

Accommodations

The bulk of the hotels in the area are chain operations, and they're all just off I-57 on exits in Bradley, Bourbonnais, and Kankakee. Rates are generally $80–100, although the Hilton has some suites that can reach $130.

The newer **Hilton Garden Inn** (455 Riverstone Pkwy., Kankakee, 815/932-4444, www.kankakee.gardeninn.com) is a business travelers hotel with rooms and suites with amenities such as coffeemakers, microwaves, minifridges, desks, and wireless Internet access. The hotel has a bar and restaurant, a whirlpool and indoor swimming pool, plus a laundry room with coin-operated machines for guests.

The 59-room **Hampton Inn** (60 Ken Hayes Dr., Bourbonnais, 815/932-8369, $89–120) has a 24-hour exercise room and offers guests continental breakfast. The **Fairfield Inn** (1550 N. Hwy. 50, Bourbonnais, 815/935-1334, $85–95) has an indoor pool and exercise room and also offers guests a continental breakfast.

Camping

There are two campgrounds at **Kankakee River State Park** (513 W. Hwy. 102, Bourbonnais, 815/933-1383) with RV and tent sites available. Rates are $20–25 per night including a $5 reservation fee.

Information

Contact the **Kankakee County Convention and Visitors Bureau** (1 Dearborn Sq., Suite 521, Kankakee, 815/935-7390 or 800/747-4837, www.visitkankakeecounty.com) for information about Kankakee, Bourbonnais, and nearby towns.

IROQUOIS COUNTY
Iroquois State Wildlife Area

Perhaps one of the state's quietest and least crowded parks, the Iroquois State Wildlife Area (2803 E. 3300 N. Rd., Beaverville, 815/435-2218, www.dnr.state.il.us) is also quite a rare sight. Totaling about 2,480 acres, the wildlife area contains prairie and sedge meadow, and the 480-acre Hooper Branch Savanna Nature Preserve, the largest single tract of native savanna left in Illinois. There you can find switch grass, June grass, and some boggy areas with plants not common in the state (such as the sundew, which eats insects). Hiking and nature trails, including a 0.3-mile wheelchair-accessible trail, weave past sand dunes and marshy areas. The site is about 15 miles east of I-57 and a mile west of the Illinois-Indiana state line.

Heartland Health Spa
Called a "destination spa," Heartland Health Spa (1237 E. 1600 N. Rd., Gilman, 815/683-2182 or 800/545-4853, www.heartlandspa.com) is a place where you retreat for the weekend, indulge in a few massages, practice a little yoga, eat fresh healthy foods, and get your hair done. The 32-acre estate in rural Iroquois County is a little oasis in the prairie. (Imagine a very, very upscale farmstead, if you can.) This is a place to go when you want to get away from work and far from a noisy crowded city. (It's in Gilman, a city of about 2,000 people.) Here guests essentially choose their objectives, such as reducing stress or to start exercising again, for their stay. Then they plan ways to meet that goal, such as signing up for group exercise classes, spending time in the weight room, swimming laps in the indoor pool, or walking or cross-country skiing along the spa's trails. The spa also has adventure programs in which instructors teach you how to walk on a cable above the ground or fly down a zip-line. Meals here are the opposite of those served at the Bayern Stube in nearby Gibson City. They're light—fewer than 2,000 calories for guys and girls—although you can ask for more if you're not calorie-counting. Rates vary but are definitely upscale. There are one-person and two-person rates, plus there's a two-night minimum stay. Rates start around $345–550 per night and can go up depending on the type of room you choose to stay in.

Bloomington-Normal

Like Champaign-Urbana to the southeast, Bloomington-Normal was first settled by hunters and fisherman and eventually farm families as people realized the prairie was fertile ground. Yankees and immigrant families established homesteads, tamed the prairie, and started shipping their grain and livestock to Chicago on new train lines. Today the twin cities of Bloomington and Normal are fairly diverse communities with a mix of university students, academics, farmers, and white- and blue-collar workers. Illinois State University is here, agricultural and automotive manufacturers are here, and the headquarters for State Farm Insurance (a company that employs about 12,000 people in the area) is here. Bloomington is the county seat for McLean, which means there's also a fair amount of government activity going on.

You'll notice the land rises slightly in this area. That's because about 15,000 years ago the last glacier in Illinois pushed and shoved enormous amounts of rocks and dirt around to create ridges, or moraines. There are four of these ridges in Illinois and one of the largest is the Bloomington moraine, which covers an area from Elgin to the Illinois River and Saybrook, a tiny town east of Bloomington-Normal. Outside the cities the area mostly comprises grain farms and a few cattle or hog farms. In recent years the county has restricted residential and commercial development on prime farmland, and in McLean County there's a lot of that. The county is always among the tops in corn and soybean production and yields.

ORIENTATION
Bloomington-Normal is where several federal interstates intersect, meaning lots of travelers and truckers stop by overnight or for a meal.

© CHRISTINE DES GARENNES

the old county courthouse, now home to the McLean County Museum of History

I-39 and U.S. 51 are the main north-south highways, with Business 51 (Main Street) slicing right through the center of the cities. I-74 runs diagonally through the region, from Champaign-Urbana and Indianapolis northwest to the Quad Cities, and it circumvents the cities to the south. Finally, I-55, the main drag between Chicago and St. Louis, also passes by Bloomington. Veteran's Parkway, Business 55, runs north-south on the east side of both towns. With that said, it's quick and easy to get around Bloomington; there are many highways you can hop on to go where you want. But in the past it prompted many businesses to move away from the downtowns. However, in recent years restaurants, coffee shops, and boutiques are choosing to locate in the downtowns.

SIGHTS
Franklin Park Historic District

One of Bloomington's favorite sons was David Davis, a local politician who went on to become a U.S. Supreme Court justice 1862–1877. His grand home, the **David Davis Mansion State Historic Site** (1000 E. Monroe Dr.,

Bloomington, 309/828-1084, typically 9 A.M.–4 P.M. Wed.–Sun. but call ahead for hours, $2) has been restored and filled with period furniture. When it was built in 1872, the home was quite fancy for the area. You can tour the interior and exterior, which includes a carriage house and gardens. Tours run every 30 minutes on the hour and half hour and last about an hour.

When you're done touring the Davis home, walk or drive through the Franklin Park Historic District (Chestnut, McLean, Prairie, and Walnut Sts., bordering Franklin Park), once a posh Bloomington neighborhood. There are a number of rambling Victorian homes, brick streets, and antique streetlamps.

Another famous family that hails from Bloomington is the Stevenson family. **Adlai E. Stevenson,** born in 1835, moved to Bloomington in his late teens, attended Illinois Wesleyan University, worked as a postmaster, and then went on to serve in Congress and as Grover Cleveland's vice president 1893–1897. Stevenson ran for president and Illinois governor unsuccessfully before retiring and returning to Bloomington. He's buried in Bloomington's **Evergreen Cemetery** (302 E. Miller St., Bloomington, 309/827-6950, dawn–dusk). His grandson, Adlai E. Stevenson II, had a distinguished political career and ended up becoming governor of Illinois. Born in 1900, he was governor 1949–1953 and ran for president against Dwight D. Eisenhower in 1952 and 1956 (the Republican World War II general defeated him both times). Former U.S. President John F. Kennedy picked him to be U.S. ambassador to the United Nations. Stevenson died in 1965 and is also buried in Evergreen Cemetery. Great-grandson Adlai E. Stevenson III, who is still alive, was also a politician, serving in the Illinois House of Representatives, as state treasurer, and as a senator from Illinois during the 1970s. He ran unsuccessfully for the presidency in the 1980s.

Miller Park Zoo

One of the better small zoos in the region, Miller Park Zoo (1020 S. Morris Ave., Bloomington, 309/434-2250, $4.50) has an impressive rainforest exhibit with exotic animals such as leopards and tigers, plus a marine mammal section and petting zoo area for children. The park opens at 9:30 A.M. daily. The buildings close at 5:30 P.M. and the grounds close at 6 P.M. Memorial Day–Labor Day. During the fall, winter, and spring the buildings close at 4:30 P.M. and the grounds close at 5 P.M.

Museums

Let your child's imagination break free at **Children's Discovery Museum** (101 E. Beaufort St., Normal, 309/433-3444, www.childrensdiscoverymuseum.net, 9 A.M.–5 P.M. Tues.–Wed. and Sat., 9 A.M.–8 P.M. Thurs.–Fri., 1–5 P.M. Sun., $4), a multistory museum packed with activities and exhibits. Visitors can don scrubs and play doctor or dentist, run or shop at a grocery store, or be a restaurant proprietor. If that doesn't keep them busy, there's a water play area, train tables, and exhibits about agriculture.

As far as regional museums go, the **McLean County Museum of History** (200 N. Main St., Bloomington, 309/827-0428, www.mchistory.org, 10 A.M.–5 P.M. Mon. and Wed.–Sat., 10 A.M.–9 P.M. Tues. year-round, 1–5 P.M. Sun. Sept.–May, $5) is one of the better ones in the state, partly because of its venue. The museum is housed in the county's former courthouse, an American Renaissance–style building featuring mosaic tiles throughout and a marble staircase. Built in 1904, the courthouse is listed on the National Register of Historic Places and is in downtown Bloomington. You'll recognize it by the copper dome. Inside, museum volunteers have collected archives from the region, including exhibits on famous folks who lived or passed through town, including Adlai Stevenson and David Davis. There's a log cabin display, farming display with an old steel plow, and in one area visitors are invited to mimic chores of the pioneers such as hauling buckets of water. Other displays show photos of the town through the years, including one depicting the devastation caused by a fire in 1900.

The **McLean County Arts Center** (601 N. East St., Bloomington, 309/829-0011, www.mcac.org, 10 A.M.–7 P.M. Tues., 10 A.M.–5 P.M. Wed.–Fri., noon–4 P.M. Sat., free) showcases regional artwork in its Spanish-style building in downtown Bloomington. You can view area landscape paintings, photographs, abstract art, and sculptures. Exhibits rotate throughout the year.

If you fly in or out of the Bloomington-Normal Airport (it's one of the best regional airports in Illinois) and find yourself with some extra time before your flight departs, or before you set off to explore after your flight in, set aside some extra time to tour the **Prairie Aviation Museum** (Central Illinois Regional Airport, 2929 E. Empire St., Bloomington, 309/663-7632, www.prairieaviationmseum.org, 11 A.M.–4 P.M. Tues.–Sat., noon–4 P.M. Sun., $4). Its collection includes vintage Cessnas, a restored Ozark Airlines DC-3, a Marine Corps helicopter, and several airplane engines.

ENTERTAINMENT AND EVENTS

Theater

The **Normal Theater** (209 North St., Normal, 309/454-9722 or 309/454-9720, www.normaltheater.com, $6) is a renovated 1937 movie theater that shows new documentaries such as *The Fog of War* (about former Defense Secretary Robert McNamara), *I'm Not There* (about Bob Dylan), foreign films, and award-winning classics such as *From Here to Eternity.* The art deco–style theater features salmon- and silver-colored seats.

Theater and music students, visiting artists, and groups perform a variety of musicals, plays, operas, music concerts, and more at **Illinois State University's Center for the Performing Arts** (School and Beaufort Sts., Normal, 309/438-2535). The center has a recital hall, studio theater, and experimental theater within its walls.

Formerly a Scottish Rite Masonic temple, **The Bloomington Center for the Performing Arts** (110 E. Mulberry St., Bloomington, 309/434-2777 or 866/686-9541, www.artsblooming.org) is a 1,320-seat theater that dates to 1921 and once hosted jazz great Duke Ellington. By 2000 the temple was showing its age, and a group of residents rallied to restore the building and revitalize the north side of Bloomington's downtown. During the Easter season, the center is home to the oldest continually running passion play in the country.

Events

The **Illinois Shakespeare Festival** (Ewing Manor, Emerson St., east of Towanda Ave., Bloomington, day box office 309/438-8110, evening box office 309/828-9814, www.thefestival.org, $14–40) is one of the best summer events in central Illinois. Produced by Illinois State University on the beautiful grounds of the Ewing Manor, the festival's professional actors present about three different Shakespearean plays (usually a mix of comedies and dramas) for a total of about 40 performances July–mid-August. Outdoor theater is also presented during the summer in the Miller Park pavilion.

Check local newspaper listings for productions, dates, and times.

Arrive early to stake out a picnic spot on the lawn, bring your own basket or buy dinner from the concessionaire, stroll through the formal gardens, and listen to the madrigal singer. Then take a peek inside the manor, where every summer staff prepare exhibits about Shakespeare, British theater, and other related subjects. Finally, take in a show under the stars.

Sponsored by the McLean County Arts Center, the **Sugar Creek Arts Festival,** held early–mid July in downtown Normal, showcases the work of about 135 artists from the region and across the country. You'll find paintings, sculpture, jewelry, and other creations for sale, plus food and live music.

SHOPPING

Virginia Redskins, also known as **Beer Nuts,** are made in Bloomington. You can stock up on them at one of the company's stores in Bloomington: the sale barn (2027 S. Main St./U.S. 51, Bloomington, 10 A.M.–5 P.M. Mon.–Fri., 10 A.M.–4 P.M. Sat., free admission) or the plant and store (103 N. Robinson St., Bloomington, 309/827-8580 or 309/829-8091, www.beernuts.com, 8 A.M.–5 P.M. Mon.–Fri.).

RECREATION

Climbing

Surrounded by miles and miles of corn- and soybean fields planted on low-lying land, Bloomington is not exactly a prime destination for rock climbers. But there is a growing and dedicated group of climbers in the state, and one of their favorite places to climb is at **Upper Limits Rock Gym** (1304 W. Washington St., Bloomington, 309/829-7255, $12–14 for climbing, $5 initiation fee, $6 per rappel). Yes, you can scale the walls of a former grain silo. The 65-foot-tall silos have 20,000 square feet of indoor climbing surface, plus there's an outdoor lighted wall. Outside is also a new "bouldering" area, for those interested in climbing without ropes in areas close to the ground. You can also rappel down the outside of the silos. (If you plan to rappel, call to make an appointment.) During the cold months the imaginative staff creates a frozen waterfall outside the silos with the sprinkler system. It's not far from Cargill's massive grain elevator complex. It's easy to confuse the two, but along the north end of one of the elevators the owners have painted the name Upper Limits. Summer hours: 4–10 P.M. Monday, noon–10 P.M. Tuesday–Friday, 10 A.M.–8 P.M. Saturday, 10 A.M.–6 P.M. Sunday. Winter hours: 4–10 P.M. Monday, Wednesday, and Friday, noon–10 P.M. Tuesday and Thursday, 10 A.M.–10 P.M. Saturday, 10 A.M.–6 P.M. Sunday.

Hiking and Biking

If it's a nice day and you've got the time (and energy), see Bloomington's sights on your bike. Follow **Constitution Trail,** a 14-mile paved trail through the twin cities, and you'll pass the David Davis mansion, Bloomington's historic districts, **Hidden Creek Nature Sanctuary** (Sycamore St., between Fell and Linden), and other city parks, gardens, and residential and commercial areas. The trail runs largely from the north to south, but there is also an east-west branch. Along the way you'll find plenty of water fountains, picnic tables, and benches. The trail, by the way, was named the Constitution Trail because the towns started planning it in 1987 when the United States was celebrating the 200th anniversary of the signing of the Constitution. The north-south trail runs from County Road 1850 North (just north of Normal) to Oakland Avenue in Bloomington. The east-west branch starts at Normal's parks and recreation office (611 S. Linden St., Normal, 309/454-9540) and ends at Towanda Barnes Road in Bloomington. The trail is accessible at several points along the way. You can park at the Hugh Atwood wayside on Robinson and Jefferson Streets; at the parking lot adjacent to the Upper Limits climbing gym; or at Normal's parks and recreation department's office.

ACCOMMODATIONS

Because several interstates run through Bloomington-Normal, there is no shortage of national chain motels at the exits.

Under $50

There's a **Motel 6** (1600 N. Main St., Normal, 309/452-0422) on the north side of the twin cities, near I-55 and U.S. 51.

$50-100

Best Western University Inn (Six Traders Circle, Normal, 309/454-4070, $67–76) is easily accessible from all three interstates that run through Bloomington-Normal: I-74, I-55, and I-39. There's an indoor pool, and pets are allowed.

In Bloomington's Franklin Park Historic District, the **Burr House B&B** (210 E. Chestnut St., Bloomington, 309/828-7686 or 800/449-4182, $60–100) has six rooms for guests, some with private bathrooms and some with shared bathrooms. The stately brick home, built in 1864, is just across the street from Franklin Park.

The **Hampton Inn West** (906 Maple Hill Rd., Bloomington, 309/829-3700 or 800/426-7866, $100) is close to Upper Limits gym and about three miles west of downtown Bloomington. The hotel has an indoor pool and fitness room, plus it offers a continental breakfast.

Over $100

Ostensibly modeled after a French castle, **The Chateau Hotel and Conference Center** (1601 Jumer Ave., Bloomington, 309/662-2020 or 866/690-4006, www.chateauhotel.biz, $99–189) is a bit different from your standard chain hotels, with some antiques and decorative touches around the hotel and in the rooms, although it's still far from the real thing. But for folks looking for something a little different, this is a good option. There are 180 rooms here, including rooms with queen and king beds and some suites with fireplaces. The hotel has a restaurant and lounge on-site, but if you want to venture beyond the hotel, the

Chateau offers free local transportation. The Constitution Trail is steps away from the hotel, so this is also a good option if you're planning to do some biking.

The three-story **Vrooman Mansion** (701 E. Taylor St., Normal, 309/828-8816, www.vroomanmansion.com, $75–125) has five spacious rooms which come with private bathrooms and are outfitted with antique furniture. The stately home, built in 1869 with additions around the turn of the 20th century, has several areas within the home for guests to read or unwind in, including a formal drawing room and music room.

FOOD
American Casual
Kelly's Bakery and Café (113 N. Center St., Bloomington, 309/820-1200, www.kellysbakeryandcafe.com, 7 A.M.–6 P.M. Mon.–Wed. and Fri., 7 A.M.–7 P.M. Thurs., 7 A.M.–2 P.M. Sat., $6) is a friendly breakfast and lunch spot that serves a variety of soups, sandwiches, and salads. The place is known for the hefty cinnamon rolls and homemade quiche, but the sandwiches are also yummy: Chicken salad croissant and the Black Russian sandwich—roast beef, turkey, and provolone on pumpernickel rye—are good bets. Soups are different every day of the week. And the cooks use local seasonal ingredients when possible. Above the restaurant, Abraham Lincoln delivered a speech to area residents after losing a campaign against Stephen Douglas for the Senate seat.

The newer **DeStihl Restaurant and Brew Works** (318 S. Towanda Ave., Normal, 309/862-2337, www.destihl.com, 11 A.M.–11 P.M. Mon.–Thurs., 11 A.M.–midnight Fri.–Sat., 11 A.M.–10 P.M. Sun., $12), located at the Shoppes at College Hills, is a large restaurant with an extensive food and beverage menu. Choose from traditional items like a spinach salad and a pastrami sandwich or some more unusual creations such as the pancetta and apple pizza, espresso-rubbed rib eye, or root beer–baked beans. They brew lagers, ales, Hefeweizen, and stouts. Try a sampler to get a taste of several different kinds. This popular place (it can get a little loud) also has live music some nights.

⑴ Lucca Grill (116 E. Main St., Bloomington, 309/828-7521, www.luccagrill.com, 3–10 P.M. Sun., 10 A.M.–midnight Mon.–Wed., 10 A.M.–1 A.M. Thurs.–Sat., $4–10) is one of those places where you can walk in as a stranger and feel at home. Lucca seems to attract quite a mix of clientele—professionals, students, and blue-collar workers. This casual restaurant and bar serves Italian-American food. Some of the food is what you would expect from an Italian restaurant: Italian beef sandwiches and fettuccine Alfredo. Then there are items such as deep-fried chicken livers (give 'em a try) and liverwurst sandwiches. You cannot beat the pasta, especially the fettuccine with spicy Italian sausage. Pizza is also a good bet, especially late in the evening.

If you're looking for a place to watch the game before or during your lunch or dinner but want more than a plate of nachos, **Swingers Grille** (1304 Cross Creek Dr., Normal, 309/829-5777, www.swingersgrille.com, 11 A.M.–10 P.M. Tues.–Thurs., 11 A.M.–11 P.M. Fri.–Sat., 10 A.M.–4 P.M. Sun., $14–25) is a good choice. Located in the lower level of the All Seasons Entertainment Center (a golf center), Swingers is part sports bar (some tables have TVs), part steak house. They cook up plates of stuffed pork tenderloin, blue cheese flatiron steak, lobster and chorizo mostaccioli (and sandwiches and salads if you're on a budget). Two of you? The restaurant offers an evening special early in the week: $35 for a shared appetizer, two entrées, and dessert. Live jazz is featured some weekend evenings.

Indian
The folks at **Puran Indian** (1704 Eastland Dr., Bloomington, 309/663-0885, http://puranindian.com, 10:30 A.M.–2 P.M., 5–10 P.M. Mon.–Fri., 11 A.M.–2:30 P.M., 5–10 P.M. Sat.–Sun., $9–13) cook up delicious curries and rice dishes, appetizers like samosas, naan and roti breads, lamb, shrimp, and chicken entrées (try the chicken vindaloo or one of the tandoori options), and there are plenty of items with

lentils, cheese, spinach, and chick peas to satisfy vegetarians. Try the mango milkshake for a complement to your meal or for dessert.

Fine Dining

The menu at the white-tablecloth **Lancaster's** (513 N. Main St., Bloomington, 309/827-3333, 5–10 P.M. Mon.–Sat., $22) changes weekly, but you can always expect refreshing seafood and meat dishes, such as lobster cakes for appetizers, lamp chops, Tuscan chicken (with tomatoes, onions, bacon, and feta), and stuffed pork tenderloin. Fine dining is rare in these parts, and Lancaster's does a good job of keeping people coming back to this intimate storefront restaurant.

Sweets

Here's your chance to be a kid in a candy shop once again. **The Chocolatier** (514 N. Main St., Bloomington, 309/821-0277, 9:30 A.M.–6 P.M. Mon.–Sat.) is an old-fashioned type of candy store: Counters are lined with dozens of glass jars filled with penny candy such as sweet tarts. It also has a selection of chocolate such as chocolate-covered strawberries and cherries, plus Italian ices.

Markets

The Common Ground Natural Foods (516 N. Main St., Bloomington, 309/829-2621, www.commongroundgrocery.com, 9:30 A.M.–5:30 P.M. Mon.–Sat., opens 7:30 A.M. Sat. summer) stocks plenty of Paul Newman's line of foods, such as organic tortilla chips, plus a small selection of fruits and vegetables grown organically on regional farms.

The Bloomington **Farmers Market** and "artists' alley" is held 7:30 A.M.–noon Saturdays at the courthouse square, mid-May–late October.

INFORMATION AND SERVICES

The **Bloomington-Normal Area Convention and Visitors Bureau** (3201 CIRA Dr., Bloomington, 309/665-0033 or 800/433-8226, www.visitbn.org) has information on the region's many lodging and dining options and attractions. Give the staff a call or visit their website and they'll send you some brochures in the mail.

If the bike ride went awry or you just don't feel well, you can visit **OSF St. Joseph Medical Center** (2200 E. Washington St., Bloomington, 309/662-3311) or **BroMenn Regional Medical Center** (Virginia and Franklin Aves., Normal, 309/454-1400).

GETTING AROUND
Air

Fares are relatively inexpensive in and out of **Central Illinois Regional Airport** (Hwy. 9, two miles east of Veterans Pkwy., Bloomington, 309/663-7383, www.cira.com), plus parking here is free. AirTran has flights to and from Orlando, Florida; Atlanta; and Las Vegas. Northwest flies to and from Detroit, and American Eagle and United Express fly planes back and forth between Bloomington and Chicago. Delta Connection shuttles passengers to and from Atlanta, and American Connection flies to and from St. Louis.

Car

Several car-rental companies have offices at the airport, including Alamo (800/462-5266, www.alamo.com), Avis (800/230-4898, www.avis.com), Enterprise (800/261-7331, www.enterprise.com), and Hertz (800/654-3131, www.hertz.com).

FUNKS GROVE

Less than 10 miles south of Bloomington near Route 66 is a historic farmstead surrounded by groves of sugar maples, big old white oaks, and Osage orange trees. This scenic corner of the world didn't belong to any old farmer. Lafayette Funk was a big-time cattle operator in Illinois, cofounder and director of the Union Stockyards in Chicago, and was involved in many other successful agricultural business ventures. Today visitors can tour the old farmstead, take a look at the family's collection of minerals, and buy syrup made from the nearby trees. The farmstead is on the east side of I-55

© CHRISTINE DES GARENNES

sugar maple grove at Funks Grove

The **Funks Grove Maple Sirup** shop (5257 Old Rte. 66, Shirley, 309/874-3360, www.funkspuremaplesirup.com, 9 A.M.–5 P.M. Mon.–Sat., 1–5 P.M. Sun. Mar.–Aug. or by appointment) on Route 66 between the towns of Funks Grove and McLean. Here the syrup is made every spring from the sugar maple trees nearby. Guided tours in February and March show how the syrup is made from capturing the sap and boiling it down. The shop also sells Route 66 memorabilia.

Nearby is the **Sugar Grove Nature Center** (follow signs off Rte. 66 to Funks Grove Rd., 309/874-2174, www.sugargrovenaturecenter.org, 10 A.M.–3 P.M. Tues.–Sat. Nov.–Mar., 9 A.M.–5 P.M. Tues.–Fri., 10 A.M.–3 P.M. Sat. Apr.–Oct.), an 18-acre parcel that is one of the largest remnants of virgin forest in Illinois (now owned by the Illinois Department of Natural Resources). It was once dominated by native white and burr oaks, but in recent decades sugar maples have been moving in as the older trees start dying. Bring your field guide. There are five miles of trails here, plus a bird-watching area in the nature center.

off the Shirley exit (just follow the signs) and the nature center and syrup shop are on the west side of I-55, just off Old Route 66.

Start your visit at the **Funk Prairie Home and Gem and Mineral Museum** (10875 Prairie Home Ln., Shirley, 309/827-6792, 9 A.M.–4 P.M. Tues.–Sat. Mar.–Dec., free). The home, built in 1864, is filled with antiques that once belonged to the Funk family. On the grounds outside are formal gardens, a water fountain, and a tennis court—not exactly your typical farmstead. The gem and mineral collection in a separate building is extensive and impressive with fluorite from southern Illinois, but also every gem and mineral imaginable from around the world. Funk's collection also includes some fossils, such as trilobites and the skull of a saber-toothed tiger. Kids will get a kick out of the fossilized dinosaur poop and the black-light room filled with glowing rocks. Another room is stocked with Native American artifacts, including arrowheads and other items found in the region. If you want to visit the museum, call ahead to arrange a time during the days and hours the museum is open.

SOUTHEAST OF BLOOMINGTON-NORMAL

Agriculture is king here. See how many grain elevators you can count while driving the 45 minutes or so between Champaign-Urbana and Bloomington-Normal along I-74. It's easy to zip along on the highway and miss what's between the two regions. But take the slower route, Highway 150, which runs parallel to I-74. You find that in the shadow of these grain elevators are towns marked by red-brick buildings and town squares that date back 100 years. Shop for antiques in Farmer City or Le Roy. Pick up a pint of strawberries at a farm market. Hike through Moraine View State Park. Farmer City and Le Roy were for many years autonomous towns home to farmers and people who worked in agribusiness. However, as the years have passed, more and more professionals from Bloomington and Champaign have settled there.

Moraine View State Park

At 1,700 acres, Moraine View State Park (27374 Moraine View Park Rd., Le Roy, 309/724-8032, www.dnr.state.il.us, sunrise–10 P.M. daily), five miles north of Le Roy, is not the largest state park in the state, but it offers a slew of activities. The center of activity is 158-acre Lake Dawson, which was created in the early 1960s when a dam was built on the North Fork, a tributary to Salt Creek, near U.S. 150 and Highway 9. Boats with engines higher than 10 horsepower need to run on an idle or no-wake speed on Lake Dawson. This means the lake is not overrun with large, loud boats zooming by, but mostly fisherman in 15-foot boats.

You can easily spend an afternoon or morning here. Start by renting a boat (you can rent rowboats, paddleboats, and canoes for $8–10 per hour) and fishing for bluegill, bass, walleye, and northern pike, followed by a dip in the lake from the park's sandy beach and a meal at the restaurant near the boat ramp. Top it off with a walk along the nature trail that winds around part of the lake. During the fall, Moraine View is a popular spot for pheasant hunting. During the winter, area residents go ice-skating and ice-fishing on the lake. In addition, park staff groom several miles of cross-country ski trails. The restaurant and concession stand operate seasonally. Swimming is allowed on the sandy beach Memorial Day–Labor Day. There is no admission fee to the park, but to swim you have to pay $1.

The park has several different types of **camping** facilities. It has 137 campsites, plus 32 primitive sites accessible from the backpacking trail called Tall Timber. Class A sites have electricity with shower. Cost is about $6–8 per night per site.

Farmer City

Farmer City's Main Street has a handful of antiques shops where you can spend hours getting lost looking at vintage jewelry, furniture, books, magazines, china, and more. Try **Farmer City Antiques Center** (201 S. Main St., Farmer City, 309/928-9210) or **Main Street Antiques** (115 S. Main St., Farmer City, 309/928-9208).

The big to-do in Farmer City is its **Scarecrow and Pumpkin Festival** held in mid-October. Residents build scarecrows and display them throughout downtown. There are a petting zoo, art show, tractor show, live music (usually country), and plenty of food.

Stop by the **Farmer City Visitors Center** (701 E. Clinton Ave./Hwy. 54, Farmer City, 309/928-2825, 6 A.M.–6 P.M. Fri.–Sun.) to pick up brochures and maps. To help set the mood as you drive through this region of the world, turn on the radio to **The Whip, WHHP 98.3 FM** (407 N. Main St., Farmer City, 309/928-9876). Disc jockeys play a blend of blues, bluegrass, and alt-country. You can hear Johnny Cash, Champaign native Alison Krauss, and blues musician Charlie Musselwhite.

PONTIAC

In a restored firehouse in downtown Pontiac, the **Route 66 Hall of Fame Museum** (110 W. Howard St., Pontiac, 815/844-5657 or 815/844-6937, www.il66assoc.org, noon–4 P.M. Mon., 10 A.M.–4 P.M. Tues.–Sat., by appointment Sun.) has an impressive collection of road memorabilia, including numerous old and new gas station signs, gas pumps, and photographs of motels and restaurants along the road (some long gone, others still kickin'). For travelers who are actually driving Route 66, this is a must-stop. Volunteers with the museum (which is run by the Illinois Route 66 Association) can chat for hours about what to see and do along the road from Chicago to California.

Clinton Lake Region

Built in the 1970s by the damming of Salt Creek, Clinton Lake is a popular spot for fishing and boating in central Illinois. A lot of folks in the region head to Clinton Lake when they want to get some boating in but don't have time to drive down to southern Illinois or north to Wisconsin. The lake and much of the surrounding land may be a state recreation area, but the land is actually owned by the utility company Exelon, which leases some of the land to the state. The southern part of the lake is good for fishing and boating. The narrower north ends are more suitable for smaller watercraft such as canoes. Exelon operates a nuclear power plant on the shores of Clinton Lake. There's one plant at the site now, but the company may build another. A few miles west of the lake is Clinton, the county seat of DeWitt. With a population of 8,000 people, Clinton is the largest town in the county. Unlike the lake, Clinton has been around for a while. In fact, Abraham Lincoln once had a law office on the courthouse square, which locals now refer to as Mr. Lincoln's Square. To get to Clinton, follow Highway 10 from the east or west or U.S. 51 from the north or south.

SIGHTS
Clinton Lake State Recreation Area
Shaped a little like a right-leaning letter U, the 5,000-acre Clinton Lake (217/935-8722, www.dnr.state.il.us) has two sides to it: motorized and nonmotorized sections. Powerboaters and water-skiers tend to stick to the south end. People canoeing or at the helm of sailboats are more likely to be found in the northern parts. If you have a canoe or kayak, launch it at the North Fork Canoe Access Area in the upper west part of the lake (off County Rd. 900 N.). Here you might find osprey and other wildlife. On the northeast side by the Parnell Boat Access Area you have access to a 10-mile trail for hiking, horseback riding, or cross-country skiing in the winter (if the area receives enough snow). There are also more trails throughout

the state recreation area, such as the 9.3-mile North Fork Trail, which winds through woods and past a restored prairie. You can fish all around the lake for just about every fish common in Illinois, including striped bass, walleye, and crappie. The lake reportedly has some of the best catfish fishing in the state. Some decent boat ramps are at the West Side Day Use and Mascoutin Access areas, both north of Highway 10. North of Mascoutin is a swimming beach and bathhouse. It's open Memorial Day–Labor Day and costs $1.

Weldon Springs State Recreation Area
A few miles south of Clinton Lake is Weldon Springs State Recreation Area (1159 County Rd. 500 N., Clinton, 217/935-2644, www.dnr.state.il.us), which was once home to a popular regional chautauqua at the turn of the 20th century. At 550 acres, it's a relatively small park. But it's accessible, and there's lots of stuff to do for people with young children or for visitors who can't spend the entire day hiking up and down ravines. Choose from several trails, none of which are too exhausting. Two good trails are the 1.3-mile Schoolhouse Trail, which has several bluebird houses placed along this mainly prairie path, and the two-mile trail around the lake. Staff groom trails for cross-country skiing in the winter. Within the park is a concessionaire that rents rowboats and paddleboats, so you can paddle out on the 30-acre spring-fed lake. (The stand also sells ice cream and other treats.) The park also has a wheelchair-accessible fishing dock, campground, playground, and picnic areas.

EVENTS
One of the big to-dos in Clinton is the **Apple 'n' Pork Festival** held annually at the end of September on the grounds of the **C. H. Moore Homestead** (219 E. Woodlawn St., Clinton, 217/935-6066, www.chmoorehomestead.org). If you don't want to eat the pig ears, you can dive

into the pork sandwiches, apple fritters, apple pie, and then wash it all down with some apple cider. In addition to apple- and pork-related food, the festival features a flea market. The homestead, which includes an 1867 Italianate mansion, a barn, and other outbuildings, has local-history and farm-machinery exhibits and hosts other traditional events throughout the year, such as classic car shows, quilt shows, and ice cream socials. The homestead is open for tours 10–5 P.M. Tuesday–Saturday, 1–5 P.M. Sunday April–December. It's a block east of Business U.S. 51 on the north side of Clinton.

SHOPPING

Clinton has a handful of antiques shops in and around town. By far the largest is the **Clinton Antique Mall** (1439 W. Hwy. 54, Clinton, 217/935-8846, 10 A.M.–5 P.M. Mon.–Sat., 11 A.M.–5 P.M. Sun.) on the west side of town, with 15,000 square feet of furniture, china, books, magazines, silverware, jewelry, and everything else you can imagine. Downtown **Memories Past Antiques** (102 Eastside Sq., Clinton, 217/935-6569, 10 A.M.–5 P.M. Tues.–Sun.) is not nearly as large but still has several dealers who set up booths inside its building, meaning there's quite a variety of china, quilts, toys, and furniture. Just around the block you'll find new home-decor items at **Loft 202** (202 Eastside Sq., Clinton, 217/935-8900, 9 A.M.–5 P.M. Mon.–Fri., 9 A.M.–4 P.M. Sat.), which not only sells things such as candles and soaps but also chocolates, penny candy, and gourmet dips.

ACCOMMODATIONS

Sunset Inn and Suites (U.S. 51 at Kleeman Dr., Clinton, 217/935-4140, www.sunset-innandsuites.com, $100–150) is an amusing roadside hotel with 41 rooms that include so-called fantasy suites—imagine sleeping in a cave with faux torches flickering or in a spaceship. Other extras include massaging shower-heads, microwaves, and minifridges.

FOOD

Ted's Garage (808 W. Van Buren St./Hwy. 54, Clinton, 217/935-8008, www.teds-garage.com, 4–9 P.M. Mon.–Thurs., 4–10 P.M. Fri., 11 A.M.–10 P.M. Sat., 11 A.M.–2 P.M. Sun., $7–17), is a retro diner that serves dishes such as "the convertible" (barbecue pulled pork) and "the hot rod" (black Angus burger). Sure, it's got the usual sides of French fries, but also sweet-potato fries and mac and cheese. Ted's also serves fountain drinks plus beer, wine, and mixed drinks.

A gift shop that doubles as a tearoom, **La Tea Da** (1100 S. Madison St., Clinton, 217/935-8855, www.lateadaclinton.com) serves tea and treats such as muffins along with a variety of teas 11 A.M.–2 P.M. Tuesday–Saturday.

INFORMATION

The Clinton Area Chamber of Commerce operates a **Clinton Visitor Center** (Hwy. 54 and U.S. 51, Clinton, 866/433-9488). Look for the white house a little larger than a toll booth, just by the antique mall.

SHAWNEE HILLS AND SOUTHERN ILLINOIS

The first settlers to Illinois did not make a beeline toward the Chicago region. Instead they headed to the hills of southern Illinois. With its green valleys, wooded ravines, and rivers teeming with fish, southern Illinois reminded the early settlers of where they came from—Kentucky and Tennessee. There was enough timber to build homes, and after coal, salt, and fluorspar were discovered, plenty of jobs. This is where Illinois got its start—in former mining towns such as Shawneetown and Elizabethtown and river towns such as Cairo and Metropolis, where steamboats carried passengers, grain, and coal to other parts of the country. There's a lot of history here—remains of American Indian villages, re-created French and British forts, river pirate caves, and memorials to Meriwether Lewis and William Clark, who recruited men and gathered supplies before embarking on their great westward journey.

The southern tip of Illinois escaped the glaciers' advances, and as a result the land is rugged and gorgeous. Its boundaries are three great rivers: the Wabash to the east, the flood-prone Ohio to the southeast and south, and the Mississippi River to the west. In addition, the Saline River charts a course about 45 miles long, southeasterly from McLeansboro to the Ohio River near Cave-in-Rock. The Cache weaves through the center part of the region, leaving cypress and tupelo swamps behind. In the midst of it all are the grand Shawnee Hills, an extension of the Ozark range, and the Shawnee National Forest. At 270,000 acres and with countless

© CHRISTINE DES GARENNES

HIGHLIGHTS

LOOK FOR ☾ TO FIND RECOMMENDED
SIGHTS, ACTIVITIES, DINING, AND LODGING.

☾ **Giant City State Park:** This popular 4,000-acre park south of Carbondale is loaded with outdoor adventure possibilities: climbing or rappelling off sandstone bluffs, hiking through ravines, and horseback riding through hardwood forests and prairie. Make it an overnight trip and stake out one of the campsites or cabins (page 358).

☾ **Little Grand Canyon Trail:** Take off on one of the best hiking trails in the state. This steep and winding trail in the heart of the Shawnee National Forest rewards hikers with views of the Big Muddy River valley, Mississippi River floodplain, waterfalls, and the occasional bobcat or snake (page 366).

☾ **Cache River State Natural Area:** In this 13,000-acre natural area, visitors can explore cypress swamps by walking on a floating boardwalk or canoeing along the quiet Cache River. Plus, learn about wetland wildlife at a visitors center or hike through bottomland forests (page 375).

☾ **Garden of the Gods Wilderness:** Millions of years of wind and rain have eroded the rocky land southwest of Shawneetown and south of Harrisburg to create startling formations. An easy 0.25-mile trail takes hikers past formations such as Devil's Smokestack and Camel Rock. For a longer, more challenging hike, nearby Lusk Creek offers twisty paths down to the forest floor (page 384).

☾ **Cave-in-Rock State Park:** Once a hideout for gangs of violent thieves in the 1800s, the cave within this state park, which is right on the Ohio River, is now a tourist-friendly destination with walking trails and picnic tables (page 387).

miles of trails, the forest is a splendid sight any time of year. Wildlife such as deer, turkeys, and ducks is abundant, making the region a favorite weekend spot for hunters from the area. Boaters cruise the Ohio River, anglers stake out spots on quiet ponds, and hikers take to the countless hills. Southern Illinois, you will find, is about driving scenic two-lane roads, spending hours hiking, biking, or canoeing, and then filling up on juicy peaches, sipping wine, and indulging in barbecue.

PLANNING YOUR TIME

Ahh. If only you had an entire month to hike through southern Illinois. With 1,250 miles of trails not only for hiking but horseback riding and mountain biking, the **Shawnee National Forest** (not to mention all the parks and natural areas outside the forest boundaries) has almost unlimited opportunities for outdoor adventure. You could pack the major sites into a week, beginning with hiking and a night or two's stay in the lodge at **Giant City State Park** south of Carbondale, followed by a walk through the cypress swamps or

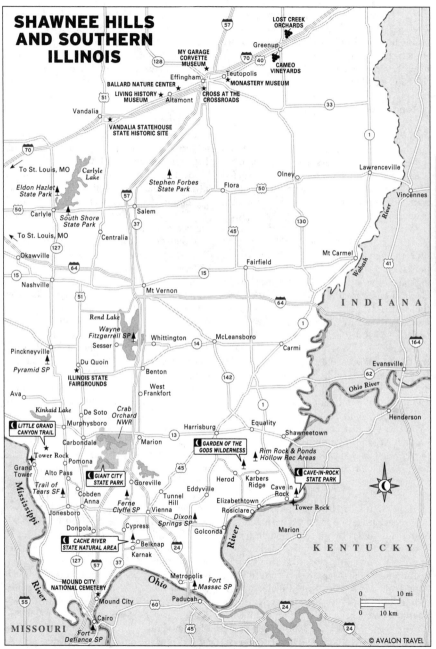

SHAWNEE HILLS AND SOUTHERN ILLINOIS

LOST CREEK ORCHARDS

Greenup

MY GARAGE CORVETTE MUSEUM

CAMEO VINEYARDS

Effingham
Teutopolis
MONASTERY MUSEUM

BALLARD NATURE CENTER

LIVING HISTORY MUSEUM
Altamont
CROSS AT THE CROSSROADS

Vandalia

VANDALIA STATEHOUSE STATE HISTORIC SITE

To St. Louis, MO

Carlyle Lake

Eldon Hazlet State Park

Olney

Lawrenceville

Stephen Forbes State Park

Flora

Vincennes

Carlyle

Salem

South Shore State Park

Centralia

Mt Carmel

To St. Louis, MO

Okawville

Fairfield

Nashville

Mt Vernon

INDIANA

Rend Lake

Wayne Fitzgerrell SP

Whittington
McLeansboro

Sesser

Carmi

Pinckneyville

Evansville

Pyramid SP

Du Quoin

Ohio River

ILLINOIS STATE FAIRGROUNDS

Benton

Henderson

Ava

West Frankfort

Kinkaid Lake

De Soto

Crab Orchard NWR

LITTLE GRAND CANYON TRAIL

Murphysboro

Harrisburg

Equality

Shawneetown

Carbondale

Marion

GARDEN OF THE GODS WILDERNESS

Rim Rock & Ponds Hollow Rec Areas

CAVE-IN-ROCK STATE PARK

Tower Rock

Pomona

Grand Tower

Alto Pass

GIANT CITY STATE PARK

Goreville

Herod
Karbers Ridge
Cave in Rock

Trail of Tears SF

Cobden
Anna

Eddyville

Elizabethtown

Tower Rock

Jonesboro

Ferne Clyffe SP

Tunnel Hill

Vienna

Rosiclare

Dongola

Dixon Springs SP

Cypress

Golconda

Marion

CACHE RIVER STATE NATURAL AREA

Belknap

Karnak

River

KENTUCKY

MOUND CITY NATIONAL CEMETERY

Metropolis

Fort Massac SP

Mound City

Paducah

Ohio

Cairo

MISSOURI

Fort Defiance SP

River

0   10 mi
0   10 km

© AVALON TRAVEL

a canoe ride in the **Cache River State Natural Area** near Belknap, a quick exploration into the former home of bandits at **Cave-in-Rock State Park** by Elizabethtown, and finally more hiking to see the rock formations at **Garden of the Gods** south of Harrisburg. If all you have is a weekend, pick one of the regions above and stay in a cabin, bed-and-breakfast, or campsite.

Access

Southern Illinois is road-tripping country; it's full of two-lane highways that cut through the Shawnee Hills or follow several rivers such as the grand Ohio. It's also got several interstates running north and south and east and west, making it somewhat of an easy area to navigate. The major highways in southern Illinois are heading elsewhere, to cities such as St. Louis, Memphis, or Nashville. I-57 slices through the center of the southern part of the state, jogging along Rend Lake and other fishing and boating areas. Just as it enters the Shawnee National Forest, south of Marion, there's a Y in the road. I-24 begins here and pushes to the southeast to Paducah, Kentucky; Nashville; and onward. I-57 is destined for Memphis. An alternative to I-57 is U.S. 51, which for most of southern Illinois follows a route parallel to I-57 about 10 miles to the west. The east-west I-64 shuttles drivers from St. Louis to Mount Vernon in the middle of southern Illinois, and then eastward to Evansville, Indiana, and over to Louisville, Kentucky. I-70 divides central Illinois from the southern region by running diagonally across the region, with St. Louis on the west, Vandalia and Effingham in the middle, and Greenup and Marshall on the eastern side.

Most of the two-lane highways and back roads in southern Illinois wind past horse farms, orchards, wooded hills, corn and soybean fields, and through one-stoplight towns. Tourism agencies have compiled road maps to the region's orchards, wineries, art galleries, and antiques shops. Maps to the **Orchard Trail, Wine Trail,** and **Art Trail** are available at most visitors bureaus. The **Ohio River National Scenic Byway** trails the river for 70 miles in Illinois, from Cairo on the southern tip of the state to the tiny Grand Chain in the southeast.

Illinois Highway 127 between Anna-Jonesboro and Murphysboro is quite the scenic route, as is Highway 146 from Dixon Springs State Park to Golconda and then on to Elizabethtown. If you plan to discover the back roads, buy a copy of DeLorme's *Illinois Gazetteer,* which has detailed information on the rural roads.

Resources

The main source of tourism information for the southern tip of the state is the **Southern Illinois Tourism Development Office** (14967 Gun Creek Tr., Whittington, 888/998-9397, www.adventureillinois.com), which is like an umbrella organization for all the other smaller regional visitors bureaus and chambers of commerce. There are two other bureaus that cover larger areas. The **Southernmost Illinois Convention and Tourism Bureau** (618/833-9928 or 800/248-4373, www.southernmostillinois.com) in Anna is a clearinghouse for information on the six southernmost counties in the state (Pope, Alexander, Massac, Union, Pulaski, and Johnson). This includes everything from the Trail of Tears region by Jonesboro-Anna to Cairo and Metropolis. The **Southeastern Illinois Convention and Visitors Bureau** (1707 E. Main St., Suite 5, Olney, 618/392-0925 or 877/273-4554, www.southeastillinois.com) covers seven primarily rural counties: Crawford, Jasper, Richland, Lawrence, Edwards, Wabash, and White. These are the counties north of the Garden of the Gods area that primarily border Indiana.

The **Shawnee National Forest** is divided into two districts: Hidden Springs (Vienna and Elizabethtown area) to the east and Mississippi Bluffs (Jonesboro and Murphysboro) to the west. The headquarters is in Harrisburg (50 Hwy. 145, Harrisburg, 618/253-7114 or 800/699-6637, www.fs.fed.us/r9/forests/shawnee), and ranger stations are in Jonesboro (521 N. Main St., Jonesboro, 618/833-8576), Murphysboro (2221 Walnut St., Murphysboro, 618/687-1731), Vienna (602 N. 1st St./U.S. 45, Vienna, 618/658-2111), and Elizabethtown (618/287-2201). The stations are staffed 8 A.M.–4:30 P.M. Monday–Friday, but sometimes you can find rangers on hand during the weekends.

Carbondale and Vicinity

The town of Carbondale was first established and settled in the 1850s, but the region had been home to human beings for thousands of years. As indicated by the blackened ceilings within rock shelters at Giant City State Park, just south of Carbondale, Indian tribes hunted and camped in the region for many years. The first white people in the area were French fur traders, followed by the British and eventually American colonists. The permanent settlers arrived from Kentucky and Tennessee, and they planted fruit trees along the hills and worked in the coal mines. After Carbondale was designated a stop along the Illinois Central Railroad, it became a transportation center for shipping fruit grown in the nearby hills and coal mined from the region. In 1866 educators founded Carbondale College, which eventually became Southern Illinois University. In its early years it was a teacher training institution. SIU was back then and still is today a large employer for the region's residents. Carbondale is home to about 25,000 people.

ORIENTATION

Carbondale is a jumping-off point to the Shawnee National Forest, just a few miles to the south, west, and east. The north-south U.S. 51 slices straight through the city and intersects with Highway 13. Hotels and motels are clustered along Highway 13 just east of downtown. I-57 is about 15 miles to the east in Marion and many businesses are located between these two cities on Highway 13. Several large lakes surround Carbondale, including Cedar Lake to the south, Crab Orchard Lake to the east, Kinkaid Lake to the northwest, and Little Grassy Lake and Devils Kitchen Lake to the southeast.

SIGHTS
Southern Illinois University

A good way to spend a rainy day or learn about the region before setting off on a hike is to pay a visit to the **Southern Illinois University Museum** (Faner Hall, 1000 Faner Dr., Carbondale, 618/453-5388, www.siuc.edu,

9 A.M.–3 P.M. Tues.–Sat., 1:30–4:30 P.M. Sun., closed university holidays, free). The museum is divided into North Hall and South Hall, which contain several galleries of rotating and permanent exhibits. Two permanent shows are *Life Through Time,* a geology exhibit, and several dioramas of pioneer life. The atrium gallery contains modern sculptures and rotating exhibits. The SIU museum has an impressive collection of prehistoric items (about 50,000 geological and anthropological objects) from southern Illinois and regions around the world, including Central and South America and Africa. It has everything from ancient Melanesian masks (from the Papua New Guinea and Fiji areas), Civil War weapons, and Anna pottery. Anna pottery, also known as Kirkpatrick pottery, was made by a pair of brothers in Anna during the second half of the 19th century. Their folk art creations (frogs, pigs, fair jugs) are a favorite among collectors. In addition, the museum has paintings, metal sculptures, and photographs. Outside the museum is a modern sculpture garden with a Japanese garden and koi pond. To get to the museum follow signs from Lincoln Drive.

After your visit to the museum, take a stroll through the campus to admire some of the architecture. Built in 1898, **Altgeld Hall** (1000 S. Normal Ave., Carbondale) is the oldest building on campus. The Gothic-revival, castle-like building comes complete with a tower and turrets. Initially a science building, it now houses the music department. **Wheeler Hall** is a Romanesque red-brick and sandstone building that dates to the turn of the 20th century. Originally the school's library, it now contains administrative offices.

Southern Illinois University (618/453-2121, www.siuc.edu) is in southwest Carbondale. Enter from U.S. 51 and follow Lincoln Drive through the campus.

Woodlawn Cemetery

One of Carbondale's claims to fame is that the first Memorial Day service was held here. On

SOUTHERN ILLINOIS

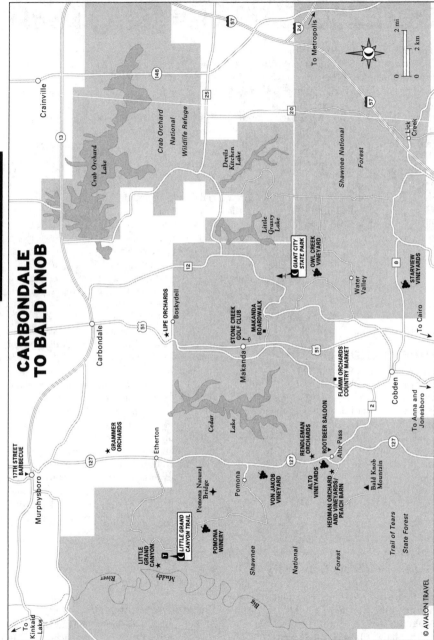

CARBONDALE TO BALD KNOB

© AVALON TRAVEL

April 29, 1866, area residents met at a church and organized a procession to the **Woodlawn Cemetery** (405 E. Main St., Carbondale), a small cemetery on a hill within the city limits. Civil War General John A. Logan, a southern Illinois native, spoke at the service commemorating area soldiers who died during the Civil War. Logan was later elected national commander of the veterans group Grand Army of the Republic, and he spearheaded efforts to establish a national Memorial Day observance, which took place May 30, 1868. Memorial Day services are held in the cemetery, now listed on the National Register of Historic Places, every year. About 400 people were buried in Woodlawn from the mid-1800s to the mid-1900s. In addition to the bodies of Civil War soldiers and other veterans, the cemetery is the final resting place for 30 freed slaves who died of smallpox. They died in Carbondale shortly after arriving in the city in 1864.

Orchards

The warm, sunny hills of southern Illinois are great for growing peaches, not to mention apples and other fruit. You'll find several orchards within a short driving distance of Carbondale. **Grammer Orchards** (144 Peach Rd., follow Grammer Rd. from Hwy. 127, Carbondale, 618/684-2471) is between Carbondale and Murphysboro. It grows peaches and apples, and because bushels of apples are kept in cold storage, you can snack on crispy apples months after the apple season has wrapped up. Run by the Lipe family since the 1880s, **Lipe Orchards** (3925 Illinois Ave./Old U.S. 51, Carbondale, 618/549-1263, www.lipeorchards. com, 9 A.M.–5 P.M. Mon.–Sat. mid-June–early Dec., extended hours during peach season) is just south of Carbondale by Giant City State Park. You can stock up on fruit such as peaches and apples, but also plums, nectarines, cider, and pumpkins.

ENTERTAINMENT

Southern Illinois University at Carbondale boasts several performance spaces. Student-produced plays, performance art, and other

© CHRISTINE DES GARENNES

an apple orchard in springtime, south of Carbondale

productions are presented at SIU's **Kleinau Theatre** (Communications Bldg., Lincoln Dr., Carbondale, 618/453-2291, tickets 618/453-5618, www.siuc.edu), a 100-seat theater in the Communications Building. The box office is open one hour before performances.

McLeod Theatre (Communications Bldg., Lincoln Dr., Carbondale, 618/453-5741, box office noon–4:30 P.M. Mon.–Fri. and one hour before shows) is the SIU theater department's 488-seat main stage. Everything from elaborate Greek drama to modern musicals has been staged in McLeod. The theater also has a small laboratory theater space. The next size up as far as theaters go is the university's **Shryock Auditorium** (618/453-2787, www.siuc.edu). Built in 1918, the renovated 1,200-seat theater hosts lectures, visiting dance troupes, musicals, and other events. (It is here where the late former U.S. Senator Paul Simon announced he was running for president in 1988.) The beautiful Roman-style theater is also the home for the **Southern Illinois Symphony Orchestra,** comprising university professors and students. Tickets for Shryock events can be purchased from Ticketmaster at 866/646-8849 or in person at the box office (9 A.M.–4 P.M. Mon.–Fri.) Phone orders for special tickets, such as groups or for patrons with disabilities, can be made by calling 618/453-2000.

The Stage Company (101 N. Washington St., Carbondale, 618/549-5466) is the local community theater group in downtown Carbondale. It presents four productions a year, plus a children's play in June.

SPORTS

Catch competitive bike racing at **Evergreen Park BMX Raceway** (2175 McLafferty Rd., Carbondale, 618/924-6862 or 618/568-1076, May–Oct.), a National Bike League–sanctioned track, on Sunday afternoons in the summer and fall. You can also watch bikers practice on Tuesday and Thursday evenings. Novice and experienced bow hunters can fine-tune their skills at **Archery International** (3002 Airport Rd., Carbondale, 618/351-1510), a national training center for archers. You can

rent equipment here and hunt for game via interactive video programs.

ACCOMMODATIONS
$50-100

Several national chain hotels are on or adjacent to Highway 13, the main east-west road through Carbondale. They include the **Hampton Inn** (2175 Reed Station Pkwy., Carbondale, 618/549-6900, $86), which has 70 rooms, an indoor pool, plus a full free breakfast; and the **Ramada Inn** (801 N. Giant City Rd., Carbondale, 618/351-6611, $89), a 65-room hotel which also has an indoor pool and offers free breakfast to guests.

$100-150

Southeast of town, on a hill above a small farm and near the scenic Crab Orchard Lake, are three cabins available for rent. The newer-construction homes at 【 **Cabin on the Hill** (2751 Dogwood Rd., Carbondale, 618/529-5667, www.cabinonthehill.com, $105–225) feature exposed knotty-pine decor, modern kitchens (stocked with coffee and coffee pots, plus cooking pans), living areas with board games and satellite television, and comfortable clean bedrooms. Down the hill the owners live on a small farm with horses, donkeys, and other animals.

FOOD
American

The Bald Knob dining room at **Giant City Lodge** (460 Giant City Lodge Rd., Makanda, 618/457-4921, www.giantcitylodge.com, breakfast, lunch, and dinner Mon.–Sat., chicken dinners only on Sun.) serves traditional dishes, such as prime rib, steaks, and a variety of seafood in a hunt-club atmosphere. It's almost worth a dinner here just to take everything in—the brick and fieldstone walls, the white oak accents. The lodge also has a cocktail lounge. On Sundays folks come from all around for the all-you-can-eat family-style chicken dinners.

At local favorite **Quatro's Pizza** (218 W. Freeman St., Carbondale, 618/549-5326, www.quatros.com, 11 A.M.–midnight Sun.–Thurs.,

11:30 A.M.–1 A.M. Fri.–Sat.), you can order chicken Alfredo or veggie and taco pizzas, but stick with the standard stuff here: cheesy, crispy, chewy pan pizza, accompanied by a pitcher of soda or beer. It can't be beat—really. Served in a casual no-frills restaurant by smiling young servers, it is so good.

Asian

Run by a friendly Laotian and American couple, **Hunan** (710 E. Main St., Carbondale, 618/529-1108 or 618/529-1109, www.hunaninc. com, 11 A.M.–9:30 P.M. Mon.–Thurs., 11 A.M.–10 P.M. Fri., 11:30 A.M.–10 P.M. Sat., 11:30 A.M.–9:30 P.M. Sun.) offers a wide range of Chinese food—dishes from Beijing, Canton, Shanghai, you name it. Hunan is a local favorite (and has been for years). Why? You can't go wrong with any of its meals (chicken, pork, duck, beef, plus plenty of vegetarian options), all under $13 and averaging about $10. It also stocks imported and domestic beer and wine and whips up lovely tropical drinks that you'll savor on a hot southern Illinois summer evening.

A little bit Thai, a little bit Japanese and Korean, **C Kaya** (817 S. Illinois Ave., Carbondale, 618/457-0968, 11 A.M.–9:30 P.M. daily) is a small locally owned restaurant that serves wonderful fresh sushi, noodle dishes, and steak entrées. Most dishes are under $10.

Mexican

The lively **Tres Hombres** (119 N. Washington St., Carbondale, 618/457-3308, lunch and dinner daily) in downtown Carbondale offers standard Mexican and Southwestern fare such as *chiles rellenos,* tostadas, huge burritos and enchiladas, and large combination platters. On some evenings, local bands kick it in gear and the margaritas start flowing. Entrées are $6–10.50.

Café

The **Longbranch Coffee House** (100 E. Jackson St., Carbondale, 618/529-4488) is one of those places where you can settle in and stay for a while reading a book, paper, or talking with a friend. The outdoor patio is especially inviting, especially on evenings

when a local band starts jamming. Beverages are the specialty—coffee, tea, smoothies, and juice—but it also has baked goods, toasty panini sandwiches, salads, and some light Southwestern-style food such as enchiladas.

Markets

Before you spend a day hiking or biking through the Shawnee hills, load up on nutritional bars, juice, fruit, and other healthy snacks at **Neighborhood Co-op Grocery** (1815 W. Main St., Carbondale, 618/529-3533, www.neighborhood.coop, 9 A.M.–8 P.M. Sun.–Fri., 8 A.M.–9 P.M. Sat.). The co-op also bakes bread daily, so you can pick up some bread, cheese, and a fresh tomato to make sandwiches for the ride.

Carbondale hosts a farmers market on the town square (Jackson and Washington Sts. at Hwy. 13) 4–6 P.M. Wednesdays May–October.

GETTING THERE AND AROUND

Regional carrier Great Lakes Airlines offers several flights daily between St. Louis and **Williamson County Regional Airport** (10400 Terminal Dr., Marion, 618/993-3353, www. wilcoairport.com). The airport is at Highways 13 and 148, about 10 miles east of Carbondale, between Carbondale and Marion.

The Illini and City of New Orleans **Amtrak** trains (401 S. Illinois Ave., Carbondale, 618/457-3388 or 800/872-7245, www.amtrak.com) stop daily in downtown Carbondale. The Illini runs between Chicago and Carbondale; the City of New Orleans links Chicago and New Orleans.

Bart Transportation (800/284-2278, www.bartshuttle.com) shuttles riders to and from Carbondale, Marion, Murphysboro, and other southern Illinois towns and Lambert International Airport in St. Louis, about two hours away.

Greyhound buses (618/549-3495, www. greyhound.com) arrive and depart from 404 South Illinois Avenue.

If you're in town and need a lift, call **Yellow Cab** (618/457-8121).

INFORMATION AND SERVICES
Visitor Information

For the scoop on hotels, hiking trails, or events, contact the **Carbondale Convention and Tourism Bureau** (Old Passenger Depot, 111 S. Illinois Ave./U.S. 51, Carbondale, 618/529-4451 or 800/526-1500, www.cctb.org).

Media

The daily newspaper for all of southern Illinois is *The Southern Illinoisan* (www.thesouthern.com), available at most convenience stores, coffee shops, and the like. The Thursday paper includes an entertainment guide supplement. Also, *The Daily Egyptian* (www.siude.com), a publication of Southern Illinois University, is published Monday–Friday and sold throughout the Carbondale area.

Hospital

If you need medical care, go to **Memorial Hospital of Carbondale** (400 W. Jackson St., Carbondale, 618/549-0721 or 866/744-2468, www.memorialhospitalofcarbondale.org).

◖ GIANT CITY STATE PARK

Giant City State Park is one of those places where you can return every year and never tire of it, where everywhere you turn you see a trail you want to explore. One of the most (if not the most) scenic parks in Illinois, Giant City is best known for its towering sandstone bluffs, some as high as 70 to 80 feet, and its excellent hiking trails. Bluffs that high may not be rare out West, but in Illinois they're few and far between. As a result, they always attract a crowd, especially the climbing and rappelling crowd. Giant City is one of the few places in Illinois where you can go rock climbing and rappelling.

Hiking

The 4,000-acre park got its name when early settlers through the area walked among the rock formations and said the experience was like walking through a giant city. To see what they were talking about, wander down (or rather, up) the one-mile-long Giant City Nature Trail. The park boasts several short (about 0.3 mile) but steep trails, including

SOUTHERN ILLINOIS

© CHRISTINE DES GARENNES

Giant City State Park

Devil's Standtable Trail, which you climb to take a look at a towerlike sandstone formation, and the Stone Fort Nature Trail, which highlights the remains of a wall built sometime between A.D. 600 and 800 by Indians during the Late Woodland Period. A solid hiking trail is the two-mile Trillium Trail, named after the many wildflowers growing along its path during the spring. The Post Oak Trail, 0.3 mile long, is wheelchair-accessible and also an excellent option if you're pushing any children in strollers. If you're here for the long haul, strap on the hiking boots and backpack and hit the challenging 12-mile Red Cedar Hiking Trail, which covers the entire park. You'll come upon a primitive campsite about eight miles into the trail. If your time is limited, climb to the top of an 82-foot-tall water tower near the lodge. The water tower has an observation platform that offers astounding views of the area.

You can't go wrong with any trail in Giant City. All are scenic, winding through dark wooded areas lush with ferns and moss growing on trees, past small ponds, scenic overlooks of the Shawnee Hills, and past rock shelters used by camping hunters for thousands of years. (During the Civil War soldiers were said to have camped in some of these shelters.)

You can pick up detailed maps of the trails at the park's newer 4,000-square-foot **visitors center** (618/457-4836, 8 A.M.–4 P.M. daily). The center has exhibits on the region's geology, a gift shop, a "discovery corner" for children, plus it shows a short film about the park's history. Pick up all your maps and brochures here.

Climbing and Horseback Riding

Other activities in the park are climbing and horseback riding. If your feet need a break from all the hiking, see the rest of the park on horseback. At the park's **Giant City Stables** (618/529-4110, 9 A.M.–5 P.M. Wed.–Mon., Mar. 15–Nov. 1) you can rent horses and take a one-, two-, or three-hour guided tour of the park. If you bring your own horse, there's an equestrian campground and 12-mile horse trail in the park. Rock climbers can head to Devil's Standtable rock and Shelter 1 bluff. No need to pay a fee or

register; just bring your own equipment and be on the lookout for poisonous copperhead snakes that like to sun themselves on the ledges. Maps to the rocks are available from the visitors center.

Accommodations and Camping

At the top of the park sits the impressive **Giant City State Park Lodge** (460 Giant City Lodge Rd., Makanda, 618/457-4921, www.giantcitylodge.com, $69–139), built by the Civilian Conservation Corps in the 1930s. The lodge contains the Bald Knob Dining Room restaurant, which serves American fare, a cocktail lounge, and a gift shop. Nearby are 34 cabins for rent. All are near the lodge high up in the hills. Take your pick from 12 one-room cabins, 18 two-room cabins, or four large bluff cabins that can sleep up to six people. They come with bathrooms, tables and chairs, and televisions, but no kitchens (although the bluff cabins have minifridges). Inside they resemble the interiors of midprice-range hotel rooms. Guests also have use of an outdoor swimming pool. Cabins are closed mid-December–February.

The **campsites** at Giant City State Park (235 Giant City Rd., Makanda, 618/457-4836) are tucked away in the northeast corner of the park near Little Grassy Lake. The 85 electric sites with showers are in one area; 14 sites for tent camping are in another, plus there are several walk-in sites for folks carrying backpacks. (The walk-in sites have pit toilets.) There's also an equestrian campground with electrical hookups in the southwestern part of the park.

MAKANDA

A tiny town easy to miss, Makanda is a treasured community of artists just outside the secondary entrance to Giant City State Park. To get to Makanda from U.S. 51 south of Carbondale, follow Makanda Road east. The main attraction in this 400-person town is the **Makanda Boardwalk,** a string of shops built in the 1890s, connected by plank boards. At 530 Makanda Road, you'll find a handful of boutiques and galleries including **Rainmaker Art Studio** (618/457-6282, 11 A.M.–6 P.M. daily), where you can browse for stone and

Makanda, a community of artists near Giant City State Park

metal creations, such as bronze and copper sculptures, jewelry, and water fountains; **Visions** (618/549-5523, 10 A.M.–5 P.M. Mon. and Wed.–Sat., noon–5 P.M. Sun.), which showcases glassware, photographs, and woodcarvings created by southern Illinois artists; and **Makanda Trading Company** (618/351-0201, www.makandatradingcompany.com, 10 A.M.–5 P.M. daily), which sells fair-trade clothing, musical instruments, jewelry, and more from Asia, Africa, and other far corners of the world.

Finally, nearby you can hunt for vintage furniture, glassware, and other collectibles at **Spider Web Antiques and Used Furniture** (4588 Old U.S. 51, Makanda, 618/457-0227, 12:30–5 P.M. Mon. and Thurs.–Sat.).

Recreation

One of the most scenic courses in the state, **Stone Creek Golf Club** (503 Stone Creek Dr., Makanda, 618/351-4653, www.stonecreekgolf.com) is an 18-hole public golf course within the Shawnee Hills, a few miles from Giant City State Park. Golfing here (the course is 6,875 yards, par

72) is not only pleasant and challenging but affordable; a round will cost you $25–42.

Accommodations

In addition to the cabins at **Giant City Lodge,** you'll find a handful of other options tucked into the hills south of Carbondale.

Set up somewhat like a duplex, the **Toolshed Corner B&B** (1420 Hall Church Rd., Makanda, 618/893-4063 or 866/300-4063, www.tscbb.com, $85–100) has two rooms available for guests, separated by a common area. Each room comes with its own queen-size bed, private bathroom, deck, and gas fireplace. The common area has a full kitchen and laundry area. Rates include breakfast.

Stone Creek Golf Club (see *Recreation*) has one- and two-bedroom log cabins available for rent on a nightly basis, in a residential area of the club. The newer-construction cabins come with fieldstone fireplaces, small kitchens (microwave and fridge), lounge chairs, and private decks. Rates are $99–129 per night. If you plan to golf, ask about its overnight golf packages.

CRAB ORCHARD NATIONAL WILDLIFE REFUGE

Developed as a refuge for waterfowl migrating along the Mississippi River Flyway, Crab Orchard National Wildlife Refuge (8588 Hwy. 148, Marion, 618/997-3344, www.fws.gov/midwest/craborchard) is an interesting site ecologically speaking (it's home to more 200 species of birds), but also historically. The area it encompasses is believed to have once been prime hunting ground for Native American tribes. As white settlers moved into the area they were also attracted to the region's vast number of waterfowl, upland game, and other animals. After years of hunting and logging altered the landscape, the U.S. government, through the Works Progress Administration, built Crab Orchard Lake in 1939 as a way to entice boaters and fisherman to the area and build up a water supply. It also planted thousands of trees. Along came World War II and plans to build two more artificial lakes for the area were put on hold as the area became the site of the Illinois Ordnance Plant, one of the Army's largest munitions plants.

After the war, the other two lakes were eventually created and the area is now being restored to more of a natural state.

The entire site is more than 43,000 acres. About half of the refuge, much of it on the eastern side, is closed to the public as a wildlife sanctuary. The three lakes—**Crab Orchard, Little Grassy,** and **Devils Kitchen**—together cover 8,300 acres. The largest is Crab Orchard Lake, popular among boaters. The other two are smaller and tend to be quiet. All three are stocked with crappie, bass, bluegill, and catfish. You can rent fishing boats at Little Grassy and canoes and fishing boats at Devils Kitchen. Because the refuge is a haven for birds along the flyway, it's a prime bird-watching area, especially during the winter. The winter population of Canada geese alone can peak at 200,000. Several hiking trails wind around the lakes, wetlands, and forests. Nearby on some of the land, cattle graze, and farmers harvest hay. Try **Little Grassy Boat Dock, Marina, and Campground** (Grassy Rd., 618/457-6655, $15–17) for tent or RV camping.

© CHRISTINE DES GARENNES

Crab Orchard Lake, popular among boaters

SOUTHERN ILLINOIS

To get to the refuge, enter from Highway 13, about 3.5 miles west of Marion. Follow Highway 148 south to the visitors center for a few miles. The center (8 A.M.–5 P.M. daily) has a few trails that lead to the lake. There is a $2 daily entrance fee assessed per vehicle, or you can pay $5 for a five-day pass.

Marion

Just off I-57 at Highway 13, not far from U.S. 51 and I-24, Marion is at the crossroads of southern Illinois and is packed with lodging options, the majority of which are situated at I-57 and Highway 13. It makes for a decent launching point if you're just looking for a place to sleep. Depending on the season and day of the week, rates at these hotels range $50–100 per night. Here's a sampling of some of the many chain hotels in Marion: **Drury Inn** (2706 W. DeYoung, Marion, 618/997-9600); **Holiday Inn Express** (400 Comfort Dr., Marion, 618/998-1220); and **Comfort Suites** (2608 W. Main St., Marion, 618/997-9133).

One of the more original lodging options in southern Illinois is the 【 **Olde Squat Inn** (14160 Liberty School Rd., Marion, 618/982-2916 or 618/922-2637, www.oldesquatinn.com, $85–100), comprising genuine log cabins from 1825 to 1874. The owners have moved the cabins from spots throughout the region to their Marion farm, restored them, added to them, and outfitted them with modern amenities, most notably air-conditioning (a must in southern Illinois in July). Choose from five cabins. All come with private bathrooms, porches, and full breakfasts for guests. The farm has a walking trail through the property.

For more information on the area, contact the **Williamson County Tourism Bureau** (Marion, 618/997-3690 or 800/433-7399, www.wctb.org).

Murphysboro and Kincaid Lake

SIGHTS AND ACTIVITIES
Kincaid Lake State Fish and Wildlife Area

Most folks headed to Kincaid Lake (52 Cinder Hill Dr., Murphysboro, 618/684-2867, www.dnr.state.il.us), about five miles northwest of Murphysboro, are on expeditions: fishing expeditions. This expansive artificial lake, at 2,650 acres, offers prime muskie fishing. From Highway 149, follow the signs to one of the many boat launches and try your luck. Created in 1958, the lake, as deep as 80 feet in some spots, has an average depth of 30 feet. The lake also has plenty of walleye, bluegill, and other fish common in Illinois. On the northwest corner of the lake is **Johnson Creek Recreation Area,** accessible from Highway 3 and Highway 151 North. The area has a boat launch, swimming area, and 20-site campground geared toward groups. Camping fees are $5–12. The beach is open 6 A.M.–10 P.M. daily May–September. In this area you'll also find **Kincaid Lake Trail,** a hiking and horse trail that snakes around the woods and lake for 16 miles. To get to the trail, also follow Highway 3 to Highway 151 North.

If you prefer smaller, quieter lakes, spend the day fishing at **Murphysboro State Park** (Hwy. 149, Murphysboro, 618/684-2867, www.dnr.state.il.us), just east of Kincaid Lake and west of Murphysboro. This artificial lake of about 140 acres is also stocked with bass, catfish, and other fish. Speaking of quiet, the park is in an oak-hickory forest, and naturalists should hike along the three-mile lakeside and forest trail at Murphysboro State Park, where you can spot wild orchids and wildflowers such as lady's slipper. The park also has a campground. There are 20 tent campsites and 54 electrical sites for RVs, plus a shower building.

Orchard and Winery

If you've never had a white peach or a sweet Mutsu

apple, drop by **Mileur Orchard** (172 Mileur Orchard Rd., 1.5 miles west of Murphysboro on Hwy. 149, 618/687-3663, 9 A.M.–5 P.M. Mon.– Sat., noon–5 P.M. Sun., July–Oct.) while driving through the area. The orchard sells white peaches, white nectarines, and some rarer varieties of apples, in addition to the standard regional favorites such as Jonagold.

About halfway between Murphysboro and Carbondale, **Kite Hill Winery** (83 Kite Hill Rd., Murphysboro, 618/684-5072 or 877/648-8725, www.kitehillvineyards.com, 11 A.M.–5 P.M. Mon.–Sat.) is one of the newer wineries in the region. It grows French-American hybrid grapes and specializes in producing white and red grape wines such as those from Chambourcin and Chardonel grapes. A tasting room is open to the public. The winery also operates a bed and breakfast here (around $115 per night) with several rooms named after grapes grown on the property. One looks out on a little lake; another has views of the rolling countryside.

John A. Logan Museum

The local hero in Murphysboro is a man by the name of John Logan, a Civil War general credited with starting Memorial Day. The John A. Logan Museum (1613 Edith St., Murphysboro, 618/684-3455, www.loganmuseum.org, $2) has exhibits on his life as a lawyer, congressman, senatorial and vice presidential candidate, orator, and lecturer, as well as displays about and artifacts from the Civil War. A walking trail from the house museum leads to the site of the home where Logan was actually born (it was in the process of being excavated) and the home of Samuel Dalton, a freed slave who fought in the Civil War and later moved to Murphysboro. It's open 10 A.M.–4 P.M. Tuesday–Saturday, 1–4 P.M. Sunday June–August, 1–4 P.M. Tuesday–Sunday September–May, or by appointment.

EVENTS

If you're looking to attend a down-home slice-of-Americana kind of festival, this is it. Murphysboro's **Apple Festival,** held every year in mid-September, is an extravaganza. There's a reason (actually several) it is the longest-running

festival in southern Illinois. There is absolutely no dull moment at the festival. Residents square off in the apple pie–eating and apple-peeling contests, bid on apple baked goods, watch area firefighters hose each other down, cheer on weekend warriors as they race lawnmowers, and get together and show off their vintage cars and motorcycles. More information about the festival is available from the Murphysboro Chamber of Commerce at 618/684-6421.

SHOPPING

If antiquing is your thing, then stopping in Murphysboro is a must. Start with a visit to **Joseph Redleggs Antiques** (1517 Walnut St., Murphysboro, 618/687-5360, 11 A.M.–5 P.M. Fri., 10 A.M.–5 P.M. Sat., or by appointment), where a bevy of antiques for sale are displayed within an Italianate Victorian home. After you've spent hours there, go treasure-hunting down the street at **George's Resale** (1324 Walnut St., Murphysboro, 618/687-1337) or **Phoebe Jane's Antiques and Collectibles** (1330 Walnut St., Murphysboro, 618/684-5546).

ACCOMMODATIONS

The quaint roadside motel, **Apple Tree Inn** (200 N. 2nd St., Murphysboro, 618/687-2345 or 800/626-4356, www.1appletree.com, about $50) has several room-size options for guests (such as rooms with one queen-size bed or rooms with three double beds). All come with handy extras such as minifridges, coffeemakers, and ironing boards. Adjacent to the hotel is an indoor pool complex with an indoor pool, sauna, and hot tub.

For more of a private getaway, book a room or cottage at **Kite Hill Vineyard B&B** (83 Kite Hill Rd., Murphysboro, 618/684-5072 or 877/648-8725, www.kitehillvineyards.com, about $115), a winery and bed-and-breakfast in rural Murphysboro.

FOOD

You know it's a good sign when a barbecue joint has trophies proudly displayed throughout the restaurant. These trophies weren't awarded for softball playing, but for Mike

Mills's mouthwatering barbecue. In southern Illinois, where barbecue stands are a dime a dozen, **【 17th Street Bar and Grill** (32 N. 17th St., Murphysboro, 618/684-3722, www.17thstreetbarbecue.com, 10 A.M.–11 P.M. Mon.–Sat.) is a standout. Mmm: Barbecued ribs, barbecued pork, beef brisket, walleye fish sandwiches, baked beans, coleslaw. Diet? Who's dieting? Top off that sandwich with a slice of cheesecake or apple pie. Sandwiches will run you about $6, a rack of ribs with two sides is $20.

INFORMATION AND SERVICES

Contact the **Murphysboro Chamber of Commerce** (203 S. 13th St., Murphysboro, 618/684-6421, www.murphysboro.com) for questions about attractions and lodging. For information on the Shawnee National Forest, stop by or call the ranger's office in Murphysboro (221 Walnut St., Murphysboro, 618/687-1731).

VICINITY OF MURPHYSBORO
Ava

About 20 miles or so northwest of Murphysboro is another small artists community. At the **Ava**

Craft Center (Main St., across from the bank, Ava, 618/426-3547 or 618/426-3054, call for hours, generally Tues.–Sat.), visitors can have a seat in front of one of several antique looms and learn how to weave for free. Braided rugs and other home-decor items are for sale. At the **Old Bank Gallery** (Main and Oak Sts., Ava, 618/426-3466, by appointment) you can admire a variety of artwork—oil and watercolor paintings and much more by local artists.

De Soto

Northeast of Murphysboro and north of Carbondale is the small rural community of De Soto, just off U.S. 51. Stop by **Ken's Reproductions and Judy's Antiques** (Hwy. 127, De Soto, 618/867-2932, 9 A.M.–5 P.M. Mon.–Sat.) to browse thousands of imported items and local antiques. Then have a slice of pie and a cup of coffee across the street at the homey **Chestnut Café** (Hwy. 127, De Soto, 618/867-2244, 6 A.M.–3 P.M. Sat.–Thurs., 6 A.M.–8 P.M. Fri.), where you can look at photographs of favorite customers placed under plastic tablecloths. The Chestnut serves what's called "heartland country cooking"—in other words, butter-rich waffles and thick slices of bacon strips. Meals are about $4.

The Big Muddy River Watershed

GRAND TOWER

The town of Grand Tower, or more appropriately, the rocks and ridges nearby, have a storied history. If you believe local legends (and there are many of them), the place is haunted. The stories go back hundreds of years, and all revolve around the giant limestone formation jutting more than 60 feet from among the rushing waters of the Mississippi River and other similar rock formations along the river. The rock in the river is called Tower Rock. The rocky ridge along the northern end of Grand Tower is Devil's Backbone, and Devil's Bake Oven is the funky formation at the end of the Backbone ridge. For centuries the rapids and whirlpools around Tower Rock have sabotaged

ships as they traveled down the Mississippi. According to Native American folklore, a pair of Indian lovers jumped to their deaths here because they could not marry. Explorers Louis Jolliet and Father Marquette wrote about their encounter with Tower Rock on their adventure in the late 1600s. They managed to maneuver around it safely. After them a group of French missionaries erected a wooden cross on top of it. The place was evil, they had heard. Bad stuff continued to happen. A tribe of Indians reportedly killed several white travelers as they came through the area in the late 1700s, prompting the lone survivor to embark on a lifelong mission to kill any Indians who were involved with the murders. River pirates often hid behind the rocks in its shelters and caves and attacked boats until the U.S. Calvary pushed them out. Later, the town grew into a shipping center and hub for iron manufacturing. Local legend says the ghost of a girl who died either from grief or illness after a man she loved left town (at the request of her father) still lingers in the Devil's Backbone area, where she and her father lived. Another version goes that she jumped off the ridge after learning the man she loved had drowned in a boating accident.

Grand Tower is no longer the shipping port or manufacturing center it once was. Visitors can see remains of the iron furnaces near the Devil's Backbone and crumbling pieces of the home where the girl supposedly makes an appearance. You can view the tower any time from the levee road. To get there follow Highway 3 to Grand Tower and follow the signs. The **River-to-River Trail** (www.rivertorivertrail.com), part of the American Discovery Trail, ends or begins here. It goes to Cave-in-Rock, clear across the state on the Ohio River.

As a short side trip from Grand Tower, drive north along Highway 3 to Gorham Road and the tiny town of Gorham. Continue to Lake Street and follow the gravel road to **Fountain Bluff** (watch for signs; it's about a mile or so southwest of Gorham). The site has several rock shelters with drawings of animals such as birds (possibly eagles or turkeys), wolves, and deer. They are believed to have been carved by the Mississippian Indians who lived in the region around A.D. 850–1200. To find the animal drawings you'll have to sort through other symbols and declarations of love carved by people in more recent decades.

OAKWOOD BOTTOMS

During the fall, tens of thousands of mallard ducks stop by Oakwood Bottoms and the **Greentree Reservoir,** a bottomland forest that provides habitat for migrating waterfowl. Walk along the 0.3-mile wheelchair-accessible trail and boardwalk, have a seat in one of the bird blinds, and scout not only for ducks but also great horned owls, pileated woodpeckers, and hawks. To get to the reservoir, follow Highway 149 west from Murphysboro to Highway 3. Drive south on Highway 3 for about six miles. There will be signs for Oakwood Bottoms; the entrance is south of Gorham.

LARUE-PINE HILLS RESEARCH NATURAL AREA

A National Natural Heritage landmark, the LaRue–Pine Hills region of the Shawnee National Forest overlooks the Mississippi River and abounds in diverse wildlife. The 2,500-acre site is gorgeous and includes pine hills to the east and the low, level Mississippi River floodplain to the west. It's another favorite among the region's hikers. But you don't even have to get out of your car to take in the splendor (although it's highly recommended). The main road through the area, called the LaRue–Pine Hills Road, climbs along the 350-foot-tall bluffs, offering several places along the way to pull off and take in views of the mighty Mississippi River.

One of the reasons people love it so is because of the wildlife. In the swampy areas, search for blooming lotus flowers, listen to singing frogs, and look for muskrats. In the hills, listen for woodpeckers and look out for bobcats and timber rattlesnakes. The LaRue–Pine Hills area is well-known for its snakes. In the spring and fall, forest rangers limit car and truck traffic to allow cottonmouth snakes (also known as water moccasins) and other amphibians to migrate from their winter homes in the limestone bluffs to the swampy areas by the river.

As far as hiking opportunities go, try **Inspiration Point Trail,** a 0.75-mile trail that begins on the bluffs and has awesome views of the Big Muddy River and, on clear days, the Mississippi. As the name suggests, this is a great trail to watch the sunset, write in your travel journal, and be inspired. But remember, snakes like this area too, so keep an eye out for them. The area has picnic sites and a campground. The **Pine Hills campground** has 12 primitive sites and is open mid-March–mid-December. Camping costs $5 per night. The two-mile **White Pine Trail** is accessible from here. It can be used for hiking and horseback riding. LaRue–Pine Hills is just east of Highway 3, about eight miles south of Grand Tower and 15 miles northwest of Jonesboro. More information is available from the **Shawnee National Forest ranger station** in Jonesboro (521 N. Main St., Jonesboro, 618/833-8576) or Murphysboro (221 Walnut St., Murphysboro, 618/687-1731).

◖ LITTLE GRAND CANYON TRAIL

One of the best hiking trails in the state (it's challenging, remote, and scenic), the Little Grand Canyon Trail in the heart of the Shawnee National Forest offers views of the Big Muddy River valley, Mississippi River floodplain, waterfalls, and thick vegetation. The loop is almost four miles long and pretty steep; you'll work your calves while hiking down and back up. But there are some stops along the way to take in the scenes, and a few overlooks. Mink, foxes, or deer might skirt across the trail in front of you. Bobcats also live among the

hills, as do cottonmouth, copperhead, and timber rattlesnakes. The snakes make their winter dens in here and migrate between the canyon and nearby Turkey Bayou.

For hiking, you have several options. The shortest option is to hike one mile to the canyon overlook and turn around. It can take you about 30 minutes back and forth, depending on how much time you spend staring out across at the maple, oak, and beech trees and at the hawks soaring through the sky. To view the Mississippi River valley will take you about an hour to hike 2.1 miles. You can hike to the cool canyon floor and return to the parking lot in about an hour. Of course, you can also hike the entire loop to view all the scenic overlooks and hike through the canyon floor. The trail starts at the top of a ridge and goes down to the canyon and along the Big Muddy River, then back up again, making a loop. The entire loop is 3.6 miles long, however there are several different options for hiking it. The three best options (if you don't want to hike the entire loop) include 1: going down to the canyon and coming back

Little Grand Canyon hiking trail

(1.5 miles), 2: going to an overlook of the canyon and coming back (1 mile), and 3: going down to the canyon and then to an overlook of the Mississippi River and coming back (2.1 miles). They all start from the same place (the parking lot at the top of a bluff), but length and sights vary according to how far along the loop you go.

To get to the trail, watch for signs to the Little Grand Canyon from Highway 127, south of Murphysboro. From Murphysboro, you'll want to go south on Highway 127 for about 5–6 miles to Etherton Road. Follow Etherton for another five miles or so. More information is available from the Shawnee National Forest's Murphysboro Ranger District at 618/687-1731.

POMONA NATURAL BRIDGE

Shaped during the course of millions of years, the Pomona Natural Bridge is a sandstone arch over a creek in a rural, wooded, and hilly region south of Murphysboro. A steep, sometimes slippery trail takes you over hills and down into the ravine to the bridge. The trail is about 0.3 mile and has a little lookout area over the bridge if you need a break from climbing up or down the incline. It also leads down to the creek, so you can get a look at the bridge from below. The bridge spans about 90 feet and is made of soft bedrock that has eroded through the years by water and wind.

It's a pretty cool sight, but if you're pressed for time, you might want to think twice. It takes a long time to get there along sometimes unmarked serpentine gravel roads. On the map it looks as if it'll take about 20 minutes from Murphysboro, but in reality it's more like 45 minutes to an hour. Signs posted along the way will point you in the right direction, but still, it's easy to get lost. If you're not rushed, no matter. The drive, along rolling hills, past oak and hickory forests and farmsteads set in the valleys, is beautiful. To get to the bridge from Highway 127, go west on Pomona Road, about nine miles south of Murphysboro and four miles north of Alto Pass. Then follow signs to the site. For more information you can contact

Pomona Natural Bridge

the Shawnee National Forest's Murphysboro Ranger District at 618/687-1731.

SHAWNEE SALTPETRE CAVE

Local blues, bluegrass, and other concerts are often held in this cave's natural amphitheater. About seven miles south of Murphysboro, Shawnee Saltpetre Cave (3747 Hwy. 127, halfway between Murphysboro and Alto Pass, 618/687-9663, $5) is an approximately 50-acre park with the amphitheater, walking trails, picnic tables, and after a string of rainy days, waterfalls streaming down from the rocks. Hours vary; call ahead to make sure the owners will be there. You can camp there for a fee during weekend events.

WINERIES

Take a break from hiking in the forest and spend an afternoon tasting wines at two wineries not too far from the Little Grand Canyon and Pomona Natural Bridge trails. **Pomona Winery** (2865 Hickory Ridge Rd., 618/893-2623, www.pomonawinery.com, 10 A.M.–5 P.M.

Mon.–Sat., noon–5 P.M. Sun. Apr.–Dec., 10 A.M.–5 P.M. Thurs.–Sat., noon–5 P.M. Sun. Jan.–Mar.), hidden in a woodsy area of the forest, specializes in wine made from fruit such as peaches, apples, and blueberries. Set in a sunny valley, **Von Jakob Vineyards** (1309 Sadler Rd., Pomona, 618/893-4500, www.vonjakobvineyard.com, 10 A.M.–5 P.M. Mon.–Sat., noon–5 P.M. Sun., extended hours in summer) offers an awe-inspiring place to taste its wines with an expansive deck that overlooks the vineyard. Von Jakob makes red, white, and blush wines, plus mead and port wines. Von Jakob was preparing to open a second winery on Highway 127 between Murphysboro and Alto Pass.

The Bald Knob Area

SIGHTS AND ACTIVITIES
Bald Knob Mountain and Cross

One of the highest hills in the Shawnee region, Bald Knob Mountain rises 700 feet above the valley floor southeast of the town of Alto Pass (about 1,000 feet above sea level). It is part of the Bald Knob Wilderness Area within the Shawnee National Forest, and neighboring mountains range 400–900 feet tall. Bald Knob, however, stands out thanks to the 100-foot-tall steel and marble cross erected on the top. The cross's story began back in the 1930s when locals began holding Easter sunrise services on the mountain's summit. The idea for the cross hatched in the 1950s, and it took about 10 years for organizers to raise money. (One of the best-known fundraisers was a poor widow farmer named Myrtle Cutts who raised pigs for the cause.) It was finally completed in 1963. Easter sunrise services are still held there every year along with events such as the blessing of the bikes and barbecue fund-raisers. A welcome center, with a gift shop and restrooms, has been added in recent years. To get to the cross, follow signs from Highway 127 in Alto Pass. Head west on Chestnut Street to Bald Knob Road for about 4–5 miles, winding up and around the mountain. For more information, call 618/893-2344. Admission is free, but donations are accepted.

Parks

If you need a few moments to stretch your legs, there are two choices in Alto Pass. The **Quetil Trail** is a short nature trail along the old Cairo–St. Louis Narrow Gauge railroad in downtown Alto Pass (just off Main Street). Then one mile east of Highway 127 and just south of downtown Alto Pass is **Cliff View Park,** a small but definitely scenic overlook on Skyline Drive. Have a seat at a picnic table, bite into a fresh peach or apple, and look out onto the horizon for Bald Knob Cross.

Horseback Riding

Southern Illinois is jam-packed with trails for horseback riding. Alto Pass is no exception. East of town **Kosmic Acres Stables and Rentals** (Hwy. 127 and Prospect Rd., Alto Pass, 618/893-2347) offers year-round riding through the Shawnee Hills and along the Little Cedar Lake spillway. Take your pick from two-, three-, or four-hour rides or daylong regional tours. Pack a lunch and tuck it into the saddlebag and you'll be set. The owner, a zoologist, will point out wildlife or signs of wildlife as you ride through the woods. Beginners are welcome, but reservations are required.

Wineries

Perhaps the most well-known of southern Illinois wineries, **Alto Vineyards** (8515 Hwy. 127, Alto Pass, 618/893-4898, www.altovineyards.net, 10 A.M.–5 P.M. Mon.–Sat., noon–5 P.M. Sun.) has been growing grapes and producing wine since 1988. Its award-winning wines vary from dry to sweet and are mostly made from grapes grown in its 10-acre vineyard. However, it also makes specialty wines such as sparkling raspberry. The tasting room and winery are just off Highway 127 north of Alto Pass. Another winery that has won awards is **Owl Creek Vineyard** (2655 Water Valley Rd., Cobden, 618/893-2557, www.owlcreekvineyard.com, noon–5 P.M. Sat.–Sun. Jan.–Apr., noon–5 P.M. Wed.–Sun. May–Dec.), a small winery in rural Cobden. You can sample wines for free in the tasting room and gift shop or spend some time outside relaxing on a picnic bench near the vineyard. In addition to selling excellent wines in a scenic setting (imagine sitting on a deck sipping wine surrounded by a pond and vineyards), **StarView Vineyards** (5100 Winghill Rd., Cobden, 618/893-9463, www.starviewvineyards.com, noon–5 P.M. Mon.–Fri., 10 A.M.–dusk Sat., noon–dusk Sun. May–Oct., noon–5 P.M. Sun.–Fri., 10 A.M.–6 P.M. Sat. Nov.–Apr.) showcases work of regional artists and hosts live music concerts outside in the summer months. Open since 2003, **Inheritance Valley Vineyards** (5490 Hwy. 127, Cobden, 618/893-6141, www.inheritancevalley.com, noon–5 P.M. Sat.–Sun. Jan.–Mar., noon–5 P.M. Wed.–Sun. Apr.–Dec.) is, like Alto Pass, easy to get to, just off Highway 127.

EVENTS

Several wineries in and around Alto Pass and Cobden hold spring tasting festivals in May and grape-stomping events in the fall. Check with the wineries or the **Shawnee Hill Wine Trail** website (www.shawneehillwinetrail.com) for dates and activities. Cobden celebrates its fruit heritage with the **Peach Festival** in mid to late August with plenty of peach treats for sale, carnival rides, and coronation of the peach queen. Alto Pass's Dog Days of Summer **Root Beer Festival** is also in mid to late August.

SHOPPING
Orchards and Fruit Markets

This is fruit country. And here it is so easy to spend an entire day hopping from one farm market to another, filling up on luscious peaches and crispy apples. Here's a sampling of the markets, farm stands, and you-pick farms in and around Alto Pass and its neighboring town to the south, Cobden.

Pick some of the freshest strawberries, blackberries, and blueberries you can imagine at **Blueberry Hill Farm** (67 Wrights Crossing Rd., just north of Cobden off U.S. 51, 618/893-2397, May–July), a you-pick berry farm just north of Cobden off U.S. 51. This author's favorite orchard is just outside Alto Pass on the way to Bald Knob Mountain: **Hedman Orchard and Vineyards** (560 Chestnut St., Alto Pass, 618/893-4923, www.peachbarn.com, July–mid-Sept.) sells peaches, nectarines, grapes, and apples from a big white barn overlooking a valley. The owners also plan to start making wine from grapes grown on their hillside. **Flamm Orchards Country Market** (8760 Old Hwy. 51, Cobden, 618/893-4241, 9 A.M.–6 P.M. daily May–Nov., after daylight saving time ends the store closes at 5 P.M.) sells fruits and vegetables, plus take-home treats such as strawberry shortcake, peach cobbler, jams, and honey. At **Rendleman Orchards Farm Market** (9680 Hwy. 127, Alto Pass, 618/893-2771, www.rendlemanorchards.com), you can load your car with crates full of peaches, sweet corn, and other produce, plus gourmet food items such as prepackaged soup mixes and jams.

Shops

Austin's of Alto Pass (595 Main St., Alto Pass, 618/893-2206, 10 A.M.–4 P.M. Sat., 1–4 P.M. Sun., or by appointment, open by chance or appointment Jan.–Feb.) is a 3,500-square-foot antiques store filled with furniture, ceramics, and other collectibles. A few miles south of Alto Pass you can gather ideas for your yard while strolling through **Fernwood Gardens** (2395 Hwy. 127, Cobden, 618/833-2162, 9 A.M.–6 P.M. Mon.–Sat., noon–5 P.M. Sun.), which has display gardens for you to admire. Fernwood sells a variety of herbs, medicinal plants, perennials, and native plants.

ACCOMMODATIONS

Your lodging options in and around Alto Pass are limited to bed-and-breakfasts—gorgeous, refreshingly affordable bed-and-breakfasts nestled among the Shawnee Hills. You'll never want to stay in a hotel overlooking the interstate again.

C **Windy Hill Acres Inn** (830 Bell Hill Rd., Cobden, 618/893-4065, www.windy hillacresinn.com, $75–130) is a renovated stone house that once stored farmers' sweet potatoes back in the 1800s. Renovated into a two-bedroom inn, the house features a living room with fireplace, a kitchen stocked with pots and pans, and beautiful touches such as queen-size sleigh beds in the bedrooms and hardwood floors.

Shawnee Hill Bed and Breakfast (U.S. 51 and Upper Cobden Rd., 209 Water Valley Rd., Cobden, 618/893-2211, www.shawnee-hillbb.com, $60–150) is a retreat-like bed-and-breakfast with a fishing pond, hiking trails to a nearby cave (where Daniel Boone reportedly signed his name in 1766), an outdoor hot tub, and antiques shopping at the owners' nearby Shawnee Hill Barn Antiques. Rooms are decorated in country style with antiques. You have the option of choosing a continental or a full breakfast.

The **Peach Barn B&B** (560 Chestnut St., Alto Pass, 618/893-4923, www.peachbarn. com, $110–115) at Hedman's Orchard and Vineyards by Alto Pass offers guests a suite in its renovated barn overlooking grapevines and fruit orchards. The two-room suite has a queen bed plus a sleeper sofa in the living room. Decorated in Swedish blue and white decor, the barn suite has nice touches such as a down comforter, robes, and radiant floor heating, which visitors will appreciate during winter visits.

FOOD

You can spend hours looking at all the stuff at the C **Northwest Passage Root Beer Saloon** (Alto Pass, 618/893-1634, 11:30 A.M.–4 P.M. Mon.–Fri., 11 A.M.–5 P.M. Sat.–Sun.), and we're not just talking about the stuff for sale (coffee, tea, spices, gourmet foods) but also the taxidermy. A staggering, impressive number of fish and stuffed waterfowl and the occasional pair of snowshoes are mounted on the walls. Have a seat at one of the tables throughout the store/saloon or at the vintage bar. (Root beer is on tap.) You can order gourmet sandwiches here such as heaping turkey clubs, but also full seafood plates featuring salmon and other fish. Dishes are about $8.

Another local institution is **Grammer's Market** (10 W. Pine St., Alto Pass, 618/893-2490, 7 A.M.–5 P.M. Mon.–Fri., 7 A.M.–4 P.M. Sat.) a general store that sells deli sandwiches (the local favorite is the "flying pig" pork sandwich). You can also stock up on drinks, groceries, and a variety of hardware tools here.

Swedish cuisine is the specialty of **Peach Barn Café** (at Hedman Orchard and Vineyards, 560 Chestnut St., Alto Pass, 618/893-4923, www.peachbarn.com, 10 A.M.–7 P.M. Sat., noon–5 P.M. Sun.), and that means warm open-faced sandwiches and lingonberry desserts as well as dishes made with peaches and other fruit grown at the orchard.

INFORMATION

The Union County Chamber of Commerce (330 S. Main St., Anna, 618/833-6311, www. shawneeheartland.com) has loads of info about the county's orchards, events, bed-and-breakfasts, and attractions.

The Trail of Tears: Anna and Jonesboro

RECREATION
Trail of Tears State Forest

The history of southern Illinois is unfortunately tied to one of the saddest chapters in the history of the United States. In 1838 the U.S. Army ordered the Cherokee, Creek, and Chicksaw Indians off their lands in the southeastern United States. They were to settle in the Oklahoma Territory, about 1,000 miles to the west, and they headed west in wagons, on horses, but mostly on foot. During the winter of 1838–1839, unable to cross the Mississippi River because of floating ice blocks, they camped in an area about four miles south of the forest. During this brutal winter hundreds died from cold, starvation, and disease. Today the forest is a quiet area with hilly forests and some prairie and low-lying areas. It comprises a total of about 5,000 acres a few miles south of Jonesboro. A walk through here will take you past oak trees, sugar maples, wild blueberry shrubs, wood violets, and possibly deer and foxes. Several miles of remote trails wind through the hills and valleys. You can bike or hike along these interior gravel roads, accessible from Highway 127 or Highway 3. The Oak Hills Nature Preserve, in the middle of the forest (and also accessible from Highways 127 or 3), has a lookout tower. There's tent camping south of the preserve. Stop by the forest headquarters (3240 State Forest Rd., Jonesboro, 618/833-4910, www.dnr.state.il.us) for maps.

Hunting and Fishing

Whether it's hunting for pheasants, shooting clays, or practicing your shot at the gun range or archery range, the privately owned **Trail of Tears Lodge and Sports Resort** (1575 Fair City Rd., Jonesboro, 618/833-8697) has a slew of outdoor activities for day and overnight guests.

Didn't bring along your fishing rod, but have the urge to fish? No license either? Fishing is easy at **Bob's Shrimp and Trout Farm** (1.5 miles west of Jonesboro on Hwy. 146, 618/833-6409), where you can rent poles and buy bait. Drop by Bob's for rainbow trout fishing in March and April. You won't need a license because it's on a private fish farm.

Orchard

Southern Illinois is famous for its sweet peaches and apples. Sample a few fruits and stock up for pies at **Boyds Orchards** (675 Sadler Rd., Anna, 618/833-5533, 9 A.M.–6 P.M. Mon.–Sat., noon–6 P.M. Sun. Sept. 1–Oct. 31). With the rope swing, barn slide, petting zoo, and maze, Boyds has become quite the tourist destination, especially in the fall during pumpkin season. You can also shop for flowers, honey, jams, and cookbooks.

EVENTS

Most of the festivals that take place in Union County, not surprisingly, have to do with outdoor activities. During the **Trail**

© CHRISTINE DES GARENNES

hiking in the Trail of Tears State Forest

SOUTHERN ILLINOIS

MUSHROOM HUNTING

Every spring, usually around the time the may-apples start poking up above the forest floor and the redbud trees start blooming, a small but devoted group of Illinoisans hit the woods in search of morel mushrooms. The mushrooms, which can range in size from a quarter of an inch to 14 inches tall, feature an oval, honeycombed cap that looks like a sponge. They're delicious and taste great simply rolled in a little flour and pan-fried with butter. A cup of smooth and mild morel mushroom soup is also a good bet.

Morel-hunting season in Illinois is mid to late April through the beginning of May. You can find morels in all regions of the state, although many people believe they are most plentiful in bottomland forests. And many mushroom hunters swear morels are most plentiful near dead elm trees, especially trees that have bark peeling off them. One of the Midwest's most popular mushroom-related festivals is the **Illinois State Morel Mushroom Hunting Championship and Spongy Fungi Festival** at the Marshall-Putnam Fairgrounds in Henry, a small town on the Illinois River, southwest of the LaSalle-Peru area. Held annually in early May, the contest attracts hundreds of mushroom hunters. On the day of the hunting contest they board buses and are dropped off at a top-secret location. They then take off in search of morels. Prizes are awarded to hunters who find the most mushrooms, plus the largest and smallest mushroom. The Trail of

© CHRISTINE DES GARENNES

the elusive morel mushroom

Tears Lodge near Jonesboro in southern Illinois also hosts a morel festival, as does the town of Shelbyville in central Illinois.

For more information about morels in Illinois, check with **Morel Mania** (800/438-8213, www.morelmania.com), a company in Magnolia that sells hunting supplies such as sacks and walking sticks, or visit the website for the state hunt, www.ilmorelhunt.org.

of Tears Rendezvous held in the Trail of Tears State Forest in mid-May, men and women camp out in the forest and reenact the Civil War and demonstrate life back in the 1800s. The forest is also the site of an early August **hummingbird festival** sponsored by the Illinois Audubon Society. During the **Union County Colorfest** in October, farm markets and shops around the county celebrate the harvest season with fun runs, music, cooking demonstrations, and more. For more information about the events, contact the Union County Chamber

of Commerce in Anna at 618/833-6311, www.shawneeheartland.com.

SHOPPING

Back in the late 1800s, the Kirkpatrick brothers manufactured pottery in Anna. Also known as Anna pottery, their work included traditional pieces such as jugs and jars, but also animal shapes that have been called everything from bizarre to whimsical. To check out some of this stoneware, buy a piece or two, or browse for other antiques, drop by **Isom's Antiques** (107 N. Main St., Anna, 618/833-3516, call ahead for hours).

ACCOMMODATIONS

Your best bet for accommodations in this area is a bed-and-breakfast or lodge, of which there are plenty.

Hunters and other outdoor enthusiasts will feel at home at **Trail of Tears Lodge and Sports Resort** (1575 Fair City Rd., Jonesboro, 618/833-8697), about nine miles south of Jonesboro on a 425-acre site adjacent to the Shawnee National Forest. The lodge itself has seven rooms, plus there's a two-bedroom cabin that sleeps four adults, and a campground. Rooms don't have telephones or televisions. But there is a gathering room with a television in it if you really want to watch something on the tube. The barn has a game room and laundry for guests, and there are showers for campers. Fees are $10 per night for tent camping, $25 for RV camping, $65–80 for a room in the lodge, and $125 for the cabin. The resort has a slew of activities for guests, such as horseback riding, shooting clays, and practicing your shot at the gun range.

◖ **Hidden Lake B&B** (433 Cook Ave., Jonesboro, 618/833-5252, www.hiddenlakebb. com, $120–175) exudes relaxation. This is a place where you just might abandon the trip itinerary and spend the days reading a book and looking out over the lawn. The 12-acre site has a private two-acre lake with a paddle boat and a little pier for catch-and-release fishing. There are flower gardens, walking paths, and a sunroom. Some of the rooms come with fireplaces, whirlpool baths, and private balconies. There are five rooms total; three are in a guest house, and two are in the main house where the owners live.

If some hotel and bed-and-breakfast rooms make you feel claustrophobic, you'll love the **Davie School Inn Banquet Center** (300 Freeman St., Anna, 618/833-2377, www.daviecenter.com, from $85), where a 1910 school building has been transformed into a bed-and-breakfast and banquet center. The ten rooms are spacious, about 850 square feet. Each one comes with a king-size bed, private bath and whirlpool tub, and sitting area. Antiques fill the rooms and hallways. (You'll also notice in places such as the hallway that a few fixtures from the school's past remain, such as the tiny water fountains.

FOOD
Barbecue
Leather-clad Harley-Davidson motorcyclists mingle with white-haired locals and visitors at ◖ **Dixie Barbecue** (205 W. Broad St., Jonesboro, 618/833-6437, 10 A.M.–8 P.M. Mon.–Sat., $5), a popular lunch and dinner spot along Highway 127. The little white building is a classic roadside restaurant. Food is cheap, simple, and comforting, such as hamburgers, ham and cheese, and the famous barbecue sandwiches. Wash down your meal with a lemonade.

American
The Country Cupboard Café and Gift Shop (169 E. Vienna St., Anna, 618/833-7827, lunch 11 A.M.–2 P.M. Mon.–Sat., dinner 4–8 P.M. Fri., $3–10) is under relatively new ownership, but the building has been a fixture in Anna for over eight decades. The big maroon barn near downtown Anna was actually the place where the local sweet potato crop was stored. Through the years it's housed many agriculturally related businesses and in recent years a restaurant that sells simple food (think chicken salad sandwiches, potato soup in a bread bowl, fried fish baskets) alongside antiques and home-decor items. Friday night dinners can include fish, fillets, and other more hefty options. The gift shop is open 11 A.M.–2 P.M. Mon., 11 A.M.–5 P.M. Tues.–Thurs., 11 A.M.–8 P.M. Fri., 11 A.M.–5 P.M. Sun. You can get coffee and dessert during those hours. If you've got a sweet tooth, try one of their cream pies.

For more homemade food, but in a rural setting, head to the restaurant at the **Trail of Tears Lodge and Sports Resort** (1575 Fair City Rd., Jonesboro, 618/833-8697, www. trailoftears.com, 5–8 P.M. Fri.–Sat., $8). It has traditional American fare, plus Cajun cooking and dishes such as catfish and even some more exotic items such as frogs' legs.

SOUTHERN ILLINOIS

INFORMATION AND SERVICES

For visitor information, turn to the **Union County Chamber of Commerce** (330 S. Main St., Anna, 618/833-6311, www.shawnee-heartland.com) or the **Southernmost Illinois Tourism Bureau** in Anna (618/833-9928 or 800/248-4373, www.southernmostillinois. com), which has information on the six southernmost counties in the state, including Union County. You can also stock up on brochures at the **Trail of Tears Welcome Center** (I-57 and Hwy. 146, Mount Pleasant, 618/833-4809), a rest area boasting a little memorial to the prized pig known as King Neptune, a Navy mascot auctioned for $19 million in war bonds during World War II.

If you're feeling ill or sprained an ankle during a hike in the Anna-Jonesboro area, contact the **Union County Hospital** (517 N. Main St., Anna, 618/833-4511, www.unioncountyhospital.com).

Lower Cache River

What makes the Cache River region such a fascinating and beautiful place is that it's at a biological midpoint in North America, where physiographic regions overlap. What this means is that as the regions (defined by terrain, soils, and wildlife) meet, they all bring a set of diverse animal, plant, and tree species. The Cache River basin is surrounded by the Shawnee Hills physiographic region (an extension of the Ozark mountain range) to the west, the Central Plateau to the north, the Interior Lowland to the east, and the Gulf Coastal Plain to the south. A dizzying array of amphibians (such as tree frogs and salamanders), mammals (beavers, mink), plants (floating emerald duckweed, buttonbush), trees (red oaks, cypress) and birds (egrets, eagles) live in the basin. As a result, it is and has been a prime fishing and hunting region. Native American tribes fished, trapped, and hunted seasonally here long before the white settlers from Kentucky, Tennessee, Ohio, and other states moved into Illinois. Back then the swamp was about 250,000 acres.

When the settlers arrived in the late 1700s and early 1800s, they focused on harvesting the thousands of mature tupelo, oak, and black gum trees in the area for timber. Lumber mills in Cairo and other towns churned out railroad ties, shipping crates, and other products. Some pioneers established farms and grew tobacco, cotton, wheat, and other crops. They dammed streams to create ponds for their livestock. Settlement in the basin area, however, was limited. The swamps and bottomland forests were ideal mosquito-breeding areas, and residents often became ill from malaria and other diseases. The threat of disease and the prospect of turning the area into more of an agricultural region prompted people to drain many of the wetlands in the early 1900s. Corn and soybeans were planted, but yields still didn't match those found in the central part of the state.

Today the Cache River region is still a stunning site, though agriculture, erosion, and development have taken their toll on the river and its inhabitants. The Cache River State Natural Area was established in 1970 to preserve and manage the region, plus several other national and regional groups have been working to acquire land and restore wetlands, control streambank erosion, and address other environmental problems. The Cypress Creek National Wildlife Refuge comprises about 15,000 acres, and let's hope it will also expand in coming years.

ORIENTATION

The Cache River can be divided into an upper region and a lower region. The narrower northern section of the river flows through hills and bluffs. The lower Cache River, where the Cache River State Natural Area is, has a wider floodplain with plenty of swampy areas, sloughs, and small oxbow lakes. It's between I-57 and I-24, south of Highway 146 and north of Highway 169, east of Highway 37 and west of U.S. 45.

The lower section is loaded with nature preserves and trails. If you're coming from the north, a good starting point is the Wildcat Bluff Access Area southwest of Vienna, which has a lookout and trail to the swamps and a huge championship cherrybark oak tree. A good place to learn about the region is the Henry Barkhausen Wetlands Center a few miles north of Karnak. Some trails in the region are more than a mile long, but most are easy, as they are through bottomland swamps and forest. Tunnel Hill State Trail skirts the southern part of the state natural area; you can reach Heron Pond, Barkhausen Center, Section 8 Woods Nature Preserve, and other natural areas from the trail. Regional roads have plenty of signs that mark popular destinations (such as Heron Pond) and driving distances.

◖ CACHE RIVER STATE NATURAL AREA

With about 13,000 acres stretching into Johnson and Pulaski Counties, the Cache River State Natural Area (headquarters 930 Sunflower Ln., Belknap, 618/634-9678, www.dnr.state.il.us) should be your first destination while visiting the Cache River basin region. The area boasts several nature preserves, accessible boardwalks, scenic overlooks, giant trees, and tiny plants (perhaps the tiniest are duckweed, little plants that float on water). Plus, more than 20 miles of trails wind through dark bottomland forests, low ridges, barrens, meadows, and other areas. You can't go wrong with any of the trails.

Heron Pond

This 75-acre nature preserve has three trails along the Cache River and to and along Heron Pond (it looks more like a swamp, actually). There are three trails: a 0.5-mile hike to the Heron Pond boardwalk; a 0.75-mile hike to the cherrybark oak; and one just over two miles to the Little Black Slough, an adjacent

© CHRISTINE DES GARENNES

cypress trees in Heron Pond

nature preserve. The Heron Pond boardwalk trail is a must-see. There you have the chance to walk into the swamp (well, above the water on the boardwalk) and get close to some several 100-year-old cypress trees and look for river otters, snowy egrets, and other animals. Along the mostly woodchip trail to Heron Pond are educational signs that point out plants, such as bloodroot, and explain their significance (Native Americans used it for dye). The cherry-bark oak tree stands about 100 feet tall with a circumference of more than 22 feet. It's pretty big. But if you're in town visiting from Oregon or Washington State, you could probably skip the walk to this tree. The area is accessible from the Belknap blacktop, just west of U.S. 45.

Little Black Slough and Wildcat Bluff

The total length of the Little Black Slough Trail is 5.5 miles. It connects with Heron Pond, Marshall Ridge, and the Wildcat Bluff. Some parts of it may challenge infrequent hikers. This trail lets you see it all. You'll climb sandstone bluffs that are a common sight in Illinois, trudge through wooded floodplain areas and through cypress and tupelo swamps, cross the Cache River on a rock ford, and hike to Boss Island. The one-mile-long lookout trail, accessible from the Wildcat Bluff access area south of Highway 146, is a hillside and hilltop trail with overviews of the river valley.

Section 8 Woods Nature Preserve

In the southwestern corner of the Cache River State Natural Area, just east of the town of Perks (and about four miles south of the town of Cypress) is the Section 8 preserve. This site also has a 475-foot-long, wheelchair-accessible boardwalk into the cypress and tupelo swamp. It leads to the state champion water tupelo tree that boasts a buttress circumference of 22.5 feet.

Wetlands Center

The excellent new **Henry N. Barkhausen Cache River Wetlands Center** (Hwy. 37 and

a birder's paradise: Henry N. Barkhausen Cache River Wetlands Center, White Hill

© CHRISTINE DES GARENNES

Perks Rd., White Hill, 618/657-2064, www. dnr.state.il.us, free) is another must-see stop for visitors to the Cache River region. A short film and several interactive exhibits explain the geologic, natural, and cultural history of the Cache River region. Take a "photo safari" and test your plant and animal identification skills. The indoor birding area is a fantastic spot to relax and watch the red-wing blackbirds and other birds dart around the pond and meadow. Head outside and take a stroll along a half-mile wheelchair-accessible trail along a newly created wetland. Have a seat on a bench and look for shorebirds and waterfowl. Adjacent to the center is the Tunnel Hill State Trail's western terminus, so after your visit you can hop on your bike and ride to the swamps. The Wetlands Center is open 9 A.M.–4 P.M. Wed.–Sun.

Canoeing

The **Lower Cache River Canoe Trail** is a section of the Cache River designated for canoeing. Paddle northeast to the state championship tupelo tree, past cypress and gum trees and the occasional river otter and egret. You can launch your canoe or kayak at the Lower Cache River Access Area, where Cypress Creek meets the Cache River. The trail, up to six miles long, has signposts with arrows and other markings that point you in the right direction, but you might want to pick up a map from the state natural headquarters office in Belknap, just in case you get lost. The canoe trail is just west of Highway 37 and north of Highway 169 (follow signs from Highway 37). If you didn't drive to the region with your canoe tied to your car's roof, look up **Land for Learning Institute** in Jonesboro (618/833-8030 or 618/967-6876, www.landforlearning.org), which offers guided canoe trips in the region.

TUNNEL HILL STATE TRAIL

Johnson County's nickname is the biking capital of the state, and that's largely because of the 45-mile-long Tunnel Hill State Trail (618/658-2168, www.dnr.state.il.us or www. ilbikecap.org), which carves a path through the county. It begins at U.S. 45 and Highway

13 in Harrisburg (where there are bathrooms, parking, and a bike rack) and continues to the Henry Barkhausen Wetlands Center west of Karnak. You'll find there are several places where you can start your ride, including Community Park in Vienna and the wetlands center. The crushed-limestone and gravel trail follows part of the old Norfolk Southern Railroad line, through fairly flat farmland, up and down the hills of the Shawnee National Forest, the bottomlands of the Cache River basin, along creeks, past ghost towns, and atop trestle bridges (one is more than 90 feet high, south of the town of Tunnel Hill). The trail's highlight is a 500-foot-long sandstone and shale tunnel built in 1872, also near the town of Tunnel Hill. **Morris Acres** (1645 Tunnel Hill Rd., Tunnel Hill, 618/658-4022) offers shuttle service on the tunnel trail for a fee.

The nine-mile section between the towns of Tunnel Hill and Vienna intersects with the **River-to-River Trail,** a 175-mile trail that connects the Mississippi and Ohio rivers (www.rivertorivertrail.org) between Cave-in-Rock and Grand Tower.

SCENIC OVERLOOK

The Nature Conservancy's **Grassy Slough Preserve** (off the Belknap blacktop, a few miles north of Karnak, 618/634-2524) has an overlook, the Jean Campbell Farwell Overlook, that offers views of an ongoing wetland restoration project. More than 2,500 acres of land damaged by drainage, farming, and logging will one day look like a cypress-tupelo swamp again.

WINERIES

Just down the road from Heron Pond, **Cache River Basin Vineyard and Winery** (315 Forman Ln., Belknap, 618/658-7023 or 618/658-2274, www.crbwinery.com, 10 A.M.–6 P.M. Mon.–Sat., 1–5 P.M. Sun.) offers wine tastings and tours of its winery. Its wines include red and white brands such as Hawk Tail Red and Cottonmouth White, named after Cache River wildlife. The winery holds events throughout the year—the wine and arts festival in July, grape stomp in July, plus barbecue dinners and murder mystery dinners. In recent years the owner has also opened a little restaurant on site called Wineaux's (get it?). Now you can dig into some ribs, try some pheasant, or nibble on a bread and oil while you sip wine from a glass. Sandwiches are also an option for lunches. Restaurant hours vary.

Opened in 2004, **Shawnee Winery** (200 Commercial Dr., Vienna, 618/658-8400, www.shawneewinery.com) is a cooperative of small regional wineries. Its shop is just off I-24 in Vienna.

FERNE CLYFFE STATE PARK

As the name implies, Ferne Clyffe State Park (one mile south of Goreville on Hwy. 37, 618/995-2411, www.dnr.state.il.us) is in a rich forested area at the southern edge of the Shawnee National Forest. Ferns abound, but so do trilliums, lilies, flowering dogwoods, and redbud trees, making this place a beautiful sight in the spring. It's also interesting on a historical level. Revolutionary War hero George Rogers Clark was said to have hiked through here with his men after securing the British Fort Massac and on his way to Fort Kaskaskia. Speaking of hiking, the park, at almost 2,500 acres, has great hiking—a total of 18 trails, from the easy one-mile loop around Ferne Clyffe Lake to the steep five-mile-long Happy Hollow Trail. (You won't be happy if you forget to bring along enough water, especially in the summer.) One of the coolest sights in the park is Hawks' Cave, a rock shelter about 150 feet long. To get there follow the half-mile Hawk Cave Trail in the northern part of the park. Follow Rebman Trail to the climbing and rappelling area. If you want to keep your visit low-key, drop a line into the Ferne Clyffe Lake for bank fishing or picnic at one of the spots overlooking the hills.

The park has several campgrounds, each geared toward a different camper. Deer Ridge has modern sites with electricity and gravel pads. Turkey Ridge is a walk-in campground with tent pads, picnic tables, and showers. The backpack campground is a half-mile hike

through the woods from Turkey Ridge. There's also an equestrian campground. Camping costs $8–15 per night.

Climbing

Learn how to rock climb at **Drapers Bluff and Vertical Heartland Climbing School** (618/995-1427, www.verticalheartland.com, open daily year-round) just south of Ferne Clyffe State Park.

ACCOMMODATIONS
$50-100

Two decent national chain hotels are on the eastern edge of Vienna, just off I-24. There's **The Limited Inn** (Hwy. 146 and I-24, Vienna, 618/658-6300, $65) with an indoor pool and continental breakfast; and the **Gambit Inn** (Hwy. 146 and I-24, Vienna, 618/658-2802, $45–61).

Camping

Tent and RV campsites are available at Ferne Clyffe State Park (details below) to the north.

FOOD
Farm Markets

You can pick up some fresh fruits, veggies, and flowers at **Trover Produce** (992 Gilead Church Rd., Vienna, 618/658-5100, open seasonally) or **Eastman Orchard and Fruit Market** (Hwy. 37, two miles north of Goreville, 618/995-2118, 8 A.M.–5 P.M. daily Sept.–Nov.).

INFORMATION

The **Johnson County Chamber of Commerce** (Vienna, 618/658-2063, 9 A.M.–3 P.M. Tues.–Sat.) operates a visitors center within a renovated train depot at Vienna Community Park, on the north side of Highway 146 just as you drive west into town. Friendly staff have brochures on nearby attractions, maps, and p hotographs of the old train depot that once stood in the area. They also sell a few gifts such as train whistles. The depot is on the Tunnel Hill Trail, and there's plenty of parking if you want to make this the launching point of your bike trip through the region.

For a regional overview, contact the **Southernmost Illinois Convention and Tourism Bureau** in Anna (618/833-9928 or 800/248-4373, www.southernmostillinois.com), which has lodging and attractions info for the Cache River area as well as surrounding counties. Another good resource is the **Shawnee National Forest** ranger station in Vienna

(602 N. 1st St./U.S. 45, Vienna, 618/658-2111, 8 A.M.–4:30 P.M. Mon.–Fri.). And for more information about the Cache River basin, you can contact staff at the **Cypress Creek National Wildlife Refuge** (Cypress Creek National Wildlife Refuge, Rustic Campus Dr., Ullin, 618/634-2231, 7:30 A.M.–4 P.M. Mon.–Fri., www.fws.gov/midwest/cypresscreek).

Metropolis

The only city named Metropolis in the United States, Metropolis, Illinois, has capitalized on its connection to the man of steel. Decades ago the Illinois legislature declared Metropolis, Illinois, as Superman's hometown. The town celebrates with a Superman festival every summer, and Jim Hambrick's Super Museum is arguably one of the best roadside attractions in the region. In addition to the Superman sights, Metropolis has the oldest state park in the Illinois, Fort Massac, a place once visited by legendary figures such as Revolutionary War hero George Rogers Clark and explorers William Clark and Meriwether Lewis.

SIGHTS
Fort Massac State Park
Almost hidden at the eastern end of Metropolis near an industrial site and shopping center is Fort Massac State Park (1308 E. 5th St., Metropolis, 618/524-9321, www.dnr.state.il.us, visitors center 9:30 A.M.–4:30 P.M. daily), which has quite a history. Shortly after you enter the park you'll see on a hill above the Ohio River a replica of an 1802 timber fort. The version you see is one of many forts that once stood guard in the area. Back in 1702 the French established a trading post in the area, and as the French took control of the region they built a fort to protect their growing territory. (They initially called it Fort Ascension.) After France and Great Britain signed the Treaty of Paris in 1763 to end the Seven Years War (locally the French and Indian War), the French surrendered territory that included the area in and around the fort. A few years later the Brits

failed to adequately supply the fort, and in June 1778 George Rogers Clark, with fewer than 200 men, was able to secure it for the American colonies. General George Washington ordered it rebuilt in 1794. In the early 1800s it was mostly a point of entry for pioneers and explorers, and it was also used as a customs office in the 19th century. Explorers William Clark (younger brother to George Rogers Clark) and Meriwether Lewis stopped by here to recruit some men for their Corps of Discovery.

Fort Massac State Park

© CHRISTINE DES GARENNES

SOUTHERN ILLINOIS

Eventually the fort was dismantled. In 1866 a man named J. C. Blair, later the dean of the University of Illinois College of Agriculture, rode by the park on horseback and thought the area would make a nice park. The Daughters of the American Revolution bought land there in 1908, and it became the first state park.

Today the park, at almost 2,000 acres, has a new fort modeled after how it may have looked when Washington ordered it rebuilt. A visitors center has exhibits on the fort's history, and there are picnic spots and hiking trails. A one-mile loop wanders through the woods, and a 2.5-mile trail follows part of the Ohio River. The park also has a campground.

Superman Sights

The **Super Museum** (Metropolis, 618/524-5518, 9 A.M.–6 P.M. daily, $3) is a maze of a museum with constantly changing exhibits that run the gamut. The owner has hundreds of thousands of pieces of Superman paraphernalia: action figures, costumes worn by television and movie actors, lunch boxes, posters, inflatables, you name it. The museum has a large shop with plenty of T-shirts and Superman and comic book ephemera. A few feet from the Super Museum is a bronze **statue of Superman** in the town square. You can't miss it.

Birdman of Alcatraz

Made famous by Burt Lancaster in a movie about life in Alcatraz, Robert Stroud was known as the birdman of Alcatraz. Stroud, convicted for murdering a bartender, was not exactly a model prisoner in his youth. But after being transferred to Alcatraz Island in the San Francisco Bay, he grew to love tending to birds. He raised hundreds of them while there and even wrote books about bird diseases. He's buried in Metropolis in the Masonic Cemetery on North Avenue.

ENTERTAINMENT AND EVENTS

Parked on the bank of the Ohio River, **Harrah's Casino** (100 E. Front St., Metropolis, 800/929-5905, www.harrahs.com, 9 A.M.–7 P.M. daily) is one of Illinois's several riverboat casinos. (It's not really a boat moving along the river, though.) This place is hopping, especially on weekend nights. There are 1,100 slot machines, 25 tables with games such as blackjack, plus three restaurants (a diner, a steakhouse, and a buffet restaurant). A new hotel is adjacent to the casino.

The big to-do in the summer is the annual **Superman Festival** held in June. In addition to the standard carnival rides and fried food, the festival has Superman-themed games, and usually former stars of Superman movies and television shows show up. Over at **Fort Massac** several reenactments and encampments are held throughout the year, including French and Indian War reenactments in mid-May and a "living history" weekend in mid-August, when participants live as if they were inhabitants of the fort.

ACCOMMODATIONS
$50-100

The **Baymont Inn & Suites** (203 E. Front St., Metropolis, 800/434-8500, $89–140) overlooks the Ohio River and is just across the street from the riverboat casino. It has an indoor pool, and rooms come with wireless Internet access and coffeemakers. Continental breakfast is included. The **Holiday Inn Express** (2179 E. 5th St., Metropolis, 618/524-8899, $80–140) and **Comfort Inn** (2118 E. 5th St., Metropolis, 618/524-7227, $65–100) are both on U.S. 45 on the east side of town by Fort Massac State Park. Each has an indoor pool and offers continental breakfast.

You can also stay at **Harrah's** (100 E. Front St., Metropolis, 800/929-5905, www.harrahs.com) beginning at around $60 for a weekday night. Expect to pay a lot more, though, if you stay on a weekend night.

Over $100

The beautiful **Old Bethlehem Schoolhouse Cottage** (6512 Old Marion Rd., Metropolis, 618/524-4922, www.bethlehemschool.com, $135) is a one-room schoolhouse renovated into a three-bedroom cottage with an eat-in kitchen and one bathroom. Tastefully decorated with antiques, the cottage can sleep up to six people (one queen, one double, and two twin beds). Outside the windows are views of cornfields and the Shawnee Hills.

Standing guard on a hill overlooking the Ohio River, the **Isle of View Bed and Breakfast** (205 Metropolis St., Metropolis, 618/524-5838, www.isle-of-view.net, $65–150) is an 1889 brick Victorian home converted into a bed-and-breakfast. There are five rooms in total, all with private bathrooms and richly decorated with Victorian-style antiques and decor. Extras, such as the two-person tubs and canopy beds, make it a good choice for couples on romantic getaways. A full breakfast is included. The hosts also offer extensive in-room dinners if you give them notice. Items on the menu could be Cornish game hens, sherried shrimp, and other dishes.

Camping

Fort Massac State Park (1308 E. 5th St., Metropolis, 618/524-9321, www.dnr.state. il.us) has campsites for RVs and tents. Fees are $8–15 per night.

FOOD

In downtown Metropolis, a block from the Super Museum, you'll find a rare sight: a cafeteria. It's not a school or retirement center, but an old-fashioned storefront restaurant cafeteria. **Farley's Cafeteria** (613 Market St., Metropolis, 618/524-7226, 3:30–7 P.M. Wed.–Sat., $7) features smiling older ladies serving big spoonfuls of green beans, creamed corn, and slices of roast beef and steaming pork. The crowd definitely leans toward the white-haired. It's a good people-watching spot.

Stock up on groceries at **Big John's** supermarket (1200 E. 5th St., Metropolis, 618/524-4096). Look for the giant fiberglass "Big John" (who, like Superman, boasts a brawny figure) grasping a bag of groceries at the parking lot entrance.

Farm Market

Faughn Farms (3059 Old Marion Rd., Metropolis, 618/524-8383, 10 A.M.–2 P.M. Tues., Thurs., Sat.) specializes in organic herbs for culinary or medicinal use.

INFORMATION

You can get lodging information from the **Metropolis Chamber of Commerce** (607 Market St., Metropolis, 618/524-2714, www. metropolischamber.com).

DIXON SPRINGS AND LAKE GLENDALE
Dixon Springs State Park

Named for the mineral springs in the area, Dixon Springs State Park (618/949-3394) is tucked off Highway 146 west of Golconda and easy to miss. It could use some updating (the roads are a little bumpy) but that doesn't matter; the park's best attraction is its geology (and for the kids, it's the swimming pool). Park your car and spend some time hiking one or both of the two trails here. Hike them both and they'll add up to less than three miles. (The park is about 800 acres.) Ghost Dance Canyon, which can get a little slippery and follows along the side of a canyon for a section of the trail, takes you past canyon walls that stretch about 50 feet high. On rainy days and some of the days

Dixon Springs State Park

thereafter, little waterfalls and rivulets come rushing down the hillsides and rocks. The wooded park is beautiful in the spring, when the oak and hickory trees have pale green buds and dogwood trees bloom cream-colored flowers. There are about 40 campsites here with electricity, plus 10 rustic sites for tents. The swimming pool is open to the public Memorial Day–Labor Day.

After your rigorous hike atop bluffs and along canyon walls, treat yourself to a hand-dipped ice cream cone at **The Chocolate Factory** (Hwy. 146, 618/949-3829 or 877/949-3829, www.thechocolatefactory.net, 9 A.M.–5 P.M. Mon.–Sat.), across the highway from the park. Then pack some fudge or peanut brittle in the cooler for the ride home.

Lake Glendale

If you need to cool off, you can take a dip in the 80-acre Lake Glendale (Hwy. 145, north of Dixon Springs, 618/658-2111), a few miles north of Dixon Springs State Park and managed by the U.S. Forest Service. The lake has a sandy beach, concession stand, shower house, and paddleboats for rent.

In the Shawnee National Forest near Lake Glendale, **Lake Glendale Stables** (201 Lake Glendale Rd., Golconda, 618/949-3737, www.lakeglendalestables.com, call for times, rides available daily, year-round) offers horseback rides by the hour or entire day, plus overnight camping trips, or lunch and dinner trips. The main attraction is horseback riding, but the owners also have a private lake for bank fishing, a zip-line swing (where you grab onto a bar, zoom down the line, and jump into the lake), and a rustic campground. In addition, there's a lodge that sleeps up to four people. It's nothing fancy—just air-conditioning, a wood-burning stove, and a kitchen stocked with dishes. The lodge is $135 per night.

Golconda

This little town on the Ohio River can be a base for your trip through the Shawnee National Forest. It has a short but reemerging Main Street with a few alternative lodging options, friendly restaurants, and a marina for boaters.

SIGHTS AND ACTIVITIES

Rauchfuss Hill is a small recreation area on a bluff above the Ohio River and is connected to Golconda marina below by a walking trail. The selling point of this state-owned park is the view of the river. It used to be called Steamboat Hill because you could watch the steamboats pass by. Now you can count the barges. There are two short trails through the area, a few picnic tables, and a few campsites. To get to the park, follow signs to the marina from Highway 146.

For a peaceful hike through river bottomland, past oak trees and ferns and through meadows, visit **War Bluff Valley Wildlife Sanctuary** (dawn–dusk daily, free) just north of Golconda. The 500-acre site, owned by the Illinois Audubon Society, boasts several mowed grass trails and hiking trails by several ponds and along Simmons Creek. To get to the site, drive 3.5 miles north of Golconda on Highway 146, take a left on Bushwack Road, and follow a gravel road for a few more miles.

Fishing and Boating

Golconda is near the Smithland Pool, a 23,000-acre area created by the lock and dam near Smithland, Kentucky. The fishing there is, well, famous. Bass? They're there. Bluegill? Yup. Catfish? You bet. If you want to give it a shot, you can rent a boat or launch your boat at the **Golconda Marina** (just off Hwy. 146, Golconda, 618/683-5875, www.golcondamarina.com, call for hours, Mar.–Nov.). Rent a fishing boat or pontoon boat here, buy some snacks, and learn about where the fish are biting. You can walk to the marina from downtown or vice versa via a highway bridge.

EVENTS

In the fall, farmers harvest not only corn and soybeans but prawns. Prawns are freshwater shrimp. And every year it seems more farmers in southern Illinois are raising them in ponds behind their houses (it's called aquaculture). In mid-September, Golconda celebrates the shrimp harvest with the **Shrimp Festival.** Listen to live music, nibble on fresh shrimp, watch shrimp being prepared in the great shrimp cook-off, and then take home some frozen shrimp to eat later.

ACCOMMODATIONS

How often do you get to stay in the house of a former lockkeeper? You can at the **Lock and Dam 51 houses** (Levy Rd., Golconda, 618/683-6702, www.golcondalockmaster-homes.com, $85–185). After they fell into disrepair from disuse, the city of Golconda bought the four buildings and restored them. Opened in 2002, the homes are decorated with 1920s antiques, plus a few modern amenities such as whirlpool tubs and pull-out couches. There are four houses in two different styles. Both have porches and offer great views of the river. And both have full kitchens that contain dishes and pots and pans. The wooden-frame houses have one bedroom with a queen bed, plus a pull-out in the living room, and a bathroom with a whirlpool tub. The brick homes have three bedrooms, plus a pull-out sofa in the living room.

FOOD
Continental

The European-styled (**Café Bella Mia** (217 E. Main St., Golconda, 618/683-2094, 11 A.M.–2 P.M. Tues.–Sat., 5–9 P.M. Fri.–Sat., $10) in downtown Golconda is a little bit of everything: bakery, restaurant, and wine bar. You can visit the intimate cream- and black-decorated storefront café for a panini sandwich and caffe latte or seafood dinner entrée accompanied by a glass of wine.

American

Dari-Barr (209 W. Main St., Golconda, 618/683-4878, 6 A.M.–8 P.M. daily, call for winter hours) is the kind of place where local farmers eat their meals of biscuits and gravy and regulars sit and drink coffee for most of the morning (and make wisecracks to the waitress). Food is cheap and good. An egg, two pieces of toast, and sausage costs about $3. Dishes also include catfish sandwiches, hot dogs, and chicken dinners.

Farm Market

For fresh-picked peaches, tomatoes, and salad mix, drop by the **Golconda Farmers Market,** held on Saturdays mid to late April–September, on the courthouse lawn on Main Street. Vendors sell 8 A.M.–noon.

INFORMATION

Before you visit, give the folks a call at **Main Street Golconda** (618/683-6246 or 888/490-2850) to get the scoop on any new lodgings, driving tips, or other information.

GETTING AROUND

A great and inexpensive way to see the Ohio River and some of the Ohio River towns is on the *Shawnee Queen River Taxi* (618/285-3342 or 877/667-6123, www.ridesmtd.com), which rolls along the Ohio River with stops in Golconda, Rosiclare, Elizabethtown, and Cave-in-Rock. It's managed by the Rides Mass Transit District and operates Tuesday–Saturday, second Tuesday in May–November 1. The river taxi seats 48 people and has bike racks. You can reserve a seat online.

MERMET SPRINGS

Illinois is hundreds of miles from any ocean, sea, or gulf. But that doesn't mean you can't scuba dive and explore the underwater world. About halfway between Metropolis and Vienna is an abandoned stone quarry that has been transformed into a scuba school and scuba adventure spot for more experienced divers. Visitors to Mermet Springs (west side of U.S. 45 between Vienna and Metropolis, 618/527-3483, www.mermetsprings.com) can dive down to depths of 10, 15, 20, and even more than 100 feet. The owners have placed things such as an old school bus and an airplane down there for visitors to explore. There's a $15 entry fee for divers, plus more if you rent equipment. Lessons are available. If scuba diving is not your thing and you're

still interested in checking out a spring-fed quarry, rent a kayak from the scuba center for $10 per hour; there's a two-hour minimum.

While you're in the area, drive through the **Mermet Lake State Conservation Area** (618/524-5577), also on U.S. 45 between Metropolis and Vienna. This area was once a cypress swamp and is now used primarily for waterfowl hunting.

Hardin and Saline Counties

One of the first regions to be settled in Illinois, the Hardin and Saline Counties region was one rich place—rich in natural resources (salt, coal, fluorite) and therefore rich with business opportunities. In Saline County, early settlers had heard from the Native Americans about the salt springs along the Saline River, and they set up operations to extract the brine from the water. This involved importing slaves from the South and ordering them to chop wood used for the process. The salt was later sold as a food preservative and an ingredient for hide tanning. To the south, towns such as Rosiclare and Elizabethtown cropped up as settlers and later immigrants from Germany, Ireland, and other European countries moved in after hearing that coal and fluorspar mines were being established. Ironworks were also constructed in the outlying areas. With the Ohio River nearby and all the steamboat traffic, perhaps it was only natural for outlaws to show up. A large dark cave now at present-day Cave-in-Rock State Park was the perfect hiding place for them. After the river gangs were kicked out, along came the bootleggers in the early 1900s. By the turn of the 20th century the region was churning out hundreds of thousands of pounds of coal. Today the salt mines and fluorspar mines are closed. Coal mining is still going on, but not at the level it was at 30 years ago.

ORIENTATION

Part of the Ohio River Scenic Byway, Highway 146 follows the river along the southeastern

part of the region. There are plenty of signs along the way to point you in the right direction, and there are a few spurs along back roads and through small towns. The north-south Highway 1 hooks up with Highway 146 and will lead you to the town of Cave-in-Rock and the state park of the same name. Highway 13 runs east-west from Old Shawneetown on the Ohio River toward Harrisburg and beyond. It's a quick smooth road. The county and forest roads are sometimes paved, sometimes gravel, and it's not uncommon for some to be unmarked. With that said, when you drive to places such as the Illinois Iron Furnace and Garden of the Gods, allow some extra time to get lost. Even navigating with a county map can be a challenge. At the top of your to-do list is a hike through the Shawnee National Forest, namely the Garden of the Gods, an area where eroded sandstone and limestone formations resemble people and creatures.

◖ GARDEN OF THE GODS WILDERNESS

More than 300 million years ago, Illinois was covered by an inland sea. Through time, sand and soil washed into the sea from rivers that flowed into it. The sand and mud settled along the shores, building up layer by layer, year after year, becoming bedrock. At one point there was a great tectonic uplift and these bedrock formations pushed up out of the water, exposing them to wind, rain, sand, and other forces. What you see during your visit to the Garden

© CHRISTINE DES GARENNES

view of the Shawnee National Forest from Garden of the Gods

SOUTHERN ILLINOIS

of the Gods country is the result of all that erosion: pretty cool-looking rock formations. The Garden of the Gods Wilderness is a 3,300-acre site southwest of Shawneetown and south of Harrisburg where a cluster of these formations is viewable from a short hiking trail. The 0.25-mile Observation Trail takes you past rocks called Mushroom Rock, Camel Rock, and Devil's Smokestack. The trail is steep but short. Nearby Pharaoh Campground has 12 tent campsites available year-round. To get to the site, follow Highway 34 south to Karbers Ridge Road (there are signs to the Garden of the Gods Wilderness). Head east for 2.5 miles to Garden of the Gods Road.

Rim Rock and Pounds Hollow Recreation Area

Rim Rock National Recreation Trail is a 0.75-mile loop on top of a bluff called the Rim Rock Escarpment. Hike through an upland forest and past a cedar plantation and then down a set of stairs into the valley. There you'll find remains of a Native American wall and a shelter bluff called Ox Lot Cave, where pioneers used to keep their oxen. From there it's on to "fat man's misery," a narrow passageway through boulders. Rim Rock and Pounds Hollow Recreation Areas are connected by Beaver Trail. On the northwestern part of the site are remains of a wall believed to have been built by Native Americans. In the southeast at Pounds Hollow Recreation Area is a 25-acre artificial lake with a beach, picnic area, and campground. You can rent rowboats and paddleboats. The area is about four miles east of Karbers Ridge along the Karbers Ridge Road.

Scenic Overlooks

Overlooking the Ohio River, **Tower Rock** (not to be confused with the Tower Rock in the Mississippi River near Grand Tower) is a small park with a trail of about 800 yards. The Shawnee National Forest manages a 25-site campground there. It is four miles south of Highway 146 between the historic river towns of Elizabethtown and Cave-in-Rock. You can drive to the top of High Knob, which has overlooks of the Garden of the Gods country.

Park here and explore about five miles of trail through wilderness. The trails here are part of the River-to-River Trail. To get there, follow Highway 34 to Karbers Ridge Road. Head east a few miles to a gravel road. There will be signs for High Knob. At 1,064 feet high, **Williams Hill** is the second-highest point in southern Illinois, after Bald Knob. It's off Williams Tower Road a few miles west of the town of Herod and Highway 34.

LUSK CREEK WILDERNESS

With 80- to 100-foot-high bluffs, the Lusk Creek Wilderness is an amazing site with challenging hiking trails and glimpses of an old Native American stone wall. Perhaps Lush Creek is a better name. An array of plants such as moss, ferns, and wildflowers thrive throughout the canyon. And as one of the least polluted waterways in the state, Lusk Creek is home to more than 20 species of fish. The creek begins just south of Delwood and zigzags toward the Ohio River near Golconda. At Lusk Creek Wilderness it carves through a 100-foot-high gorge which you can see by hiking along a two-mile trail. Along the trail you'll find remains of a Native American stone wall, thought to have been built sometime between A.D. 600 and 900 by Indians of the Late Woodland Period. The wall may have been built for defense, ceremonial, or hunting purposes. (Charging buffalo would have stumbled over the wall and down the cliff.) A footpath leads to a rock shelter called **Indian Kitchen,** 70 feet above the canyon. Views from here are unbeatable. Lusk Creek Wilderness is a few miles northeast of Eddyville and Highway 145. Watch for signs.

BELL SMITH SPRINGS

Another gorgeous wilderness site, Bell Smith Springs has the distinction of being a U.S. Park Service National Natural Landmark. Four creeks meet in the canyon here where hundreds of species of plants and animals live. Walk among beech and tupelo trees. Listen for pileated woodpeckers and tanagers. Several

Lusk Creek, one of the least polluted waterways in the state

© CHRISTINE DES GARENNES

trails ranging 1.5–3.2 miles in length meander through the area, atop canyons and down in the canyons. They are all interconnected, so you can hike a total of eight miles if you want. A highlight is a natural stone bridge that spans 125 feet and has a 30-foot-high arch. Other discoveries are rock formations such as the Devil's Backbone (not to be confused with the Devil's Backbone in Grand Tower on the Mississippi River) and remains of an old gristmill. There is a campground here, called Redbud, which has 21 tent sites available for $5 per night. Drinking water is available.

To get to the site from Harrisburg, follow Highway 145 south to Delwood about nine miles. Then take Forest Road 402 for four miles to Forest Road 447 and continue to Forest Road 848. Go southwest on Forest Road 848 for a few more miles. If you're coming from Vienna, follow U.S. 45 toward Ozark. Signs will point you east on forest roads to the recreation area.

SALINE COUNTY STATE FISH AND WILDLIFE AREA

West of the tiny town of Equality and southeast of Harrisburg is a peaceful hidden park on a quiet lake, the Saline County State Fish and Wildlife Area (85 Glen O. Jones Rd., Equality, 618/276-4405, www.dnr.state.il.us). This is a good spot for bank fishing. The lake is stocked with bluegill, bass, and other fish. You can rent fishing boats from the concession building, and there are two boat docks. (The lake has a 10-horsepower engine limit.) In addition, the park has several scenic picnic spots and plenty of lakeside campsites. The park is about four miles south of Highway 13. Four trails totaling seven miles wind around the 1,270-acre site.

C CAVE-IN-ROCK STATE PARK

Like most caves, Cave-in-Rock was an ideal hiding place for outlaws. This large cave on the Ohio River has had quite a chilling history. Samuel Mason, once a soldier for George Washington during the Revolutionary War, was one of the more notorious inhabitants of the cave. He and his gang in the late 1790s

Cave-in-Rock State Park, on the Ohio River

© CHRISTINE DES GARENNES

SOUTHERN ILLINOIS

were said to have lured unsuspecting travelers to the cave, then robbed them, beat them, and maybe even murdered a few. After Mason's gang disbanded, the Harpe brothers, who were convicted of murder in Kentucky (and somehow escaped execution) took refuge in the cave and used it as their headquarters for more murder and mayhem. Now the worst activities that occur in the cave are visitors writing their names into its walls. The cave and surrounding area are part of Cave-in-Rock State Park (1 New State Park Rd., Cave-in-Rock, 618/289-4325, www.dnr.state.il.us). A set of stone stairs leads down to the cave and a small beach. There are also two trails that follow the river and cut through the woods. Several picnic tables are placed throughout the nearby wooded valley, and there are tent and RV campsites.

ROSICLARE SIGHTS
American Fluorite Museum

Rosiclare, now a town of about 1,200 people at the edge of Shawnee National Forest, was once a major mining town in the region. Calcium fluoride, barite, and calcite were all mined here at one time (the peak was 1910–1945). An excellent museum about that mining history is the American Fluorite Museum (Hwy. 34 and Main St., Rosiclare, 618/285-3513, 1–4 P.M. Thurs.–Fri. and Sun., 10 A.M.–4 P.M. Sat., Mar.–Nov., $3). Open since 1997, it's housed in the former office building of the Rosiclare Lead and Fluorspar Mining Company and is run by former miners and volunteers. The focus of the museum is fluorspar, or fluorite, the state mineral. Made of calcium fluoride, the brittle mineral comes in a variety of colors, including purple, blue, yellow, green, and white. In ultraviolet light the mineral is fluorescent. There's plenty of fluorite in the museum, including a giant hunk placed in the middle of the room. When the sun shines on it at various angles, it's quite a dazzling sight. The museum also has petrified wood, galena lead, calcite needles, and other gems and minerals on view. Visitors can pick through the ore piles near the museum and buy some fluorite for about $1 per pound.

Illinois Iron Furnace

Northeast of Rosiclare is another example of the region's industrial past. The Illinois Iron Furnace is a re-created furnace modeled after the one that stood in the same spot in the mid-1800s. The original stone furnace was built in 1837, and production started two years later. Workers burned about 1,800 bushels of charcoal (gathered from area hills) each day to fuel the furnace. Then, iron ore from the area was smelted with limestone to draw out the slag, or impurities. The end product was something called pig iron, oblong pieces of iron shipped to manufacturers. The furnace could produce nine tons of pig iron each day. Eventually, as iron production shifted elsewhere, locals blew up the furnace to get the stones. It was declared beyond repair in the mid-1960s, but locals raised some money and rebuilt it. The 42-foot-high stone furnace is tucked away in the hills off a scenic back road near the babbling Big Creek. To get to the site, follow signs north from Highway 146 in Rosiclare or Elizabethtown.

© CHRISTINE DES GARENNES

Illinois Iron Furnace, near Rosiclare

ACCOMMODATIONS
Cave-in-Rock State Park

Perched on a high bluff within **Cave-in-Rock State Park** (618/289-4545, Mar.–Nov., from $69) are four lodges, each with two units. Each suite has a private bathroom, private deck, and living room area. You cannot beat the view from up here.

Garden of the Gods Area

In the heart of the Garden of the Gods region, **Rim Rocks Dogwood Cabins** (Pounds Hollow Blacktop, 618/264-6036, about $100) offers two rustic cabins. Each cedar cabin comes with a screened-in porch, a loft sleeping area, bathroom, full kitchen (stove, fridge, microwave), and some extras such as DVD players. Outside each cabin is a fire ring, picnic table, and flower gardens. It's one of the best spots to stay if you're doing some serious hiking in the region and do not want to camp.

Elizabethtown

Built in 1812 and listed on the National Register of Historic Places, the **Grand Rose Hotel Bed and Breakfast** (10 Main St., Elizabethtown, 618/287-2872, www.rosehotelbb.com, $95) is one of the oldest hotels, if not the oldest hotel, in Illinois. Facing the

Ohio River, the white-painted building with its porches and gazebo offers incredible views of the river valley. Perched on a limestone bluff, the hotel has five rooms, outfitted with classic bed-and-breakfast furniture (four-poster beds, sleigh beds), and some modern touches such as flat-screen televisions. If you don't stay here, at least drop by and take in the view from the gazebo on a rock above the river.

Across the street and also overlooking the river is the **River Rose Inn** (1 Main St., Elizabethtown, 618/287-8811, www.riveroseinn.com, $85–125), another bed-and-breakfast with a large front porch accented with hanging flower baskets. The 1914 Greek Gothic home has four guest rooms in the house, plus a little cottage adjacent to the main house. Rooms come with private bathrooms.

Harrisburg

Chain hotels include **Comfort Inn** (100A E. Seright St., Harrisburg, 618/252-2442, $70–100) and the **Super 8** (100 E. Seright St., Harrisburg, 618/253-8081, $55–80). There's also an inexpensive bed-and-breakfast in town, the **Lafayette Inn** (202–204 W. Poplar St., Harrisburg, 618/252-7599, $72–84), which is just off Highway 13 near downtown.

Camping

Cave-in-Rock State Park (Hwy. 1, Cave-in-Rock, 618/289-4325, www.dnr.state.il.us) has 25 tent campsites and 34 electrical sites for RVs. Fees are $8–15 per night.

The Shawnee National Forest has several campgrounds in its eastern district. Most are unbeatable private wooded tent sites with drinking water, fire pits, and vault toilets. Fees are $5 per night for tent camping. Area campgrounds include **Rim Rock Recreation Area,** which has 76 campsites available April–mid-December; Redbud campground in **Bell Smith Springs Recreation Area** with 21 tent sites; and Pharaoh Campground in the **Garden of the Gods Wilderness Area** with 12 tent campsites available year-round. For more information on camping in the forest, call the Hidden Springs Ranger District at 618/658-2111.

FOOD

Cave-in-Rock and Elizabethtown

During the winter, dining options are limited. But once the trees start flowering and the weather warms, a great seasonally operated restaurant opens for business: **Kaylor's Restaurant** (Cave-in-Rock State Park, 618/289-4545, 8 A.M.–9 P.M. daily Mar.–Nov., $6–12), which specializes in Southern-style cooking such as fried chicken and catfish. Otherwise, when you're in town November–March, drop by the casual local joint **Gee Jays** (downtown Cave-in-Rock, 618/289-5000, 7:30 A.M.–8 P.M. Mon.–Thurs., 7:30 A.M.–9 P.M. Fri.), where you can fill up on a cheeseburger and fries or a chicken sandwich for a few bucks.

Harrisburg

You know the food must be good at **The Barb BQ Barn** (632 N. Main St./Hwy. 34, Harrisburg, 618/252-6190, 6 A.M.–8 P.M. Mon.–Sat., 10:30 A.M.–2:30 P.M. Sun.) when folks start heading there in the early hours of the morning; yes, for breakfast.

The family-friendly **Morello's** (217 E. Poplar St./Hwy.13, Harrisburg, 618/252-2300, 11 A.M.–9 P.M. Mon.–Thurs., 11 A.M.–11 P.M. Fri.–Sat., 4–9 P.M. Sun.) is ostensibly an Italian restaurant with pizza, garlic bread, and Caesar salads, but it does have a little bit of everything on its menu, including steak. A popular spot on weekends, expect to wait a few minutes for a table.

INFORMATION

For information on exploring the **Shawnee National Forest** in the Elizabethtown region, you can call the regional ranger at 618/287-2201.

SERVICES

Harrisburg is billed as the gateway to the Shawnee National Forest. It's a good place to stock up on food supplies, film, or other gear at the several grocery and department stores in town. They're all clustered along Highway 13 and U.S. 45.

SOUTHERN ILLINOIS

Rend Lake Region

Stretching over about 19,000 acres, Rend Lake is one big lake. But it's not a giant circle of a lake; instead, it's shaped somewhat like a hand holding its fingers up in a peace sign. It's got plenty of quiet little bay areas for fishing or snoozing in the sun in the back of your boat. Built by the U.S. Army Corps of Engineers in 1970, the lake (formed by damming the Muddy River) acts as a reservoir for the area. The whole construction project was envisioned after a drought in the 1950s. Most of the people who gravitate to Rend Lake are boaters and anglers. This is definitely fishing country—some would say it offers the best crappie fishing in the state, not to mention bass, catfish, and bluegill fishing.

Before you visit, drop by the **visitors center** (10 A.M.–5 P.M. daily end of May–mid-Aug., 10 A.M.–5 P.M. Sat.–Sun. Apr.–end of May and mid-Aug.–end of Oct.) on the main Rend Lake Dam Road on the south side of the lake. It's accessible from I-57 and Highway 14. You can pick up lake maps, get directions to campsites, get recommendations for the best times to fish, and more. Plus there's an aquarium stocked with fish found in the lake and a terrarium with snakes.

SPORTS AND RECREATION

There are two major sites for recreation at Rend Lake: **Wayne Fitzgerrell State Park** (11094 Ranger Rd., Whittington, 618/629-2230, www.dnr.state.il.us) on the east side of the lake, and **Rend Lake Recreation Complex** (south of Hwy. 154, look for the giant water tower masquerading as a golf ball and tee, Golf Course Dr., Whittington, 618/629-2600, www.rendlake.org), also on the east side of the lake. In addition, all around the lake the Army Corps of Engineers has day-use parks, campgrounds, and boat launches.

Boating and Fishing

As mentioned, Rend Lake is teeming with bass (there's a white bass fishery at Rend Lake), bowfin, white and black crappie, channel catfish, and bluegill fish. As you drive around the lake,

you'll see one turnoff after the other for boat ramps, or day-use areas where you can pick a spot along the edge of the lake and cast a line. If you're not hauling your own boat along on this trip, you can rent fishing boats and pontoon boats at the **Rend Lake Marina** (Rend City Rd., 618/724-7651), in the southwest corner of the lake in the Sandusky Creek Day-use Area. The area is accessible from Highway 154 or Rend Lake Dam Road. Or if you have your own boat, you can rent a slip. To use the boat ramp will cost a few bucks. Remember, you'll need to buy a fishing license.

Hunting and Shooting

Most of the hunters in the Rend Lake region are there for the upland game (pheasants, quail, and the like). The **Rend Lake Conservancy District** maintains a prairie and wooded hunting preserve on the south side of the lake for such game; it's open to members of the public with the proper permits. Over in **Wayne Fitzgerrell State Park,** a controlled pheasant hunt is held each fall. Enthusiasts might be interested in the dog field trials also held in the state park, where you can watch or enter your dog in hunting contests.

Otherwise, if you want to practice your shot or if you don't want to go after an actual animal, the Rend Lake Recreation Complex has skeet and sporting clay stations near the clubhouse. No traipsing through mud or tall grass; the paths are paved and guided by lights. The district can help you get the right license, pair you up with a hunting dog or dogs, and even outfit you in some camouflage clothing. For more information, call 618/629-2368.

Golf

On the southeast side of the lake you'll find the **Rend Lake Golf Course** (Golf Course Dr., Whittington, 618/629-2353), a 27-hole public course. There's also a lighted driving range and pro shop.

Swimming

You can sun yourself, get your toes wet, or practice handstands under water at two public swimming beaches on Rend Lake. **North Marcum Beach** is on the east side of the lake off Highway 37 by Benton. The **South Sandusky Beach** is on the west side of the lake off Rend City Road. There's a $1 per person swimming fee or $4 per car. Kids 12 and under are free. Beaches close at 10 P.M.

Hiking

Because this is primarily a boating, fishing, and hunting area, your hiking options are limited to a handful of trails in Wayne Fitzgerrell State Park and a few in the Army Corps of Engineers' day-use areas. The trails are fairly easy and short, none more than a mile long. Two options are the Blackberry Nature Trail, a 0.75-mile trail by the Sandusky Creek Day-use Area, and the Rend Lake Hiking Trail, a 0.75-mile wheelchair-accessible concrete trail that connects the South Sandusky Trail with the Sandusky Creek Day-use Area.

ENTERTAINMENT AND SHOPPING
Art

Set on a 90-acre site, the **Cedarhurst Center for the Arts** (Richview Rd., Mount Vernon, 618/242-1236, www.cedarhurst.org, 10 A.M.–5 P.M. Tues.–Sat., 1–5 P.M. Sun., free) has an outdoor sculpture park with a walking trail, a collection of American paintings (including works by John Singer Sargent and Mary Cassatt), and a performing arts center. In addition to the permanent painting collection, the center organizes rotating exhibits, indoor and outdoor musical concerts, a craft fair, lectures, and more.

Run by the Illinois State Museum and just off I-57, the **Southern Illinois Artisan Shop and Visitors Center** (14967 Gun Creek Tr., Whittington, 618/629-2220, www.museum.state.il.us, 9 A.M.–5 P.M. daily Apr.–Dec., 9 A.M.–5 P.M. Tues.–Sat. Dec.–Mar., free) is a great find with rotating exhibits of glasswork, sculptures, paintings, and photography,

all by regional artists. It's not strictly a museum, though: There's lots of original artwork for sale. The center often holds workshops and demonstrations.

Winery

Focusing mainly on red and white grape wines, but also selling some rosés and apple wines, **GenKota Winery** (301 N. 44th St., Mount Vernon, 618/246-9463, www.genkotawine.com, 10 A.M.–6 P.M. Mon.–Thurs., 10 A.M.–7 P.M. Fri.–Sat., noon–6 P.M. Sun. Apr.–Dec. 31, 10 A.M.–6 P.M. Mon.–Sat., noon–4 P.M. Sun. Jan.–Mar.) has a gift shop and deck that overlooks the vineyard. GenKota Winery is near the intersection of I-57 and I-64, just east of Mount Vernon.

ACCOMMODATIONS
Under $100

Louise Harrison, sister of the late great Beatle George Harrison, used to live in Benton. Back in 1963 he visited her while she was living with her husband in a 1930s cottage-style house. Louise no longer lives in Benton, but the current owner has transformed the house into a little Beatle-o-rama, saving it from being demolished for a parking lot. The result is the comfy **Hard Days Nite B&B** (113 McCann St., Benton, 618/438-2328, www.harddaysnitebnb.com, $80). There are four rooms, each one named after a member of the band. As you might expect, there are a few photographs and posters of the band and its members hanging in the rooms.

$100-150

At **Rend Lake Resort** (11712 E. Windy Ln., Whittington, 62897, 618/629-2211 or 800/633-3341, www.rendlakeresort.net, $65–130) you have your pick of more than 100 cabins. (They're called cabins, but they are really modern, clean cottages.) The resort is in Wayne Fitzgerrell State Park, and all units are within a short walking distance of the lake, a swimming pool, two resort restaurants, a fishing and boating pier, tennis courts, and horse-riding stables. Some rooms have fireplaces and whirlpool tubs. Others are

SOUTHERN ILLINOIS

wheelchair-accessible. In addition to the cabins, there are units the resort calls "boatel," which essentially means they're right next to the lake and have decks looking out on the water. Rooms are also available in the lodge adjacent to the dining room, which serves everything from shrimp to quail.

Seasons Lodge (Rend Lake Recreation Complex, Golf Course Dr., Whittington, 800/999-0977, www.rendlake.org, $65–148) looks and feels more like a large modern country home than an actual hotel. There's also an outdoor swimming pool. Depending on what day of week you stay and whether or not you opt for features such as a fireplace in your room, room rates can vary quite a bit. Dining is also on-site.

Camping
If you're traveling in an RV, you're in luck. Around the lake there are hundreds of sites with electrical hookups. The Army Corps of Engineers has campsites in North Sandusky, South Sandusky, and South Marcum. Fees range from $12 for a walk-in tent site to $40 for a double family site with electrical hookup. Camping is allowed May 1–October 31. To make a reservation, you'll need to call the Reserve America reservation service at 877/444-6777 or www.reserveusa.com.

A cheaper option is staying at **Wayne Fitzgerrell State Park** (11094 Ranger Rd.,

Whittington, 618/629-2230, www.dnr.state. il.us), where there are 243 electric sites and 40 tent sites. Fees range $6–15 per night. Only 31 of the sites can be reserved; the others are available on a first-come, first-served basis.

FOOD
As the sun sets over the lake, sip some wine and sink your teeth into a lobster tail at **Rend Lake Resort** (11712 E. Windy Ln., Whittington, 618/629-2211 or 800/633-3341, www.rendlakeresort.net, 7 A.M.–9 P.M. Sun.–Thurs., 7 A.M.–10 P.M. Fri.–Sat.) in Wayne Fitzgerrell State Park. The resort has two restaurants with extensive menus: Reilley's Lounge is more casual, and Windows is the fancier restaurant with lake views. It serves breakfast foods, sandwiches, ribs, fried chicken, you name it. Windows's buffets always draw a crowd. A seafood buffet is on Friday nights, and a prime rib and pasta buffet is on Saturday nights. An average entrée is $15.

At **Gibby's on the Green** (Seasons Lodge/Rend Lake Resort, Golf Course Dr., Whittington, 618/629-2454, www.rendlake. org, breakfast, lunch, and dinner daily) you can order traditional American meals such as bacon and eggs and pancakes for breakfast, an Italian beef or fried-cod sandwich for lunch, and for dinner beef tips or rainbow trout. Sandwiches are around $5; dinner entrées are about $10–20.

Perry County

Although Perry County has had salt mined there, been home to successful meat-packing plants, creameries, and plenty of farms, its history is linked to coal. Situated above coal veins, Perry County started seeing coal mines and coal-related businesses established beginning in the mid to late-1800s. They thrived through the first half of the 20th century, but activity slowed down significantly in the 1970s through the 1990s after the Clean Air Act modified pollution rules and the high-carbon coal of Illinois

was no longer in demand. Anyone in town will tell you the local economy took a hit. Today Perry County is a largely rural county with livestock and grain farms. The hidden gem of the area is Pyramid State Park, a vast park with dozens of trails for mountain biking, hiking, and horseback riding.

SIGHTS AND RECREATION
Pyramid State Park
The beauty of Pyramid State Park (1562

Pyramid Park Rd., Pinckneyville, 618/357-2574, www.dnr.state.il.us) is that it's one of the state's underdeveloped parks. At 19,000 acres, it's also one of the largest. Most of the roads are gravel and the campsites are pretty rustic (meaning no electrical hookups). Almost 17 miles of hiking and horseback-riding trails encircle lakes, wrap around hills, and extend into the woods. A rarity in Illinois, there's a rough 12-mile trail that mountain bikers are welcome to explore. For a change of pace, the park has several areas where you can just sit at a picnic table or at the edge of a little lake and watch deer come out to eat in the evening or beavers as they build a dam. Several little lakes, such as Reed Lake, Heron Lake, and Marsh Lake, are scattered throughout the park, as are boat launches. Lakes have a 10-horsepower engine limit, but who needs an engine? Bring your canoe and slip into one of the lakes (Lost Lake, maybe?) and count how many times you see a fish jump. Park entrances are off Galum-Church Road and Pyatt-Cutler Road, about a mile west of Highways 127 and 13.

Perry County Jail Museum

Ostensibly a jail museum, the Perry County Jail Museum (108 W. Jackson St., Pinckneyville, 618/357-2225, 8 A.M.–4 P.M. Mon., 8 A.M.–noon Wed. year-round, 10 A.M.–3 P.M. Sat. Apr.–Dec., donation) is also a repository of sorts for local-history artifacts and a community center. (On Mondays quilters come and work in one of the front rooms.) Built in 1871, the building was initially a county jail building, one of many throughout the state where the sheriff lived adjacent to the jail and the sheriff's wife cooked for the prisoners. It remained a jail for more than 100 years, until 1987. During your tour you'll walk through the jail, inspect the drawings of cartoon characters and weapons on the walls, check out all the drug paraphernalia seized through the years, and investigate a part of the old shower area where a man once did escape by digging a hole (he was captured). The other rooms of the building, former offices and bedrooms, are stocked with local-history items. One room

has been converted into a one-room country schoolhouse, another highlights the area's coal history, and another features posters from old county fairs and packages from the old Blue Bell packing plant (as tour host Eunice said, if you've never tasted a Blue Bell wiener, you've never tasted a wiener).

EVENTS
Du Quoin State Fair

Even if you're not in town during the Du Quoin State Fair (U.S. 51, just north of Hwy. 14, Du Quoin, 618/542-1515, www.dnr.state.il.us, fairgrounds open at 10 A.M. daily), which takes place at the end of August and early September, if you love art deco, take a tour of the fairgrounds, first established in the 1920s. The grounds include livestock barns, a grandstand, concession stands, and other outbuildings. About 400,000 people come to the fair every year for its agricultural events, food, music concerts, and races. One of the main events of the fair is the World Trotting Derby, a horse-racing event.

Du Quoin State Fairgrounds

Farm Festival

Ever see an antique steam thresher perform its magic? It's a sight to see. The **American Thresherman Association** (Pinckneyville Fairgrounds, Hwys. 154, 127, and 13, 618/329-5573, www.americanthresherman.com) sets up camp for a show during the third weekend in August. The fest includes demonstrations of these magnificent (loud, smoky) machines harvesting wheat and other crops. Admire the vintage steam- and gas-powered plows and tractors, chat with some of the collectors (who can talk for hours about their machines), and watch other demos such as a blacksmithing workshop. There's also a good old parade through Pinckneyville.

SHOPPING

Downtown Pinckneyville and Du Quoin have several antiques shops, such as **Pinckneyville Antique Mall** (7 E. Jackson St., Pinckneyville, 618/357-8963) and **White Rabbit** (109 S. Walnut St., Pinckneyville, 618/357-8630).

ACCOMMODATIONS
Under $50

The **Mainstreet Inn** (112 S. Main St., Pinckneyville, 618/357-2128 or 800/455-7378) is a good bargain. The motel has 27 single or double rooms. Each comes with a desk, chair, alarm clock, and television. There is no continental breakfast, but coffee is always brewing at the front desk.

$50-100

If you don't have any plans to visit Du Quoin, you should at least come to the town for a stay at **C Francie's Bed and Breakfast Inn** (104 S. Line St., Du Quoin, 618/542-6686 or 877/877-2657, www.franciesinnonline.com, $70–115), a real treasure of an inn. The five rooms are gorgeous, but there are two spots to relax that make this inn stand out: an expansive front porch looking out onto an equally expansive front lawn, and a back deck overlooking gardens and more green lawn. The house, which sits on three acres, was built in 1908 as a home for orphaned children. But

don't imagine any kind of sparse whitewashed accommodations. Extras include wine in the evening and wireless Internet access throughout the house.

Another inn with plenty of room to wander is the **Oxbow B&B** (3967 Hwy. 13/Hwy. 127, Pinckneyville, 618/357-9839 or 800/929-6888, $65–80), which is situated on a 10-acre site with gardens and several sitting areas. A remodeled barn contains a hot tub and pool. Yes, a pool in a barn. The bed-and-breakfast has five rooms and one barn suite in a separate building. A full country breakfast is included.

Camping

Pyramid State Park (1562 Pyramid Park Rd., 618/357-2574, www.dnr.state.il.us) has several rustic campgrounds (no electricity) for tent camping, backpack camping, and people traveling with their horses. Some sites are hike-in, and others have tent pads with car or truck access. Fees are $6–8 per night.

FOOD

A southern Illinois tradition, **Alongi's** (18 W. Main St., Du Quoin, 618/542-2468, www.alongis.com, 11 A.M.–10 P.M. Mon.–Thurs., 11 A.M.–11 P.M. Fri.–Sat., 11 A.M.–9 P.M. Sun.) is an old-school Italian restaurant with quite the following among locals. It's been run by a local Italian family for decades. The menu is impressive, with panini sandwiches for under $6, pastas around $10, and an a surprising array of seafood dishes, including a lovely tilapia with artichokes, tomatoes, and olives in a white wine and butter sauce.

INFORMATION

Du Quoin and Pinckneyville have chambers of commerce where you can find out more information about lodging or attractions: **Pinckneyville Chamber of Commerce** (2 S. Main St., Pinckneyville, 618/357-3243, www.pinckneyville.com) and **Du Quoin Chamber of Commerce** (20 N. Chestnut St., Du Quoin, 800/445-9570, www.duquoin.org).

Carlyle Lake Region

Topping out around 26,000 acres, Carlyle Lake is just humongous. Like many of the state's big lakes, Carlyle is artificial (in fact, it's the largest reservoir in the state). Thousands of years ago and up until about 50 years ago, the region looked quite different. The Kaskaskia River flows southwest through here, and Native American tribes often traveled along its shores and in canoes from villages upriver south toward the town of Kaskaskia, where the river meets the Mississippi. An old buffalo trace passed through here, which the Indians and eventually pioneers followed. The trail ran from the salt mines near Shawneetown by the Ohio River to present-day Edwardsville. It became a popular trail because there was a natural rock ford in the river by the present-day town of Carlyle and eventually a bridge was built over it to accommodate more traffic. (The General Dean Bridge, as it is now called, is a suspension bridge listed on the National Register of

Historic Places. It's just north of U.S. 50 at the Kaskaskia River, before you enter the town of Carlyle. You can walk over it.)

This area was great for hunting and fishing, but the river often flooded, which became a problem as farmers started growing corn, wheat, and other crops. After a series of floods from the 1920s to the 1940s, a local attorney named Eldon Hazlet proposed a major damming project to control the river. After several years of raising money and soliciting Congress for the funds, the project was completed in 1967.

Carlyle Lake is shaped like a right-leaning kidney bean. The town of Carlyle, where you'll find grocery stores, hotels, and a few restaurants, is on the southern tip of the lake, just south of the dam. The Army Corps of Engineers has several recreation areas around the lake where there are boat launches and picnic tables. In addition, the Illinois Department

SOUTHERN ILLINOIS

© CHRISTINE DES GARENNES

Carlyle's historic General Dean Bridge

of Natural Resources has two state parks here. Eldon Hazlet State Park on the southwest shore, the larger and more developed of the two, has cottages for rent, a campground, an outdoor swimming pool, and several trails. South Shore State Park is across the lake from Eldon Hazlet in the southeast corner. It also has boat launches and camping but tends to be a little less crowded. Something to keep in mind: The eastern massasauga rattlesnake, an Illinois endangered species, lives in the Carlyle Lake area. This reclusive snake with black and brown spots on it tends to stick to the marshy areas around the lake. It's poisonous; if you get bitten, you probably won't die from it, but you should seek medical attention.

The **Carlyle Lake Visitor Center** (Dam West Recreation Area, Lake Rd., Carlyle, 618/594-5253) has displays on the dam's history, info on what kind of fish and animals are in the area, plus plenty of brochures and maps. It's open 10 A.M.–6 P.M. Saturday–Sunday April–May and in September except Labor Day weekend. It is open daily 10 A.M.–6 P.M. June–early September. The visitors center occasionally offers walking tours of the dam during the summer. The Carlyle Lake 24-hour information line is 618/594-4637.

CARLYLE LAKE FISH AND WILDLIFE AREA
Dam West Recreation Area
Just north of the town of Carlyle, off Highway 127 and County Road 1430N, is Dam West Recreation Area, where you'll find the visitors center, a large sandy swimming beach, boat launches, and nature trails. The Little Prairie Nature Trail is a 0.75-mile trail through woods and prairie adjacent to the dam area. You'll walk among such prairie grasses as little and big bluestem, and Indian and switch grass. The wood-chip and grass trail is an easy quiet walk. There's also a short hiking trail, the Willow Pond Nature Trail, near the visitors center. The beach is big and faces northeast, so it's a good place to soak up some morning sun. Bank anglers tend to stake out spots early in the Dam West area to fish for walleye, largemouth bass,

bluegill, white bass, and crappie. It costs $1 to use the beaches, which close at sunset. There is also a $3 boat-launching fee. The Army Corps of Engineers manages several other recreation areas on the lake, including **Keyesport Recreation Area** in the middle of the lake on the west side (east of Highway 127). It also has a marina, boat ramp, beach, and picnic area. It tends to be a bit less crowded than Eldon State Park and Dam West Recreation Area.

Eldon Hazlet State Park
Eldon Hazlet State Park (20100 Hazlet Park Rd., Carlyle, 618/594-3015, www.dnr.state. il.us) is one of the state's most popular parks. And why not? It's a family-friendly kind of place with activities for people of any age and fitness level, with large campgrounds for groups, RVers, and tent campers, as well as modern cottages, an outdoor swimming pool, several trails, boat launches, picnic areas, and playgrounds. The 3,000-acre park has tallgrass prairie, hardwood forest, and low brush areas. Throughout the park grow wildflowers, such as purple coneflowers, and several bluebird boxes have been installed near the trails in an effort to attract songbirds back to the area. There are nine miles of trails through here, many of them winding through wooded areas of the park and along the shore. The Cherokee Trail is one of the best. You'll walk under tall oaks and hickory trees, by a little cemetery with graves more than 150 years old, and by the lakeshore. Some trails are off-limits during pheasant-hunting season. Check with the ranger before you go hiking during the fall.

Boating is the big thing to do at Carlyle Lake. Within Eldon Hazlet State Park are three free boat ramps. The Peppenhorst Branch small boat launch is just south of the camp store and swimming pool in a quieter area of the park (it's easy to miss). If you have a small canoe or sailboat, this is a good spot to launch it. You can also come here to watch herons fishing or look for waterfowl that stop by the backwaters of the lake during the spring and fall. Hunting for deer, pheasants, doves, and some waterfowl is allowed in some

SOUTHERN ILLINOIS

© CHRISTINE DES GARENNES

observation area at Eldon Hazlet State Park

areas of the park during the season, which runs typically early November–mid-January. Permits are required from the office. The park is on the west side of the lake, about three miles north of the town of Carlyle, east of Highway 127.

South Shore State Park and Coles Creek Recreation Area

Across the lake from Eldon Hazlet Park is South Shore State Park (County Rd. 2200E, north of U.S. 50, Carlyle, 618/594-3015, www.dnr.state.il.us), a narrow 800-acre park in the southeast corner of the lake. It's a good spot for a short picnic on the shore or a walk along the 0.75-mile walking trail. As with many parks and areas near Carlyle Lake, bluebird boxes have been mounted here. There's a boat ramp for smaller fishing boats and canoes, and spots for bank fishing. Hickory Hollow Camping Area has 33 sites. North of South Shore State Park is the Army Corps of Engineers' Coles Creek Recreation Area, which has a beach on one of the lake's little bays, a boat ramp, plus camping with showers. It is just off County Road 1500N.

Carlyle Lake State Wildlife Management Area

On the northern tip of the lake is Carlyle Lake State Wildlife Management Area (618/425-3533), an area of about 9,600 acres that includes woods, wetlands, grasslands, and farmland. A good spot for bird-watching, the northern region is home to ducks, eagles, herons, turkeys, and doves. Up here there are several boat ramps for canoes and smaller fishing boats. The northernmost ramp, called the Hitogi Access Area, is on the Kaskaskia River off County Road 700N. There is parking for the wildlife area off County Road 450N, a few miles east of Highway 127; and off County Roads 450N, 500N, and 525N, a few miles west of U.S. 51.

SPORTS AND RECREATION
Boating

At **Carlyle Lake Rentals** (West Access Marina, 1422 Lake Rd., Carlyle, 618/594-4480) you can rent pontoon boats and houseboats. Pontoon boats costs $40 per hour and houseboats cost $150 per hour. Plus you will pay for gas. The houseboats come with extras such as grills, dishes, CD players, microwaves, and have an upper deck with a slide.

Carlyle Lake Wet Bike Rentals (Dam West Recreation Area, 618/594-8680, www.clwetbikes.com, sunrise–sunset daily May 1–Sept. 30) rents personal watercraft. Rates range $50–60 per hour depending on how long you rent. You pay for gas.

Amusement Park

Practice your batting and minigolfing skills at **Fisherman's Cove** (4211 N. 12th St., Carlyle, 618/594-2972), which also has bumper boats, go-karts, and other games. It's just off Highway 127 north of Carlyle.

ACCOMMODATIONS
$50-100

Microtel Inn and Suites Mariner's Village (1 Resort Dr., Carlyle, 618/594-7666, $65–85) is within a short walk from the Dam West Recreation Area and the beach, dam, marina, and trails. Take your pick from one of 65 rooms (singles, doubles, or one-room suites) in the hotel, or rent a log cabin (see the *$100–150* category for more information about the cabins). Guests have use of an outdoor swimming pool.

The cottages at **Eldon Hazlet State Park** (two miles east of Hwy. 127, Carlyle, 877/342-8862, www.carlylelakecottages.com, $96–115) are surprisingly affordable and pleasant. The 20 lakefront cottages, set in a less crowded area of the park, come with private boat docks and fish-cleaning stations. Inside, the living is pretty easy, with satellite television, gas fireplaces, and minikitchens with stoves, microwaves, and refrigerators. A short distance down the road the state park also has an outdoor swimming pool and campground store with groceries. Three cottages are wheelchair-accessible. There's parking outside the cottages if you bring your own boat.

The **Super 8** (1371 William Rd., U.S. 50 and Hwy. 127, Carlyle, 618/594-8888, $55–75) in Carlyle is a newer building with an indoor swimming pool. No fancy soaps or lotions here, but rooms are clean and the hotel is a short drive from the lake.

$100-150

The five cabins for rent at **Microtel Inn and Suites Mariner's Village** (1 Resort Dr., Carlyle, 618/594-7666, $120–160) are steps from the lake and the Dam West Recreation Area, meaning you can walk to the beach, dam, marina, and trail. The cabins come in two different styles: two-level lofts and one-level ranch-style cabins. Both styles can sleep up to six adults, and they include a gas fireplace, porch, bathroom, and heating and air-conditioning. They're not in a secluded area, but behind the hotel and near the marina, so if you're looking for privacy, you're probably better off renting a cottage at Eldon Hazlet. Still, they offer a nice alternative to standard hotel rooms. There is a five-night minimum for cabin rentals Memorial Day–Labor Day.

On the northwest side of the lake, about six miles from the Dam West Recreation Area, is **Hickory Shores Resort** (21925 Dove Ln., Carlyle, 618/749-5288, www.hickoryshoresresort.com, cabins $90–225), which has 148 campsites ($20–29), more than 12 cabins that sleep four people, and a few others that sleep up to 10. This is a recreation complex, complete with swimming pools, fishing ponds, tennis courts, miniature golf, and a recreation building with table tennis. Cabins have full kitchens, porches, fire pits, and picnic tables, and they come with air-conditioning.

Camping

The Carlyle Lake region has more than 600 campsites, about half of which are in the Eldon Hazlet and South Shore State Parks. **Eldon Hazlet State Park** (2100 Hazlet Park Rd., two miles east of Hwy. 127, Carlyle, 618/594-3015, www.dnr.state.il.us) has 328 camp sites. You can reserve sites 1–65; the others are available on a first-come, first-served basis. Fees range from $7 for tent camping only to $11 for those with electrical hookups. A majority of the sites are occupied by RVs. Tent campers can park by the RVers, but there are plenty of walk-in tent camping areas. This means you park your car in a lot and then carry your stuff to sites about 100 yards away. In the middle of the park is a camp store. Scattered throughout are playgrounds.

Hickory Hollow Camping Area at **South Shore State Park** (618/594-3015, www.dnr. state.il.us) has 33 sites near the lakeshore. No electrical hookups or showers here, but you could probably run to Eldon Hazlet if you need to shower. Fees are $7 per night. The park has a boat ramp for smaller fishing boats and canoes.

FOOD
American
Near but not on the lake, the **Dockside Diner** (Lake Rd., at the entrance to the Dam West Recreation Area, Carlyle, 618/594-4657, 6 A.M.–9 P.M. Sun.–Thurs., 6 A.M.–10 P.M. Fri.–Sat.) has a solid array of Midwestern cuisine: omelets and pancakes, Reuben sandwiches, fried walleye, and hot dogs. Sandwiches are around $6; dinner entrées such as ribs or fried walleye fillets with sides range $7–18. It serves breakfasts, lunches, and dinners. If you plan to spend a day on the lake, staff can prepare picnic baskets for you.

The black-and-white-themed **Fifties Cruisers Diner** (911 Fairfax St., Courthouse Sq., Carlyle, 618/594-5940, 10:30 A.M.–8 P.M. Mon.–Thurs., 10:30 A.M.–9 P.M. Fri., 7 A.M.–9 P.M. Sat., 7 A.M.–8 P.M. Sun.) in downtown Carlyle is a fun local gathering place that also has solid American eats: BLT, ham and cheese, and meatball sandwiches, plus basic breakfasts of eggs, meat, and toast. Breakfast and lunch costs around $5. Most dinners are around $8; however, a handful of entrées cost more, such as a 12-ounce rib eye for $15.

During the summer months you can grab an ice cream cone or sundae at **Scoops** (491 Fairfax St., Carlyle, 618/594-8799, 11 A.M.–8 P.M. Mon.–Thurs., 11 A.M.–9 P.M. Fri.–Sat., noon–8 P.M. Sun.) before heading to the beach or back to your boat.

Markets
Stock up on water and other essentials at **Carlyle IGA** (1110 S. 12th St., Carlyle, 618/594-3415) or **Super Valu** (U.S. 50 and Hwy. 127, Carlyle, 618/594-3522); both are full-service grocery stores.

INFORMATION
The city of Carlyle has a handy website (www. playandstaycarlyle.com) that contains updated lists and links to information about the lake and places to eat and stay. More information is available by contacting the city at 850 Franklin Street (618/594-2468). You can also pick up lake and area information in the **Carlyle Lake Visitor Center** (Dam West Recreation Area, Lake Rd., Carlyle, 618/594-5253).

CENTRALIA
A town rooted in oil and coal production and home to a state prison, Centralia is not exactly one of the top tourist destinations in the state. But it does have a great balloon festival every year, nice parks, and friendly restaurants that serve satisfying food.

Sights and Activities
For an admission fee of about $2, cheer on hot air balloon races or watch balloons glow in the evening as brass or bluegrass bands play. The **Centralia Balloonfest** (Foundation Park, Pleasant and McCord Sts., Centralia, 618/352-6789, www.centraliail.com), held in mid to late August, features a car show, fireworks display, cardboard boat races, and other fun events.

At the 235-acre **Foundation Park** (McCord St./Hwy. 161 and Pleasant Ave., Centralia, sunrise–11 P.M. daily, free) you can hike through restored prairie, visit a little chapel in the woods, or stop by a memorial for a 1947 mining accident in the area that killed more than 100 miners.

Food
Centralia's streets are dominated by casual national chain restaurants. But here are two good places to go to if you're looking for local color and you're in the mood to eat food that will fill you up. Load up your tray with napkins when you go to **Burger Haven** (U.S. 51, Centralia,

11 A.M.–8:30 P.M. Mon.–Thurs., 11 A.M.–9 P.M. Fri.–Sat., $4), where the cheese oozes down the sides of hamburgers and the chili is piled on top of cheese fries. This locally owned drive-through and sit-down restaurant offers burgers, hot dogs, fries, and ice cream.

The fare at **Centralia House Restaurant** (111 N. Oak St., Centralia, 618/532-9754, www.centraliahouserestaurant.com, 11 A.M.–2 P.M., 4–10 P.M. Mon.–Fri., dinner only Sat., $8–20) tends to have a New Orleans touch to it, such as a Creole shrimp entrée. Although many of the dinners cost around $20, you can still find a sandwich (try the andouille sausage sandwich) for about $8. Dress is casual in this historic restaurant facing the railroad tracks. The atmosphere is dark and clubby, with big booths and stained-glass windows.

SALEM

Most visitors to Salem, a town of about 8,000 people, don't venture beyond the gas stations or hotel rooms. Situated where I-57, U.S. 51, and Highway 37 meet, Salem is often dubbed the "Gateway to Little Egypt." Folks stop by here briefly on their way to southern Illinois or beyond. But drive a short distance west of the interstate and you'll find a lively little coffee house where you can order a latte. Drive a bit further and you can get a history lesson or two in William Jennings Bryan.

William Jennings Bryan Sights

The orator is perhaps most famous for his role as one of the prosecutors in the John Scopes Trial, the so-called Monkey Trial of 1925, in which teacher John T. Scopes was taken to task for teaching evolution in a Tennessee school. (Scopes, in an interesting twist, was also a Salem native.) Bryan, a three-time-nominated presidential candidate, was born in a modest house in Salem, now the **William Jennings Bryan Birthplace Home** (408 S. Broadway, Salem, 618/548-2222, noon–4:30 P.M. Mon., Wed., Sat., free). Bryan was born in the white clapboard house in 1860. His father, Silas, was a lawyer, judge, school superintendent, and state senator. Later Bryan would become a lawyer

himself, U.S. secretary of state, and crusader against evolution theory. About a mile or so away is a statue honoring Bryan at **Bryan Memorial Park** (North Broadway and Millett Dr.). Created by Mt. Rushmore sculptor Gutzon Borglum, the statue was dedicated by former U.S. President Teddy Roosevelt in 1934.

Stephen Forbes State Park

The highlight of the 3,100-acre Stephen Forbes State Park (6924 Omega Rd., Kinmundy, 618/547-3381, www.dnr.state.il.us) is its 200-foot-long beach, a rarity in central and southern Illinois. The 500-plus-acre lake is stocked with a variety of fish and is a popular destination for fishing. (There's a relatively new marina with a bait shop and restaurant.) The campground offers a "rent-a-camp," where you pay a few bucks to use the park's eight-person tents (along with cots, lights, and other camping tools), or you can stay in a two-room cabin with bunk beds. Otherwise, the park has 115 campsites with electrical hookups and 10 walk-in tent campsites for visitors wanting more rustic accommodations. The park is 14 miles northeast of Salem.

Shopping

South of town in the middle of an industrial and agribusiness district is the **Rusty Nail** (1101 S. Broadway, 618/548-3034, Salem, 10 A.M.–6 P.M. Tues.–Sat., 1–4 P.M. Sun.), a gift shop and antiques shop where you can find new and vintage garden accessories, from the practical, such as watering cans, to the not-so-practical, such as lawn ornaments.

Accommodations

Because it is situated where U.S. 50 meets I-57, Salem has a number of national chain hotels in its town, all of which are near these main thoroughfares. They include the **Comfort Inn** (1800 W. Main St., Salem, 618/548-2177, $68–130), which has an indoor swimming pool and continental breakfast; and **Super 8** (118 Woods Ln., Salem, 618/548-5882, $70), which also has continental breakfast. The Super 8 will accept pets.

Washington County

Once a posh destination for the wealthy and even a gangster or two, Okawville (pronounced "O-ka-ville") is now a quiet rural community. Like many other towns in Washington County, about an hour drive southeast of St. Louis, Okawville and nearby Nashville have German and Polish roots. In the late 1800s Okawville sprang up from relative obscurity after mineral springs there were reportedly found to possess curative powers for people suffering from arthritis and other ailments. The Original Springs bathhouse, listed on the National Register of Historic Places, still stands as a main attraction in the county (although it's a little fading and in need of the remodeling it has been undergoing). In addition to the bathhouse, the towns have a few small local-history museums and antiques shops.

OKAWVILLE
Original Springs Bathhouse

Saddle and harness shop owner Rudolph Plegge needed water for his business, so he dug a well, as most business owners would do. But his kettles were leaking and he wondered if something in the water was causing the corrosion. He hired a firm to test the water and discovered it had lots of potassium, zinc, iron, iodine, calcium, magnesium, and other minerals. He shifted entrepreneurial gears and partnered with a local farmer who had worked in mineral baths in Europe. In 1868 they opened a bathhouse, now called the Original Springs (506 N. Hanover St., Okawville, 618/243-5458). They spread the word that folks suffering from arthritis and other rheumatoid conditions could alleviate their symptoms by soaking in their waters. Soon other hotels and bathhouses popped up in the area, and Washington County became bathhouse central. In 1893 a fire destroyed Plegge's building, but it was rebuilt the same year. This building still stands, although it has been remodeled several times throughout the decades. And another phased-in renovation is planned by the current owners.

(A good idea, because the hotel was showing its age with peeling paint and sagging floors.) Today the hotel still offers pampering services (massages, manicures, pedicures, body wraps) at nonexclusive prices. Spa admission is $15 for hotel guests and $23 for those not staying at the hotel. The hotel has a swimming pool, steam rooms, game room, restaurant, and 33 guest rooms. Stop by the restaurant if you're interested in seeing the building but not a massage or mineral bath soak.

Museums

Okawville has two museum complexes. The **Schlosser Home, Harness Shop, and Laundry** (114 W. Walnut St., Okawville, 618/243-5694, noon–4 P.M. Sat.–Sun., most afternoons Mon., Wed., Fri., $2 donation) is a collection of several buildings (a home, laundry building, outhouse) set up as if they were operating at the turn of the 20th century. The house is nice enough, but how often do you get to see what a laundry shop used to look like 100 years ago? It's like an earlier version of today's dry cleaners. Ironing boards are set up and several irons (made of real iron) are placed nearby, as if a worker had just taken it off the stove to cool. A few blocks away is the **Dr. Poos Home** (202 N. Front St., Okawville, 618/243-5694, open by appointment, donation) a pink Second Empire building once home to the local medical doctor. Built in 1888, it was actually originally designed to be a bathhouse. For a glimpse of Okawville's intriguing past, call the Okawville Chamber of Commerce and arrange a tour. The home has plenty of photographs of Okawville back when it was the place to be.

NASHVILLE
Rainbow Ranch

Yes, zoos are fun, but at the Rainbow Ranch (9906 Hwy. 15, nine miles west of Nashville, 618/424-7979, 9 A.M.–5 P.M. Wed.–Sat., noon–5 P.M. Sun. Apr.–Oct., $3) you can get up close and personal with the animals—llamas, sheep, cows, peacocks, a pot-bellied pig, and "Simon, the Kissing Camel." Bring shoes or boots that you can get muddy (and put in a plastic bag in the trunk of the car after your visit) at this petting zoo and exotic animal farm.

Log Chapel

Reportedly the smallest chapel in the world at about 96 square feet, the log chapel at the Little Nashville Truck Stop (I-64 and Hwy. 127, 618/327-3700) was built in the 1980s as a place for weary travelers to take a break from the road and read Bible passages carved into wood. Supposedly you can fit about 10–18 people inside; someone did get married here. It's open all the time.

Washington County Conservation Area

A 1,440-acre retreat south of Nashville and I-64, the Washington County Conservation Area (18500 Conservation Dr., Nashville, 618/327-3137, www.dnr.state.il.us) has a great

seven-mile hiking trail around the 248-acre Washington Lake and through hardwood and pine woods. It's also a great park for fishing if you prefer quiet lakes. Rent a fishing boat with a trolling motor or drop a line from the fishing pier. Boats rent for $20 for a six-hour period or $36 for 12 hours. A few private, wooded RV and tent campsites overlook the lake. The park is just east of Highway 127 between Nashville and Pinckneyville.

Accommodations and Food

Within walking distance of downtown, the **Nashville Motel** (346 E. St. Louis St., Nashville, 618/327-4472, under $50) is a small white motor lodge with clean rooms. Over by I-64, the newer **U.S. Inn Best Western** (11640 Hwy. 127, Nashville, 618/478-5341, about $50) has an outdoor swimming pool, a laundry room for guests, free high-speed Internet access, and offers guests a continental breakfast.

Washington County Conservation Area (18500 Conservation Dr., Nashville, 618/327-3137, www.dnr.state.il.us) has tent and RV

Washington County Conservation Area, near Nashville

© CHRISTINE DES GARENNES

camping, rustic sites with pit toilets, and a modern shower building. Some sites overlook the lake. Rates are $8–15.

Northwest of Nashville, it seems the entire town of Addieville (which has a population of less than 300) hangs out at the **Eagle's Nest** (120 W. Front St., Addieville, 618/424-7777, food 11 A.M.–10 P.M. daily, bar open later). Given its proximity to St. Louis, perhaps it's not surprising that Addieville residents are fans of St. Louis sports teams: The walls of the Eagle's Nest are plastered with St. Louis Cardinals and Blues paraphernalia. The food here is solid too, focusing on seafood (the walleye platter is a good bet) and red meat, such as prime rib.

INFORMATION

Staff at the **Nashville Chamber of Commerce** (247 E. St. Louis St., Nashville, 618/327-3700) or **Okawville Chamber of Commerce** (P.O. Box 345, Okawville 62271, 618/243-5694) are eager to talk with visitors coming into the area, so give them a call before you swing by.

Vandalia

Home to the oldest surviving Illinois capitol building, Vandalia is a good place for amateur historians and Lincoln fans to visit. So the town lacks the quaint shops, galleries, and restaurants of other historic towns in Illinois, such as Galena, but the building is remarkably well-preserved. You can easily imagine newly elected state representative Abraham Lincoln walking the halls and sitting at the desks taking notes.

SIGHTS
Vandalia Statehouse
State Historic Site

Springfield has not always been the capital of Illinois. Before Abraham Lincoln and a group of legislators dubbed the "Long Nine" lobbied to move the capital to Springfield, it was in Vandalia, a bustling town on the Kaskaskia River. (And before Vandalia, it was the town of Kaskaskia on the Mississippi River.) Dominating downtown, the Vandalia Statehouse State Historic Site (103 W. Gallatin St., Vandalia, 618/283-1161, typically 9 A.M.–5 P.M. Wed.–Sun. Mar.–Nov., 9 A.M.–4 P.M. Wed.–Sun. Nov.–Feb., but call ahead for hours) is a large white federal-style building. It's the oldest surviving Illinois capitol building. State government was headquartered here 1820–1839.

The first capitol building was a plain two-story frame house. State officials met here but conducted the bulk of their work in their homes or other buildings. After this building burned down, they hurried to build another one in 1824. Ten years later the quickly built structure had sagging floors and other construction defects. So they planned for another building. What visitors see today is the third building, finished in 1836. This one, while built much more solidly, as you will see, would not serve as the capitol for long. Three years later the capitol was moved to Springfield, thanks in part to Lincoln, who did serve here as a young legislator.

The building has been wonderfully preserved, and it does look the way you might imagine it would have looked while legislators were in town. The secretary of state's office and treasurer's office contain period furnishings of large desks lined with tall half-burned candles, ledgers and books, and quill pens. The second floor, featuring original hardwood flooring, contains the state senate and house of representatives chambers. If you're in the area during December, stop by for the candlelight tour.

Fayette County Museum

More local historic photographs and documents on Vandalia can be found at the Fayette County Museum (U.S. 51 and Main St., Vandalia, 618/283-4866, 9:30 A.M.–4 P.M. Mon.–Sat. year-round, 1–4 P.M. Sun.

© CHRISTINE DES GARENNES

Vandalia, the state capital before Springfield

Apr.–Dec., donation), less than a block north of the capitol building in a former Presbyterian church. The collection includes a printing press used in the Vandalia capitol building and Civil War uniforms.

SPORTS AND RECREATION
Skydiving

Each year about 12,000 people jump out of the Cessna planes run by **Archway Skydiving** (Vandalia City Airport, Airport Rd., I-70 Exit 61, Vandalia, 618/283-4973, www.archway skydiving.com), a local skydiving school where an episode of MTV's adventure reality show *Road Rules* was once filmed. After spending about 15 minutes in the plane, you'll jump out of an airplane at 4,000–14,000 feet. The trip down takes about six minutes. You can jump with someone in a tandem setup or by yourself. Dives for beginners start around $169, with discounts for college students.

Outdoor Recreation

Ramsey Lake State Park (one mile west of U.S. 51 on County Rd. 2900N, Ramsey, 618/936-2469, www.dnr.state.il.us) is a 2,000-acre park that appears geared toward sportsmen. Long before it became a state park, the area was popular among hunters of raccoons and foxes. Today, during the fall, you can hunt for deer, pheasant, and believe it or not, squirrels. For the most part though, most of the park's attraction is its lake and the fishing opportunities. Drop a line for bluegill, largemouth bass, and other Illinois fish. What's great about Ramsey is that it's one of the quieter lakes; gas motors are not allowed (although anglers are allowed to troll for fish using an electric motor). Park staff maintain a boat ramp and dock and rent rowboats for a few dollars. In addition to fishing, you can ride horses or hike along a 13-mile horse trail that winds through the park. There is also a campground with 95 sites. Half of those are in an area called Hickory Grove, where the sites are more rustic (no running water or electricity), but quieter, more secluded, and in a wooded area. The other sites have electricity, a bathhouse with showers, and tend to be frequented by RVs. Nightly camping fees range $6–15.

If you're interested in speedboating, head to **Vandalia Lake** (Hwy. 185, four miles northwest of Vandalia, 618/283-4770). You'll have to buy a $10–15 day pass from Vandalia's city hall (219 S. 5th St.) or at the marina (4–6 P.M. Mon.–Fri., 10 A.M.–7 P.M. Sat., 11 A.M.–6 P.M. Sun.). The marina also sells bait. The lake is stocked with bass, catfish, and bluegill. There's a wheelchair-accessible fishing pier near the marina, which is just inside the main entrance from the highway. To the left of the lake's entrance is **Jaycees Beach** (noon–5:30 P.M. Mon.–Fri., 10 A.M.–6:30 P.M. Sat., 11 A.M.–6 P.M. Sun.), where everyone goes swimming. There's a bathhouse with showers and plenty of picnic tables in the area. A lifeguard is on duty during the day.

INFORMATION AND SERVICES

The **Vandalia Tourist Information Center** (1408 N. 5th St., just off I-70 and U.S. 51, 618/283-2728), staffed by cheery locals, has tons of brochures and magazines about regional attractions as well as some from throughout the state. There are restrooms too.

Feeling ill? The **Fayette County Hospital** (7th and Taylor Sts., Vandalia, 618/283-1231) serves the region surrounding Vandalia.

The National Road: Effingham to Greenup

EFFINGHAM

Who and what you'll find in Effingham are 100 percent Midwestern: a museum devoted to Corvettes, a giant cross on the side of the highway, and anglers spending a Saturday on the lake. At the intersection of I-57 and I-70, Effingham is a crossroads town, and the majority of the economic activity is at the exits of these interstates, focused around hotels and chain restaurants. Around 12,000 people live here. They work in manufacturing (printing or painting), agriculture (either on the farm or for an ag-related business), or the service industry. The town was established and grew in the mid to late 1800s after several rail lines sliced through town. Effingham is still a railroad town; freight trains pass daily, and two Amtrak trains stop by each day. Thousands and thousands of travelers, truckers, and other people zip by Effingham daily, one of the reasons why a group of folks chose the city as the site of a massive cross.

Sights and Activities

Situated at the edge of an industrial park, just off I-57/70, **The Cross at the Crossroads** (Exit 159, I-57/I-70, 217/347-2846, www.crossusa.org, 10 A.M.–7 P.M. daily, free) is a towering, glaring white structure that attracts everyone from truck drivers to minivans full of

Effingham's Cross at the Crossroads

U.S. 40: THE NATIONAL ROAD

In 1806 Congress authorized money to build a road that would extend from Cumberland, Maryland, to the Northwest Territory. The first federal highway, the National Road would become the route most pioneers followed to the west, earning the nickname "the road that built a nation." Until the steamboat and railroad era in the 1850s, the National Road was the major east-west thoroughfare for stagecoaches and covered wagons. With the development of the automobile, the National Road became U.S. 40, a two-lane highway. In Illinois, U.S. 40 stretches for about 150 miles from the state line to East St. Louis. The highway still exists, but now it's overshadowed by I-70, which also moves in a southwest diagonal across the state.

The National Road in Illinois does not pass any mountains or canyons, but it's still an awesome drive. It's a nostalgic route through the core of Middle America. You'll drive through towns like Greenup, dubbed the "city of porches," with its antiques stores and winery; quiet Teutopolis, site of an old monastery; Altamont, with its homespun farm museum; Vandalia, where Abraham Lincoln served as a state legislator; and finally Collinsville, home of the giant Brooks Catsup bottle (a water tower). Travel the road by yourself or with a group of other two-lane-road enthusiasts. The National Road Association of Illinois (217/849-3188, www.nationalroad.org) organizes the **National Road Festival** every year in mid-June. Several communities along the road host ice cream socials, garage sales, music concerts, and car shows.

---

families. The cross itself is nearly 200 feet tall and 113 feet wide and was completed in 2001. You can't actually go inside the cross or climb to the top, but you can stand below it or sit at one of the many benches arranged in a circle at its bottom. Surrounding the cross are polished granite stones with the Ten Commandments carved into them. During your visit, orchestral music booms out of speakers (made to look like granite rocks). At the visitors center, you can watch a short film about how the regional foundation built the cross. A visitors center on the site sells religious items. A chapel is planned to be built in the future.

The motto of **MY Garage Corvette Museum** (at Mid America Motorworks, 1 Mid America Pl., 17082 N. U.S. 45, Effingham, 217/347-5591 or 800/500-1500, www.mamotorworks.com, 8 A.M.–5 P.M. Mon.–Sat., free) should be "all Corvettes, all the time." You've got rare racecars and show cars so polished they look brand new—as if they had never been driven before. Detailed displays accompany the cars, complete with mannequins dressed in attire appropriate to when the car was developed. The shop stocks parts and accessories for collectors. Mid America Motorworks hosts several car shows throughout the year, including a Corvette fest in mid-September and a Beetle FunFest in early June.

Got an urge to fish? Launch your boat at **Lake Sara** on Effingham's northwest side. You can park your truck and slide the boat into the lake at **J&J Marina** (8641 E. Marine Dr., follow Beach Rd. from 1600th Rd., rural Effingham, 217/868-2791). A launch will cost you $4. Near the marina is a public beach, south of Moccasin Road and off Beach Road.

Accommodations and Food

A cluster of national chain hotels and motels is near the I-57 and I-70 exits in Effingham. One good option is **Comfort Suites** (1310 W. Lafayette Ave., Effingham, 217/342-3151, $68–130), which has an indoor pool, offers continental breakfast, and allows pets. On the outskirts of town are two cottage and campground options. **Anthony Acres Resort** (15286 N. Resort Rd., Effingham, 217/868-2950, www.anthonyacres.com, $57–125), a fishing resort, has motel rooms near Lake Sara. (Request a room in the newer motel building.)

It has a boat dock and a little sandy beach for guests. **Camp Lakewood** (1217 W. Rickelman Ave., Effingham, 217/342-6233, www.camplakewoodcampground.com, Mar.–Nov.), has sites above 33-acre Lake Pauline, also a fishing lake. There's no sandy beach, but there is a boat ramp, which campers are free to use. The woodsy campground is mostly populated by people staying in RVs, although there are some tent sites. The campground rents rowboats.

Slide into a pea-green booth at **Betty's Café** (125 E. Jefferson St., Effingham, 217/342-3584, 6 a.m.–2 p.m. Mon.–Fri.) and you'll swear you were being transported back several years (maybe even decades). At this mom-and-pop coffee shop a plate of eggs, potatoes, and toast will set you back about $3. A noontime meal of meatloaf? About $5.

Information

If you have any questions about the area, the staff at the **Effingham Chamber of Commerce and Convention and Visitors Bureau** (903 N. Keller Dr., Effingham, 217/342-4147, www.effinghamchamber.org) should be able to help.

Getting There

Effingham has an **Amtrak** station downtown (401 W. National Ave., Effingham, 800/872-7245, www.amtrak.com). The City of New Orleans, Illini, and Saluki trains each stop here once daily. They all go to and from Chicago. **Greyhound** (2500 N. 3rd St./U.S. 45, 217/342-4075) buses stop at the McDonald's on U.S. 45.

ALTAMONT

A small but dynamic farming community, Altamont (population 2,283) is just north of I-70 and west of Effingham on U.S. 40, the National Road. It's a delightful town with a few surprises: an old church that hosts lively bluegrass concerts, a nature center with beautiful, quiet walking trails, and a hometown café.

Sights and Activities

Ballard Nature Center (5253 Hwy. 40, Altamont, 618/483-6856, free) is a real gem, especially if you are looking for an easy peaceful hike. No bicycles, all-terrain vehicles, or horses are allowed on these trails. There's no hunting ever, and pets must be leashed. Sure, there are a lot of rules, but when you walk along the trails—through restored prairie, past wildflowers, a wetland, woods, or above a creek—you'll hear only the sound of your feet crunching on wood chips or stepping on the occasional twig. (OK, and maybe some woodpeckers, squirrels, and the wind rustling through the wheat.) Because of the quietness of this place, birding is big here. You can look for birds while walking on one of the trails or have a seat in the newer nature center and watch as the birds feed outside the picture windows. Staff have placed several binoculars near the window for guests to use. Along the trails are several signposts that illustrate which creatures, plants, or flowers you might encounter on your walks. All in all, it's a welcoming place, with a few treasures, such as a tiny cemetery that dates to the 1800s. The trails are open

Ballard Nature Center, Altamont

© CHRISTINE DES GARENNES

SOUTHERN ILLINOIS

dawn–dusk daily. The visitors center is open 8 A.M.–4 P.M. Monday–Friday, noon–4 P.M. Saturday, 1–4 P.M. Sunday.

It's called the **Altamont Living Museum** (102 S. Main St., Altamont, 618/483-3333, www.altamontlivingmuseum.org), but basically it's a community center. The 1912 church (with dazzling Tiffany stained-glass windows) hosts bluegrass concerts every Tuesday evening, plays and musicals by local actors, lectures or discussions about topics such as World War II, local art shows, and other concerts by area musicians.

Get your road-trip food—creamy ice cream and crispy French fries—at the **Dairy Bar** (600 S. Main St., Altamont, 618/483-5656), a red-and-white-striped building just south of the National Road.

TEUTOPOLIS

The monks are long gone, but you can learn about their presence in Teutopolis, a town of about 1,600 people just east of Effingham, at the **Monastery Museum** (adjacent to St. Francis church, 110 S. Garrett St., Teutopolis, 217/857-3586, 12:30–4 P.M. first Sun. of the month Apr.–Nov. and by appointment, $3). Exhibits highlight the history of the Franciscan monastery that was built 1858–1904. Items on view include vintage bibles, clothes the monks wore, and furniture from the monastery. Additional museum displays are about the region's agricultural history. Behind the museum is a park with a few religious statues, a grotto, a playground, and basketball courts.

GREENUP

Billed as the "village of porches," Greenup has become somewhat of a burgeoning tourist destination. Just off the National Road, south of I-70, and along the rambling Embarras River, the town boasts a winery, a covered bridge, a restored train depot, and a handful of antiques shops and restaurants. It also claims a Lincoln connection. On their journey from Indiana into Illinois, Lincoln's family reportedly camped for a few nights in Greenup.

OLNEY'S WHITE SQUIRRELS

An oil-drilling town in the state's sparsely populated southeastern corner, the town of Olney continues to attract curious visitors every year for its high population of white squirrels. In this town the white squirrels (technically they're albino gray squirrels) have the right of way. A badge with an image of the white squirrel is featured on the City of Olney's uniforms. And white-squirrel-crossing signs are dotted throughout town. The squirrels have been in town at least since 1902, when according to local lore one or two area farmers reportedly caught albino squirrels and then displayed them for visitors to see. Later they were released in town, and one thing led to another. Today the white squirrel population is estimated at around 120.

The squirrels are all over town, but the most common place to see them is at Olney City Park, just off Highway 130. More information is available from the **City of Olney** (300 S. Whittle Ave., Olney, 618/395-7302) or **Olney and the Greater Richland County Chamber of Commerce** (201 E. Chestnut St., Olney, 618/392-2241, www.olneychamber.com).

Sights and Activities

The tasting room at **Cameo Vineyards** (400 Mill Rd., Greenup, 217/923-9963, www.cameowine.com, 10 A.M.–5 P.M. Tues.–Sat., noon–5 P.M. Sun.) could be one of the best that Illinois wineries have to offer. In a turn-of-the-20th-century barn, it overlooks a vineyard and has cozy chairs and a roaring fireplace. The wines are pretty grand too.

On your way out to the winery, drive through the **Cumberland County Covered Bridge** (Cumberland St., one mile west of Greenup, 217/923-9322). This 200-foot-long bridge over the Embarras River was built recently to resemble bridges that were once common throughout the region.

© CHRISTINE DES GARENNES

Greenup, "the village of porches"

SOUTHERN ILLINOIS

Continuing the rural theme, stop by **Grissom Lost Creek Orchards** (Hwy. 130, 1.5 miles north of Greenup, 217/923-3736, 9 A.M.–6 P.M. daily spring–fall) to stock up on apples, peaches, plums, nectarines, and melons. At Lost Creek Orchards you can find about 100 different varieties of apples (including heirloom varieties) beginning in August and continuing through November. The store also sells cider, homemade jams, and crafts. During the fall, **Earthborne Farm** (754 County Rd. 1625E, Greenup, 217/923-3035, 5–10 P.M. Fri., noon–10 P.M. Sat., noon–8 P.M. Sun. Oct.) opens its gates to the public for its pumpkin patch, petting zoos, and straw maze. The farm is 0.5 mile west of Greenup off Highway 121.

The Greenup Depot (204 W. Cumberland St., Greenup, 217/923-9306, noon–4 P.M. Tues.–Sun., free), which dates back to the 1870s, is currently being restored to reflect its past. It is open during restoration, and visitors can tour the waiting room and view model trains and displays of antique railroad tools.

Antiques

Stroll through downtown Greenup on Cumberland Road and peek inside some of the antiques shops. The mazelike **Greenup Antiques Mall** (15 E. Illinois St., Greenup, 217/923-9322, 9 A.M.–5 P.M. Mon.–Sat., 11 A.M.–5 P.M. Sun.) is a musty old shoe factory packed with furniture, including pie safes and bedroom bureaus, antique kitchen utensils, farm tools, records, dolls, and glassware. **Cumberland Road Collectibles** (100 W. Cumberland St., Greenup, 217/923-5260, 9 A.M.–5 P.M. Wed.–Sat., noon–5 P.M. Sun.) has posters, magazines, books, advertisements, china, and an assortment of collectibles. **The Tin Ceiling** (101 W. Cumberland St., Greenup, 217/923-3877) sells a variety of antiques, from affordable to high-end, including primitives, furniture, and garden supplies.

Accommodations and Food

The **Daisy Inn** (315 E. Illinois St., Greenup, 217/923-3050, about $130), a big white farmhouse, is within walking distance of downtown

Greenup's shops and restaurants. It has one-bedroom cottages with full kitchens. The 29-room **Budget Host** (716 E. Elizabeth St., Greenup, 217/923-3176) has rooms for about $50.

The Stockyards (119 S. Kentucky St., Greenup, 217/923-9367, food 4:30–9 P.M. Tues.–Thurs., 11 A.M.–9 P.M. Fri.–Sun., lounge open later) cooks up black Angus steaks and dishes such as beef and noodles and ham loaf.

Information

The village of Greenup maintains a helpful website, www.villageofgreenup.com, that lists area attractions and contact information for area lodging and dining.

Moonshine

After receiving national attention for its out-of-this-world burgers on television shows such as *CBS Sunday Morning,* Moonshine (6017 E. 300th Rd., Martinsville, 618/569-9200, lunch Mon.–Sat.) has been transformed from a local secret to a tourist destination. You may even see a tour bus parked outside. No matter how popular it gets or how many people they feed, the owners, Roy Lee and Helen Tuttle, are still cooking up thick juicy Moonburgers and cold-cut sandwiches for a few bucks. Once a country store, Moonshine has antiques scattered about among benches and picnic tables. This is a rural community, and people eat early here; order by 12:30 P.M. or you might not get a burger.

BACKGROUND

The Land

Right smack in the middle of the Midwest, Illinois is considered part of a transitional region, the land between the eastern forests and the treeless central plains. It's not as hilly and woodsy as Ohio, not yet level and expansive as the Nebraskan plains. Most folks, when they think of Illinois, think of the central region: cornfield followed by soybean field, followed by a slight slope in the land, followed by grain elevator. Illinois's nickname, after all, is the prairie state.

Much of the state's midsection is flat, but there's so much more than level farmland in Illinois. There are savannas, grasslands, wetlands, upland and bottomland forests, craggy ravines, sandy dunes, lofty sandstone bluffs, waterfalls, sinkholes, and limestone caves. Rivers, such as the Illinois, Sangamon, and Rock, crisscross the state with woods clustered along their sides. The grand Mississippi River lines the western border. To the southeast are the Ohio and Wabash Rivers. And let's not forget Lake Michigan, which plays prominently in the northeastern part of the state.

Much of Illinois's topography—the rich farmland in the central region, the myriad lakes in the northeast, the sandy dune region along parts of the Illinois River—were produced by glaciers thousands of years ago. The only regions spared from advancing and retreating

© CHRISTINE DES GARENNES

ILLINOIS STATE SYMBOLS

- **Bird:** cardinal
- **Animal:** white-tailed deer
- **Insect:** monarch butterfly (seen May to October)
- **Fish:** bluegill
- **Reptile:** eastern painted turtle
- **Amphibian:** eastern tiger salamander
- **Tree:** white oak
- **Flower:** violet
- **Prairie grass:** the towering big bluestem (recognizable by its turkey foot-like top)

- **Mineral:** fluorite, found in southern Illinois
- **Soil:** the dark and rich drummer silty clay loam (it's why so much of the central part of the state is cropland)
- **Fossil:** tully monster, a soft-bodied carnivore with a long tail and fins
- **Slogan:** Land of Lincoln
- **Dance:** The square dance (thank you, Governor Jim Thompson)
- **Snack food:** popcorn (could it be anything else?), grown on tens of thousands of acres in the state

glaciers were the far northwest corner of the state by Galena (called the Driftless Area), the far southern tip of the state in the Shawnee National Forest, and Calhoun County in west-central Illinois. These areas are hilly, full of caverns, ravines, eroded sandstone bluffs, and other stunning geological landmarks.

FORMATION

Rewind time to 150,000 years ago and most of Illinois was covered by ice. The glaciation was massive. It stretched across 85 percent of the state, in some places as thick as 2,000 feet. This glacier, called the Illinois, pushed as far south as the northern edge of the Ozark Range to Carbondale.

The second glacier that shaped the state's topography was the Wisconsin glacier about 18,000–12,000 years ago. It reached across the northern and east-central part of the state and is credited with creating Lake Chicago (later Lake Michigan) and the Chain O' Lakes in Lake County. The Wisconsin glacier also had a significant influence on shaping the Illinois River valley. About 12,000 years ago, massive amounts of melting glacial water poured down the valley, eroding the surface and river channels. Westerly winds blew sand and soil throughout the region and formed dunes around modern-day Havana and surrounding areas. As a result of the flood, water filled lakes around the Illinois River. And over time, these lakes slowly filled up with sediment, and some became marshes and wet prairies.

After the Wisconsin glacier retreated, the state had areas of boreal forest found now in northern Canada. Through time the climate warmed, and the forests gradually shifted to bottomland forests, savannas, and prairies. Up until the 1800s when the white pioneers started moving in, the state was chock-full of oak groves and prairies, and native forests in the north and south. Gradually settlers cut the trees for timber and drained the wet prairies for farming. Forests, which once covered 42 percent of the state, now comprise about 5 percent of the terrain. When French explorers arrived in the late 1670s, the prairie covered about 23 million acres of the upper two-thirds of the state. Now you'll find about 2,200 acres of native prairie. Most of the remaining native prairie is near the Mississippi and Illinois Rivers.

GEOGRAPHY

Stretching about 385 miles from north to south and 218 miles wide in the center of the state, Illinois is diverse, not only in topography but also in climate and flora and fauna. It's a fascinating state to tour. Based on the state's geology, glacial history, soil compositions, and animal and plant habitat, scientists have recognized 14 natural divisions in the state. They include the Driftless Area in the northwest, the Rock River hill country near Freeport and Oregon, the Northeast Moraine surrounding Chicagoland, the Grand Prairie in the central part of the state, the Southern Till Plain in the south-central part of the state, and the Wabash Border division along the eastern part of the state. In the far southern region of Illinois are the Shawnee Hills and the Coastal Plain divisions. West from the Shawnee Hills is the Ozark division, just east of the Mississippi River. The Mississippi River runs through four natural divisions in Illinois: the Upper Mississippi River and Illinois River bottomlands, the Illinois River and Mississippi River Sands, the Middle Mississippi Border division, and the Lower Mississippi River Bottomlands east of St. Louis. Finally, there's also the Western Forest near Galesburg and Carlinville.

Here's a look at some of the more prominent divisions. The Driftless Area is a small corner in the northwest near Galena, often cited as one of the most scenic areas in the state. The glaciers skirted around this region, and as a result the area is much more rugged. The highest point in the state, Charles Mound, is here (not in the Shawnee Hills to the south, as one might think). For a good look at the geology of this area, hike through **Apple River Canyon State Park** near Millville to admire the cliffs and flora such as wood violets and ferns. East of the Driftless Area is the **Rock River Hill Country** near the towns of Freeport and Oregon. The scenic Rock River rolls through this area, through hills, limestone, sandstone bedrock, pines, and more ferns.

The Northeast Moraine division around Chicago consists of the dune habitat along Lake Michigan (visit **Illinois Beach State Park** to see this), the scrub oak forests and marshes surrounding Chicago, moraines formed by

© CHRISTINE DES GARENNES

The state is a leading producer of corn.

glaciers piling up rock and debris, and lakes and bogs formed by retreating glaciers. (Don't miss **Volo Bog** near Ingleside.) The northeast is home to many lakes created by the glaciers. The Chain O' Lakes region, just south of the Wisconsin border, is a prime example and popular for boating and fishing.

As you move south, the **Grand Prairie** includes the flat, rich farmland areas in central Illinois, with some marshes, scrub oak forest, and the Shelbyville and Bloomington moraines (yes, there are some hills!).

Bordering the eastern part of the state from Danville and south to the Shawnee Hills is the Wabash Border division, which includes the magnificent and sometimes underrated **Vermilion River** system. To the south are the Wabash and Ohio River valleys. This region is marked by thick deciduous forests, sandstone ravines, more marshes, and river floodplains. Take a canoe ride down the Middle Fork River while you're along the eastern edge of the state.

Farther south is the **Shawnee Hills** region, which teems with outdoor opportunities. Hikers and bikers, get ready to salivate; you'll see one bluff, ravine, and stream after the other. The fall brings out many apple pickers and leaf peepers. Next door to the Shawnee Hills (and often lumped together with the region) is the Coastal Plain, famous for its bottomland forests of cypress and tupelo tree swamps in the **Cache River** area. Although untouched by the glaciers, this region was still affected as flood waters surged in the area creating swamps. Believe it or not, this is the northernmost extension of the Gulf Coastal Plain.

The Mississippi River and Illinois River corridors are divided into several sections: The Upper Mississippi River and Illinois River bottomlands near Alton and Père Marquette State Park have bottomland forests, bogs, backwater lakes, and bluffs; the Middle Mississippi Border section and Lower Mississippi River Bottomlands division are also referred to as the American Bottoms. This low-lying area is east of St. Louis, near Cahokia, and frequently floods. It has rich farmland, wet prairies, marshes, and few trees.

Rivers

With the exception of the northeastern part of the state, Illinois does not have many natural lakes, compared with Wisconsin or Minnesota. But we do have rivers, from major commercial river ways such as the Illinois to scenic rivers such as the Vermilion, perfect for canoeing. The major river basins in the state include the Illinois, Rock, Kaskaskia, Big Muddy, Wabash, and Ohio Rivers. The Illinois drains an area 250 miles long and 100 miles wide—quite a large part of the state. The Wabash River, about 475 miles long, moves in a southwesterly direction across Indiana and along part of Illinois's eastern border. It leads into the Ohio River, which also borders Indiana in the southeast corner of the state. The flooding-prone Ohio has several shallow sloughs where people harvest mussels for pearls. Also on the eastern edge of the state near Danville is the Middle Fork, a National Scenic Waterway popular among canoeists. The Sangamon River dominates much of the central region of the state. It's about 225 miles long and flows south and west from McLean County in the central part of the state to the Illinois River. The Fox River is in the northern part of the state and flows south from southern Wisconsin to the Illinois River. It's a good river for fishing and has many multiuse recreation trails along its banks as well as towns such as Elgin, Batavia, Geneva, and St. Charles. Other important rivers include the Kankakee, Chicago, Du Page, and Des Plaines.

Natural Resources

Coal is a dominant natural resource in Illinois and for many years drove the state's economy. Illinois coal, which has a lot of sulfur in it, has been mined in the south and along the upper Illinois River valley. Most of the state's coal dates to the late Paleozoic Era, around 300 million years ago, when Illinois and most of the United States was covered alternately by a tropical sea and wet tropical forest. Through time the sea advanced, retreated, advanced, retreated, and so on. These cycles went on for many, many years. Coal occurs in layers or seams underground that vary in width from three quarters of an inch to 15 feet thick. Each layer represents a swamp at the edge of the ancient shallow sea where the water levels rose and fell.

Other natural resources include, oil, lead, and fluorspar. Commercial oil production dates back to the turn of the 20th century, but it really kicked into high gear in the 1950s and 1960s, when the state produced about 80 million barrels a day. Today that figure is closer to 10–12 million barrels per day. Most of the oil wells are in the south-central and southern part of the state.

Galena dolomite in the northwestern part of the state contains minable lead. The Sac and Fox Indians were believed to be the first to mine lead near Galena. The town really came into being in the 1820s, and mining occurred for about 30 years until the California gold rush lured miners westward.

Fluorite, or fluorspar, the state mineral, was mined in the south near Rosiclare. Made of calcium fluoride, fluorite is brittle and comes in a variety of colors, including purple, yellow, green, and white. In ultraviolet light, it's fluorescent. Fluorite production peaked about 1900–1945, when it was in demand for processing steel, aluminum, and other materials because it helped to remove impurities during steel production. Most of those mining operations have since shut down.

Earthquakes

No, this isn't California, but don't be surprised if you feel the ground shake while traveling here. Earthquakes are rare in Illinois, but not unheard of. Southern Illinois is part of the New Madrid seismic zone, which snakes through the area from northwest of Memphis, Tennessee. The Wabash Valley Seismic Zone also runs through the eastern part of the state. On April 18, 2008, after 20 years of relatively quiet earthquake activity in the state, a quake registering 5.2 on the Richter scale struck near West Salem, a tiny town northeast of Mount Vernon and southeast of Effingham. People awoke to the tremors as far west as Kansas City and as far north as Chicago and even Wisconsin. Pictures fell off walls, some loose bricks fell from building facades, and at least one porch in southern Illinois collapsed. A week later the roof of a high school auditorium in Urbana, 140 miles north of the epicenter, collapsed, and engineers later blamed the quake for causing it. Prior to the April 18, 2008, quake, a 5.0 earthquake occurred in 1987. Based on research at the U.S. Geological Survey, there's a 25–40 percent chance an earthquake of 6.0 or higher will occur in the next 50 years. In December 1811 and January 1812, Illinois, Arkansas, and Missouri were rattled by a series of quakes estimated to be 7.5–8.0 in magnitude. The chance that will happen in the next 50 years is about 7 percent–12 percent, according to the survey.

CLIMATE

The beauty (or frustrating thing) about Illinois's climate and weather is its variability. Take a recent week in January. One day the temperature climbed to a near-record high of 50°F; the next day it dived 20 degrees to near-normal temperatures. Sure, the state does see sunny, 70°F days similar to those in San Diego (Illinois has about 220 sunny days a year). But the next day it could be cold and rainy. This phenomenon is fairly common throughout the Midwestern states, and Illinois has a standard Midwestern climate: four distinct seasons with winters that can get pretty wet and cold and summers that can turn hot and humid.

Remember, Illinois is nearly 400 miles long from north to south. That means in April and October, highs can be in the low 60s in northern Illinois and in the low 70s in southern Illinois. Winter is shorter and warmer in southern Illinois compared with the northern section of the state. When it's snowing in Chicago, the southern part of the state may see freezing rain, sleet, or rain. Northern Illinois will have about 10 days below zero in a typical winter, whereas southern Illinois will have one day below zero.

In the summer southern Illinois is definitely more humid and sticky than Chicago.

NORMAL HIGH AND LOW TEMPERATURES

	Chicago	Springfield	Carbondale
January	31/16	33/17	39/21
April	59/40	63/42	66/42
July	85/66	87/66	88/66
October	63/45	67/44	69/43

Temperatures are in degrees Fahrenheit.

But the north is certainly not immune from heat waves. Warm temperatures can get not only uncomfortable, but dangerous. A heat wave in 1995 claimed the lives of about 739 people in Chicago. Since then, whenever temperatures rise and humidity gets stifling, cities open "cooling centers" in places such as libraries and schools and invite the public to chill out there. When traveling through Chicago, remember it's a few degrees cooler by Lake Michigan in the summer and a few degrees warmer in the winter.

Illinois receives about 40 inches of precipitation in a year, about seven inches of which is snow or sleet in the winter. The wettest months are in the spring and summer. Floods, caused by heavy spring rains and melting snow, occur throughout the state, particularly along the Mississippi, Illinois and Sangamon Rivers. When you visit parks in the floodplains after a string of rainy days, it's a good idea to call the rangers ahead of time to check on road conditions. One of the more destructive floods in Illinois was in 1993, when the Mississippi River flooded not only because of major spring rains but heavy rains through the summer. Illinois and several other states were hit hard as levees failed. Towns and farm fields were not just soaked, but completely inundated in water. In Grafton, for example, flood stage was 18 feet, but a record was set at 38 feet. Then, in late spring 2004, the Des Plaines River, which flows through the western and northwestern suburbs of Chicago and drains into the Illinois River, rose above its banks, flooding basements and causing street closures in Gurnee and other towns.

Thunderstorms and Tornadoes

Watching a thunderstorm roll across the prairie is an awesome sight. A tornado is another story. Illinois averages 28 tornadoes each year, so it's a good idea to learn a little about them and recognize the signs of a developing tornado. In Illinois the tornado season generally runs March–May, but technically, tornadoes can pop up at any time of the year. Most form 3–7 P.M. All areas of the state are susceptible to tornados. From 1995 to 2003, Illinois had 561 tornadoes and 10 deaths due to tornadoes. In 2006 a record 124 tornadoes were reported in the state.

Thunderstorms in Illinois usually form in warm, humid conditions as an eastern cold front moves in. A storm that produces a tornado will often be accompanied by hail and high winds. Tornadoes are essentially windstorms with twisting funnel clouds, formed when cool air moves above a layer of warm air. Think of them as rotating columns of air that reach down from the thunderstorm to the ground. Tornado watches are issued when conditions are favorable for the development of a tornado. If you're traveling through the state in the spring and the skies turn stormy, turn on the radio or television to keep tabs on the weather alerts.

When a tornado watch is issued, that might

be a good time to think about where you are, and find out if there is a basement nearby and how to get there. A tornado warning is issued when a funnel cloud has been sighted or detected by radar. Usually the air becomes very calm before a tornado hits. Sometimes you won't see a tornado, but flying clouds of debris. When a tornado warning is issued (you'll hear the sirens in towns or hear a warning on the radio), move to a basement or the lowest floor. If you are not in a building with a basement, move to one of the interior rooms, away from windows. According to the Federal Emergency Management Agency you should avoid being in buildings with wide-span roofs; that includes auditoriums and shopping malls. If you're in a car and in the path of a tornado, get out of the car. A tornado, in which winds can reach 300 miles per hour, can pick up your car and flip it through the air. If you don't have time to get to a building, move away from the car and to the closest low-lying area you can find. Tornadoes often shift direction; they don't always move in a straight path.

FLORA AND FAUNA

Because of Illinois's location near several biomes—the eastern deciduous forest, the southern coastal plains, western great plains, Ozark uplift, and the boreal forest—many animal and plant species thrive in the state. Discover songbirds and migratory birds, snakes, white-tailed deer, prairie chickens, native wildflowers, oak and hickory forests, bald cypress swamps, and more.

Flora

In 1820, Illinois had 22 million acres of prairie. How much native prairie exists now? About one-tenth of 1 percent, or 2,200 acres. In recent years, however, residents have grown more fond of native prairie grasses and wildflowers. Rehabilitated prairies now dot the Illinois landscape, from large projects such as the **Midewin National Tallgrass Prairie** near Wilmington and many local in-town prairie plots. Prairies are amazing communities, home to hundreds of plant species, including tall grasses such as big and little bluestem, switch grass, prairie

phlox, found in Illinois woodlands in the spring

dropseed, and Indian grass, which can grow up to 7 feet tall, as well as flowers such as purple and yellow coneflower, rough blazing star, and butterfly weed.

When hiking through the woods in state forests and parks, you'll likely spot the petite state flower, the wood violet, growing on the forest floor. Trilliums, bloodroot flowers, Dutchman's britches, and phlox are also common across the state.

The state tree is the towering white oak, which can shoot up 80–100 feet tall and grow several feet wide. It's a strong tree; the pioneers used it to build furniture and fences. Common in many state parks, such as **Starved Rock State Park,** the white oak's leaves turn a brilliant red in the autumn (check out **Morton Arboretum** in Lisle to witness this display).

Other native trees found throughout the state in parks and towns are hickory trees, sycamores, white cedars, walnuts, and redbuds. The bald cypress is most often found in the southern part of the state, but since it grows in swampy areas, you can find it in wet pockets across the state. It's most common in the Cache River State Natural Area in the far south. Tupelo is also common in the far southern tip of the state in the Cache River basin. The sugar maple, native to the eastern United States, is common in the northern part of the state. Its sap is collected in the spring and used to make syrup. Funks Grove, just south of Bloomington, is home to a sugar bush, and you can buy syrup there in the spring.

Fauna

About 600 different species of vertebrate animals, including almost 300 species of birds, can be found in Illinois. Because the state is situated along the **Mississippi Flyway,** a migration route millions of birds follow twice a year, birders can catch sight of species that don't normally make their homes in Illinois, plus plenty of geese and swans. In river valleys and creeks, look for the little blue heron, wood duck, loon, and the tern, which can be found along sandbars near rivers. The great egret hides out in the state's wetlands from spring

Canada geese – they're everywhere.

through fall. The gray falcon, a large white raptor with brown specks on its wings, makes its home in Illinois during the winter.

The prairies teem with meadowlarks, woodchucks, box turtles, monarch butterflies, and red-winged blackbirds. The rare metalmark butterfly lives in wetland areas. Upland game such as the prairie chicken, grouse, and wild turkey roams the prairies and grasslands. Throughout the state look for Baltimore orioles, the common blue jay, the robin, and the cardinal, the state bird. The male cardinal is a deep red, and the female is a light reddish-brown. You can see cardinals throughout the year. Robins migrate, but some stick it out during the winter and survive by eating berries. The great horned owl is common in the state. The short-eared owl, much rarer, tends to stick to the grassland areas of the state.

The white-tailed deer is common in every county, even Cook County, where Chicago is. Be on the lookout for deer while driving in rural areas (they like to eat the grasses along the highways), but especially during the fall hunting season when they might be fleeing hunters. Also prevalent in all regions is the eastern cottontail rabbit, a brown short-eared rabbit known for its fluffy little tail. There's also no shortage of Canada geese, thanks to the many reservoirs and ponds in subdivisions and shopping centers.

There are about 200 fish species in Illinois. The state fish is the bluegill, but you will also find many other kinds in the rivers and streams of Illinois, many of which are also common in other Midwestern states. They include the large and smallmouth bass; walleye; sauger; yellow perch; yellow, white, and striped bass; a variety of catfish and trout; carp; muskie; northern pike; green sunfish; white and black crappie; and salmon.

Four of the snake species found in Illinois are venomous: the northern/southern copperhead, the cottonmouth water moccasin, the timber rattlesnake, and the massasauga rattlesnake. All of the poisonous snakes in Illinois have elliptical pupils, a pit on each side of the head (this helps them sense heat), and a row of scales under their tails. Chances are you won't run into any of these guys while out and about. None are aggressive, and most bites occur when a person steps on the snake, picks it up, or forces it into a corner. Snakes can bite when they feel threatened, so if you see a snake, leave it alone.

Aside from the occasional haughty goose, hungry raccoon, or tom turkey looking for a mate, the animals you'll encounter in Illinois are far from aggressive. You're more likely to cross paths with a painted turtle, spring peeper, or common garter snake. You won't see any American bison (except for maybe on a farm), American black bears, cougars, mountain lions, elks, or white-tailed jackrabbits. These were all once part of the Illinois landscape before white settlers started plowing the prairie, building towns along the river valleys, and setting off on hunting parties.

History

EARLY NATIVE AMERICANS

The first people to live in Illinois, or at least spend part of the year hunting or gathering here, are believed to be descendents of the folks who hiked across the Bering Strait. The original explorers made the trek about 15,000–20,000 years ago when waters receded and revealed a land bridge connecting Asia and North America or modern-day Russia with Alaska. By the time their descendents arrived in Illinois it was probably around 10,000 years ago. These early tribes followed herds of animals, such as bison, stopping in places such as the **Modoc Rock Shelter,** a sandstone bluff near Prairie du Rocher in southwest Illinois. A National Historic Landmark, the shelter was used by hunters beginning around 8,000 years ago.

As the years passed, the climate warmed and the native hunters may have cut down on the amount of traveling they did, perhaps migrating twice a year in the fall and spring. As they lived in more permanent locations they started cultivating plants such as squash for food, and making tools and bowls that they could keep since they didn't move around as much.

The early inhabitants of Illinois were **Woodland Indians.** The Woodland Period can be divided into the Early, Middle, and Late Periods, ranging from about 3,000 to 1,250 years ago. The Early and Middle Woodland Indians were hunters and foragers and grew corn, pumpkins, and other vegetables. They also built small animal-shaped burial mounds. By the Late Woodland Period, people had begun to settle in larger villages in the Illinois and Mississippi River valleys. And by A.D. 700, a new group emerged called the Mound Builders.

The **Mound Builders,** such as those who lived near Cahokia, were the main people living in Illinois from A.D. 700 or 900 to 1400. This is considered the Mississippian Period.

THE MOUND BUILDERS

You've probably heard of Black Hawk, the Sauk Indian Chief who fought against the U.S. over land in northwest Illinois and southwest Wisconsin in the 1830s. But before the Sauk and the tribes that preceded them – the Il-lini and the Iroquois – there were the Missis-sippian Indians, the mound builders. Back around A.D. 1100, near modern-day Cahokia by the Mississippi River and near Lewis-town by the Illinois River, were thriving cit-ies where thousands of people traded with other cultures, grew corn, hunted deer, and held religious ceremonies. They built earthen mounds to hold those religious ceremonies, to bury important members of their city, and to house rulers. By 1400 most of the cities had disappeared for reasons archaeologists are still trying to figure out (war, famine, or overpopulation are some theories). As the state developed, many of these mounds were plowed over. But there are two places in Il-linois where you can see remaining mounds and learn more about the prehistoric Indian cultures that lived here.

Cahokia Mounds, a UNESCO World Heri-tage Site, is a 2,200-acre park with about 69 mounds near Collinsville. You can walk past many of these mounds and hike the largest, Monks Mound. With a base of 14 acres and a height of 100 feet, it's the largest Indian mound north of Mexico. Nearby is Woodhenge, a calendar made of wooden posts, and a visi-tors center with displays about the city.

Dickson Mounds, a museum and park with mounds near Havana, highlights the mound-building culture that lived about 1,500 years ago in the Illinois River valley, including at the site of the museum. Excellent museum displays explain the state's geography and its history going back thousands of years.

These villages, which in some cases had as many as 10,000–20,000 people living in them, were mainly in the Mississippi and Illinois River valleys. The villages comprised open plazas, farm fields, plus several earthen mounds built for village religious and govern-mental leaders. Residents raised crops, hunted, gathered, and honed their pottery, weaving, and tool-making skills. Based on items exca-vated from some mounds, historians believe the Mound Builders traded with other tribes in North America. When residents died, they buried them in mounds. It's not clear where the Mound Builders came from, or whether they were related to Maya or Aztec Indians, or any other tribe. These cultures eventually disappeared around 1500, probably because of disease, war, overcrowding, or other reasons. Although many of their mounds were even-tually plowed over for farming and develop-ment, thousands of mounds can still be spotted throughout the state, namely **Cahokia Mounds** east of St. Louis near Collinsville, and **Dickson Mounds** by Havana.

By 1500, about 8,000 Native Americans were living in Illinois, the majority of whom were **Illiniwek.** The Illiniwek or Illinois Indians spoke the Algonquian language and were di-vided into several tribes, including, but not lim-ited to the Cahokia, Kaskaskia, Michigamea, Moingwena, Peoria, and Tamoroa tribes. They lived throughout the state but were centered around the Peoria area. Illiniwek were, for the most part, peaceful and friendly to the early white explorers. They worshiped a great spirit called Manitou and hunted and grew corn, squash, and other crops.

In the mid-1600s, the Iroquois Indians made their way west from the eastern United States, such as New York. They moved into the northern part of Illinois and clashed with the tribes living there. The Iroquois were said to be strong warriors and often allied with other tribes to fight against the whites. In 1680 the Iroquois attacked Illinois Indians living in vil-lages along the Illinois River and toward the Mississippi River.

The Illinois not only had to contend with

the Iroquois encroaching on their territory, but the Sauk and Fox Indians who came from the north (such as Wisconsin) and claimed territory between the Mississippi and Rock Rivers. (Before living in Wisconsin, the Sauk hailed from regions along the St. Lawrence River, but were pushed out of there by the Iroquois.) The Sauk eventually allied with the Potawatomi Indians and pushed the Illinois Indians farther south in the state.

Other early Indians included the Shawnee, who lived in southern part of the state, and the Miami, who lived for a time around Chicago.

THE FRENCH ARRIVE

The land in and around Illinois became French territory in 1671 thanks to a declaration made in the French trading-post town of Sault Sainte Marie in modern-day Michigan's Upper Peninsula. That is when the governor of New France (territory that included the Great Lakes region and other parts of Canada) claimed that all the interior land of North America was property of France. With that said, the first white men to explore the Illinois region were the French—French fur traders, missionaries, explorers, and soldiers. The French, who came from French Canada via the Great Lakes and rivers, had a hold on things in Illinois for about 100 years, beginning from the late 1600s.

One famous pair of French explorers was missionary **Father Jacques Marquette** and fur trader **Louis Jolliet,** who traveled through Illinois in 1673. They came down from St. Ignace in the Upper Peninsula and journeyed through Wisconsin and down the Mississippi River. From there, they made it as far as the mouth of the Arkansas River before heading back north and east on the Illinois and Des Plaines Rivers, eventually to Lake Michigan.

Meanwhile, traveling French fur traders were busy trapping animals and trading with the Indians. After the fur traders set up posts, settlements cropped up around those trading posts. And along with the settlements came missionaries. One of the earliest missions and settlements was Cahokia near East St. Louis and the **Church of the Holy Family** mission, founded in 1699.

Another important pair of explorers were René-Robert Cavelier Sieur de La Salle and Henri de Tonti, who voyaged down the Illinois River and built Fort St. Louis (near present-day Utica, now called Starved Rock) and Fort Crèvecoeur near Peoria (in present-day Creve Coeur) in 1680. La Salle promised the Illinois Indians in both areas that the French would help protect them from the Iroquois. While Tonti was on a trip to visit the Kaskaskian Illinois Indians at Starved Rock, some Frenchmen ransacked Fort Crèvecoeur, stealing ammunition and other supplies, before taking off. After hearing about what happened, Tonti decided to bring whatever was left at Fort Crèvecoeur to Starved Rock. Both the Iroquois and Illinois Indians were fuming mad with Tonti, who they saw as a traitor. A fight ensued, the Kaskaskian village was burned, and the Iroquois took over. Tonti managed to escape.

Illinois officially became part of the French colony of Louisiana in 1717 and almost 14 years later was named a province of the kingdom of France in 1731. After the city of New Orleans was established in 1718, trade picked up along the Mississippi River, and more French people, traders, farmers, and land speculators started trickling into the region. To protect their territory, in 1720 the French erected **Fort de Chartres** on the banks of the Mississippi River, about an hour south of present day Collinsville. Fort de Chartres would become the seat of French government in the Illinois country for a while.

Into the late 1740s and early 1750s, the British began expanding their territory in the New World. The Ohio Land Company, comprising a group of Virginia land speculators, planned to establish villages in the Ohio River valley. And the French felt threatened. In response, the French built more forts and revamped their current ones. As more Brits moved west, it was inevitable the two countries would clash over land. The **French and Indian War** lasted 1754–1763. The Illinois Indians allied with the French, and the Iroquois partnered with the British. After seven years of war, France ended up ceding its land east of the Mississippi to Great Britain in 1763 in the Treaty of Paris. Illinois now belonged to the king of England.

At the time France was handing over some of its land to Great Britain, Ottawa Indian Chief Pontiac from Michigan led several attacks against white settlers, particularly the British. Pontiac and his Indians later settled in Illinois near the Illinois River and claimed they would make peace with the Brits. But then in 1769 Pontiac was killed near Cahokia by a Peoria Indian (Peorias were part of the Illini nation, who allied with the French). Seeking revenge, tribes loyal to Pontiac, including the Ottawa, Chippewa, and Potawatomi, streamed into the area and drove a band of Illinois Indians to the top of a rock above the Illinois River near La Salle's fort. The Illinois ran out of water and food, and many eventually died. The rock is now called **Starved Rock** and is home to a popular state park.

REVOLUTIONARY WAR, LEWIS AND CLARK, AND BLACK HAWK

In the years after the French and Indian War, Illinois was still considered a wild, desolate place, deep in the interior of the continent. Only a few thousand Frenchmen and women lived here, and many of them ended up crossing the Mississippi into Missouri after the territory was ceded to the Brits. Meanwhile tension was brewing out East. The American colonists had had it with British attempts to control and tax them, and they declared independence in 1776.

While most of the Revolutionary War battles were in the east, Illinois did see some action. Virginian **George Rogers Clark,** stationed in Kentucky, learned from spies that the British had not bothered to safeguard some of the Illinois forts where they stored military supplies. Patrick Henry, then governor of Virginia, delegated Clark to be leader of the colonists' efforts to wrestle control of the west from the Brits. In 1778 Clark and about 200 of his comrades set off and took control first

of Fort Massac, near present-day Metropolis, and marched on northwestward to Kaskaskia, Cahokia, Prairie du Rocher, and back east to Vincennes (on the Illinois and Indiana border), and others. Of these forts, Vincennes was later recaptured by the British. And in the winter of 1780, Clark led another scraggy group of fewer than 200 men to reclaim Vincennes. For 22 days he and his men trudged through the cold and wet Little Wabash River valley before tricking the British into surrendering. That hike across Illinois became known as the Impossible March.

After the American colonists won the war, Illinois settlements became part of Virginia. And in 1784 Virginia ceded Illinois to the U.S. government. Illinois, along with Wisconsin, Michigan, Indiana, and Ohio, officially became part of the **Northwest Territory.** Surveying of the territory began. A few adventurous souls started moving into Illinois, most of them into the southern towns of Cairo, Shawneetown, Cahokia, and Kaskaskia. It wasn't until **Jean Baptiste Point du Sable** arrived in Chicago that the region started to grow as a settlement. Du Sable was a black trader from the Caribbean who traded with the Indians in the area about 1779–1800.

In 1795, probably a few years before Du Sable left Chicago for other business opportunities farther west, a group of Indian tribes signed the **Treaty of Greenville** with the United States. In the treaty, and many other treaties that followed, the tribes gave up much of their territory to the United States. One parcel transferred to the government was six square miles near the mouth of the Chicago River. Later, it would become the city of Chicago. By 1800 only a few hundred Illinois Indians remained in the region; most had moved west of the Mississippi River. In 1803 the U.S. Army built **Fort Dearborn** near the mouth of the Chicago River to protect the new territory, a region that was becoming more of a trading and transportation center.

When Thomas Jefferson became president of the United States in 1801, much of the west was still uncharted territory, explored largely by French fur traders and Spanish explorers. He thought it was about time a team of Americans hit the road, so to speak, and write home about it. The chosen men? **Captain Meriwether Lewis and William Clark** (George Rogers Clark's younger brother). Before setting out on their famous journey westward, Lewis and Clark spent about six months in Illinois recruiting men and stocking supplies. In November 1803 they arrived at Fort Massac, then went on to Fort Kaskaskia, Cahokia, and finally Wood River. At Wood River they established **Camp River DuBois,** believed to be north of the present-day town of Hartford. (Hartford, north of East St. Louis, has an extensive interpretive center about the men and their travels.) It was from this camp that they embarked on their trip westward.

Not long after Lewis and Clark completed their expedition, the United States found itself edging closer to war with Britain again. In 1812 the relationship between the two countries was strained as they butted heads over maritime trade rights, the Canadian territory, and many other issues. At the same time, the Americans' relationship with Native Americans in Illinois was also strained as some tribes allied with the British. After the British captured the American post at Mackinac, Michigan, the U.S. government ordered soldiers and their families at Fort Dearborn in Chicago to leave. As soldiers and their families left town, they were attacked by Indians (which tribe it was is up for debate). About 60 Americans were killed during the incident, called the **Fort Dearborn Massacre.** The Indians burned the fort, which the Americans later rebuilt in 1816 and the Army used until the mid-1830s. Around that same time, the Potawatomi signed away their land in northern Illinois and were forced west.

In the spring of 1832, under the leadership of **Chief Black Hawk,** the Sauk Indians crossed the Mississippi River and moved into northwestern Illinois. The Sauk had lived in the region and in southwestern Wisconsin several decades earlier, but were forced into Iowa because of an 1804 treaty (which Black Hawk disputed) in which they gave up some territory east of the river. The Sauks' return made settlers jittery, and white residents formed militias. (Abraham Lincoln was among the men who signed up.) Black Hawk's route in Illinois roughly followed the Rock River northeastward. Early on in the journey, he realized the Sauks could not live peacefully with the white settlers and decided to go back across the Mississippi. However, several skirmishes occurred, and before they knew it they were at war with the United States.

One episode that stands out in Illinois history took place in May 1832 south of Rockford at a place now called **Stillman's Run.** Black Hawk reportedly sent some scouts to Major Isaiah Stillman's militia to make peace, but none of Stillman's men spoke Sauk. They ended up attacking the Sauks. Black Hawk's men retaliated, frightening the militia and prompting them to flee. It was a short-lived victory. More militia and eventually U.S. troops pursued Black Hawk and his tribe into Wisconsin, where they were defeated in the Battle of Bad Axe. Not long afterward, other Indian tribes, such as the Winnebago, Potawatomi, Ottawa, and Chippewa ceded their land to the U.S. government and agreed to move west of the Mississippi River.

STATEHOOD AND SETTLEMENTS

Illinois became a state in 1818; it was still quite small, however, population-wise. It was actually the smallest state to be admitted to the union. In 1820 there were about 55,000 people living here. New residents initially came from the southern states such as Kentucky, Tennessee, and the Carolinas. Most settled in the southern third of the state because the hills reminded them of home. They chose towns such as Shawneetown in the southeast near the salt mines and Kaskaskia to the southwest along the Mississippi River. (Kaskaskia, the first capital, would eventually be washed away by frequent floods.) It was easier to live in the south than in the prairie or northern region. The ground was not as wet as in the prairies to the north, where people often got sick from living near mosquito-infested wetlands. There was plenty of timber to harvest, animals to hunt, farmland to plant corn, and opportunities to make whiskey. Early residents of Illinois were frontiersmen, subsistence farmers, veterans, miners, and land surveyors.

When the Erie Canal was finished in 1825, people from the East Coast could travel westward from the Hudson River at Albany to Lake Erie and to the Great Lakes. The opening of the canal spurred the development of Midwestern states such as Illinois and cities such as Chicago and Milwaukee. Chicago went from a sleepy trading post to a bustling center of commerce. People began to flock to Illinois. In the mid-1800s, several ethnic and religious groups arrived in Illinois with grand hopes that they could prosper here free from prejudice. These groups included the Mormons, who settled in Nauvoo in the west, and shortly after them, the French Icarians, who also settled in Nauvoo; and the Swedish immigrants known as Janssonists, who established **Bishop Hill**, now a state historic site, also in the western part of the state.

As steam travel continued to develop, talk surfaced about connecting the Great Lakes to the Illinois and Mississippi Rivers via canals. Real-estate developers poured into Chicago and other towns. During this time Galena and Jo Daviess County in the northwest of the state started prospering as a hub for lead ore mining, farming, and steamboating. By 1830 about 157,000 people were living in the state. Another boom to development was the opening of the **Illinois & Michigan Canal** in 1848, which would link the Great Lakes to the Mississippi River. The massive capital improvement project cost about $6 million at the time.

As the canals sparked development in the northern part of the state, the railroads were responsible for jump-starting hundreds of towns throughout Illinois. First came the Galena and Chicago Union railroad in 1848, eventually connecting Chicago with the lead mines in Galena to the west. The **Illinois Central,** begun in 1851, set off a development boom.

The line would connect Cairo at the southern tip of the state with Galena in the far northwest, with several branches to other cities, including Chicago. Towns such as Champaign, Rantoul, Pana, Mattoon, and many others sprung up around the Illinois Central depots. Once the railroads were in place, farmers realized they didn't have to be subsistence farmers but could sell their grain and livestock at the Chicago markets. Travel was also much more of a speedy and pleasant experience. People didn't have to travel great distances on stagecoaches, which often became stuck in the thick deep prairie soil.

LINCOLN, SLAVERY, AND THE CIVIL WAR

One of the many families who moved to Illinois in hopes of seeking good affordable farmland were the Lincolns. Twenty-one-year-old **Abraham Lincoln** moved into the state from Kentucky in 1830 along with his father, Thomas, and stepmother, Sarah. Lincoln eventually set out on his own, working as a flatboat pilot, surveyor, merchant, and eventually politician. He spent quite a bit of time in New Salem, a town along the Sangamon River, just northwest of Springfield. There he toyed with several jobs, among them postmaster and clerk at a general store. But it was there he read books (including law books) and toyed with the idea of becoming involved in politics.

He was elected as a state representative in 1834 and spent time between New Salem and Vandalia, the second capital. He passed the bar exam and received a license to practice law. His law offices were in Springfield, but he also traveled quite a bit on the Eighth Judicial Circuit court, trying cases in county courthouses throughout the state. Lincoln then went on to serve a term in the U.S. House of Representatives beginning in 1847. He didn't run for a second term and instead chose to return to practice law in Springfield.

During the next 10 years slavery would become more of a contentious issue not only in Illinois but throughout the country. Illinois was torn. Many northern Illinois residents came from the northeastern United States and were against slavery. Illinois's southern neighbors of Kentucky and Missouri permitted slavery. Considering that many southern residents of Illinois hailed from the Southern states, perhaps it was not surprising that many residents there supported slavery.

While some French settlers brought slaves with them to Illinois and there were slaves working in the state, such as at the salt mines in Gallatin County, slavery was not common in Illinois. The **Missouri Compromise** in 1820, which allowed slavery in Missouri, banned it in Illinois and other states included in the Louisiana Purchase. Just because slavery was illegal in Illinois, the living was definitely not easy for its black residents. They could serve in militias and testify in court, but they had no right to vote. Slaves who had escaped from the South tried to escape through Illinois to Canada, but they risked being kidnapped. Abolitionists also didn't have it easy. **Elijah Lovejoy,** who published an antislavery newspaper in Alton, had his printing presses destroyed several times by mobs. Eventually he was murdered in 1847. Lovejoy's death shocked and incited other abolitionists in the state to stand up against slavery's supporters. **Underground Railroad** stops were established throughout the state, particularly in and around Jacksonville.

In 1850 a U.S. senator from Illinois, **Stephen A. Douglas** (known as the "little giant" for his small stature and his power and influence in politics), proposed a solution to the question of slavery in the country. In the Compromise of 1850, Douglas said states should decide themselves whether or not slavery was legal or illegal. The proposal didn't move forward, but a few years later the **Kansas-Nebraska Act** did. The 1854 act left it up to the two territories (Kansas and Nebraska) to decide if slavery would be allowed or not. The act outraged slavery opponents, the Republican Party was born, and Lincoln readied himself for a return to politics.

After Republicans nominated Lincoln as a candidate for the U.S. Senate, he and his opponent, Douglas, toured the state during the summer and fall of 1858 and debate the issue of slavery and other topics. The **Lincoln-Douglas debates** were held in Ottawa, Freeport, Jonesboro, Charleston, Galesburg, Quincy, and Alton. Lincoln lost the race, but his performance at the debates brought him national attention. Republicans later nominated him as their presidential candidate, and he was elected president of the United States in 1860.

Not long after Lincoln took office, the Civil War began. No Civil War battles were fought in Illinois, but about 250,000 men and boys from Illinois fought in the war, among them Galena resident Ulysses S. Grant, who would become general and eventually U.S. president. The state was also home to several prisons that held Confederate soldiers, among them Rock Island in the Quad Cities and Fort Douglas in Chicago. Many hospitals, such as one near Cairo, cared for the wounded. Like many states in the country, when the conflict finally ended in 1865, Illinois did not come out unscathed: About 34,000 Illinois soldiers died in battle or from disease. And less than a week after the Confederate General Lee surrendered at Appomattox, the state, and the country, would lose their beloved leader.

On April 14, 1865, John Wilkes Booth aimed a pistol at Lincoln's head in Ford's Theatre in Washington, D.C. Lincoln died early the next morning. After lying in state in the nation's capital, Lincoln's body was placed aboard a funeral train headed back for Illinois. The train chuffed through several states, including New York, Ohio, Indiana, and along the way stopped at over 100 towns where Americans would assemble to play music, read poems, sing songs, and weep over the loss of their president. After arriving in Springfield, Lincoln was ultimately buried in Oak Ridge Cemetery, where his body remains.

INDUSTRIALIZATION AND MODERNIZATION

The latter part of the 19th century was a busy one for Illinois. New settlers drained wetlands and established farmsteads. In 1865 the Union Stock Yards opened on the southwest side of Chicago, and trading grain futures at the Chicago Board of Trade became more formalized. Manufacturing—steel, glass, farm tools, pearl buttons, lumber—was big. Textiles and food-processing businesses boomed. Gas, oil, and minerals were discovered and mined throughout the state. Steel rail lines were developed in Chicago, and more rail lines were added throughout the state. **Cyrus McCormick** built his mechanical reaper factory in Chicago. **George Pullman** launched his Pullman Palace Car company.

The **Chicago Fire** in October 1871 destroyed much of downtown Chicago and the north side. But Chicagoans pulled themselves up by the bootstraps, and architects such as Daniel Burnham, Louis Sullivan, Jens Jensen, and Frank Lloyd Wright swooped in and redesigned the city. Chicago, not to mention the entire state, was proud of itself, especially in 1893 when the city hosted the world's fair, the **Columbia Exposition.**

In response to the growth of factories and the influx of workers, workers' rights became a hot-button issue around the state as working conditions, as described in Upton Sinclair's book, *The Jungle,* were not exactly favorable. Strikes, protests, and riots were not unheard of. During **The Haymarket Riot** in 1886, several police officers were killed when a person or group of people threw a bomb during a protest against police violence. While employees were striking at the McCormick reaper factory, demanding an eight-hour work day, police shot several workers. Workers at Pullman's factory went on strike in 1894 after Pullman reduced wages but did not reduce rent on the company-owned houses. Skirmishes between protesting miners and managers and scabs were also common in southern Illinois. Some progress was made. Mother Jones rallied miners, seamstresses, and others and fought for workers' rights. Jane Addams founded the **Hull House** in 1889 in Chicago to help the poor and uneducated. The state shortened the women's work day to eight hours, passed laws limiting child labor, and organized schools.

As the business climate in Illinois expanded, the population ballooned and more people moved to the urban centers. Yankees flooded Chicago, as did European immigrants such as Germans, Irish, and Scandinavians, followed by immigrants from southern and Eastern Europe. By 1900, the state's population swelled to about 4.8 million people. Along with the immigrants who came to Illinois looking for good jobs came Southern blacks. But the state was not always a welcoming place. The 1908 Springfield race riots, brought on after a white woman said a black man had assaulted her (a statement she later retracted), several black and white people were killed and many shops and homes burned. Stunned and urged to act, several people met in New York to discuss what happened, eventually forming the **National Association for the Advancement of Colored People.** In the 1917 race riot in East St. Louis, sparked after factories invited blacks to move to town and work there, 48 blacks and nine whites were killed. Chicago was also fast becoming a tense, segregated city. From 1910 to 1920 the city's black population doubled to 109,000. Most blacks settled together in the city's south side neighborhoods. In 1919 a black boy drifted into the white swimming area on the lakefront and drowned after a white youth threw a stone at him. The killing sparked days of riots throughout the city and elsewhere in the United States.

Yes, the first few decades of the 20th century were quite violent. Shortly after Prohibition, a man named Alphonse Capone joined the Chicago mob's bootlegging, gambling, and brothel businesses. When Capone's boss was shot and killed, he took the helm of the organization, known as **The Syndicate.** Capone ran speakeasies, racetracks, and dance clubs. Capone was responsible for the St. Valentine's Day Massacre in 1929, when his strong-arm men killed off rival gang lord Bugs Moran. Although never arrested for murder or bootlegging, he was nabbed on income tax evasion charges and sent to prison on Alcatraz Island in California. He died in 1947, and many attribute the cause to complications from syphilis. He's buried in Mt. Carmel Cemetery in Hillside, west of Oak Park.

Later Chicago and many other towns became preoccupied with World War II, sending hundreds of thousands of young men to fight in it and modifying factories to produce supplies to help with the cause. One of the biggest contributions to indirectly ending the war happened in 1942 beneath the University of Chicago's Stagg Field. It was there that Enrico Fermi and other scientists conducted the first nuclear chain reaction.

THE MID- TO LATE 20TH CENTURY AND CONTEMPORARY TIMES

Following a trend that occurred throughout the country from the 1950s onward, rural residents moved to the cities, and the populations of the rural counties aged and dwindled. The federal highway system rendered two-lane highways such as Route 66 obsolete. Chicago became even more of a transportation hub for the Midwest as semitrailers roared along the highways and more freight train lines came in and out of the city. Richard J. Daley was elected mayor of Chicago in 1955 and became known as a builder mayor, approving and overseeing dozens of modernization projects, including the high-rise housing projects on the west and south sides that are now being torn down.

Segregation occurred somewhat reluctantly around the state, and clashes between blacks and whites were not uncommon. In the town of Cairo, for example, many white businessmen closed up shop and left town rather than have blacks as customers. Cairo and many other towns, such as East St. Louis, Peoria, Rockford, and Elgin were the scenes of race riots in 1966

and 1967. In April 1968, after Dr. Martin Luther King Jr. was assassinated, National Guardsmen flew in after more riots exploded in Joliet, Alton, Maywood, Carbondale, and other areas.

Despite the racial tension, the state was a melting pot of people, art, and ideas. Architect Mies van der Rohe's glass and steel skyscrapers changed the look of Chicago. Carl Sandburg and Gwendolyn Brooks penned moving prose and poetry. Blues musicians such as Buddy Guy made Chicago a destination for budding musicians. Toward the mid-1970s, though, things began to change. After six terms in office, Daley died of a heart attack in December 1976. The oil embargo and inflation put a damper on the economy. New regulations in the Clean Air Act prompted many coal mines and plants to shutter. Farmland prices crashed in the mid-1980s, causing many farmers to file for bankruptcy and sell their farms.

Like many other states, Illinois, for the most part, recovered. While many coal-mining towns continue to struggle and people look elsewhere to find jobs in manufacturing, tourism, or in prisons, most of the state's towns and residents thrived in the 1990s. New businesses were launched, everyone's stock portfolios were in the black, and everyone rallied around Michael Jordan and the Chicago Bulls. The economic downturn in recent years has caused a few folks to suffer. State spending for education and research is not at the level teachers, parents, or students would like; tuition at most universities is up; capital improvement projects have been delayed; and Illinois has lost quite a few soldiers in the war in Iraq.

Government and Economy

GOVERNMENT

Illinois is solidly Democratic. In all presidential elections since 1992, the state has gone to the Democrats. This is largely because of the power of Chicago, where the Dems dominate. But out in the burbs (particularly those in Du Page County) and in most rural parts of the state, the Republicans hold power in village halls and at county board meetings.

In 2007 Illinois had a Democrat in the governor's house, a Democrat-controlled general assembly, and Democrats in charge of most statewide offices. You'd think all would be well, and the different government branches and agencies would be able to work together. Not so in Illinois. To start with, since he took office in 2003, Governor Rod Blagojevich, who is from Chicago, has been criticized for not spending enough time in Springfield. Even though the capital is Springfield, many state bureaus and departments have offices in Springfield and Chicago. It's not uncommon for downstate residents (generally anyone living below I-80) to complain that Chicago politicians run the state. So a governor who doesn't spend a lot of time in Springfield rubbed some legislators and voters the wrong way. And in the ensuing years a feud developed between Blagojevich and the current and longtime speaker of the house, Mike Madigan. Finally, Blagojevich campaigned on cleaning up Springfield and ending pay-to-play politics in Illinois. But some of his fund-raisers and friends have been on trial for being involved in just those kind of games.

Illinois voters are a tough crowd, quite a bit cynical and mistrusting of state and local government. Maybe it has to do with the scandals, the allegations of patronage, the embezzlements, and the bribes that have plagued the state since its early days. During the Prohibition era there was Big Bill Thompson, Chicago's mayor, who unabashedly hung out with Al Capone and his buddies. In the 1950s the state auditor and several others pleaded

Illinois State Capitol complex in Springfield

COURTESY OF SPRINGFIELD AREA CONVENTION AND VISITORS BUREAU

guilty to embezzling money from the state. In the 1980s the U.S. attorney's office was busy investigating voter fraud. In the 1990s the FBI's Operation Silver Shovel uncovered widespread political corruption in Chicago's city hall. Also in the 1990s, Illinoisans saw their longtime U.S. Senator Dan Rostenkowski head to the big house, where he served time for mail fraud. In recent years the U.S. attorney's office has been handing out indictments in the licenses-for-bribes scandal in which staffers of the secretary of state's office reportedly issued commercial truck licenses to people in exchange for political contributions. In 2006 former Republican governor George Ryan was found guilty in a federal corruption trial for essentially steering state contracts to friends. A year later he started serving his 6.5-year jail sentence. In 2008, one of Governor Blagojevich's key fund-raisers was on trial for essentially using his influence to secure seats on state boards in exchange for kickbacks or campaign donations.

There have been some bright spots in the state's political history. The late bow tie–wearing U.S. Senator Paul Simon, a newspaper publisher turned politician, had admirers from both sides of the aisles. The late former president Ronald Reagan, who was born in Tampico and raised in Dixon, is beloved here. Republican Governor Jim Thompson, who served 1977–1991, was criticized for his pork barrel politics, but his terms in office were relatively free from scandals. U.S. Senator Barack Obama, the charismatic politician from Chicago, is also adored by Democrats and has even impressed a few Republicans.

As for the nuts and bolts of government in Illinois, the governor is Illinois's chief executive officer, elected for a four-year term. The lieutenant governor and other constitutional officers, such as the attorney general, secretary of state, treasurer, and comptroller, are also elected to four-year terms. The Illinois Supreme Court has seven justices who serve 10-year terms. Three of the justices hail from Cook County, which is the first district, plus four others come from four districts across the state. Appellate and circuit court judges are elected for 10- and four-year terms respectively.

The Illinois General Assembly has 59 senators and 118 representatives, a majority of whom are from Chicago and its collar counties. In 2003 Illinois voters elected a Democrat to the governor's office and enough Democrats into the state senate and house that both chambers would be controlled by the Democrats, for the first time in almost three decades. Two senators represent Illinois in the U.S. Senate and 20 representatives from Illinois are in the U.S. House of Representatives.

ECONOMY

In 2006 Illinois's gross state product was close to $590 billion, the largest among Midwest and Plains states. If Illinois were a country, its economy would rank as the 23rd largest. The three main drivers of Illinois's economy are manufacturing, agriculture, and industrial production. Chicago is a hub for the transportation industry (including truck, train, airline, and bus companies), as well as insurance (Aon) and consulting companies (Accenture).

MAJOR COMPANIES IN ILLINOIS

The following companies are headquartered in or have major offices in Illinois:

- Abbott Laboratories
- Accenture
- Allstate
- Archer Daniels Midland
- Baxter International
- Boeing
- Caterpillar
- Encyclopedia Britannica
- John Deere
- Kraft Foods
- Mars
- Midway Games
- Playboy
- Rand McNally
- Sara Lee
- Sears
- State Farm Insurance
- Tribune Company
- Walgreens
- Wm. Wrigley Jr.

Peoria is known for equipment manufacturing (Caterpillar), Decatur for grain processing (ADM), Bloomington for general manufacturing, health care, and insurance (State Farm) jobs, and Champaign-Urbana for University of Illinois jobs and health care employment. East St. Louis is home to iron and steel production.

About 12 percent of the state's workforce is employed in manufacturing, a number that is declining. Companies in Illinois make tractors, electronic equipment, computer chips, pharmaceuticals, food, and more. The major names in manufacturing are Caterpillar, General Electric, Illinois Tool Works, and John Deere. Other large employers in the state are Motorola, Abbott Laboratories, and Kraft Foods. Most manufacturers are located in the northeast part of the state. In recent years, as is the trend across the country, the state's manufacturing sector has dampened somewhat as tire manufacturer Firestone closed shop in Decatur, Maytag closed a plant in Galesburg, Mitsubishi scaled back its workforce in Bloomington, and Motorola laid off employees to save costs.

A bright spot in the state's economy has been agriculture. Although the number of families who live and work on farms has declined, the size of farms has been growing steadily, and Illinois has for years been first or second (usually with Iowa) in corn and soybean production. When you travel outside of Chicagoland, particularly in September and October, and see all the towering grain bins and piles of corn, you realize this is a big agricultural state. Large farms grow corn and soybeans throughout the state, a lot of wheat is grown in the St. Louis metro-east area, and another grain, sorghum, is found mostly in the south. Dairy farms are in the northern hilly part of the state, particularly near the Wisconsin border. Fruit orchards, including peach and apple, are concentrated in the southern third of the state. Illinois is also a top producer of pumpkins (in and around the Morton and Peoria area) and watermelons (grown in the areas with sandy soils). Illinois is not just big in terms of crop output; it's huge in corn processing and soybean milling, largely because

© GEOFFREY POCIASK

An operating oil derrick is a common sight in southern Illinois.

of Archer Daniels Midland in Decatur and Bunge in Danville. The grains processed there are made into everything from corn syrup for sodas to soy protein for vegetarian burgers.

In the southern part of the state, coal mines have dominated the economies of several local towns for many years. (A quick look at a map of this region yields names such as Coalton, Coal Valley, Carbondale, and Carbon Cliff.) However, the economic climate for coal in Illinois has changed dramatically in the last 15 years. The Clean Air Act amendments passed in 1990 had quite an effect on industry in Illinois. In fact, the state estimates coal production and industry sales in Illinois dropped by one-third because of price competition and the move from high-sulfur coal to low-sulfur coal. You see, Illinois coal is bituminous and has a lot of sulfur in it. After the act, many mining companies in Illinois shifted their attention to coal beds out West where the coal does not have such a high sulfur content. But the coal industry in Illinois is not dead. About one eighth of the country's coal reserves are under Illinois, and underground coal beds cover about 65 percent of the state. About 33.5 million tons of coal is still mined each year in Illinois. (Much of it goes to produce electricity for Illinois utilities.) And in recent years, researchers have unveiled promising technologies that could reduce the harmful pollutants emitted when high-sulfur coal is burned. In addition to coal, Illinois has oil reserves and is home to four oil refineries. These refineries produce more gasoline than any other Midwestern state. (Their production levels, however, do not nearly meet the state's demands.)

The State of Illinois employs the most people in the state, followed by the federal government (including postal workers), the Chicago Public School District, and the city of Chicago. The state's largest private employer is Wal-Mart, which has about 40,000 employees in Illinois. Other top employers include Jewel-Osco (a grocery chain), Caterpillar, United Parcel Service, Advocate Health Care (an HMO or health maintenance organization), and State Farm Insurance. The state's unemployment rate was around 4.5 percent during the late 1990s and climbed gradually to about 6.5 percent in 2002. By early 2005 it had dipped to 5.9 percent and continued to decline before increasing again. In spring 2008 it was hovering around 5.4 percent, at the time lower than Michigan's and Ohio's unemployment rates, but higher than Iowa, Wisconsin, and Indiana. Unemployment rates tend to be higher in Illinois's downstate counties where mining and manufacturing jobs have dwindled.

The People

Throughout your adventures in Illinois, you'll meet some pretty humble, practical people— people who will gladly offer you directions to their favorite coffee shop or bar or engage you in conversation and complain about the weather or the Chicago Bears. During the fall it's not uncommon for farmers to get together and harvest the fields of a neighbor who has fallen ill. Instead of waxing poetic about their volunteer efforts, they're more likely to shrug it off, saying, "Well, the beans have to be cut sometime," or "He'd do it for me if I were sick." Although technically a Midwestern state, Illinois also has an easygoing Southern feel in its downstate towns, where many residents have roots in Tennessee and Kentucky.

SETTLEMENT AND IMMIGRATION PATTERNS

In the biased opinion of this writer, Illinois has the most fascinating mix of residents compared with any other Midwestern state. We have people from every ethnic background and racial makeup in towns across the state, not just in Chicago. We have Nobel Prize–winning scientists, internationally known artists, cunning

IT'S "IL-LI-NOY," NOT "IL-LI-NOYS"

Illinois is squarely in the Midwest. But driving through the state, from Rockford in the north, Springfield in the center, and Carbondale to the south, you'll hear a range of accents. Essentially, northerners' speech will sound more nasal and staccato. Head south and you'll pick up more of a drawl, which becomes more pronounced the farther south you go.

The Chicago accent is perhaps the most mimicked accent in the state. Remember that *Saturday Night Live* sketch in which Mike Ditka-like actors cheer on "da Bulls an' da Bears"? The *a*'s were long, and the pace staccato. Some folks do talk that way. Born-and-bred Chicagoans will pronounce words such as Pulaski (as in the street named after the Polish general) with an accent on the *a*, i.e., "Pu-LAY-ski." Most Chicagoans will pronounce the city's name as "Shi-CAH-go" or "Shi-CAW-go." Mayor Richard Daley, by the way, whose family is from the south side, has a solid Chicago accent.

As you travel south, more and more people speak with a drawl and Southern accent. In the central region of the state, such as Springfield, Bloomington-Normal, and Champaign-Urbana,

you'll notice that in-town residents have no sign of a drawl. But those who live just a few miles from the city outskirts have a slight Southern accent. In the southern part of the state, from Marion and southward, you'll notice that along with the Southern accent there often comes a friendly, casual Southern attitude. Don't be surprised when gas station attendants, wait staff, and others slip in a "sweetheart" or "honey" when they thank you for your business.

Some final words on pronunciation. Because the state was first settled by the French, many town and place names bear French names. Illinois is the French word for the Native American Indians who lived in the state when the French fur traders arrived here. But of course, Illinois is not pronounced as the French would pronounce it. Instead, it's "Il-li-NOY" (ignore the *s* at the end). Around the state there are a number of place names that are pronounced nothing like the way you might think they would be. Marseilles is "Mar-SALES." Okawville is pronounced "O-ka-ville." Vienna is "Va-YAN-a." And Cairo is "CA-ro" (like the syrup).

---

developers, smart and some might say smarmy politicians, homespun country folk, wealthy businessmen, migrant workers, inventors, copycats, do-gooders, poets, curmudgeons, conservatives, liberals, independents, and everyone in between. On a tour of the state you could meet a couple whose family has farmed on the same land for five generations, an immigrant couple from Southeast Asia who runs a hotel in a small southern town, and an East Coast transplant who never planned on staying in Illinois for more than a few years but found himself making a home in the state for several decades. We make up quite a collage.

From its early beginnings, Illinois never really belonged to one particular group of people. Settlement started with the French, followed by the Brits and the American colonists. The early arrivals were explorers, fur trappers, farmers, land speculators, and people seeking religious

freedom. After the Native Americans, the first group to put down roots in Illinois was the French. The French settlers lived mostly in the southwest part of the state. Some towns and buildings there still bear French names. The first Americans to build homes in Illinois were from the southern states, such as Kentucky and Tennessee. Through the state's early development, American colonists from the Southern states stuck to southern Illinois, and Yankees—people from the Northeast—focused on the Chicago region. Political and philosophical clashes between these two groups occurred often, especially over the issue of slavery.

In the mid-1800s, as steamers and railroad travel became more available to the Midwest, immigrants came mainly from Germany, Ireland, England, and a few other European countries. They came here directly from their homelands and from other states, probably after reading promotional literature about the cheap fertile land available here. In the 1830s German immigrants from St. Louis and Cincinnati settled in and near towns along the National Road, such as Effingham and Teutopolis. Chicago was also heavily German, although not as much so as Milwaukee to the north. Norwegians clustered in villages along the Fox River. The Swedes were mostly in the western part of the state, such as Bishop Hill.

Between 1890 and 1914, another wave of immigrants entered Illinois, this time from countries in eastern and southern Europe. This group included Poles, Italians, and Ukrainians. After World War II and into the second half of the 20th century, immigrants to Illinois originated from Central and South America, Asia (including Southeast Asia), Eastern Europe, and some from Africa. While their point of arrival is almost always Chicago, some of the immigrants migrate to other towns in the state where the cost of living is lower and jobs are available. These cities and towns include Moline, Peoria, Carbondale, and Champaign-Urbana, which has a number of international undergraduate and graduate students studying and living in the area.

According to the U.S. Census, almost 90 percent of Illinoisans are native to the United States, with 20 percent claiming German ancestry, 12 percent Irish ancestry, 8 percent Polish, 7 percent English, 6 percent Italian, and 2.4 percent Scottish-Irish. English is spoken everywhere, but there are pockets on Devon Street in Chicago where you'll hear Indian and Pakistani languages. Along South Halsted Street you can pick up Greek phrases. In some of Springfield and Champaign's restaurants and ethnic stores you'll hear Korean, Mandarin, or Russian being spoken. In Amish country near Arcola and Arthur, you might catch the Amish farmers speaking German.

The state has a sizeable Jewish population estimated at 270,000, ranking the state seventh in terms of numbers of Jewish people. Most live in and around Chicago, particularly the north shore suburbs of Skokie and Highland Park. However, some Jewish communities can be found in central Illinois towns such as Bloomington and Champaign.

STATISTICS

In the state's very early days, most of the population centers were in the south, such as near Cairo and Shawneetown. That has changed drastically since the 1800s, and Chicago is now where most people live. Of the state's estimated 12.8 million people, about 85 percent of them live in urban areas, and more than 65 percent of the state's residents live in Chicago and its surrounding suburbs. Cook County itself has 5.3 million people. Chicagoland (Cook and the surrounding collar counties) is the only region in the state where visitors might feel crowded. Here you will often encounter long lines at tollbooth plazas, museums, and cafés.

About 71 percent of the state's residents are Caucasian, about 15 percent are African American, close to 15 percent are Hispanic, and a little more than 4 percent are Asian. In line with the national trend, it was the Hispanic category that saw the most population growth 1990–2000.

Chicago is a youthful town; college graduates and young professionals are the majority of residents in neighborhoods such as Wicker Park and Wrigleyville. While Chicago and some large towns such as Champaign, Urbana, and Bloomington have a fair share of young adults, the average age of people in the rural counties keeps creeping higher, following the trend across the country. According to the U.S. Census about 70 percent of state residents are 21 years old or older. Illinois's population is fairly evenly distributed among men (49 percent) and women (51 percent).

Compared with national averages, Illinoisans are doing fairly well on a financial and educational level. About 12 percent of Illinoisans live below the poverty level. About 85 percent have a high school degree or higher, and almost 29 percent have a bachelor's degree or higher, both a bit higher than the national average. The home-ownership rate is around 70 percent, compared with the 69 percent national average.

ATTITUDES

At some point on your trip through the state you may hear a Chicagoan poke fun at downstate Illinois, alluding to their unsophisticated ways, their being out of touch with the latest trends (whether that trend is in real estate, fashion, or what have you). If you're in the south, chances are someone will refer to the know-it-all northerners and their obsessive consumerism. These jibes are nothing new. For almost 200 years it has been the case: north versus south in Illinois. And that probably won't change any time soon. Just where is that dividing line between northern and southern Illinois? That varies depending on who you talk to. For some people, "downstate" is anything outside the Chicago region. For many people, though, it's anything south of I-80.

Northern Illinois residents tend to be more diverse politically as well as racially and ethnically. Chicago is without a doubt a global city. World travelers live and work there. But it still has a colloquial feel to it, and people can't stop comparing it to New York and Los Angeles. It's the third-largest city in the country, and yet residents and members of the media (including print, television, and radio) always seem to get overexcited when Chicago is mentioned in national media or when a celebrity visits and dines in a local restaurant.

As you travel south, you'll notice people dress more casually and seem less hurried. They tend to be more conservative and religious. More folks (but not all) talk with a slight drawl, which intensifies the farther south you go. People are curious about visitors. If you walk into a local café, they'll all stop to look at you. But once you say hello and engage someone in conversation, you could while away the morning or afternoon chatting with him or her.

The phrase "Midwestern values" gets thrown around a lot, especially during election seasons. Just what this word implies probably varies with the speaker. Generally you'll find Illinoisans are a welcoming, engaging, loyal, practical bunch. We donate to charities, try to recycle, and make sure the kids are getting a good education. Illinois is predominantly Christian with a mix of Protestants, particularly Presbyterians, Methodists, Baptists, and Lutherans, and a good number of Catholics. Protestants and Catholics are the major religions, but in recent years a growing number of nondenominational churches have cropped up in the state. Mosques and synagogues are also found in most major towns. There's definitely a conservative religious contingent in the state (you'll notice several areas have quite a few Christian radio stations), but it probably does not have as many conservative or evangelical communities as the Bible Belt states.

Race relations have come a long way since the riots in the early 1900s and in the 1960s. Kids ride the buses together and attend schools together. Several nonprofit organizations around the state promote equality and diversity through school and workplace education. Most communities have human relations committees to iron out issues. Things aren't sparkling, though. In 1999 in Decatur, several black students were expelled for fighting at a football game. The action of the predominantly white school board was considered severe by many throughout the state, including the Reverend Jesse Jackson of Chicago, who led a march in the city to protest the school board's decision. In addition, Chicago and many other cities such as Rockford and the Champaign-Urbana region remain fairly segregated. In Chicago blacks tend to live in black communities on the south and west sides. Latinos live with Latinos on the southwest and northwest sides. People of different races may work together, but they don't always live in the same neighborhoods.

Arts and Culture

MUSEUMS

From folksy Raggedy Ann and Andy Museum in Arcola to the Museum of Contemporary Art in Chicago, Illinois has a vast array of museums, large and small, with collections that run the gamut. Museum Campus in Chicago is a trio of world-class museums: the Field Museum of Natural History, Adler Planetarium, and Shedd Aquarium. A few blocks away from those three museums is the Art Institute of Chicago with its famous French impressionist paintings and architecture collections. In Hyde Park to the south is the kid-friendly Museum of Science and Industry. And in Chicago's neighborhoods are a range of ethnic museums also worthy of a visit, such as the National Museum of Mexican Art and the Swedish American Museum Center.

One of the newest museums to open in Illinois is the long-awaited and much-anticipated **Abraham Lincoln Presidential Library and Museum** in Springfield. With a price tag of more than $100 million, this complex at more than 200,000 square feet has everything a Lincoln fan or historian could imagine, with exhibits that chronicle his life from his childhood to his time in the White House and assassination in Washington, D.C. Also in downstate Illinois, the University of Illinois at Urbana-Champaign has a few museums visitors might want to check out, including the Krannert Art Museum, which shows traditional and contemporary art, and the Spurlock Museum, which houses history exhibits from around the world.

Illinois has dozens of other lesser-known museums scattered throughout the state. These tend to be run by local residents or groups and highlight local history, or a private collection of items someone or a group of people have amassed through several decades. One gem of a museum is the **Under the Prairie Frontier Archaeological Museum** in Athens, where owners have discovered and artfully arranged artifacts, such as a kettle, a tin cup, or part of

an oxen shoe that date from before the Civil War. In a small town surrounded by fields of corn and soybeans, the **National Museum of Ship Models and Sea History** in Sadorus is a find with a large collection of models in a renovated storefront. **Shea's Gas Station Museum** in Springfield takes a nostalgic look at Route 66 and two-lane highway travel. Travelers who collect vintage postcards will get a kick out of the impressive **Curt Teich Postcard Archives** in the Lake County Discovery Museum in Wauconda. The collection comprises about 10,000 postcards depicting rural and urban scenes in Illinois and the Midwest, but also from more than 80 countries.

HISTORIC TRAVEL

Illinois, the "Land of Lincoln," will not disappoint visitors who want to follow in the footsteps of the state's famous son, **Abraham Lincoln.** Lincoln spent some three decades here, from his early 20s to his early 50s. As a young man looking to find work and eventually as a lawyer on the circuit court and a politician, Lincoln traveled a lot throughout the state. And you can bet anything he touched, any building or room that he walked in, any town that he traveled through, if it's still around and someone knows about it, there's a plaque or sign marking the significance. There's no shortage of Lincoln sites in Illinois.

The must-see Lincoln sites are his home in Springfield and the surrounding historic district, the new Lincoln museum and library, his tomb in Springfield's **Oak Ridge Cemetery,** plus **Lincoln's New Salem,** a recreated village northwest of Springfield. This is where he worked as a postmaster and in a general store and taught himself law. In addition, you can visit the sites around the state where Lincoln debated with **Stephen A. Douglas** issues such as slavery. The **Lincoln Log Cabin State Historic Site** in Lerna, south of Charleston, is where Lincoln's father and stepmother lived. This sometimes-overlooked site is a living history farm and has informative exhibits on the Lincoln family and their backgrounds. In the former lead-mining town of Galena, you can visit the home of former president and Civil War general **Ulysses S. Grant** and stay or dine in the **DeSoto House Hotel,** where Abraham Lincoln and others have stayed.

For Native American history, one of the best sites in the state is **Cahokia,** a UNESCO World Heritage Site near East St. Louis. From about A.D. 900 to 1400, members of this thriving Indian village traded with other cities miles away, cultivated corn and squash, and built extensive earthen mounds, dozens of which still remain in the area. Northeast of Cahokia in the Illinois River Valley are remains of more mound cultures. The **Dickson Mounds Museum** near Havana highlights the histories and contributions of these people. The **Center for American Archeology** in Kampsville organizes archaeological digs of such sites for amateur historians.

Although many buildings associated with Illinois's French and British past are long gone, you can visit the site of some of their forts, which have been rebuilt. Both empires built these forts to protect their Illinois territory, which in the 1700s and early 1800s was considered a remote and wild place. In the Mississippi River floodplain near Prairie du Rocher is **Fort de Chartres.** Several forts were actually built here, beginning in 1720. The massive stone fort you visit today was built to resemble the fort built by the French in the 1750s. Some archaeological remains of the original forts are on view there. Several forts also once stood in **Fort Massac State Park** overlooking the Ohio River near Metropolis. First the French built a fort there, followed by the British and finally the Americans. Virginian George Rogers Clark overtook the British fort during the Revolutionary War. During the Civil War the Illinois Calvary camped there. A replica of the American fort is on the site today, and a reenactment of life in the 1700s is held in the park every fall.

Even if you're not Mormon, chances are you'll be fascinated with a tour of Nauvoo on the western edge of the state. Joseph Smith and his followers settled here in the 1840s and left behind a remarkably well-preserved village. The **Joseph Smith Historic Site** consists of several original settlement buildings, including Smith's former home, and shops such as the post office, blacksmith shop, gun shop, and more. Also included in the site is the Smith Family Cemetery. The Historic Nauvoo Visitors Center fills you in on the history of the village, temple, and the Mormons, as does the recreated **Nauvoo Illinois Temple.** Steps from the temple, downtown Nauvoo has shops and restaurants for visitors. And a short drive eastward is the **Carthage Jail,** where Joseph Smith was killed by a mob.

Two organizations you might want to become familiar with are the **Illinois State Historical Society** and the **Chicago History Museum.** The state society (210½ S. 6th St., Springfield, 217/525-2781, www.historyillinois.org) publishes a number of books related to Illinois history and the glossy bimonthly magazine *Illinois Heritage,* which you might want to look for in a local bookstore or order from the society before your trip through the state. The society also publishes the scholarly *Journal of the Illinois State Historical Society.* **The Chicago History Museum** (Clark St. at North Ave., 312/642-4600, www.chicagohistory.org) has several rotating and permanent exhibits that may focus on a person (such as Stephen Douglas or Lincoln) or an event in history related to the city or state. The store has vintage photographs, posters, and a great selection of books for sale.

FESTIVALS

There's always something going on in Illinois, no matter what time of year. There are the traditional events such as Fourth of July and Memorial Day parades held in most towns. And there are the nontraditional ones, such as Morton's Punkin Chuckin' contest, where participants shoot pumpkins out of cannons.

Whatever event it is, most likely it involves eating. We Illinoisans like to eat and drink. We like to listen to music. We like a parade. We like silly contests. Oh, and we like to eat. Here's a sampling of just a few food-focused festivals in Illinois: the Arthur cheese festival, the horseradish festival in Collinsville, the strawberry and chocolate festivals in the Historic Village of Long Grove, the crab festival in Alto Pass, and of course the sweet-corn festival held in just about every rural town where someone grows corn. The mother of all food festivals is the enormously popular Taste of Chicago, where you can try hundreds of dishes from the city's restaurants.

Plenty of hot dogs and popcorn are on hand at the Illinois state fairs, held at permanent fairgrounds in Springfield and Du Quoin. These fairs bring in nationally known music acts, plus they feature 4-H and other agriculturally focused exhibits. On a smaller scale, dozens of county fairs and farm shows are held all summer long throughout the state. They tend to include tractor pulls, demolition derbies, carnival rides, and plenty of food and beer tents. Stop by a county fair and you can learn how to raise a sow, goat, or other farm animal. The summer months are packed with music and art festivals, including Chicago's world-famous Blues Fest, Peoria's riverfront blues festival, Custer's Last Stand Art Fair in Evanston, and Galena's Festival of the Performing Arts. Summer is also a time for many antique car shows, which pop up in many towns. One not-to-miss road party is the International Route 66 Mother Road Festival in Springfield.

Naturalists will enjoy solstice and equinox festivals at Cahokia Mounds near Collinsville, Lombard's lilac festival, and bird-watching events held in the cool months in towns along the Illinois and Mississippi Rivers. In late November and early December tree-lighting ceremonies are common throughout the state. Several towns hold outdoor markets and ethnic festivals around the holidays. Chicago's Christkindlesmarkt always attracts large crowds for its German crafts, warm cider, and stollen. For that quiet hometown feel, head to Bishop Hill's Lucia Nights, a Swedish festival of lights in mid-December.

SHOPPING

Variety, variety, variety. Whether you're hunting for a sleek outfit for a night on the town, a rare book from the late 19th century, or a ceramic dish circa 1950, you can satisfy your shopping impulses in Illinois. Chicago's got it all—expensive clothes and accessories, antiques, and kitschy collectibles. But don't forget to scour shops around the state. You might be surprised by the deals and oddities you could find in the barn turned antique store or tucked in the back of the storefront space on Main Street.

Chicago and Vicinity

State Street (otherwise known as "that great street") and **Michigan Avenue** in Chicago's downtown have long been the shopping hubs for the city. Department stores Marshall Field's and Carson Pirie Scott and ritzy boutiques such as Tiffany and Company line these shopping districts. Both are vibrant throughout the year, but effervesce during the holiday season with one elaborate window display and busking musician after the other. Upscale galleries are common in the **River North** neighborhood just north of the Chicago River and west of the Gold Coast. Funky boutiques are dotted throughout **Wicker Park, Bucktown,** and **Andersonville.** In-vogue fashions and home-decor shops are common in the gentrified neighborhoods of **Armitage** and **Southport.** Megamalls are mostly installed in the suburbs, such as the huge **Gurnee Mills** in Gurnee and **Woodfield Mall** in Schaumburg.

Antiques, Arts and Crafts, and Flea Markets

You won't have to hunt long for antiques or works by local artists. Several Illinois towns have charming main streets lined with storefront shops and galleries. Wilmington and Lincoln are well-known for their bevy of antiques shops. The Fox River cities of St. Charles and Geneva have dozens of upscale art and antiques stores. You could spend hours in the mazelike **Illinois Antique Center** in an old warehouse on Peoria's riverfront. For arts and crafts, the former Swedish colony of **Bishop**

ILLINOIS WINE

In recent years the Illinois wine-making industry has really taken off. Ten years ago the state was home to a handful of vineyards and wineries. Now there are dozens. Illinois wineries are run by families who have been crafting wine for decades – they're retired teachers, former livestock farmers, you name it.

Illinois wines are primarily made from red and white French hybrid grapes such as Chambourcin and Traminette, grapes that are suited to the varied Illinois climate. Some vintners make wine from Illinois-grown fruit, such as peaches, apples, and berries. Bottles usually cost under $20.

The bulk of the state's wineries and vineyards are in the south. Grapes do well on the hillsides and in the mild climate there. While in southern Illinois, pick up a map of the Shawnee Hills Wine Trail (www.shawneewinetrail.com), which directs visitors to five different wineries around the Pomona and Alto Pass region. Two good bets in southern Illinois are Von Jakob Vineyards near Pomona and Cameo Vineyards in Greenup. In addition to the Shawnee Hills wineries, you'll find wineries within an hour's drive from Chicago, such as Lynfred in Roselle and Glunz Family Winery and Cellars in Grayslake. In the far northwestern part of the state are the scenic Galena Cellars Winery in Galena and Massbach Ridge Winery in nearby Elizabeth. Both are set amid the rolling hills and near bustling small towns.

New wineries seem to open annually. To get the latest scoop on where to go, check with the Illinois Grape Growers and Vintners Association's website, www.illinoiswine.com. Most wineries are open to the public according to set hours, and a few are open by appointment.

Hill has shops that sell handcrafted furniture, home-decor items, clothing, and jewelry. The streets of **Galena** are also lined with artisans' shops run by friendly potters, weavers, and the like.

In addition, the **Illinois State Museum** highlights the work of some of the state's best artisans at the Southern Illinois Artisan Shop near Benton and the Illinois Artisan Shop in the James R. Thompson Center in Chicago. At these shops you can learn about basket-weaving and quilt-making as well as buy some of these items. Other handmade items can be found in Illinois's **Amish country** near Arthur and Arcola, where downtown and homestead shops sell furniture, plants, produce, and everything you can imagine. Seeking bargains? The towns of **Sandwich** and **St. Charles** in the northern part of the state both hold regular flea markets in the warm months.

FOOD

To be honest, it'll be tough to travel through Illinois if you're limiting calories and fat. As noted earlier, Illinoisans love to eat. We like doughnuts, pizza, hot dogs, fish sandwiches, steaks, you name it. Here are a few common dishes in Illinois. First off is the **Chicago-style pizza.** Chicago-style pizza tends to be very cheesy and is usually a few inches thick. The crust, made of pressed dough, is topped with thick mozzarella slices followed by other toppings (popular choices are sausage or spinach), and then it's all topped with a layer of chunky tomato sauce. **Chicago-style hot dogs** are all-beef wieners loaded with green relish, chopped onions, sliced tomatoes, serrano peppers, yellow mustard, and a dash of celery salt. They're usually served in a poppy-seed bun.

Outside of Chicago, the **horseshoe sandwich** is a common menu item, especially in Springfield, where it supposedly was invented. Every restaurant, bar, or drive-in has its own version of the horseshoe, but essentially it's an open-faced sandwich with 2–3 pieces of toast layered with your choice of meat (hamburger, ham steak, turkey, corned beef, you name it), then topped with a pile of French fries, and on top of that melted cheese. What kind of cheese sauce it is varies by restaurant.

Some places pour the cheese over the meat and then dump the fries over the sauce. Basically a horseshoe hits the spot after you've spent the day walking, hiking, biking, swimming, or engaged in some other type of activity for a long time, or after a night of partaking in more than a few drinks.

Food Markets and Farmers Markets

Illinois has about 200 regularly scheduled farmers markets throughout the state, held in places such as downtown parks and church or city hall parking lots. (Chicago alone has more than a dozen markets.) Here you can find seasonal produce, from apricots to zucchinis, plus flowers, locally raised meats, and sometimes local artists playing music or exhibiting their creations. Check with the local visitors bureaus to find out about days and times the markets are held, typically on Saturdays May–October. In addition to the markets, several farms organize stands where you can buy a peck of apples or they allow you to pick your own strawberries or pumpkins, such as at Eckert's in Belleville or Curtis Orchard in Champaign. Farm stands are common in southern Illinois, where the sunny hills make prime spots for growing fruit trees. You can find dozens of apple and peach stands on the outskirts of towns such as Carbondale and Alto Pass in and near the Shawnee National Forest. Area visitors bureaus have orchard maps to help you navigate your way through the region.

ESSENTIALS

Getting There and Around

BY AIR

Chicago's **O'Hare International Airport** on the northwest side is by far the busiest airport in the state and usually the busiest or one of the busiest in the country. It can handle nearly 1 million flights in a year. O'Hare is connected to the city via the Blue Line train, plus dozens of cabs and hotel shuttles are often lined up in the arrival and departure areas. On the southwest side of Chicago is **Midway International Airport,** a hub for economy carriers such as Southwest Airlines. It's linked to the city by the Orange Line train. A third regional airport is proposed in Will County to the south, near Peotone and Monee.

Flying into Rockford is another option if you're visiting the Chicago region. About 80 miles from Chicago, the Rockford airport (officially called the **Chicago Rockford International Airport**) has flights to and from cities such as Ft. Lauderdale, Florida; Las Vegas; Denver; and Myrtle Beach, South Carolina. Parking there is free. Regional carriers such as American Airlines and Delta fly into smaller airports such as the **Central Illinois Regional Airport** in Bloomington-Normal, which also offers free parking; Springfield's **Capital Airport;** the **Greater Peoria Regional Airport;** and the **University of Illinois's Willard Airport** in Savoy. The airlines serving these smaller airports tend to change frequently, so be sure to check back to the airline or airport website. Otherwise, if you plan to explore the southern and central regions, consider flying into St. Louis or even Indianapolis and then renting a car from those airports.

BY TRAIN

Illinois is lucky. Several **Amtrak** (800/872-7245, www.amtrak.com) lines crisscross the state, with Chicago's Union Station serving as a regional hub for many of these lines. Most of the trains run daily; however, sometimes they're subject to delays as they often yield to heavy freight traffic. You can hop on one of several "Superliner" trains. The **California Zephyr** train runs from Chicago west to Princeton and Galesburg before moving on through Iowa, Nebraska, Colorado, Nevada, and finally to Emeryville, California. The **Southwest Chief** links Chicago to Los Angeles, with stops in Illinois in Naperville, Mendota, and Princeton. The **Texas Eagle** connects Chicago with San Antonio via the Illinois towns of Joliet, Pontiac, Normal, Lincoln, Springfield, and Alton. The famous **City of New Orleans** train connects Chicago to New Orleans and stops in towns primarily along the eastern part of the state, such as the university towns of Champaign-Urbana and Carbondale.

Several other in-state and regional trains include the **Ann Rutledge,** which goes between Chicago and Kansas City, and the **Hiawatha,** which carries passengers between Chicago and Milwaukee. The **Lincoln** train runs daily between Chicago and St. Louis, with stops in towns such as Dwight, Bloomington, Springfield, and Alton. The **Illinois Zephyr** train links Chicago and Quincy, with stops in towns such as Naperville, Princeton, Galesburg, and Macomb. **Illini Service** ties Chicago with Carbondale, with stops in towns such as Kankakee, Gilman, Rantoul, Mattoon, Effingham, and Du Quoin. Other Midwestern cities served by Chicago trains include, for example, Detroit and Indianapolis.

Before you take one of the congestion-plagued interstate highways in the Chicago

The Blue Line train connects O'Hare Airport to Chicago.

region, check to see if a Metra train line runs to or near your destination. **Metra** (312/836-7000, www.metrarail.com) has 12 train lines that cover all of Chicagoland and more. They stretch all the way north to Kenosha, Wisconsin; Fox Lake (by the Chain O' Lakes State Park); northwest to Harvard and Woodstock; and south to University Park. Metra train rides cost a few bucks each way, and Metra has special unlimited weekend fares that run about $5 per person. Plus the trains are almost always on time.

BY BUS

Greyhound (general info 800/231-2222, Chicago main station 312/408-5800, www.greyhound.com) serves 31 cities in Illinois with several stops in Chicago (in addition to the main bus terminal building downtown on Harrison Street). Buses go to most of the other major towns and cities in Illinois, such as downstate cities like Mattoon and Carbondale, and west to Galena and Moline. Not all cities have actual bus terminals, but buses will stop at places such as designated motels along highways. Hours at these terminals are always subject to change, so call ahead. Fares are usually around or under $30 for one-way trips, with discounts given to passengers booking a week in advance. Discounts are also available to seniors, students, and others. Greyhound also offers Internet-only and companion fare specials.

Other private bus companies operate in some central and southern towns, mostly to shuttle people back and forth to major airports in the region, such as the Chicago airports and those in St. Louis and Indianapolis. Check in the regional chapters for information on these companies.

BY CAR

Illinois is definitely a road trip–friendly state. Thanks to the Eisenhower freeway system, several interstates carve paths through the state, making it possible to zip through, stopping only at toll plazas or truck stops. Bring some quarters. A few tollways cross our state (I-80, I-90, and I-294). Fares vary, but tolls are generally $0.80 a shot (although crossing the Skyway bridge, which links Chicago to Indiana, will cost a few bucks per car). Residents and long-term repeat visitors might want to invest in an I-PASS for about $40 (800/824-7277, www. getipass.com). Tolls for I-PASS holders are generally $0.40 or $0.50 per toll booth.

If you're going long distances, say from Chicago to Carbondale, and have no plans to stop in between, the interstates are efficient. But if you have time, veer off them for some two-lane highway journeys through the main streets of small towns or the hilly roads through orchard country in the south. The mother of all two-lane highways, **Route 66** begins at Chicago's lakefront and winds southwest toward St. Louis, mostly along I-55. Follow the **Great River Road** along the Mississippi River from East Dubuque all the way down to the southern tip of the state. The **Dixie Highway** (also known as Route 1) follows the eastern edge of the state through the Vermilion and Wabash River valleys. The **National Road** (or U.S. 40) cuts through the center of the state and takes you through many farming regions. The **Ohio River Scenic Byway** snakes along the great Ohio River in the south and southeastern part of the state past quaint and historic river towns such as Elizabethtown and Golconda. All these historic highways are marked with signs that point you in the right direction.

The **Illinois Department of Transportation** releases road conditions on its website, www. gettingaroundillinois.com, and records them on the hotline, 800/452-IDOT (800/452-4368). For road conditions, lane closures, and other information on the tollways, call 800/ TOLL-FYI (800/865-5394).

Recreation

RESOURCES

Illinois has nearly 100 state parks in just about every region of the state, from the expansive Jim Edgar Panther Creek site in the center of the state to the small but scenic Apple River Canyon in the northwest. One of the best things about the state parks is that admission is free, no catch. Camping fees are nominal. **The Illinois Department of Natural Resources** (1 Natural Resources Wy., Springfield, 217/782-6302, www.dnr.state.il.us) manages the sites, some of which feature historic lodges (such as

Père Marquette in Grafton) in addition to the standard hiking trails, lakes, rivers, and picnic and camping areas. The website contains information, including maps, on every state park in Illinois. The DNR publishes the glossy *Outdoor Illinois* magazine, which costs $15 a year. You can subscribe online or look for it in libraries and bookstores.

Another glossy magazine for naturalists is *Illinois Steward,* published quarterly by the University of Illinois Extension. This one has more of a focus on environmental and natural-

BEST TRAILS

BEST HIKING TRAILS, BY REGION

- **Collar Counties:** Volo Bog.

- **Northern:** Apple River Canyon State Park, Moraine Hills.

- **Great River Valleys:** Mississippi Palisades, Starved Rock, and Père Marquette State Parks.

- **Grand Prairie:** Kickapoo State Park, Lake Shelbyville.

- **Shawnee Hills and Southern Illinois:** Rim Rock National Recreation Trail, Little Grand Canyon.

BEST BIKE TRAILS, BY REGION

- **Chicago:** Lakefront Trail

- **Collar Counties:** Salt Creek Trail, near west suburbs; Green Bay Trail, northern suburbs.

- **Northern:** Hennepin Canal.

- **Great River Valleys:** Sam Vadalabene Trail, Illinois & Michigan Canal Trail.

- **Shawnee Hills and Southern Illinois:** Tunnel Hill State Trail.

© CHRISTINE DES GARENNES

Mississippi Palisades State Park has some challenging hiking trails.

history issues important to the state. You can also find it at most libraries and bookstores, by calling 217/244-2851, or by visiting the University of Illinois Extension website, www.extension.uiuc.edu, and searching under "Publications." The cost is $20 for one year.

HIKING

Through river bottomland forests, restored prairies, or old-growth forests, Illinois has a network of trails throughout the state for hikers with varying degrees of ability. The southern and northern part of the state, where most of the hills are, have the most challenging trails. The central region has trails through restored prairies, offering opportunities for bird-watching and scouting for wildflowers. In the south, you can test your calf muscles by hiking along **Little Grand Canyon** by Carbondale. The steep four-mile loop has several scenic overlooks of the Illinois version of the Grand Canyon. Nearby **Giant City State Park** has short nature trails, such as the Stone Fort Trail, which are less than a mile, or the 16-mile Red Cedar Hiking Trail winds around the exterior of this beautiful park. To the east of Giant City, hike past the remains of a Native American village and an ancient rock shelter at **Lusk Creek Canyon,** east of Eddyville. The **River-to-River Trail** is a vigorous 175-mile-long trail through Illinois that connects the Mississippi and Ohio Rivers. Try a 12-mile section from Panthers' Den to Giant City State Park or a six- to eight-mile section from the Godwin Trail to the LaRue–Pine Hills State Recreation Area on the Mississippi River.

In the northwest part of the state, the Apple River has carved 250-foot-high cliffs through limestone and bedrock. Admire the geology of the driftless region by hiking through the 300-acre **Apple River Canyon State Park,** which has short trails through bottomland and upland forests. Like Giant City State Park, **Starved Rock State Park** near Utica has a wide variety of trails for hikers of any level. There are 13 miles of trails in total at Starved Rock, from the 0.3-mile Starved Rock Trail to the 4.7-mile Illinois Canyon Trail. You'll scale cliffs, maneuver along canyons, and view the Illinois River from on high.

Trails in the central part of the state are more level but no less scenic. One of the newest places to go walking is **Midewin National Tallgrass Prairie** near Wilmington. Once the site of an Army ammunition plant, Midewin offers miles of mowed-grass trails for hiking. The entire site is about 19,000 acres; however, a little more than 7,000 are now open to the public. (More land is expected to open as the U.S. Department of Agriculture's Forest Service cleans and rehabilitates the land.) Moving southwest along the Illinois and Sangamon River valleys you'll find 24 miles of rough trails for hiking or mountain biking at **Jim Edgar Panther Creek State Fish and Wildlife Area** near Chandlerville. For more rustic trails (and by rustic I mean not pavement or asphalt), head to **Sand Ridge State Forest** near Forest City. Situated along the Illinois River, the state forest has 44 miles of hiking trails, each ranging in length from about 1.5 miles to 17 miles. **Pyramid State Park** in south-central Perry County is another quiet park with about 20,000 acres to explore, with 17 miles of hiking and horseback-riding trails.

BIKING

Illinoisans love to bike. And why not? There are lots of trails to choose from, and they're all accessible and fairly easy to navigate. Most of the state's bike trails are converted railroad beds with asphalt or crushed-limestone bases. And with the exception of the trails in southern Illinois, most trails wind through flat terrain with occasional sets of rolling hills, tunnels, or railroad trestles.

In the northeastern part of the state Chicago's **Lakefront Trail** runs along the lakeshore for about 18 miles, past landmarks such as the Shedd Aquarium and the Museum of Science and Industry, sand volleyball courts, marinas, and sandy beaches. West of Chicago the 60-mile-long **Prairie Path** traverses a former railroad bed past Wheaton, Naperville, and many nature preserves. For a glimpse of the tony north shore suburbs, pedal along the **Green Bay Trail,** which follows the Metra line starting near Shorewood Park in Wilmette to Lake Bluff.

On the western edge of the state, the **Sam Vadalabene Bicycle Trail** connects the classic Mississippi River town of Alton with Père Marquette State Park. It follows the Great River Road for about 20 miles. Another trail along the Mississippi River is the **Great River Trail** in the northwestern part of the state. It winds for almost 63 miles from the Quad Cities to Savanna to the north. You'll pass the Rock Island Arsenal and several locks and dams. One of the newest (and probably less crowded) bike trails in the state is the 96-mile **Hennepin Canal State Trail,** which carves a north-south path through the north-central part of the state through and near towns such as Bureau Junction, Princeton, Sheffield, Mineral, and Geneseo. And the **I&M Canal State Trail** or Illinois & Michigan Canal connects Rockdale, southwest of Joliet, to the LaSalle–Peru area, just west of Starved Rock State Park. That trail also follows one of the state's canals north of the Illinois River.

At the far southern end of the state, **Tunnel Hill State Trail** challenges riders for 45 miles from Harrisburg to Karnak. Pedal through tunnels, over trestles, and along the bottomlands of the Cache River basin. A short spur introduces visitors to the Cache River State Natural Area with its cypress and tupelo swamps. Also in the southern region is **Pyramid State Park** near Pinckneyville. Fat-tire riders will never want to leave this 19,000-acre rustic park, which has a network of trails, including a 12-mile mountain-bike trail through woods, meadows, and past small lakes.

WATER ADVENTURES
Canoeing and Kayaking
Most visitors tend to think of Illinois as a water-deficient state. And compared to some of its neighbors to the north, such as Wisconsin and Minnesota, it is. But you might be surprised by the opportunities we have for paddling through quiet sloughs, along a national scenic river, and yes, even the **Chicago River.** Strolling through downtown Chicago early on a weekend morning, take a few minutes to peer over the Madison Street Bridge or any other bridge in the Loop. You could stumble upon a curious sight: people kayaking along the Chicago River. Yup, those are actually kayakers. In recent years paddling the Chicago River has become a fairly popular way to see the city. Visitors can also have a go at sea kayaking on Lake Michigan, which you might be surprised to learn can become quite rough on windy days. Or for a quieter, calmer canoe ride in the Chicago region, head to the **Skokie Lagoons** near Evanston. The Chicago area has quite a few clubs plus outfitters where you can rent and buy equipment, such as Chicago River Canoe and Kayak in Evanston.

If you're looking for a challenging paddle along churning rivers and rapids, two popular rivers downstate are the **Middle Fork National Scenic River** or Vermilion River near Danville and the **Kankakee River** near Bourbonnais and Kankakee. The ultimate canoe tour in Illinois can be found in the extreme southern part of the state in the Cache River region. There you'll glide through cypress and tupelo swamps and past orchards while tree frogs sing. You can't beat it.

Before setting out on a canoe or kayak adventure, check out Illinois Paddling's website (www.illinoispaddling.org), which has links to several regional clubs and outfitters. Members are working to develop and expand canoeing and kayaking opportunities in Illinois.

Boating
For more fast-paced boating action, you can find several public boat launches and piers along the shores of Illinois's many lakes. Because of the way the glaciers carved their way through the state, the naturally occurring lakes are in the northern part of Illinois (such as **Chain O' Lakes** at the town of Fox Lake), and the artificial lakes are in the central and south-central part of the state. The artificial lakes, such as **Carlyle Lake** (at the town of Carlyle), **Clinton Lake** (at Clinton), **Lake Shelbyville** (at Shelbyville), and **Rend Lake** (south of Mount Vernon), are huge and tend to attract people who are boating for sport or who are fishing. The largest artificial lake is Carlyle Lake at 26,000 acres.

Before launching into an Illinois lake or river, you need to register and have a title for your boat (for more info, contact the Illinois Department of Natural Resources at 217/557-0180 or 800/382-1696). You'll also want to find out if there are any restrictions related to horsepower. Some lakes, for example, are restricted to boats with electric trolling motors. The DNR has a list of those lakes. If you aren't hauling your own boat around the state, you can rent anything from a paddleboat to a fishing boat with a 10-horsepower engine. **Eagle Creek Resort** on Lake Shelbyville, for example, rents personal watercraft, and **Golconda Marina** in the southern part of the state rents pontoon boats.

FISHING
If you have a rod, bring it along on your trip through Illinois. The state has numerous accessible lakes, rivers, streams, and ponds for fishing. And fishing licenses are easy to get and cost just a few bucks. You can land a hefty chinook salmon while on a thrilling charter ride on **Lake Michigan** or a try for a channel catfish in the **Illinois River valley.** There are about 1.6 million acres of surface water and 26,000 miles of streams in the state, filled with trout (lake, rainbow, and brown trout), perch, muskies, walleyes, catfish, plus the usual crappies and sunfish. Salmon and trout are common

in Lake Michigan, and muskies and bass are stocked in the big inland lakes such as Lake Shelbyville. Catfish and walleye make their home in the streams and rivers.

Fishing licenses are available from the Illinois Department of Natural Resources (888/673-7648), bait shops, harbors, sporting goods stores, and some gas stations. You can buy a 24-hour license, 10-day license, or an annual one. Daily licenses are about $6 for residents or nonresidents. Nonresidents can get a 10-day license for $13. An annual license for residents is $13 and $24.50 for nonresidents. You don't need one if you are under age 16 or are disabled. If you fish for salmon or trout in Lake Michigan, you'll need a stamp.

The Illinois Department of Natural Resources publishes a fishing regulations handbook, available at most bait shops, harbors, and visitors bureaus. In addition to basic information on licenses and size limits, the handbook also includes the department of health's fish consumption guidelines, which might come in handy if you decide to fish in Chicago's harbors. In addition to the handbook, a great Internet resource is www.ifishillinois.org, which has a roundup of where to fish, lists of local tournaments, and weekly fish reports for lakes and rivers in regions around the state. The DNR's Division of Fisheries manages several hatcheries throughout the state, including the **Little Grassy Fish Hatchery** in Makanda and the **Jake Wolf Memorial Fish Hatchery** in Topeka. These are open to the public.

If you have some time, take off on a half-day or daylong charter fishing trip on Lake Michigan to fish for salmon and trout. Dozens of charter boat companies offer trips launching from Chicago's harbors and the north shore marinas in Waukegan and Winthrop Harbor. These trips can run several hours and cost several hundred dollars, but they're usually quite an adventure. (From the shore, you might not realize Lake Michigan can kick up some tough waves pretty quickly. If you're prone to seasickness, don't forget the Dramamine.) For a list of charter boat companies, contact the Waukegan Charter Boat Association (103 E. Madison St.,

Waukegan Harbor, Waukegan, 847/244-3474, www.wcba.info); North Point Charter Boat Association (North Point Marina, 701 North Point Dr., Winthrop Harbor, 800/247-6727, www.salmonoid.com/npcba); or the Chicago Sportfishing Association (www.great-lakes.org/il/fish-chicago/index.html), which represents tours that embark from several of Chicago's harbors.

HUNTING

Although primarily liberal and democratic Chicago tends to dominate the cultural and political landscape of Illinois, visitors and new residents are often surprised to discover that a devoted hunting (and pro-gun) subculture exists in the state, particularly in the rural counties in central and southern Illinois. Perhaps not as ingrained into the way of life as in, say, Wisconsin or Michigan, hunting is something many residents do throughout the year. With the growing popularity of commercial game preserves and resorts, hunting as a pastime may continue to expand.

Essentially there are four hunting categories in Illinois: deer and turkeys, migratory fowl (such as Canada geese and doves), upland game (such as quail and pheasant), plus trapping for fur animals such as foxes, raccoons, and even squirrels. Hunting for wild turkeys is fairly popular and done in all regions, especially in the north in the spring. The deer season in Illinois runs from early October to early January, with separate weeks set aside for hunting with bows or shotguns. You can hunt deer in virtually all regions of the state.

Many state parks and wildlife areas are open for hunting, in addition to about 50 hunting preserves (which are mainly for hunting upland game and fowl), which you'll find in just about every region except Chicagoland. Fees vary according to the preserve. Some have set fees based on the time you spend in the preserve (half-day versus full-day hunting trips) or based on the amount of birds the preserve releases for you to go after. A list of preserves is on the Illinois Department of Natural Resources website (www.dnr.state.il.us).

A seasonal hunting pass for residents is $7.50. For nonresidents, a five-day pass is $28.50. Seasonal passes are also available. In addition to these fees, you'll have to buy permits specific to the animal you're after (deer, turkeys, etc.), and permit fees can range from about $10–200 depending on the animal, whether you are an Illinois resident or not, and whether you choose to hunt with a shotgun or a bow and arrow. The Illinois Department of Natural Resources' *Digest of Hunting and Trapping Regulations* contains comprehensive information about fees and rules of hunting in Illinois, plus maps of public hunting areas. You can download it from the website www.dnr.state.il.us, pick up a free copy in most sporting goods shops, or call the DNR's regional offices: Sterling (northern), 815/625-2968; Bartlett (Chicagoland), 815/675-2385; Clinton (central), 217/935-6860; Alton (southwest), 618/462-1181; Benton (southern), 618/435-8138; and Chicago, 312/814-2070. For special hunting permits call the DNR at 217/782-7305.

GOLF

If you're a newcomer to Illinois links, a good place to begin your search for a course is the **Chicago District Golf Association** (main office at Midwest Golf House, 11855 Archer Ave., Lemont, 630/257-2005, www.cdga.org). This organization is not just about Chicago courses, but it's an association of golfers and 350 clubs in Illinois and parts of Wisconsin, Michigan, and Indiana. It publishes course information (ratings, yardages, fees, etc.) online and in their bimonthly magazine, *Chicago District Golfer.*

As far as top courses in Illinois, here's a sampling: the Glen Club in Glenview (on the grounds of the former Glenview naval base); Cog Hill in Lemont; Medinah Country Club in Medinah, near Bloomingdale; Lake of the Woods County Park golf course in Mahomet (a refreshingly hilly course in the middle of flat land); Ironhorse Golf Course in Tuscola; the Den at Fox Creek in Bloomington; and Eagle Ridge Resort in Galena.

BIRD-WATCHING

Whether you stroll through the prairie, river bottomlands, or atop sandstone cliffs, you will encounter and hear a variety of birds. Birding is a popular pastime in Illinois, and the **Illinois Audubon Society** (217/544-2473, www.illinoisaudubon.org), an organization that actually predates the founding of the national society, is active in protecting the state's flora and fauna, particularly birds. It maintains several wildlife sanctuaries in the state, mostly in the central and southern region. One is the Robert Ridgeway Grasslands adjacent to Prairie Ridge State Natural Area near Newton. Members also often organize bird-watching and counting trips to areas around Illinois.

Towns along the Mississippi and Illinois Rivers, such as Havana and Alton, are often destinations for birders. Migratory birds, eagles, and other raptors congregate along those rivers in the winter and towns such as Havana hold bird-watching events. Some good spots include locks and dams along the rivers, trails within the Upper Mississippi River National Fish and Wildlife Refuge south of Savanna, Delbar State Park north of Oquawka, and the Chautauqua National Wildlife Refuge near Havana. If you like to look for birds with others, you can join organized tours held throughout the year at parks such as Starved Rock State Park near Ottawa or Midewin National Tallgrass Prairie by Wilmington. Take a short drive through the western town of Griggsville and you'll see why it is considered the purple martin capital of the nation. Houses for these mosquito-eating birds line the streets and front- and backyards of the town's residents. Birders will want to check the Nature House Showroom, where you can buy houses for purple martins.

OTHER OUTDOOR RECREATION
Skiing

If you're itching to shush down some slopes, you won't have to drive out of state. Illinois is certainly not Colorado or New Hampshire, but there are a few hills where skiers get their kicks. Many offer great opportunities for beginners or intermediate skiers who want to brush up on their skills before heading elsewhere. One option (and perhaps the best one in the state for downhill skiing) is **Chestnut Mountain Resort** near Galena. Otherwise, novices and snowboarders can try **Villa Olivia** in Bartlett, **Four Lakes Villages** in Lisle, or **Ski Snowstar** in Taylor Ridge near the Quad Cities. If you want to slow things down, Illinois has plenty of spots for **cross-country skiing,** especially in the state parks in the north. Stick to parks in the north, such as **Blackwell Forest Preserve** in Warrenville near Chicago and **Kankakee River State Park** in Bourbonnais. Snow often doesn't stick around long enough in the central and southern regions to make for a good cross-country skiing base.

Caves

Illinois has several hundred caves throughout the state, but the only one open to the public is **Illinois Caverns State Natural Area** in the southwestern part of the state near the tiny town of Redbud. Considered a wild cave (no electricity down here), Illinois Caverns has six miles of trails for visitors to explore. You'll trudge through mud and jostle around stalagmites and stalactites (those icicle-like formations common in caves). Visitors are required to explore in groups of four or more, wear boots and a hard hat, and carry three sources of light (i.e., a waterproof flashlight) per person.

Climbing

The outcropping and hills of southern Illinois make for some excellent rock climbing, especially for novices and climbers wanting to perfect their bouldering skills. You can climb at the following state parks: **Ferne Clyffe** and **Giant City** (both of which are in southern Illinois), and **Mississippi Palisades** in the northwest corner of the state. When you can't go outside, head to **Upper Limits** in Bloomington where old grain silos have been converted into climbing gyms.

Accommodations

HOTELS, MOTELS, AND BED-AND-BREAKFASTS

Rates for hotels vary widely throughout the state, the most expensive ones being in downtown Chicago, although there are some pricey resorts and inns in Galena and the Geneva area also. Midweek prices tend to be lower than weekend rates. Summer rates are almost always higher than those in February or March, when not many people, except business travelers, are visiting the state. If you reserve a hotel room with a credit card, you should be able to check in any time of night. But most hotels will give away your room if you don't show up by 6 P.M. and haven't given them a credit-card guarantee. Most bed-and-breakfasts require two-night stays on the weekends, and if you cancel, usually it needs to be done a week or so in advance; otherwise you may lose some money.

On the **Illinois Hotel and Lodging Association** website (www.stayillinois.com), you can type in your destination and date of arrival and departure, and the server will check availability for all hotels, inns, and bed-and-breakfasts in the area.

The **Illinois Bed and Breakfast Association** (888/523-2406, www.go-illinois.com) publishes a helpful online guide and color booklet listing bed-and-breakfasts in the state. It includes lists of bed-and-breakfasts by region, plus info such as whether the inn or bed-and-breakfast is pet-friendly, child-friendly, or wheelchair-accessible. The site also keeps a log of specials going on at bed-and-breakfasts around the state.

CAMPING AND CABINS

Do you want to walk a half mile through the woods and then camp in a tent? Hook up your RV in a park alongside several other trucks? How about renting an air-conditioned cottage in the woods? In other words, how close to

© CHRISTINE DES GARENNES

Giant City State Park, south of Carbondale, offers camping, cabins, and a historic lodge.

nature do you want to get? Illinois has plenty of camping options. This is a big RV state, and the **Illinois Campground Association** (866/895-2267, www.illinoisgocamping. com) can help you choose where to park your truck. It lists campgrounds and RV parks online (through the National Association of RV Parks and Campgrounds website) and through a guide you can find at most travel information centers.

Otherwise, contact the **Illinois Department of Natural Resources** (1 Natural Resources Wy., Springfield, 217/782-6302, www.dnr. state.il.us) to find out about its campgrounds, which vary from modern sites with electric hookups and shower buildings to remote hike-in sites where you haul in your tent and supplies by yourself. Camping fees at Illinois state parks range about $6–20 per night. Some state parks offer what's called "rent-a-tent," where for an extra fee you rent equipment such as the tent and flashlights for the night. Others have full-fledged cabins or cottages,

complete with air-conditioning and heaters, such as Starved Rock State Park near Utica and Eldon Hazlet State Park on Carlyle Lake. Then there are the historic state park lodges, many of which were built more than 50 years ago by the Civilian Conservation Corps. Two personal favorites are the Père Marquette State Park lodge overlooking the Mississippi River and the Giant City State Park lodge tucked in the Shawnee Hills.

Finally, there are 12 campgrounds in the **Shawnee National Forest.** Many are rustic (with pit toilets), but Oak Point Campground at Lake Glendale Recreation Area and Pounds Hollow have shower buildings. The forest is divided into two districts: Hidden Springs (Vienna and Elizabethtown area) to the east and Mississippi Bluffs (Jonesboro and Murphysboro) to the west. For more information on camping, you can contact the headquarters in Harrisburg (50 Hwy. 145, Harrisburg, 618/253-7114 or 800/699-6637, www.fs.fed.us/r9/forests/shawnee).

Tips for Travelers

HEALTH AND SAFETY
Plants, Bugs, and Animals

There are no lions, tigers, or bears (wild ones, anyway) in Illinois, but there are a few critters you'll want to keep an eye out for. First, the mosquito: The **West Nile virus** was first detected in Illinois in 2001 after a laboratory confirmed two dead birds found in Chicago had the virus. Since then, the virus has been detected in all 102 counties (in birds, horses, and people). In 2002 the state registered more people sick and dead from the disease than any other state (that year 66 people died from the disease). The number of people infected who fall sick varies every year. Compared with 2002, in 2007 there were 101 people who came down with the virus, four of whom died. Because people can get the virus by being bitten by an infected mosquito, the Illinois Department of Public Health recommends people apply an insect repellent with 25–35 percent DEET. Mild symptoms include fever and muscle aches; severe symptoms include a high-grade fever, dizziness, convulsions, and a whole slew of other unpleasant things. More information is available by calling the **West Nile Virus State Hotline** at 866/369-9710.

Critter No. 2: the tick. Although more of a risk in the northeastern United States than in Illinois, **Lyme disease** is something to think about when you're hiking through the woods or through areas with tall grasses. Illinois does have deer ticks, which can transmit the disease. Symptoms can include (but are not limited to) a ringlike rash around the bite (which gradually gets worse), fatigue, and dizziness. Check your hair and clothing for the insects after your outdoor adventure. You can use DEET to ward off ticks. As for other possible outdoor risks, if you develop a rash from **poison ivy** or **poison sumac,** pick up some cortisone cream from the nearest pharmacy. It should be available without a prescription. Illinois has a handful of poisonous **snakes,** including the northern/ southern copperhead, the cottonmouth water

moccasin, timber rattlesnake, and massasauga rattlesnake. Most live in specific areas of the state and don't really want to encounter humans. If you see a snake that could be poisonous, leave it alone. (For more information, see *Fauna* in the *Background* section.)

Severe Weather

Any time from spring through summer when it looks wicked outside (dark skies, shifting winds, hard rain), turn on a radio or television to listen for any weather alerts. Major towns have tornado sirens that will go off in case of a tornado warning. But if you're in a rural area, get out of your car and head to a low-lying area. But don't take cover under a viaduct. If you're in a building without a basement, head to the interior of the building, away from windows. (For more on tornadoes, see *Climate* in the *Background* section.) Also, use common sense when boating and golfing. Lightening does strike the ground, and it can kill people. If it looks as if it's going to storm, hop back onto the golf cart or turn the boat toward the marina. Don't go raising your irons or fishing rods to the sky.

GAY AND LESBIAN TRAVELERS

Not surprisingly, gay and lesbian visitors should feel quite comfortable traveling through the city of Chicago. Throughout the rest of the state, however, how the natives receive you can vary from warm to cool. Generally the slightly more progressive college towns and larger cities such as Springfield and Champaign-Urbana are more accepting of gays and lesbians.

In Chicago, the North Halsted and Broadway neighborhood is home to many gay-owned businesses, clothing and accessories stores, and bars. Andersonville, also on the far north side, is another gay-friendly neighborhood. As far as Chicago resources, there are several options. **Windy City Media** (5443 N. Broadway, Chicago, 773/871-7610, www.windycitymediagroup.com) publishes the weekly *Windy City Times* newspaper, *Nightspots,* a weekly entertainment guide, plus other publications. They also have a bar guide online. You can pick up their publications at most convenience stores and book shops. Another resource is the **Chicago Area Gay and Lesbian Chamber of Commerce** (3656 N. Halsted Ave., Chicago, 773/303-0167, www.glchamber.org), which lists events for the gay community on its website.

"Reeling," Chicago's **International Gay and Lesbian Film Festival** sponsored by the Chicago Filmmakers and held usually in early November, is always a big hit. But the biggest gay and lesbian event in town every year is **PRIDEChicago,** held the last weekend in June. The parade and rally through the North Halsted neighborhood always attracts hundreds of thousands of people, gay and straight.

TRAVELERS WITH DISABILITIES

Visitors traveling in wheelchairs will find that most modern buildings (museums, restaurants, hotels) are accessible. The older historic sites might be technically "accessible," but you'll have to enter through a rear entrance or other type of entrance and exit. Always check about wheelchair access with historic inns and bed-and-breakfasts.

If you're planning to travel to Chicago, there are several organizations that will help disabled visitors and residents navigate the city. Almost all of the **Chicago Transit Authority** buses are wheelchair-accessible, plus dozens of elevated train stations are wheelchair-accessible with elevators. Another option for getting around the city is the **CTA's Paratransit Service,** which offers door-to-door service for a fee. You'll need to apply and make reservations, but it's a handy service to have if you plan to stay in Chicago for a while. For information on any of CTA's programs, including the Chicago Taxi Access Program, which offers taxi rides to people with disabilities at reduced rates, contact the **Regional Transportation Authority** at 312/663-4357, TTY 312/913-

3122, www.rtachicago.com. Otherwise you can reach the CTA at 312/681-3098 or TTY 312/681-3099. A list of accessible elevated train stations can be found on the CTA's website, www.yourcta.com. The site also has downloadable brochures for disabled people about getting around Chicago.

A new guide to the city of Chicago was recently published thanks to the mayor's office, the accessibility advocacy group Open Door, and the state tourism bureau. Check it out online, www.easyaccesschicago.org, or request a copy by calling the tourism bureau at 800/2-CONNECT (800/226-6632). It contains, among many other tips and information, helpful links such as a listing of hotels with wheelchair accessible rooms with roll-in showers and other features.

Other sources for information include the **City of Chicago Mayor's Office for People with Disabilities** (312/744-6673 or TTY 312/744-7833, www.cityofchicago.org). For a national perspective on this topic, contact the **Society for Accessible Travel and Hospitality** (347 5th Ave., New York, NY, 10016, 212/447-7284, www.sath.org).

The **Illinois Department of Natural Resources,** through its Disabled Outdoor Opportunities Program (618/439-9111, www.dnr.state.il.us), organizes special outdoor recreation events throughout the year for people with disabilities. The department also waives fees for hunting and fishing licenses for people with disabilities. Several state parks have wheelchair-accessible fishing piers and nature paths.

SENIOR TRAVELERS

Seniors can receive discounted admission at many of Illinois's museums, play performances, and even restaurants, golf courses, and other places of business. Remember to ask for the discount, though. In addition, if you're a member of the **American Association of Retired Persons** (601 E St. N.W., Washington, DC 20049, 888/687-2277, www.aarp.org), don't forget to ask at the hotel or rental car company for a discount, usually around 10 percent.

Elderhostel (11 Delafayette Ave., Boston, MA 02111-1746, 877/426-8056, www.elderhostel. org), a national nonprofit organization, holds daylong "day of discovery" events in cities around the country, including in Illinois.

TRAVELING WITH CHILDREN

If you are of the minivan set, Illinois has lots of stuff for you to do with your kids. First, there are more than a dozen children's museums in the state, from the multileveled Children's Museum of Illinois in Decatur to the small but growing Orpheum Children's Science Museum in Champaign. Check with the national **Association of Children's Museums** (1300 L St. N.W., Suite 975, Washington, DC 20005, 202/898-1080, www.childrensmuseums.org) for a list of museums in Illinois. There are also several water parks and theme parks to keep them entertained, from Six Flags Great America

in Gurnee to Magic Waters near Rockford. For a list of water parks in the state, consult the **World Waterpark Association** (8826 Santa Fe Dr., Suite 319, Overland Park, KS 66212, 913/599-0300, www.waterparks.com), which not only contains information on the major sites but also on some of the smaller, but just as refreshing, pools owned by park districts. While in the Chicago region, pick up a free copy of *Chicago Parent,* a monthly magazine that is a great resource for visiting and resident parents. There are several kid-focused travel guides to Chicago, such as *Frommer's Chicago with Kids, Fodor's Around Chicago with Kids,* and *The Lobster Kids' Guide to Exploring Chicago.*

To keep the kids entertained in the car, buy a copy of *Illinois Jeopardy: Questions and Answers About Our State* by Carole Marsh, published by Gallopade International in 2000. It's a trivia book for kids in 4th–8th grades.

Information and Services

MONEY

Generally you should be able to find automated teller machines throughout the state in banks, gas stations, and grocery stores. Usage fees will vary; the average is $1.50, plus any charge you have to pay to your home bank. You can change money and cash checks and traveler's checks at currency exchanges, which are in most major cities.

Sales taxes vary according to city and county, but it's generally around 6.5 to 7.5 percent, except in Cook County, where it's higher. Chicago sales tax is a whopping 10.25 percent. The state hotel tax is 6 percent, plus many counties and cities have additional hotel and motel taxes (taxes that usually fund convention and visitors bureaus). Expect gas prices around Chicago and the major interstates to be higher than in other areas.

Tipping

A standard tip at a restaurant is 15 percent. Giving 20 percent is not uncommon if you've

had over-the-top service or are particularly generous. The tip amount is not included on the bill unless you are a large party of more than 8–10 people. Most restaurants automatically include the tip for big tables. Shoe shiners at the railroad station expect tips (10–15 percent is acceptable), as do the folks who offer to carry your bags from your car to the ticket counter at airports (they're called skycaps). Tipping is optional for taxicab service. A tip of 10–15 percent is a nice gesture.

MAPS AND TOURIST INFORMATION

The Illinois Bureau of Tourism (800/226-6632, www.enjoyillinois.com) stocks several rest stops across the state with tons of free maps, brochures, and coupons. Here's a list: I-24 (called Fort Massac, one mile north of the Kentucky state line); I-55 (called Homestead, eight miles north of the I-70 interchange); I-57 (called Trail of Tears, 32 miles north of the Missouri border); I-57 (at Rend Lake);

I-57 (called Prairie View, 27 miles north of Kankakee); I-64 (called Gateway, 25 miles east of St. Louis); I-70 (called Silver Lake, 27 miles east of St. Louis); I-70 (called Cumberland Road, seven miles west of the Indiana state line); I-74 (called Salt Kettle, seven miles west of Danville); I-80 (called Mississippi Rapids, near the Iowa border); and I-90 (called Turtle Creek, two miles south of the Wisconsin border). There's also a tourist information center in the **Chicago Cultural Center** (78 E. Washington St., Chicago).

Instead of buying a map, order a free one (regular version or large print) from the Illinois Department of Transportation's website, www.dot.state.il.us, or by writing the department at IDOT, 2300 S. Dirksen Pkwy., Springfield, IL 62764.

For more detailed information on back roads and topography, buy DeLorme's *Illinois Gazetteer,* available at most bookstores. Also, the **Illinois Geological Survey** publishes an array of topographic maps and geology field guides, some of which focus on a particular region or natural area in the state, such as Illinois Caverns State Natural Area. To review its guides and maps for sale, contact the survey's public information office (1816 S. Oak St., Champaign, 217/244-2414, www.isgs.uiuc.edu).

MEDIA
Newspapers
The two Chicago daily papers, the *Chicago Tribune* and the *Chicago Sun-Times,* are available in most towns around the state, in addition to Chicago and the collar counties. Most visitors bureaus and chambers of commerce have links to local papers. You can also check the website of the **Illinois Press Association,** www.il-press.com, which has links to regional and local newspapers.

Magazines
The Tribune-owned *Chicago* magazine (www.chicagomag.com) covers the Chicago social, political, dining, and cultural scene, plus some statewide issues. It's available in stores throughout Chicagoland, plus in bookstores downstate.

The University of Illinois at Springfield publishes the monthly magazine *Illinois Issues* (http://illinoisissues.uis.edu), which objectively explores a range of statewide issues, including political, economic, historical, and social matters. You can find it at bookstores and libraries around the state, particularly in the central region.

INTERNET ACCESS
Speedy and free wireless Internet access is available at most coffee shops around the state, and more and more truck stops along the interstate highways. If you have a Wi-Fi–enabled laptop, all you have to do is have a seat at one of the tables to pick up the signal. Chains such as Panera Bread (in most Chicago suburbs and some downstate communities such as Champaign-Urbana) and Krispy Kreme doughnut shops offer Wi-Fi, as do many public libraries. The website www.wififreespot.com lists such places.

Whether or not they have Wi-Fi, DSL, or dial-up, just about every public library has Internet access. You'll have to sign in and might have to wait your turn (especially if you drop by after school or early in the evening), but it's free. Internet cafés can also be found around the state, from Chicago to little Savanna. Otherwise you can always rent a computer workstation at Kinko's locations around the state. Finally, don't forget to ask about access at your hotel or bed-and-breakfast. Most hotels, whether they are national chains or locally owned, offer Internet access free or at a nominal charge to their guests.

TIME ZONES
Illinois is in the central standard time zone, one hour behind New York (which is on eastern standard time), two hours ahead of Los Angeles, and six hours behind Greenwich mean time. The dividing line between central standard time and eastern standard time is along most of the Illinois-Indiana border. Illinois participates in daylight saving time by setting

clocks one hour ahead at 2 A.M. on the second Sunday in March. We switch back to standard time by turning the clocks back one hour at 2 A.M. on the first Sunday in November.

BUSINESS HOURS

Typically your locally or independently owned boutiques and shops are open 9 or 10 A.M.–6 or 7 P.M. Monday–Saturday. Malls and shopping centers are open later, until 8 P.M. or 9 P.M. Monday–Saturday. Sunday shopping hours are typically 11 A.M.–5 or 6 P.M. Most of the shops in Chicago's Loop don't stay open past 5 P.M. on weekdays. Restaurant hours vary depending on the region and the season. Some close on Mondays or Tuesdays or reduce their hours on those days. Museum and historic site hours can run the gamut, especially November–March. Post office hours also vary according to the town. In big cities, you can bet the branches there are open later than in rural towns. Most are open 8 A.M.–5 P.M. Monday–Friday and 8 A.M.–12:30 P.M. Saturday. The big holidays are New Year's Day, Easter, Thanksgiving, and Christmas. Just about everything is closed on these days. Tourist attractions tend to stay open on Memorial Day and Labor Day. Illinois celebrates a few obscure holidays, such as Casimir Pulaski Day, held on the first Monday of March. Chicago public schools shut down in honor of this Revolutionary War hero, but most businesses are still up and running.

RESOURCES

Suggested Reading

LITERATURE

Algren, Nelson. *Chicago: City on the Make.* Chicago: University of Chicago Press, 2001. Or *The Man with the Golden Arm.* New York City: Seven Stories Press, 1999. Algren eloquently illustrates life in Chicago's Polish ghetto.

Masters, Edgar Lee. *Spoon River Anthology.* Urbana: University of Illinois Press, 1993. American poetry at its best. Masters, who was born in Kansas but grew up along the Spoon River in northwestern Illinois, chronicles life in small-town Illinois.

Sandburg, Carl. *Chicago Poems.* Mineola, NY: Dover Publications, 1994. Or *Cornhuskers.* Bridgewater, NJ: Replica Books, 2003. These contain classic Sandburg poems. They're lyrical, poignant, beautiful, and accessible portrayals of everyday people and everyday things.

Sinclair, Upton. *The Jungle.* Tucson, AZ: See Sharp Press, 2003. This version is a reprint of the original uncensored edition from 1905. If you didn't read it in high school (or haven't read it in a while), pick up this masterful portrayal of the Chicago stockyards, which also touches upon issues such as race, workers' rights, immigrants rights, and much more.

Wright, Richard A. *Native Son.* New York City: Perennial Harper Collins, 1998. A page-turning tragic story about Bigger Thomas and life as a black man in 1930s Chicago.

PEOPLE

Addams, Jane. *Twenty Years at Hull House.* Champaign: University of Illinois Press, 1990. Originally published in 1910, this book includes her thoughts on public and social policy, autobiographical notes, and stories about her experience at the complex to help poor and immigrant families in Chicago.

Higdon, Hal. *Leopold and Lobe: The Crime of the Century.* Champaign: University of Illinois Press, 1999. An account of the crime and the trial from the 1920s of two rich boys who killed a fellow boy and thought they could get away with it.

Royko, Mike. *Boss: Richard J. Daley of Chicago.* New York City: Plume Books, 1998. Originally published in 1971, when Daley was still at the helm, this is a classic book about Chicago politics. Royko takes a hard look at the Democratic machine that dominated and still dominates Chicago politics and how Daley conducted business in city hall.

Royko, Mike. *One More Time: The Best of Mike Royko.* Chicago: University of Chicago Press, 2000. The best essays and columns about Chicago people and politics by Royko, a longtime *Chicago Tribune* columnist.

Russo, Gus. *The Outfit: The Role of Chicago's Underworld in the Shaping of Modern America.* New York City: Bloomsbury, 2001. Not only do you learn about Al Capone here, but meet Frank "The Enforcer" Nitti and Mooney Giancana. The book spans about 60 years and includes stories about Chicago's beer wars during the Prohibition era and modern off-track betting and casino gambling ventures. With black-and white-photographs.

Sandburg, Carl. *Abraham Lincoln: The Prairie Years and the War Years.* Edison, NJ: BBS Publishing Corp., 1993. This is the ultimate Lincoln book. The second part of this two-volume biography won Sandburg the Pulitzer Prize.

HISTORY, POLITICS, AND ECONOMY

Angle, Paul M. *Bloody Williamson: A Chapter in American Lawlessness.* Champaign: University of Illinois Press, 1952 and 1992. The late state historian Paul Angle dives into the history of what was once one of the most notoriously bloody counties in the state: Williamson County in southern Illinois. Now a quiet rural county, Williamson once was the scene of several murders among rival gangs, violence between striking coal miners and the strikebreakers, and violence between the Ku Klux Klan and bootleggers.

Biles, Roger. *Illinois: A History of the Land and Its People.* DeKalb: Northern Illinois University Press, 2005. Finally, a comprehensive history of the state and its colorful people. Biles begins with the Native Americans and continues with the French explorers, describes the Illinois frontier, the Civil War era, all the way into the 1960s, the Daley era, and contemporary times. Includes sidebars on various towns around the state, and some photos and maps.

Clark, George Rogers. *The Conquest of the Illinois.* Carbondale: Southern Illinois University, 2001. Written 1789–1791, and reissued by SIU a few years ago, this book, in Rogers's words, describes what Illinois (and the Illinois Indians) were like before the state became a state. With plenty of footnotes with background information about historical events and people.

Hartley, Robert E. *Lewis and Clark in the Illinois Country: The Little-Told Story.* Westminster, CO: Xlibris and Sniktau Publishers, 2002. Before they set off on their westward expedition, Meriwether Lewis and William Clark spent six months in Illinois November 1803–May 1804. This book sets the stage for that endeavor, recounting how they recruited men and gathered supplies. It also provides a look into the makeup of the Illinois country, its early settlements of Cahokia and Kaskaskia, and touches upon its early history, such as the forays of George Rogers Clark (William's older brother) in the state.

Hill, Libby. *The Chicago River: A Natural and Unnatural History.* Chicago: Lake Claremont Press, 2000. A fascinating look at the history of the river, beginning with geologic prehistory from millions of years ago, through the creation of the Illinois and Michigan Canal, the Sanitary and Ship Canal, and modern efforts to keep the river clean.

Jensen, Richard J. *Illinois: A History.* Champaign: University of Illinois Press, 2001. In one of the few books about the prairie state's beginnings, Jensen writes in somewhat of an academic style about the early years of statehood through modern times, particularly focusing on the clashes between traditionalists in the south and so-called modernists in the north during the Civil War era.

Klinenberg, Eric. *Heat Wave: A Social Autopsy of a Disaster in Chicago.* Chicago: University of Chicago Press, 2002. In 1995 a deadly heat wave struck Illinois, hitting Chicago hard. There were power outages and reduced water pressure because of opened hydrants, hospitals were overwhelmed with cases of heat-related illnesses, and an estimated 739 people died. Klinenberg examines what happened, the city's response, who died (mainly the poor, the elderly, and people who lived alone), and the societal implications of the event.

Terkel, Studs. *Working.* New York City: New Press, 2004. The original Terkel, a Chicago institution, talks to people about what they do and what they think about their jobs.

Tilley Turner, Glenette. *The Underground Railroad in Illinois.* Glen Ellyn, IL: Newman Educational Publishing Company, 2001. Organized in question and answer format, with maps and historical and contemporary photographs.

Whiting, Biloine, and Melvin L. Fowler. *Cahokia: The Great Native American Metropolis.* Champaign: University of Illinois Press, 1999. This book not only discusses theories about the people who lived at this Native American village near the Mississippi River, but about all the modern development, archaeological research, and other activities that have occurred since the tribes disappeared hundreds of years ago.

GEOLOGY AND NATURAL HISTORY

De Vore, Sheryl. *Birding Illinois.* Guilford, CT: Falcon Publishing, 2000. This paperback guidebook, a little less than 300 pages, is divided by region and lists the top birdwatching sites in the state, as well as nature preserves, rookeries, and more. It also includes plenty of maps and illustrations of birds, plus background information about the habitats of Illinois birds.

Jeffords, Michael R., Susan L. Post, and Kenneth R. Robertson. *Illinois Wilds.* Urbana, IL: Phoenix Publishing, 1995. A beautiful book with color photographs and essays about the state's geography and natural wonders. Divided into 15 regions, from the unglaciated woods in the north to the coastal plain forests of the south, the book explains how the state looks the way it does with its flat midsection, eastern forests, and bluff-filled northwest. With stunning photographs of green caterpillars, mushrooms, bluffs, and more.

Wiggers, Ray. *Geology Underfoot in Illinois.* Missoula, MT: Mountain Press Publishing, 1996. An engaging book that traces the state's history back to the most recent ice age and millions of years before that. With illustrations and travel tips, this is a great resource for anyone interested in how the Illinois landscape came to be.

ART AND ARCHITECTURE

Clayton, Marie, ed. *Frank Lloyd Wright Field Guide.* Philadelphia: Running Press, 2002. About 100 Wright creations are highlighted here, with aerial, exterior, and interior photos. A great guide for folks who know about Wright's body of work; buildings are organized by his different periods, such as Prairie and Usonian. A thick book with a small, trim size, it can fit into your purse or backpack.

Kanfer, Larry. *Prairiescapes.* Champaign: University of Illinois Press, 1987. Champaign resident and photographer Larry Kanfer captures the beauty of the prairie with 101 photographs of mostly rural scenes in east-central Illinois: corn and soybean harvests, abandoned farmsteads, foggy winter mornings on country roads. Kanfer has several other coffee-table books featuring Midwestern landscapes.

Lowe, David. *Lost Chicago.* Avenel, NJ: Wings Books. An amazing compilation of the city's treasures now tragically gone from the landscape. The stockyards, fairs, movie palaces, amusement parks, mansions—they're all here in black and white photos, with essays on the history of the city.

O'Gorman, Thomas. *Frank Lloyd Wright's Chicago.* San Diego: Thunder Bay Press, 2004. A slick coffee-table book, this book is arranged chronologically, from Wright's earliest designs to the late ones. Buildings are not limited to Chicago but also include estates in the suburbs as well as in Michigan and Wisconsin.

Schulze, Franz, and Kevin Harrington. *Chicago's Famous Buildings.* Chicago: University of Chicago Press, 2003. A guide that you can slip into your backpack while touring the city. The guide, which has maps and black-and-white pictures, covers well-known and not-so-well-known buildings downtown, plus some key historical buildings in the surrounding suburbs, such as Oak Park and those on the north shore.

TRAVEL AND FOOD

Avis, Ed. *The Lobster Kids' Guide to Exploring Chicago*. Montreal: Lobster Press, 2001. Small, convenient guide for parents.

Davenport, Don. *In Lincoln's Footsteps: A Historical Guide to the Lincoln Sites in Illinois, Indiana, and Kentucky*. Black Earth, WI: Trails Media Group, 2002. Another easy-to-follow guide with maps, practical info, and historical summaries of Lincoln's movement through the state.

Pohlen, Jerome. *Oddball Illinois: A Guide to Some Really Strange Places*. Chicago: Chicago Review Press, 2000. A lighthearted look at the state's kookiest attractions (people included).

Post, Susan L. *Hiking Illinois*. Champaign, IL: Human Kinetics, 1997. Easy to use with detailed maps and trail information, this book outlines 100 day hikes in regions throughout the state. Hike details include information about the region's topography, plant life, and nearby attractions. Pages are perforated, so you can tear them out and carry the maps in your pocket or pack.

Shepard, Robin. *The Best Pints and Breweries in Illinois*. Madison: University of Wisconsin Press, 2003. The perfect book for those who enjoy a good brew. Shepard writes about 36 top-notch pubs and breweries in the state, with an explainer about how beers are made and a guide to rating beers.

Svob, Mike. *Paddling Illinois: 64 Great Trips by Canoe and Kayak*. Black Earth, WI: Trails Media Group, 2000. A large paperback, this easy-to-use book is a must-have for paddlers. It comes with maps.

Internet Resources

Illinois Bureau of Tourism
www.enjoyillinois.com

The statewide source for attractions, lodging, dining, and recreation. Links to local visitors bureaus.

Chicago Convention and Visitors Bureau
www.choosechicago.com

A guide to the city, with helpful calendar of events and themed itinerary suggestions.

Chicago Tribune
www.chicagotribune.com

The city's major daily newspaper.

Chicago Sun-Times
www.sun-times.com

The other major daily newspaper (this one is tabloid-size).

Chicago Magazine
www.chicagomag.com

Fashion, cultural events, restaurants, and some politics.

Illinois Historic Preservation Agency
www.state.il.us/hpa

Information about all state historic sites.

Chicago History Museum
www.chicagohistory.org

The website offers a good primer on the city's colorful history; the museum on Chicago's north side is even better.

Frank Lloyd Wright Preservation Trust
www.gowright.org

Frank Lloyd Wright sites in Oak Park and Chicago.

Springfield Tourism Bureau
www.visit-springfieldillinois.com

Helpful guide to Springfield and surrounding area.

Abraham Lincoln Presidential Library and Museum
www.alplm.org

A comprehensive look at Lincoln, his family, and his legacy.

Looking for Lincoln
www.lookingforlincoln.com

Abraham Lincoln sites in central Illinois.

Route 66 in Illinois
www.illinoisroute66.org
www.il66assoc.org

Trip suggestions and information about current and past roadside attractions and restaurants.

Illinois Department of Natural Resources
www.dnr.state.il.us

State park, camping, and fishing information.

Illinois League of Bicyclists
www.bikelib.org

Trail information and links to maps.

Shawnee National Forest
www.fs.fed.us/r9/forests/shawnee

U.S. Forest Service website for Shawnee National Forest.

Getting Around Illinois
www.gettingaroundillinois.com

Construction and roadway information from the Illinois Department of Transportation.

Index

Map Index

www.moon.com

DESTINATIONS | ACTIVITIES | BLOGS | MAPS | BOOKS

MOON.COM is all new, and ready to help plan your next trip! Filled with fresh trip ideas and strategies, author interviews, informative blogs, a detailed map library, and descriptions of all the Moon guidebooks, Moon.com is all you need to get out and explore the world—or even places in your own backyard. As always, when you travel with Moon, expect an experience that is uncommon and truly unique.